THE COMMUNIST INSURRECTION
IN MALAYA
1948-1960

MALAYA

THE COMMUNIST INSURRECTION IN MALAYA

1948-1960

ANTHONY SHORT

CRANE, RUSSAK & COMPANY, INC.
NEW YORK

First published 1975 by
Impulse Publications Ltd.,
28 Guild Street, Aberdeen

Published in the United States by:
Crane, Russak & Company, Inc.
347 Madison Avenue
New York, N.Y. 10017

Library of Congress Catalog Card No. 73-93384

ISBN 0-8448-0306-5

Printed in Great Britain

PREFACE

Not long after I joined the University of Malaya in the middle of 1960 an agreement between the University and the Government of Malaya was reached that I should write, for publication and without censorship, the history of the communist insurrection in Malaya: generally known in Malaya as 'the Emergency'. To this end I was provided with every assistance by the Malayan Government, the most important of which was full access to their confidential and secret papers. The British Government, after some initial encouragement, chose to be bound by what was then the Fifty Year Rule and the result, I feel, is that I have probably missed the top five or ten per cent of the sources that are in London. Critical papers, however, had a habit of turning up in not so important files but, quite apart from this serendipity, the compensating advantage was that I had to look a lot further and a lot deeper than I might otherwise have done.

The manuscript, of which the first three chapters are presented here in an abridgement, was handed over to the Malaysian Government in October 1968 and for the next three years I waited for publication or some indication of their intention. Eventually I was told that it was not to be published; since then, and in spite of my offers to remove what might be thought of by the Malaysian Government as any matters of genuine security, it has been described as top secret and subversive and I have had reluctantly to conclude that it stands no chance whatever of being published by virtue of the original undertaking. Since then also the manuscript was read and accepted by Oxford University Press but I was then asked to regard my contract as invalid because, in their opinion, the copyright did not belong to me. This was not my Counsel's opinion on the matter nor that of my publishers and we offer it now for what it is: an account which, while not 'official', is as close as it has yet been possible to write.

It is to me a matter of the greatest regret that the government of Malaysia which I believe is still fundamentally tolerant should object to an account based on evidence that is presumably not yet in dispute. As far as security is concerned I do not think that it contains anything that could jeopardise the lives of men or women or those of their families nor anything by way of hitherto secret techniques, plans or assessments that might now be of direct advantage to those who might seek to overthrow a democratic state.

That is not to say however that this is a history free from all account of human error. It may be that, in juxtaposition and selection, I have failed to give due weight and consideration to one or other or more of the many sides involved. The very sensitive may regard it as anti-Malay, anti-Chinese or anti-Indian. It can equally well be regarded as anti-British. It may also be reckoned to lack the insights that a Malay, a Chinese or an Indian author could have provided and against this charge I have no defence. It can also be argued perhaps that it is too concerned with the framework of 'colonial' decisions and activities and again I would have to agree or plead that, for me, and making certain large assumptions about Malayan political *stasis*, these were the important data that helped to explain the course of the insurrection and its ultimate failure.

There have been many published stories of the Emergency and the jungle war—too many, perhaps, written by Europeans and from a European standpoint—but for the time being this may be the last to have had the advantage of classified information. What one may hope for now is that the Malaysian Government, at least for its own satisfaction, will commission Asian scholars to examine the record so that this account can, if necessary, be corrected. Whether it is or not I suspect that it may now be out of humour with the times and that, with much of South-east Asia today nominally at peace, there is for many people an understandable weariness with such narratives of insurrection and a longing for fundamental and common causes to emerge that will hold good at most times and in most places. For them, I fear, this book may be a disappointment. I have tended to treat Malaya as a singular case and have, I suppose, concentrated on the particular at the expense of the general. This is not to deny that comparisons can and should be made with the experiences of other countries in South-east Asia, their insurrections, emergence, and ability to survive civil and military disturbance. As a basis for such comparisons, however, I have sought to provide data and some comment on what, I think, were the most important features.

King's College, Aberdeen.
October, 1973.

ACKNOWLEDGMENTS

The first, in my list of acknowledgments, is of my debt to John Bastin who, as Professor of History in the University of Malaya, initiated this study and has sustained me over ten years with his interest and advice; and to Sir Alexander Oppenheim who, as Vice-Chancellor, enlisted the support of the government of Malaya. To the latter, my debts are obvious: to the Ministers concerned, to the permanent officials in what was then the Ministry of Internal Security, and to the many serving officers of government, civil and police, who gave me their assistance, time and experience. In particular, in the Ministry of Internal Security, Frank Smith, Dato Nik Daud, Samad Ismail and Yvonne Koudelka (née Noronha); at Police Headquarters, Richard Craig, P. Seenivasagam, Richard Mooney and Paul Barnes; the Commanding Officer of the Senoi Pra'aq, M. Ruslan bin Abdullah; and the Head of the Department of Psychological Warfare, Mr. C. C. Too. In Malaya my principal recorded conversations were with Dato Haji Bangs, J. R. H. Burns, Richard Buxton, Chan Chulia, Dato J. S. E. Crawford, Sir Claud Fenner, Charles Gamba, Tim Hatton, Douglas Hyde, Cyril Keele, Allington Kennard, the late Senator Khaw Kai Boh, Charles McLane, the late Mrs Dorothy Nixon, P. P. Narayanan, Richard Noone, Peter Setchell, Tan Sri Mubin Sheppard, Michael Stenson, Andrew Taylor and the Honourable Tan Siew Sin.

In Singapore, George Bogaars, Richard Corridon, Gerald de Cruz, George Thomson, K. G. Tregonning who was kind enough to allow me access to the Tan Cheng Lock papers and, especially, Yoong Siew Wah.

In Bangkok, Frank Brewer and the late Moreton Horsley. In New Delhi, the Director of the Indian Intelligence Bureau, Sri B. N. Mullik, and Sri A. C. M. Nambiar, both of whom went to great trouble on my behalf.

In the United Kingdom and Ireland I talked or corresponded with Noel Alexander, John Barnard, John Brazier, Richard Broome, Hugh Bryson, W. L. R. Carbonell, the late Francis Carnell, Richard Clutterbuck, Charles Corry, John Dalley,

ACKNOWLEDGMENTS

Bernard Davis, John Davis, A. H. Dickinson, the late H. K. Dimoline, H. H. Facer, E. B. de Fonblanque, Lady Gent, David Gray, John Gullick, A. W. D. James, Dato J. N. McHugh, Desmond O'Duffy, J. B. Prentis, Harvey Ryves, the late F. W. Spencer Chapman, Ian Wyllie and Sir Arthur Young.

In the United States, Basil O'Connel and Oliver Wolters.

For their assistance in compiling this work I was fortunate to have the services of J. B. Perry Robinson in London; Jack Humphrey, Margaret Clark and especially Margaret Lee (and Tommy) in Kuala Lumpur; Miss Joan Roberton and Michael Dyer in Aberdeen. Also the library staffs of the University of Malaya, Aberdeen University and, in London, the Ministry of Defence and the Press Library of the Royal Institute of International Affairs.

Professor Wang Gung-Wu and my former colleagues and students in the History Department, University of Malaya, have helped in various ways; so have Frank Bealey, Michael Leifer, Peter Calvert, Alistair Maclean and Christopher MacLehose: not least with their encouragement.

To the Police Field Force, the Jungle Warfare School and the Senoi Pra'aq in Malaya: my thanks and hope that I was not too much of an encumbrance.

I have a particularly large debt and wish to record my appreciation of the kindness of Sir David Watherston, former Secretary for Defence, later Chief Secretary, and Guy Madoc, former Director of Intelligence, Federation of Malaya, who, at the end, read the entire manuscript and made many useful suggestions.

Finally, my thanks to Paul Harris and the Master of Forbes, who made it possible; and to Agnes, who bore it with her usual patience and love.

CONTENTS

	Page
Preface	1
Acknowledgments	3
Foreword	7
Glossary	9
Introduction	11

THE UPTURNED HIVE

| 1. | Prologue | 19 |
| 2. | Towards a Revolutionary Situation | 34 |

THE ARMED STRUGGLE BEGINS

3.	The Onus of Responsibility	65
4.	The Pattern of Attack	95
5.	Government Maintained	113
6.	Government Constrained	149

ORIGINAL PROBLEMS

7.	The Squatter Problem	173
8.	The Assault Renewed	206
9.	The Briggs Plan	231
10.	Community Politics	254
11.	Slack Water	275

SECOND OPINIONS

12.	New Orders (1): The MCP	309
13.	New Orders (2): Government	322
14.	Battle Defined	345

COURSE OF BATTLE

15.	The New Villages	391
16.	Battle for the Mind	416
17.	Aborigines and the Deep Jungle	439

CONTENTS

Page

EVAPORATION

18. Negotiable Terms? 459
19. Fight to the Finish 472
20. Conclusions 496

Appendix 507
Bibliography 509
Index 515

FOREWORD

Many books have been written about the so-called Communist Emergency in Malaya. The numerous eye-witness accounts of the 1950s, of which the late Brigadier Richard Miers' *Shoot to Kill* (London, 1959) is possibly the best, gave way during the 1960s to more reflective studies such as Edgar O'Ballance's *Malaya: The Communist Insurgent War, 1948–1960* (London, 1966), and Major-General Richard Clutterbuck's *The Long Long War: The Emergency in Malaya, 1948–1960* (London, 1967). At the same time there developed a noticeable tendency to generalise and theorise about the relevance of the Malayan experience to combating Communist infiltration elsewhere in South-east Asia, notably in Vietnam. Mr. Short rightly eschews an attempt to draw any such lessons in this book. He has instead set himself the task of writing an account of the Emergency from a strictly historical point of view, indeed, one may say, from a professional historian's point of view. The result is a book of outstanding quality which lifts the study of the Malayan Emergency on to an entirely new plane and, as such, makes an important and significant contribution to the historiography of modern Malaysia. The author has had the considerable advantage of access to restricted records in Malaysia which have not been available to others, but he has nowhere breached the confidentiality of those records insofar as they relate to persons. Indeed, he has sustained throughout his book such obvious impartiality that one can only wonder on what possible grounds the Malaysian Government decided to prohibit its publication. The resultant delay in arranging publication in the United Kingdom, exacerbated by the decision of Oxford University Press to withdraw from its contract with the author, has meant that the public has been denied for more than five years the opportunity of reading what is unquestionably the most authoritative and balanced book on the Communist Insurrection in Malaya.

John Bastin
Former Professor of History, University of Malaya
School of Oriental and African Studies
University of London

GLOSSARY/ABBREVIATIONS

ACA	Adviser on Chinese Affairs
AMCJA	All Malayan Council of Joint Action
API	Angkatan Pemuda Insa'af (Youth Movement for Justice)
asal	aborigine (guerrilla term)
attap	palm thatch
BA	British Adviser
BDCC	British Defence Coordinating Committee
belukar	thick (secondary) jungle
BMA	British Military Administration
CCP	China Communist Party
CDL	China Democratic League
CIS	Combined Intelligence Staff
CPI	Communist Party of India
CPO	Chief Police Officer (State)
DWEC	District War Executive Committee
Exco	Executive Council
FARELF	Far East Land Forces
FMS	Federated Malay States
IMP	Independence for Malaya Party
jelutong	wild rubber
kampong	village
kati	$1\frac{1}{3}$ lb.
kepala	head man
KMT	Kuomintang
kongsi	Chinese 'collective'
ladang	clearing
lallang	elephant grass
Legco	Legislative Council
MCP	Malayan Communist Party
MCS	Malayan Civil Service
MNP	Malay Nationalist Party
MPAJA	Malayan Peoples Anti-Japanese Army
MPIEA	Malayan Planting Industry Employers' Association

GLOSSARY/ABBREVIATIONS

MRLA	Malayan Races Liberation Army
Mentri Besar (MB)	Chief Minister
Min Yuen	'Masses Organisation'
mui-tsai	'little sister'
OCPD	Officer Commanding Police District
OSPC	Officer Superintending Police Circle
PMFTU	Pan Malayan Federation of Trade Unions
padi	rice
penghulu	village headman
pikul	$133\frac{1}{3}$ lb. : 100 katis
rentis	narrow boundary clearing
San Min Chu Yi	KMT Youth Corps
SCA	Secretary for Chinese Affairs
SC's	Special Constables
SEP	Surrendered enemy personnel
SF	Security Forces
SWEC	State War Executive Committee
TOL	Temporary Occupation Licence (land)
triad	Chinese secret society
UMNO	United Malays National Organisation
UPAM	United Planning Association of Malaya

INTRODUCTION

It is now sixteen years since Malaya became independent and over thirteen since the Emergency was officially declared at an end. It is possible therefore to see the events of 1948 to 1960 in better perspective than could have been done when the dust had barely settled.

The problems involved in overcoming the Communist Terrorists were without precedent, and many lessons had to be learned the hard way before the tide turned in the government's favour. It was a long drawn-out campaign and victory came only after many years of anxiety, frustration and despondency. The fact that it did come in the end is something of which all of us who were concerned with the government's effort can feel justifiable pride. There is the conviction too that the campaign was one of great historical interest, of which an account, based on the official records, should be preserved.

This is what Mr. Short has given us. He is particularly well qualified to undertake the task. As a historian he has the approach of a professional. In addition he has the advantage of having seen service himself in Malaya in the Army during the early stages of the Emergency, and more recently of having spent a considerable period at the University in Kuala Lumpur. As the result of his careful research, in Malaya itself and elsewhere, we now have, for the first time, a book which provides a balanced picture, both of the background before the Emergency broke out and of the subsequent campaign. He deserves the warmest gratitude and congratulations of all those who love the country and its people.

The early chapters are rightly devoted to the paramount importance of the part played by the Malayan Communist Party in the series of events leading up to the murders in June 1948 when a State of Emergency was officially proclaimed. It was, as Mr. Short says, a Communist insurrection. It is perhaps useful to reflect on some of the other circumstances which were occupying the attention of the government at the time.

Looking back on the immediate post-war years, it is remarkable that there was not greater trouble. Among the legacies of the

Japanese occupation were wide-spread malnutrition; a demoralised police force; acute tension in some areas between Malays and Chinese, culminating in massacres in a few instances; and government services whose senior (European) members had been seriously depleted by internment and retirement and by the fact that no recruitment, either in the UK or in Malaya, had been carried out during the war.

In addition to this, politics had, for the first time, emerged on a national scale. The proposal of the British Government to the Malay Rulers that they should sign new treaties, replacing the separate pre-war agreements with each of the Malay States, and setting up a Malayan Union, had been reluctantly accepted by Their Highnesses in the atmosphere of relief which prevailed during the first few months after the war had ended; but it had stimulated resentment among Malays throughout the country on the grounds that it put greater power in the hands of the British Government. Led by Dato Onn, who formed the United Malays National Organisation (UMNO), they had demanded a reversal of policy, and negotiations, which took up much of the attention of senior government officers in Kuala Lumpur, continued from mid-1946 until a new Agreement creating a Federation of Malay States was signed in January 1948, only a few months before the Emergency broke out. One of the results of this was that, in each of the nine Malay States, new government machinery under a Malay Chief Minister (Mentri Besar) had to be set up. These State Governments had had no time effectively to find their feet before all the problems and pressures of the Emergency were thrust upon them.

As Mr. Short has described, the initial effort, which the MCP launched in June 1948, failed to achieve its purpose, and they withdrew into the jungle in 1949 to prepare themselves for a second attempt. This pause had the immense advantage that it gave the government time to get itself better organised—though in retrospect much more could have been done. An example is the Squatter Committee Report on which no action was taken for well over twelve months after its publication early in 1949; until in fact Lieutenant-General Sir Harold Briggs made it one of the corner-stones of his operational plan in 1950.

The most critical period of the whole campaign came, as Mr. Short points out, at the end of 1951 and in the early months of 1952. The High Commissioner, Sir Henry Gurney, had been murdered, Sir Harold Briggs' appointment as Director of Operations had expired, and Colonel Gray was removed from his post as Commissioner of Police following the visit by the new Colonial

INTRODUCTION 13

Secretary, Oliver Lyttelton. Yet, despite the general feeling of depression, and his severe criticism of the dichotomy in the system of administration and command, Lyttelton found nothing fundamentally wrong with the policies that were being followed either in the political or in the operational field. What he diagnosed was a need for the concentration of authority in one man, who should be given all the resources he required to push the government's total effort 'over the hump'.

The British Cabinet endorsed his recommendations. The arrival of Sir Gerald Templer in February 1952, and his obvious determination to get to grips with the situation, put new life into the scene so that the atmosphere of gloom rapidly dispersed. On the operational side, he endorsed the Briggs plan of resettlement in New Villages and gave it fresh impetus; he was successful too in obtaining more troops. On the political side, he continued Gurney's policy of appointing prominent Malayans as 'Members' of Government, responsible to him for the affairs of some government Departments, answering for these Departments in the Legislative Council, and so representing a step on the road to more democratic institutions and to eventual independence. A new, and immensely important move, as Mr. Short describes, was the introduction of elected Councils in the New Villages. By the end of 1952 the climate had radically changed for the better, and although progress in this type of warfare is inevitably slow, it was by then clear that the government had a strong chance of winning.

As things went on improving, so there was growing pressure from the Malays for a greater share in the government, and for a clear statement of the British Government's intentions on the issue of independence. It had been held as almost axiomatic by the government in London that the Emergency must be cleared out of the way, before consideration could be given to any further political changes; but as time went on, it was increasingly realised in Kuala Lumpur that this attitude could not be maintained without serious risk of losing the goodwill of some of the influential Malays. Strong representations were made to London, but it was not until the latter part of 1954 that a statement was made by the Colonial Secretary in the House of Commons, promising independence once the Emergency had been brought to a successful conclusion. I was fortunate in witnessing at first hand the remarkable effect that this undertaking made on some of the Malay Members of Government. They had not been unco-operative before, but they became positively enthusiastic about affording the government every assistance in their power to end the Emergency with the least possible delay. The first elections to the Federal Legislative Council took place in 1955 and Independence came on August 31st 1957.

With the lapse of time since all these events took place, it is possible to draw certain conclusions, and to give credit where credit is due. First, although it was recognised almost from the start on the side of the government that the struggle was a political one, and that the purpose of the terrorists was to make Malaya into a Communist State, the full implications of this took some time to learn; for example, that operations must be truly 'combined', with the armed forces, the police and the civil administration each playing their appropriate part in a completely integrated plan. Again, it was only slowly realised that the winning of the hearts and minds of the people, so that they would be an asset to the security forces and not a liability, was absolutely vital to success. Here the magnificent part played by the Malays deserves the highest praise. The terrorists were largely alien Chinese with no loyalty to Malaya, and the very few Malays and Indians among them attracted negligible support from their own people. When men were wanted in large numbers as Special Constables or for the expansion of the Police Force or the Malay Regiment, there was always an ample supply of willing volunteers. At the other end of the social scale, the Rulers, and Malays in senior appointments, gave their unstinted support to the government's measures—even more whole-heartedly, as I have said, after independence had been promised.

Yet without the resources of men, money and equipment which Britain placed at Malaya's disposal, without the leadership provided by British officers, both civil and military from the High Commissioner and GOC downwards, without the brilliance of the senior Europeans in the Special Branch whose expertise was responsible for the intelligence which was so essential to successful operations, and without the heroic resistance put up by European planters and miners, it is certain that the Communists would have been successful. Mr. Short has of course described the part played by the planters, and often their families as well, but it is worth repeating the point that if they had not remained on their estates, under conditions of isolation and almost intolerable strain, with their lives at risk at any time of the day or night, large areas would have come under the control of the terrorists, and the economy of the country would have been crippled.

It follows that, if the Communists had been successful, the Malays would have found themselves under the control of an alien régime. No doubt some Quislings would have emerged, but this would not have altered the basic fact that the Malays would have lost the

INTRODUCTION 15

power to decide the future of their own country. Their own leaders, who have proved so successful since Merdeka in 1957, had not at the time in question served the apprenticeship which would have enabled them to guide the nation to victory over an experienced and ruthless enemy. It would be a mistake to imagine that the massive surrenders, which took place after Merdeka, in 1958 and 1959, would have happened earlier if independence had come earlier; the terrorists' leaders could and would have prevented them.

What can one say of the Malayan Chinese? The educated class, including those with business and other financial interests in Malaya, were of course anxious that the government should win. They had no sympathy with Communism. With their background, however, they could see more clearly than others the dangers that threatened South-east Asia in the future, and in particular the dominating influence that Communist China would be likely to wield once the colonial powers withdrew. They did not wish to come out into the open for fear of possible repercussions on their families perhaps many years ahead. Traditionally, too, no one of any education or substance in the old China joined the Police or the Army, so they resisted the government's attempts to recruit Chinese into these organisations. There were, however, two directions in particular in which the Malayan Chinese were able to make a most effective contribution to the government's effort; these were in the non-uniformed sector of the Police Force, notably in Special Branch, where their work was invaluable, and in such departments as the Emergency Information Services. After its formation they were able too to defend the new villages in which they lived, by becoming members of the Home Guard.

Mr. Short has placed emphasis, again absolutely rightly, on the importance of the battle for the minds of the people, meaning particularly the Chinese. There were a number of reasons why the Malayan Chinese were vulnerable to MCP propaganda. In the first place it came from people of their own race, and all Chinese share a natural pride in the culture and traditions of China. Secondly, the 'Overseas Chinese', even though in no sense Communists themselves, greatly admire the achievements of the People's Government in making China a world power. Thirdly, as Mr. Short explains, the Malayan Chinese were in many ways cut off from contact with the Malayan Government. All this made the task of countering MCP propaganda an exceptionally difficult one.

It has to be remembered that the Malayan Chinese came originally from different parts of China and had carried local loyalties and languages with them to Malaya; it was for this reason that Sir

INTRODUCTION

Henry Gurney gave all the support he could to the creation of the Malayan Chinese Association, in the hope that it would focus, on the country of their adoption, the allegiance of those who had settled permanently in Malaya.

As the first elections drew nearer, Tunku Abdul Rahman saw the importance of the MCA as a means of broadening the base of UMNO's purely Malay appeal. Dato Onn's attempt to get UMNO to admit other races to its ranks had failed. So the Tunku formed the Alliance, of which UMNO and the MCA were the first members, joined later by the Malayan Indian Congress. This gave the MCA a standing which it would not have achieved otherwise, and meant that a reasonable number of Chinese were elected to the Federal Legislative Council in 1955. But the MCA has never had deep roots, and its aims have had only limited success. The alliance with UMNO too has not led to any noticeable rapprochement between the two races. The serious racial riots of May 1969, in Kuala Lumpur were terrible examples of this, but it is encouraging that there has been no recurrence of violence since then.

During the years since the Emergency ended, Malaya—now of course Malaysia—has made outstanding progress under its independent government. It is difficult now to remember the dark days of ambushes and murder, and the extensive restrictions which had to be imposed through food control and in other ways, including detention without trial. But it is undoubtedly the case that today's prosperity has been built on the victory won in the campaign of 1948–60, towards whose successful outcome the efforts of all the races in Malaya contributed.

David Watherston
Former Chief Secretary
Federation of Malaya

Harbury
August, 1973

The Upturned Hive

I

PROLOGUE

It may be argued that the origins of the insurrection in Malaya should be sought in the economic and social conditions of the time, in political disturbances, in the repressive acts of government and in the experiences of the Malay and the Chinese communities during and after the war. These arguments have their place; and while it cannot be denied that upheavals of some kind would have occurred in its absence, the presence of the Malayan Communist Party—its membership, its experience, and its objectives—ensured that when it began, formally, in June 1948 it took on the shape of a Communist insurrection. It is to this party and its organisation that we turn first.

Communism
Communism in Malaya had a precarious existence before the Second World War. Institutionally, it suffered a series of disruptions at the hands of government while numerically it was so small that it stood in constant danger of being wiped out by vigorous police action. Racially, it was almost entirely Chinese.[1] Ideologically, it was subject to alternating phases of Chinese and Comintern influence; to Trotskyist or left-wing adventurist deviationism; and the rigid formalism which sought a proletarian oasis in the ideological desert of Asian peasantry.[2]

Communism as a self-conscious political ideology can be said to have arrived in Asia with the second congress of the Communist International, held in July and August 1920. In February 1922 the first Congress of the Toilers of the Far East was held in Petrograd and was attended by representatives from South, East and South-East Asia—including Indo-China and the Philippines —but both in representation as well as in the stirring manifesto to the Toilers of the East in which the various colonial possessions were enumerated, Malaya, at least in that respect, was conspicuously absent.

[1] Non-Chinese membership of the Party and its ancillary bodies never exceeded 10 per cent.
[2] See J. H. Brimmell *Communism in South East Asia*, London, 1959; and Charles B. McLane *Soviet Strategies in Southeast Asia*, Princeton, 1966.

Well before any practical interest was shown by the Comintern or the Soviet Union in Malaya, the China Communist Party had already begun its activities. Even before the death of Dr Sun Yat-Sen in 1925 Malayan communism, like Chinese communism, had been nurtured within the ranks of the *Kuomintang*. After his death, Singapore was the focus of both Malayan and Indonesian communism and the South Seas branch of the China Communist Party was formed there in 1925. Its political organisation was disrupted by a series of police raids but the Nanyang General Labour Union, founded in May 1926, and communist in origin, did not suffer the same disasters as the political apparatus and, both in Singapore and later in the Federation, was by far the more resilient of the two if only on account of its numbers. By 1928 the Nanyang Communist Party was virtually in abeyance: with no money, no spirit and nearly all the original members of its Provisional Committee gone. In April 1930 it was decided, in place of the general South Seas organisation, to create a specifically Malayan Communist Party and a Malayan General Labour Union. Both of them now came under the direct control of the Pan Pacific Trade Union Secretariat in Shanghai, which was itself the control organ of the Comintern's Far Eastern Bureau, and a member of the French Communist Party arrived in Singapore to help with reorganisation. After his arrest—and the subsequent arrest of Ho Chi Minh in Hong Kong—practically the whole of the Comintern's Far Eastern Bureau was destroyed; and while this marked the beginning of the lean years for the Malayan Communist Party—arrests, purges and internal dissensions—it meant that they were more active and eventually more successful in their search for viable local causes.

These were to be found in two sources; first, the world economic depression; second, the cause of Chinese nationalism in its anti-Japanese form. In the labour disturbances of 1936 and 1937 the MCP was able to exploit genuine grievances, to set up strike committees, to organise sympathy strikes, large demonstrations and even the elements of an insurrection in the Malayan collieries at Batu Arang, Selangor.[3] Although, as a result of these disturbances, there was a marked reluctance on the part of non-Communist workers to come into conflict with authority or to join the various unlawful labour unions which were being rigorously prosecuted by the police, they were nevertheless ready

[3] See also J. N. Parmer, Chinese Estate Workers Strikes in Malaya in March 1937 in C. D. Cowan (ed.) *The Economic Development of South-East Asia*, London, 1964.

PROLOGUE

to show their political feelings by joining anti-Japanese associations and were enrolled in what were supposed to be 'vocational' Anti-Japanese National Salvation Associations. These had their origins in a parent organisation controlled by the CCP in China; and the nominal reconciliation of the CCP and the KMT in the face of the Japanese invasion in 1937 helped to re-establish the MCP's claim to the allegiance of Malayan Chinese and the direction of the Malayan branch of the Anti-Japanese Association was again in the hands of the communist party.

With the outbreak of war in Europe in 1939 the MCP brought itself into line with international communist policy which changed after the German invasion of Russia in 1941. This, however, as might have been expected, was a tactical move rather than a long-range policy and the Party's principal objective remained: the expulsion of the British from Malaya and the institution of the dictatorship of the proletariat.

Resistance

When the Japanese invaded Malaya in December 1941 the MCP were, for the moment, in an unusually strong position. Their offer of assistance to government was now accepted and ten days after the invasion began the MCP agreed to provide as many Chinese communists as could be accepted at the 101 Special Training School organised by the late Lieutenant-Colonel Spencer-Chapman; and agreed further that, after training, they could be used against the Japanese in any way that was thought fit.[4] In the event, it was possible only to organise sporadic acts of sabotage as the British armies retreated and to send up four 'stay-behind' parties in the closing stages of the war; and in the case of the first three groups contact was then made with the local MCP organ-

---

[4] Spencer-Chapman has provided the classic account of personal resistance in Malaya: *The Jungle is Neutral*, London, 1957. For other limited but first-hand accounts see *No Dram of Mercy*, by the late Sybil Kathigasu, GM, who with her husband treated wounded guerillas and resisted Japanese torture, London, 1954. *Pai-Naa*, the story of Nona Baker, MBE—probably the only Englishwoman to be a card-carrying member of the MPAJA Old Comrades' Association. By Dorothy Thatcher and Robert Cross, London, 1959. *Singa: the Lion of Malaya*, by the late Gurchan Singh, who organised a clandestine news-service in Occupied Malaya, Kuala Lumpur, n.d. D. Holman, *Green Torture*, London, 1962.

See also two books by Chin Kee Onn: *Malaya Upside Down*, Singapore, 1946; and *Ma-Rai-Ee*, London, 1952. Mr Chan Chulia of Ipoh was kind enough to show me an unpublished manuscript based on personal experiences, *Behind the Guerrilla Front*.

isation and recruiting was organised by them. From the original groups of between thirty and sixty men (the total number of graduates from the 101 School was approximately two hundred) numbers increased five-fold and more, but from the very beginning theirs was a touch and go existence. It has been argued, somewhat unconvincingly, that a third of the entire guerrilla force was lost in the first eighteen months of the Japanese occupation;[5] but whether or not this is so the political leadership of the MCP certainly suffered a series of disasters in 1942.

By the middle of that year the whole of the Central Committee of the Singapore Communist Party had been wiped out by the Japanese and the Central Committee members from other states were arrested by the Japanese as they arrived in Singapore. On September 1st 1942 a meeting had been arranged between top MCP and MPAJA leaders throughout Malaya and was to take place in a small Chinese squatter settlement by the side of the Batu caves, a famous limestone outcrop a few miles from Kuala Lumpur. Loi Tak, the Secretary-General of the Party, who had called the meeting, was known to be in Kuala Lumpur and although his failure to arrive on the eve of the meeting, when most of the work on finalising the resolutions was to have been done, occasioned some surprise, the forty-odd guerrillas and Party leaders were hardly prepared for the attack that was launched on them at dawn the following day. The Japanese had, in fact, surrounded the area with several battalions of troops and, in spite of some heroic resistance—there were many subsequent accounts given of a girl with a tommy gun who fought the Japanese to the end—only a small but unknown number had escaped. Eighteen were killed, including four political commissars of the First, Third, Fourth and Fifth Regiments, and the three Regional Committee members : most of them, it is said, members of the 'Old Guard' of the Party. Others were captured and by April 1943 none of the Central Committee members who were elected into office during the sixth and seventh Expanded Conferences of 'Central' were left apart from Loi Tak.

It says much for the resilience of the MCP that it was able to survive these disasters and to continue as the directing force behind the bulk of the resistance groups. The numbers in communist-led 'patrols' or camps at least until the closing months of the war were probably between two and a half and three thousand but of these, it was estimated by the first Force 136

[5] Gene Z. Hanrahan, *The Communist Struggle in Malaya*, Institute of Pacific Relations, New York, 1954.

liaison officers, probably no more than four or five in any particular camp were members of the MCP. Nevertheless, within the jungle camps, the very long periods of inactivity gave the MCP its greatest opportunity of providing an ideology that was fashionable, exciting and not altogether unrealistic. The resistance, in fact, acted as a political hot-house for Malayan communism and where, operationally, it was of immanent rather than immediate importance, politically, the MCP was thinking of itself as at least an element in the government, at one stage removed, of Malaya. In February 1943 for example, the MCP issued its nine-point '*Anti-Japanese Programme*' : its first policy declaration since that of 1940 which was aimed at the expulsion of British imperialism. Its first objective was to drive the Japanese fascists out of Malaya and establish the Malayan Republic; and while, presumably after the war, it looked forward to co-operation with Russia and China in supporting independence struggles in the Far East, it was an open question whether or not its post-war existence would be in concert with or in opposition to the colonial regime.

This was one of the political factors which had, perhaps of necessity, to be overlooked by both sides when at last sufficient contact had been made between Force 136—the South-East Asian division of the Special Operations Executive—and the leadership of the MCP. On the evidence that has been seen the actual agreements entered into between the Force 136 members, acting as representatives for Admiral Mountbatten, and the MPAJA/MCP were entirely straightforward. No political promises were made on either side but the MCP agreed to follow the instructions of the Allied Commander-in-Chief insofar as military operations in Malaya were concerned; and this co-operation would continue so long as the military authorities were responsible for peace and good order in Malaya. In return, according to the eye-witness account, the SEAC representatives agreed to supply arms, finance, training and medical treatment.[6]

It is sometimes assumed that as a result of this agreement large-scale co-operation began between Force 136 and the MPAJA. This is not, in fact, so, although, in the first instance, it was due to the limited range of aircraft flying from India and Ceylon and the difficulties of effecting submarine rendezvous points. It was only in the concluding months of the war, as a new mark of Liberator was introduced and the dropping zones of Force 136

[6] See also F. S. V. Donnison *British Military Administration in the Far East, 1943–46*, London, 1956, pp. 380–1.

moved southwards down the peninsula, that comparatively large numbers of British liaison officers, radio operators and Gurkha support groups began to arrive. Although Victor Purcell puts their number at three hundred, only eighty-eight British officers in fact arrived by air, practically all of them between May and August 1945, and it must be remembered that for more than three years the MPAJA were fighting practically on their own. One of the consequences was a profound lack of intelligence, both political and military, that found its way back to Allied Headquarters; and the fact that most of the MPAJA patrols had no Allied liaison officers or support enhanced their opinion that they were fighting single-handed.[7]

Many features of the Emergency were prefigured in the resistance to Japanese occupation. First, there was the mixed composition of the MPAJA. A hard core of MCP; those who were fighting for a republic; and those who were fighting the occupying forces. To this must be added an element of banditry, whether in the irregular forces who professed any allegiance to the KMT or in the MPAJA itself, and a belated but rapid development of armed Malay units. Second, the support of the Anti-Japanese Union, or, in its later form, the *Min Yuen*, which was essential to the maintenance of the armed guerrilla camps; and the possibilities of this support which were inherent in the enormously augmented squatter population : those who had been driven by the rigours of the occupation to the jungle edge in order to grow food and subsist. Third, hatred, and later, as their power evaporated, the contempt that was felt for the mixed forces of the police. Fourth, the cultivation of friendly contacts with

[7] Similarities with the Yugoslav resistance suggest themselves; but where, in Yugoslavia, the decision to support the Partisans may have been critical, in Malaya, Mountbatten's proposal on August 4th 1945 to the Chiefs of Staff that he should be released from any obligations to the *Kuomintang* had no immediate effect. The closest support between Force 136 and Malayan resistance groups was established in upper Perak with the Malay Resistance Group known as *Ashkar Melayu Setia* (Loyal Malay Army) in December 1944. Subsequent contact was also made with another Malay resistance group in Pahang, *Wataniah*, where through the tireless efforts of Yeop Mahidin and under the nominal command of the Sultan of Pahang himself, they were expected by September 1945 to reach a strength of seven hundred. Separate *Kuomintang* Chinese resistance forces were also to be found in upper Perak, again with British liaison officers, and before the Japanese occupation had ended the ideological clash between them and the MCP had reached the level of open warfare and it is almost certain, although again hard to substantiate, that the greater part of whatever fighting the MPAJA did was with the KMT resistance rather than with the Japanese.

aborigines; and a strictly 'correct' attitude that was taken towards them. Fifth, a mixed relationship—or at least a mixed opinion of the relationship—with the civil population. On the one hand, Chinese guerrillas could count on racial and patriotic support and the relationship was close enough for Chinese in remote settlements to bring their legal and domestic problems to the guerrillas for settlement. On the other hand, where necessary, the guerrillas did not stop short of extortion, intimidation and terrorism : activities which increased as Japanese power declined and British Government was still a long way off. Lastly, the limited experience of the MPAJA in conducting guerrilla warfare but the almost unlimited possibilities that were open to them to maintain or refurbish their activities should they decide to do so.

The Politics of Violence
When the war ended the MCP found itself for the first time, and *de facto*, a legal organisation. Most of its prestige, however, was the after-glow from the resistance; and its political efforts were, in their way, as dispersed as they had been before the war. Apart from the MPAJA Ex-Comrades Association, which was a useful continuing organisation, they managed to penetrate the only non-communal party, the Malayan Democratic Union, to the point where two of its communist and most active committee members had brought its policy into line with that of the MCP;[8] and the Malayan Nationalist Party, it was believed by the Malayan Security Services, had been formed in part at the suggestion of the MCP, who supported it financially and dominated the organisation in at least one state.

The premise of organised political activity in post-war Malaya was, of course, independence : when, for whom, and on what terms. On the first point the proposals for Malayan Union were

[8] Recent correspondence on the relationship between the MCP and the MDU derives from an article by Yeo Kim Wah, 'A Study of Three Early Political Parties in Singapore, 1945–1955'. *Journal of Southeast Asian History*, Vol. 10, No. 1, March 1969. See letter from Gerald de Cruz, *Journal of Southeast Asian Studies*, Vol. 1, March 1970, pp. 123–5, and a reply from Yeo Kim Wah, *JSEAS*, Vol. 1, No. 2, September 1970, pp. 150–55. One is reminded of the apparent non-communist and anonymous companion of André Malraux in 1944 who said, 'I must tell you that at the national level the Resistance movements have been infiltrated through and through by the Communist Party ... of which I have been a member for seventeen years'. *Anti Memoirs*, Bantam, New York, 1970, p. 95. See also Gordon P. Means' *Malaysian Politics*, London, 1971, ch. 7, 'The Radical Nationalists, 1945–48'.

indefinite.[9] But on the second and third they envisaged an improvement in Chinese status which, ironically, created, instead of Chinese support, overwhelming Malay opposition that crystallised in the formation and dominance of UMNO as the Malay political party.[10] Many of the established leaders of the Malayan Chinese community spent the war years outside Malaya and had to start again from scratch; and to the extent that Malayan Chinese politics was an extension of the politics of mainland China, a conflict was in train between communist and KMT supporters. Both, it must be remembered, were capable of violent anti-imperialism but in the post-war years the violence was seen in an internecine contest, particularly between the rival youth groups: the *San Min Chu Yi* on the one hand and the New Democratic Youth League on the other. Both were competing for the allegiance of the Malayan Chinese, the majority of whom were now found to have been born in Malaya, but neither offered much in the way of a distinctively Malayan programme although it can be argued that to a large extent the colonial format precluded such programmes or parties.

In any event it is seldom remembered to what an extent Malaya seemed a prey to endemic disorders; and a good case can be made out to support the argument that government was never properly re-established after the war. Nor was this limited to the months immediately following the Japanese surrender, when the MCP paid off its scores with collaborators and political enemies, when the dismal catalogue of Sino-Malay massacres began, invulnerability cults revived and fears were raised of a holy war. The presence of numerous bodies of uniformed men and the keynote of violence in so many political speeches both created and reflected the conditions in which numerous acts of violence occurred. As late as 1948, for example, one finds on January 16th a report that six Chinese and two Indonesians had been arrested in what the *Straits Times* called the notorious Scudai/Pontian area of Johore. They had been carrying two Lewis guns, five hundred rounds of ammunition and two hundred and fifty thousand dollars in Indonesian banknotes, probably forged. On April 10th it reported that an Assistant Superintendent

[9] An account of *The Malayan Union* is given by James de V. Allen. Yale Southeast Asian Studies Monograph Series, No. 10, 1967. It is challenged by M. R. Stenson 'The Malayan Union and the Historians', *Journal of Southeast Asian History*, Vol 10, No. 2, September 1969.

[10] Gerald Hawkins 'Marking Time in Malaya', *International Affairs*, January 1948.

of Police had been killed in a raid against bandits near Grik. Three days later there were eighteen arrests in Perak, including three key men, and a great deal of political information is said to have been revealed. On May 10th, anti-bandit operations were continuing in North Perak. On the 28th, an abandoned camp for forty was destroyed north of Baling and a dozen hand grenades were recovered.

These acts, violent though they were, were an improvement on the situation in 1947. To take some examples from that year: in February forty Chinese bandits raided Klian Intan, shot a customs officer and Chinese villager and then pillaged the whole village itself. In March, two hundred and thirty illicit weapons and ten thousand rounds of ammunition were recovered from a dump nine miles from Kuala Lumpur. In May, bandits threatened to decimate Klian Intan unless the village paid a ransom of thirty thousand dollars. A week later, the Kuala Lumpur–Penang night mail was derailed. Eight people were killed. In June, police and twenty bandits were engaged in an hour-long shooting battle near Grik. The following day police discovered another large arms dump in Johore. In September, three police and six civilians were killed and fourteen wounded when bandits ambushed two buses and an escorting lorry-load of policemen, again near Klian Intan. There was a slight variation later in the month when bandits in Japanese uniform terrorised an estate near Rengam in Johore. In October, a European planter was killed and his wife injured by bandits, again in central Johore.

Over much of Malaya it follows that not only was government unable to maintain law and order but it was, in fact, sharing power and in some areas was certainly no more than first among equals. In particular its problems centred on the police force which had practically disintegrated in Malaya at the end of the war and after initial and almost crippling disabilities, not least being the loss of its agents and its criminal records, was only slowly and painfully being rebuilt. It was, therefore, barely equipped to deal with the politics of violence at a time when Malaya was suffering the delayed effects of war. The upheavals that would have followed British defeat and expulsion had been largely suppressed in the time of the Japanese occupation. Now that they were under way, political movements were largely communal, and the only one that was not lacked, for this reason, any solid basis of support. In all of this the MCP may be seen as the principal beneficiary: more particularly when it could claim to have organised a syndicalist alternative to government in the economic and political power of its General Labour Unions and Federations.

Unions or Soviets?
The labour situation in pre-war Malaya was distinguished by its comparative tranquility. One reason for this, apart from the fact that the Malay peasantry, the most insular element in the labour force was largely unaffected by political movements derived from economic conditions, was that capitalist enterprise in Malaya depended almost entirely on contract labour. Rubber estates, tin mines and construction work were all served by a flow of immigrant labour which was subject to the simple controls of the tap and the plug. In spite of certain requirements of the Indian Government and fluctuating attitudes of the Chinese authorities and political parties there was, as far as Malaya was concerned, an almost inexhaustible supply of labour from India and China. More important than this, however, was the contract system on which this supply was based, which made it possible in time of depression to repatriate redundant workers. Thus, in spite of residual unemployment, deliberate under-employment and the feeling of many employers that a pool of unemployment should be created, the greater part of the unemployed immigrant labour pool was drained off when times were bad rather than be allowed to remain and stagnate.

As far as employers were concerned this was a fortunate hydraulic system but it was also largely fortuitous. The war, of course, made it impossible for this system to work and perhaps the most fundamental social and economic change to be found in post-war Malaya was the relative immobility of a large part of its labour force. The position of labour was enhanced by the needs of economic recovery, as well as world demand for rubber and tin, and there was, in the poverty, inflation and near famine of post-war Malaya, as well as in the organisation and direction of largely unorganised labour, one of the greatest of the MCP's opportunities to influence government and perhaps to change the course of Malayan history.

By October 1945 the MCP had created, as a matter of high priority and without legal restraint, the General Labour Union in Singapore; and similar organisations were eventually set up in all the states of Malaya as well. In this bid to replace the pre-war pattern of triad, guild and union with its own network of all-purpose associations the MCP was very largely successful and it was also to succeed in harnessing the forces of Indian radicalism in many parts of the country. The formation of individual communist unions in many of the smaller towns often involved little more than nailing up a board which proclaimed the union's existence; and as premises were generally shared with the MCP or the local branch of the Anti-Japanese Army Ex-Comrades' Association, there was, at least physically, no doubt about the closeness between the two. As Stenson puts it, 'The original organisers of the various branch General Labour Unions and later of the state and Pan-Malayan organisations were invariably MCP appointed officials who were able to perpetuate their own oligarchy';[11] and his comment on the Pan-Malayan General Labour Union is that it 'remained an essentially vanguard organisation, directed by the highly disciplined MCP members who had founded it'.[12]

In Singapore, the organisers of the General Labour Union, once established, spent most of their time in securing the political underpinnings for their activities and over the country as a whole there were manifest expectations, certainly on their part, that the General Labour Unions were a force to be reckoned with in Malayan politics. The first demonstration of their power was seen in the organisation of the Singapore general strike of January 29th–30th 1946, and the occasion was to demand the release of a former general secretary of the Malayan People's Anti-Japanese Union in Selangor who, after three trials, had been convicted of extortion from a former Japanese callaborator a month after the war had ended.[13]

The strike affected 150,000 workers and although violence itself was comparatively rare the threat was freely used by some 3,500 organised intimidators provided by the General Labour Union propaganda section. A fortnight later, on the anniversary of the fall of Singapore, a rally was organised to 'observe' a day of national humiliation and in a clash with police, who fired eighteen rounds, two Chinese were killed and several wounded: among them the MCP's open representative in Singapore.

Victor Purcell, himself a witness to these events, reckoned that they had been a trial of strength and that the issue had been simply whether the country should be ruled by the British Military Administration or by a small group of extortioners and intimidators.[14] For the moment the issue might seem to have

[11] M. R. Stenson *Industrial Conflict in Malaya*, London, 1970, p. 102.
[12] Stenson, *op cit*, p. 101.
[13] For details, see F. S. V. Donnison, *op. cit*, pp. 389–91.
[14] Purcell, *The Chinese in Malaya*, London, 1948, p. 275.

B

been settled but the strength of the General Labour Unions was largely untouched and their methods unchanged. In a letter to the Assistant General Secretary of the TUC in London in July 1946, the then Trade Union Adviser for both Singapore and the Malayan Union left no doubt that the General Labour Union was not only controlled by the Communist Party but was completely undemocratic both as to constitution and organisation.

> It is difficult to give you a clear picture of the situation as it exists at the moment. The real tragedy is of course the ruthless intimidation and pressure that is brought to bear on some of the small potential Trade Unions who are just growing up, whereby, the GLU insists that some of their nominees should be on the Trade Union Committee, that they must either pay heavy application fees to the GLU or let the GLU run the organisation. Their tactics are subversive in the sense that men are forced to come out on strike on direct instructions from the particular State General Labour Union and the picketing is generally carried out by young Indians, late members of the Indian National Army, and Chinese, members of the ex-guerrilla forces.

Overall government policy after the war was to encourage the growth of what were called 'moderate' and 'responsible' trade unions. The existing framework and the ultimate authority of colonial government were assumed; and while it appeared that there was no objection to unions having political purposes *per se*, nor to political contributions, Kuala Lumpur had taken its cue from London on the possibility of criminal conspiracy,

> If, after the first stage (of the strike), looking at the *actions* and *intentions* of any particular body of men involved—the leaders perhaps, or any other men taking an active part in it—you find, again as a question of fact, that the object is to overthrow the government, to coerce the government, and to obtain a new change in the law by unconstitutional means, then I think that an indictment lies against those men for criminal conspiracy.[15]

and, to this end, were concerned to reduce the political power and purpose of the General Labour Unions and Federations of Trade Unions; to transform them, if possible, into unions resembling those in the United Kingdom; and, if not, to render them illegal. The prospects of transformation were not good: as may be seen in this widely quoted excerpt from the Awbery-Dalley report by

[15] The Attorney-General, Sir Hartley Shawcross, in the debate on the Trades Disputes Act in 1946. *H. C. Deb.*, Vol. 419, col. 80–92.

two visiting British trade unionists, one of them a Labour MP, who condemned the Federations of Trade Unions in the first place for having, by origins and in object, no useful trade union function.

> They call strikes but pay no strike pay or similar benefits; frame demands but carry out no negotiations, preferring to remain in the background and to act as the 'power behind the throne' by pushing forward union leaders who may interfere with and often intimidate. They claim to give unions advice and help, but in practice they leave the officers of affiliated unions to do the negotiations and then prevent settlements being made when, as is usually the case, they disagree with the provisional agreement arrived at. The genuine union authority and the members themselves are disregarded throughout these skirmishings.[16]

What was unfamiliar to Awbery and Dalley and, they thought to many of their readers, was the manner, extent and success of intimidation and how successful violence and the threat of violence had been; but it was, by these methods, that the rubber estates and many of the tin mines of Malaya offered the best prospect of a rural Communist revolution. It would not be peasant Communism in that the workers concerned were part of the non-attached 'hydraulic' labour force of Indians and Chinese rather than indigenous Malay peasantry. Its revolutionary fervour and organisation might not match that of Singapore or even Penang, but, by virtue of their isolation and their spread over the length of the country they reduced the power of government, soldiers and police to a problem of manageable dimensions.

For months the poverty of post-war Malaya had cried out for political capitalisation and even when the situation began to improve there were always the possibilities to be exploited of capitalist contradictions. If it is argued that Malaya was prey to endemic disorders after the war, there is no reason why labour should be considered immune. In many ways the possibilities of coercion, intimidation and violence were greater here than elsewhere but the fact that any of them occurred or that disputes flared up into violent clashes between labourers and police cannot of themselves be taken as evidence of constant communist intervention. In many cases strikes originated as genuine industrial disputes even though many of them were a matter for subsequent political capitalisation by the MCP, while it would be absurd to

[16] *Labour and Trade Union Organisation in the Federation of Singapore.* HMSO, Colonial, No. 224, London, 1948.

ignore wages and prices. There is also more than a suggestion at this time of bloody-minded or incompetent employers, some evidence of 'capitalist contradictions' and, together with an often exaggerated sense of independence, an approach to self-governing estates. Ofter this was a result of intransigence on both sides. In Malacca, for example, and particularly in the Machap area which was regarded as a stronghold of communism, some Chinese employers evidently welcomed the prospect of a violent showdown with their labour force but on the other side labourers flatly refused to become redundant. On one estate notice had been given several months running but had not been taken as labourers had refused to go. Absentee landlords were part of the problem but dereliction of duty on the part of the management, from which even large European companies were not exempt, gave more immediate point to the question that was being asked on some estates—'Are managers necessary?'

By August 1947 estate managers in the Malacca area were complaining that their estates were now controlled by the labourers and that unless government took strong action labour would soon control the whole country. This was not for the moment an argument that was accepted by government who, at this stage, was still able to particularise items of violence on estates and to hold detailed inquiries. Nevertheless, the violent incidents and incipient riots were increasing, many of them concerned with the lingering influence of the Indian National Army that had fought with the Japanese and had been raised and based in Malaya and Singapore, and in particular the challenge of the *Thondar Padai*, a sort of ragged militia that drilled with sticks and clubs and which often functioned as a militant temperance society. Thus, speaking of a strike on a Malacca estate in April 1948, the Assistant Commissioner of Labour described it as a battle to decide whether the Indian National Army or the management controlled the estate; and there were many more instances featuring *Thondar Padai* in both Malacca and Johore.

Conditions in 1947 were probably nowhere near as anarchical as some estate owners made out but in 1948 the volume of industrial unrest grew steadily, first, through what might be described as natural causes—low wages in the planting industry—and then combined in the second quarters with other factors to produce a crescendo of strikes. More important, it became increasingly clear that the pattern and form of violence was changing and in particular, that it was more widespread and that it did not now stop short of murder. Disputes now developed through a series of

PROLOGUE 33

affray, strike and lockout: a pattern that was increasingly common and one which stretched the limited police force to the utmost. Whether all this approximated to the creation of rural soviets remains an open question. Probably not: and certainly not as part of a comprehensive plan. Nevertheless, it was one of the reasons, if not the principal reason, which led government to tighten up its union regulations and thus to intensify the open challenge to its authority. The MCP, for its part, was unlikely to evacuate its position of strength in the unions and its union-controlled labour and in any case by this time had taken its major political decision. The struggle was now to be concentrated in the masses: a decision which was ideologically correct but which was to transform them into a battleground rather than an army.[17]

[17] The two principal works on the post-war labour situation in Malaya, Charles Gamba, *The Origins of Trade Unionism in Malaya*, Singapore, 1962, and M. R. Stenson, *Industrial Conflict in Malaya*, London, 1970, are both sympathetic to the idea that it resulted in a self-igniting revolution. Gamba implies that it was the result of the repression of a legitimate labour movement. So, perhaps does D. J. Blake in his review of Gamba (*Malayan Economic Review*, October 1963, pp. 91–103) who regards the strike primarily as an organisational technique. Stenson appears to proceed from the *a priori* assumption that, after the Japanese surrender, 'the time was surely ripe for an MCP-led war of national resistance' (*Repression and Revolt*, Papers in International Studies, South-East Asian Series, No. 10, Ohio University, 1969, p. 1); suggests that 'the MCP had begun to appreciate the pointlessness of peaceful constitutional agitation' (*Industrial Conflict in Malaya*, p. 178); and regards the conflict as that 'between one form of authoritarianism and another' (*Industrial Conflict in Malaya*, p. 233). For the context of communism in Malaya and Singapore, see J. M. Van Der Kroef, *Communism in Malaysia and Singapore: a Contemporary Survey*. The Hague, 1967.

2
TOWARDS A REVOLUTIONARY SITUATION

Perhaps the greatest anticlimax in the Second World War was the way in which the war against Japan ended. Two atomic bombs and a massive bombardment of Japanese home islands, notwithstanding, throughout the whole of South-east Asia—Burma and the Philippines excepted—Japanese forces stood, apparently intact, at the time of the Imperial rescript ordering surrender. For most of South-east Asia memories of the war itself were the visible defeat of the European nations at the hands of an Asian power; and nowhere was this memory more vivid, or the sense of anticlimax greater, than in Malaya.

The fall of Singapore in 1942 was the greatest single defeat ever sustained by Britain in the history of her empire. As far as Malaya was concerned it was one in a series of defeats that had begun within a few days of the Japanese landings and which had, at times, turned the retreat down the peninsula into little more than a rout. This, together with the loss of two capital ships and the destruction of the RAF, was a comprehensive defeat viewed from any angle and one that was unmitigated by the superiority in numbers of the British forces. When British troops did return to Malaya, after an absence of three and a half years, it was in a series of unopposed landings on the west coast which, from all accounts, would have been a shambles had the Japanese not surrendered already, and which did nothing to restore the prestige of the colonial power.

For the Malayan Communist Party, immediate policy was determined by the fact that it did not oppose the resumption of colonial government. The idea that it should do so had in fact been canvassed in the closing stages of the war amongst sections of the Anti-Japanese Army; and in Johore, in particular, suggestions had been made that all the Force 136 officers who were attached to AJA guerrilla units should be killed and that the forces of reoccupation should be presented with a takeover of power as a *fait accompli*. As it was, in many parts of Malaya, and not only the remoter ones, the local and in particular the Chinese population professed to treat the Anti-Japanese Army as their liberators. Triumphal arches were erected to the particular regiments and in many places it was anticipated that the reoccupation forces would be from the Chinese army. In the remoter parts of Malaya—Pahang, for example, and parts of Perak—it is important to remember how little impact the allied victory had made. A former AJA guerrilla and later Secretary of the Town Committee of the MCP in Singapore mentioned that the only troops he saw on the reoccupation were Indian, of whom he did not have a particularly high opinion, and that no British forces had been in evidence. This argument did not of course apply to Penang or Singapore, both of which were soon crowded with allied warships, including battleships and aircraft carriers, but outside the main population centres it was probably true to say that amongst the guerrillas at any rate there was a sense of enormous possibilities.

A hundred and thirty years earlier, a series of battles in eastern Germany following an equally disastrous retreat, had shaken the hold of Napoleon in Europe. In a somewhat romantic expression, the Battle of the Nations at Leipzig marked a stage in the destruction of the Napoleonic empire; from it dated the sense of national possibilities which was ultimately to replace the 'geographical expression' of conservative statesmen in Europe. In a sense, the series of Japanese triumphs that followed from Pearl Harbour represented the Battle of the Nations in Asia. It was, to be sure, a vicarious battle as far as most of the peoples of Southeast Asia were concerned. What mattered most in the long run, however, was the challenge to European omnipotence and the destruction of colonial regimes which, though they may have involved the possibilities of modification, seemed destined to last for ever.

After the fall of Singapore things could never be the same again if only because the myth of European invincibility had been shattered. Having decided, however, to acquiesce in the resumption of colonial power—and it seems likely that the sudden end to the war took the MCP as much by surprise as it did SEAC— the MCP was now committed, at least for the moment, in the abeyance of pre-war legislation, to a new role as a more or less constitutional party. The definitive act took place in December 1945 when the MPAJA laid down the greater part of its arms. In fact, a greater number of arms was surrendered than had been supplied by allied forces during the war but a detailed analysis reveals interesting discrepancies. For example, while there was a surplus of almost 700 rifles and over 1,000 shotguns, representing weapons which the guerrillas had acquired for themselves, there were deficits varying from 300 to over 400 in each of the categories for stens, carbines and pistols.[1] When the remainder of its weapons were buried in secret arms dumps this was an almost symbolic act. For the time being and on the political level the MCP was prepared to function in a more or less constitutional role and for almost three years it existed as a quasi-legal party. Whether more or less depended upon its degree of success, the temper of its members, and the formulation of ideologically correct objectives. In any event its successes in the field of trade unions tended to obscure the need for a constitutional role although, as they developed, their political function was obvious. For the former members of the Anti-Japanese Army—veterans as well as the 'coffee shop revolutionaries' who jumped on the band-wagon in the closing months of the war—the Ex-Comrades' Association served to maintain their interests, but, from the start, had an equally obvious political complexion. For some ex-guerrillas it was difficult, by this fact alone, to obtain employment but if this was, in some cases, an insult to genuine ex-servicemen it should also be remembered how much time and effort was made by a sort of continuing organisation of Force 136 officers to find employment for its Malayan members. In this it was seldom helped by the Ex-Comrades' Association. There were many instances when the Association made it difficult and even impossible for its members to accept employment and out of the $350 gratuity that was paid to demobilised guerrillas the guerrillas themselves would sometimes be left with only a fraction of this amount.[2]

One of the deductions that was made by the Ex-Comrades' Association was for payment to guerrillas who were unknown either to Force 136 or to the post-war British administration.[3] Together with their arms dumps and the possibility of remobilising the anti-Japanese guerrillas they offered an alternative form of

---

[1] All bren guns, 102, that were supplied by Force 136 were recovered. These were unpopular on account of their weight but were probably the most effective single weapon in jungle fighting.

[2] There is an interesting and apparently quite widely held belief among Malayan Chinese that it was this derisory amount—some £45—that government offered which provided the starting point for the guerrillas' discontent.

[3] In Malayan intelligence sources, in particular the Basic Paper on the MCP, these guerrillas are referred to as 'the secret army'. Whether they were any more secret than by virtue of the fact that they were unknown remains doubtful.

power but for the moment, and perhaps even 'objectively', one may consider the prospects for the Malayan communists as a political party.

In the first place their programme and promises catered for the backlog of political demands. If independence was the unspoken premise of all post-war political activity in Malaya, and could later be inferred from the liquidation of the Indian Empire, nevertheless the British Government was remarkably modest in its proposals for Malayan independence. The Malayan Union proposals of January 1946 mention 'that political adjustment which will offer, through broad based institutions in which the whole community can participate, the means and prospect of developing Malaya's capacity in the direction of responsible self-government'. Even under the Federation Agreement of 1948 the election of members to the several legislatures—'as soon as circumstances and local conditions will permit'—was only part of a progress towards eventual self-government.

In the meantime the MCP could claim that it was the patriotic party: insofar as it had fought against the Japanese. That it was the democratic party: insofar as it had fought against Japanese 'fascism' and had been supported by the allies. It could also argue that it was the only party that catered for or was in touch with the Chinese masses; and if residual Malayan Chinese support for the *Kuomintang* belied this it could at least claim to represent a large part of the Malayan Chinese population: the part, that is to say, which neither wanted nor was allowed to offer allegiance to Malaya. It was also well equipped for politics which had more than an element of violence, although this is not to say that it had a monopoly of revolutionary potential in Malayan politics at the time.

Conversely, it may be argued that the MCP's political record after the war did not accord with the political possibilities (rather than objectives, which need only to be formulated, or aspirations, which should be articulate) of the masses of Malayan Chinese. Political status would have been a bonus for the Malayan Chinese but it was something that few of them were prepared to work for even if they had the time or the money. A pre-war and 'westernised' Chinese community leader such as Tan Cheng Lock might extol the virtues of *jus soli* but there was little evidence that the bulk of Malayan Chinese wanted to be treated in this way and, even if they did, whether they were amenable at this time to a political party whose only programme could be that of multi-racial partnership. While the primacy of the Malay political awakening is acknowledged and the leaderless state of the Chinese community conceded, the fact is not always recognised that the allegiance of Malayan Chinese was, at best, in a transitional stage. Until it was, demonstrably, to Malaya and not to China they had little hope of securing the status and rights of citizens. At least, that is, by a constitutional process which was itself of unknown length but this was not the only course open and for those who thought in more immediate terms the MCP offered the short cut of an equalitarian republic.

There were, broadly speaking, two ways in which this could be achieved. First, as a political party with a programme that transcended its appeal and limitations as an essentially Chinese party. There was some evidence of this in the activities of API/MNP but although both had a socialist content they were essentially Malay/Indonesian nationalist parties as far as their mass support was concerned, no matter what their origins and the undoubted support they received from the MCP. Similarly, the Malayan Democratic Union and the AMCJA were essentially 'liberal' parties, no matter how much they were infiltrated and influenced by the MCP, and were certainly not reliable Communist 'front' organisations. The MCP might, itself, have adapted to the practices of representative government but would have been a rare and somewhat ambivalent phenomenon in South-east Asia: a constitutional Communist party. In any case it could be argued that there was no representative government in Malaya: in which case, the MCP could revert to what was perhaps a more congenial role, namely, that of a party whose objective was to obtain power through revolution.

To take advantage of the political situation, however, which was not altogether unfavourable, the MCP needed the strength of its limitations. If one of the determinants of its policy was how firmly British power had been re-established in Malaya the second, and even more important, was the extent and effectiveness of its own power. Far more than the MCP acknowledged, save in one respect, the war had been a traumatic experience. For years afterwards, and even after the insurrection had begun, fresh discoveries were made of party members who had collaborated with the Japanese during the occupation and had betrayed the Party to a greater or lesser extent. The two outstanding instances of wartime betrayal had been of the Singapore Town Committee and the greater part of its organisation and the even more catastrophic disruption of the Batu Caves meeting in 1942. Betrayal had begun to be suspected but in September 1945 a denunciation of Loi Tak, the Secretary-General, as a traitor to the Party during the Occupation which appeared in a Penang newspaper was regarded as incredible: and was in any case written by a member of the MCP who was known to have been an agent of the Japanese Kempeitai during the Occupation in Singapore. Loi Tak's exploits during the war, when he regularly managed to drive out of Singapore in a Japanese car in order to make contact with guerrilla units in the Federation, had become a legend in the Party and in a campaign at the end of 1945 Loi Tak's role as supreme leader of the Party was made known publicly and he was hailed as the deliverer and preserver of the MCP. Nevertheless the ugly rumours that Loi Tak had betrayed the Party to the Japanese continued and gained in strength when they came to the attention of Yeong Kuo, a member of the Central Standing Committee from Selangor who had practically been banished to Penang by Loi Tak himself. After apparent consultation with other Central Committee members Loi Tak found himself relegated to the Political Bureau and debarred from the Organisation Committee which, under Yeong Kuo, became responsible for the actual organisation of the Party itself. By October 1946 Loi Tak was being criticised not only for his lack of ability as an orator but also, significantly, for his lack of knowledge of written Chinese characters.

Loi Tak, although he spoke the language, was not Chinese. An Annamite, he arrived in Singapore in the early 1930s with a dazzling reputation. He was a representative of the Third International: he had studied communism in Russia and France; had assisted the Vietnamese Communist Party in its early struggles; and had served on the Shanghai Town Committee of the China Communist Party. He also spoke French as well as English. His immediate success, for which an internal history of the MCP gives him credit, was to resolve the Party crisis of 1936 in an intensive six-month 'offensive against the opportunists' but it was not long after this that Special Branch managed to arrest and banish the whole of the Central Committee whereupon Loi Tak assumed the leadership of the Party.

This was a brilliant success: not only for Loi Tak but also for the Singapore Special Branch who had brought him to Singapore. Before embarking on this career Loi Tak was a French intelligence agent in Indo-China, had been 'blown' and was acquired by a Special Branch officer in the course of a visit to Saigon. After the fall of Singapore and capture by the Japanese Loi Tak became a Japanese agent and it was, as such, that he arranged for the liquidation of the senior Party members in Singapore and in the Batu Caves 'massacre'. During the Japanese occupation he was in the singular position of Secretary-General of the MCP; agent for the Japanese; and in contact with British officers of Force 136. Loi Tak was obviously cautious enough not to throw in his lot altogether with the Japanese for none of the original trio of Force 136 officers, whose elimination would have been of immense value to the Japanese, was betrayed and only one Force 136 officer was lost: apparently having delayed his departure after warnings that the Japanese were in the area.[4] After the war and the Japanese occupation, which he seemed miraculously to have survived, Loi Tak resumed his contacts with Special Branch in Singapore. One could hardly expect a formal record of all the subsequent transactions; but the ones that exist are curiously impalpable and remote: hardly what one would expect of a highly efficient and presumably ruthless double agent. It can only be assumed that the material facts transmitted were never committed to paper. Even so, the air of mystery in which he thrived, indeed that was essential for his survival, is hardly dispelled by the record of his dealings with Special Branch.[5] Nevertheless, and the degree of control notwithstanding, the installation of Loi Tak as Secretary-General of the MCP and the maintenance of contact with him ranks as one of the more notable successes of British intelligence although it may well have led to a certain complacency and the confusion of darkness when, as it were, the light at the top of the stairs went out.[6]

Criticism of Loi Tak within the MCP came to a head in early 1947. Accusations of dictatorship, an incompetent Central Com-

[4] How much information he had to 'feed' the Japanese, or possibly something more, is suggested by the enigmatic reference in the *Basic Paper* (p. 37) 'whether he would have been able to safeguard the allied landings on the beaches whose locations he had betrayed was never put to the test'.

[5] One suggestion, hardly surprising, is that he was of increasingly nervous disposition; and after one secret meeting in Singapore was frightened out of his wits when his contact, presumably to establish bona fide credentials, ordered the chauffeur to illuminate Loi Tak in the car headlights. It is hard to believe on the *prima facie* evidence alone that he was entirely reliable at any particular time. It is, incidentally, extremely difficult at this distance to establish even the year in which he arrived in Singapore. 1932 and 1934 seem to be the principal probabilities.

[6] It is of interest perhaps to note that two other Asian Communist leaders, Ho Chi Minh and P. C. Joshi, Secretary-General of the Communist Party of India, have also been accused of being enemy agents. In Tsarist Russia Stalin too seems to have had an ambivalent relationship with the Secret Police.

mittee that was afraid to criticise his bad leadership and right wing policies which were bringing the Party to ruin were heard at a meeting of 'Central' in February 1947; and after another meeting of 'Central' on February 28th it was agreed that the discussions should continue in a week's time when the whole question of criticism of members of 'Central' should be thrashed out and special attention given to the supervision and security of the Party's arms. Loi Tak had himself given instructions for the concentration of arms dumps; and that night three of them were discovered by the Selangor police. On March 6th, in an atmosphere of mounting tension, the Central Committee assembled as arranged, five miles outside Kuala Lumpur, but Loi Tak failed to appear and the MCP never saw him again.[7]

The Wright Case
The MCP reacted to the disappearance of Loi Tak with a mixture of fury, confusion and despair.[8] Owing, apparently, to a clerkly solecism in which Loi Tak was taken as the Chinese pronunciation of a European name 'Wright' this was one of the aliases which Loi Tak adopted and by which he was known in the Party. After his disappearance in March it took 'Central' until December 1947 'to complete their work of investigating, tracing and probing into his history, his way of life, his activities within the Party and his contacts with various quarters'. The result was the statement on the *Wright Case* that was generally released on May 28th 1948 and which was designed as much to meet the surge of criticism within the Party as it was to pronounce anathemas upon the former Secretary-General. The fact of Loi Tak's defection had been released slowly from the previous July when cadres of State level were told to February 1948 when the news was broken to District level cadres and State Party organs.

In its statement Loi Tak was described as an internal traitor and the greatest culprit in the history of the MCP. But from the opening paragraph 'Central' was concerned with the questions that had been asked since news of his defection became known.

[7] He remained in hiding in Singapore until the following August when he went to Hong Kong. From here he went to Siam and the MCP subsequently received a message that said the account had been settled. Apparently, a killer squad from China had followed his movements but it is not known for certain where he was killed. From time to time reports reached Malayan intelligence of Loi Tak manifestations: that he was again active in Siamese Communist circles.

[8] There is some evidence to suggest that the majority of 'Central' were in favour of an immediate resort to arms.

'How did he infiltrate into the Party and how did he build up his own position?' 'Why was it that despite our great trust in him during the anti-Japanese days, his background was still not disclosed in the early post-war period, and he was still re-elected Secretary at the eighth Central Enlarged Conference?' 'Why did he escape?' 'How did Central handle the case after his escape?' 'Why was his case disclosed so late?' 'What sort of a person was he after all?' 'Were his henchmen still in the Party after his escape?' 'Who should be responsible for his case?' 'How shall we prevent the recurrence of such a case in future?'

In answer to these questions and charges 'Central' threw all the blame on to Loi Tak. He was, they said, 'a one man Central'; 'an internal renegade and traitor' and one who was guilty of 'individual conspiracy with the enemy'. Specifically, he had surrendered to the enemy, betrayed the revolution and embezzled the Party funds, both during and after the Japanese occupation. His Comintern claims and alleged Chinese experience were exploded but, specifically, his treachery was only established in this document for the period of the anti-Japanese war. After the war, he was accused of making an essentially 'running dog' policy, treacherous to the cause of the revolution; but while it could be clearly seen that he had been collaborating with the Imperialists to sabotage the revolution, 'Central' admitted that there was, at the moment, no way to investigate his pre-war activities, 'yet it is estimated that the possibility of his having intrigued with the Imperialists was very great'.

Although Loi Tak was presented as the scapegoat and the architect of all the Party's misfortunes it is evident that, a year after his disappearance, 'Central' at any rate were still fighting a rearguard action. Although they absolved themselves from responsibility and indeed claimed credit for his exposure, it was obvious that Loi Tak's defection had potentially catastrophic effects upon the Party.

> It is very unfavourable to the Party that at present there are certain comrades who are inclined to be over-suspicious of the Party and so begin to mistrust one another. Just because Loi Tak was an internal traitor, they cast their suspicion, without facts that are substantiated, on other comrades as being internal traitors as well, and even talk about the existence within the Party of internal traitors. This is actually spreading an atmosphere of terror, merely increasing the mutual mistrust within the Party, shaking the revolutionary faith of comrades, and weakening the

directing influence of the Party, which may result in the ideological disintegration of the Party.

In part, at least, the reaction against Loi Tak was a reaction against 'Central' and in order to eliminate 'internal traitors' if not to 'chastise' Central, there were demands that 'comrades of the Party Central be taken to various States for scrutiny'. 'Central' itself reacted to the charges that there was lack of democracy within the Party with the charge that this was an attitude of extreme democracy which would never help strengthen the Party organisation.

Rather, it tends to weaken the Party leadership, relax the Party discipline, spoil the order of the Party and promote confusion within the Party, turning the Party into a weak, incompetent organisation until it collapses and dissolves.

The specific, in this case, was 'democratic centralism' : 'the alltime principle of the Party organisation', but this was no more than an organisational principle. Something more was obviously needed to restore the confidence of the 'comrades (who) think that our past work was done in vain, that we have to start everything all over again now that we revert to the position in 1938'.

In fact, by the time this Paper was issued the Party had already changed course and the Emergency was no more than three weeks away. The Loi Tak Paper had particularly criticised his 'running dog' line, his surrender to the enemy politically, and what was presumably his decision that the anti-Japanese army should be disbanded : something which the Standing Executive Committee of Central had opposed. The main problem arising out of the Loi Tak case, according to Central, 'was whether or not, after the incident had been discovered they were determined to liquidate it (especially its running dog line), to rectify their own mistakes and to push the Party forward with a spirit of loyalty to the proletarian cause'. At the same time it seems the problem had been solved.

Fellow comrades, we have already done so, and we should feel happy about it.

Calcutta: the uncertain trumpet
In the course of the Loi Tak investigations the newly-appointed Secretary-General of the MCP, Chin Peng, seems to have extended his inquiries, via Hong Kong, to the Chinese Communist Party and it is in these contacts with 'international Communism', or what one may think of as the main stream of Communism, that the origins of the Malayan insurrection have been sought.

This apparently was the second time personal contact had been established with the CCP in Hong Kong : but on neither occasion was there unqualified support for the launching of an armed struggle. The advice on the first occasion, as it was given to and reported by Loi Tak himself, may be somewhat suspect, although it is at least internally consistent. In conversations between Loi Tak and Leng Goan, representative of the South-China Bureau of the CCP and General Fong Feng of the CCP Central Committee, the latter, amongst other things, advised the MCP that they could expect no help from the CCP; that Malaya must depend upon the British Communist Party for any assistance; that a united front should be organised; that while the Labour Government was in power in Britain the MCP should work for self-government by constitutional means, always ensuring that the Chinese element dominated; and that, in short, the MCP should not embark upon an armed insurrection.

On the second occasion, sometime in 1947, Chin Peng is supposed to have made contact again with Fong Feng and Leow Cheng Chi and the result seems to have been a brief letter from Chou En Lai which Chin Peng brought back with him to Malaya. In it, Chou En Lai is said to have pointed out that the general conditions in semi-colonial countries were ideal for armed struggles; but he added that he was not fully conversant with conditions in Malaya and was therefore unable to say whether the time was ripe for the MCP to launch its armed struggle. That was something to be decided in the light of prevailing conditions.[9]

There were other, more routine, international contacts in 1947 and MCP delegates went to Prague to the World Federation of Democratic Youth, meeting Soviet officials in Paris en route, and in January an Indian and a Malay delegate, Balan and Rashid Maidin, had been at the 'Empire' Communist Conference in London.[10] The latter had returned from London very disappointed with the lukewarm interest of the British Communist Party in Malayan affairs; but even after the great shift in Soviet policy later in the year the Prague delegates apparently received no encouragement for armed revolution in Malay.

At no time up to the outbreak of the various insurrections in South-east Asia—Indo-China, Burma, the Philippines, Malaya

[9] In an earlier version Chou is said to have told an MCP emissary simply that in a colony bloodshed was the only means of achieving Communist revolution. *Basic Paper*, p. 42.

[10] Which, incidentally, was in favour of 'immediate and unequivocal independence for India, Burma and Ceylon' : Malaya was not included.

and Indonesia—was there any clear cut and public call from the Soviet Union for the launching of an armed struggle.[11] But an end to wartime allied co-operation and a formal announcement that the world was divided into two camps was given in a major Soviet policy speech in September 1947. Speaking in Poland, Andrei Zhdanov, widely regarded at the time as Stalin's heir apparent, may only in fact have affirmed the course that had already been set but it is at least possible to read into his speech a plea to the Communist parties of the world to come to the aid of Russia in Europe. Support for this Eurocentric contention may be seen in part 4 of Zhdanov's speech where it is argued that Communists had the special historical task of leading the resistance to the American plan for the enthralment of Europe; and although there was a crisis in the colonial system it was, in a throwback to Leninist argument, represented as the potential weakness of western capitalism. If the purpose of the anti-fascist camp, which included those fighting for national liberation in the colonies and dependencies, was to resist the threat of new wars and Imperialist expansion, to strengthen democracy and to extirpate the vestiges of fascism, the chief danger to the working class at the time lay in under-rating its own strength and over-rating the strength of the enemy. Concessions to the new course of the United States and the Imperialist camp might encourage its inspirers to be even more insolent and aggressive. The Communist Parties must therefore head the resistance to the plans of Imperialist expansion and aggression along every line.

Zhdanov's speech was printed in the first number of the Cominform paper, *'For A Lasting Peace, For A People's Democracy!'* in November 1947, and the 'two camp' theme was the one which dominated the Calcutta Conference of February 1948 sponsored by two Communist controlled associations—the World Federation of Democratic Youth and the International Union of Students: the Conference of Youth and Students of South-East Asia Fighting for Freedom and Independence. In the meantime, with a shift in Soviet writing on colonial policy to take account of the Zhdanov line, there was still no endorsement for an armed struggle in Asia against either colonial or bourgeois regimes; but, perhaps because of the time, the place, the title and the participants, revolutionary enthusiasm became only the slightly less dominant motif of the Calcutta Conference.

[11] An excellent analysis of the developments of Soviet policy, together with the developments in the countries of South-east Asia themselves, is given in Charles B. McLane *Soviet Strategies in South-East Asia*, Princeton, 1966.

In a most interesting paper on the Calcutta Conference that deals with its origins and place in the development of Communist policies Ruth McVey makes the critical point that while the Conference did not openly declare for insurrection its mood was one of extreme belligerence towards colonial rule.[12] The main report on the opening day of the Conference was given by a Vietnamese delegate, Le Tam, and, in a sense, set the tone for the entire Conference. He described the anti-Imperialist struggle as having reached its highest form in the armed struggles of Indonesia and Vietnam and, as McVey points out, the fact that the Vietnamese delegation consisted of officers of the Vietminh may have had much to do with the military emphasis of the speech. There were, however, many events and manifestations other than the formal Conference sessions and on at least one occasion—a procession and speeches to mark 'the day of revolution of the Indian Navy' two years earlier—it offered encouragement to militant action.

> Soviet youth are watching with deep and heartfelt sympathy the armed struggle which the youth of different countries in South-East Asia are waging for their independence. They have our full support in the struggle.[13]

For the most part, however, the Conference may be said to have adopted a permissive attitude towards the armed struggle and, as McVey points out, it is notable that none of the Calcutta meeting reports in any way discouraged armed action against the Imperialists.[14]

> Indeed, the main point made by the Conference—that there could be no compromise in the struggle against Imperialism—could have led easily to the conclusion that the only remaining path was that of armed struggle. This may not have been the intention of the Soviet Union, since the adoption of the two-camp doctrine elsewhere did not result in violence but in political non-co-operation and economic sabotage. Nonetheless, the militant tone displayed by the Calcutta Conference may well have given encouragement and added prestige to the more extreme elements among the South-East Asian Communists. Later, when the Communists of Malaya, Burma and Indonesia came to realise that they had no

---

[12] Ruth D. McVey, *The Calcutta Conference and the South-East Asian Uprisings*, Cornell, 1958 (mimeo).
[13] *A History of the Communist Party of India*, Vol. 2, 1947–1951, Indian Intelligence Bureau, New Delhi, 1964.
[14] McVey, p. 16.

TOWARDS A REVOLUTIONARY SITUATION 47

prospect of gaining power peacefully, they could look back to the Conference's declarations as an ideological justification for their decisions to try the way of violence.[15]

At the very least the Calcutta Conference provided a forum for the discussion and 'correct' understanding of the Zhdanov line and the Soviet view of world affairs. If, however, it is denied that any sort of instruction was issued to South-East Asian Communist Parties to introduce the armed struggle—and on balance this seems to be correct—then a much more likely forum, namely the Second Congress of the Communist Party of India, must not be ignored. This took place directly after the Youth Conference, from February 28th to March 6th, and where the earlier Conference catered for the more or less enthusiastic amateurs of revolution, the CPI Congress was for the professionals. Of principal importance as far as domestic Communism in India was concerned it was the occasion for the indictment, replacement and abasement of the CPI Secretary-General, P. C. Joshi, but it is worth noting that the Indian political situation was analysed in the context of an impending clash between the rival camps of capitalism and Communism. Lawrence Sharkey, President of the Australian Communist Party, referred to it as the coming war, and, in general, it was the foreign Communist Parties that pressed the CPI to organise an armed revolution against the Indian National Government. Indian Intelligence sources singled out Chinese and Mongolian delegates as being particularly lavish with this advice but, on the whole, the most militant line was taken by the Yugoslav representatives, Dedijer and Zokovic, who were reportedly also the Cominform delegates.

Considerable prestige seems to have been attached to the Yugoslavs at Calcutta and, at a time before the split between Yugoslavia and the Soviet Union, they were not only ideologically sound but represented a semi-peasant state that had created a socialist revolution through force of arms.[16] Although they were later to be stigmatised as 'leftist-opportunists' it has been argued that because the Russians themselves did not have an agreed strategy for the Indian situation the result, whether intentional

[15] Ibid.
[16] Thus, the new Secretary-General of the CPI Ranadive based his economic analysis of the situation on Kardelj. In a later recantation Bhowani Sen acknowledged the influence of the two Yugoslav delegates who had criticised the draft political thesis and argued that the Indian revolution, like Yugoslavia's, was a one stage socialist revolution. 'Along with other members of the Central Committee I accepted this formulation uncritically.'

or not, was that guidance of the CPI fell to the Cominform and thus to the Yugoslavs.[17] One of them (Zokovic) certainly ridiculed the CPI for having missed the bus. There was no doubt, he said, that the Cominform was going to capture China and immediately afterwards Burma and India; and while Indian comrades could rely on the Cominform for arms, money and other resources they should make haste to cultivate the Indian 'tribals' in both the east and the west.[18]

Like the Youth Conference that preceded it the Calcutta Congress of the CPI was offered frequent glimpses of the apocalypse and was certainly not immune to enthusiasm. In an atmosphere of mutual encouragement the Secretary-General of the CPI spoke of an economic crisis of gigantic magnitude and argued that the post-war revolutionary epoch had brought the colonies to the path of the armed struggle. In India the Party took up the cause of what had begun as an entirely indigenous and largely non-Communist struggle in Telengana but, rather ironically, when it took advantage of the resistance to the feudal regime and Telengana became the war cry it was urban struggle—short, violent, unco-ordinated—rather than a peasant guerrilla revolt that became the general pattern. In part, perhaps, this is a reflection on the fact that parties which have their existence in the realms of intellectual violence must always have their members who are ready and willing to take up arms. This does not mean that the policy of indigenous Communist parties hovers constantly on the brink of insurrection; and even when the situation boils over into an armed struggle its plans, in the case of both India and Malaya, seemed to be of an *ad hoc* nature.

Students of the CPI have argued that it is at least possible that Yugoslav directives triggered Communist guerrilla-style revolution throughout South-east Asia[19] but while the importance of Yugoslav influence is acknowledged one may doubt the existence of 'directives', asking in any case why they should have been obeyed and even if one assumes that the two Yugoslav delegates to the CPI Congress were in fact the Cominform representatives one might inquire further whether there was any such thing as an agreed Cominform policy for South-east Asia: assuming for

[17] Gene D. Overstreet and Marshall Windmiller, *Communism in India*, University of California Press, 1959, p. 270.
[18] By the middle of 1947 the Yugoslav Communist Party had already begun arguing for more militant policy. Evidence of 'leftism' is given in Overstreet and Windmiller, *op cit.*, p. 258 f.n.
[19] Overstreet and Windmiller, *op cit.*, p. 274.

the moment that there was no clear line of Russian policy. In the history of the Asian revolutions of 1948 Calcutta sounds an uncertain note and, while the Conference and the Congress between them may have promoted delusions of Jericho among the participants, the individual Communist Parties of South-east Asia still had a lot of hard marching to do before the walls of capitalism and colonialism came tumbling down. The similarities in the pattern of revolution are there; but so are the anomalies; while a hundred years before a simultaneous outbreak of revolutions throughout Europe in 1848 was an even more gigantic coincidence.[20] In any case it would seem important to look at the decisions which were taken by the individual communist parties. One returns therefore to the MCP and its critical meetings in Singapore.

Critical Path

Lee Soong (Lee Siong), the MCP representative at the Calcutta Youth Conference, who had been chosen to attend because he spoke good English, returned to Singapore on March 22nd 1948. He came by boat from Rangoon where he had attended a Communist sponsored Congress of the All Burma Peasants' Union, and thus had no part in the Fourth Plenary Session of the Party Central meeting which ended the day before he arrived in Singapore. The Fourth Plenary meeting of the MCP, together with the Fifth which was held in May, are the turning point in the MCP's post-war history. It is arguable which of the two is the more important; and although it is sometimes assumed that the Fifth being later, was the decisive occasion there seems to be more evidence to suggest that the principal decisions were taken in March. In their documentary form, however, the importance of both meetings seems to be by way of ideological preparation rather than a clear-cut decision to begin the armed struggle although on the understanding of at least one of those who was present the Fourth Plenary was meant, at any rate, to indicate an unmistakable changeover to the armed struggle. The documents of the Fourth Plenary meeting are in three parts.[21] In the

---

[20] And even forty years before that, in Spain in 1808, with curious spontaneity risings broke out in town and village as though a great synchronised movement had been arranged. H. Butterfield, *Napoleon*, London, 1939.

[21] *Regarding the Decisions on Rectification of the Party. The Political Line of the Party. The Current Situation in Malaya.* I am particularly grateful to Mr. Yoong Siew Wah, of the Singapore Special Branch, for providing me with a new and full translation of the Fourth and Fifth Plenary Session documents.

third, *The Current Situation in Malaya*, there is a particular concern to identify the Labour Government in Britain as irredeemably imperialist; to speak in the name of the people;[22] and to identify the contradictions between British Imperialism and the people. These contradictions 'were continuously deteriorating and becoming more and more acute' and the logic of history, as well as theory, suggested the proper course.

> Owing to the fact that the economic condition is worsening, that the people are leading an increasingly wretched life and that British Imperialists are implementing fanatical policies, the masses and society are no longer the same. They generally demand struggle and are not afraid of the attack by the British Imperialists. The masses are also aware that it is futile to hold talks and that a united struggle must be launched and determined action be taken so as to carry on the struggle persistently.

More precisely

> We are facing a new situation of a mass struggle which demands that the Party must determinedly undertake to mobilise the masses to launch the struggle and must firmly and courageously lead them to move forward for the purpose of achieving victory in the struggle.

To some extent this was a conventional assessment and one which was consistent with the shift in analysis and policy of the Soviet Union and the communist parties that had been represented at Calcutta. In its paper, *The Political Line of the Party*, however, the change in policy may be attributed to the MCP's internal history and in this particular paper one may see the Party doing its best to recoup the situation after the Wright fiasco. The postwar political line of the Party was condemned as 'the right-inclined doctrine of abandonment', 'right-inclined opportunism', 'the rearguard policy' and 'the policy of patience'.

> The line of right-inclined doctrine of abandonment is manifested in abandoning the programme of national independence, in making unprincipled concession to the British Imperialists, in carrying out unprincipled compromise of the reactionary political parties, in carrying out unprincipled appeasement with the petty

---

[22] 'The people will be more and more disillusioned.' 'The Labour Party Government has run counter to the demands of the people.' 'The people are further disillusioned.' 'The people's indignation is aroused.' 'The People's Democratic Movement.'

bourgeoisie political parties, and in not daring to resolutely lead the masses and to mobilise the masses in launching the struggle.

Among other mistakes that were noted was that of demobilising and disarming at the end of the war: 'abolishing the military struggle'; a defensive rather than an offensive policy towards British Imperialism—to whom concessions were useless; limiting the struggle to lawful and peaceful assembly, strikes and protests; and in not daring to go all out to mobilise the masses and launching the struggle. In short, the MCP had not fulfilled its role as the vanguard of the proletariat and in a sense it had betrayed the Federations of Trade Unions by not acknowledging leadership. Again in retrospect but with obvious reference to future rectification, the Party condemned itself for ignoring the political possibilities when the Japanese surrendered, for not creating local governments so that a republic could have been set up immediately and in trying to fight a war without bloodshed and in preserving its strength by resorting to defence.

The main fault in the past to which the MCP admitted was in losing its class basis and blurring its class viewpoint. In the future the new political line was to be built upon proletarian leadership with the strength of workers and peasants as its foundation. A general mobilisation of the masses would then carry out a resolute struggle to defeat the policy of the British Imperialists. Struggle, in this case, embraced peaceful as well as violent measures and if it perhaps implied the use of limited force, and was to this extent ambiguous, there was little ambiguity in the simple statement that

> 'to fight for national independence, an armed struggle will be inevitable and will constitute the most important form of struggle'.[23]

---

[23] Nevertheless another version of the Fourth Plenary meeting suggests a lingering uncertainty.

'Under this new circumstance, the peoples of the colonies cannot but adopt a new method of struggle, i.e. to establish a united front with the workers and peasants of the lower class as a basis and to discard and attack the minority of wavering upper class elements who were otherwise likely to become turncoats. In most cases, while following the policy of carrying out resolute and extensive mobilisation of the broad masses and of taking practical action to repulse Imperialism in order to fight for full national liberation and independence it is impossible to avoid or to do without the armed struggle (the people's revolutionary war). That is why the armed struggle has its particularly important significance.'

52   COMMUNIST INSURRECTION IN MALAYA

The question now arises: who was responsible for this change of policy? And one may first consider the evidence of external influence. Lee Soong, it will be remembered, did not return to Singapore from Calcutta till after the critical decision had been taken. In any case he was comparatively junior—certainly no higher than a State Committee Member in rank—and of little or no account apart from this.[24] A much more likely courier, if there was one, was the President of the Australian Communist Party, Lawrence Sharkey, who arrived in Singapore on his way back from Calcutta on March 9th and did not leave until March 20th. Much of this time was spent with MCP members; he attended the Fourth Plenary meetings; and his influence on the 'armed struggle' decision is accredited from two sources.[25] Sharkey himself, although creating the impression of a man of some standing, whose advice would be listened to by the MCP, was somewhat evasive about the nature of this advice, and while he may or may not have told the Australian Communist Party on his return that he 'took full responsibility before the international movement' for his activities in Asia, only committed himself publicly to support for the Malayan struggle for national independence. The question of when they should have started an armed insurrection, or whether they should have started one at all and how they should have carried it out, was a matter for the Malayans themselves.[26] Whether or not Sharkey was mainly responsible for the Fourth Plenary Conference Paper on The Current Situation, all accounts suggest that he advised the MCP

---

[24] He was another of those suspected of betraying the Party during the Japanese occupation, is said to have been dismissed in February 1949, but was later reinstated. He became a guerrilla in Johore and was a 'cultural instructor' when he was killed by Security Forces in 1954.

[25] The secondhand source is Hor Lung, the Central Committee member who surrendered in 1957. He says that Sharkey's opinion was that only by continuing the armed struggle could the revolution in Malaya be achieved. Siew Chong told Hor Lung that the opinions of Sharkey and Chou En Lai encouraged the MCP to make their big decision. Australian Intelligence, quoting an unknown source, believe that Sharkey criticised the MCP for losing a good opportunity after the liberation and said the MPAJA should never have been demobilised.

[26] *Tribune* (Sydney), August 14th 1948. A former Australian Communist, Cecil Sharpley, says that Sharkey told the National Congress of the Australian CP in May 1948 that he had been commissioned by Cominform representatives at 'the CPI Congress to convey decisions to the MCP. It was therefore no coincidence that only a few months later the Communists began open revolt in Malaya.' Cecil Sharpley, *The Great Delusion*, London, 1952, p. 111.

TOWARDS A REVOLUTIONARY SITUATION

to give up the constitutional struggle: something which the Australian Communist Party was going to discard and which would be a mistake for the MCP to continue.

Events in Australia were later to belie Sharkey's boast of revolutionary action but it is perhaps worth considering that he was temperamentally ill-suited to a constitutional struggle, admired the organisation—and success—of the Chinese and Vietnamese Communist Parties, and on many occasions professed his utter contempt for the Communist Party of Great Britain: not least, one suspects, because it was British. Whether or not he was conveying Cominform directives was perhaps a less important consideration than the fact that this was Sharkey's *second* visit to Singapore and contact with MCP leaders; and that on his way *to* Calcutta he had spoken in similarly violent terms of the need to attack British Imperialism—Britain, on his account, being on her last legs—urging that the MCP, which was militarily equipped to launch an armed struggle, should not lose the opportunity of doing so. In any event there are equally important sources which contradict the opinion of Sharkey's influence and while he was listened to attentively his opinions, for such they were, were not particularly important.

What seems more likely is that Sharkey provided useful but by no means indispensable encouragement for a course which, now apparently ideologically correct, was an approach to impending armed conflict. At first sight this might seem surprising in that the MCP, which was only now beginning to get over the post-Wright tasks of Party reorganisation, had as its new Secretary-General someone who, at least comparatively, was reckoned to be a moderate.

Chin Peng, with a distinguished resistance record that had earned him an OBE, was twenty-six when he became Secretary-General of the Party in 1947. Since his appointment he had been largely concerned with the reconstruction of the Party after the Wright incident and although undoubtedly efficient it is possible that his age and comparative inexperience told against him. One curious impediment to the spread of MCP influence was that Malayan Chinese who were sympathetic to the cause of the Chinese Communist Party and were impressed by its cumulative successes were spreading the idea that the revolution in Malaya was no longer necessary because once victory had been attained in China, Malayan Chinese could then return to their homeland or, alternatively, a Chinese Communist Government would use its power to protect the overseas Chinese. This was only one element in the declining support for the MCP, important in that there was at least latent hostility between the China-oriented China Democratic League and the young, comparatively poor and uneducated leaders of the MCP. C. C. Too, now head of the Federation Psychological Warfare Service who had first-hand experience of Chinese politics and affairs at this time, singles out the low calibre of MCP leaders as one reason for the general collapse of the 'masses struggle' in this period. He holds that very few of them being English educated, it was impossible to infiltrate English educated government service officers: thus depriving the Party of an important field of influence. Other sources of MCP weakness at this time which might not otherwise be apparent are, according to Too, their alienation of the sympathy and support of the petty bourgeois and national capitalists by the huge extortion rackets that followed the Japanese surrender. Internally, an unequal distribution of these extortion proceeds caused considerable discontent while reduced unemployment consequent upon reconstruction and the revival of local industries reduced the Party's appeal and the defection of many fulltime 'professional' Party workers—in many cases presumably because they obtained better employment—seriously affected recruitment and the mobilisation of open support.

There had, moreover, been a growing dichotomy between the MCP, particularly in its Loi Tak phase, and the Federations of Trades Unions with the latter achieving far greater success through its militant policies. The decision taken at the Fourth Plenary session and the MCP's adoption of a generally militant policy meant that the two were now reconciled and the MCP could rest assured that it had re-established itself on a proper class basis.

> In the implementation of a new MCP policy Singapore was the scene of most of the immediate labour unrest, and the Indian labour supported the Chinese movement. From April 5th to 12th the PMFTU held its annual conference in Singapore, at which all the regular Communist leaders were re-elected to office, and a policy of complete self-reliance and disregard for official mediation in labour disputes was adopted for the future. Throughout the month there was trouble first in the rubber factories and then at the Harbour Board, where the Singapore Federation of Trades Unions backed a serious strike during which hand grenades were thrown on several occasions, and attempts were made to stab a Chinese mandore and labourer. Workers at the Tai Tong Rubber

TOWARDS A REVOLUTIONARY SITUATION

Factory staged a sit-down strike, and there was attempted arson at the Joo Lim Saw Mill. Labour became increasingly truculent, seditious pamphlets were published threatening a 'bloody struggle against the British Imperialists' and preparations were made to defy the Colonial Secretary's ban on May Day processions. When, as a result, permission already granted for a May Day assembly was cancelled, the labour leaders thought twice, and May Day passed without incident, and without a procession. On 11th May the Bin Seng Rubber Milling Factory was burnt to the ground a few hours before some of the workers who had been on strike were to have returned to work. The fire caused a million dollars damage.[27]

The principal elements in this increasing violence in Singapore were the Singapore Harbour Board Labour Union Executive Committee within which there was an organ of the MCP—the Secretary of the Union Lam Chun Fuk and Ho Ah Chung—which was directly under the Singapore Town Committee;[28] and the Singapore Workers' Protection Corps, an organ which had been in existence since November 1946, was organised in teams of 10 and had, as the last of its stated objects, the extermination of all worker-traitors who were detrimental to the interests of the working class. The Singapore Harbour Board Labourers' Union was raided by the police on April 14th—lists of members, receipt books and so on were seized—and on April 29th four members of the Union Committee were convicted of assisting in the management of an unlawful society. On May 1st, in place of the mass demonstrations that had been planned and the banning of which, according to several former Communists, contributed greatly to the frustration of MCP plans, an MCP May Day manifesto warned the workers that acquiescence in government repression meant death: if they wanted to exist the only way open was to struggle. Rhetoric and translation on one side, however, this manifesto cannot be described as a specific incitement to revolution although it could well depend on how literally the advice was taken. But in an atmosphere of increasing tension, encouraged as well as alarmed by developments in the Unions, the MCP now set its foot firmly on the path towards insurrection.

The Fifth Plenary session of the Central Committee took place

[27] *Basic Paper*, p. 45.
[28] (According to Teh Ah Meng, Secretary of the Town Committee of the MCP, although Lim's file gives no indication that he was an MCP member or under direct contact and guidance).

in Singapore on May 10th 1948. It was convened hurriedly to review the latest situation and was the last occasion on which 'Central' met before the declaration of a state of emergency. Its decisions may be variously interpreted[29] but it was in one sense a declaration of defensive war, an unmistakable call to clear the decks for action, a confession of constitutional failure in that the political struggle was now taken on to another level but, at the same time, it was to be a graduated political struggle rather than a *coup d'état* or recognisable revolution. Above all, it was a decision to attack through the workers and as long as the MCP was not allowed to use trade unions as its main weapon in the struggle against government then conflict was inevitable. As 'Central' presented its case it was the British Imperialists who were attacking the Revolution, not only suppressing the people by law but actively preparing to use force. They had combined with all reactionary forces—Dato Onn was specifically mentioned—and the fact that they were implementing 'such a maniacal and persistently uncompromising policy' showed that this was their attempt to impose a final solution.

> Under the increased exploitation and oppression and even the use of violent attacks of the British Imperialists, the working classes launched a general strike struggle, followed also by an outbreak of peasant struggle in certain places. The working classes displayed exceptional valour in the struggle: it does not only dare to resolutely use the strike weapon but also to ignore and struggle against the British Imperialists, seeing through their plot of deceptive improvements and utilising its own united strength and violent tactics to counter-attack the enemy. It realises that without resolute action, concerted struggle and the use of violence when necessary it will not be able to repel the enemy and achieve victory. It requests the Party to lead in the carrying out of the struggle and not to be hesitant in compromising.

> No concessions would be made on either side and while this was still not the decisive struggle stage and still not the time to mobilise the whole population for rioting—it was time instead to persist in the mass struggle and lead the struggle to its high tide—there could be little doubt of the eventual outcome.

> On the other hand, the masses *cannot tolerate British Imperialist suppression* and their reactionary laws and ordinances any longer

---

[29] See, for example, Michael Stenson, *The 1948 Communist Revolt in Malaya: A Note on Historical Sources and Interpretation. A Reply by Gerald de Cruz.* Institute of Southeast Asian Studies (mimeo), Singapore, 1971.

and want to use action to smash their reactionary legal restrictions. Therefore the people's legal status with the British Imperialists (laws) is extremely shaky and the significance of a lawful struggle has become very small. It is wrong to place hopes in utilising a lawful struggle to drive back the British Imperialists reactionary policy and slowly push forward the revolution. This will actually facilitate their attack and obstruct the masses' advance.

Under such circumstances, although the British Imperialists will certainly immediately carry out an overall attack and sweep away the people's legal status and rights, the possibility of using terrorist tactics and carrying out an overall suppression exists. Thus, on the one hand the leading of the masses' struggle must be continued whilst on the other hand, adequate preparations must be made to meet with such a new situation.

Developments in the present situation are pressing and urgent. Developments in the struggle in all places are happening one after another and not concurrently. As long as there is no pause, there will be progress not retrogression. But in the entire situation, if the struggle became more violent daily and developed forward, then the tide of the masses' struggle would rise daily. At the same time, when the struggle became more acute, the use of violence in the struggle between the British Imperialists and masses would increase and would turn into a violent clash. Under the violent suppression of the British Imperialists, the masses' struggle would positively develop into a national revolutionary war.

Up to this point Central's opinions were to be transmitted in writing to the State Town Committee who would then relay them orally to all members as their own views. The second part of the Fifth Plenary meeting decisions was entitled *Regarding Decision on Struggle Strategy* and was itself in two parts. It was admitted that open activities of the MCP had been contracting daily and the written instructions were that 'secret leading organs and organisational nucleus of the masses of the lower tier should be set up to strengthen the actual leadership of masses in various places'. The main plan was to divert the Central leadership and the main work to 'the lower stratum'. Cadres were to be reduced and States themselves were to decide whether or not to dissolve the open Party organisation. Unlawful tactics should be adopted, arrest avoided, and court trial rejected in order to preserve the cadres. In particular, Indian cadres who might be attacked were to be withdrawn first, if necessary transferring them to other States. Developments in the trade union struggle would inevitably become more violent, brutal and acute each day. The main political objectives of the struggle were not only to improve livelihood but to attack the British Imperialists, train workers, resolutely lead them to the road of violent action and to use violence against violence to facilitate the co-ordination and development of the future struggle. This was to be the direction in which the trade union struggle would develop and if a favourable result was not achieved at first, and if the workers were willing they could resume work and be prepared to launch the struggle a second time. In all this the Party was not to act as the 'tail' of the masses.

> During the struggle if the British Imperialists utilised troops and police for suppression, and when the degree of the workers consciousness and struggle resolve have grown to the stage when they want to use violence or accept it, the Party should, without hesitation, lead the workers to use violence to retaliate at the enemy.

One of the basic policies of the Party was to undermine the enemy's economic production. The main objective was to use this weapon to support the Trade Union struggle but

> when using the tool of violent destruction of enemy production, natural resources or commodities, consideration should be given to the workers support (to be carried out only when workers participate spontaneously or express sympathy; it is wrong to carry out destruction indiscriminately whether or not with the workers' support), the repercussions on the livelihood (like the destruction of tanks or reservoirs which will greatly effect the production of the general masses, and should not be carried out at present) of the general masses (mainly the workers and peasants) and politics (like the burning of certain commodities would cause a fire calamity, and if it would cause unfavourable repercussions it should not be done).

These instructions were fairly explicit but the first part, the 'struggle form' was left blank. More precise instructions on organisation were given verbally and throughout May, but particularly in the middle of the month, there was a great deal of activity amongst the open MCP organisations, the disappearance of many of them, and cumulative evidence which suggests that instructions were being obeyed. For example, according to a member of the Central Committee who surrendered,[30] the State Committees were

[30] Hor Lung.

instructed that they should form mobilisation sections to deal with all problems connected with the armed struggle and that violence could be used against the opposition from then (mid-May) onwards.[31] In the middle of April security instructions regarding documents, photographs and records had been sent to all MPAJA associations.

On 5th May an Executive MPAJA Council meeting was held in Kuala Lumpur. District MPAJA Ex-Service Comrades' Associations were told to compile fresh records of all members, including those who had left the Associations, and this re-registration was completed in June, by which time large scale mobilisation was well under way in Perak and Johore and was imminent in Selangor. On 11th June an emergency meeting in Kuala Lumpur was attended by Selangor, Pahang, Perak and Negri Sembilan MPAJAESCA leaders who were told to sell all property, destroy all records and prepare for evacuation to the hills. Government's expected ban on the MCP was to be the signal for all-out mobilisation.

At the same time a rather hasty internal re-organisation was going on within the MCP. Preparations for local representatives meetings, which were to have elected the MCP leadership, were dropped—or rather instructions were given that they should be dropped—and detailed instructions were given for the security of members. The Selangor State Committee, for instance, met on May 14th when the State was subdivided into small areas, members appointed to their specific posts and leaders instructed to be ready to go to ground by May 31st. At the same time ranking MCP members, including two on the Central Committee, who were known or were suspected opponents of the armed struggle policy were jettisoned by the Party and by the beginning of June policy was being already put into practice.

On June 4th the High Commissioner's despatch to the Colonial Office mentioned twelve serious incidents, including nine murders and three attacks on European estate managers, involving grievous hurt that had occurred recently in Penang, Perak,

---

[31] In its explicit instruction, *Regarding the Peasant Struggle* the fifth Plenum laid down that 'when dealing with reactionary village chiefs, corrupt officials, running dogs, local bullies (including reactionary gangsters) in rural villages (we) should wrest the initiative and use positive action to attack (or paralyse their purpose or role, or drive them away, or eliminate their king pins, and win over the neutrals in their middle or lower strata); passive precaution is bad for it will bring about losses to ourselves.

Selangor, Negri Sembilan and Johore. Where industrial disputes had been the occasion sometimes, according to the despatch they had been of a quite trivial nature but violence had followed if the labourers' demands had not been met immediately. One case in Penang involved the murder of an Indian merchant who had given evidence in court of attempted intimidation and in Negri Sembilan there were two cases on estates of the murder of witnesses in intimidation prosecutions in 1947. At this stage, however, Government was not touching the MCP as such but was putting the blame on the Pan-Malayan Federation of Trade Unions which was now to be proscribed, as a Federation, by the Trade Union Amendment Bill which was read on May 31st. On the same day the communist Union organiser in Perak, R. G. Balan, was arrested and the MCP position in the unions was beginning to crumble away.[32] On another front, the MCP had formally taken over ownership of the *Min Sheng Pao*, the Chinese paper with the biggest circulation in the Federation, on June 1st. The editorials were considered to be increasingly inflammatory and the editor, Liew Yit Fan, a Eurasian, former political secretary of the Second Regiment AJA and 'open' representative of the MCP in the middle of 1947 was arrested on June 9th on a charge of sedition. As far as ordinary members of the MCP were concerned, and in particular those who might still be awaiting the call to action, the *Min Sheng Pao* was the voice of the Party. Its editorial of June 15th entitled 'Complete Exposure of the Cruel Countenance' probably removed all doubts about the 'present situation'. The people of Malaya, it said, were now facing a new situation and difficulty which they must have the courage and ability to face.

> 'We must intensify our unity and strengthen our mobilisation to answer Imperialism's fascist rule with our own heroic and stubborn struggle and action. Imperialism wants to suppress our struggle for better living conditions with guns and knives and we must answer it with more vigorous and larger scale unified struggle. Imperialism declared Trade Unions to be illegal (or any other organisation to be illegal) and not allowed to remain in public: then we are not afraid of being illegal and strongly determined to turn underground and to carry out secret activities. Imperialism wants to arrest the leaders of the workers and the responsible members of the people's organisations: then they must

---

[32] When he was arrested Balan was within 6 hours of taking to the jungle; and was to have gone by car to Johore.

use every method to protect the safety of our personnel. Imperialism orders its running dogs and their followers to oppress us : then we will use the same method against them. All in all, for the sake of our lives, we cannot procrastinate any more nor can we give in any further but to fight our way out through struggle.

Today the British Imperialists' cruel fascist countenance has been completely exposed. Imperialism is fascism and their violence and outrages are the same as those of Japanese. The people of Malaya can never forget the bloody role of the Japanese fascists. At the same time they will remember the methods used against the fascists.

The Armed Struggle Begins

3
THE ONUS OF RESPONSIBILITY

Until, on the one side, three European planters were murdered on June 16th, 1948 and, on the other, the government declared a state of Emergency, in three stages over this and the following two days, the approach to this impending conflict can best be seen as a jig-saw puzzle of interlocking actions and intentions on the part of government and the MCP. It was a most untidy beginning to a state of emergency. Neither Government nor the MCP appeared anxious to accept the firm responsibility for declaring war upon the other; and, treated as an exercise in diplomatic history, perhaps in the Taylorian fashion, one might be tempted to argue that it was something of a miscalculation if not an outright mistake. Even more than in the Origins of the Second World War was timing important. Precipitate action on the part of government would provide the MCP with *ex post facto* justification if not a *casus belli*. The MCP, on the other hand, having taken its decision, at least in principle, to begin the armed struggle and having at the most encouraged and at the least done nothing to discourage the climate of violence, indeed Armageddon, amongst its members and supporters had now to seek a favourable occasion on which its revolutionary theory might be translated into practice.

The Approach to conflict (i) Consultations and Decisions

The first meeting in the series of consultations and decisions leading immediately to the declaration of a state of emergency was held on May 21st 1948. It was called by the Chief Secretary of various heads of departments and it included the Commissioner of Police, the Commissioner for Labour, the Acting Attorney General, the Acting Secretary for Chinese Affairs, the Registrar of Trade Unions and the Trade Union Adviser. The purpose of the meeting was 'to consider the numerous and recent manifestations in Malaya of what appeared to be a general increase of Communist propaganda in many parts of the world, as well as in Malaya; and the steps which should be taken by government to strike at organisations indulging in anti-government activities and to restore public confidence in the government's ability to protect them from intimidation and lawlessness.' At the suggestion of the Chief Secretary, the meeting considered in turn the incidents which had taken place within the past few weeks, many of which seemed to spring from industrial disputes, in order to see if there was any common pattern and controlling source. In short, what the meeting was looking for was evidence against the MCP although the occasion was not unconnected with the fact that in ten days' time the matter was due to be raised in the Legislative Council when it would be alleged that Europeans including women and children were leaving estates on account of the number of incidents which had already occurred.

On the subject of industrial unrest itself, it is interesting to note that both the Trade Union Adviser and the Commissioner for Labour, who did not normally always see eye to eye with each other, agreed that the employers would have to take at least part of the blame for the occurrence of strikes. The causes given were, in the south, the employer's refusal to pay in future for 'spot marking'; dissatisfaction with the MPIEA rates of pay; and the lack of uniformity among the employers on the question of granting a holiday with pay on May 1st. These were grievances which the PMFTU had exploited with alacrity; and what was alarming to the Trade Union Adviser was the amount of unruliness and intimidation which accompanied the strikes: due, he thought, to the successful way in which law and order had been flouted. Only the third of the Labour/Union triumvirate, the Registrar of Trade Unions, is on record as saying that there might have been a central organisation behind the disputes and that the PMFTU, for example, had circulated instructions to unions telling them not to follow the Registrar's instructions regarding the non-payment of contributions to the Federation and, generally, to oppose his enforcement of the Trade Unions Ordinances. The Commissioner of Labour believed that developments then taking place were the results of the PMFTU meeting in Singapore in April, when a general anti-government campaign was decided upon, and that on particular estates, for example the Socfin estates in the neighbourhood of Slim River, the New Democratic Youth League was an organising power. There was a brief but minor difference of opinion between the Commissioner for Labour and the Trade Union Adviser as to whether Balan's power was waxing or waning in Perak but it is another point of interest that no one contradicted Brazier when he said that the Federations of Unions, losing power and short of funds, were getting desperate.[1]

Three possible lines of action were then discussed. First, whether to deal severely with the *Min Sheng Pao*, whose general attitude towards the government was considered to have become intolerable. Second, whether to attack the NDYL wherever a search warrant could be obtained. Third, whether to take such action as was possible under the Societies Legislation against the PMFTU. Discussion of the *Min Sheng Pao* case was inconclusive. It was argued that this paper (the voice of the MCP) consistently misrepresented every action of government. There were many instances of scurrilous articles, some of which might amount to criminal libel. It also had the biggest circulation of any Chinese paper in the Federation. The possibility of cancelling the paper's licence was thought to be too drastic a step, at least, until the Editor had been given a preliminary warning, and it was thought better, in any case, to get a conviction in court for criminal libel. Discussion of the NDYL was brief. No one offered any recommendations and the Commissioner of Police simply undertook to go into the question of whether an application for a search warrant for the Slim River branch of the NDYL would be likely to yield results. He himself apparently had no views on the matter.

What took up the greater part of the discussion was consideration of the PMFTU. Could they be prosecuted for a pamphlet which had been printed for them in Tamil by the *Min Sheng Pao*? Would government agree to the Registrar of Trade Unions' suggestion that a simultaneous raid on the headquarters of the PMFTU in Kuala Lumpur and of the Federations in each of the states be made with a view to action against them as unlawful societies under Section 21 of the Societies Ordinance? (The question whether such raids would have been illegal does not seem to have been considered.) Would the amendment to the Trade Union Ordinance be put through on May 31st and would the Registrar of Trade Unions be able 'to jump on the PMFTU and the State Federations immediately'; and if not, what sort of action could the Registrar take against the Federations under the two-thirds rule?[2] Which, until the amending bill was passed, was only an interim measure in that the Registrar's decision could be the subject of appeal. Would the confidence of the country as a whole and in particular that of labourers in outlying districts be

[1] R. G. Balan was one of the most successful communist union organisers in Malaya. His rivalry with the Trade Union Adviser was conspicuous.
[2] *Infra* p. 91

restored by the presence of small bodies of troops who might be sent to various parts of the country as part of a training exercise? To all of these proposals the meeting gave its approval although only in the case of the PMFTU can this be regarded as a mandate for definite, if not urgent, action.

Ten days later, another side to the question of lawlessness among labour was put at a meeting of the Legislative Council, but here again, although the discussion ranged wider, there was little sense of urgency certainly on the part of some Asian members, and although the debate took place on a motion for the adjournment as a matter of urgency—the first in post-war Malaya—the only definite proposal to come out of it was for a Commission of Inquiry. The motion for the adjournment, which was moved by Mr. V. M. Menon, a trade union representative on the Legislative Council, was not so much an attack upon the incidence of industrial disputes 'With attendant crimes' as it was a defence of labour.

> What I have in mind in moving this motion this morning was to have a debate and find out the real culprit behind the whole trouble, to find out the right person and not the wrong person, as often happens in the case of Indian labourers. They are today made the scapegoats, and the whole brunt of the government onslaught in curbing lawlessness in industrial front falls unfortunately on the back of these men, who are really misguided and misled in many ways, and I therefore suggest, in view of the serious situation now prevailing, that a commisssion of inquiry be appointed to go into the matter and arrive at some form of solution.[2]

It was the seconder of the motion, Mr. A. W. Wallich, who was then Chairman of the FMS Chamber of Commerce, who took the opportunity for a vehement denunciation of

> a campaign originating outside this country and directed by forces who have their headquarters outside this country and by individuals who are not genuine labourers and with little, if any, interest in labour except as a medium for subversion and intrigue.[3]

Wallich denied that 'the series of outrages which has spread over this country in the last few weeks' was the manifestation of discontented and oppressed labour.

> Is it really the discontented labourer who of his own accord proceeds to arson and sabotage and murder? Is it the hired thug,

[2] *Proceedings of the Legislative Council of the Federation of Malaya* (First Session) February 1948–February 1949. B.244.
[3] *Ibid*. B.245.

THE ONUS OF RESPONSIBILITY

> the petty gunman? No, it is not. Those are the people who are pushed by inflammatory speeches in the hope of reward into the front line. Behind, in the shadows, skulk the professional sedition-mongers. What do they represent, when they demonstrate under a foreign flag; their speeches and their pamphlets are one long incitement to violence and anarchy; their salutation is the clenched fist. They represent a tyranny as complete, as unscruplous, as sinister as that of Nazi Germany.

and where Wallich implied, Dato Onn, the *Mentri Besar* of Johore, was more specific,

> The time has now come when the Federation Government should firmly show by its action that it will have no truck with Communism in this country, that every step possible, every power that this Council can give, should be given to the police and to others to maintain that law and order, to see that law and order is maintained in this country and that Communism is eradicated, and those responsible for bringing that ideology into this country are banished for ever. I would request further that such action should be taken not only against the people who advocate Communism, but also against every foreigner, against every alien who comes to this land to agitate, to create trouble and to instigate the people. The fullest use of the law should be made to seek these people out and to send them back to their own country to ferment trouble there.[4]

These speeches, and those of the other official and employers' representatives, were unqualified in their denunciation of Communist subversion but others, from Asian representatives,[5] and Mr. P. P. Narayanan,[6] were more concerned that labour should be defended and that government should dispel the feeling in the working class that there was a kind of unholy alliance between it and the employers.

> Had it not too often occurred, when an employer hears anything which is unpleasant to his ears—something which he does not like —that he should immediately telephone to the seat of government? If only the workers of the country could be made to feel that their interests are just as safe in the hands of the employers as they must be safe in the hands of government, then most

---

[4] B.248.
[5] Mr. R. Ramani, subsequently, as Senator Ramani, Malaysia's representative on the Security Council.
[6] Later Secretary General of the National Union of Plantation Workers.

undoubtedly they would never become the tools, willing or unwilling, of any element of local, national, or international communism or whatever you call it.[7]

With the beginning of a state of emergency little more than a fortnight away this record of the Legislative Council debate showed that there was at least an incipient division of opinion between those who maintained that the biggest and most powerful subversive element in the working classes was the denial of a living wage,[8] and those who drew attention to the record of strikes, violence and political murder. There was no agreement on action between Asian and European, employer and employed, and in his concluding remarks, the High Commissioner Sir Edward Gent, as president of the Council, perhaps trod more softly than he might otherwise have done. In his view, the situation was that of a war of nerves by forces of disorder against the return of peace and law throughout the world. Allowances were made for the past, but trade unions who were under pressure from those who would subvert them to their own ends were receiving and would receive the support of government. Individuals were promised protection against criminal action, actual or threatened, and banishment would, if necessary and in consultation with His Majesty's Government, be employed against British citizens.[9] A commission of inquiry was rejected. No other action was announced except that there would be no hesitation in seeking further legal powers in advance of their actual requirements.

[7] Mr. R. Ramani B.252.
[8] Mr. M. P. Rajagopal.
[9] Gent's statement on the Banishment laws was, on the face of it, a good deal less than clear. 'Operating in this country, we have two different laws of banishment. This country has become a political entity—the Federation of Malaya—but in Penang and Malacca where the Straits Settlements Ordinance applies, a British subject cannot, under that law, be banished. In the Malay States where the former Federated Malay States Enactment has been applied, any person may be banished. This difference represents, and has for many years represented, the concern of His Majesty's Government to preserve in British territories the rights and liberties of those who can claim British nationality. I know of no change in that policy, and in the partnership here established between His Majesty and Their Highnesses the Malay rulers in the Federation the policy of the Government of the Federation and of His Majesty's Government has been to observe the limitation on the banishment of a British subject in respect of the Federation as a whole. In all respects, offenders who are British subjects are subject to the jurisdiction of the courts no less than other residents in the Federation.' If the purpose of this statement was to announce that British subjects could *not* be banished then the last sentence robbed the statement of its meaning and *vice versa*.

If the Legislative Council debate of May 31st gave the impression of a certain complacency on the part of government, Emergency measures were, within a matter of days, under active consideration and although, prior to the actual declaration of a state of Emergency, the important decisions were taken in the week or so between the 4th and the 12th of June, it is perhaps a matter of speculation whether these decisions were themselves critical. Two points stand out. First, that the enemy had not been identified; second, that the High Commissioner and, as at this time he does not appear to have been disassociated from these views, the Commissioner General as well, were unable or unwilling to act without the authority of the Colonial Office. Probably the first consideration applied. In his dispatch to the Colonial Office of June 4th Gent gave an account of the debate in the Legislative Council of May 31st. Government, he said, were severely criticised for not taking sterner action and stronger powers to suppress lawlessness and criminal intimidation and it was asserted that lack of such action had led to suspicion that government was unable to stop it. Having summarised the situation,[10] Gent went on

> My information from police and security services is that all but one of these incidents are direct consequence of policy recently adopted by PMFTU of extreme action against authorities including non-co-operation by labour with any attempts at conciliation in labour disputes. As you are aware PMFTU is one of principal organisations through which the Communist Party exercises its influence and I am convinced that its recent decisions are part of intensified drive now being made by Communists throughout Southeast Asia. Situation has undoubtedly very serious symptoms and is likely to deteriorate sharply unless those responsible for present policy of violence can be dealt with and confidence of public restored.

The measures which Gent proposed were essentially prophylactic. A show of force; passing the Trade Union Amendment Bill through all its stages; and to request the British Government to reconsider its complete prohibition of banishment with every category of British subject. The first was to provide intensive police mobile patrols, road blocks, and police raids on certain suspected offices including PMFTU branches. Only if the PMFTU raids were designed to provide evidence for their proscription could these be regarded as other than purely deterrent

[10] Supra. p. 70.

measures. Government, said Gent, agreed with those members who saw the Communist Party behind the various recent disturbances; but the intention of government was not to proscribe the Party, nor was it announced as the breaking up of the Federations of Trade Unions, but Gent gave notice that he would press for the restoration of the deleted sub-section in the Trade Union Amendment Bill: a sub-section which had been deleted on Colonial Office instructions.

Gent's policy at this time was to deal with lawlessness through the use of banishment orders. The use of banishment powers to deport Chinese and other non-British subjects had proved an effective weapon in dealing with gangs of robbers and extortioners and criminal intimidation. But, he went on,

> the policy of not banishing British subjects has however become known and on account of their immunity British Indians have increasingly become prominent as leaders in recent months in disturbances accompanied with threats of violence. When as usually happens, criminal charge of intimidation or the like cannot be taken to court for lack of evidence, only alternative methods of dealing with such persons are (i) banishment, (ii) an order under the Restricted Residence Enactment. Latter alternative as law stands at present is unsatisfactory.

At that time 84 banishment orders had already been completed. Three hundred and forty orders had been approved but a further 366 banishment cases were still being considered and orders had not yet been given. In spite of the backlog the extension of the Banishment Ordinance was intended for the selective removal from the country of those who were suspected of subverting existing law and order.

> I regret that I must ask you therefore whether decision conveyed in your secret despatch no. 18 of 16th December 1947 can be reconsidered and the banishment of British subjects from the Malay States be permissible for at the very least an emergency period of say two years. No amendment of the law in Malay states is involved. In practice only Indians are likely to be involved. Present situation can be remedied only by firmest action in dealing with persons responsible for unrest and widespread intimidation and by exercising powers of an emergency character.

On June 8th a meeting took place at King's House, Kuala Lumpur, between the High Commissioner and European repre-

THE ONUS OF RESPONSIBILITY

sentatives of planting, mining and commercial interests.[11] Representations of this kind had been made, both in London and in Kuala Lumpur, at least since 1947; are recorded as having gone on until 1950; and may, of course, be assumed to have been a more or less permanent feature of government where large colonial interests were at stake. In London, the British Association of Straits Merchants had taken the initiative in March 1947 in addressing the Colonial Secretary on the matter of growing labour unrest throughout Malaya and later that month representations were made in person at the Colonial Office. The Malayan interests suggested more attractive terms for the police force; the Colonial Office were, they said, well aware of the problem. Now, more than a year after that polite and rather innocuous meeting in London, the President of the United Planting Association of Malaya asked, point blank, exactly what the government was doing to restore the situation. When the Commissioner General had broadcast two days before it had seemed to Mr. Facer that he had said subversive forces of Communism must be stamped out in Malaya; but he was corrected by the High Commissioner who, while assuring the deputation that there was no failure on the part of government to understand the seriousness of the threat, emphasised that Mr. MacDonald had referred to the reduction of those Communist agitators who were using the gun and the knife. As far as the delegation was concerned law and order might be restored if the government were to use the Banishment Ordinance against British subjects as well as against aliens and if the withdrawn amendment to the Trade Union Ordinance were reintroduced. Three of the delegation's remaining four points were precautionary—that there were enough police, that they had proper instructions, and that ample military aid was at hand—and the last, at once confident and naïve, was that government was undertaking suitable counter-propaganda, particularly against the allegations of the extreme left wing that labour conditions were appalling : which, they said, was palpably untrue.

In reply to these points, Gent gave some idea of his own difficulties as High Commissioner. The physical and practical difficulties of catching the terrorists were very great. Immediate and complete success could not be expected. He was holding daily conferences with the Commissioner of Police and his other

[11] On June 11th Asian members of Council met Gent but apparently at the latter's request. They gave him some idea of the difficulties facing *bona fide* union officials, but their advice, e.g. adult education was hardly suited to a crisis.

advisers. Urgent cables for radio equipment for police cars had been sent. The Commissioner of Police had been authorised to secure more transport for his force and as far as military aid was concerned the GOC had never yet failed to provide support and assistance. It had to be remembered, said Gent, that the present garrison in Malaya consisted mainly of Gurkha troops, many of whom were not yet fully trained; and the government of Nepal, in making the Gurkha troops available for Malaya, had stipulated that they were not to be used for strike breaking and internal trouble, which ought to be handled by the civil police. The troops could only be used for proper military action in aid of the civil power; but this had not been a manifest handicap hitherto. On the matter of the Trade Union Ordinance it should be noted, said Gent in a pointed reference to the Colonial Office, that there was strong opposition from certain quarters and it had been necessary therefore to withdraw the amendment for further consideration. In regard to banishment the difficulty was that there were two sets of laws in two different parts of the Federation. Strong representations had already been made to the Secretary of State for permission to banish anyone against whom sufficient ground existed from the Malay States; but while this made it appear that the approval of London was all that was needed for success in this venture, the Attorney-General was more pessimistic. He stressed that evidence against the person concerned was essential. A man could not be banished unless there was something concrete against him. The courts were still open to a banishee by a writ of *habeas corpus*, and it was most important that the High Commissioner should have sufficient evidence for making a banishment order. The matter of evidence was also raised in the case of the *Min Sheng Pao*. Sedition was a difficult crime to prove and unless there was a cast iron case the Attorney-General said it would be folly to risk a prosecution which failed. The most effective way of dealing with it would be to get the necessary evidence upon which the Editor could be convicted and sentenced to a substantial term of imprisonment. If, however, the paper continued to be seditious—how long this implied long run would be the Attorney-General did not say—then there would be a strong case for withdrawing its licence.

The Commissioner of Police was equally pessimistic on the subject of evidence. During the past few months very little evidence of intimidation had been received by the police yet there was no doubt it was going on on a large scale. In an implied criticism, or perhaps a counter-attack, he said that police were not called in until there was serious trouble on an estate and then they were told plenty of stories of systematic intimidation of labour which had been going on for weeks previously. Apparently estate managers had not thought it worthwhile to report the matter earlier. Asked whether he had sufficient police to deal with the present situation, the Commissioner replied that he had but that of course he could not say whether this would be the case if the situation deteriorated seriously in the future. Mr. Wallich, the Legislative Council member who had asked the question, pressed the point. Would not the Commissioner of Police consider that 1,000 Gurkha police would enable him to cope with the situation immediately and satisfactorily? At present, said the Commissioner, he considered that he had sufficient forces at his disposal. In fact, he still had a considerable reserve of police under his command who were not required at present but, in any case, he suggested, it was not possible to increase the existing force immediately. If the situation seriously deteriorated he would require military aid. Yet the Commissioner admitted, there was reason to believe that there were some dumps of arms in various parts of Malaya which the police had not yet succeeded in locating. Recently, the police had succeeded in recovering 300 weapons from one such cache; but he had reason to believe that the number of people with illicit arms had considerably decreased. Nothing was said about the police radios which had been asked for earlier and Mr. Wallich, for whom this was the third conference on the maintenance of law and order which he had attended in the last eighteen months, might be forgiven his question, 'Was there a crisis or not?'

If there was a crisis, then two points stand out. First, the comparative helplessness of government. Playing by the existing rules, government appeared powerless to deal with a situation of lawlessness : in face of intimidation, the law itself was paralysed. Intimidation of witnesses made court proceedings a farce. Until the Trade Union Amendment was passed, the Communist unions were impregnable. And if the banishment laws needed evidence, i.e. witnesses in order to make them work, then whether they were applied according to London rules or Kuala Lumpur needs was quite immaterial : they would almost certainly fail in their purpose. The second point is that what might, conveniently but erroneously, be called the 'settler interest' had no more idea than government how the problem was to be solved. Specifically, and on two occasions, Mr. Facer said, and was not contradicted, that he was not in favour of banning the MCP : it was both impossible and impracticable. Malayan planters, miners and commercial interests had been making representations on lawlessness since 1947 and had succeeded in raising a fox or two even if they did not actually cry wolf. It is hard to see what could have been done in 1947 except (i) banning the MCP and (ii) proscribing the greater number of trades unions. In view of London's opposition to the Banishment Ordinance, not to mention the necessity of evidence, it is hardly likely that this could have been used. Nor the more drastic, if not Draconian measures which were proposed which seemed to rely heavily on corporal punishment.

On the morning of Saturday, June 12th, an extraordinary meeting of the Executive Council was held in Kuala Lumpur. In searching for evidence of complacency on the part of government, three possibilities suggest themselves. First, the statement of the Commissioner of Police that in Johore the police had been reinforced, military assistance was available and the morale on the estates was said to be improving. Second, the statement of the Commissioner for Labour that in the previous month only 155,000 man days had been lost compared with 271,000 in August 1946 (chosen presumably as the high water mark of labour unrest) and that the situation was improving. Third, a remark of the High Commissioner, which seems in retrospect to have been unduly optimistic, that it remained to re-establish, where it had been shaken, the mutual confidence between employers and their labour forces, especially on estates, or to demonstrate the reality of that confidence if it had not been shaken. At the same time, while he did not reply to some of Mr. Wallich's specific proposals, the High Commissioner revealed that other measures were in train. A Printing Presses Bill was already before the Council; and now, for the first time, there was mention of a Sedition Bill and an Emergency Regulations Bill. These were described as precautionary measures but in the meantime there had been no reply from the Secretary of State in London to a request for banishment of British subjects and the restoration of the excluded clause from the Trade Union Amendment Bill.

For Mr. Wallich, the Secretary of State in London was the villain of the piece; and by going counter to the considered advice of Council and public opinion he must be responsible for the consequences. Wallich again contended that the present situation would never have arisen had the advice of unofficial counsellors, himself presumably included, been taken at the time of the Kedah riots in February 1947 but the present remedies which he suggested were that maximum sentences, including flogging, should be imposed for the illegal carrying of arms; and that bail should be refused in certain cases and that various security arrangements should be improved on estates. Two Asian members of the Executive Council, Dato Onn, the *Mentri Besar* of Johore, and Dr. Ong Chong Keng, of Penang, who was shortly to be murdered, although not apparently a victim of Communist terrorism, both argued in favour of banning the MCP. The ordinary public, said Dr. Ong, considered that government was too soft: a point that reinforced Colonel H. S. Lee's opinion that the public, though shocked by violent crime, had now become innured to it. This was not a unanimous opinion: for Mr. Menon, a Trade Union member, while agreeing that strong action should be taken, pointed out that not only had government been slow in acting but employers had also been slow in raising wages. Certain disturbances, he argued, had not been the fault of the Communist Party, nor of gangsters, but of irresponsible estate managers. Mr. Menon wanted a detailed report. The Commissioner for Labour undertook to prepare one.

(ii) Failure of Intelligence?
The situation on the eve of the Emergency was that, on the government's side, the High Commissioner was giving full consideration to proposals to ban the Malayan Communist Party while, on the other side, the Party itself, fearing that it was to be proscribed, was making plans to go into hiding.[12] The question now arises: was the government warned? If so, when, of what and by whom? What indications were there of an insurrection— as opposed to more or less indiscriminate lawlessness? What action (*a*) was taken? (*b*) could have been taken? (*c*) should have been taken? It is now practically an article of faith amongst many former members of the Malayan Civil Service, police officers, planters and other expatriates that the government knew all along that an insurrection was coming; that it had received adequate warning from its intelligence services; that it chose, in its blindness, to ignore these warnings; and that the insurrection was as much an act of folly on the part of government as it was a manifestation of the irremediable violence of Communism on the other. It is against this background that the record of the Malayan intelligence services and their forecast of events for 1948 will be examined.

[12] According to the Acting Chief Secretary written on the morning of the Sungei Siput murders.

In June 1947 the GOC Malaya, Lieutenant-General Galloway, had discussed with the High Commissioner the effects of a reduction in the military garrison between October of that year and March 1948. The coming shortage of troops was the result of the running down of the Gurkha battalions and the interim period until the young entry began to take effect. It was recognised as an interim period and the GOC was not unhappy about it and was indeed confident that the army would support the police in adequate numbers where and when they were likely to be required. There were, however, certain contingent circumstances on which this depended and the first of these was Intelligence.

> The need for the highest grade intelligence system so that we all know before hand what is likely to happen and can take steps to meet events without being 'surprised'. I think this is working well, though of course the military contribution is fading out.

The other contingencies were army mobility and what the GOC called 'the need for the strongest timely action against malcontents, agitators, agents and the like, who were clearly out for mischief and who, if left at large, will undoubtedly make the task of the reduced forces more difficult if/when it comes to restoring law and order'. One of the last papers in the phasing out of military security intelligence (shortly to be merged in a joint intelligence committee) which took political and economic factors into consideration, was the forecast for the six months from October 1947 when Malaya would have a reduced garrison. The interest of this paper, apart from the generous entitlement of economic influences, itself a reflection of the times, is the order of priorities affecting the internal security situation.

(a) Economic, particularly the availability and price of rice and the state of the rubber industry.
(b) The growth of Communist influence.
(c) The resurgent nationalism of all Asiatic peoples.
(d) The maintenance of law and order.

The Police, according to this paper, would not be capable of dealing with unrest on more than a local scale until March 1948. The objective of the Malayan Communist Party was to 'preserve and gain time to conserve and increase the strength of the party and to work hand in hand with the people until the right moment arrives to accomplish the revolutionary mission'.[13] The infrastructure was already being built in labour and youth movements. The next stage was the calling of a general strike; but as the present period was one of consolidation the present plans did not apparently call for a country-wide strike until, at the earliest, the beginning of 1948. The general conclusion was that it was unfortunate that the reduction in the rice ration, with its accompanying rise in the cost of living, had coincided with a crisis in the Malayan rubber industry, at a time when the military garrison was about to be reduced.

> The body most likely to take advantage of this favourable moment was the Malayan Communist Party, whose aim is the eventual overthrow of the present administration, by violence. The party may well make use of the Nationalist influence in order to gain its ends. But Communist policy does not involve the calling of a general strike except at a time of governmental weakness, or when an immediate political advantage is likely to be gained by a threat of force. This was the case in Burma and may prove to be the case in Ceylon. Also, it is known that present plans do not allow such a course being taken in Malaya during 1948.

Nevertheless it was a matter for consideration whether certain favourable circumstances would induce the MCP to advance the moment for the achievement of 'the Communist revolutionary mission'; and these were

- (a) a labour force discontented by higher cost of living and lower wages.
- (b) a reduced military garrison whose efficiency might be impaired by reason of its dependence on an administrative machine, which in turn was dependent to a large extent on civilian labour.
- (c) any hesitation on the part of the civil authorities to make use of force sufficiently early for the maintenance of law and order.

The emphasis on general economic political and social conditions was something that was continued in the internal security reports of the Malayan Security Services. The MSS was headed by Lieutenant-Colonel John Dalley, a pre-war police officer who had raised and served with Dalforce, the group of young Chinese

---

[13] In this paper 'from information available'. In an MSS paper 'according to top secret sources'. In fact, almost certainly according to Government's top secret source at this time: Loi Tak.

Communists which had fought so heroically in the defence of Singapore and upon whom the Japanese took a terrible retribution. Designed as a sort of super intelligence organisation, MSS was, in fact, supernumerary, at any rate to the police force and in particular the CID. Its role was non-executive: to arrest someone, the authority of the CID was needed. Individual states were accredited with a Security Liaison Officer who worked closely with the CID. In the state of Perak in 1947 the CID itself was staffed by two detectives, one Malay and one Chinese, and one clerk. In other states the CID did not exist as a separate entity as late as 1948. A Deputy Director of the MSS was to be found in Kuala Lumpur. The Director himself was based on Singapore.

Before the war, Colonel Dalley had been responsible for the disruption of a Malay political organisation, *Perisoc*, which the government had considered to be subversive. Dalley's memory is said to have been prodigious; and during his internment he was apparently given to recalling the names of many of his Malay political opponents and musing on their present and future activities. After the war, Malay political activities and their affiliation with Indonesia, became something of an obsession for Dalley. Pride of place in the MSS reports was always given to Malay political activities and although, in general, the impression of omniscience was created—reading these reports one has the impression that political activists had hardly blown their noses before MSS heard of it—there is, in spite of a great mass of undigested detail, surprisingly little information regarding the intentions and capabilities of the post-war Malayan Communist Party. And this was precisely the information that government needed. Writing to General Galloway to discount the military appreciation of a country-wide strike in early 1948, the High Commissioner said that the present situation was admittedly far from being clear cut and free from obscurity and only a fuller knowledge of the Communist Party's present-day activities in Malaya and of development in other parts of Asia would enable a forecast to be made with any degree of reliability.

Two days before the Emergency began, on June 14th 1948, Colonel Dalley put his name to a paper (MSS 988) on the internal security of Malaya. It began

> At the time of writing there is no immediate threat to internal security in Malaya although the position is constantly changing and is potentially dangerous. One of the major problems con-

THE ONUS OF RESPONSIBILITY

fronting security administration is control of immigration from China, Java, Sumatra, Siam and India.

A number of useful analyses of the various communities and political movements in Malaya was contained in this paper which, by virtue of its breadth, was essentially discursive, hypothetical rather than analytical. The specific paragraph on the Communist Party read

> The immediate intention of the Communist Party is (i) to obtain complete control of labour through trade unions and through this control disorganise the economic life of the country. It is estimated that the Communist Party now control or have a strong influence of 65–70 per cent of organised labour in Malaya, and that intimidatory methods can cause a partial stoppage of essential services and productive activities throughout Malaya. There are signs that through the activities of the KMT/UMNO and certain Muslim organisations, the Communist Party is losing ground in the labour field and it is unlikely that the Communist Party will attempt a full-scale trial of strength unless they feel that their recent setbacks demand a display of authority to prevent any further weakening of their influence.

Whether or not the MCP would attempt a full-scale trial of strength was therefore an open question : a toss up in which either result would prove Dalley right. Exactly the same inference could be drawn from his forecast of industrial action.

> A general strike is not imminent, nor can one be forecast in the near future, providing the present political situation remains, but a change in the political situation in China and intensification of Russia's present policy, or political developments in the NEI or Siam may provide an opportunity or necessity for the Communist Party to call a general strike, in which case military aid will be necessary to safeguard essential services and to assist the civil police in protecting workers in vulnerable points.

The second purpose of the MCP was

> to create such a state of lawlessness and anarchy as to cause the general public to lose confidence in the government. There are indications that the Communist Party is already attempting to do this through its control over ex-MPAJA members and infiltration into Chinese secret societies.

Nevertheless,

> providing the present police drive against existing gangs is successful, and providing the police can recover most of the arms and

ammunition now available to the Communist Party it is unlikely that military aid will be required to assist the civil police if the immigration of undesirable Chinese and the smuggling of arms into Malaya can be prevented.

although there was a further consideration that the maintenance of police morale and loyalty might be affected by internal political developments and developments in the Netherlands East Indies.

The problem of having Dalley as an intelligence adviser was that he nearly always hedged his bets. Nevertheless, in this particular paper he probably came as near to giving an unequivocal answer as he had ever done.[14] The question was 'Is the threat to internal security *now* great, middling or negligible'? The unequivocal part of the answer reads

> Internal security today presents no problem for which a solution cannot be found.

although it goes on to the emendation

---

[14] Two papers seen subsequently in a Commissioner of Police (Personal) file modify but do not overturn this opinion. On June 12th Dalley sent a letter to the Chief Secretary in Kuala Lumpur accompanying documents found on a Chinese detained on suspicion in Johore (on April 14th). It pointed out a reference to action against 'running dogs' and sabotage. Two days later, on June 14th, Dalley referred to his earlier letter and said that information had been received from a very delicate source

> to the effect that in the present political struggle against the British Government the MCP have decided to adopt a policy of disturbance in both the Federation of Malaya and Singapore. The MCP have decided to carry out a plan of violence and arson, including the burning and looting of godowns, killing of capitalists and property owners, with a view to bringing economic chaos to the European merchants of Malaya. This, according to the MCP, will lead to unemployment and economic unrest among the masses and a state of unrest will then prevail. The responsibility according to this source, for the murders and arson on rubber estates in the Federation of Malaya lies with the MPAJA which is now known as the Liberating Forces and is directed by the MCP.
>
> 2. The same source reports that in Singapore a joint organ of the Waterside Workers Unions has been organised with a view to secretly organising the responsible working personnel in the various Waterside Workers Unions with a view to putting up concerted opposition to any attempt by Government and merchants in cutting handling charges. It is reported that one of the methods they will adopt in their campaign will be the destroying and looting of godowns on the Singapore water front.
>
> 3. The information contained in Para 1 above has not as yet been substantiated by documents or other sources. The information in Para 2 has however been confirmed by five other separate sources which have all stated that the SFTU is responsible for the formation of the joint organ of the **Waterside Workers Unions**.

THE ONUS OF RESPONSIBILITY

But the danger today increases as long as the power of the Communists increases. The threat in the event of open conflict with Russia or China will give rise to difficulties which might endanger the whole field of security.

Conflict with Russia or China was a future contingency. In the meantime, and in the existing situation, it is obvious that in this paper Dalley had no inkling of the MCP's plans for the armed struggle. After the Emergency had been declared Dalley implied that it was a result of preventable acts. The paragraph which said that there was no immediate threat to the security of Malaya was, he said, accurate at the time; and one could not foresee at that time the failure to take action which would have prevented the present state of affairs. Even allowing for the fact that this paper was drafted in May, records of a meeting with the Joint Intelligence Advisory Committee on June 9th, exactly a week before the Emergency began, cast some doubt on Dalley's role as the victim of events which government were unwilling or unable to control. This, the seventh meeting of the committee, was still primarily concerned with the frontier area: and even when a Frontier Force was discussed Dalley took the opportunity to propose a special striking force to be available, not in the event of a Communist insurrection, but in the event of a Malay attack upon the Chinese or of serious religious trouble. If Dalley had received any indication in the first week of June that the Communist insurrection was imminent this would surely have been the occasion to bring it to the attention of a wider audience. In the event, discussion of general lawlessness and Communist activities was relegated to Any Other Business and the meeting which had begun at 10.30 ended at 12.15.

Even more revealing are the lurid forecasts that were made in the June issue of the MSS monthly intelligence review. This paper was written on June 30th and page 2 of this two-and-a-half page report contains the most astonishing series of errors from what was an intelligence rather than a clairvoyant organisation.

(1) that the Communist Party was short of funds and that the probabilities were that they would engage in blackmail and kidnapping as well as robbery in order to obtain funds and food supplies
(2) that provided efforts were made to cut off supplies from squatter areas the insurgents would have to come out in the open to get their food supply

(3) the indications are that after attacks on managerial staff on plantations and mines government officials would be assassinated in an attempt to create a state of anarchy throughout Malaya
(4) during the early stages there has been arson and the indications are that extensive sabotage will follow
(5) there are also indications that another line will be the instigation of Sino–Malay enmity which was to take the form of provoking the Malays to attack the Chinese.

Of these five predictions the last three were totally wrong. The first was half-right and the second devoid of any practical application. They seem to have been, not so much more or less intelligent guesses of what might happen, as intimations of Armageddon.

> We can then anticipate even more intensive sabotage of essential installations, the cutting of communications and raids on small towns and villages by the armed and trained bands of Communists who will hide in the jungle.
>
> It is not only in Malaya that the Communists are organising a reign of terror. In areas in Java they have already begun. They have plans ready to start a reign of terror in Sumatra, and the indications are that trouble may soon break out in Siam.

As significant in its way as this mistaken forecast was the twenty page paper that accompanied it—*Malay and Indonesian Communists*. MSS monthly intelligence reviews always began with a survey of the Malay situation and even after the insurrection had been on for a month Dalley was still devoting almost as much space to Malay, as to Chinese Communism. By way of vindication, he argued that during the last few months there had been indications and information from many sources that the Communist Party in Malaya had been preparing for a critical period. Perhaps if an external factor were introduced it would provide further vindication for what might be thought of as a purely domestic analysis. Dalley argued

> There are clear indications that the change from the constitutional policy of the Communist Party in Malaya to a policy of violence was directed from some outside source.

To which he adds the gratuitous and unenlightening observation

> There is every indication, however, that the implementation of this new policy is being directed by the Central Executive Committee of the Malayan Communist Party.

THE ONUS OF RESPONSIBILITY

In view of the forecasts[15] which, after the event, look uncommonly like guesses, it is hardly surprising that MacDonald came up to Kuala Lumpur especially to urge new intelligence organisation. There is no doubt that MacDonald had little confidence in the judgments of Kuala Lumpur. On July 6th he told the Colonial Office, in support of an opinion that the Communists had started their campaign of violence about a year too early, that if the police and top civil authorities in Kuala Lumpur had continued to underestimate the dangers as gravely as they did during the past year, the MCP might very greatly have increased their 'fifth column' in the Federation. To a considerable extent, said MacDonald, we are groping in the dark. The intelligence service, for various reasons, have not succeeded in getting more than a fraction of the information about the enemy's strength and plans that we should like.

In an earlier Commissioner General's conference (June 20th 1948) Gent had complained of the absence of any reliable basis on which to estimate the worst case that the authorities might reasonably have to meet. There was, he said, no information as to the number of organised guerrillas with whom the government had to contend; to what extent they were armed and equipped; or who were their real leaders and directors. In fact, no reliable estimate of the potential forces opposing the government, nor of their plans nor of the identities of the leaders and lieutenants of the present insurrection. Which the Under-Secretary, Singapore, explained by saying that the MSS was not only short of agents but also seriously short of clerical staff but, he added, the Director of MSS had not asked for further finance.

---

[15] Another, which did not materialise, 'We can anticipate that they (the MCP) will now attempt to drive labour off mines and estates by intimidation.' With the declaration of a state of emergency Dalley's forecasts became even more alarming. On July 2nd the Secretary of State for the Colonies cabled the Commissioner General

> I have seen a signal from Chief of Intelligence Staff, British Pacific Fleet to C-in-C British Pacific Fleet, dated June 26th which quotes head of Malayan security services as giving an appreciation of future moves of Communist party in three phases ending with a general strike throughout Malaya and Singapore followed by a march on Singapore and declaration of Malayan Republic on August 3rd.

The Secretary of State was understandably perturbed. On June 22nd Dalley told a meeting at which MacDonald, Gent and Gimson, the Governor of Singapore, were present, that there was now information from a reliable source of the general intentions of the communists: there was reason to believe that general directions had come from Russia through Bangkok.

The onus of responsibility, however, did not fall entirely on the MSS. It may well have been a mistake to divorce the security services from the police but although in theory they worked alongside one another at this time of crisis neither seems to have benefited from the other's intelligence. Where the Director of MSS had little idea of the MCP's plans, the Commissioner of Police had even less idea of their order of battle. All he was able to tell the conference on the 20th was that the police had identified four major gangs each comprising possibly forty or fifty persons. To which there was a sharp rejoinder from Mr. Macdonald that he would regard that as a very serious underestimate.

To offset this evidence of ineptitude at the top credit should be given to reports that were definitely submitted by officers in lower levels of police and intelligence. Two of these stand out. First a report from Mr. Khaw Kai Boh,[16] Local Security Officer in Perak, which was submitted to the Director of MSS on May 22nd 1948. Khaw's argument was that the MCP had already launched a programme, in which all means were being used, to bring the rubber industry to a standstill. The evidence of arson, murder, abduction and strikes was collated and he believed that 'eradication of labour thieves, running dogs and undermining elements' on page 1 of the PMFTU's official May Day programme was now being taken literally by the MCP and its supporters. Perhaps even more important was the fact that this coincided with

> the very latest report that many ex-members of the MPAJA have been called up to return to the hills for training to form a Special Corps to provide the 'strong arm' for labour disputes and to deal with the reactionaries—labour thieves, running dogs and undermining elements. One unconfirmed report stated that the MPAJA organisation in Sungei Siput has been disbanded, its furniture sold and its members returned to the hills in the Sungei Siput district for training.

This report was sent to Dalley with an accompanying note from the senior MSS officer, Ryves, who said

> It stands out a mile that we are approaching an extremely critical period. The MCP has launched its big campaign and unless swift and drastic action is taken the position in this country is going to be absolutely intolerable.

[16] Later Minister for Local Government and Housing.

THE ONUS OF RESPONSIBILITY 87

In early June[17] the OC Detectives, CID, Kuala Lumpur, submitted a report on the political aspect of violent crime in the state of Selangor. It was, he said, due to a very large extent to Chinese members of the MCP and the China Democratic League. Much more important, was the schedule drawn up at a meeting in the middle of April that was held near Kajang.

A Suicide Squad of Ex-Killers and former members of the MPAJA was to be formed at once.

Arms kept underground since the reoccupation were to be held in readiness for action.

Steps were to be taken to stop all work on Estates, Mines and other businesses throughout the State.

The Labour Leaders were to organise strikes which were to be maintained.

Intensive Anti-Chiang, KMT, Anti-British, and Anti-Police, government and Upper Class Propaganda was to be inaugurated at once. Employers unwilling to fall into line with impossible demands which would be presented by Labour Unions were to be murdered.

Government Leaders and important Non-Official Leaders of the Community who spoke against the Communist Party were to be murdered.

A Campaign against Police interference, and the use of Military and Police Forces, in settling strikes was to be inaugurated.

Police Officials and Detectives who became too active in fighting the campaign were to be murdered.

The invincibility of the Europeans was to be shown up once and for all, and Managers of Estates and Mines who were prominent in failing to comply with the demands of their Labourers were to be beaten up or murdered.

In cases where the Labourers themselves were not willing to co-operate, but preferred to go on working, Spokesmen, Kepalas, or even Labourers who spoke against striking were to be murdered, thus intimidating the balance of any Labour Force who wish to go on working.

Labour Leaders on the various Mines, Businesses, and Estates were to be told that if they experienced any difficulty in their work of forcing strikes, they could depend on the active co-operation of the Suicide Squads, who should be sent for, and the Suicide Squads themselves would murder any opposition to the Labour Leaders.

[17] The report is dated June 14th but Dalley claims it was in the hands of the Commissioner of Police on June 9th.

One or two of these items—for example the murder of government leaders—are probably better thought of as aspirations than distinct objectives but it was, nevertheless, a remarkably accurate forecast of the shape that the armed struggle was to assume. The trouble was that it derived from KMT sources. And to it was attached an application from the Commissioner of Police to banish about eighty members of the China Democratic League who were held to be among those responsible for the outbreak of violent crime in Selangor. Dalley, very properly, objected to the banishment of the KMT's political enemies on those grounds alone.

> The greatest care has to be taken with information from KMT sources because we have discovered from experience that the KMT is continually trying to persuade the government in Malaya, through MSS and Police, to take action against the CDL, the consequences of which would in some measure justify the frequent allegations that the Malayan governments are in alliance with the KMT in Malaya.

Dalley and his local representative argued against banishment without close enquiries and individual identification by the police, more particularly it seems because there was in fact no suggestion that the eighty men listed were to form part of the killer gang already referred to. The matter was taken to the Chief Secretary on June 15th and Bryson, the Acting Chief Secretary, argued on the side of Dalley, putting the case to the Commissioner of Police that if he failed to get his evidence except against a small number of men the effect of having to release most of them would have a very serious effect on the position generally. The Commissioner favoured their arrest as a prelude to obtaining sufficient evidence for banishment orders. Bryson feared that it would precipitate the MCP's plans to go into hiding: an important difference of opinion, even though it may now seem academic, but on the following day the Sungei Siput murders were to put the whole train of events in motion and questions of mover and moved were forgotten.

If one accepts as a fact that there was a failure of intelligence then the following imperfect epilogue may be offered. It is drawn, by analogy, from a remarkable article that deals with American intelligence forecasts at the time of Pearl Harbour in 1941 and the Cuban Missile Crisis in 1962.[18]

[18] 'Cuba and Pearl Harbor: hindsight and foresight,' Roberta Wohlstetter, *Foreign Affairs*, July 1965.

THE ONUS OF RESPONSIBILITY

For the layman, the feeling persists that there must be some marvellous source that will provide a single signal, a clear tip-off that will alert the American forces and tell them exactly what to do. Unfortunately, there is no instance where such a tip-off arrived in time, except perhaps in the Philippines in 1941, when General MacArthur had a minimum of nine hours' warning between his knowledge of the Pearl Harbor attack and the initial Japanese assault on his own forces. The news of the attack on Pearl Harbor clearly did not tell him what alert posture to take, since his planes were found by the Japanese attackers in formation, wing-tip to wing-tip, on their bases.

Instead, said Mrs. Wohlstetter, we must wait for a number of signals to converge in the formation of a single hypothesis about the intentions and actions of an opponent. This is a necessary but slow process.

It is true for both Pearl Harbor and Cuba that we had lots of information about the approaching crisis. In discussing this information it will perhaps be useful to distinguish again between signals and noise. By the 'signal' of an action is meant a sign, a clue, a piece of evidence that points to the action or to an adversary's intention to undertake it, and by 'noise' is meant the background of irrelevant or inconsistent signals, signs pointing in the wrong directions, that tend always to obscure the signs pointing the right way. Pearl Harbor, looked at closely and objectively, shows how hard it is to hear a signal against the prevailing noise, in particular when you are listening for the wrong signal, and even when you have a wealth of information. (Or perhaps especially then. There are clearly cases when riches can be embarrassing.)

In spite of its shortage of officers and agents there was plenty of evidence for the general intentions of the MCP, very little for its precise objectives. As in the case of Pearl Harbor and Cuba, although obviously not of the same magnitude, there was the same 'cry wolf' phenomenon : an excess of warnings, false alarms, and attendant fatigue and lessening of sensitivity; and probably a mistaken estimate of the adversary's willingness to take risks. The results were not dissimilar.

Defense departments and intelligence agencies, of course, continually estimate what an opponent can do, may do, intends to do. They try to gauge the technical limits within which he is operating, to determine his usual ways of behaviour, under what conditions he will probe, push or withdraw. They try to measure what risks he will take, and how he might estimate the risks to us of countering him. Much of this work by American analysts is sound, thorough, intelligent, frequently ingenious and sometimes brilliant—but not infallible. Unhappily, any of these estimates may be partly, but critically, wrong. A wealth of information is never enough.

But two simpler explanations are to hand. First, that until March 1947 government derived its knowledge of the MCP from the highest possible source; having, as they thought, commissioned the architect, there was less urgency about examining the actual foundations of the building. Second, that the Malayan Security Services could not reveal a precise plan for a Communist insurrection before the State of Emergency was declared because this plan did not exist. In any case, from the Communist standpoint it had, tactically, to be presented as a defensive action : retaliation against outrageous and intolerable government provocation. The most likely signal was the banning of the MCP. In its absence, the Declaration of a State of Emergency did almost as well.

(iii) *Definitive Acts*
On the policy-making level government was beginning to change course but on another level challenge and response was played out in a series of actions taken by both sides. Over a year before, in April 1947, the Chief Secretary of the Federation had set out the general policy line on the matter of the coercion of government by the MCP acting through Communist-controlled unions. In the first place the proper method of dealing with the problem was to increase the effectiveness of the control over registered trade unions to take action where breaches of the law occurred. In the second place, where influence was exerted through intimidation and extortion such cases were to be dealt with before the courts and it was believed that exemplary sentences by convictions in open court would have 'an excellent and deterrent effect'. In the time that had elapsed it had proved almost impossible to deal with intimidation and extortion in open court through lack of witnesses but it was felt that to some extent the problem could be dealt with by setting the unions on a legal course although to do this obviously required further legislation. The history of this legislation seems to have followed a desultory course involving Singapore and the Federation as well as the three government departments concerned and the recommendations of a Governor's

Conference on November 1946 did not approach a practical outcome until early 1948 when it had originally been proposed to submit a bill, on a Certificate of Urgency, to the Federal Council meeting at the end of April. The first reading of this bill to amend the Trade Union Ordinance was not taken until the Council meeting on May 31st when there were still differences of opinion between Kuala Lumpur and London. The principal provision of the bill, however, was to limit the formation of Federations of Trade Unions to unions of a similar trade, occupation or industry; while another provision made a conviction for certain criminal offences—notably extortion and intimidation—a bar to holding trade union office. The bill became law on June 12th but not before the Colonial Office had queried it in some of its particulars and suggested that, in the circumstances, the High Commissioners might want to defer the whole bill for further examination.[19] At this point, however, government wanted to move fast and on June 3rd it was decided that notices were to be served on the Pan Malayan Federation of Trade Unions and the State Federations that their applications for registration had been refused on the grounds that they were Federations of Trade Unions of all trades rather than of similar ones.[20] The additional ground was given in some cases that two-thirds of the officers of the Federation were not actually employed in the trades and industries with which the Federation was connected and in July, when the Emergency had begun, a further Amendment to the Trade Union Ordinance required all officers of trade unions, except the secretary, not actually engaged or employed in the industry, to have had at least three years' experience in it.

Two days before this decision was taken a riot had broken out on an estate in Johore in which eight labourers had been killed by police. The background to this dispute was familiar: disagreement on 'spot marking'; the whole labour force given notice; and the reaction in which the estate labourers went on tapping and sold the proceeds themselves.[21] By mid-May 100 police were disposed on another estate in Johore where another big strike was in progress, but the most serious development was reckoned to

---

[19] Secretary of State to High Commissioner 30.5.48.

[20] Appeals were to be lodged within one month. The penalty, curiously enough, was limited to a fine of $500.

[21] In the absence of the manager it was presumed that the labourers had taken over the estate. It was surprising however that even though, in the haste of his departure, the manager had not locked up the office, nothing had been stolen.

be in lower Perak where R. G. Balan, a skilful communist union organiser, was running government officers ragged. Eighty-five strikes were recorded in Perak during 1948 and nearly all of them in the first six months of the year and the most serious of these were attributed to Balan,[22] but the strikes and wholesale evictions on Klapa Bali and Lima Blas estates were reckoned to be Balan's last success for he was arrested on May 30th.[23] In these particular events the frequency of contact between Indian labourers and the Chinese New Democratic Youth League was noted and there was increasing certainty that the strikes were being directed by the MCP in one form or another. A member of the MCP who was captured in Perak in early July admitted that the Rubber Workers' Union was the chief cover for the MCP in Perak but at the end of May and early June it was only suspected. When the Perak Rubber Workers' Union offices in Ipoh were raided in early June the purpose of the raid was to secure evidence on which to cancel the union's registration and as the documents seized were reckoned to incriminate it in a campaign of intimidation and sedition the president and secretary of the union were banished. Perak police had earlier raided other union offices at Chemor and Sungei Siput in search of information on the murder of a Chinese rubber factory manager. The general effect of these raids was a feeling of unrest with strikes both in progress and threatened.

Even before June however there was an increase in the number of political murders and attempted murders which, as the ultimate form of intimidation, may be thought of as self-defeating in its particulars but generally effective. On May 25th the Commissioner of Police reported two cases of murder on Negri Sembilan estates within the previous 48 hours. Three Chinese who within the last six months had appeared as complainants in court charges of intimidation against Labour Union officers were shot to death and the previous day had seen another case of a European estate manager being stabbed. On June 2nd an armed clash took place in Selangor between police and what was probably a Chinese lynching party and in the week from June 7th in Johore alone there were reports of armed robbery, two

---

[22] The Labour Department Annual Report for 1948 devotes three pages to Balan's activities.
[23] The estates seemed to have been fertile ground for disorder with an obstinate manager whose qualities were said to be better suited to a military training school. Balan himself was arrested under one enactment, held under another and was detained for 10 years.

THE ONUS OF RESPONSIBILITY

attempted murders—one European manager and one assistant Chinese manager—and the murder of three Chinese contractors.

Declarations of government policy presumably left the lawbreakers in no doubt of impending action against them although it can perhaps be argued that each side was screwing up the pressure against the other. Apart from the condemnation of the MCP in the Legislative Council debate on May 31st, and a suggestion that they should all be banished, the Commissioner General's broadcast on June 6th referred to the outbreak of lawlessness and violence that was inspired by Communist agitators and on June 9th government could be said to have gone on to the political offensive against the MCP with the arrest of Liew Yit Fan, the editor of *Min Sheng Pao* which had formally been taken over by the MCP on June 1st. By June 11th police were stopping and searching traffic on the roads and on June 12th three Chinese *Kuomintang* leaders were shot dead in their homes in Central Johore. On the 13th in a press conference which, at least according to the *Min Sheng Pao,* threatened fire and the sword the High Commissioner said that in the wave of violence 'in certain parts of Malaya' there had been at least thirteen serious incidents including ten murders and three attacks on European estate managers. Still there was no formal declaration of war on either side, at least as such, although this was the particular day on which the PMFTU and the State Federations of Trade Unions were notified that their registration had been refused.

On the morning of June 16th two events which took place within half an hour of each other on estates in the Sungei Siput area of Perak seemed to determine the subsequent course of events : either in themselves or in their consequences. Companies of Gurkhas had already been called out in the Sungei Siput area but it was thought that a military presence would have a stabilising influence on what would otherwise have been a volatile situation. The area itself was afterwards reckoned by guerrillas to be one of the best organised and toughest of the MCP districts and this is perhaps the reason why three European estate managers there were executed in cold blood. A detailed account of the murders may be found in Miller, *Menace in Malaya*,[24] but the events on Elphil and Sungei Siput estates could, one feels, have occurred in any one of a dozen places. Their apparent significance lies in the fact that that evening a State of Emergency was proclaimed in several districts in Perak and Johore. The following

[24] H. Miller, *Menace in Malay*, London, 1954.

D

day a State of Emergency was extended to the whole of Perak and Johore and on June 18th a State of Emergency was proclaimed for the whole of Malaya. Police raids on MCP offices began on June 17th, large-scale arrests were made on June 21st and on July 23rd the Malayan Communist Party, the AJA Ex-Service Comrades' Association and the New Democratic Youth League were declared to be illegal organisations. By then, however, this was something of a self-evident truth.

4

THE PATTERN OF ATTACK

It is, after the event, somewhat easier to deduce the pattern of Communist insurrection in Malaya than it was to anticipate either its strategy or tactics at the time. Both reconstruction and intentions are and were subject to various frailties. The former, in that the extrapolation of ideology with events does not add up to a plan of campaign. The latter, often in the early days the subject of wrong guesses when deductions were made about what the guerrillas *ought* to do, carried the implicit assumption, not only that the enemy were acting on a predetermined if general plan of battle, but also that there would be little divergence between plans and execution.

Considered in retrospect, the assault had two conditions of success. The first, and also the minimal objective, was the general disruption of the country: more particularly, of the economy and the government. On mines and estates, it was anticipated that the managers would desert; and that the labour force would pass under Communist control passively, in that they would provide food, intelligence and moral support and actively, in that they would themselves be transformed into guerrillas. Effective government would come to an end with the assassination of its officials; government would no longer be obeyed; taxes would no longer be paid. The ultimate objective was victory and the takeover of power: something that would be achieved through the defeat of British and local armed forces and the destruction of their will to fight.

The immediate concern of the MCP, however, was mobilisation. This was in three phases. In May and early June the hard core of the MCP assault force, many if not most of them not publicly identified as Communists, disappeared from public view. These were the professional revolutionaries who were drafted into the mobile units of the Special Service Corps or *Lau Tong Tui*. A more pointed description, based upon their function, was 'killer squads' who usually operated in groups of four or five and whose principal purpose was murder. The second phase was a preparation to move on the part of the open members of the MCP and their affiliates. In Selangor, for example, an emergency meeting of the MPAJA leaders was held on June 11th under the presidency of Lau Yew, president of the MPAJA Ex-Comrades' Association, at which the instructions of the Central Committee were given. These were to prepare to sell all property owned by the Ex-Comrades' Association; to destroy all records, lists of members and documents, and to prepare for mobilisation and evacuation to the hills; and that henceforth all instructions and orders were to be given verbally. The third phase would come when, as a result of increasing government pressure, the sympathisers, the nervous and the would-be revolutionaries in approximately the one week on either side of the declaration of a state of emergency took up arms against the government. Again taking Selangor as an example it was believed that five hundred men could be mobilised and armed in that state within three days of the order being given. But in other areas, notably Johore, the mobilisation was much more haphazard and some would-be Indian insurgents from Singapore—conceivably because they were Indian rather than Chinese—spent two or three weeks camping on the jungle fringes before they made contact with organised guerrillas.

It was in part due to this phased mobilisation—which was to be contingent on the banning of the MCP and the attempted arrest of its open members—that the insurrection began at half-cock. Although the dating on various telegrams, signals and reports is not always easy to establish, and can therefore not be taken as entirely reliable, it would seem that after the Sungei Siput murders on June 16th there were four more killings on the 18th and then there was nothing until June 26th when eight more murders occurred and the 27th, when an attack in force was made on the Kuala Krau police station in central Pahang. It was therefore practically ten days before the insurrection got into its stride and it is arguable that these ten days were of critical importance for government. By the time the large-scale attacks developed and there was anything like a strategic purpose to which the MCP were working the counter-measures were already under way. The insurrection did not come as a surprise; without surprise it had lost its first chance of success. The MCP had now to undertake the transition from a quasi-legal political organisation whose strength lay principally in the labour unions and Ex-Comrades' Associations to an entirely clandestine association in the towns; a covert but manifest force in the villages and scattered Chinese peasant areas, which were open to sporadic visitations by government security forces; and the mobilisation, training and supply of a regular guerrilla army. The first two levels could be, and were, often maintained by 'legitimate' occupation; but once armed and in the jungle, as part of what was hoped to be the main striking force, the supply problem was crucial. It was for this reason that probably the majority of the guerrilla camps in use during the early part of the insurrection were within commuting distance of sympathetic squatter areas. The basic requirements of the guerrillas were rice, weapons and ammunition. The jungle could supply none of these; and there were obvious physical limitations upon the distance and frequency of carrying, say, a forty-pound bag of rice to a jungle camp. In practice, guerrilla camps relied almost entirely upon squatters for their daily supply of food and when a unit moved it carried little more than enough for the journey. Dumps of food were found which could supply a hundred men for twenty days but guerrilla units did not normally hold more than a ten days reserve and if they were cut off from their normal source for much more than a week, then they would have to move out: usually towards another squatter area.

The camps themselves varied both in size and quality. Many of them were reactivated MPAJA bases, particularly those which had had no Force 136 liaison officers, but given their ease of construction, where simple resting places could be built in a matter of hours and even elaborate facilities such as parade grounds and lecture halls could be perfected within a month or so, it is not surprising that active insurgent areas were established with camps of varying degrees of permanence. In the first month of the emergency a combined police and army patrol found this typical camp in Selangor. It was approached by a path through *lallang*, past some empty squatter shacks, and then into thick *belukar* where there was a small lean-to shed which acted as a supply point. From here the path led up a hillside through virgin forest along a narrow and recently stamped out track travelling approximately north for a distance of about one and a quarter miles. The going was extremely difficult and the track in places was almost perpendicular in a five- or six-hundred-foot ascent. The first sign of a camp was a well-concealed sentry post overlooking the track and a *rentis* in which the bamboo and undergrowth had been cut off at the roots, in fact below the ground, and all bamboo and brushwood removed so that the actual *rentis* appeared to be a natural clearing and not likely to arouse suspicion. Dry sticks had been placed on the trail so that anyone coming along it would step on them and announce their presence.

A hundred and fifty yards further up the track was a second sentry post; three hundred yards beyond that the camp itself was reached.

This was incomplete; but accommodation had already been built for approximately a hundred men. It was built by experts. The actual buildings consisted of lean-to sheds constructed from *attap* and bamboo which had been collected from the nearby forest and cut from over an area of approximately three acres in order that signs of clearing could not be observed from the air. The buildings were situated on the hillside at five different points and the intervening jungle between each shed left standing so that it was impossible to see more than one shed at a time. Observation from the air was impossible as the high undergrowth and trees had not been disturbed. A kitchen had been built in a hollow and dry wood, broken small and completely covered with *attap*, had been stacked so that, when building fires, no smoke would be observed from the hillside or from the air. Latrine pits had been dug some distance from the camp and were provided with the comparative luxury of bamboo seats. Inside each living shed a bamboo sleeping platform had been constructed together with bamboo chairs and tables. A good water supply had been laid on and had been piped through hollow bamboo from a mountain stream some distance away. The approach to the camp from the track had been carefully screened and no part of it could be seen from more than five yards away. On the farther side of the camp the track continued for some distance and two more sentry posts were sited to cover it. Another sentry post was provided at a vantage point about a hundred yards from the camp itself from which the whole of the Ampang valley, and its numerous squatter population, could be observed. The nearest squatter huts were in fact about a mile away from the camp and the guerrillas drew their supplies from them and their well-stocked vegetable gardens. Other supplies were purchased in nearby villages and kampongs and left at a staging point where they were picked up.

Once in their camps the guerrillas were practically immune to surprise attack—the one described, at Ampang, was only found through a captured guerrilla—and in the event of an attack it was normal practice for the sentry to fire warning shots, possibly hold up the attack for a minute or two, and the whole camp would disperse and rendezvous later at secondary camp sites which were sometimes as close as half a mile to the original base.

Before considering the approach to large-scale guerrilla operations, it is perhaps worthwhile looking at a representative phase of the initial attack: the middle of July 1948. In the week ending July 15th, the first covered by the new Combined Intelligence Staff Summary,[1] the guerrillas had launched only two large-scale attacks and murders committed by the Special Service squads had declined compared with the previous week. In Johore there were four murders and attempted murders during the week: a vegetable gardener killed by four armed Chinese—possibly for refusing to supply food to guerrillas camped nearby; the second, on the same day, when two Chinese shot and seriously wounded a Chinese schoolmaster; the third, when a party of fourteen Chinese stabbed a man, whose brother was a KMT member, to death; and the fourth when the proprietor of a medicine shop was shot and badly wounded by an unknown number of assailants. Apart from this the only other incident reported was a desultory night attack on a police station in which only a few shots were fired but there were also reports of small groups of men, who were probably Special Service squads, visiting estates in search of managers and conductors. Movement of guerrillas was reported from various areas but at the time only five guerrilla units were identified: and then only by locality rather than designation.

In Negri Sembilan and Malacca, where the MPAJA had been practically driven out during the war, no major guerrilla activity was expected by government except in two localised areas but an increasing number of reports was received during the week. In the event, apart from Special Service squads searching for estate managers, the only incident occurred when a Tamil estate conductor was shot dead by a small group of Chinese on an estate near Seremban. To the north, Selangor was the scene of what, in its repercussions on public confidence and potential economic importance, came to be regarded as a major incident of the emergency. At seven o'clock in the morning of July 13th five groups of guerrillas converged on Malaya's only coal mine at Batu Arang. Serious labour troubles had taken place at the mine both before and after the war and the area was to be the scene of a particularly severe combing out by government forces later in the year. The air of industrial violence was maintained on this occasion as some of the guerrillas were identified as employees although only a few were actually in uniform. One party went into the town and while some men engaged the police station

---

[1] Up till then the Intelligence Summary had been an army one, produced by Malaya District.

others went and killed three KMT men, a mining superintendent and a lorry driver, who had apparently been selected beforehand. Fifteen minutes later the Kuala Lumpur train was met by a group of some forty men who held up the station staff, paraded the passengers and robbed them of valuables and the stationmaster of a first-aid box. Meanwhile a bus from Kuala Selangor was halted by rifle fire outside the town and the driver wounded, while three demolition parties visited two of the outlying open-cast mines where they damaged excavator equipment and damaged the generator. A truck was also burnt out and some four thousand detonators stolen. Estimates of enemy strength varied considerably, but the attack was certainly well planned and well co-ordinated and could not have been accomplished by less than eighty men. On the same day a gang attacked the small village of Ulu Yam and killed two male Chinese and one woman. The rest of the village took to the hills. In Kajang, a hot bed of guerrilla activity, a Chinese vegetable seller was shot dead in the market place in the middle of the morning. No one in the town remembered seeing it happen.

In Perak, the main event of the week was an attack on the Langkap police station which took place at one o'clock in the morning. Like the attack on Batu Arang, it was well planned, but was driven off with only two police constables wounded. Road blocks were established by the guerrillas on access roads and driving through one of them a special constable was killed in the process. A wooden bridge and two smoke houses on an estate were burned down; a Chinese KMT member was murdered; an attempt was made to murder an estate manager in an ambush. In Kedah and Perlis robbery and rape distinguished the attacks made by armed Chinese which seems to suggest that these were bandits rather than guerrillas. As in Kelantan, another state which bordered on Siam, there were vague reports of troop movements back and forwards across the frontier and of large but unspecified concentrations of guerrillas. From Trengganu there was the report of a spirited affray which involved an unarmed Danish estate assistant, three armed Chinese, fisticuffs, shotguns and flour bags. Pahang was more serious. Three people, including a European planter, were killed in one ambush in which another European was reported missing. A KMT *kepala* was reported missing from the same area—Sungei Lembing—and while he might have been kidnapped for ransom, the Summary provided the reminder that two Chinese who were earlier kidnapped from Jerantut were later found hanging from trees with their bodies

THE PATTERN OF ATTACK

riddled with bullets and their throats cut. Packing sheds and smoke houses were burned down on two estates; a Chinese contractor and a Chinese labourer were murdered.

In its minor particulars the following week, ending July 22nd, was much the same. Reports from many states of movement of parties of armed men; more or less fortuitous ambushes; and premeditated arson and killing. Johore and Perak were each estimated to have five or six hundred guerrillas under arms but in both states in this particular week they seemed more concerned with training than with offensive operations for in neither state were murders reported. In Selangor, however, the Officer Commanding the Police District of Mantin and three constables were killed in a jeep ambush; a Chinese schoolmaster with KMT affiliations was shot dead near his school north of Kajang; and on the next day two families of planters belatedly evacuating their bungalows after repeated requests from the police, were ambushed and although a Malay special constable driver showed conspicuous bravery in driving through in spite of his wounds, a child died. This particular ambush of women and children might, according to the Intelligence Summary, have been unintentional; but, it points out, it could have been a reprisal because earlier in the week five Chinese women were killed during a battle in the Kajang area not far away.

This had been the major encounter in the first month of the Emergency and a major setback for the guerrillas. On the morning of July 16th a small mobile squad of detectives led by an energetic and effective police officer surprised three guerrillas in a hut three miles from Kajang. Two were killed and one captured together with six women who were also in the hut. An attack was then mounted by an unknown number of guerrillas and they, in turn, withdrew in the face of a police counter-attack. In this encounter six guerrillas were killed; and so were five out of the six women originally found in the hut. One of these was Liew Yau (Lau Yew), a member of the Central Military Committee of the MCP and President of the MPAJA Ex-Comrades' Association.

The presence of Liew Yau, nominally one of the highest ranking military members of the MCP, so close to Kajang, may be accounted for by the fact that the town itself had strong Communist connections. Miller, however, suggests that Liew Yau had been presiding at a meeting of some of the most important men of the Central Executive Committee of the Party. They were, he says, planning to concentrate a very large force of Communist troops in order to capture Kajang, occupy it, and make it the headquarters of the anti-British campaign. Reinforcements were to come later from Negri Sembilan and Pahang.[2] Given the ideological confidence of the MCP at this time, this might seem to be possible although the evidence of Batu Arang, the week before, where the guerrillas made no attempt to hold the town although the whole area was one of considerable Communist sympathies, suggests that the guerrillas recognised their own strategic limitations; and as Kajang was little further away from Kuala Lumpur than Batu Arang one wonders whether the guerrillas would ever have hoped to have held it against government forces. Or, indeed, have been able to 'liberate' it.

In a remoter part of Malaya in this particular week, however, the hypothesis became a limited fact. Gua Musang is a small town on the southern border of Kelantan and Pahang. In 1948 it was the last station on the old East Coast railway. From the north it could be approached from Kota Bharu by road 44 miles to Kuala Krai, then eight to ten hours by river to Bertam and from Bertam the old bed of the railway could be used for motor transport if it was available. In the first month of the Emergency it now seems obvious that the whole area, Bertam—Gua-Musang—Pulai—Merapoh, was ripe for a liberated area. The police in Bertam were there in name only: sullen and out of uniform. The village itself was deserted and all the villagers were living on rafts below the kampong and across the river ready to slip away at a moment's notice. It was estimated that 2,500 Chinese lived in the area and only a handful of Malays.

On July 1st, when there was a clear threat of armed attack, the police post at Gua Musang was reinforced by one inspector and four police constables, making a total strength of fourteen. They were armed with six stens, thirteen rifles and three revolvers. Their ammunition consisted of twelve sten magazines, 600 rounds of .303 and fifty rounds of revolver ammunition. There was no wireless but the *Penghulu* of Pulai had been given a bicycle so that he might send a message rapidly to Gua Musang in the event of there being armed insurgents in the area. When the attack came, spearheaded by guerrillas but including large numbers of the inhabitants of Pulai, the police inspector at Gua Musang was captured at dawn on a ruse, escaped, went back to the police station and organised token resistance. The police sergeant in the post said they would all be killed by grenades that were being

[2] Miller, p. 95.

THE PATTERN OF ATTACK

thrown from the cliffs of the huge limestone outcrop which dominates Gua Musang—the nearest in fact landed fifty yards away—the inspector took his advice and surrendered the post, his men and his arms. None of them had been wounded; but each of them on surrendering was given $20 and a cup of coffee by the insurgents.

As soon as news was received of the occupation of Gua Musang a relief force set out from the south but was ambushed two miles south of Merapoh and the Major commanding the force and six men were killed. A stronger force eventually reached Gua Musang which had been held for five days and after a brief battle the guerrillas and their supporters retired.[3] During its brief 'liberation' it seemed that little happened in Gua Musang except the collection of taxes and contributions but if more guerrillas had been available the area could certainly have been held for far longer and heavier casualties would almost certainly have been inflicted on the relief force. As it was, the capture of Gua Musang was something in the nature of a gigantic confidence trick. The *Penghulu* of Pulai—a Chinese—himself took part in the attack on the police station and he and his villagers had been told that Kuala Lumpur had already fallen to the guerrillas and that Gua Musang was one of the last government outposts that remained to be captured. Like many other inhabitants of areas where government existed in name only the villagers of Pulai were told that the aircraft which they had seen belonged to liberating Chinese armies: a point which it was impossible for them to verify until they were strafed by obviously hostile aircraft. On the retaking of Gua Musang many of the temporary insurgents from Pulai melted away into the jungle and almost a year later negotiations were going on for their surrender.

Gua Musang was both an illustration and an example to the guerrillas. In the first place it was an illustration of the general strategic principles which underlay the insurrection. These were derived without modification from the works of Mao Tse Tung

---

[3] Spitfires were used quite effectively at various stages of this action—though not at the critical one where Shaw Force was ambushed—and there were reports that their low flying had prevented a much larger ambush which had been laid on the river and which might well have wiped out the police and military parties. It was unfortunate, however, that they destroyed one of the larger buildings which turned out to be a small mosque that had been built during the virtual occupation of the area by guerrillas during the war.

and their wholesale application to Malaya must be regarded as an act of faith rather than of intelligence. Liberated areas could either be captured; or they could be taken over by default of government. In China, on account of its size and bad communications, a dense peasant population was the foundation on which a Communist army was able to build firm bases. Malaya was a comparatively small country and the populated areas were served by communications which, while they may have been bad on the east coast, allowed access in a matter of hours rather than days or weeks. Gua Musang was nevertheless something of an encouragement to the MCP, whose own designation changed from Malayan People's Anti-British Army to Malayan Races Liberation Army, and who were always and understandably attracted by the idea of establishing areas which they themselves controlled. One of the few decisions that was taken by the Central Committee in 1949 was to set up three main bases, each in the nature of a liberated area. In the North, the obvious choice was the Malaya/Siam border area, in the area of the Betong salient, and the Eighth Regiment from Kedah/Perlis made a half-hearted attempt to establish themselves there. The main base that was chosen for the central area of Malaya was to have been somewhere in the Kelantan—Pahang—Perak watershed: in all probability somewhere near Gua Musang. In October 1948 the Fifth Regiment from Perak had marched over the mountains into Kelantan in the wettest season of the year, found that it was wet and uncomfortable, and that there was not much to eat and had decided, therefore, to march back again into Perak. The original idea for the Southern base was that it was to be near Broga on the border of Negri Sembilan and Selangor but this was dropped in favour of south Pahang: in the Tasek Bera, one of the fresh water swamp areas of Malaya. The tribulations of the Fourth Regiment on their march into this area from Johore, their experience on arrival similar to that of the Fifth Regiment and their straggling return to Johore, eventually led to the demotion and surrender of the regimental commander; but this is something that may be considered under the heading of defection rather than defeat.

In one sense therefore, the strategy of the liberated area was a failure. But in another, more modest sense, it was also more capable of realisation. Little attention seems to have been paid at the time to an important exposition of peasant Communism that was recovered after Tan Kan, the president of the All-Johore Labour Union, was killed in a gun battle north of Segamat in

Johore in early July.[4] Tan Kan's argument was that British control over the countryside was deteriorating.

> The running dogs of imperialism—the reactionary KMT SMCYYC (the Kuomintang youth corps), contractors, detectives, and informers, traitors and others—fearing that the strength of progress in the farming villages will be exploited by the Party for an attack, are beginning to run to the towns and their base.

Conversely, he asserted that

> the general masses of labourers . . . without security for their lives are beginning to leave the factories for the farming villages

and this two-way traffic had already set the stage for a confrontation between imperialism and its running dogs on the one hand and a liberation army on the other.

> The main production of the British imperialists, rubber and tin, have already become stagnant. Most of the rubber estates and tin mines, especially rubber estates, have stopped work on a general scale, and workers have run to the farming villages. There is a shortage of labour, and this threatens the economic resources of British imperialism. To restore its rubber and tin production, British imperialism has to resort to further widespread ejectment of farmers by forcing them to move out of their houses so that when these farmers are desperate they will have to move into rubber estates and tin mines to restore its rubber and tin production and to satisfy its economic exploitation on the workers and the farmers.

In Tan Kan's opinion this reactionary purpose could be frustrated in two ways. First the peasant farmers—'and other non-propertied classes'—had to resist eviction. Second, after the eviction of managers and staff, rubber estates were to be organised on a co-operative basis. The first argument was calculated to appeal to Chinese squatters who might have been expected to resist removal and resettlement as the English peasantry resisted enclosures; but was likely to break down in practice unless the MCP could provide arms and a stiffening of regular guerrillas when the physical confrontation with government forces actually occurred. Estates, on the other hand, offered considerably more

---

[4] Possibly because it went through the Intelligence files headed 'Found in a short pants pocket in Tan Kan's room'.

scope and with a sufficiently militant labour force on sufficiently remote estates rubber production would have been seriously curtailed. In theory, Tan Kan argued for 'self-tap and self-sell' in which the labour unions would replace the normal machinery of management. In practice this, too, was likely to break down unless outlets could be found for selling the product of estates under such new management; but as a theory in which it was assumed that, if estate workers behaved in this way, numerous and presumably self-sustaining liberated areas would have been created it had a certain attraction.

In fact, the insurgents' principal hope of success in this early phase of the insurrection was to reduce the government and the extractive economy in the countryside and to create self-sustaining areas. Some potential headway at least was made in the reduction of government when a small number of indefensible police posts was closed down in Kedah; but in their battle, now undisguised, to win control of the rubber estates there was an even greater prize to be had. Some aspects of this battle will be considered later but for the moment the point to be made is that a number of estates—between twenty and over a hundred—came under varying degrees of Communist control. A few European estates were temporarily lost. Managers left remote and extremely dangerous positions and one, who received considerable publicity, declared that he was on the Johore guerrillas' black list, was given a police escort to the Singapore airport, and retired to Australia. Some managers did not bother, prudently, to visit outlying and particularly dangerous divisions of their estates. That tapping continued there was known; and so was the destination of its product. Instances, however, where such control was relinquished were comparatively few on European estates and they seldom occurred when the comparative advantage was enjoyed of armed managers and assistants and the presence of an increasingly large body of Malay special constabulary who served not only as estate defence forces but also as personal bodyguards. Asian—which meant principally Chinese—owned and managed estates fared far worse both for arms and special constables and it may be variously argued that this was either cause or effect of many of them giving up control of their estates to the MCP either through absentee managers or working arrangements with the guerrillas which would overlook the abnormally low official yields on tapping.

While much of their policy never attained to the coherence of Tan Kan's arguments, at the tactical and *ad hoc* level the insur-

THE PATTERN OF ATTACK

gents were often surprisingly effective. For example in the approach to open conflict with government the MCP's argument to encourage ex-Anti-Japanese Army recruitment was severely pragmatic. Their argument was that if members of the MCP and ex-members of the MPAJA allowed themselves to be arrested they would be banished to China and killed on arrival by the *Kuomintang* government.[5] On the other hand, if they struggled and fought against the British, though they might lie on the battlefield, there was a chance of their gaining independence, eventually taking their place alongside Indonesia, Burma and Indo-China. It was better to fight and live than to be arrested and killed.

After the assassination of their enemies it was usual for killer squads to leave pamphlets and slogans on and around their victims. The following is an example from a village in Negri Sembilan.

'Rotten-staff of the people. Pho Tee Lai's crime is as follows:

1. On 20th May he advocated armed strength to oppose democratic people and he also destroyed the public educational organ.

2. On 3rd July he secretly made the people sign their names in a petition against not a few of MCP elements and in a certain house where there were arms. Further, he led British Imperialists to arrest the people. This connivance with the British Imperialists is destructive to the people's rights and privileges. He is a running-dog.

3. He protects unwholesome elements and becomes their informer. He is not loyal to the local people. We must exterminate this evil and running dog for the people whose rights and privileges he sells to the British imperialists.

1. 'Exterminate Labour-robbers and universal increase of wages.
2. 'Down with demagogues, corrupt officials and running dogs.
3. 'Less rent and less interest.
4. 'Protect Security of Labourers' representatives.
5. 'Freedom for sale of cereals (padi)
6. 'Abolish high taxation and various collections of revenue.
7. 'Safeguard freedom of organisation by the peasants.

[5] The Commissioner General's visit to China was used to support this contention: 'He had reached agreement with the KMT Government for a mass deportation of Communists from Malaya.'

8. 'Increase rice ration and reduce its official price.
9. Oppose removal of families (from one place to another).
10. 'Safeguard Liberty and Rights of Labourers.'
11. 'Freedom for tilling the land.'

                          Malayan People's Self Protection Corps.

In Perak in July 1948 the *Lenin Publishing Press* set out the *Lines of Propaganda in Connection with the Expansion of the Army* which was straightforward anti-imperialist argument. British imperialism was one of the most ruthless of all imperialisms: it had killed thousands and tens of thousands of the Malay brethren and had taken Malaya forcibly by 'oppressive inducements and violent oppressions'. The right of ownership of every inch of land had been taken. Almost all large mines, estates, trusts, business concerns, factories, communications, wharves, naval bases, etc. were in the hands of or managed by British imperialism. All political, economic, national defence, foreign affairs, internal administration and other matters were controlled by British imperialists. The lives and properties of the Malayan people were completely in the hands of British imperialism as it sucked dry the blood of the Malayan people. When the Japanese bandits attacked Malaya British imperialism failed in its responsibility to protect Malaya and without opposition surrendered to the Japanese allowing them to slaughter several hundreds of thousands of the Malayan people. After the war it had returned to Malaya by chance, snatching the fruits of victory from the people and forgetting all gratitude and discarding all loyalty. Now it had become a satellite of American imperialism actively preparing for war, opposing the people and suppressing the liberation movement of the colonial races. In its place it plotted with Fascist accomplices, the secret service of the Kuomintang Conservatives, Royalty and territorial chiefs and the reactionary capitalist class: all of which pointed to the fact that the British Government in Malaya had turned Fascist. Workers on strike had been slaughtered. Farmers had been driven from their homes at the point of the bayonet. Federations of trade unions were declared illegal, old comrades of the MPAJA had been arrested, newspaper offices raided, passers-by searched and detained, people banished, tortured and imprisoned and ultimately slaughtered with guns and knives. Government policy was one of insatiable economic exploitation on behalf of the United States, and those who submitted became the everlasting slaves of the enemy. Armed struggle was the only alternative. The liberation army comprised the best of the people : brave, intelligent, self-sacrificing. The end of imperialism was at hand and with the MCP in the vanguard it would be overthrown forthwith in Malaya.

As the pattern of attack developed and the campaign, on both sides, took shape, the two critical states appeared to be Johore in the south and Perak in the north. Both states were able to concentrate large numbers of guerrillas for comparatively short periods; and while concentrations of up to 400 were infrequent, there were occasions when the guerrillas mustered up to 150 men for attacks on rubber estates although they seldom used their numerical advantage if engaged with Security forces. In Johore, the Kulai and Poh Lee Sen areas began as guerrilla strongholds and in October 400 guerrillas were scheduled to receive three months training at a camp in the Tengkil area. In the event this never took place for lack of supplies soon forced them to disperse and return to their earlier locations. In central Johore there were few, if any, large groups of guerrillas although, qualitatively, those based on Yong Peng and Kahang in particular were notably determined. But it was in north Johore that the guerrillas had their greatest chance of success in 1948, not only because they were well established where security forces were particularly thin on the ground, but also because of their domination of the Chinese squatter areas. The Combined Intelligence Staff admitted that they knew very little of what was going on in the area and even thought it possible that some part of it might already have been liberated by the guerrillas. When large scale operations began, patrols on the Muar-Lengga road were preceded by strafing attacks from the air, and in the Panchor area at least, the clearing operations had little effect.

In all three areas of Johore guerrilla activities and policy began to be affected from October by comparatively large scale army operations. By December guerrillas in the Kota Tinggi area of south-east Johore had been sufficiently put out by three operations mounted by the Inniskillings to begin desultory movement towards Gua Musang via Kuantan : although it is not established whether this was a result of an order received or whether Gua Musang had by this time become a sort of Communist Shangri-La. By the end of December, in the Bekok area of north Johore, a group of seventy guerrillas had broken up and was moving north west; and in January 1949 the headquarters of the north Johore brigade moved into south Pahang as a result of harrying from the Security Forces.

This trend continued during the first six months of 1949 which were characterised by the movement of large guerrilla units northwards and on into south Pahang. Early in January orders were received from command section to move into Pahang for training and immediately reports began to come into government intelligence that various units were preparing or had already begun to head north. Lam Swee, for example, with 120 men and Foo Chee Hwa, with 80, who had been hiding in the Kulai/Poh Lee Sen area since November moved first to Layang Layang where they remained for four days. Lam Swee then moved off with a party of 100, followed by Foo Chee Hwa. They left outside workers and messengers behind but three weeks later word came from Lam Swee that the food situation was very poor in the Labis area and the remaining guerrillas were to proceed direct to Pahang via an aborigine village near Paloh. Upon reaching Paloh, however, this group was attacked by security forces and dispersed. They managed to regroup and went on to Labis where they found that Lam Swee and Foo Chee Hwa had already departed for Pahang and all available guides had gone with them. They were thus forced to stay in the Labis areas as a result.

Meanwhile, in the Hailam Kang and Kota Tinggi sectors of Johore security force operations had been mounted against the squatter areas and mining *kongsis* located there. The biggest operation by far was the one at Hailam Kang squatter area which began at dawn on January 19th 1949 and ended at half past five on the same evening. 650 people were rounded up and sent to Majeedi detention camp and 144 houses were destroyed. This drastic action and subsequent patrolling broke up one of the two most dangerous units in southern Johore which had hitherto used the squatter area as a safe place of operations and sent them fleeing to the north and north-west. After this operation there remained only several small units, generally eight to ten men, who would leave the area during military operations then return to their area once things had quietened down.

Some reports of guerrilla flight were obviously exaggerated—for example the Kahang gang had obviously not gone to Siam as was earlier reported—and it is evident that those who were driven from the south tended to settle down almost as soon as favourable conditions were encountered. It is possible, however, that some of the groups encountered by Gurkhas in the Seligi area of north Johore, where they were living off the aborigines, were protecting a trail north to Pahang rather than enjoying the (comparatively)

THE PATTERN OF ATTACK 111

good life.[6] But whatever the degree of movement that is allowed, it was as a result of military pressure. Which was not the case in Perak.

Perak guerrillas at the outset of the insurrection were under two commands, north and south, and consisted of six units in Taiping, Sitiawan, Ipoh, Tapah, Bidor and Pusing. One of their strongest areas, however, was Sungei Siput and an index of this strength was that by early August only one estate smoke house was said to have been left standing. Information on guerrilla movements was supposed to have been surprisingly good but a lack of troops prevented effective follow-up on a large scale. Concentrations of up to 500 seem to have built up occasionally, almost always in the hills which overlook the small towns strung along the road of the southern Kinta valley, but hardly any large scale attacks were mounted by the guerrillas in Perak itself. Instead, they moved over the central mountain range for Kelantan where they were to set up a liberated area—again, Gua Musang and Pulai were the areas mentioned—but the collapse of this project saw their return to Perak where they tended to disperse. By May there was another large scale movement north and north-east to the wild country of northern Perak, if not to the safety of the Thai border, which was almost entirely free of security forces. Unlike Johore, therefore, which had seen a forced movement of 'main forces', guerrilla movement in Perak had been largely deliberate and even where there had been large scale security force operations—although at this time the army was particularly thin on the ground in Perak—this led to a regrouping of forces rather than a withdrawal from the area.[7] What can be said of these first twelve months, however, is that there was a tendency for guerrilla main forces to move out of their state or into deeper jungle. To this extent their initial plans and attack had been disrupted and their initial chance of success had been lost. In early 1949 there were several reports of low morale, certainly among new recruits to the main force, and this was perhaps one of the factors which contributed to the comparative lull in their attacks in early 1949; February, March, April and June in particular. This was a period of transition in which the main forces retired and the recruitment of large scale *Min Yuen* or 'Masses Organisation' got under way.

---

[6] The Gurkhas reported a large guerrilla unit moving north along a well-defined path which continued towards Pahang.

[7] It was a contradiction therefore when intelligence reports from Perak said, 'In spite of successful and continuous harrassing of known CT gangs, they have never moved from their area'.

Increasingly, the *Min Yuen* took over the duties of the main force and when their organisation was perfected they became not only the essential Communist infra-structure but also an auxiliary fighting unit which was often more effective and more ruthless than the main force itself.

5
GOVERNMENT MAINTAINED

On July 4th 1948 the Federal Executive Council was told for its secret information that 'there is no prospect at present of military reinforcements from abroad.' A year earlier the GOC Malaya, Lieutenant-General Galloway, had written to the High Commissioner pointing out a weakness in the Malayan garrison that was likely to last for several months as the Gurkha battalions ran down and their numbers were not filled by the 'young entry'. In General Galloway's opinion this underlined the importance of intelligence, mobility and timely political action, but when a state of emergency was declared the military weakness remained. The actual number of battalions available in Malaya when the Emergency was declared varies according to source. According to the Director of Operations in 1957 there were only ten infantry battalions in the country, but a public and remarkably informative booklet, *Communist Banditry in Malaya*, lists the following units that were stationed in the Federation in June:

North Sub-District
   Second Battalion, King's Own Yorkshire Light Infantry
   1/6th Gurkha Rifles
   2/2nd Gurkha Rifles
   1st Batt. the Malay Regiment
   2nd Batt. the Malay Regiment

Central Sub-District
   2/6th Gurkha Rifles
   1/7th Gurkha Rifles
   2/7th Gurkha Rifles
   26th Field Regiment, Royal Artillery

Johore Sub-district
   1st Batt. Seaforth Highlanders
   1st Batt. Devonshire Regiment
   1/10th Gurkha Rifles

and more troops were made available immediately from Singapore district. Apart from certain discrepancies—for example the Devonshire Regiment was stationed in Singapore when the Emergency was declared—it is important to note that neither account gives any indication of the state of training: particularly of the Gurkha Rifle battalions. Almost all the battalions were under strength when the insurrection began and remained so for at least eighteen months afterwards,[1] while the Gurkha battalions still included large numbers of recruits. In the air there was similar weakness. Offensive capability was limited to one squadron of Spitfires and, more dubiously, a squadron of Sunderland flying boats; and while, presumably, the Photographic Reconnaissance squadron of Austers could have been pressed into service, their official role, like that of the sole Dakota transport squadron, was non-combatant.[2] The police, too, were slightly under strength, but with a force of 9,000 they greatly outnumbered the army.

On the ground, these resources were spread very thin. In Johore, for example, a state bigger than Yorkshire and almost the size of New Jersey, with an area of 7,300 sq. miles and a population of 730,000, the army dispositions on the 1st of July were a squadron of the RAF Regiment, consisting largely of Malays, at Segamat; a company of Seaforths at Muar and a platoon at Labis; a mobile company of Seaforths at Kluang; and another company at Kota Tinggi less a platoon at Mersing. In the south, there were only three platoons of Ghurkas and a reserve of 100 which also furnished the static guards for the Commissioner General's residence at Bukit Serene. Given these numbers, one way in which commitments could have been balanced against resources would have been to reduce commitments. And in the event, certain police stations, principally in Kedah, were in fact closed down but Government chose, perhaps unconsciously, to maintain its presence throughout the Federation although there were many areas, notably where squatters were concentrated, in which its writ did not and perhaps never had run. In June 1948 the weakness was there: but on both sides. The guerrillas were unable to take advantage of the situation but it is arguable that they might have done more had the government's immediate priorities been different.

On June 22nd MacDonald was in Kuala Lumpur for a meeting which included Gent, Gimson, the Governor of Singapore, the GOC Malaya and the heads of the Police and Intelligence

[1] In the middle of 1949, for example, the Suffolks were 250 under the charted strength of 637.
[2] In fact, between July 1948 and March 1949, when additional air-striking power was available, only eight tons of bombs were dropped and less than 140 rockets fired per month.

GOVERNMENT MAINTAINED   115

services. It was clear at the outset of the Emergency that with the existing regular forces government could not even begin to defend the country's estates and mines: and it is equally apparent that this was regarded as the first priority. The question was, should they make the attempt? MacDonald was concerned with the immediate future: a matter of the next two weeks. Gent, the GOC and the police were all thinking of perhaps a few months. No one, incidentally, considered that it might go on for years, and there were no plans to deal with this eventuality. General Wade, the GOC, had probably not asked for reinforcements; nor had Langworthy, the Commissioner of Police, and the problem was to distribute what they already had.

After some rather inconclusive discussions, in which it was noted that Colonel Dalley had prescribed the operations that were needed by government forces rather than answer the question what operations the guerrillas were likely to undertake, Macdonald intervened to say that he did not consider that sufficient stress had been laid upon the importance of keeping the rubber estates, tin mines and transport systems under protection. One of the first objectives of the enemy was to disrupt the economic life of the country and labour was already in a nervous state and suffering from a great measure of intimidation. In MacDonald's view it was essential to keep the economic life of the country going and this postulated an extensive commitment for the provision of static guards on plantations and mines. In spite of this it was obvious that the deputy Commissioner of Police in the Federation took this threat lightly. Planters, he said, had been advised to form their own defence units and steps were being taken to issue arms to them. Managers were being urged to remain on their estates and if necessary to send their women and children to places of safety. MacDonald, however, emphasised that confidence could only be restored if parties of troops or police could be made available to all the estates and mines: a commitment that was both urgent and immense and one that would hardly have been met, as someone suggested, by enrolling all respectable citizens as special constables.

From the record of this conference it is equally obvious that it was only MacDonald's insistence that kept the question of an immediate and large-scale commitment to defend the country's principal economic resources alive. No one had prepared any figures of the numbers of guards that were required for estates and mines, but MacDonald thought that a guard of about ten men would be required on each and he had heard that there were about 3,000 rubber estates alone in the Federation.[3] It was, nevertheless, agreed that the whole country was not yet affected and the conference therefore decided, on a rough guess, that at least 10,000 men would be required for static guard duties if all estates, not only those that were European owned, mines, business houses, depots and so on were to be protected. This would, in effect, have taken up the whole police force of the Federation; and when asked how many men he could spare for the job the Deputy Commissioner of Police said certainly not more than 1,000 and probably only 750.

It was at this point that the difference of opinion began. It was no doubt desirable, said MacDonald, not to use the regular army for the purpose of static guard duties but it seemed that no other manpower would be available. The police force could not be substantially expanded in a very short time and it therefore seemed necessary to call upon the army for these duties until confidence could be restored and other devices, such as the organisation of a special constabulary, could be satisfactorily dealt with. It might therefore be necessary to require the army to undertake these tasks for a matter of three or four weeks. Dalley was the first to oppose this suggestion; Macdonald lowered the time limit to perhaps two weeks; and the Deputy Commissioner of Police said that the GOC Malaya's Operation Order No. 4 seemed to imply that troops were not to be used for static guard purposes. Gent went even further. The discussions, he said, were unrealistic. The defence of every plantation and mine, European and Asian, central and remote, seemed to him to be impossible. Even 100,000 troops would not prevent the murder of individual estate and mine managers and their assistants at some hour in the twenty-four if they were going to keep on their job. The line to be taken was to employ the emergency powers to the fullest possible extent and to go on rounding up suspects. The police and the army should continually be on the offensive in as large numbers as possible and available fully-trained police and troops should be used to the least possible extent necessary on static jobs. The main campaign must be directed to an active, offensive routing out of suspects.

Gent asserted and repeated that the important thing was to capture the comparatively small number of individuals who were causing all the trouble and when the GOC Malaya arrived in the meeting, he, too, said he was tremendously averse to using

[3] It is interesting to note that this figure—3,000 × 10—eventually became the ceiling for the number of Special Constables guarding estates.

trained troops for static guard duties except where it was absolutely essential. The only way to deal with the present state of affairs was by strong offensive measures. These would keep the enemy on the run so that their communications, sources of supply and higher direction broke down. He appreciated the feelings of individual planters; but offensive action would produce immediate and satisfactory results for them. There was no possibility of the army providing 10–12,000 men for guard duties, in addition to those required for offensive action, and in any case he could not agree that troops should be dispersed throughout the country in penny packets.

Confronted by this weight of opinion, MacDonald was deferential to the military view but affirmed flatly that it was essential to maintain the economic life of the country and to restore morale. He also took the lead in suggesting that not only should there be a central planning committee which should report within twenty-four hours and whose views should be considered without delay by the Defence Co-ordination Committee in Singapore in the presence of the High Commissioner and the Governor of Singapore but, in addition, every State and Settlement should be directed to set up its own security committee of officials and unofficials which would be responsible for planning and directing operations. MacDonald's initiative went still further. There must, he said, be complete co-ordination, a proper appreciation, and plans including a full statement of the reinforcements, if any, of manpower and equipment required.

Gent's reaction, if one may attempt to vivify the minutes, seems to have been violent. Operations in Malaya were his authority and not MacDonald's but the Commissioner-General sought not only to reverse his own priorities but also to hold him accountable to the British Defence Co-ordination Committee in Singapore. The minute records:

> The *High Commissioner* stated that he must make it quite clear that, so far as the Federation was concerned, full reponsibility remained with him, and that he could not have his discretion or authority tied by a need, in any emergency, for the consent of the Committee which had just been mentioned. So far as he was concerned, the measures he had in view would be put into operation and could not be dependant upon the consent of or direction from the Committee, if he felt it necessary to take decisions immediately.

On the same day that this conference was held in Kuala

Lumpur a delegation which described itself as 'representing all Malayan interests' called on the Colonial Secretary in London to tell him 'that their experience over the last two years has completely undermined their confidence in the High Commissioner's ability to handle the present situation.[4] In a long and critical editorial on July 1st the *Straits Times* referred to strong pressure from unofficial quarters, especially the planters, for the appointment of a new High Commissioner but it discounted Gent's personal unpopularity among the European community.[5] Given that this pressure existed it hardly seems to have been decisive: at least in June 1948. Curiously enough, when Gent was first notified verbally by MacDonald that someone else was needed as High Commissioner, the reason given was that he had not won the confidence of the Asians. This notice was given on the 3rd or 4th of May 1948; had been discussed in London in the previous January; but no decision had been taken until mid-April.[6] It may well be that these representations from British economic interests in Malaya predisposed the Colonial Secretary, even a Labour Colonial Secretary, against the High Commissioner. But it seems more likely that his dismissal was occasioned by MacDonald and followed immediately upon the confrontation which took place in the conference at Kuala Lumpur on June 22nd. In the Commissioner General's telegram,[7] between June 22nd and June 25th, to the Secretary of State he reported that Gent's reputation was very much worsened by the Emergency; that he was the stumbling block to quick action; that he had been ignoring MSS warnings (on the advice of the police); that there was no co-ordination for planning at the beginning of the Emergency; that he was pushed

---

[4] This delegation was organised by the Rubber Growers' Association and the United Planting Association of Malaya and those invited to attend were the Eastern Exchange Banks Association, the British Association of Straits Merchants; the Rubber Trade Association of London; the Malayan Chamber of Mines; and the Association of British Malaya. In the event the Incorporated Society of Planters and Glen Line were also represented. An anodyne Press release was issued afterwards which had been agreed by the Colonial Office with a few members of the delegation.

[5] This editorial was a far stronger indictment of Gent than its front page of June 17th under the famous headline 'Govern or Get Out'. It referred to 'day-long arguments at King's house with angry unofficial deputations' and its view was that Gent had not taken a sufficiently far-sighted or realistic view of the violent elements in the Federation or of the armed challenge to the planting and mining industries and to constitutional government.

[6] An unconfirmed report says that Gent's dismissal was being discussed in the Colonial Office as far back as September 1947.

[7] No. 82.

into decisions by unofficials and by the Services; that he had delayed taking emergency powers and using them; and that he admitted the police high command was unable to cope with the situation but had taken no action to remedy this defect. Seven telegrams later, on June 25th, MacDonald asked for Gent's resignation to be requested at once. The Commander-in-Chief (General Ritchie) reported that all soldiers had lost confidence in Gent, the AOC, Air Marshal Lloyd agreeing, and that planters in Johore as well at Dato Onn were always asking that he should go. On June 26th Gent received a telegram from the Secretary of State telling him to come home at the earliest opportunity. It was suggested that he should return 'for health reasons' but Gent rejected this in favour of 'consultations' and it was understood that he would resign upon arrival in London.

Gent left Singapore at midnight on June 28th. He was delayed for twenty-four hours in Colombo because the RAF in Singapore had not obtained clearance in advance for the plane to continue through to London and was there transferred to a York freighter aircraft. On the morning of July 4th the York was in collision with another aircraft near London, crashed, and the High Commissioner was killed.

His death was an occasion to redress the balance of opinions. Even before he died Asians were defending him where Europeans attacked. On the day Gent was killed MacDonald conveyed a message to the Colonial Office from Tan Cheng Lock asking that Gent be reinstated; and an Indian member of the Legislative Council, Mr. S. O. K. Ubaidullah, had tabled a motion that Sir Edward, who enjoyed the confidence of the Council and the popularity, especially among the Asian population, was indispensable to effect the Emergency regulations and to secure the co-operation of the people of Malaya. Most of his friends, it was said, were among the poor; and in an outspoken letter to the *Strait Times* Mr. Tan Siew Sin said that Sir Edward Gent would probably be alive today but for his courage and determination to obey his conscience in his dealings with the local-born community and that in the eyes of the majority of his countrymen he committed the unpardonable sin of treating the Asians as if they were human beings: a remark which predictably brought down the wrath of some of Sir Edward's fellow-countrymen.[8]

---

[8] A minor curiosity is that the late Sultan of Perak, at one of the post-war constitutional conferences, had apparently asked that Gent should be appointed the first High Commissioner of the Federation. *Legco Proceedings*, February 1948–February 1949, pp. B 371–72.

For a man who had won a DSO for his command of a regular battalion in 1918 at the age of 23 it is rather surprising that a prominent European civilian in Malaya should have described him as 'a good staff officer but certainly no regimental officer'; and for a man who had earlier won the MC, courage was hardly in question, nor even acts of civil courage. It was Gent who, having achieved the reputation of father of the Malayan Union and who, in a sense, was sent to Malaya to make it work, came to the conclusion after two months that the scheme would not work and recommended that it should be scrapped in favour of a Federation.

That he did not act was probably a calculated risk. The country had been on the verge of terrorism for the last two years or more. Whether it was the natural aftermath of war, defeat and occupation as well as chaotic social and economic conditions, or whether it was to be laid at the door of political parties and particularly the MCP, was something that remained to be seen. To destroy the MCP before its intentions were unmistakably known might have brought immediate advantages, but in the long run, as the typical act of a repressive colonial regime, it would have been to court political disaster. The MCP did not make up its mind, in stages, more than three months before a state of emergency was declared. As long as it was acting through the trade unions it would have been difficult if not impossible to destroy the one without the other and until the MCP had unmistakably shown its hand overt action against it was suspended. The danger was that when the insurrection began events would move so fast and government would move so slowly that the situation would be out of hand.

In organisation alone, the government was suffering from grave disadvantages when the insurrection began. It was, in fact, an acting government. In early July, as the minutes of the Executive Council show, the country was without a High Commissioner. Sir Alec Newboult, the substantive Chief Secretary, was now the Officer Administering the government. There was an acting Chief Secretary; an acting Attorney General; an acting Financial Secretary; and an acting Commissioner of Police. The GOC Malaya, Major-General C. H. Boucher, had assumed his position only a few weeks before.

Perhaps the most serious lack of an experienced and substantive officer, next to the High Commissioner, was that of a Commissioner of Police. Mr. Langworthy, the former Commissioner, who had been in bad health for some time, resigned almost as soon as the Emergency began; but while he was still Inspector-

GOVERNMENT MAINTAINED

General Designate of the Gold Coast, Colonel W. N. Gray was invited to visit Malaya in an advisory capacity. Colonel Gray, a former Royal Marine officer, had until very recently been Inspector General of the Palestine police and made his report with the knowledge of counter-terrorist operations in the last months of the British mandate in Palestine. Having made his report Gray was then recommended to the Colonial Secretary to be the new Commissioner of Police.[9]

Gray returned to Malaya as Commissioner of Police in the middle of August 1948, but it was not until October 6th that a new High Commissioner, Sir Henry Gurney, was installed. Sir Henry had also seen out the end of British Administration in Palestine, as Chief Secretary, and it was remarkable that the end of the British commitment there was followed so soon by the beginning of a similar commitment in Malaya.[10] Publicly, their appointment, and particularly that of Gurney, was greeted with caution and it was argued that it was unwise to bring in newcomers to what was assumed to be an unfamiliar situation. Privately, but based upon the same premise, the fears were more forcibly expressed: that Malaya would become a second Palestine. Apart from the prospect of terrorism and internecine warfare, the Malay rulers and *Mentri Besar* were reported to be protesting against Gurney's appointment on the ground that *he* would think Malaya was another Palestine: that is to say that Malaya was a country in which both communities had equal rights; and that they should have been consulted beforehand.[11] A threat was made to boycott Gurney's installation in the same way as, without precedent, the Malay rulers had boycotted Gent's installation at the head of the Malayan Union, but in the event all the states were represented except Johore.

In the absence of a High Commissioner and a Commissioner of Police it is perhaps surprising that the conduct of emergency operations got under way so smoothly. Meetings of the Local Defence Committee were held at King's House every morning at 8.30 and lasted from two to three hours. These meetings were largely discursive and in the afternoons their ideas and decisions

---

[9] C-G to S/S tel. 148 of 19.7.48.
[10] Other names that had been mentioned included Lord Milverton, General Nye and Sir Alexander Grantham, the Governor of Hong Kong.
[11] There had of course been nothing like a Balfour Declaration; but with the largest Chinese population in South East Asia it might pardonably have been assumed that Malaya had become the national home of the Nanyang Chinese.

were implemented by the Internal Security Committee. The first meeting of the new Internal Security Committee was held on June 25th. On the 28th a special section of the Federal Secretariat was created to deal with internal security and was placed in charge of Mr. D. C. Watherston who became Secretary for Internal Security and later Secretary for Defence and Internal Security. He was to act as Chairman of the Internal Security Committee which was set up to co-ordinate action between the police and other civil government departments and the military. In particular it dealt with urgent requirements of all kinds for the police, some of which could be obtained from military authorities or from other government departments. At its daily meetings in June, for example, it was concerned mainly with telecommunications, wireless sets, stores, arms and ammunition. It started off by meeting every day at 2.30; in July it met every two days and from August, when it seemed that immediate requirements were being met, until December it met once a week.

The records of the Internal Security Committee show that it was essentially an administrative body. It dealt with essential but low level routine matters—barbed wire, planter's weapons, estate security, the accommodation of special constables—and handled, on a federal basis problems which for the most part originated with the states themselves.[12] Two points stand out in restrospect. First that it was largely concerned with the security of European property. Second, and more important, that it made no attempt to direct emergency operations on either the civilian or the military level.

The basic document on which emergency operations were based at this time was a circular from the High Commissioner to all departments of government on June 19th instructing them to give 'all assistance to the police' in combating the disturbances. How this was interpreted in the states seemed to depend largely on the temperament of the Chief Police Officer; and in Pahang, in particular, there seems to have been an approach to almost absolute power. Perry Robinson observes that in most areas it cut the civil, i.e., non-police officials off from the emergency and thereby discouraged the civil population from doing anything to help.[13]

[12] The committee was composed, at a typical meeting, of the Secretary, Defence and Internal Security (Chairman); the Deputy Financial Secretary; the Principal Assistant Secretary, Internal Security; the Secretary, United Planting Association of Malaya; a representative of the FMS Chamber of Mines; the Deputy Commissioner of Police; four Service representatives; and an MCS officer as secretary.

[13] J. B. Perry Robinson, *Transformation in Malaya*, London, 1956. p. 166.

Another consequence, which will be considered later, is that it laid the way open to uncertainty and dispute in areas where the army were operating with the police but it may also be seen as stemming from the government's basic decision that the country was not to be given over to martial law, which many of its critics, European and Asian, demanded, and that civilian control over military and para-military operations was to be maintained. The army, therefore, was regarded as acting in support of the civil power and, as such, was to operate within a quasi-legal framework. In practice, however, and in particular in the critical few months before Gurney arrived and in which the pattern for emergency operations was formed, the Commissioner-General's influence was of outstanding importance. With a roving commission in the Federation rather than fixed responsibilities he was able to visit many estates, particularly in Johore, visits which are still recalled as inspiring confidence, and his opposition to more or less indiscriminate use of air power, for example in loosely-authorised air strikes, helped to mould a pattern which was seldom followed in other colonial counter-guerrilla operations.

In practice, and on the state level, the conduct of operations was usually a straightforward matter and uncomplicated by questions of authority and its delimitations. In Johore, discussion and action on security problems were dealt with by the State Liaison Committee which held its first meeting on July 1st in the office of the British Adviser. It consisted of the Chief Police Officer who acted as chairman; Dato Onn the *Mentri Besar*; the British Adviser; Brigadier Hedley, who commanded the local military forces;[14] the Chairman of the Johore Planters' Association; and the Secretary to the British Adviser who was himself the Secretary of the Committee. This, as it was pointed out, was an advisory rather than an executive committee but it provided a pool of information on which members could draw in their individual executive capacities. *Ad hoc* conferences were also held. For example, on July 8th, over twenty representatives of Chinese Associations in Johore held a conference with the *Mentri Besar* and the British Adviser.[15] Where advice was sought—for example

---

[14] Johore Sub-District; at this time under the command of GOC Singapore.
[15] One of the purposes of this meeting was to impress upon the Chinese community the necessity of refusing any aid to the terrorists and of giving more co-operation and help to government. But it is worth noting that the second purpose was to reassure the Chinese community who had expressed fears of a deterioration in Sino-Malay relations resulting from present terrorism.

from the Brigadier on whether armed guards generally had power to shoot to kill when guarded places were approached by unauthorised persons—it was either given or else referred to the competent authority.[16] Members of the committee retained the right to reject advice,[17] and each maintained the competence of his own individual executive capacity. In practice, in Johore, the committee tended to defer to the opinions of the army representative in the early stages but were very much aware of the importance of the opinions of the *Mentri Besar*, Dato Onn who, as leader of UMNO, was also the foremost political figure in the Federation. His explosion on the matter of not arming all special constables, his allegations of mistrust of the Malays, and his threat to broadcast to his community to withdraw from the scheme were all sure to be heard immediately in Kuala Lumpur, if only in the British Adviser's report. Reports were received and considered from administrative officers, instructions for alarm systems, defence plans for estates and methods of substituting bamboo stakes for barbed wire were passed on and opinions—whether Palestine Police sergeants should be posted singly or the number of special constables should be doubled—were passed back to Kuala Lumpur. Two problems remained: whether or not it was an executive committee and whose authority was to prevail in the conduct of operations.

New Forces
Special Constables

In retrospect, the raising of special constabulary was the largest, the most ambitious, and possibly the crucial task undertaken by government in the opening phase of the insurrection. The idea arose of providing armed guards on rubber estates, which were reckoned to be the primary target; it was discussed in the first few days of the emergency; decided upon on June 24th; and on June 26th embodied in the Essential Regulations and published

---

[16] In this case the CPO. Some of the decisions were rough and ready: for example the Callus Index. Brig. Hedley brought up the question of squatters who, judging by the appearance of their hands, were not manual labourers. It was agreed that the military could arrest them, if they could not give a satisfactory explanation, for subsequent interrogation by police.

[17] The Adviser, Chinese Affairs, (who doubled up as Deputy Commissioner for Labour) wanted more troops posted to the towns as part of a plan for getting information from the Chinese community. The Brigadier refused. Although bodies of troops had been stationed recently in Muar, Renggam, Kluang and Layang Layang, no more information had been coming in.

as a second supplement to the Government Gazette. The original intention was that it should be a force some ten to fifteen thousand strong, but at its peak, in late 1952 and early 1953, its numbers exceeded 41,000 men. Within three months the original figure had almost doubled and nearly 24,000 men had been enrolled. Their initial and often rudimentary training was carried out by twenty-five training teams provided by the army, by the police, by officers seconded from civilian government departments, and by estate managers and tin miners themselves. Later, with the arrival of Palestine Police sergeants, their training was put on a more formal basis, but in the first couple of months, the wonder was, not only the speed with which such large numbers were raised, but that they maintained themselves as an effective deterrent on so many estates.

Recruitment was voluntary: anyone acceptable to the Commissioner of Police or CPO other than members of the Forces. Guards who were already employed on estates and mines might be enrolled as special constables subject first to screening. Preference was given to those already trained in firearms and many of the original members were drawn from former Volunteers, Police, and ex-members of the Malay Regiment and locally enlisted personnel of the Imperial Forces. The enrolment and organisation of SCs was a State responsibility under the control and direction of the CPO but further assistance could be provided by government. For administration purposes European officers were released from other departments and seconded to CPOs and altogether fifty-two were seconded and officiated as staff officers until the arrival of the Palestine police. By the beginning of August the *ad hoc* arrangements involving officers seconded from civil departments of government were beginning to be phased out. In the critical period of two months fifteen thousand special constables had been screened, enrolled and documented. In practice, these civilian staff officers had succeeded in raising a force which was larger than the regular police at a time when the police themselves were fully occupied. By the end of August the special constabulary passed over to police control and Gray's first HQ policy instruction as Commissioner of Police was on the assumption of these responsibilities by the police. Many of the initial problems had still to be overcome. Quite a number of them arose from the infusion of what had started out as privately raised state forces into what the new Commissioner of Police had very definitely decided was to be a reserve police force to be organised on a uniform basis.

Even before the formal declaration of the Emergency, many estates and agency houses had been recruiting defence forces which were both armed and paid for by them. Harrison and Crosfield, with the assistance of Colonel Dalley, had been recruiting in Singapore—some, apparently, rather dubious characters—and these they were paying at the rate of $120 a month. The uniform rate that was now agreed on for special constables was only $70 a month and while payment was now assumed by government, forces that were maintained over and above those allocated had to be paid for by estates. The allocations for estates and mines were decided, nominally, by OSPCs but in practice often by the SC staff officers, and this led to frequent complaints that estates were not receiving sufficient numbers. There were counter arguments that by paying over and above the authorised $70 a month some estates, and probably many, were buying protection at the expense of others. Questions were also raised as to how the allocated SCs were being used.[18] With so many special constables as yet untrained[19] it was hardly surprising that estates should have attempted to maintain as many guards as possible; and that they should have sought a weapon for every man. With an initial shortage of weapons the policy was that the number of rifles issued per estate should not exceed one and a half times the number of guard duty posts, i.e. one rifle per post with a 50 per cent reserve and not one per special constable. What this meant, in effect, was that only one man in three had a rifle, and this, with a normal rota of eight hours on in twenty-four, meant that only those actually on duty would be armed. This was essentially prophylactic and was hardly designed to counter an attack in force when all available men might have been needed for defence. At the same time, it was thought to reduce the danger of losing weapons to the guerrillas who might more easily have acquired them from SCs who were off duty.

Almost all the special constables who were recruited were Malays. This fact was significant in itself, reflecting a loyal support in the face of very real danger which surprised and gratified the country's European administrators and business interests. The

---

[18] At one estate, in Johore, in the Yong Peng area, one manager with a force of thirty special constables withdrew twenty-five of them for the protection of his bungalow at night while five men left to guard the smoke house were augmented by up to a platoon from a co-operative local battalion in time of expected trouble.

[19] At the beginning of August only half of them had received individual arms instruction.

number of special constables killed in 1948 was barely exceeded by the number of regular police who were killed—37 to 45—and over the Emergency as a whole their casualties were even greater: 593 dead and 746 wounded compared to the police figures of 511 dead and 701 wounded. Nevertheless, the fact that one community was being armed rather than another created some apprehension amongst Malayan Chinese.[20] On Chinese estates the marked absence of special constables and of any scheme to provide them was creating a doubly uneasy situation. On July 15th representatives of European planters and rubber interests called on the Secretary for Internal Security to inquire what government proposed to do with regard to Asian estates and mines. They felt that the situation now that the European estates and mines were being taken care of was becoming a trifle delicate and it was time that the government formulated its policy on the matter. This raised a difficult but important problem. The dilemma was stated in a minute that was put up to the OAG.

> We have reason to believe that some Chinese mine or estate owners are paying protection money to the Communists. To offer to arm guards on Chinese estates and mines therefore is to take a very grave risk, and yet to leave them entirely without protection would almost certainly result in a further lowering of Chinese morale and those now on the fence would be driven off to the enemy's side.

The suggestion was that there should be a meeting with the Malayan Estate Owners Association and Chinese Chamber of Mines representatives and that they should be told quite frankly what government's fear was, viz., that until the Chinese generally could show that they were solidly behind government, the issue of arms was a risk which could not properly be taken. However,

---

[20] The *Straits Times* in an editorial (5.7.48) criticised a suggestion which Sir George Maxwell, former Chief Secretary, had made urging that Malays, and only the Malays, should be armed to combat the present threat to the country. Sir George's remarks, in a letter to the *Daily Telegraph* (1.5.48) were somewhat ambiguous. 'If they (the Malays) were provided with ordinary shotguns . . . the change in the internal security of Malaya might be almost instantaneous.' But it could be argued that he was more concerned with avoiding the situation after the Japanese invasion Dec. 1941 when the GOC issued an order of the day which said '. . . from the civilian population, Malay, Chinese and Indian, we expect that patience, endurance and serenity which is the great virtue of the East and which will go far to assist the fighting men to gain a final and complete victory.'

if plans for arming Chinese special/auxiliary police in towns and villages proved successful there would be a rise of Chinese morale which would justify issuing arms to estates and mines.

At the end of the year the dilemma was unresolved. The opinion of the Commissioner of Police[21] was that it would be unwise in the extreme to arm a large number of Chinese at that stage for it was difficult if not impossible to distinguish between loyal citizens and bandits and their fellow travellers. Security forces must not be hampered by doubt whether armed Chinese were friend or foe. Experience had shown that Malay special constables would not stay on estates and mines which were purely Chinese except where it was possible to provide adequate supervision as had been done in areas where mines were concentrated, for example, in Perak. Moreover it was abundantly clear that protection money was being paid by a very large number of Chinese-owned estates and mines and it was illogical for government to provide further protection to those who were so doing. Because of these considerations CPOs were instructed that they would only provide special constables for guard purposes on Chinese-owned properties when a request had been made and CPOs were completely satisfied that the Chinese owner and/or his staff were giving such assistance to the security forces as was within their power. The criterion, in fact, was whether the Chinese owners or staff were prepared to give information concerning the guerrillas and, in particular, information regarding the payment and collection of protection money. The vicious circle was maintained. Absentee owners and managers were unlikely to return to their estates without protection. That protection was never complete; and the chances of murder and the destruction of property—chances that would be increased if it were known that information was being supplied to the police—as well as possible self-incrimination continued to be offset against contributions in cash or kind which was the premium of insurance with the insurgents.

Auxiliary Police
Alternative and informal Chinese proposals for the arming of their own community will be considered later but on the formal level Chinese recruitment for the Auxiliary Police was discouraging. In early August Negri Sembilan reported that there was still only one Chinese auxiliary policeman in that state and in Sep-

---

[21] Police Headquarters Policy Instruction No. 10, December 23rd 1948.

tember (3.9.48) the Chief Secretary told the Secretary for Chinese Affairs the Chinese response to the Auxiliary Police recruiting call had been so poor that he personally thought that they could put the file away. In his opinion the majority of Chinese estate and mine owners didn't want to be protected by armed guards and to issue weapons to them would be just another way of handing them over to the bandits.

The proposal to establish an auxiliary police force had been made in May; but the provision already existed under BMA regulations for an unpaid special constabulary although this seems to have attracted little support. With the insurrection under way there was an obvious need to raise a voluntary auxiliary police force to relieve the regular police in both towns and villages. The specific duties that were envisaged in the memorandum on the auxiliary police force were patrols both on foot and in vehicles, certain static guard duties and the training of recruits both in the auxiliary police and the special constabulary. By October 1948 12,000 auxiliary police had already been recruited, 15,000 by the end of the year and the astonishing peak figure of almost 100,000 in September 1951. Translating these figures into recruitment and establishment in 1948 there was a small but definite commitment of Chinese in the larger towns but nine-tenths of the Auxiliary Police were at this stage '*kampong* guards' and consisted of rural Malay volunteers. The offer of Chinese Chambers of Commerce to act as recruiting agents had little effect and although, at a later stage, Auxiliary Police units consisted entirely of Chinese in some of the smaller towns of Malaya, there was very little Chinese commitment at this point to take up arms voluntarily in support of the Federation Government.

Regular Police
Including recruits in training, the strength of the regular Federation police in June 1948 stood at almost 10,000. On June 28th the Deputy Commissioner of Police reported to the Executive Council the intention to increase the permanent strength of the police by one thousand men: ten per cent. A fortnight later Gray advised the Council that he would recommend an increase of seventy-five per cent.[22] One of the first things to be done was to reduce the training programme for recruits from the normal twelve to an emergency five months; and for immediate needs

---
[22] On the same day (12.7) MacDonald's telegram to the Colonial Office said that the aim was only 3,000 extra police and part of that would be Auxiliary police.

the government turned to former members of the Palestine Police many of whom, fortuitously, were on demobilisation leave in Britain. The possibilities of such recruitment had been discussed in early June but the first request seems to have been made, again by Macdonald, for 200 Palestine police on June 26th.[23] A small advance party left Britain for Malaya on August 5th and chartered aircraft brought in the first 200 by the end of the month. A total of 500 eventually arrived and after some acrimonious discussion on their tasks and seniority it was accepted that their principal role was that of training special constables in the defence of estates and mines. In this capacity they were invaluable as a leavening of experienced NCOs in the mass of inexperienced special constables but they were, at this stage, only a marginal reinforcement to the regular police.

In almost every mention of Malaya's post-war police force reference is made to its demoralisation under the Japanese occupation and the slow processes of recovery. How slow that recovery was and how difficult it would be to build on the existing foundation can be seen in Gray's report to Gurney shortly after he had arrived in Malaya which should have jolted government out of any feelings of complacency.[24] It was a comprehensive indictment. General efficiency, said Gray, could be judged by the fact that in the middle of August 1948 no steps had been taken to ensure that police headquarters and headquarters of states and settlements functioned throughout the twenty-four hours. These establishments and their telephone systems closed at 6.30 p.m. daily until 8 a.m. the following day and throughout week-ends from Saturday mid-day until Monday morning. There had been no clear cut and well understood chain of command in the force. No broad or explicit policy directives or instructions had been issued to the force by police headquarters on major points of action to meet the emergency quite apart from other important matters affecting the control and operation of the force as a whole. Security of information, documents and conversation was neither observed nor understood. Morale in general was not high and there existed considerable distrust and open criticism of senior government and police officials although there was a pride in the old traditions of the force which was particularly noticeable at ceremonial parades and functions at which all ranks were astoundingly good. Training on lower levels was good but rigid. At higher levels it hardly existed. Promotion appeared to have

[23] Gray had suggested 300 when he met the Executive Council.
[24] November 30th 1948.

been based upon Apostolic succession regardless of efficiency except in cases of quite remarkable ineptitude. There was very little promotion and in the inspectorate and rank and file hundreds of cases were outstanding. The organisation, establishment and staff of police headquarters was totally inadequate and authority so centralised as to make it impossible for the functions of a headquarters to be performed. From accounting, which was neither properly understood, nor controlled, to wireless, which was nonexistent, the deficiencies of the system were exposed and the only aspect in which criticism was moderated was in regard to the original draft.[25]

In the first twelve months of the emergency the police had to deal with three main problems. First, the establishment and maintenance of viable police stations in order, at the least, to dispute territory with guerrillas and their local supporters. Second, to adapt its normal peacetime role so as to provide a major striking force. Third, to train the vastly expanded numbers of the regular and ancillary police. In Kelantan, for example, the Commissioner of Police authorised the construction of five new police stations during his visit in December 1948 and a strengthening of many of the rural posts either by re-siting, reinforcement or the construction of small police barracks. The installation of wireless equipment was essential if these and other isolated stations were to give warning of attacks made upon them; but even before it arrived there were less than half a dozen instances of heavy attacks or the over-running of small police stations.

The provision of jungle or 'anti-bandit' squads of police was eventually to involve a major reorganisation but there was an obvious shortage when they might perhaps have been used with most effect: that is to say in the period of guerrilla mobilisation in the squatter areas and jungle fringes. By the end of July Selangor maintained a force of 90 men based on a nucleus of a 40-man flying squad. This did not operate outside a fifteen-mile radius of Kuala Lumpur and in any case had hardly any experience of map reading. In Kedah, as in Perak, police had conducted para-military operations since well before the emergency began, but the only regular squad was based on Sungei Patani and numbered 20. It, too, was a short range group and, being composed of Malays, Chinese and Indians, had particular

---

[25] Two consequences may be seen in Gray's opinion of the police force which he had come to command. First, a determination to overhaul the system, if necessary with outside help. Second, the dismay of the existing senior but discredited officers.

difficulties of rationing.[26] At the end of the September the Perak police, one of the most enterprising contingents, were using eight jungle squads, some of them reinforced by auxiliary police, with an average strength of nine or ten men per squad.

Irregular Forces
In the early days of the emergency there was both the need and the opportunity for a great deal of flexibility in the raising of forces. One of the most interesting of these, about which unfortunately little information is available, was *Ferret Force*. This was originally both proposed by and designed for the former Force 136 officers who were still in Malaya and whose first-hand knowledge of the guerrillas and their operational areas was one of the most valuable intelligence sources of the day and was also to have considerable operational value. As a result of discussions between J. L. H. Davis, R. N. Broome and R. G. K. Thompson, a memorandum was submitted for a special jungle force of twenty operational units of 15 men each. Apart from suitable military and police officers there were a number of ex-Force 136 officers with the required knowledge and experience, in particular knowledge of a local language and of local conditions, and it was reckoned that half the patrol would consist of troops or police. The rest of the patrol was to consist of local Asians who would be hand-picked by the unit commander himself.[27] The purpose of this long-range jungle group was to go and live in the jungle, to establish good relations with the aborigines and locate and destroy the guerrillas either by themselves or in conjunction with regular forces. To maintain itself the patrol would live on a basic rice diet and if supply drops were necessary rice had the advantage that it could be dropped 'free fall' : that is to say, without parachutes.

These proposals were largely accepted at a meeting on July 6th at HQ Malaya District and it was decided to establish offensive bases from which 14 to 15 men would operate. Malay and Gurkha infantry battalions were to provide eleven out of the fifteen men in a team and the balance was to be made up of Dyaks from Borneo, who would be used as trackers and who should be accompanied by a European known to them, interpreters, and the whole to be led by Force 136 officers. Instead

---
[26] Although numbers of Sikhs were used in these jungle squads it was reckoned that the religious problems of a Sikh diet were insuperable for prolonged patrols away from their normal food supply.
[27] Former guerrillas and Chinese detectives were envisaged.

GOVERNMENT MAINTAINED

of the proposed location in Perak it was to be based on Port Dickson[28] but the groups were to be put in where needed.

For various reasons which included administrative problems, the dislike of the services for 'private armies' and the change in composition from that originally envisaged, the four Ferret groups were ending their operations by November. They were, however, the first real jungle fighters that the Emergency produced and with more official encouragement might have achieved far greater successes. Lessons which they learned the hard way, for example about the maximum weight of wireless sets and generators that could be carried for long distances, took a long time to be appreciated by the army and the police and the former in particular took a very long time to establish their own long-range jungle groups.[29] If it had been possible, John Davis's proposal of the experiment of a Chinese jungle squad might have paid the greatest dividends. The advantage of having soldiers and policemen of the same race and with an intimate knowledge of the bandits was obvious but the only Chinese, said Davis, who had this knowledge and who were willing to work as private soldiers were the rougher and 'Chinese-minded' type as opposed to the Malayanised English-speaking Chinese. This proposal does not seem to have been accepted as such although in January 1949 a squad of Chinese under an MCS officer was operating in Perak dressed in guerrilla uniform. Their role was part intelligence gathering, part *agent provocateur*.

In addition, civil liaison officers were recruited and numbers of Borneo and Singapore constabulary were seconded but it was a pity perhaps that government did not act on a proposal to establish jungle units of about twelve men, namely one European, one Chinese interpreter and ten Sarawak Iban for jungle penetration of up to three or four months and to disrupt relations between guerrillas and aborigines. This was a sensible suggestion and took some important facts into account, for example, that the aborigines regarded the 'three stars'[30] as their friends, having saved them against the depredations of the 'twelve stars'.[31] Also that the

---

[28] Presumably because this was the Headquarters of the Malay Regiment.
[29] There were other experiments on a smaller scale. Within a week of the beginning of the emergency, G. R. Leonard, Game Warden in Pahang, and F. A. Olsen, proprietor of a sawmill in Johore, had become ASPs and had begun reconnoitring the Bahau area. Olsen had been with Force 136 in Bahau during the Occupation. One discouragement to this sort of operation was the bill for $400 which one well-known rubber company submitted for board and lodging: the estate having originally asked for protection.
[30] MPAJA guerrillas. [31] KMT guerrillas.

aborigines' religion made them fear a violent death as the greatest of all misfortunes.

Frontier Force
The question of the defence of Malaya's northern frontier had been discussed off and on since October 1947. The frontier, except for the few customs and immigration posts on the main roads and railway, was completely open and sectors of it had been dominated by guerrillas usually of the Kuomintang variety, ever since the war ended. The dangers, when the emergency began, were not only of the movement of guerrillas backwards and forwards across the frontier but the smuggling of arms from Thailand which, given that smuggling is, was and perhaps always will be rampant with whole networks of smugglers' paths available, would have been almost impossible to prevent. As an emergency measure, the Local Defence Committee had agreed at the end of June that a special auxiliary frontier force—under police control—would be required. The GOC, however, had rather different ideas in that he envisaged a permanent military frontier force which could be used instead of regular army field units both to police and protect the northern frontier.[32] When a committee deliberated on the raising of a frontier force it considered and disposed of numerous possibilities: Gurkhas, Punjabis and Pathan, Chinese, Lushais, Chins, ex-Palestine Police officers and practically anyone who was militarily employable. All these were rejected and the committee came to the somewhat surprising but unanimous decision that the obvious answer would be, not to provide an auxiliary police force, but to raise an additional battalion of the Malay regiment.

This proposal fell into abeyance and when a frontier force was eventually raised, in 1949, it was firmly back in police hands. It was, primarily, a territorial force. The detailed knowledge of the terrain and of the inhabitants living in this frontier zone was considered to be essential and recruits were usually men from the border areas and *kampongs*. They were to remain in the area, as opposed to the regular police where members were liable to periodic transfer to any part of the Federation. The force was to consist of 600 men who, although under contract, were under the command of the CPOs of the border states (Kedah/Perlis,

---

[32] The GOC, perhaps with the events of December 1941 fresh in his mind, had, according to his public pronouncements, something like a preoccupation with the northern frontier and the possibility of 'the enemy receiving massive reinforcements' across it.

Perak and Kelantan) and came under the existing police organisation in order to ensure the most efficient flow of information and complete co-operation and unity of command. Despite the organisational relationship they functioned more as armed constabulary than as normal police. They were stationed at police posts on the frontier and in depth, as opposed to 'a somewhat amorphous body' patrolling the entire border zone and ignoring state boundaries. The guiding principle was that a detachment should be capable of patrolling its area adequately and, if necessary, defend itself against superior forces until aid arrived. Emphasis was placed on physical fitness, local knowledge and ability to speak some Thai or Chinese (however, of the 189 recruited in Kelantan, only seventeen possessed any knowledge of these two languages) and the educational standard was generally overlooked. A total of eight new stations and one post were built and twenty-four existing stations were enlarged or rebuilt to accommodate frontier force personnel.

Army
From the public statements that were made, both in Britain and Malaya, there can be no doubt that both governments were either complacent or dishonest about the need for immediate military reinforcements from Malaya. In London Lord Listowel told the House of Lords that there was reason to believe that the military forces then in Malaya would provide 'all the strength that the civil power required to back them up'; and the Minister of Defence, Mr. A. V. Alexander, in a bad-tempered reply which evaded the question whether he could give stronger assurance that he had the matter well in hand in Malaya, deprecated Members' attempts to give him advice which should come from the Commander-in-Chief. In Malaya, the Army insisted that it had enough troops—which was at best arguable—and, specifically, that it had sufficient armoured cars—which was manifestly untrue as there wasn't a single armoured car squadron in either Malaya or Singapore. The effect of this assurance was rather spoilt some three weeks later when it was announced that the first armoured car regiment, the Fourth Hussars, was coming to Malay and that the Inniskillings were embarking from Hong Kong in the next few days. In October there was an even greater surprise when three battalions of the Brigade of Guards arrived in Malaya : the first time that the Guards had ever served abroad except in war. By the end of the year there had in fact been a fifty per cent increase in the number of battalions serving in

Malaya—fifteen compared to ten—and two additional squadrons, one fighter, one light bomber, were also in action by the middle of 1949.

Operations
The Army's plan of operations at the beginning of the campaign was rather vague. At least, this was the impression given at the highest level. The GOC Malaya, General Wade, talked about 'organised drives' which would achieve great and satisfactory results in a short time.[33] But if this did not work, and if extensive operations were needed in a number of different parts of Malaya then perhaps a whole division would be necessary. Whether this division would be used in 'sweeps through scores of miles of mountainous jungle' was not made clear; but it was noted that the Japanese army had never solved the problem and comparatively small bodies of wartime guerrillas had evaded capture with little difficulty. Within a few days of the beginning of the Emergency General Wade was succeeded by General Boucher; and it is difficult to repress a shudder of apprehension that the battle was about to be lost when one reads the press reports of the government's counter-guerrilla operations at the time. To begin with, the army in general and General Boucher in particular seemed to be looking at matters from a formal military point of view. General Boucher, for example, seemed to have something of a fixation with the possibility of guerrilla reinforcements: from somewhere north of Malaya—which he thought could be prevented, at least from the sea; from Indonesia—which he thought unlikely; and even airborne reinforcements from Siam to be parachuted into Malaya—about which he professed some concern.

This first indication that he was thinking in terms of large-scale war was reinforced by the report of July 10th that insurgents were preparing to filter into Kuala Lumpur: which had brought the statement from Boucher that Spitfires, firing rockets, would be used against these concentrations. The *Financial Times*, again on July 10th, spoke of fighting that was raging near Kuala Lumpur; and carried with it Boucher's comment, 'We are dealing with it on battle lines'. On July 27th General Boucher outlined his plan to members of the Legislative Council.

> My object is to break up the insurgent concentrations to bring them to battle before they are ready, and to drive them under-

[33] June 24th.

ground or into the jungle, and then to follow them there, by troops in the jungles, and by police backed by troops and by the RAF outside of them. I intend to keep them constantly moving and deprive them of food and of recruits, because if they are constantly moving they cannot terrorise an area properly so that they can get these commodities from it; and then to ferret them out of their holes, wherever these holes may be.

Looked at in the light of subsequent events, this would seem to be the formula which guarantees a long-drawn-out guerrilla war. The idea that if guerrillas are constantly on the move they are unable to stop to pick up food is now known to be extremely optimistic; and the idea of sweeping guerrillas back from the shores of government and economy was almost as futile as the exploits of Mother Partington were absurd.[34] It was not realised at the time that approximately a thousand hours of patrolling would be needed to eliminate each guerrilla; and in any case neither the army nor the police had the capability of mounting jungle operations. While in the jungle fringes, which is as far as they were likely to be driven in this early phase, the guerrillas would be supplied with food, intelligence and recruits and as long as they were able to stay together in reasonably large groups —anything between twenty and fifty—they would be able to emerge at unknown points and mount their attacks.

The headline of this report, characteristically, was 'Boucher Promises More Toughness' but, in fact, this was in response to the demands that had been made by other members of the Legislative Council and the 'toughness' to which Boucher referred was that the squatter problem would have to be faced and solved —which would mean great hardship to certain squatter areas— and that there must be official control of rice, proper means of identification by registration and adequate control of the frontier and the coast. General Boucher said nothing of martial law—a point which one must consider wholly in his favour as there were certainly vociferous demands made for it—and the events of the preceding fortnight, which included Batu Arang and Gua Musang, suggest that something more may be said in favour of his plan of campaign. Operating on minimal intelligence—after three months only six units in the enemy order of battle had been identified—with no fixed lines, understrength and under-

[34] Mother Partington, a legendary Devonian figure of the nineteenth century, was renowned for her morning exercise of sweeping the waves back into the sea: an exercise which was of limited value in that, to state the obvious, the waves depend for their strength upon the sea itself.

trained battalions,[35] a large part of available forces diverted for static defence and with the constant possibility of large-scale attacks, it is hardly surprising that there was a reluctance to break up units below the company level.[36]

One of the first lessons to be learned from these early operations was that 'sweeps' were largely ineffective. An analysis of operations, and the lessons to be learned from them, at the end of October 1948 said, categorically, that 'the value of large and elaborate sweeps is doubtful'. And this was something that was to be repeated, at least by the police, at the state and federal level.[37] Nevertheless, by the end of the year as more troops became available large-scale operations were launched under particular code names, notably in Johore and Selangor, and although they may have cleared certain areas temporarily, they did not succeed in bringing the enemy to battle.

In any event these large-scale operations, involving concentrations of troops, were limited to certain areas. Other states, such as Pahang, were starved of troops and here, apart from police who, as in Kedah, had been closing down certain stations, one

---

[35] The greater part of one British battalion learned 'on the job'. Before their first haphazard operations the majority if not the whole of certain rifle companies had never been in the jungle, even on training exercises. What would have happened on more than one sortie if, without scouts, brenguns, wireless or water bottles, they had encountered experienced or well-led guerrillas hardly bears thinking about.

[36] In what appears to have been the standard work on the subject of guerrilla warfare—Colonel C. E. Callwell *Small Wars. Their Principles and Practice*, London, HMSO 1906—the entire weight is on bringing large forces of the enemy to battle. It also emphasises the importance, whether in South Africa, the Sudan, Dahomey, Algeria or India, of large-scale 'sweeps' against the enemy. The third edition, 1906, had the Boer war as a recent experience to go on; but there is only the most perfunctory reference to experiences of guerrilla warfare in the Philippines at the end of the Spanish-American war. Here, as in other historical instances, it was simply noted that *guerrilla* warfare was very unfavourable to regular troops and that it had often been found impossible to avoid being ambushed from time to time. There was no suggestion that regular troops should themselves adopt the guerrilla style of operations.

[37] In his speech to the Legislative Council on July 27th the GOC offered a rather curious justification. While admitting that press reports such as 'Large sweep in Johore. No success' were partially true he said they did not take into account the experience which the troops carrying out that operation had gained nor the fact that these areas were at least cleared, that it was now known that there were no insurgents in them, nor had any insurgent camps been left behind.' Insurgents who had moved out could, once the troops had gone, move back and the building of new camps did not take long.

battalion (the Malay Regiment) was spread over an area of fourteen thousand square miles—and this in November 1948. The CPO of Pahang reported on December 1st that so far they had been very much on the defensive. The British Adviser, a short while earlier, said he thought the situation was deteriorating and there was some danger of a 'liberated area' in central Pahang. From Selangor the CPO reported that in spite of the fact that they had changed over from large sweeps to small wandering patrols and ambushes they needed more troops: as many again as they had already. It was amazing, however, how few troops were operational from among two battalions: and although the Guards Brigade were detailed for their move to Malaya on or about the 12th August they were not ready for operations until December 8th—four months later.

Civil Control and Powers of State
Six months, more or less, from the beginning of the campaign both sides had reached a climax. In the case of the insurgents, a decrease in their activity began in December 1948 and the fact that they had failed to secure obvious objectives meant that, in reality, they had to move into a second phase: that of regrouping and retraining. Simultaneously, however, the security forces were approaching maximum strength and full deployment; but this was a situation which gave rise to as much concern as congratulation. On January 11th 1949 the GOC told a conference of sub-district commanders and the Commissioner of Police he had informed the High Commissioner that their own forces were fully deployed and that the maximum military effort had now been reached. Any increase in momentum therefore had to come from the police and the 'civil' [*sic*].

In mid-1947 the GOC's appreciation had stressed the importance of intelligence. In mid-1948 an absence of worthwhile intelligence not only reduced the value of the forces that were available when the insurrection began but, when reinforcements did arrive, they were often still unable to be provided with military targets. Intelligence organisation was generally and for a long while regarded as the government's Achilles heel in its counter-guerrilla operations. Early recognition of the weakness had come on July 2nd when Macdonald attended a meeting of the Internal Security Committee in Kuala Lumpur especially to put forward the view of the Chief of Staff that an improved intelligence organisation was required. This view, obviously reflecting the opinions of the British Defence Co-ordination

Committee, resulted in the creation of a Combined Intelligence Staff—MSS, Police and Services—to be responsible to the Local Defence Committee. It is not altogether clear from the MSS orders embodying this directive (8.7.48) what this meant, but, on the highest level, it is evident that it reduced the powers of the Director of MSS; while on the state level intelligence centres were to be set up and attached to the CPO's headquarters. Police and army were to pass their information to the nearest police headquarters; and the order was to go into immediate effect.

This reliance on the police for additional momentum seems not to be commonplace. It was significant at the time for Boucher's acceptance of the campaign as a joint responsibility. This had not always been the case. In the interim period between the departure of Gent and the arrival of Gurney it may not be true to say that there was a struggle for the direction of operations but the field was certainly open for local initiative. Gray in particular, newly arrived, was under a certain amount of pressure to put the police under the army and this was something that was being experienced at lower levels too. Thus in a meeting held at HQ Malaya District on August 20th 1948, Gray, while admitting the interim weaknesses of the police force,[38] hoped that, if possible, the putting of the police under the Army Act would be avoided. The summary of decisions taken at this meeting leaves one in doubt whether the army was, as the GOC claimed, operating in support of the civil power. It was decided, conditionally, that the Federation police should not be placed under the army—if it could be avoided. At the same time, it was also decided that operations were to be carried out on a combined police-army-air plan—under the army commander. Ambiguities here were similarly unresolved in what might be called the constitutional structure of operations where the civil control of the emergency seems, in at least one instance, to have been rather a threadbare concept.[39]

Gurney's arrival in November helped to resolve the issue of control of operations. From the beginning, he emphasised the importance of the police and realised as well as argued that the

[38] It was not reckoned to become effective until the first six months of 1949.

[39] Discussing the destruction of villages for security purposes the Johore State Liaison Committee minutes record

"It was made clear that the decision whether the village was to be destroyed or not must rest with the police/military. The Adviser on Chinese affairs would then have to explain to the villagers the reason for the destruction."

brunt of the emergency must rest upon them. Gurney had been Chief Secretary in Palestine with Gray as Inspector-General of Police and although they were not always to agree in the troubled years to come they enjoyed each other's mutual confidence and support. The new High Commissioner brought with him new emergency regulations, some of them drawn from his Palestine experience, but a large number were already in force when he arrived. An examination suggests that they represented a balance between an incipient police state[40] and a determination to preserve the rule of law. The first tendency may be seen in the provision to detain up to a period of twelve months, later increased to two years; while the second was reflected in the cumbersome processes by which captured guerrillas were tried and convicted on the charge of carrying arms; a process which originally involved the evidence of soldiers or policemen who were present on the occasions, usually pitched battles, on which the technical arrests were made.

Using the Essential Regulations Proclamation of the former British Military Administration a number of Emergency measures ultimately extending to the whole of the Federation were taken between the 16th and 18th of June 1948. These gave the police extraordinary powers of search, detention, curfew, the control of movement of persons and traffic, and re-introduced the death penalty for the simple, unlawful carrying of arms. These were supplemented by bills that were taken swiftly through the Legislative Council at its first post-emergency meeting on July 7th and occasioned practically no discussion at the time. Among the bills to receive a first and second reading that day was the Printing Presses Bill which meant that the printing and publication of newspapers would henceforth require a permit from the Chief Secretary.[41] Terminologically, the acting Attorney-General succeeded in squaring the circle—there was to be no repression of the press: but a control of certain organs which did not share our ways of life and thought—but, as with most of the emergency legislation, much depended on the way in which these extraordinary powers were exercised. For example, correspondents, at

---

[40] One of the three measures that would probably qualify without reservation for those of a police state was 17C which provided that detainees whose appeals had been rejected or who had not appealed could be deported ('repatriated' was the word used) by order of the High Commissioner in Council—provided that they were not Federal Citizens or British subjects born in Malaya. A qualification which excluded the majority of Malayan Chinese.

[41] An enactment which remained in force.

their own risk, were allowed to accompany numerous military operations; but had to submit their reports for clearance afterwards. Initially, this was a security measure but it could also be used as a means of censorship and from time to time there was a certain amount of bullying of reporters and papers who for one reason or another did not submit their reports for prior clearance.[42] Probably the two most important enactments were those concerning detention and national registration. By the end of 1948 over 5,000 people were held under detention orders: a number which flooded the gaol at Seremban and occasioned the opening of various detention camps. The manner in which this regulation worked and the process of appeal will be considered separately. Generally speaking, those who were detained fell into three categories: security risks—by virtue (or its absence) of their previous association; individual suspects for which the police could not find sufficient material evidence for the courts; and what might be called territorial suspects—those who lived in areas which were known or might reasonably be supposed to be providing assistance for the insurgents.

National registration was not only a way of distinguishing the law-breaking from the law-abiding—in principle a separation of the carded from the uncarded—but also, by its individual identification, a significant enumeration both for government and the subject. For government, because it was made aware of its responsibilities to unknown numbers of subjects. For the subject, because he was made aware of the presence of government. Sociological implications were of less immediate importance than political. Details of a form of national registration were agreed on in September. By the end of 1948 work had been completed in only two limited areas: (*a*) a 'sealed' belt about 20 miles wide along the Siamese frontier—where only Chinese were registered at first, and (*b*) the Settlement of Penang where all residents were registered. Inconvenience and antipathy to government sometimes made the beginning of registration schemes look like an incipient disobedience campaign; and when properly organised and enforced by government its disruption was sought by the

---

[42] Apart from the unintentional disclosures of operational plans and intentions there were sometimes exciting and 'human interest' stories which went up to or over the brink of disaster. The *Mentri Besar* of Johore, Dato Onn, complained, for example, of the publicity that was given to the arrival of a younger brother of a Johore planter whose name was high on the MCP murder list. Again, publication of the name and address of a sole Perak witness of a killing became his death warrant.

GOVERNMENT MAINTAINED 143

guerrillas themselves. Villagers were warned not to register, to tear up their identity cards if they were issued, and, finally, attacks were made on both registration teams and, as an easier target, the commercial photographers who were supplying identity snapshots.

Towards the end of 1948 Chief Police Officers were asked whether they thought further legislation would be necessary to increase police efficiency. On the whole, they did not seem to think so; and while many if not most of them realised the difficulties of getting on terms with the Chinese community there were one or two who suggested a more cautious approach to what they described as further 'punitive measures' against the Chinese as a whole.[43] It could hardly be said however that other communities were exempt and many Malays felt that the detention of Ishak bin Haji Mohammed, the President of the Malay Nationalist Party, was designed to curb both the left wing opinions and Malay nationalism that found their expression in this party. Some of the evidence at least on which he was detained seems rather flimsy; and the MSS representative for Selangor/West Pahang was hardly the best source for what was going on in Singapore although it was on this, an apparent commitment by an API representative that the MNP would throw in its lot with the Communist Party and the suggestion that arrangements were being made to train API youths in Johore in guerrilla warfare, which ranked as material evidence against Ishak.[44]

Confidence returns
Under a certain amount of prompting from the Colonial Office,

---

[43] Most Chinese might legitimately have two or three aliases or alternative spellings of their name: a point that underlines the difficulty and importance of registration. Which gives some point to an interesting compilation of Emergency Regulations and a more detailed treatment of some of its aspects —Roderick Renick, *Emergency Regulations of Malaya: Background, Organisation, Administration, and Use as a Socialising Technique*, unpublished M.A. thesis, Tulane University, in which his argument is that 'in reality they were used to circumscribe the activities of the Chinese segment of the population'.

[44] In fact, the material evidence presented above shows that while Ishak may have been in company with MCP representatives at a meeting in Temerloh his own speech was vague to the point of being innocuous. In the press release issued on the occasion of Ishak's detention the government claimed to hold evidence that he had been working with Communist elements for the overthrow of government and the establishment of an alternative government by force. But it was qualified by the remark that he was doing this 'in his private capacity'.

representatives of His Majesty's Government produced a series of papers in early 1949 which attempted to put the course of the Emergency so far into some sort of perspective. The High Commissioner's Dispatch No. 1 (8.1.49) to the Colonial Secretary went into considerable detail of the local forces that were to be raised and the costs that would be involved. It was now considered that the basic peace-time garrison, hitherto laid down as a minimum of 15 major units, was too low and that a second brigade group of the Malay Regiment should be raised and not merely another two battalions. There were also proposals, never implemented, to raise six heavy anti-aircraft regiments as part of the volunteer forces of the Federation and Singapore, but the emphasis was placed on a long-term policy of building up a strong, regular police force on modern lines capable of maintaining internal security without the assistance of the armed forces. An expansion of 200 in Special Branch and the Criminal Branch of the CID was recommended; although to obtain as many qualified Chinese as possible it was recognised that the rates of pay for detectives would have to be considerably increased. It was considered essential that the police should operate and maintain their own signals equipment; that there should be an increase of 25 Asian officers and 25 European cadets; and that a total of 27,000 weapons would have to be purchased to replace the great majority of arms at present on loan to the regular police and special constabulary from the army.

All of this was a significant detail but the paper's principal importance lay in its basic assumption. This set out the requirements envisaged in relation to two anticipated phases of the campaign.

> Phase A—from the beginning of 1949 until the final defeat of the militant Communists as an effective force; Phase B—the period following Phase A in which the internal security has been restored to the extent that it is no longer necessary for Imperial troops to be permanently deployed on operations in aid of the civil power.

Phase A was taken as lasting for the whole of the year 1949. There were no factors visible in the internal security situation, said Gurney, that would indicate either a shorter or a longer period for this phase although developments might occur at any time which would affect the estimate. For the purpose of planning, it was the best that could be given. Phase B was taken to extend from the beginning of 1950 to the end of 1951, and it was, therefore, assumed that the guerrillas would have been largely destroyed by the end of the year and, second, that emergency operations could be handled entirely by local forces within three years. Having regard to British and Gurkha battalions Commander-in-Chief Far East Land Forces went even further: he hoped for a reduction in these units from the middle of 1949.

Again at the request of the Colonial Office the High Commissioner in his dispatch No. 5 (30.5.49)[45] set out some more considerations on the emergency which, like its predecessor, was to be used by the Overseas Defence Committee as a basis for general guidance to Colonial governments. Here again, the emphasis on police rather than troops was carried to the point of suggesting that no more troops were needed and it questioned the belief—'which appears still to be held in some quarters'—that a Communist threat to internal security was the sort of situation that called for the dispatch of a brigade of troops. The High Commissioner did not commit himself in this paper to any forecast for the future. It was a paper that was concerned with what should be done to *prevent* an emergency or cut it down in first bloom rather than a plan of action to deal with it in the long run. Its optimism, if present, was assumed and had, in any case, been preceded by the burgeoning confidence of the Commissioner General.

Mr. Macdonald's dispatch to the Colonial Secretary (20.4.49) went beyond those of the High Commissioner both in space and time. He was concerned, as he put it, with both the wider theatre aspects and also with the long-term view. He agreed with Gurney that the restoration of law and order was basically a police task rather than a military campaign; and that the nature, both of the operation and the country, precluded any spectacular successes or rapid or sudden conclusions. He, more than Gurney, stressed the importance of intelligence

> Even now, however, our knowledge of the men forming the enemy high command, their identity, location, organisation, and intentions, together with their order of battle, remains far from satisfactory. A much greater intelligence effort in the form of interrogation centres, translating facilities and so forth should be made with the primary object of identifying, locating and if possible capturing the enemy's leaders, without hampering the intelligence required in the field.

[45] Now upgraded to Top Secret.

but on the whole he agreed with the High Commissioner's assessment.

What is remarkable, however, is the optimism that was drawn from roughly the same premises and a comparable vagueness on future courses of action. Militarily, said Macdonald, the bandits were already beaten in Malaya in the sense that they could not hope to succeed in their objectives. It was to be expected that the Malayan bandits would continue the struggle long after it became apparent to them that locally they were beaten; but his concern was with the new penetration of the labour movement rather than with successful Communist guerrilla warfare. Like Gurney, and in response to a Colonial Office inquiry, he believed that the turning point of the campaign had already occurred.

Why this should be so is not altogether apparent.[46] Militarily the current assessment was based on *A paper on the security situation in the Federation of Malaya*, April 5th 1949, which had been prepared by the Commissioner of Police and the GOC Malaya and subsequently transmitted by the High Commissioner as Dispatch No. 4. The basis of confidence here was that bandit activity had decreased from the end of 1948; that it had been difficult for them to make any sustained large-scale and co-ordinated effort; and that the initiative had passed to the security forces. Amongst other things this paper recommended that 'the bandits must be continually harried and pursued by intensive patrolling; something that would entail much more jungle work and the formation of many more jungle squads'. Macdonald, however, stated categorically 'sufficient forces with the right type of jungle training are available for this task'—the task referred to being the pursuit and extermination of guerrillas

---

[46] The Colonial Office, however, were looking for something that would enable them to strike a confident note. A telegram to the High commissioner, 28.3.49, reads:

> As you know planting and mining interests here have been showing marked uneasiness in the past six weeks. Carefully worded statements in parliament have gone some way to allay this uneasiness, and the Minister of State's statement of 23rd February made a generally favourable impression ... You will, of course, appreciate that the situation in Malaya will influence London investors when the loan comes on the market and although you will now have learnt that it will not be possible to float the loan before mid-May at the earliest you will no doubt bear in mind when formulating statements on the situation from now on the effect these statements may have on the success of the loan.

A reminder which no doubt provides a simple Marxist explanation for official confidence in the second quarter of 1949.

GOVERNMENT MAINTAINED

who were expected to move gradually into the undeveloped country north-east of the main mountain range from Pahang northwards and also into northern Perak.

In none of the four papers cited was there any expectation that the situation might deteriorate to the point which was reached in the early months of the emergency; or that a whole new range of civil measures might be needed before the guerrillas would be deprived of the civilian support on which they depended. The enormous importance of the Chinese community was acknowledged—Macdonald described them as the crux of the problem—and in particular, that of the Chinese squatters. But it was assumed by the Commissioner of Police, the GOC, and the Commissioner General that the way to deal with them was, through the collective detention and deportation of squatter areas which were known to be supporting the guerrillas, under the most drastic of emergency regulations: 17D. 'Repatriation' —something of a euphemism—was apparently the only course that was considered by Macdonald for there was no mention of resettlement: something which was at least considered by Gurney[47] even though the difficulties, at this time, were manifest;[48] and while political considerations were not underrated they were, at least in the army/police paper, regarded simply as a factor of cumulative success rather than something that might also be part of a vicious circle.

> For political reasons and to help the government to swing Chinese opinion further towards the positive pro-government and pro-law and order attitude, it is essential that the security forces continue and intensify their activities. Their efforts will not produce a quick decision unless the government's measures to swing Chinese opinion in our favour are quickly successful.

The possibility that the failure to produce a quick decision would swing Chinese opinion in favour of the guerrillas, or at least away from government, was apparently not considered; but Gurney ended his first dispatch with uncharacteristic foreboding. 'If,' he said, 'by the end of 1949, we have not restored peace and security to this country, we shall have failed and, perhaps, if my appeal in this dispatch is unsuccessful, for the lack of a comparatively small sum of money.'

[47] In the note accompanying dispatch No. 4 (11.4.49).
[48] 'The reluctance of many Malay district officers and *penghulus* to do any more than is strictly necessary where Chinese is concerned put more of the burden on the police.'

This, then, was the situation towards the end of what government considered to be the first and successful phase of its counter-guerrilla operations and policy. Strategically, it was assumed[49] that the states and settlements of Johore, Negri Sembilan, Malacca, Penang, Kedah and Perlis were all comparatively clear of active guerrillas.[50] Many of the problems of the insurrection had been identified and some of the solutions foreseen. Government had not broken down; the economy was, surprisingly, still intact; large numbers of men had been armed, if not fully trained; and civil measures were being put into effect. A campaign had been mounted and sustained which, although extensive, had not been allowed to interfere too much with the normal working of government. The police, assisted by the armed services, were dealing with the situation and a compartment of government was, in turn, dealing with administrative and logistic problems.

Such was the situation as it might be seen on the level of formal and official analysis. Whether this analysis would meet the reality of a developing situation would depend, in part, upon the answer to four questions. First, if the guerrillas were not objectively defeated in 1949 had government any idea how the campaign was to be won? Second, had they the means and the proper sense of urgency? Third, had they the resolve? And fourth, if this turned out to be more than political banditry, had they any idea how to treat with a community from which most of the insurgents were drawn?

[49] Gurney's note, 11.4.49.
[50] The main operations of the next stage were to be in Pahang, Perak, Selangor and, to a lesser extent, Kelantan and Trengganu.

6
GOVERNMENT CONSTRAINED

To say of any war or campaign at its outset that there were shortages and mistakes is to make no great contribution to its history. Nevertheless, it may be worthwhile considering the nature of these shortages, of men, material and ideas, for the effect they had upon the subsequent development of operations and the time that it took to make up these deficiencies. Mistakes are of a more subjective consideration, and are in any event better indicated by the political pressures which they created. A third consideration is the context in which the insurrection began : of time, place and spirit.

Bearing in mind the intensity of operations of the mid-fifties, it can be argued that for the first three or five years of the Emergency there were insufficient forces at the government's disposal. For months there was a desperate shortage of both police and army in the east coast states although, perhaps, for the sake of public confidence, the GOC usually managed to give the impression that everything was going well. Mention has already been made of the situation in Pahang; and in the coastal town of Kuantan there was particular cause for alarm. In July (10.7.48) the CPO Pahang signalled Kuala Lumpur.

> With reference to General Boucher's assurances in the press that the military in this country are in sufficient force, have sufficient transport, and sufficient arms, I beg to differ, and would point out that (i) when asked to send military to Kuantan, they sent by air only two platoons of untrained men, (ii) the Malay Regiment tell me themselves that their main difficulty is shortage of transport, and (iii) when a Gurkha platoon arrived in Kuala Lipis recently to guard the gaol the first thing their young officer did was to ask whether he could borrow some Sten guns from the police as they had only rifles.

An earlier signal to Kuala Lumpur had taken three weeks to surface and a reply to be sent. Fifty recruits were promised for August 1st; additional arms were sent; and the CPO was told finally, 'You have now all the military that can be spared for

Pahang' (14.7). On July 11th the CPO had requested armoured cars in order to keep the roads open.

> After the ambush and killing of Mr. Jennings, the Javanese and Chinese at Batu Sawah on 9.7.48, no one is willing to travel by road between Kuantan and Sungei Lembing, and the only answer is to have constant armoured car patrols along this road. Can General Boucher assure us that armoured cars will be sent to any particular area on request.

Two days later he sent another signal, already mentioned

> At present, the police in this state are powerless to protect life and property (13.7).

and received the following signal from the Commissioner of Police in reply

> Your request for armoured cars for patrols in Pahang is out of the question. Of the fifteen in the country twelve are army operational and three are replacement, so army says: none are available.

The situation had improved somewhat by August but more troops were urgently needed. In Trengganu, incidents at two mines early in the month had again stretched the CPO's reserves to the limit; and although he thought he would be all right if there was no further trouble, there was an obvious strain on resources where, in the absence of communications, investigations took officers away from headquarters from three to four days and the CPO himself had no deputy. Many fixed points needed guards; but in Trengganu the whole police force of under 400 men was not enough for this task alone. A hundred special constables and a hundred and fifty auxiliary police had been recruited; and this, so the CPO said, pretty well exhausted the local supply of suitable and reliable persons. Such operations as were undertaken in Trengganu were little more than expeditions to show the flag. The Royal Navy did this, no more and no less, on the coast; and a platoon of the Malay Regiment could hardly have done more in the 24 hours it spent in the state before returning to Kuala Lumpur. The remoteness of Trengganu was maintained by the absence of any aerodrome. The absence of troops was hardly made up by the strength of the police jungle squads and although here, as in many other states, the police were fortunate in being able to call upon officers with former military experience[1]

---

[1] Among them an ex-Gurkha Assistant Superintendent; and an RASC transport company captain, an ex-commando and an ex-2i/c of an infantry battalion who were cadet officers.

GOVERNMENT CONSTRAINED 151

the entire state had only one jungle squad of fifteen men in operation at any given time until late in 1948. In September/October a company of Gurkhas carried out a ten day sweep with almost negligible results; and the absence of troops generally was having its effect upon the civil fabric of the state.[2]

At the end of October the CPO Trengganu signalled Kuala Lumpur

> With the knowledge and approval of both the *Mentri Besar* and the British Adviser I today sent you a signal requesting immediate military assistance of at least two companies of infantry in order to try to restore confidence among the kampoung Malays, and to prevent a serious Sino-Malay flair up.

The major incidents reported in Trengganu show that up to October it was Chinese who were the victims of terrorism. But from October onwards, it was the Malays who were being murdered.[3] The possibilities of communal massacre were too recent to be dismissed; and there were sporadic but continuous reports that the 'invulnerability cults' were once again being followed. Less dramatically, there were reports that many Malays in areas of racial tension were leaving their homes and with the *padi* harvest due in November this foreshadowed not only serious loss for the Malay community if it were abandoned but a positive gain for the guerrillas if they were to take it over. Similarly, where there were less opportunities of alternative employment, a successful attack on an estate could have serious consequences. The following assessment was made on the spot after an estate smoke house had been burned down.

> The working of the estate is of course impossible now. This means that approximately 600 labourers will probably be out of work. The Malays had already begun to go back to their *kampongs* last night and there were many on the roads this morning with their *barang*.[4] As regards Chinese, about 130 in number, I have asked Mr. Sorenson to suggest to them most strongly that they proceed to Dungun and apply to be taken on by the Bukit Besi mine which

---

[2] On July 10th the GOC was quoted in the *Straits Times* as saying that the attack on Kerteh estate in Trengganu was made by insurgents who had landed by junk from Siam; a remark which caused consternation in the state as neither the *Mentri Besar* nor the CPO had any knowledge of this.

[3] One was beheaded; and a man, his wife and child were all murdered in another *kampong*.

[4] Belongings: luggage

is now recruiting labourers. I feel that such a large body of Chinese thrown out of work is a menace and that it might well be that they would join the gangsters. Mr. Sorenson is flying to Singapore on Thursday to see the East Asiatic Company. I think he is going to advise the company against rebuilding the smoke house immediately and to leave the estate on a care and maintenance basis until the trouble has died down. He asked me if government could guarantee to protect the smoke house, etc. if it were rebuilt. I told him that the only scheme for protection was a special constabulary. In the present state of affairs he did not seem anxious to keep the estate going by arming 50 or so of his own men, his reason being that the presence of arms in any number on the estate would be an attraction for the gangsters to visit again to replenish their armaments. He said that he would require at least that number to protect the estate adequately, and if he did arm such a number of men, only a few of them could be trusted not to deliver their arms over to the gangsters if intimidated. He said that the only way the estate could be adequately protected was by a large body of police or soldiers. I had to inform him that this was out of the question at present.

By the beginning of November refugees were in Kemaman town in sufficient numbers that the Chief Social Welfare Officer was making funds available from his below-the-line emergency account to deal with destitution; but at the end of the month, in what might have been an agonising decision, the GOC cabled the *Mentri Besar* of Trengganu that he could expect no troops, particularly during the monsoon season, unless there was a definite operational target.[5]

Even where operational targets were thought to exist they were seldom hit hard. In part, this was due to the deployment of forces. If it was the purpose of large scale operations to bring the enemy to battle on favourable terms, they did not succeed. But in part the failure was due to the normal difficulties of articulated vehicles in an emergency: the component parts were going in different directions. The extent of disagreement should not be exaggerated and very often a working relationship obtained between the three instruments of government: civil, police, and army. But the reports of disagreement that continued to come in revealed deep

[5] The situation in Trengganu was sufficiently bad for the British Adviser at least to consider the possibility that it might become a liberated area; although, unless it was within striking distance of some vital spot, this might well have been a self-defeating exercise for the guerrillas.

GOVERNMENT CONSTRAINED

divisions of opinion and approach which had not been properly bridged. In Kedah, there was serious disagreement between the police on the one hand and the *Mentri Besar* and the British Adviser on the other on action to be taken against squatters. They were agreed that certain squatter areas should be cleared but where the CPO was in favour of either a resettlement scheme or temporary accommodation the British Adviser and the *Mentri Besar* wanted to destroy houses and crops and leave the squatters to fend for themselves. In Parit the District Officer, on his own initiative and unknown to the police or army, arranged an air strike direct with the RAF. Most of the disagreement, however, was between the police and the army. In Perak a police report said of Colonel X that he

> has been seven days in Malaya and is fully prepared to deal with the present situation which he considers can only be met with fire and slaughter. He has been in India and assumes that Chinese react in a similar way to the Indian.

This same colonel was apparently restrained only with difficulty from setting off to burn and shoot up certain areas which he said were full of communists and it required the authority of his brigadier and an experienced MCS officer to restrain him. The same colonel said that as he was obviously senior to the local police officer, he should direct and initiate all operations; and there is no doubt that there was a great deal of unilateral army action. In spite of the complaint, from Pahang, that the army had been much too keen on acting the role of amateur detective to the exclusion of their main function—which was presumed to be the support of the police in an operational capacity—the results of the army acting on their own intelligence and intiative were sometimes disastrous. There were a number of cases where the army had, in fact, declined to have police with them on a patrol or operation; and certain officers had sent documents direct to their own intelligence officer and refused to show them to the police. In Kedah, a battalion of the Malay Regiment, having said that they would be ambushing paths in a particular area, in fact laid their ambush on a main road and when a Chinese clerk was returning to his estate in the late evening on a motor cycle he was shot dead.

Probably the most persistent trouble involved the destruction of property and after renewed representation to the Commissioner of Police from the deputy Chief Secretary the following directive was sent

> In view of the recent reports concerning the destruction of houses by security forces in the course of operations in squatter areas I am directed to request that the attention of all CPOs may once again be drawn to the policy which has been laid down in this matter. Only such dwellings as are known to belong to or to be frequented by bandits or in which arms, equipment, or incriminating documents are found are to be destroyed and there should be no wholesale destruction of dwellings by way of reprisals against a particular community. If it is decided to effect the removal of all occupants of a particular area on grounds of strong suspicion that the area in question is being used as a bandit base, this should be achieved by a properly prepared compulsory evacuation in conjunction with the state authorities after they have made the necessary preparations for receiving and placing the population elsewhere. (16.11.48)

OCPDs, at least in Pahang, were warned that they were not permitted to delegate their authority to a subordinate and must themselves carry the full responsibility for any buildings which were destroyed by the police. But the problem was certainly not resolved as between the police and the army. The CPO Pahang reported to the Commissioner of Police (9.11.48)

> I am afraid we shall have a lot of trouble regarding this question of burning down of buildings by the military. OCPDs are the only people allowed to seize and/or burn down buildings, and the military know this, though it has come to my knowledge that the military fully intend to burn down any buildings which they consider are being used or have been used by bandits without waiting for the instructions of the OCPD. In a recent conference between the *Mentri Besar*, the BA, General Boucher, Brigadier Erskine and myself, General Boucher mentioned the fact that it was not proposed to obey this law, and that you would fully support him in this. It is going to cause a lot of trouble if the military fail to obey the law in this respect.

As far as the actual conduct of operations was concerned both the army and the police were under fire from civil administrators. In a note which had been asked for on police and army co-operation in Kedah (October 1948) it was said that liaison between departments responsible for anti-guerrilla operations was negligible despite the efforts of individual police officers to co-operate with the army. Even between the two infantry battalions operating in the state there was said to be little liaison other than through the occasional police officer who had dealings with both of them: so much so that in the worst hill area in the Baling district, where both units were operating, neither dared go beyond the fringes of the bandit-occupied zone for fear of running into the other since neither unit had any knowledged of the movements of the other. One battalion was at least operating regular patrols, often with inadequate guides, in the hope of seeing guerrillas but it was indicative that although guerrilla movement was almost continuous in the area only one had been caught in recent weeks. Other factors gravely handicapping these patrols were lack of local knowledge and a lack of attached Chinese. Just as important was the fact that companies were switched periodically on a general post principle and on other occasions were moved well away from headquarters thus making administration, already difficult, doubly so. The observer, himself a former officer and MC, commented on the youthfulness and generally low quality of the battalion; and after months of training troops were fitter but in no way better for they still committed all the elementary mistakes, at least when on the move.

The police, more closely observed, were more heavily criticised. Police stations in the frontier zone were manned almost entirely by town Malays from elsewhere who were re-posted as a rule after some months. They were too inexperienced and frightened of the jungle to be of much use for anti-guerrilla operations. Uniformed police officers appeared to withhold information obtained in an anxiety to make personal efforts to use the information themselves. The gap between the CID and uniformed branch was particularly noticeable; little attempt was made to collate or check information as it was received; effective interrogation was submerged in a surfeit of form-filling; information always went up, and never down, and the man on the spot who had to use the information, was usually the last to receive it.

After allowances are made for local conditions, which might not have applied throughout Malaya, the picture that remains is of a disarticulated government framework, a feeble nervous system, and a series of spasmodic movements. The army was still organised on the battalion basis which was top heavy for the essentially police role which they were at present required to fulfil. Both they and the police lacked the intelligence that was essential for effective operations and, in its absence, metaphorically and often actually rode to the sound of the guns. Committed to a policy of keeping the enemy on the move they were themselves condemned to incessant movement and for the most part did not even begin to build up that local knowledge of what was later called 'framework operations' and which was to be the backbone of the military effort.

The problem of sympathetic detonation
To appreciate the physical forces that were involved in the insurrection it is necessary to set off the opening phases against a background of a turbulent Asia. As far as Malaya's three Asian communities were concerned, even the smallest, the Indian, newly divided by the transfer of power to the two successor states, felt the pull of a triumphant nationalism that could now be invoked as the precedent for independence. More important, however, were the centrifugal forces that threatened to pull the major communities apart. The close relationship between left-wing Malay nationalism and the newly emerging state of Indonesia has already been considered and Indonesia's renewed struggle for independence in December 1948, where even the conservative English newspaper of Malaya condemned the Dutch 'police action' added another variable factor to the equation of Malayan loyalty. To considerations of when Malaya should receive its independence was now added the affinitive sympathy of the Malay peoples and the undifferentiating popular suspicion of two apparently aligned colonial powers. For many there was at least the romantic attraction of union with Indonesia: a concept which sometimes overshadowed the expectation that, for obvious reasons, there would be a gradual rather than an immediate progress to independence. Thus, when the Commissioner-General in a broadcast in the middle of January spoke of eventual self-government for Malaya Asian newspapers in Malaya wanted a date to be set and *Utusan Melayu* spoke pessimistically and even despairingly of a period of a hundred or even three hundred years.

For many, however, the tide of events a little further away suggested that this period would be much shorter. By the end of 1948 Chiang Kai Shek's nationalist armies were already in a process of disintegration and the Chinese Communists stood at the gates of Pekin. For a while it was hard to appreciate the immensity of the impending Communist victory but the Malayan Chinese could be counted among the most interested and realistic observers.

Drift towards communalism
From the beginning of the insurrection the situation within Malaya alone was sufficient to create a good deal of tension

GOVERNMENT CONSTRAINED

between the Malay and Chinese communities. Most apparent was the racial composition of the combatant forces: armed Chinese guerrillas and numerous Chinese supporters on the one side, Malay police, soldiers and special constabulary on the other. Superficially, this could be and often was taken as the general alignment of the two communities: the Chinese were supporting the insurrection, the Malays were resisting it. The fact that so many leaders of the two communities should call so often for others to trust them was perhaps in itself a sufficient indication of the dangerous lack of trust that existed but there were more positive signs of the unsettling effect which the Emergency was having upon Malayan society.

For the Malays the strength of nationalist feeling which was particularly noticeable from September onwards showed itself in demands for the restoration of the *former* status of the Malay states. Dato Onn, the mainspring of Malay nationalism as well as the chief minister of Johore, warned that Malaya was not to be treated as a colony—an assumed status which seemed to have affected the attitude of some 'colonial' officials—and proposals were aired for the revival of the Johore Military Forces which would obviously not have an entirely ceremonial role. The more extreme attitudes adopted by the Malays themselves were expressed in Malay papers: *Majlis* in the Federation, *Utusan Melayu* in Singapore. It is perhaps worth making the point that in September 1948 the Federation of Malaya was only six months old. The Constitution had already been changed once since the war and the new one seemed open to specific emphasis and even amendments. The extreme statement of Malay opinion, often expressed by *Utusan Melayu*, was that Malaya belonged to the Malays: an argument which principally though not entirely was directed against the Chinese. Thus it was objected that there were too many Chinese consulates in Malaya—representatives, that is, of the Chinese Nationalist Government—and it was feared that the Chinese Government might take advantage of the existing state of emergency to assert the rights of Chinese. Where Malays were counting their numbers in the forces fighting the terrorists, the Chinese consuls, said *Majlis*, were busy calculating the amount of Chinese losses and the total of Chinese casualties.

Some idea of the dilemma of the Chinese side may be seen from one of several political ventures of Mr. Tan Cheng Lock. The Malayan Chinese League, of which he was founder, was pledged to work for collective advancement of the Chinese as well as for communal harmony; but these aims were somewhat ambiguous, if not, at this time, irreconcilable. Both Chinese language papers and the *Malaya Tribune*, in which there was a substantial Chinese interest, continued to express their disappointment at the constitutional changes and argued that the rights and privileges of the Chinese did not measure up to their contribution to the country's development. Their report, for example, that the Federation Government would supply the Chinese Consul-General with information on detainees under article 7 of the Sino-British Treaty of 1943, may have been designed as reassurance to the Chinese community that their interests were being looked after. At the same time it gave the impression that they might owe allegiance to a different authority. The fears of the two communities were mutual: that the Chinese were unassimilable and that the Malays were implacable. Evidence of communal clashes—for example when Chinese houses were burned down as a retaliation for the kidnapping of Malays—were a reminder that there was always the danger of a flash point. Chinese papers would protest; Malay papers would warn of 'strong retaliation' if the provocation continued. To some extent, popular feeling was damped down by the creation of a Sino-Malay goodwill committee which, after a meeting with the Commissioner-General in February 1949, became the Communities Liaison Committee, but there were tart replies and refusals from some State governments to entertain such ideas.

On the constitutional level both communities sought to insure their position. There was a good deal of support for the proposal that Dato Onn should become the deputy High Commissioner—and, after Gent's death, that he should be appointed as the new High Commissioner—and the movement for Penang's secession from the Federation, narrowly defeated in February by 15 votes to 10, was an ominous crack in the federal structure. It put the question in sharp and immediate terms: would the Federation be maintained? Doubts whether the country would hold together were less urgent but equally manifest in the criticism that was expressed of the increasingly authoritarian pattern of government and, while comparatively restricted, they were the more important for their articulate expression of the disenchantment of those who might be expected to see the advantages of colonial government.

The doubt which at least they implied was whether the existing government was worth defending. For those who valued the comparatively liberal tradition of British colonial government, circumscribed though it was and only a pale reflection of the metropolitan artefact, there were many causes for alarm. The pressure for summary trials; proposals to establish censorship; to reduce trade union activities;[6] and the support of one English language paper, the *Malay Mail*, for the idea of public executions. Already there was a feeling among some expatriates, again expressed by the *Malay Mail*, that the country was at war: all those who are not with us are against us. The possibility that some people who might have done no active harm would be ejected from Malaya was of minor importance compared with the task of rooting out the terrorist menace in the country.

Perhaps the most striking criticism of the early infringement of liberties was made in the Legislative Council by an Indian member, Mr. R. Ramani. After allowance is made for some exaggeration, topical literary allusions and rhetorical effect, it remains a powerful indictment of the 'new despotism of the executive and the newer despotism of the police'.[7] The Bar Council of Malaya had stated that it was its aim to maintain under all circumstances the rule of law and the principles of personal freedom which had hitherto been the heritage of those who live under the Common Law. Speaking as a lawyer himself, Mr. Ramani doubted whether that high ideal had in fact been upheld. Emergency Regulation No. 17, which dealt with detention, was compared to the notorious wartime regulation 18B in Britain—and an odious comparison at that. Even more than the grounds on which a man was detained, Mr. Ramani objected to the grounds on which a detainee might appeal.

> He is supposed to state the grounds of his objection without knowing a word about why he has been detained; and then what happens? This notice goes to the Advisory Committee, and then the Advisory Committee writes to him in another printed form. They don't, even then, tell him the grounds of his detention. They tell him that his application will be heard on such and such a date, at such and such a place, at such and such an hour, and then go on to say sapiently these magic words: 'the grounds for making a detention order against you were that you were suspected

---

[6] On which government policy was that while existing unions might continue—the Communist unions having disappeared—nothing should be done to encourage the revival of trade unions at this stage
[7] According to Mr. Ramani it took one senior officer four days to find someone in the lock-up in the Campbell Road police station in Kuala Lumpur.

of having recently acted or—mark these words—*of being likely to act* in a manner prejudicial to the public safety or good order.'

Approach to a counter-terror
A proper evaluation of Malaya in a state of emergency would seem to require dovetailing accounts of jurist, psychologist, sociologist and novelist. It would have to describe, in theory and in practice, what happened when the rule of law gave way to a twilight zone somewhere between peace and war and the thought and action of men who found themselves in it. It is not enough to say that Malaya was in a state of war because the special category of guerrilla warfare blurs nearly all the distinctions by which war is normally characterised. There were no fixed lines, seldom a set piece battle, no decisive military encounters, no enemy-held cities, towns or even villages which might be captured. Greatest and most exasperating of the problems facing the security forces was that of identifying the enemy: who and where were the combatant troops.

In view of the exceptions that will be recorded it must be stated here that while the acts of lawlessness on the part of security forces appear to occur mainly in the first twelve months or so of operations the impression derived, second-hand from the available papers and more limited first-hand experience, is that both police and army were attempting to operate within the framework of the law, that people were not shot out of hand as a matter of policy, and that where this happened it was the exception rather than the rule. It will be argued that there was nothing like the bankrupt strategy or routine brutality of either the first or second Vietnamese wars in which villages that were no longer governed were to be destroyed together with their civil population and prisoners and suspects were to be tortured and maimed as a matter of course. And it will be argued further that what is remarkable in the brutalising conditions of guerrilla warfare is that in Malaya there are so few accounts of atrocities even in the vast quantities of captured and surrendered Communist papers.

But in the early stages of the campaign, and indeed whenever contact took place in inhabited areas, there was the perpetual dilemma inherent in first contact. With incidents or information pointing unmistakably to the presence of guerrillas in a particular area, how, in the few seconds of confusion when figures are running from huts into jungle does one decide to open fire or not? If one does not, the best that can happen is that a possible enemy may escape. With a small patrol, what is equally likely is that they themselves will be attacked if they have, in fact, succeeded in surprising a guerrilla group. But, unless they are uniformed or obviously armed, there is no guarantee that the people who are running are guerrillas or wanted criminals rather than very frightened men and women who may or may not be willing or unwilling guerrilla supporters.

Almost every other situation report at the beginning of the emergency recorded the shootings of men who ran out of huts, were challenged and failed to stop. Too often, no weapons, ammunition or anything else in the least way incriminating, either materially or in oral evidence, was ever found. In November the CPO Johore was particularly concerned with the situation in which suspects were shot while attempting to escape.

> I can find no legal justification for the shooting, whether under the normal laws or the emergency regulations, unless the incident occurs in a protected place or during curfew hours.

So far it seemed that magistrates had brought in verdicts of justifiable homicide; but the CPO thought that would not always be the case and that some major scandal might result. Later that month, at the CPO's conference in Kuala Lumpur, the CPO Johore again raised the matter with the Commissioner of Police and added that in many cases he considered a small number of rounds of ammunition were planted on the bodies afterwards to justify the shooting. Sometimes this small act of meanness was unnecessary. Some coroners, it seems, declined to hold an inquest under the emergency regulations and merely accepted the military statements and recorded a verdict of justifiable homicide. Almost a year after the event, the troubled conscience of a Ferret group officer, who was then studying Chinese in Macao, prompted him to write about another incident that had taken place in Johore in November 1948. On this occasion, a Ferret group patrol, led by two aborigine guides, came across two midde-aged Chinese near some squatter huts in a small Chinese rubber holding. They were identified by one of the aborigines as Communist agents— one had organised supplies, the other acted as porter—and both were arrested. What exactly happened then is not clear from the exchanges of correspondence and the attempts that were made to secure statements from two Malay eye-witnesses—one of whom, a private in the Malay regiment, was then in a mental hospital for observation—but one of the Chinese was shot and killed either by the officer himself or on his orders.

Yet another tragedy from Johore was the case of a Malay special constable who was killed by Gurkhas in June 1949. The military operation did not go entirely as planned; there was failure of liaison, and mistaken identification when the manager of the estate and his four special constables exchanged fire with a patrol of Gurkhas, each under the impression that the others were guerrillas. What was particularly alarming in this case was the self-satisfied tone of the battalion's own board of inquiry. The account given by the OSPC Kluang differed materially from the evidence that was accepted by the board and the glaring discrepancies and mysterious disappearance of identification marks such as a *songkok*[8] and armband would have aroused the suspicion of even a Mississippi jury. Nothing that was said in extenuation at this board challenged the evidence that the special constable, with his hands up and his rifle on the ground, was mortally wounded from a distance of two yards : a point on which the board did not bother to comment.

In individual instances brutality can perhaps be put down to the exigencies of a combat situation but it is the early approach to the problem of the rural Chinese, and those who were undoubtedly supporting the guerrillas, that a series of punitive acts took on the aspect of a counter-terror. Again, individually, they may have been compounded of exasperation and error and while there is no evidence that they had any direct snowball effect there was an unmistakable hardening of certain official attitudes, a feeling that desperate situations required desperate remedies, and a growing tendency to treat this as a normal part of security operations. In the series of actions in which large numbers of homes were burnt—Jalong, Kachau, Lintang and Tronoh being particular examples of concern—the Kachau case, while it may not have been entirely representative, affords some insight into the despotic nature of certain operations.

The village of Kachau in Kajang police district of Selangor consisted of some fifty houses and shops and some six hundred inhabitants. Large quantities of arms had been dropped on the outskirts of the village late in the war and its staunch support of the guerrillas during both the Japanese occupation and the Emergency earned it the title of 'Little Yenan'—in honour of the early refuge and stronghold of the Communist armies in China. It was, as everyone from the Colonial Secretary downwards

[8] Malay brimless hat.

pointed out after the event, a notorious area.[9] There was no doubt that guerrillas had operated in and around the village which, without a police station, must be reckoned to have been largely under Communist control.[10] Various incidents had taken place in the area, among them the killing of an eight-year-old English boy when he and his family were being evacuated in July, and on two nights, October 31st and November 2nd, attacks were made on a mine and a rubber estate which resulted in considerable damage by fire.

At 2 o'clock on the morning of November 2nd guerrillas had burned down the smoke house and rubber store of Dominion estate, half-a-mile from Kachau village. By dawn Kachau village had also been burned to the ground. In various government files a series of explanations was offered for why and how this happened. What is most interesting, and alarming, is the difficulty at the time of finding out exactly what had happened. There was no doubt of the concern and general disapproval of civil government but it was not until three years later that the efforts of the Assistant Commissioner of Police, Mr. Dobree, uncovered what for the moment stands out as the definitive account of what happened and the falsehoods in the accounts that were given at the time. What is also of interest is the discrepancy given in various accounts as attempts seemed to have been made to cover up what had happened. For example, in what purported to be an appreciation of information and operations in the general Kachau area—unusual in that appreciations are usually made before rather than after an operation—the Staff Officer Operations, Selangor, maintained that the officer concerned had 'acted firmly on his conviction and information and burnt several wooden houses believed to have harboured bandits. In doing so the conflagration spread and a large portion of the village was destroyed.'[11] It went on, 'This hard blow has had a most deterrent effect on this area and is generally felt by the lower classes

---

[9] The Colonial Secretary, Mr. Creech Jones, in replying to a question from the Communist Member, Mr. Piratin. His answer may well have been based entirely on the information that was given to the Colonial Office but this did not prevent it being wrong on three material points: that the inhabitants had been warned; that they were given ample time to remove their belongings; and that the relief measures of the social welfare department were not required 'because the people found shelter with their friends'. H.C. Deb. January 26th 1949.
[10] When a guerrilla camp was located near Kachau in October, paper bags were found bearing the names of Kachau shops.
[11] 4.11.48.

up there to be a lesson for their disinclination to help government.' In his report a few days later, however, the OCPD Kajang, who was actually responsible, made no pretence that the village had burned down by mistake.

> After the attack on Dominion estate, it was decided to burn down the village and verbal approval was given by the CPO Selangor. The inhabitants of the village were called out and were told what was to happen and were warned that they had two hours in which to get out their personal belongings. Space in a safe area was allocated for their belongings to be placed but many were stubborn and did not comply. The village was burned down approximately two and a half hours after the order had been given to evacuate.

In forwarding this report, the Deputy Commissioner CID, having decided that the police were fully justified in destroying the village, had an explanation for the slowness with which the villagers removed their possessions. They delayed as long as possible, he said, probably hoping that their friends the bandits would attack and stop the operation. The claim for compensation which, at least in part, seems to have occasioned these reports, was dismissed by this officer as 'sheer impertinence and whoever is responsible for putting this forward should be questioned as to whether his allegiance is to Malaya or to the MCP. The only welfare I would recommend to the dispossessed villagers is the hospitality of a detention camp. Having backed the wrong horse they now want their money back.'[12]

There the matter rested: at least in this particular file in the Commissioner of Police's secret registry. But among the claims entered were two from Chinese villagers of Kachau who had rendered considerable personal assistance to the security forces during active operations in the months preceding the destruction of their village. Three years after the claims were filed the Secretary of Defence took refuge in two Emergency Regulations, 18A and 18B, which were published less than a fortnight after the village was burned down and which were doubtfully interpreted to give retrospective legality to the action.[13] In settlement

---

[12] The application of some of his remarks was not altogether clear. 'Those who are not helping us should be considered as enemies of the state and banished and this particularly applied to those complacent and comfortably prosperous persons in the towns who speak publicly on matters they know nothing about.'

of the original claim of $26,000, now increased to a round $30,000, he was prepared to offer an *ex-gratia* payment of $10,000; appropriately enough to be made from Secret Service funds.

It was at this point that Dobree took the case in hand. In the intervening three years the officer who was responsible had left the police. No records whatever were available in the office of the CPO Selangor or the district police headquarters in Kajang, but depositions were taken and a very different account emerged.

> Mr. X (the OCPD) and his party then went to Kachau village. On arrival of the Kajang jungle squad Mr. X gave instructions that all the inhabitants of the village were to be awakened and were to be told that the village was to be destroyed by fire and they were allowed thirty minutes in which to remove their personal property from the building. It was then about 5 a.m.
>
> The villagers managed to remove some of their property from the dwellings and this they placed on the roadway in the village. But by the time Mr. X gave the order to set fire to the village, there was still a great deal of moveable property left in the dwellings.
>
> The village fired. Daybreak had not yet come. Nothing was left of the village when the flames had subsided, and even the moveable property which had been placed on the roadway by the villagers caught fire and was destroyed.
>
> On orders of Mr. X the villagers were informed that they could now go where they wished but they should not return to Kachau. They were then left entirely to their own devices and Mr. X and his party returned to Kajang.

For one person at least the Kachau incident might be said to have had a reasonably happy ending.[14] Whether even this would have been achieved without the dedication of one officer is perhaps open to question. At the time, the incident provoked a sharp reaction from civil government and, in particular, dis-

---

[13] The two regulations read in conjunction gave an OCPD power to destroy buildings or structures; it did not authorise the destruction of anything else. Dobree, whose integrity shines through a tissue of lies and evasions, argued therefore that if an OCPD destroyed movable property, i.e. the contents of buildings or structures, either wantonly or by accident, then government was liable for payment to the owners thereof the full value of the moveable property as destroyed.

[14] As soon as the $30,000 claim was met in full, other claims followed headed by one for $80,000 from a lady who was another former resident.

approval from Watherston and the acting Chief Secretary. The latter minuted

> I agree with Mr. Watherston's para 2. The action taken by the police savours of a reprisal and cannot be justified. It embarrasses the state government, retards the implementation of the government's policy in regard to the clearing up of squatter areas and in its carrying out is inhumane since no arrangements are made beforehand for the reception to other areas of the evicted persons.

The action was, it was agreed, contrary to police policy and a CP's directive which had only recently been published. The High Commissioner himself, while showing signs of exasperation with the Chinese community,[15] had it conveyed to the Commissioner of Police that he was 'not at all satisfied that the government cause is helped by adopting methods likely to make criminals and CTs out of people who are deprived of their livelihood and suffer destruction of their property'. Both at the time therefore and in its belated restitution government admitted that the burning of Kachau was a wrongful act. Without being vindictive it might have been expected that some comment or caution would have been made to the officer who was responsible for this destruction. That he should have resigned from the police force a year later without a single mention or adverse comment on this incident is a sad reflection either of an over-extended police force or an action that was itself considered unremarkable.

In any event, the seriousness of this action was soon overtaken by the most murderous five minutes of the campaign. On December 13th it was announced briefly that on the previous day 24 bandits were killed at Batang Kali in Selangor. That 24 guerrillas should have been killed in combat was in itself remarkable but the reticence shown by the army in acclaiming what should have been a considerable victory made it even more so. For ten days there was no further statement. Two days after the incident a police inquiry began but for ten days no statement was issued although it soon became obvious that the 24 had been killed in what were at least unusual circumstances. The general implication of a further statement issued on January 4th was that the 24 Chinese were shot by a patrol of the Scots Guards while trying to escape. The GOC explained to a press conference the deadliness of modern automatic weapons when fired at short range but

---

[15] Both in his internal comments on Kachau and in a dispatch to the Colonial Office: 2.12.48.

the fact that out of a group of 25 there were no wounded and only one survivor begged a number of questions.

It would perhaps be too romantic to move from the Zola-esque topic of Kachau to the long silences of Batang Kali but the latter were indeed remarkable as was the curious remoteness of the dead. There were no photographs, no names and no evidence that they were suspected guerrillas. The official account of what happened has never been withdrawn but to this day different accounts are given in the village of Ulu Yam Bahru, which is where many of the men came from. The 25th man, the sole survivor, is now dead, but the evidence, while it may be circumstantial, seems to be based largely on the accounts of the men's families who were not far away when the shooting occurred. What emerges from the villagers' accounts is a far more complex story which begins with the earlier ambush and killing of a lieutenant and a special constable, the arrest of a guerrilla supplier, and his arrival on Sungei Remok estate with a combined army and police patrol. They encountered two young Chinese carrying padi who were accused of supplying the guerrillas, denied it, and were shot on the spot. The following morning a lorry carrying tappers and rice arrived at these remote labour lines. The detained guerrilla supporter picked out a woman guerrilla supplier and the women were divided into two groups, some returning to the village, but the families of the men staying on. Troops then proceeded to burn down the labour lines and in so doing a number of detonators which were stored there, illegally no doubt but used for fishing purposes, exploded. The troops, outnumbered and thinking they had been ambushed, panicked and began shooting. The Chinese started running but at such close quarters all of them were killed by rifle and automatic fire. The unsolved mystery is what happened to the twenty-fifth man. According to the manager of Sungei Remok estate he was taken behind the smoke house, on the previous day, threatened with a sten gun and frightened out of his wits. In the 'oral tradition' of Ulu Yam Bahru there were many references to a man who, also on the previous evening, had had a revolver pointed at his head and the trigger squeezed three times. On each occasion nothing happened and the officers, apparently impressed by the man's luck or the omens, had granted a *de facto* reprieve.

Considering the stories that must have been current in the area within hours of the event the moderation of the Chinese press is little short of astonishing. The *China Press*, for example, asked simply that the bodies should be examined and that eye-witnesses should give first-hand accounts, although in Singapore the *Nanyang Siang Pau* warned that if the military and police were to continue treating Chinese in the manner of Kuala Kubu (the town nearest to Sungei Remok estate) the consequences would be disastrous. It is hardly surprising that Asian papers in Malaya were not satisfied with the government's account but in spite of what had happened it is surprising to find that the Malaya Tribune group of Mr. Tan Cheng Lock could still find time to remember the Scots Guards sergeant and his patrol 'men under great tension, outnumbered two to one, and in fear of their lives'.

Among the consequences of this event it may be noted that the first resort of the families of the dead men was the Chinese Consul-General: that because of the curfew the bodies were left unburied for three days;[16] and that the MCP had been presented with 24 martyrs.[17]

Note: The Batang Kali Incident
Since this account was written the question of what happened at Batang Kali was re-opened on the initiative of a London Sunday newspaper. On February 1st 1970 *The People* devoted the whole of its front and two inside pages to a report which had taken its staff eight weeks to compile. The starting point, apparently, was when *The People* challenged Mr. George Brown's suspicion that, *à propos* the My Lai massacre, 'there are an awful lot of spectres in our cupboard, too'. Among those who read this challenge was a Scots Guardsman who had been a member of the patrol. Eventually, he and three other members of the patrol swore statements on oath to the effect that the twenty-five Chinese had been massacred and that they were not attempting to escape.

On February 4th, the Secretary of State for Defence, Mr. Dennis Healey, said in the House of Commons that there was a direct conflict of evidence as to what had happened; that he was treating the matter with concern and urgency; and that he would consider whether the matter should be referred to the Director of Public Prosecutions for further investigation. In Malaya, a man came forward to say that he was a survivor of the shooting;

---

[16] It was the manager of the estate who applied for permission to bury them.
[17] 'Bodies lying in the wilderness and crying aloud to heaven for justice'—reference in a quasi-Communist account of post-war Malayan history published by the Manyang Geographical and Historical Society, Nanyang University, Singapore, and banned in the Federation.

both he and a former special constable who said he had guided the patrol denied that there had been an attempt to escape. A number of questions remain unanswered—not least being the orders and purpose of the patrol—and the answers are difficult to re-construct after more than twenty years. Most of the evidence today is probably in the files of Scotland Yard, whose investigations were conducted by a Detective Chief Superintendent. In June 1970 it was announced by the new Conservative Government in London that the matter had been dropped. Incredible in its official explanation from the beginning, it was discreditable at the end. Batang Kali remains as the gravest, not least because it is the most exceptional, suspicion on the conduct of the British Army in Malaya.

Original Problems

7

THE SQUATTER PROBLEM

Resettlement of the rural Chinese was an emergency measure that grew into the major policy, executive and fiscal concern of the Malayan Government and, arguably, into the largest development project of modern South-East Asia. The process has been closely studied and the success has been given widespread citation. As a technique and a precise ordering of affairs it was eventually to become a formula for double fences 'between thirty-five and forty-five feet apart, the outer to consist of eight-foot barbed wire cross mesh with twelve-inch spacing and the inner a six-foot barbed wire double apron fence'. Vegetables and crops were to be grown between the fences, provided they were not more than two feet high, but 'under no conditions were tapioca, yams, tobacco, cereals, climbing beans and cucumber to be grown'.[1] It was also to be used as a model for the immensely efficient and successful, but limited, resettlement of Sarawak Chinese since 1965 as well as hopelessly misapplied by the Diem Government in South Vietnam where it degenerated into a shibboleth and catchpenny phrase.[2] In Malaya, it was conceived in uncertainty, carried in indifference and born in haste. Its early years were marked by bitterness, recrimination and hostility but out of these feelings and the mistakes which were made there came a social transformation in the hundreds of new villages that were governed, viable, and secure.

In 1948, however, the rural Chinese in Malaya constituted a state without a state. Leaving aside the second part of this ambiguity which may be taken to imply the absence of Malayan citizenship, when the State of Emergency was declared the government soon realised that it governed only part of Malaya. That part in general, where there were towns, large villages, and a predominantly Malay population. Its writ did not run among the rural Chinese and, in particular, those who were loosely described as 'squatters'. How many squatters there were, where

[1] Emergency Operations Council Directive No. 6, *Emergency Directives and Instructions*, 1956
[2] Milton E. Osborne, *Strategic Hamlets in South Viet-Nam*, Cornell University, 1956 (mimeo).

they were and what they were was information which government suddenly and urgently needed. And which, except in a very few areas, it did not have. Government had now to contend with a quantity that was unknown except insofar as it felt the burden of an unassimilated squatter population. Now that the storm had broken this dead weight would be unable to maintain its stable position through inertia; and, unsecured by even the minimal attachments to law and order, it would constitute a danger that was at least as great as the mutiny which had already broken out and might even sink the ship itself from within.

One of the earliest assessments of the Chinese squatter problem was provided, significantly, by the Adviser on Chinese Affairs in Perak, in September 1948.[3] Significant in that the Chinese Affairs advisers, the remnants of the pre-war Chinese Protectorate which since the war had been disestablished in the interests of uniform government, were foremost among the few civil officers of government who were at all in touch with the rural Chinese.

In Perak, and no doubt in other states, there was in 1948 an administrative no man's land, which, under the influence of Communism, threatened to become a vast sprawling state within a state extending over huge areas of what were once Forest Reserves, Malay Reservations, Mining or Agricultural land and considerable areas of privately owned estates, particularly European, which were felled during the Occupation. It was usual to ascribe this huge administrative vacuum to the 'grow more food' policy of the Japanese during the Occupation when a free for all policy of indiscriminate and illegal land acquisition was both permitted and encouraged by the occupying power. But this was not the fundamental cause of the problem; land hunger which resulted in the illegal occupation of land by Chinese farmers and their families was already becoming a problem before the war. All the Japanese Occupation did was to accelerate a movement which was already gathering momentum.

After the war, government, torn between the wish to encourage food production as much as possible and the desire to prevent squatters from doing further damage to the soil and forests, had on the one hand failed to make any plans for governing the areas occupied by squatters in places where they were not doing any immediate harm and on the other hand failed to take the drastic steps where real damage was being done. The main reason for

[3] Upon which the following description is largely based.

this was that government had not filled the administrative vacuum. Great tracts of land miles away from the nearest police station, school or district office had been opened up in areas without any communication with the outside world other than jungle tracks. The staff of the Forestry Department, adequate enough to cope pre-war with the problem of controlling forest checking stations and seeing that timber cutters cut down the right trees in the right place, was quite insufficient to cope with the problem of a huge Chinese peasant population opening up forest reserves whenever it liked. The same was true of the District Offices and the Agricultural Department. The pre-war administrative machine was by its very construction incapable of meeting the new situation. The result had been that government's writ did not run over wide areas of the country, although, had the full significance of the problem been realised earlier, adequate steps might have been taken which would have had the effect of squeezing out the influence of Communism in many if not all the areas.[4]

The problem being stated, what was the solution? In the simplest form there were only two alternatives: to control the squatters or to deport them. Beginning with the second alternative the ACA Perak insisted that distinctions be made and that the squatters as a whole should not be victimised because of the misguided activities of a few of their numbers. Squatters were of different kinds. He divided them into five groups:

(a) Squatters who possess a Temporary Occupation Licence[5] (TOL) or otherwise in lawful occupation of their land and who were situated in areas round towns and villages where they could be policed and controlled. Many of these had been on their holdings for years;
(b) Squatters holding TOLs, etc. in more remote areas not at present under proper administrative control;
(c) Squatters who had settled within easy access of towns but without any legal title to the land occupied by them;

---

[4] As a field officer ACA Perak questioned the need for large numbers and heavy expenditure in centralised government as well as providing a modest local example for Professor Parkinson in Singapore. '... it is incredible to me that it is now found necessary to have a Secretariat consisting of some 25 officers when before the war the Federal Secretariat and Secretary to the High Commissioner's office combined was staffed by 7 men. Had half the present Secretariat officers been distributed among the component states of the Federation together with their clerical staffs the administrative vacuum could have been filled and the present Emergency would not have arisen.'
[5] Of indefinite duration but renewable every year.

(d) Squatters in remote areas who were occupying plots of land in jungle felled during the Occupation;
(e) Squatters occupying similar areas where the Administration through lack of adequate staff had failed to stem their advance.

Of these groups it was the last two which constituted the problem. The ACA Perak was opposed both to their deportation and resettlement. Either one, he said, if taken on a large scale would only afford the Communists a mass grievance to exploit and instead of eliminating them by either means the wisest course would be to bring the administration to the squatters. Summing up his recommendations they were:

1. That deportation or removal to other areas of squatters should not be resorted to as a general policy;
2. It should be reserved for the comparatively few areas where there is a hard core of Communism and where the insurgents were receiving the whole-hearted support of the squatters, freely given and not the result of intimidation, or areas where squatters were occupying hill slopes or other places where their activities were causing serious damage or where they were in a Malay Reservation which was urgently required for the settlement of Malaya. Deportation or removal to be resorted to only after a most careful inquiry;
3. The position of squatters in remote areas even where they had no legal justification for their existence should be legalised either by TOLs or even a title. Such areas should be opened up by the construction of roads. This should start at once. It would facilitate rather than hamper police and military action and would go hand in hand with the registration of all Chinese in these areas. Administration should follow without delay and a great field of social experiment will be opened up.
4. With regard to forest conservation, the policy should be directed towards the prevention of further expansion rather than the reforestation of areas already cut out. This would probably require a considerable increase in the number of forest guards. It was suggested that Malay Special Constables, when the crisis is over, might be given priority of consideration.

Of these four recommendations, numbers two and three are the most important because of the assumptions which they contain. Whether wholehearted support for the guerrillas was freely given or the result of intimidation was a nice distinction. One may ask how much it mattered when the object was to deny support to the guerrillas and whether it had any more than moral validity when it was a question of action, and immediate action at that. Again, the third recommendation that squatters in remote areas should be given a legal settlement to their land and that the areas should be opened up by road may have been all very well but this was a long range development programme rather than an emergency operation.

A year later, incidentally, the Perak State Squatter Committee provided a very thorough report. But again it hardly touched on the security aspect of resettlement and gave no hint of urgency. Resettlement, if the Perak report was to be implemented, would have been done on a very sound basis, like a good slum clearance and re-housing scheme, but it is open to question whether government had sufficient time at its disposal. Both the report of the Chinese Adviser in Perak and the Perak Squatter Committee emphasised the administrative rather than the protective aspect of the squatter problem and it seems to be significant that another Chinese Affairs officer and Chinese scholar saw the Emergency first as a land problem, that is to say alienated squatters who had not been allowed by Malay states to have land; second, as a security problem; and third as a problem of local government. The sequence is important and it is certainly *not* the sequence that was adopted by the states who were faced with the need for emergency action. In these and other reports there was a tendency on the part of Chinese Affairs officers to treat the squatter problem as a major undertaking of government and to stress the land issue. There was a clear-sighted appreciation of the problem but it was one that created immediate difficulties while at the same time it could be argued that it did not address itself to the immediate problem: which was to break contact between the squatters and the guerrillas.

Before dealing with it as a question of land, and therefore a matter for the States, resettlement will be considered from the Federal standpoint. What was probably the first meeting specifically to consider the squatter problem was held between representatives of the United Planting Association of Malaya and Malayan Estate Owners' Association and presided over by the Chief Secretary. This meeting had originally been convened by Sir Edward Gent 'partly in order to soothe the ruffled feelings of UPAM' who had been pressing the government for some eighteen months to take action in dealing with squatters on the seventy thousand acres or so of their estates which were needed for replanting. The UPAM interest was in a simple legal procedure to cover proceedings against groups of persons occupying privately owned land instead of against each individual as was then necessary under the law. When the meeting was held Gent was already dead and the case for action on the Federal level went by default. It was agreed simply that State and Settlement governments should examine the question of squatters as it affected their own territories and the only directive that was minuted from the Chief Secretary was whatever might be inferred from his statement that 'failure to dislodge these people would provide a bad example for the future and the problem would grow into an even more serious one'.

From now until September 1948 there seems to have been no premeditated action to deal with squatters; and even legal proceedings, for which the Solicitor-General had been asked to prepare draft legislation for the benefit of land owners, were dropped on the suggestion that they should not be used until the present state of lawlessness had ended. On September 12th, as a result of the Commissioner General's initiative, a conference was held at Bukit Serene which foreshadowed drastic action against Chinese squatters. There was, said the Commissioner General

> No doubt that the right policy from the long term view would be to get rid of as many squatters as possible in a selective process, by methods which would incite as little adverse comment from China and from the world at large as possible. If it were possible to get rid of 25,000–50,000 Chinese within the next six or twelve months, the racial problem in the Federation would be eased. On this basis a large number of good squatters would be allowed to remain and given some sort of temporary title for suitable land.

In Singapore the Colonial Secretary reported that the GOC Singapore, General Dunlop, regarded many of the squatter locations in Johore as enemy areas virtually under Communist control. Nevertheless, he said, it would not be practical politics to deport all squatters. Mass deportation would create political difficulties and the process would therefore have to be based on selection. How this selection was to be done was less obvious; but on an *ad hoc* basis it was obvious that the banishment procedure would not work. In addition to the clerical work involved, the Secretary of State had insisted that banishment cases except those concerning criminals should be reviewed by a judge of the Supreme Court as well as Exco. In Singapore, on the other hand, it seemed that people were being detained under a warrant from the Colonial Secretary which stated that they were detained unless prepared voluntarily to return to their own country.[6]

From this conference, as from the one in July, there emerged neither decisions nor definite policy line. But they did nevertheless see the genesis of the Squatter Committee.[7] MacDonald had originally asked for a special committee to conduct an urgent investigation and report within two months. In the event, the report of the Committee was not made until January 10th 1949 and in the meantime not only were matters firmly in the hands of the various States but other means were being taken in an attempt to secure a *de facto* solution of the problem. In one of its more extreme forms the attitude of the Malay States towards large, unassimilated minorities of rural Chinese was presented by the Government of Kedah. A report from the British Adviser warned that

> the *Mentri Besar* and Malay authorities were getting restive about the passive attitude adopted towards squatters because nearly all land in Kedah is in Malay reserve and apart from resenting the contempt of the authority of the State, they feel that the Chinese, who already hold the commercial life of the State in their hands, are becoming also a resident peasantry.

After referring to various depredations made by the squatters the British Adviser did not take up too much time in a search for a solution. He had decided, *a priori*, that it would be impossible to provide camps for more than an infinitessimal number of squatters and their dependents and therefore

> the answer appears to be to destroy squatters' huts and leave them to fend for themselves—this is unpleasant in every way but it seems to me that there is no other way out.

An alternative view was expressed at meetings in the State Security Committee that were held in Negri Sembilan in October and November in which the committee stated and restated its view that the only way to deal with the trouble was to deport as many squatters as possible from the country. But the definitive statement of this uncompromising point of view came in a personal

---

[6] The Singapore Government was prepared to pay the cost of their passages.
[7] The decision to create this committee was apparently taken at the Commissioner General's conference; but in the letter (9.10.48) to all *Mentri Besar* propriety demanded that it be put in the form of a suggestion.

letter from the *Mentri Besar* of Kedah to Sir Henry Gurney on November 6th 1948.

> I am given to understand by the Police that an ugly situation may develop in the Weng, Klian Intan, Kroh area which comprises part of the Baling district and a small subdistrict of Perak, which is for Police purposes controlled by Kedah.
>
> The attitude of this Government is that under no circumstances can alternative areas of State land be given to Chinese squatters evicted from existing areas of illegal occupation. All State land, except a relatively small area near the Siam border, which is also a potential source of danger, has been constituted into Malay Reserves so that unless these Reserves were cancelled no permanent occupation rights could be given to Chinese.
>
> Cancellation of Malay Reserves would be looked on with extreme disfavour by His Highness and by the Executive Council. Unlike Selangor and Perak, this State has, up to the present, a very high preponderance of genuine Malay population. The proportion is not less than 3/4. This Government is anxious that this state of affairs shall continue and Kedah remain a genuine Malay State and that State land be maintained for the expansion of the existing Malay population.
>
> The operations on the Weng road and ultimately elsewhere must necessarily result in eviction of large numbers of squatters and their dependents, perhaps not less than 15,000 people, though we can make no accurate estimate. Camps are no solution because, as we cannot ultimately settle them in Kedah, the matter of finding accommodation, quarters, etc. would be no passing phase but a question of almost infinite duration. Nor is it possible to employ these people, of whom only a small proportion would be working males, on constructional works. There is in my view one answer only and that is that the Police and Military take the line which has, I believe, been followed elsewhere, eg Palestine and N.W. Frontier, etc., of burning out squatters and leaving them to work out their own salvation, i.e. by going into settled areas, towns, and so on, or into other and temporarily less objectionable squatter areas or, best of all, slipping over the Siamese frontier.
>
> We have, I consider, no moral obligations to the Siamese in this matter. I suggest, therefore that this treatment is applied to certain squatter areas as test cases to see if any problems involving large scale relief measures do in fact arise. It is my opinion, owing to the self-reliant character of the Chinese, that it may well be found that no problems do actually arise.

There is of course the alternative of repatriating squatters in bulk to China and this, if administratively possible, is naturally the solution most acceptable to this Government.

Gurney did not reply to this letter himself; but it nevertheless brought a sharp reminder 'that His Excellency's view is that the State of Kedah cannot divest itself of responsibility towards squatters who may, as a result of operations by Security Forces, be evicted from the land which they are occupying'. As it happened, no operations were envisaged in Kedah that would result in the eviction of 15,000 squatters but in the case of Perak, where the State government had gone ahead with its own scheme of *ad hoc* resettlement in October, it led to a notable clash between the Federal and State authorities. For all its comparatively restrained expression this was a head on collision on the issue of state rights. Perak denied that the squatter was a Federal problem and defended its right to take such action as was deemed necessary. No sooner had the eviction of Chinese squatters from Sungei Siput begun than the acting CPO told the *Mentri Besar* that he had been instructed by the Commissioner of Police that no further evictions of squatters were to take place without the consent of the Federal Government and the Commissioner of Police. To which the *Mentri Besar* had reacted by placing the matter before His Highness in Council, the Council advising that all matters which under constitutional agreements properly came within the function of the State should by right be dealt with by the executive authority of the State. Advice to which His Highness agreed accordingly. And in practice, the *Mentri Besar* insisted, the eviction of squatters from State land was a matter for magisterial action at the instance of the Collector and the police must therefore assist the Collector if the magistrate so ordered. And so 'the consent of the Federal Government and of the Commissioner of Police . . . would not therefore appear to be required'.

The Federal Government was obviously embarrassed by Perak's precipitate action; but, at the same time, it was one of the few states that had done anything to deal with the squatter problem; and after a month had passed Gurney minuted that the Federal attitude towards Perak in this matter should be one of encouragement rather than coercion. At the level of the *Mentri Besar* this meant admiration for 'the initiative and vigorous steps which have been taken by Perak government', concern for resettlement or future livelihood of evicted squatters and a reminder of the wider issues involved if squatters were to be repatriated. On the level of communication with the British Adviser, who had also identified himself with the interests of the State to which he was accredited, it meant concern that the Sungei Siput operation would be extended over wider areas still in the near future and, specifically, that evicted squatters should not be homeless on their arrival in resettlement areas.

Who actually took the decision to conduct the October clearance operations in both Perak and Selangor is not altogether clear. The fact that operations began at Batu Arang and Sungei Siput on successive days suggests some central direction; and in his letter to the BA Perak of October 29th the Acting Chief Secretary said

> I should add that officially we have heard nothing in Kuala Lumpur regarding the continued eviction of squatters and presume that you will be notified before any action is taken by the Security Forces. The GOC however states that in order to clean up the areas entirely and successfully the operations must continue.

and one must therefore assume that they took place with at least the cognisance of the GOC, General Boucher.

As an experimental model the removal of squatters from Sungei Siput via Ipoh to Pantai Remis in the Dindings area of Perak was a scheme of limited application. As the Deputy Commissioner of Labour noted in the week's Situation Report (8.11.48).

> Removal of squatters from Sungei Siput to Lumut carried out successfully. This one solution of the problem, only applicable to the type that cultivates land as his main source of livelihood. But many squatters engaged in industry squat mainly because there is nowhere else to live. They do little cultivation and it is useless to remove them to a place where they cannot get work.

What would happen if there was little or no provision for evicted squatters was to be seen in the aftermath of the clearance at Batu Arang. A camp that was erected at Morib was filled with dependants and destitutes left after the operation; was condemned by a European business representative on Exco as a concentration camp; and closed after three months. The operations at both Sungei Siput and Batu Arang resulted in a lamentable loss of life. At Sungei Siput, a baby died in the evacuation; and at Batu Arang some elderly Chinese women seem to have been accidentally shot. Complaints were made immediately at the State level—an answer to a question from the Perak Adviser on Chinese Affairs revealed that at Sungei Siput the squatters had two hours in which to assemble all their belongings—and on the Federal level attempts were made to regulate the actions both of States and security forces. Three decisions were taken on matters of principle. First, serious objections were registered to taking powers for the detention of women and children. Second, it was decided that sweeps of squatter areas by police and military should avoid the destruction of houses apart from those known to belong to bandits. And the third, recommendation of the Local Defence Committee (23.8.48) was that no one should be removed from squatter areas except those required by the police for detention or screening.

The fact that the Federal Government was reluctant to take wholesale action against squatters who, although suspected, were not convicted, did not mean that they had exhausted the possibilities of dealing with squatters at this level. Some of them were no more than conjecture. For example, transfer to Borneo and a partial solution to the shortage of labour there. A rather crude proposal by the Incorporated Society of Planters that estates should have first pick of their evicted squatters—'anyone subsequently not reporting for work to be repatriated'—revived memories of the pre-war hydraulic labour system in that surplus labour, now a problem, should be drained off, but this was dismissed by government as being so naïve as not to require a detailed answer.[8] There remained incidental pressure and what might perhaps be called general moral suasion that led to a certain amount of voluntary repatriation to China—although it seems that many of those who went carried legal certificates of re-admission with them—but there can be no doubt that the normal way of breaking squatter-guerrilla contact at this time was by arrest and detention.

In spite of its ambiguous title—Operation Frustration—a number of Communists and at least potential guerrillas were arrested in the early days of the Emergency and before the MCP had completed its mobilisation. Apart from this, there was an increasingly large number of arrests made on suspicion; and although the staff seldom existed for systematic interrogation,

---

[8] This proposal, in a modified form, appeared as an editorial in *The Planter*, February 1949, but was perhaps vitiated by its easy assumption that squatters might be converted into tappers to whom there would be no need to allocate fertile land for crop production.

arrest did at least provide the opportunity; and, in any case, in the twilight zone between peace and war, there was a tendency to detain those who were young, able bodied and obviously hostile. It was at one time suggested in the Executive Council that in areas where shooting incidents occurred suspicion should be translated into guilt and fifty young men should immediately be seized and deported: an action which, although only a pale reflection, was close enough to Japanese procedure for the proposal to be condemned and quashed. Emergency regulations made it possible to detain suspects for six, then twelve months and finally two years. By July approximately 1,500 had been detained and at the end of August of 4,500 arrested, 2,700 were still in detention.

Numbers such as these placed a considerable strain upon the country's existing prison accommodation. Seremban gaol, where many of the detainees were held, was full to overflowing: and this before any attempt had been made to get on terms with the bulk of the rural Chinese guerrilla supporters. There was little doubt that almost the entire population of many rural areas were guerrilla supporters. In a state of war they would probably have been regarded as a suitable target for offensive action: a logical extension which did so much to increase the support and improve the cause of the insurgents in Vietnam. Once it was accepted that these areas were, in the main, hostile then government faced the immediate problem of whether they should be detained, deported or dispersed. Sir Alex Newboult, the Chief Secretary who was acting as interim head of government, announced himself before the end of August in favour of large scale repatriation; but under the existing Aliens Enactments and Ordinances the procedure against individuals was so cumbersome that it would almost certainly have broken down with the numbers involved in 1949 and the early 1950s. As it was, the Executive Council favoured voluntary repatriation of those who were detained but if this were the only procedure open it would almost certainly have brought the administrative machinery to a standstill, even with these comparatively small numbers, and still have remained entirely ineffective in dealing with the very large numbers of rural Chinese who were known to exist.[9] As it was, the names of those to be banished from the Federation were presented and approved individually by the Executive Council and

---

[9] An early estimate of the numbers involved from a 'knowledgeable member' of Exco was between fifty and a hundred thousand. Those who were eventually resettled numbered more than 500,000.

it is hardly surprising that new legislation got under way almost as soon as Gurney arrived.

Voluntary repatriation was a failure. It was offered as an alternative to detention for those who did not object to their detention in the first place. Under the existing procedures those who were detained had the right of lodging an objection but the hearing of these objections was to be a continuous problem over the next few years. Even when the committees were only advisory the burden of providing evidence for deliberation was so heavy that it was decided in September 1948 to put it last on the list of CID priorities. In the state of Perak alone out of the first 700 detained, only two failed to lodge an objection and it was therefore impossible under the law as it stood even to offer the alternatives of repatriation.[10]

In its early efforts to deal with disorder the government was skating around the thin edges of the law in its quasi-legal procedures. In Singapore they were challenged in spirit and in detail. In the Executive Council it was implied that the appeals against detention were so impeded as to be *ultra vires*. In the Colonial Office there were reservations about the need for new legislation. Even within government itself a reminder was necessary that it had no legal powers to deal with the dependents of those who were actually to be repatriated. What took place was essentially executive action and was designed to meet not only long term considerations of security in hitherto ungoverned squatter areas but some more immediate problems as well. For example, a good deal of suspicion attached to squatter areas where there were large numbers of women, many of them pregnant, children and old people but practically no men between the ages of 15 and 45. This could be explained by the men having found employment elsewhere but it was obvious that in many cases guerrillas were abandoning their families who were expected to provide rather than receive support.

Rather than replace it, the Squatter Committee report in January 1949 and the notable inactivity which ensued, probably tended to encourage executive action against outstandingly dangerous squatter areas. The Squatter Committee consisted of one

---

[10] Another way out of detention was by release on bond. This was favoured by certain State governments, not by others, but by March 1950, according to the Commissioner of Police, it had gone too far. The result of releasing certain detainees was reckoned to be more dangerous than releasing captured guerrillas for information often dried up completely in the areas to which they returned.

Chinese, three Malay and five European officials under the chairmanship of the Chief Secretary. Its approach to the problem was common sense and remarkably liberal but there were one or two important ambiguities and omissions. Taking the only example of resettlement that had occurred over the previous six months, that of the Sungei Siput squatters, the Committee did not regard it as a success. But when it remarked, of displacements of this kind,

> it could only be accomplished at considerable expense to the Government—an expense which the country could ill afford if it were multiplied by a large number of such operations on an extensive scale.

it was by no means clear whether this referred to the comparatively long distance resettlement from Sungei Siput to the Dindings or to resettlement in general. Similarly, having acknowledged that the squatter problem was one that should be regarded from the long term aspect of land policy and the short term aspect of security, its recommendations dealt entirely with the first point. These were, in summary,

1. That wherever possible squatters should be settled in the areas already occupied by them;
2. That where settlement in existing areas was not possible, an alternative suitable area should be made available for resettlement;
3. That, if the squatter should refuse settlement or resettlement on the terms offered, he should be liable to compulsory repatriation;
4. That emergency measures to deal with the security problem of certain areas should be supported by administrative measures designed permanently to re-establish the authority of government;
5. That legal means should be introduced to provide for the eviction of squatters by summary process.[11]

These recommendations fell largely within the sphere of State and Settlement governments. Two months went by while the Federal authorities waited to see what action the State governments would take. In March, a politely urgent letter from the Chief Secretary pressed the States for their acceptance in principle of the Squatter Committee's recommendations and at the end of

[11] Report of committee appointed by His Excellency the High Commissioner to investigate the squatter problem, Kuala Lumpur, 10.1.49.

May, with action still hanging fire, the High Commissioner addressed the following letter to the *Mentri² Besar*

> I do not wish to appear to intervene in any way in the administrative problems of state governments, but it may be useful to them to know what considerations appear to me to need special attention with the object of getting speedier action to end the emergency.
> (ii) The reasons why the Emergency is dragging on are mainly two : the first, Communist successes in China have given a boost to bandit morale and checked a willing co-operation against local Communists. Secondly, the squatter problem.
> (v) I am fully appreciative of the great deal of thought and time already devoted to the problem of how finally to break the contact between squatters and bandits, but we are not going fast enough. It is only by State governments themselves that the necessary action can be taken. Powers have now been provided by emergency regulations for eviction and resettlement. Police are ready with funds for new police stations. I have discussed with all the *Mentri² Besar* and British Advisers ways in which the Malayan Chinese Association can help. Police, army and royal air force are now at full stretch. Great pressure is being exerted. But the effects of their operations will be only temporary if we do not at once show the potentially loyal squatters what we can offer them in the way of a peaceful livelihood free from intimidation. I am therefore particularly anxious that just at this time full first priority should be given to resettling or administering squatters because unless things go more quickly in this direction I shall have no alternative but to call off some of the more severe operations of the security forces which I am reluctant to do.

This letter followed what, from the High Commissioner's point of view at any rate, must have been an unsuccessful conference with the *Mentri² Besar* and the British Advisers which had been held to discuss the squatter problem a fortnight earlier. Gurney had made several of these points in the course of this conference but in the circular to all British Advisers he expressed his concern at the delay which was taking place in most States and Settlements in actually giving effect to the constructive recommendations of the squatter committee report.

> For your own information (the BAs were told) the High Commissioner feels unable to authorise any further operations under ER

17D outside Pahang, at least until state and settlement governments have taken some positive action either to resettle or administer squatters who are at present occupying land unlawfully and are a menace to security. He therefore asks that you will do everything you can to bring home to the state government that these constructive measures are its responsibility and the absence of them is one of the principal factors underlying the continuance of the emergency and consequent expenditure thereon.

There has perhaps been in some states a tendency to leave the squatter problem largely for the police and security forces with a view to removal and repatriation. This negative process can no longer be continued by itself and it is now time for state administration to tackle the problem positively and constructively.

It is against this background that the operations under Emergency Regulation 17D must now be considered. This regulation, which was published on January 10th 1949, gave the High Commissioner the right of ordering collective detention; and that any person so detained, other than a Federal citizen or British subject, might be ordered by the High Commissioner in Council to leave and remain out of the Federation. The grounds for such detention were that the High Commissioner should be satisfied that they aided, abetted or consorted with the bandits, suppressed evidence relating to the unlawful possession of arms, persistently failed to give information to the police concerning bandits or persistently failed to take steps to prevent their escape. The regulation seems to have had its origins in a Local Defence Committee meeting of October 8th 1948 in which the Chief Secretary instructed police to build up case files against bad areas with a view either to registration or screening or, where there was a strong case against an area and the numbers involved were not too great, to deporting all inhabitants. Towards the end of December, when it was hoped to deploy more troops and to step up the tempo of counter-guerrilla operations, action against squatter areas in which their support organisation was concentrated became a civil priority. In two areas, in Johore and Pahang, it looked as if a 'liberated area' was in the making; while in a third and particularly squalid squatter concentration it was evident that one already existed part of the time.[12] The difficulty of using the existing leglisation which allowed for individual detention was not only that Committees of Review Advisory Committees, not to mention the Chief

[12] That part, in an area that was accessible only by rail, when the afternoon train had gone through and before the following day's train arrived.

Secretary, were unlikely to agree to the detention of women and children but that if the occupants of these squatter areas were detained the existing detention camps would be filled within a few weeks. The simple alternative was to remove the squatters from Malaya altogether; and the only appeal would be on the grounds that the person to be deported was not an alien or did not live in the area concerned.

It was conceived as a limited operation. The Commissioner of Police expected that 20,000 people would be removed over six months and Watherston, less sanguine, thought that there might be some chance of shipping people away as fast as they were brought in. Lists of squatter areas that were thought to be particularly dangerous were drawn up in the separate states and on January 7th 1949, three days before the regulation was announced, Gurney notified the Colonial Office of his intention. It was implied both privately and publically that 17D would be supplemented by measures on which the Squatter Committee was already deliberating,[13] and two days after the regulation was passed the first operation was carried out in the Kajang area of Selangor.

From the first, these were operations in which security overrode all other considerations. Only the Commissioner of Police and his Secretary knew the names of the squatter areas on the black list and the decision whether or not the inhabitants of a particular squatter area were to be removed rested with the Commissioner of Police, the High Commissioner and the Attorney General. Once a decision was taken it was a matter for the police and army alone and, as Malaya District Headquarters informed its Brigadiers, 'at this stage, civil government will NOT be informed.'[14]

Six of these operations were carried out in the first three months of 1949—in Selangor, Johore, Negri Sembilan and Kedah. After the seventh, the revolt, which one suspects was endemic in the lower levels, had reached the highest levels of the Federal Secretariat. It was led by Edgeworth David, Deputy Chief Secretary,

[13] In the words of the press release, 'the government wishes also to make it clear that these plans for dealing with certain specific areas are to be supplemented by other positive measures for meeting the legitimate needs of other areas, which have been and are being investigated by the Federal Committee on the squatter problem as a whole'.
[14] Linguistic analysis aside, the imperative mood of this army directive was not reassuring. 'This period of discomfort (for squatters) can, however, be cut down by civil departments ensuring that when they are *ordered* (author's italics) to stand by, everything is prepared for immediate action as soon as they are given the area concerned.'

who was to succeed Watherston as Secretary for Defence, with a powerful and moving indictment of both the concept and process of 17D operations. It stemmed in part from a recent visit to Hongkong which had brought home to him how the action must appear to the outside world.

> Much has been written about the inhumanity of mass transfer of population during the war in Europe and except for the smaller scale on which we are working it is difficult to distinguish the circumstances which attend the removal of our Chinese repatriates . . .
> With the best will in the world realities have fallen far short of intentions. Operations have been planned entirely by the Police and Military who are only concerned with the objective of denying the particular area to the bandits and not with the fate of the wretched people who are being transplanted from their homes and forcibly removed for ultimate dispatch to China where the majority arrive in a state of destitution.
> There have consequently been many administrative hitches. In the first two operations the people did not understand what was happening and consequently did not even think to remove their few personal belongings before it was too late. Compensation is more apparent than real. The original instruction was that compensation should only be paid for pigs; this was based on the assumption that pigs would be the only property of any value possessed by these people. The forced mass collection and disposal of pigs inevitably results in the amount realised being only a fraction of the true market value of the livestock *in situ*. Many of the squatters however have put their labour and means into other channels, e.g. fish ponds and crops of various kinds. In such cases they receive nothing at all in return for these assets. Personal possessions in the form of household moveable property are also largely a dead loss. Bicycles and sewing machines have been collected by the police and subsequently sold off at the nearest police station at a forced sale, realising the type of prices fetched by a sale of lost property. Some of the property is probably never salvaged at all, part of it may be looted, part of it finds its way somewhere where it never comes to light.
> To sum up on the material side there is no question that to all intents and purposes these people who have in many instances spent years building up their small livelihood and establishing their homes are at a moment's notice evicted from their homes (which are destroyed behind them) and deprived of all their

THE SQUATTER PROBLEM

property and assets for which in some cases they receive nothing and in a few cases hopelessly inadequate compensation.

Then there was the personal side.

Particularly in the earlier operations most of the families were incomplete. The majority of the able-bodied men were missing. This may have been because they were away with the bandits; it may also have been in many cases because their place of work was elsewhere and they either had no accommodation at their place of work for their families or had placed them in the country to do market gardening to augment the family income. In such cases the family in custody is theoretically given the option of being accompanied by the husband or missing member of the family. In some instances partly due to an imperfect appreciation of what is going to happen they refuse; only when they actually come to be shipped do they fully realise the implication and by that time it is too late. In cases where they elect to be accompanied by the missing members of the family, the latter have to be traced. If they can be traced they are expected to come voluntarily straight into detention prior to embarkation to China. They may have lived in Malaya for twenty years, they may be Malayan born, they may have personal and business interests which they cannot wind up at a moment's notice. Again with the best will in the world the net result is often a permanent separation of families.

Finally there was the actual repatriation.

Apart from the difficulties at the other end which force us to land these people far from their homes in a condition of complete or semi-destitution and in a war-torn China where some may be left to starve and not reach their villages at all, there are many administrative slips; families are inadvertently embarked in different ships; the last consignment to Port Swettenham from Kluang included a woman nine months pregnant; persons sent to the wrong destination. Such errors should not occur but in fact they do and bearing in mind that the vast majority of the people concerned are women and children, however strong the conception of collective guilt put forward in justification there is no question that these operations involve a degree of very severe hardship and inhumanity which is very difficult to defend.

Two practical objections were that the squatter did not know what to do; and the alienation of the Chinese generally.

At present there is no official guidance whatsoever as to what these squatters are to do. If they stay where they are they run the risk of being picked up and deported with all the hardship that entails; if they move—as they are moving—to the towns and safer areas they are chivvied and harassed, but no one to tell them what they can do and where they can go.

So long as we continue to pursue this policy we are also engendering increasing bitterness among the influential Chinese. They are genuinely ready now to assist but cannot achieve anything without a lead and help from the authorities.

Finally

I realise that there are political difficulties in a matter so closely concerning Sino-Malay relationships but I do most earnestly suggest that when this policy of mass eviction and deportation was embarked upon the practical difficulties of moving thousands of people and of arranging for their reception in China as well as the degree of human hardship involved were not fully appreciated and the experience of the last three months emphasises the need for reconsideration of this policy and of a more constructive approach to the problem without further delay.

David's attack was supported by D. C. Watherston, the Secretary for Defence, who argued that the time had come to think of other than the purely operational aspect and that quicker and possibly even spectacular results might be achieved by constructive rather than by purely repressive measures. Civil officers, said Watherston, should be consulted before and not after operations. Police and military should attempt to conserve rather than destroy realisable squatter assets.[15] More discretion would have to be used in deciding who was to be repatriated. For example, he said, we should *not* in the last resort repatriate a destitute woman of thirty with five young children even though it is impossible to trace her husband, unless we can be reasonably satisfied that she has relatives or close connections in China.

There was also the physical problem of where both the collectively and individually detained were to be kept in custody.

---

[15] 'The attitude of one battalion commander can be judged by his apology to his troops for the length of the operation at Jemantar which, he alleged, was due to the repatriation officer's instructions that "much more padi had to be collected which would otherwise have been destroyed". It is so much easier to destroy!'

O'Connell, the outspoken Deputy Commissioner with the CID, warned that the lock-ups, gaols and camps were overflowing. The first new camp might be ready in two months: meanwhile, squatter operations had closed down. The accommodation for arrested persons, said O'Connell, 'was now WORSE than that experienced by internees under Jap regime'. At least one detention camp had become a forcing house for Communism and in the gaols themselves the Communist detainees were corrupting what the Commissioner of Prisons called the honest criminals. In the camps especially, as Watherston pointed out, enforced idleness provided a wonderful opportunity for the dissemination of Communist doctrine and was also physically bad for people who were accustomed to hard labour.

To these attacks the Commissioner of Police offered an essentially pragmatic defence. 17D operations, Gray said, were the only single measure devised and used against armed Communism in Malaya which had achieved marked and indeed spectacular results in the task of restoring law and order. They had produced badly needed information of great value and had severely damaged the bandit effort, morale and support. Of this there could be no doubt. He conceded that there were objections. There was some political difficulty 'in that politicians and so-called leaders may have some grounds for complaint'. Hardship and suffering was caused and sometimes presumably to innocent or helpless people. And there was some danger that state governments might not be so energetic as they might otherwise be in tackling resettlement problems if 17D operations were carried out. Nevertheless, and in spite of particular arguments—one rather curiously dismissed as that of 'a Chinese scholar' and the other because 'he was in the unfortunate position of having to deal with the human problems in detail'—Gray contended that the majority of administrative officers and others would be found to be in favour of many more such operations and 17D should remain as a sword of Damocles over non-co-operative areas. To the extent that Gray favoured a continuation of the operations he was defeated in principle but in practice successful. At a meeting on June 1st 1949 with the High Commissioner in the chair, the top members of the civil administration—Chief Secretary, Attorney-General, Secretary for Defence and Chinese Affairs—were all strongly opposed to their continuation; and with the dissent of the Deputy Commissioner of Police it was decided that there should be no further operations under 17D except in Pahang. Where CPOs wanted squatters areas to be cleared they should bring pressure to bear on the state governments for quick action under the new Emergency Regulation 17E.

Emergency Regulation 17E had introduced some welcome flexibility to squatter removal operations but in practice 17D continued at irregular intervals until October 1949 and was not limited to Pahang. In June there were two principal operations in Pahang, followed by two more in August and October. In the meantime, however, three more operations took place, one in Kedah near the Siamese border and two in Selangor. A total of 6,343 people were detained in all the sixteen operations that took place in 1949 but almost six months after the last of the 1949 series over 4,000 were still in detention. Not only had the original total of 20,000 been discarded but the estimated repatriation rate of 2,000 a month had also broken down.

As a supplement to 17D—and, insofar as it was integrated in the civil administration, an alternative—Emergency Regulations 17E and 17F which were introduced in May and August were protective rather than punitive; 17E was held to be suitable in dealing with areas of unlawful occupation where removal could be effectively compelled 'without the element of surprise and the backing of force which were necessary for the success of operations in places cleared under Emergency Regulation 17D'. This empowered the Ruler in Council in each state to issue eviction orders requiring all unlawful occupants of land in specified areas to leave those areas and proceed to specified places after a minimum of one month's notice. For it to work, it meant that eviction orders had to be coupled with simultaneous measures for immediate resettlement in areas under effective administration. Which meant the opening up and administration of new resettlement areas. Which meant, in turn, action by state governments. Where action on a smaller scale was needed 17F gave power to *Mentri*[2] *Besar* and Resident Commissioners to order individual squatter families to move from one place to another or to restrict the residenc of a family within a limited area. This was to enable them to move the isolated squatter into an established area or to be regrouped into a compact community under effective administration. Again, it was a responsibility for the state governments, many of whom were still considering the implications of the original Squatter Committee Report.

The first reaction when the Report was considered at a meeting of the Executive Council (21.2.49) was that the committee had not taken into consideration the different local conditions obtaining in each state and settlement or, for that matter, variations within the states themselves. The greatest single stumbling block was land tenure and while there was no objection to legalising the squatters' holdings in specific areas if, in the circumstances of the case, this was considered appropriate, it was argued that the recommendations of the committee on the terms of settling the squatters would upset the whole system of land tenure and, in any case, the council had already passed a ruling whereby temporary occupation licences should not be issued to non-Malays within a Malay reservation.

Leaving aside the varying attitudes of the Malay state governments towards their rural Chinese population, there were obviously serious objections to the activities of Chinese squatters simply as peasant farmers. In the first place, it was held that they were not genuinely landless peasants. In Kedah, for example, it was argued that the squatters were nowhere engaged in good productions. They were actively and increasingly interested in two main cash crops—tobacco and tapioca—and in the latter case were mainly financed and encouraged by mill owners most of whom lived in Penang. Kedah was in fact prepared to regularise the position of long-standing Chinese residents in certain areas where they were growing crops other than tobacco and tapioca by the issue of temporary occupation licences. In Negri Sembilan there was much illegal felling and planting with bananas which was financed by wealthy Chinese in the towns (they may indeed have been wealthy but the word tended to acquire a pejorative sense) and this presented its own problems with soil exhaustion and erosion. From Negri Sembilan the British Adviser reported frankly on the problem and the equally frank attitude of the *Mentri Besar.*

> I know from conversation that I have had with the *Mentri Besar* that his attitude is : 'These people have made nuisances of themselves. Why should we give up good Malayan land for occupation by them, when such land is likely to be needed for future expansion by the Malays? The only sensible method is to deport them.' I have tried to make him understand the physical impossibility of such action and that it has been difficult to find shipping accommodation even for those whom we have already detained. To which he replies that if they *must* be resettled it is impossible to do so in Negri Sembilan.

As for the squatters in Malay reservations. Whatever we may

feel about this matter, there is no doubt that the Malays feel very strongly that they should be removed. I recently managed to tone down a resolution in the council here which demanded complete and immediate eviction of all non-Malays in Malay reservations.

At the end of March 1949, after another representation from the Federal Government asking the states to take their decision on the Squatter Report for fear of increasing communal feelings, the approximate situation was that four states had accepted or approved—Johore, Selangor, Pahang and Perlis; one, Kelantan, accepted with reservations; another, Trengganu, was non-committal on the grounds that there was little illegal occupation within that state; Perak was going ahead with its own squatter report; while Kedah and Negri Sembilan had rejected the report altogether.

On May 17th 1949 a meeting was held between the High Commissioner, Chief Secretary, *Mentri² Besar*, Resident Commissioners and British Advisers specifically to discuss the squatter problem. Gurney began by saying that he was being pressed by police and military for more 17D operations but that he was reluctant to agree until some constructive action had been taken in the matter of resettling squatters. He identified the particular problems as administration, land and expenditure and the action that was necessary was a vigorous approach at the lowest possible level, a selection of suitable sites for settlement, and the decision whether or not the states would accept an offer of help from the Malayan Chinese Association. The latter was to involve government in a dreadful tangle but for the moment Gurney's argument was that it would be difficult to finance the schemes from public funds and that government would in any case be open to criticism for providing money to settle squatters when many Malay settlements urgently required costly development. Almost the only general agreement reached in the conference was on this point of MCA assistance. It was the opinion of the *Mentri² Besar* that it was undesirable for government to incur any obligation towards the MCA by the acceptance of financial contributions but there was no reason why the MCA should not afford direct assistance to the squatters themselves in material, transport, subsistence and even in payment of their Land Office fees. In the statements made by the various *Mentri² Besar* on the attitude and progress of their states there was both an absence of commitment and a tendency to underestimate the size of the problem.

Kedah, however, was now the only state still opposed to resettlement in principle and practice and its attitude remained that of a custodian of a Malay reservation. Its distinction was enjoyed because Negri Sembilan had changed its mind about resettlement and its *Mentri Besar* announced not only that it was looking for land for the purpose but that the state agreed to give the matter priority. After this sudden but apparently total conversion it was unfortunate, a month later, that the British Adviser had to record the *Mentri Besar*'s 'quite genuine disappointment' at the refusal of the Federal authorities to consider the release and resettlement of squatters who had been removed in a 17D operation. 'He felt,' wrote the BA, 'that a grand opportunity for restoring some morale to the Chinese has been lost by the refusal to permit resettlement.' And one doubts whether he was satisfied with the reason that was given in this and other instances: that no exceptions could be made.

Johore's attitude towards the squatters had from the first been exceptional. Where other states such as Perak or Kedah had emphasised that it was a state matter, whether they were in favour of squatter resettlement or not, Johore had urged that it was a matter of Federal responsibility and expenditure. Although the financial arrangements, involving tripartite collection and distribution between the state, the MCA and the Federal authority was a subject of endless discussion, Johore was the second state to attempt a proper settlement scheme and the first to tackle it in detail. In November 1948 a proposal had been made by the CPO Johore for squatter resettlement at a point along the Kota Tinggi-Mersing road and this, at Mawai, was the point that was eventually selected. In June 1949 a committee under the chairmanship of the *Mentri Besar* decided to recommend to the state government that an area of state land should be examined with a view to its being used for squatter resettlement. Its selection was due first, to its natural boundaries and ease of access which would make security control less difficult than in a more isolated area; second, to the absence of large tracts of alienated land thus making the whole area available for resettlement; and, third, to a favourable situation of undulating land with few hills and many streams. After inspection and soil analysis, work began on the construction of huts and central buildings at the end of August and two months later the first party of 16 detainees arrived from Majeedi detention camp in Johore. In November they were joined by their families and by the end of the month 300 people were in the area and Majeedi camp had been cleared of all squatter detainees suitable for resettlement. As the first and largest resettlement scheme in Malaya up to the time of the Briggs plan the Johore Government made an increasingly large investment of all factors of production in the Mawai scheme. Perhaps the most important of these were land, or its promise, and the factor, part labour, part enterprise, that was represented by government officers.[16] As the Administrative Officer/Collector of Land Revenue put it in his first report,

> All the settlers so far have been 'detained squatters' released from a detention camp, and in some cases it has been necessary to break down an inherent distrust of government and all that government does. The promise of a permanent title to their land within the not too distant future has done more than anything else to encourage them. The constant presence of police, settlement officers, the visits of other officers and talks to the *Kepalas* have convinced the majority that government is sincerely interested in their welfare.

But the initial handicap was in many cases enormous.

> Some of the settlers arrived in the area with money, the amounts in their possession varying between $10 and $500. Many had no money at all and few possessions. None had been allowed to bring any agricultural implements and few had household equipment. Some had received compensation for goods and crops which they had lost but the majority had not. Many had received chits when they were arrested which had not been honoured. This meant that a penniless person required about $30 before he could even start to work his lands. The settlement shop arranged to give credit to that amount but it became obvious that no business man could give credit to this extent when no repayment whatsoever could be expected for six months at the very least. The Squatter Resettlement Committee therefore decided to give each person who had no money the sum of $30 and various smaller amounts to people with money; thus no family started in debt. This action has helped to remove many doubts in the minds of the settlers as to the intention behind the scheme.[17]

---

[16] The whole of the resettlement scheme in Johore was directed by the Commissioner for Lands and Mines.
[17] The settlers in the Mawai area came in the first place from Hylam Kang, Johore and Batu Caves, Selangor. The majority of people from Hylam Kang had received some compensation at a reasonable rate. The majority from Batu Caves had not.

Another difficulty was that of families who were without ablebodied men. Out of a total of 326 people, of whom 171 were male, only ten men were between the ages of 20 and 40; and the fact that almost half the population were under the age of 15 naturally made a school an imperative consideration although this was still in the planning stage.

Who was to maintain squatters here and elsewhere before they became self-sufficient turned into an argument that continued for the better part of two years. The parties involved were state governments, Federal government and the MCA, and the problem originated in Johore although it was here part of the tangle of general responsibility and expenditure for resettlement. Drawing on local sources as well as on Singapore Chinese the Johore MCA was prepared to help financially in the resettlement of squatters. The Johore State Government however was unwilling to receive funds direct from the MCA, wished to have the money routed through Federal channels and, in any case, wanted a Federal guarantee of $400,000 before they would begin resettlement. An ungenerous summary of the situation is that while neither the Johore Government nor the Federal Government were willing to accept money from them direct, they both thought that the MCA should contribute towards the cost of resettlement. On the other hand, the MCA only disclaimed obligation when the question was put to them direct and otherwise allowed the assumption of their covenanted assistance to pass unchallenged. What seems to have happened was that at the meeting of *Mentri² Besar* in May 1949 it was assumed that the MCA (*vide* the remarks of the MB Selangor) would provide direct assistance in materials, subsistence, etc.; that the MCA, unwilling to accept a fixed commitment, temporised in its response; and that in the meantime government went ahead with its advances to state governments for the maintenance of squatters on the further assumption that this money would be recouped in whole or in part from the MCA. Large promises became large expectations and somewhat credulous assumptions[18] perhaps tended to be forgotten when amounts were minuted in figures. Acrimonious exchanges on one side, the beginnings of resettlement were hindered, but perhaps not seriously, by disagreement over the burden of responsibility and although the Federal Government had a good case against providing subsistence to those squatters whose unlawful activities had got them into serious trouble, in

---

[18] For example of the SCA.

practice the amount turned out to be far more than the funds which the MCA provided and was therefore met from government funds. In practice, too, although it was still in principle an open question whether this was a matter of land or federal security, the Federal Government was largely committed through the provision of funds for access and security roads, police stations, drainage, and other expenses necessary for the security of the area or its administration or to make it suitable for cultivation, including the cost of clearing if the work could not be done by the squatters themselves.[19]

One state that had insisted on going its own way on resettlement, even to the extent of drawing up its own squatter report, was Perak. Although only dealing with a single state, seven months were to elapse between the decision to appoint a committee and its report on October 28th 1949; and while there is no doubt that it was a very thorough piece of work, in emphasising the administrative rather than the protective aspects, it gave no hint of urgency or the security problems involved. It was, however, an indication of the rich variety of squatter cultivation and types within the state and it was careful to distinguish between the types of settlement that would be necessary for industrial, fishing and urban squatters. Probably the greatest single problem which Perak faced was the 90,000 out of a total of 130,000 squatters who were estimated to be living on mining land and who, in the interests of future mining operations, could therefore not be given permanent title. Recognising the importance of security of tenure and as part of a process of converting the squatter into a settler Perak preferred the alternative to Temporary Occupation Licences of Entries in the Mukim Register (EMR) although it was prepared in special cases to recommend TOLs even in Malay Reservations. This was obviously a most important decision and was a result of the committee's down-to-earth conclusions that large scale repatriation was both impracticable and inexpedient. Perak, said the Committee, must solve its own squatter problem within its own boundaries; and, provided that he was properly administered, the state was prepared to take the Chinese squatter on trust.

As a decision in principle this was obviously an important step forward in that it was freely taken by a committee in which there was a Malay majority. Nevertheless it revealed that not only was its only emergency settlement at Pantai Remis 'a very doubtful

---

[19] Letter from Chief Secretary to MB Pahang, 24.3.50

scheme' but that a 5,000 acre pre-war padi irrigation scheme at Changkat Jong had been abandoned by security forces soon after the outbreak of the emergency because they were 'in insufficient strength to exercise control of the area'.

Perhaps the most important event in 1949 as far as the future of Malayan squatters was concerned took place, ironically enough, in China itself. With the rapid advance of the Chinese Communist armies and the consequent loss of territory, cities and ports by the Kuomintang the end was in sight of the temporary arrangements for the repatriation of Malayan Chinese that had been made with the Chinese Nationalist Government. Growing difficulties were encountered from the middle of 1949 and by September the whole repatriation process came to a standstill. With the end of what might be called the 'China solution' the future of 17D operations lay entirely in Malayan detention camps; and if the indefinite detention of the large and potentially enormouse squatter population was impractical as well as abhorrent an alternative solution had to be found. By October 1949, and in many cases well before it, almost all of the States had accepted the need for permanent settlement of the rural Chinese; but although it might be said that in physical terms alone a crisis had been reached there was little time left in which to do anything about it in 1949. The year, in fact, was distinguished by the failure of resettlement. It was the year of the locust, of reports laid, deliberations delayed and decisions barely put into effect. Although statistically and categorically the point may be hard to establish it would appear that more squatters were detained and deported under 17D than were resettled in the whole of 1949. Many of the schemes—which were only schemes—mentioned by the High Commissioner in his speech to the Legislative Council on November 15th did not go into operation until the turn of the year and although the figures given—mostly for March 1950 —in the Legco paper *The Squatter problem in the Federation of Malaya in 1950* suggest that more than 10,000 squatters had been resettled there were probably only half as many at the end of 1949: fewer than the 6,000 removed under 17D when these operations came to an end in October 1949.

The repatriation crisis made a decision on the squatter future imperative. At a meeting at King's House on October 7th to discuss detention camp problems it was agreed that, since there was little hope of large scale repatriation, squatters against whom as individuals the police had no specific grounds for detention should be released in various categories and that the settlement should take place on a concentrated basis. Resettlement was to begin in Johore, Negri Sembilan and Selangor of the twenty-five per cent of squatters who were to be released by the end of 1949 and a further fifty per cent by the end of the first quarter of 1950.[20] Four months later, in February 1950, a detailed report by the Secretary for Chinese Affairs on resettlement that was actually in progress in the various states showed that, with the conversion of Kedah, the states were now unanimous in their acceptance of the principle but that much more thought would have to be given to the practice. It was not enough simply to bring squatters under control. They needed help in establishing themselves, as well as adequate supervision, and this was not simply a part-time job for District Officers. In a long and critical account of the situation in Negri Sembilan it was said that squatter policy there had been based solely upon the principle of denying food and support to the bandits and that the actual movement of squatters had been planned in only two districts, and here at the insistence of the security forces. In Perak, not only had the State Executive Council still to consider its own squatter report but in Pantai Remis no new squatters could be accepted for at least six months, while in Changkat Jong there was no possibility of resettling anyone from outside until the end of the year. But effective resettlement was now beginning and armed with a brief setting out the stages by which it was approached, the decisions that had been taken, and the scope of existing regulations, the High Commissioner appeared at a meeting of the British Defence Co-ordination Committee, Far East, on February 20th 1950, to discuss the squatter problem. Having been dealt with so far by the civil authorities largely as a military matter it was now about to be dealt with by the military themselves as a civil operation. Three months later, in the same committee, the new Director of Operations, Lieutenant-General Sir Harold Briggs, was to present a combined civil and military plan for the elimination of the Communist organisation and armed forces in Malaya that would largely depend upon the effective resettlement of the rural Chinese.

Note on the origins of the squatter problem
The real cause of the post-war squatter situation, it was argued by the Perak Adviser on Chinese Affairs, was to be found in the

---

[20] Subject to certain conditions, it was agreed that 'divided families'—one of the most tragic aspects of detention under 17D—should also be released.

slump and the Immigration policy which was its outcome. As a result of widespread unemployment during 1931-32, thousands of unemployed Chinese males, mostly from mines and estates, were repatriated while those who remained in employment had their wages reduced to below subsistence level. These and many others who were out of work but who preferred to remain in Malaya, took to vegetable gardening in order to support themselves and their families if the latter were in Malaya. At the same time the intake of male immigrant labour from China was severely curtailed by the introduction of a quota system so that the supply of labour could be adjusted to the demand. The quota, however, did not apply to females or children with the result that the sex ratio among the Chinese population, which stood at somewhere round 5 females to 10 males in 1931, rose to something like 10 females to 11 males in 1947. This great change in the sex ratio has resulted in a great increase in the Chinese population and what amounted to a complete social revolution.

The slump gave a boost to small scale intensive cultivation. It was therefore not surprising that Chinese labourers who during the 'thirties had realised the security from starvation to be obtained by cultivating a vegetable garden tended to settle their wives, mothers and children on the land as and when they arrived. There was no room for all of them in the towns as these were already becoming overcrowded. Chinese labourers and their employers clung to the *Kongsi* house system of accommodation,[21] a survival of the days of indentured labour, so that it frequently happened that the wage earner continued to live in his place of employment and settled his family on the land, often but by no means always in the vicinity of his place of employment. The stage was therefore set for a great increase of internal population pressure due to the rapid levelling of the sex ratio through the uncontrolled influx of females and children, the consequent increase in the birth rate, insufficient urban accommodation and shortage of land suitably situated to support the new Chinese peasant population.

In the opinion of Perak's Adviser on Chinese Affairs, the Administration had to take a large portion of the blame for the subsequent malevolent influence of Communism among squatters. The 'back to the land' movement among Chinese labourers during the 'thirties had not quite got beyond administrative control by the

[21] And still do. Even academic observers would have noticed this prevailing system in the various building phases of the University of Malaya: simple wooden huts that provided barrack accommodation for male labourers.

end of 1941 and Government, by the introduction of the Changkat Jong Padi Scheme, had at least started an experiment in Chinese land settlement which one may presume might have been extended in an orderly fashion but for the Japanese Occupation. Malay feeling, however, had always viewed Chinese settlement on the land with misgivings while the Chinese themselves, until the Occupation, showed no great inclination to grow padi in Malaya. They preferred to plant such crops as vegetables, tapioca and tobacco which gave a better return in cash for their efforts. Shortage of rice during the war and its high price since (particularly on the black market), however, had for the time being made it worth their while to plant padi and in some areas, such as between the Jalong and Lintang roads near Sungei Siput North, they were said to be raising two crops a year. But it was to be expected that once the price of rice dropped the Chinese would turn to more profitable crops.

During the enemy occupation, the resistance movement gained considerable support from the squatters in food, shelter and recruits. After the return of the Civil Government they were not slow to champion the cause of the small Chinese farmer whenever the Administration made any attempt to move squatters from hill slopes where by planting tapioca they were causing dangerous erosion or from estates where they had been permitted to settle during the war or from any other land where they were a nuisance. The Communists cashed in on the feeling of insecurity among farmers caused by government's rather puny and negative efforts to control them; puny and negative no doubt because shortage of food still made it imperative to encourage food production to keep down the cost of living. In Perak the two Communist associations with most influence on the squatters were the Sago Workers' Union and the Farmers Association. Through the medium of the latter they were able to exercise great influence on squatters who were cultivating land without any title in remote forest reserves, in unoccupied Malay Reservations and on private land.

It was already common knowledge that the KMT guerrillas had set up what was in fact a local government among cultivators in the Lenggong area where they collected taxes, settled disputes and even tried and punished people. It was not improbable that in other areas of Perak the Communists had been doing much the same thing ever since the re-occupation, indeed it was more than likely, especially in areas where official interference has been met with violence such as in areas near Sungei Siput where a

THE SQUATTER PROBLEM

Malay Settlement Officer and an Assistant *Penghulu* were murdered, in Langkap where the Chinese Settlement Officer was murdered and in the Tronoh area where two Forest Rangers were slain. All these slayings occurred since June 1st but they were symptomatic of general Communist influence.

8
THE ASSAULT RENEWED

In spite of numerous reverses and their general retraining policy the offensive potential of the guerrillas was never seriously impaired throughout the year 1949. Even in the first half of the year, which gave the government some cause for optimism, the guerrillas maintained a comparatively high rate of attacks and incidents; and in the second half of the year there was an average of one major incident per week. The majority of them were road ambushes: of police, army and planters. Casualties varied from one or two to more than twenty and were inevitable as long as security forces travelled in 'soft' vehicles. Terrorist attacks were also made on civilians; and in two notable cases casualties were extremely high. At Kampar, when a grenade was thrown into a circus tent, four civilians were killed and forty-five wounded. In another Perak incident, this time in Ipoh, a booby trap was set off during a burial in a Chinese cemetery which resulted in three dead and seventeen wounded. On balance, however, it was thought that a campaign of attrition by the security forces had meant a good deal of harrying of the guerrillas. Certainly in northern Perak a newly-formed guerrilla independent company lost its company commander and ten other men in the first two months of its existence; and an even greater loss, also in Perak, was the death of Lau Mah, a member of the Central Committee, who was killed in December. The death of Lau Mah was a considerable setback for the Fifth Regiment but there was very little else to show for an operation mounted by three battalions whose purpose was to destroy this itinerant regiment which shuttled backwards and forwards from Perak into Kelantan and which had little difficulty in extricating itself from the snare which had been laid.

Another independent company, the 26th, under Chin Nam, featured in a large scale attack on the small Pahang town of Kuala Krau on September 11th. Part of this company had arrived from Johore under Lam Swee earlier in the year and began a series of attacks by overwhelming the railway station, killing two European engineers, and dominating the town for several hours although they were unable to capture the police station. This in particular of the guerrilla operations mounted in Pahang suggested that the MCP were still flirting with the idea of liberated areas, although how relevant the experience of the Chinese Communist Party was to Malaya and how closely the Chinese pattern was to be followed were the questions that never really seem to have been answered by the MCP. The ultimate relevance was accepted; but the solution was reached as much by a multiplication of negatives as by a firm adherence to the stages of the Communist revolution in China. In the long run it was accepted that a permanent base was essential for victory in the revolutionary war when the British imperialists would be driven out of Malaya; but the principle of the CCP 'that it is impossible to maintain a long term war without bases' although generally correct, was held not to apply exactly to Malaya. This principle was to be modified to read 'it is possible to maintain a long-term war with a good number of temporary bases throughout the country'; but, as with equality, some of these bases were obviously more temporary than others. Considering the obvious risks attendant upon the capture and the attempted holding of a township such as Gua Musang or Kuala Krau—something which they never seriously attempted—the MCP fell back upon the organisation of support at what might be called the subcutaneous level. This was the import of Central Committee directives of December 1949, *Supplementary opinions of the Central Politburo on 'Strategic Problems in the Malayan Revolutionary War'*. It was a caution to the Party not to isolate itself from the masses nor to cut off its own supply lines by going too deep into the jungle; and the emphasis was on the creation of a *Min Yuen* infrastructure without which the main force units would be helpless.

> Temporary bases would first be set up among the *Min Yuen* territories; *Min Yuen* work would be expanded with increased activities, radiating spearheads into enemy-held territories, so that an intermeshing of territories would be the result, from which further enlargement of the points of the spearhead would bring about entanglement and encirclement of the enemy and their bases of communication and centres. This sort of tactic could lead to extremely fluid situations in a difficult period for the MRLA, but it could be done.

Although a somewhat pessimistic document as far as achievements were concerned[1] this was compensated by ideological confidence. The Party possessed certain advantages, most important

---

[1] The following tendencies were to be corrected:
(i) Pessimism about the present lack of bases, dispersion of armed units in

of which was the support and confidence of the people during the anti-Japanese struggle. The declaration of a state of emergency and the imposition of Emergency Regulations had caused a lot of public discontent and had elevated the political consciousness of the masses: both of which favoured the MCP. In an earlier appreciation, *June Resolutions of the Central Politburo, 1949* it was argued 'that the expenses required for complete removal of the masses from MCP influence was too great at present for the enemy to carry out such a drastic measure'—although the enemy might still decide to do it—but on the whole it was more pessimistic than the appreciation given six months later. Both papers stressed the importance of keeping the initiative—something that preoccupied the Security Forces as well—and when, in June, the advice was to launch attacks in order to raise morale and increase prestige, with the emphasis on active leadership and pushing the masses into the struggle, the December paper had settled on the slogan 'Strategically defensive, tactically aggressive'.

One of the conditions of which the MCP would have liked to take more advantage was the existence of a 'feudal state' in which the masses could be incited into overthrowing their feudal masters and setting up the inevitable 'liberated area'. The MCP, reluctantly and somewhat curiously, came to the conclusion that this situation did not exist in Malaya and one can only assume that this was an opinion born of a comparatively unsuccessful experience with Malay guerrillas. In many ways, however, to the MCP this could have been a very valuable adventure. It took place and was to continue in Pahang, a state in which the dismal poverty of the Malay riverine *kampongs* was reinforced by many determined Chinese guerrilla supporters. As far as the Malays were concerned, there were echoes of the Pahang rebellion of the 1890s, a strong tradition of disaffection and a sizeable population of recent Indonesian origin. In the opinion of the District Officer Temerloh it was more a case of profitable banditry than Communism in his district; but the fact that Malays were in arms against the government was, potentially, perhaps an even greater problem than that of an essentially Chinese insurrection. Cer-

    small groups and worry that the enemy would chase the masses away and thus cut the source of food supplies.
(ii) The idea that the masses did not like, neither would they accept, the People's Administration and that the present war was not a 'People's War'.
(iii) The feeling that MCP activities were not seriously embarrassing the government.

tainly the GOC thought a dead Malay terrorist was worth seven or eight Chinese and it was noted that the Army, though very proficient at dealing with Chinese Communists, was not very certain how to deal with Malay bandits whose habits were very different from their Chinese counterparts. For example, there was little evidence that purely Malay groups lived in jungle camps: they normally ate and slept in the *kampongs* where the inhabitants were forced to look after them on pain of death. They had also a reasonable number of active sympathisers and supporters in most *kampongs* who, as in Chinese squatter areas, provided a first class intelligence service.

The situation was, in fact, identical with the Communist-dominated Chinese squatter areas: demoralisation of village headmen and bandit visits far more frequent than those of the Security Forces. Indeed, the District Officer Temerloh was convinced that if a number of bandit incidents over the past three months were analysed his district would show up as one of the two worst in Malaya. The contention that the Army, i.e. the British battalions were almost useless in dealing with Malay banditry was confirmed by the British Adviser, Pahang. Malay banditry, he said, was too interwoven into the pattern of the countryside to be capable of being unravelled by 'foreign' forces: 'We are, in fact, trying to cut our golf green with a scythe rather than a small, fine mowing machine.' What was needed was a Malay Ferret Force: about fifty stout-hearted local Malays, hand-picked, and made to swear an oath of loyalty upon the Koran. An estimate of four to five months was given as the time needed in which to clean up Malay terrorism; and in August 1949, exactly five months later, Wan Ali, the Malay bandit insurgent was killed after an operation somewhat similar to the one that had been proposed. Malay *kampong* guards in the Jerantut area were given the credit and a reward of $10,000 was paid. In February 1950 a second leader of the Malay guerrillas, Wahi Annuar, surrendered and by this time, the Tenth Regiment had practically ceased to exist. One reason for this was the intensive operations carried out by Gurkhas in Pahang and another was that when the Chinese guerrilla organisation in the State contracted, the Malay units were left as a sort of husk which was soon and fairly easily cracked by security forces.[2] Real integration between Malay and Chinese

[2] A third reason was the role of the Sultan of Pahang, foremost among the Malay rulers in Emergency activities, who secured great personal allegiance from his Malay subjects. Attempts were also made to counter Communist influence by reasserting the primacy of religious duties.

guerrillas seems to have been rare; and the fact that food presented a problem in mixed camps suggests that many of the Malays must have been 'unreliable' in that they were Muslim first and Communist second. Malay guerrillas, as individuals and in very small numbers, continued their activities until the end of the Emergency, particularly in the east coast states, but with the elimination of the Tenth Regiment in 1949 the threat of a multiracial 'People's War' dwindled away and the MCP was again subject to its racial limitations.

At the same time as the Tenth Regiment was breaking up, Indian Communism suffered a severe setback in the loss of two of its leaders, Veerasenan and S. A. Ganapathy. Veerasenan, who had joined the guerrillas, was shot dead on May 3rd, 1949; and on the following day Ganapathy was hanged for illegal possession of arms. Ganapathy had been prominent in post-war union politics as the President of the Pan Malayan Federation of Trade Unions. His capture in possession of a revolver, while providing sufficient legal grounds for his execution, aroused protest on account of his standing both as an Indian and a trade unionist, not to mention doubts as to whether the death sentence was mandatory in this case. Pre-war Indian communism in which Ganapathy had been involved, was largely independent of the MCP and Ganapathy himself had had a chequered career. Apparently influenced by pre-war terrorism in India, he had moved from the self-styled Indian Communist Party, Malaya, to the Indian National Army of Subhas Chandra Bose which was formed after the surrender of Singapore. While in the INA Ganapathy had at some point resumed his earlier affiliation and shortly before the end of the occupation he was arrested by the Japanese for spreading Communist propaganda. Involved in the tortuous but volatile union and Communist politics of the post-war period he had joined the guerrillas at the beginning of the Emergency and although it is not recorded that he took an active part in guerrilla attacks there was little doubt first, that he was armed; second that he was at least 'consorting' with guerrillas; and third that he had taken part in a meeting in Johore in November 1948 when it was arranged to kill an Indian clerk against whom a complaint had been laid. The law, however, was concerned only with the first point and the public issue was whether or not Ganapathy's revolver was to be his death warrant. A great deal of interest in the case was aroused in India, particularly in Madras; but Mr. Nehru's reported remark 'that the Malayan government had acted with extreme folly' brought its own reactions in Malaya, particularly from Malays but also from Indians who deplored the intervention in what was essentially a Malayan concern. It should perhaps be remembered that this was a time at which Indians as well as Chinese were being deported from Malaya and the conditions of Indians living in Malaya was a lively concern of the Indian government. Indian estate labourers were now in a particularly parlous and confused condition. Estate managers might argue that everything would be all right provided they got on with their work and did not get mixed up with bandits but with their unions disappearing overnight, excited by the realisation of Indian independence but uncertain of their place in Malaya and, like Chinese squatters, subject to the pressure of security forces and guerrillas alike, the unsecured mass of Indian estate labour was both an opportunity for Communist guerrillas and a challenge to the existing government.[3]

In spite of these setbacks to its two minor racial components, the decline in its fortunes and a not altogether planned reduction in the level of its attacks, the hard core of the MCP insurgents as well as its organisation came through the year 1949 largely unscathed. By early 1950, retrained, regrouped and revitalised by a change of political climate, the main force guerrillas were ready to step up their activities. Most important, their civil support had been reorganised and was, at this time, probably equal to that of government in the matter of supplies and superior in the matter of intelligence.[4]

From June until December 1948, guerrilla incidents averaged a little over 200 a month. This was reduced to an average of less than a hundred a month by the middle of 1949, since when there was a steady increase in incidents of all types to over four hundred a month. Major incidents reached their peak during the first week of September 1950, with a total of 65, seventeen more than the previous peak. On the whole, road ambushes offered the guerrilla the greatest possibilities both of inflicting casualties and of securing weapons and while, from September 1949 to February

---

[3] Shortly before being deported to India in 1950 the founder of the Indian section of the MCP, at the end of a 50 page deposition to Special Branch re-affirmed that the housing and sanitation that he had seen on most estates in southern and central Malaya was bad.

[4] A former Director of Intelligence has pointed out that I should stress that this superiority 'was of an essentially local and low-level character; there was no penetration of S/F plans and the like'. But to take a particular point, large ration orders with local contractors gave a good indication of impending large-scale operations.

1950 road and occasional rail ambushes averaged about seventeen per month, the figure rose to an average of fifty-six a month between March and September 1950 with a peak of over one hundred in the latter month. Estates and mines offered static targets but attacks were rarely pressed home and the Politbureau's December 1949 directives were to choose 'battles of annihilation' which included the capture of weapons rather than 'battles of attrition' which only inflicted damage. The advice seems to have been taken to heart for in the first seven months of 1950 security forces lost more weapons than in the whole of the preceding year—a total of 362—and this included the loss of sixty automatic weapons. On balance, however, the guerrilla losses in weapons exceeded their gains although the figures given seemed to indicate, for the guerrillas, a potential rather than an actual loss. Thus, from June 1948 until July 1950 the total number of weapons recovered is given as over 5,000; 675,000 rounds of ammunition; and over 2,000 hand grenades. Much of this would appear to have been recovered from guerrilla arms dumps which the government, almost always on information, broached first, although the fact remains that by the beginning of 1950 the guerrillas were short of weapons and attempted, quite successfully, to redress the balance.[5]

Features of the renewed guerrilla offensive were the attention that was now being paid to the railways—twenty-five attacks on trains and rail jeeps in the first seven months of 1950 compared with four in the whole of 1949—and the more effective if not widespread use of hand grenades.[6] Looking at the overall situation the Joint Intelligence Advisory Committee reported to the Federal War Council in October 1950 that there had been a gradual improvement in MCP organisation, leadership and military tactics and the existing MCP policy of extended activity, unless checked, was likely to cause a serious breakdown in civilian morale. On the basis of order of battle, documents, statements,

---

[5] Sir Robert Thompson, *Defeating Communist Insurgency*, London, 1966, p. 40, gives alternative figures which may possibly exclude both weapons that were recovered from arms dumps and those that were stolen rather than captured. They are 1948 (six months): lost 100; recovered 497. 1949: lost 214, recovered 930. 1950: lost 551; recovered 650.

[6] Under jungle conditions grenades that had been supplied or acquired during the war were now very unreliable. Many were thrown which failed to explode. It is possible that quite a number of those used in 1950 were acquired during the year: 88 up to the end of July compared with 16 in 1949.

size of camps and so on it was estimated that the main force of the Malayan Races Liberation Army was now between 3,000 and 3,500 although this did not take into account any reserves, unidentified units or guerrillas in South Thailand. In addition it was estimated that there were about 1,200 armed ancillary units— variously known as defence corps, district units or armed work forces—but no attempt was made to estimate the numbers of the *Min Yuen*. One point of interest and alarm was the balance between guerrilla losses and recruitment. Guerrilla losses in 1949 were thought to have been as much as 25 or 30 per cent of the total number while overall recruitment was no more than 5 to 10 per cent. But in south and central Johore, where the security forces were thin on the ground during the first half of 1950, it was estimated that MRLA strength increased by 25 to 30 per cent although this was partly attributed to existing formations returning to the area. In Kedah, the figures for casualties and recruitment were put, respectively, at 8 and 18 per cent; while even in Selangor, where it was thought there had been a reduction in strength of about 20 per cent during the past two years this had probably been offset by increased recruitment to and organisation of the *Min Yuen* groups, both armed and unarmed.

One fact that seems to emerge from this and tends to be confirmed from later experience is the inverse ratio between recruitment and the presence and activity of security forces. Where army and police were present in large numbers and, more important, engaged in successful operations recruiting for the guerrillas and their helpers fell off. Where they were not much in evidence and after successful guerrilla attacks there was a jump in recruitment.[7] What was of greater importance to the outcome of the struggle however was the state of public, and particularly Chinese, confidence not only in the ability of the government to counter guerrilla operations but also in British intentions regarding Malaya and its future. From this, there emerged a minor saga of the appointment of Communist Chinese consuls.

At first sight, it might appear that Britain's recognition of the Chinese People's Republic on January 6th 1950 was a perfectly straightforward event and, if it was a recognition of a new balance of power in Asia, people in Malaya should have treated it as no more than recognition of an accepted fact. But in Malaya the recognition of Communist China introduced a new factor into the internal balance of power for, on precedent alone, recognition

[7] It was also noted that *Min Yuen* activity increased considerably when there was a guerrilla main force unit in the area.

carried with it the Chinese right to appoint consuls in Kuala Lumpur, Singapore and various other towns of Malaya. Even the Nationalist government, although increasingly distrained, had sought to preserve the national integrity of Chinese in Malaya and had in various ways encouraged and required Malayan Chinese to think of themselves as inalienably Chinese. Even more important than the preservation of Chinese citizenship were the claims that were advanced by the Nationalist Chinese Ministry of Education and the Overseas Affairs Commission to complete control over the curriculum and management of Chinese schools: something that extended to the approval of text books, the training and appointment of teachers, the payment of grants in aid, and the visits of inspecting officials from China. Local Chinese consuls were charged with carrying out the orders of the Chinese government and although the straitened circumstances of the KMT government after 1945 meant that the claims fell into abeyance after the war, there was a strong possibility that they would be reasserted once there was a firm government in Peking. At the end of 1949, however, this appeared to be a secondary consideration in determining British policy. The most important issue was recognition of the new Chinese government and the exchange of representatives; and for this none too solid achievement the Foreign Office in particular seemed willing to pay a high price. Thus it was that at a conference held at Bukit Serene, the Commissioner General's residence in Johore, in November 1949 the balance of diplomatic opinion was that Chinese Communist Consuls would have to be accepted in Malaya. Under no illusions about the consequences

> It was appreciated that Chinese Communist Consular Officers would promote the spread of Communism by underground methods through clubs, associations, schools etc; that they would attempt to affect clandestine contact with local Communist parties and to use their privileged communications for subversive purposes.[8]

it was nevertheless surprising that the conference sought only to be able to expel any consular official guilty of improper practices without delay. From subsequent telegrams it appears that the High Commissioner had opposed the idea, but although the Commissioner General attempted to set out the significance and limitation of such appointments it did little to stem a growing crisis of confidence. Considering the damage that might have been done

[8] Macdonald to Foreign Office, 14.11.49

THE ASSAULT RENEWED

before consular officials were found guilty of improper practices, and the diversion of security forces that would have been needed to prevent contact between them and the guerrillas, the objection by the Malayan government was hardly surprising. How much more would it be therefore for Malayan Chinese, with hostages of families and property in China, who would have been open to surveillance, pressure and blackmail by uncommonly close representatives of Chinese Communism against whom the Malayan government was fighting.

As confidence in the intentions and sanity of the British Government drained away, opposition within government grew. Watherston, returning to Malaya after an absence of four months, sent a strong protest to Gurney pointing out, amongst other things, that if the Communist consuls were appointed they were likely to arrive just at the time when government was organising its Anti-Bandit Month in which they hoped to enlist the co-operation of the public, Asian as well as European, in a way that had not been attempted until then. Their acceptance, he said, might have a serious, if not a disastrous effect on government's efforts and at the very least result in a setback from which it would take a very long time to recover. 'It is a matter of the confidence of the Chinese public in the government and unless we possess that confidence we cannot hope to bring the campaign to a successful conclusion.' Outside King's House opposition grew. The Emergency Chinese Advisory Committee reported the widespread uneasiness that had been created by the recognition of the Peking Government which was thought to be premature and unwise. The C-in-C FARELF was firmly opposed. 'Ridiculous that we should permit such a substantial reinforcement to reach our enemies while we are pressing for additional help for ourselves'; and in Perak, as Gurney reported to the Colonial Office, Mr. Leong Yew Koh, with considerable courage and while still suffering from injuries received from a Communist bomb outrage, had proposed a motion against the appointment of a Chinese consul in Perak which was carried unanimously.

The rising tide of official opposition in Malaya may be seen from telegrams that were sent to London. Macdonald said the issue of Chinese consuls had become the touchstone of 'our ability and determination to protect those people who were willing to co-operate in defeating the terrorist menace', while Gurney conveyed the opinion that the arrival of consuls would be tantamount to reinforcement of a division of troops for the bandits and its interpretation 'as an act of weakness amounting in present circumstances to suicidal folly'. In reply the Foreign Office urged consideration of the wider issues. In their telegram to the Commissioner General (6.4.50) the issue of accepting Communist consuls was made out to be one on which, incredibly, turned the fate of Hong Kong, open support of Ho Chi Minh and open subversion in South-east Asia. To which was added the Foreign Office view from Peking 'Any attempt to exclude Chinese consuls from Malaya might result in the Chinese Government breaking off present discussions and refusing to agree to establish diplomatic reations', sensitivity to accusations that Britain was pursuing a hypocritical and two-faced policy, and the singular opinion of the British Consul in Nanking who reported indignantly to the Foreign Office that the Chinese Government was not a Communist Government and they resented the imputation that it was.

In the event, Gurney's argument that no Communist consul should be appointed in Malaya for the duration of the Emergency was successful.[9] But not before the Singapore Teachers' union had proposed that they should take over the control of education in the Colony; a former publisher of the *Nan Chiao Jih Pao*, a Singapore Chinese left-wing daily, and now deputy chairman of the Commission of Overseas Affairs in Peking, had spoken of consuls as the agents for his Commission; attempts had been made to sell a Chinese business man $500 worth of Chinese victory bonds: the entry fee to the illegal Friends of New China Society; and the same *Nan Chiao Jih Pao* had warned the Colonial Government that unless it inclined towards new China by changing its policy it was doomed to fall before the onslaught of the peoples.

Against this background it is surprising that so many Chinese volunteered for Malaya's extended 'Anti-Bandit Month' which began in late February 1950. A tendency having been noted on the part of the general public to contract out of the Emergency towards the end of 1949, in December the High Commissioner told the Legislative Council of the government's intention 'to mobilise on a voluntary basis over a period of about a month all the civilian resources that can be made available to assist the security forces in an intensified combined operation'. It is not clear what achievements were expected from this temporary mobilisation but the obvious intention was to commit as many people as possible to the government cause. Figures variously given

[9] According to Sir David Watherston, to whom I am indebted for this information, Gurney informed the Colonial Office that he would resign if any consuls were appointed.

as a quarter and a half a million people eventually volunteered to take part in this exercise which resulted in a great deal of activity. Certain government departments were to be closed down and the High Commissioner, at least, saw no incongruity in their organisation 'on a voluntary basis' for employment on supplemental police duties. Large amounts of *lalang* that would facilitate ambushes on dangerous roads were cleared away and even the most senior government officers were to be seen taking their part at the road blocks in and around Kuala Lumpur. Had it been possible to put trained men into the field immediately, then the operations for which they were required—squatter administration and resettlement, enforcement of registration of labour, assistance with screening and closing of guerrilla communications and sources of supply—would have been given a considerable boost. But there was an obvious limitation on what could be achieved by unskilled labour and the Commissioner of Police, for one, was reluctant to divert his men, already in short supply, to what he considered to be marginal tasks and was rather chary about the whole business.

Whether Anti-Bandit Month, in fact, boomeranged—as the *Straits Times* alleged—is, however, open to question. The basis of the *Straits Times* allegations was that it had led to an increase in bandit activities. Certainly the figures for major guerrilla incidents rose from 92 in February to 123 in March and fell away again to 82 in April 1950; an even more impressive figure is that total Security Forces casualties over the same three months read 51 : 103 : 69. But as far as incidents are concerned, the statistics reflect a general increase in guerrilla activity from February 1950 onwards and a more than proportionate rise in guerrilla casualties. In March 1950 the guerrillas suffered their third highest number of killed for the campaign so far and for both sides the figure of 103 for total casualties was exactly equal : a balance which often tilted in the guerrillas' favour in the months that were to follow. Where the *Straits Times* may unexpectedly have been right about the boomerang effect, was in the matter of European opinion. For many Europeans Anti-bandit Month was the touchstone of Chinese loyalty. Echoing the High Commissioner, *The Planter*'s editorial for January 1950 affirmed that there was to be no compulsion under the new campaign : it was to be an absolute volunteer effort. But it went on 'We would suggest that just as in England during the war, when a careful look-out had to be kept for fifth columnists, so we in Malaya must treat any man, whatever his caste or creed, who does not volunteer his services to the maximum during Anti-Bandit month as suspect.' Where the purpose of Anti-Bandit Month had been to unify the country against the insurgents, and while it had undoubtedly succeeded in securing a great deal of public commitment, one effect was a tendency to use it as a simple test of loyalty; and from it there came an increasing impatience with what was thought to be the overall Chinese commitment as well as a resistance to any criticism from that quarter, constructive or otherwise, of Emergency Regulations in particular or policy in the conduct of operations in general.[10] What can hardly be confirmed or denied, but which may nevertheless be true, is that a more powerful influence on Chinese commitment at this time and upon the one critical contribution which they could make, was the effect produced by the return to their villages of detainees who had been released because of insufficient evidence on which they could be held or tried. Reports which were coming in from State police officers at this time of the reprisals that were being taken and engineered, sometimes in collaboration with the local *Min Yuen* and even small squads of the MRLA main forces led, as the Commissioner of Police reported, to a complete drying up in the flow of information.

As the evidence of a renewed guerrilla assault began to mount in early 1950, government had to contend not only with the assault itself and a renewed sense of public disaffection but a certain lack of confidence and strains within the Administration as well. The latter showed up particularly in Perak which, together with Johore and Pahang, bore the brunt of the renewed attack. The principal grievance here was that 1949 had been the year

---

[10] According to either the High Commissioner or the Commissioner of Police (the paper has no mark of origin) it took almost eighteen months before the leaders of the Chinese community gave their open support to the government campaign.

The leaders of the Malayan Chinese Association have come off the fence publically. In November the President of the Association, Tan Cheng Lock, made an anti-Communist speech in Penang and on 22nd of December in Legislative Council two leading Chinese members, Yong Shook Lin and H. S. Lee spoke for the first time with decision on the government's side against banditry. These signs of confidence reflect also the brighter prospects of political agreement between the Malays and Chinese on the Community's liaison committee [*sic*] and the universal wish to build up among the Chinese of Malaya a Malayan consciousness. One instance of this was to be seen in the Chinese support for the bill introduced into the Legislative Council in December and now passed providing for the prohibition of the display of foreign national emblems, including the Chinese flag, which had hitherto been much in evidence on all public occasions in Malaya.

of wasted opportunities. The majority of troops had been withdrawn from Perak in September 1949 when the security situation was comparatively good. But in December, a major operation which had been planned for north Malaya was postponed for lack of troops; and towards the end of January 1950, the security situation began to deteriorate very rapidly. In part this was attributed to a planned counterblast to Anti-Bandit Month and in part to a reorganisation in guerrilla leadership. Whatever the cause it led to a serious drop in public morale and even police morale was said to have deteriorated in certain areas. Many of those who were employed directly on anti-bandit operations were described as 'tired and at the end of their tether' and with a shortage of troops such that only one company of the Coldstream Guards was available for the whole of the Perak South police circle, including the Cameron Highlands, there was little prospect of the Army providing relief. The CPO Perak wanted 50 more jungle squads—a hundred per cent increase—and retraining of the existing squads which, it was admitted, could not be considered a hundred per cent efficient.

Among the points in the CPO's review which he gave to the Perak state security committee in February 1950 was the ominous report that 'the killer squads had closed in and were now operating very close to Ipoh itself'. The Perak government's alarm at the deteriorating situation in the State was communicated on the same day to the Secretary for Defence in Kuala Lumpur and was followed by representations from the Perak District Planting Association along the same lines, with the addendum that estates production was seriously affected. On submitting these points for consideration by the Commissioner of Police, the Secretary of Defence was given cold comfort in return. What the Commissioner of Police said may have been true but it was hardly encouraging. There was, he said, little one could say except that the situation in Perak was known to have deteriorated in recent weeks; a battalion of the Malay Regiment had been deployed there in mid-February; the police were doing all they could with the resources available; and that the situation might deteriorate even further. Replying to the Perak government the Secretary of Defence was rather more hopeful about the situation than this but a few days later Gray forwarded him an even bleaker account of the situation from a tin miner in Batu Gajah.

Such areas of Perak as I know and particularly this one, are going very rotten politically. The local village and *kampong* talk, more or less openly, goes like this: 'The government is getting weaker and weaker—Communism which is to liberate us all is triumphant in China and will shortly be the same in Siam and then here. Russia has the biggest and best bomb. This government is terrified and has recognised Communism in China and will shortly hand over to Communism here or will have power wrested from it by the liberating armies. Anyway they admit that they will be compelled to leave this country in a few years.' And it goes on: 'Do you want to be a man marked as a running dog, a helper of Imperialism and if you do not want to be tortured and have your throat cut, you had better help the liberating army and the people's government now.' Documents taken off the bodies of the last two bandits killed, spoke contemptuously of the security forces available here, saying 'There is nothing to fear by us, the red-faced barbarians can only muster a force thirty strong in the whole area.'

All this is having a great success and it is manifestly true to the local man because we have only thirty jungle squad men here and until last week had had no troops here for a year or more—not one.

When Abu Bakar (police SPO) was killed the rumour in the town was that the jungle squad and the OCPD had been killed and that the hour of liberation had struck—the result was that half the village came out of their shops to jeer at the Police. I do take in all seriousness a very poor view of things. It is far worse politically than July 1948. Most people then were still on the fence. Now there is little doubt whose side they are on.

In its overall policy rather than in individual operations there were few positive acts and little imagination on the government's part in 1949. Overall, there was an impression of complacency and reliance upon conventional methods. One area in particular where this was evident was the government's attitude towards surrender terms and although it did take the positive step of offering surrender terms on September 6th 1949 there is a latent suspicion that the step might have been taken with greater advantage in the preceding fifteen months. In October 1948 the *Straits Times* had suggested an offer of clemency to terrorists who surrendered voluntarily; and if, as Negri Sembilan planters alleged, counter propaganda had been practically nil and ineffective,[11] the *Straits Times* point, that with a guerrilla it was a question of 'a noose or nothing', was well taken. In 1948, however,

[11] *Straits Times,* November 7th 1948.

the Government said the time was not yet ripe for an announcement of amnesty terms and it used the rather curious argument that the guerrillas were evidently short of food and ammunition.[12]

The question of timing the announcement of an amnesty was obviously important but hardly one for which there was a definitive answer. If surrender terms had been offered too early, for example when the insurrection was still under way, they would probably have been taken as a sign of government's weakness although it might be argued that this was the sort of gesture that could be afforded early on in the campaign by a really strong government. On the other hand, the longer the announcement was delayed the more convinced would guerrillas become, even those who were barely convinced at the outset, that there was no alternative but to go on fighting. In any case, it was important to identify the particular group of insurgents who might be expected to respond to an amnesty; and this, realistically, was given as the rank and file of the MRLA by two MCS officers with first-hand experience of guerrilla and long-range operations.[13] There were already indications that certain of the rank and file would surrender even without terms if they could get close enough to civilisation to make a break; but the killer gangs were unlikely to surrender as they were the hard core of the guerrillas and the *Min Yuen* were unlikely to do so until they were sufficiently hard pressed or compromised—which they were not, as yet. Political considerations suggested that there should be a quiet amendment of Emergency Regulations to exempt those who surrendered from a mandatory death penalty and this, although it was a public intimation, was the form in which the amnesty was offered for those who had not been guilty of a violent crime. Those who professed to believe that the insurrection was something of a mistake, itself the product of those who were misguided, as well as those who believed that a large part of the guerrilla forces were simply waiting for the opportunity to surrender were perhaps disappointed at the total number of surrenders for 1949 : 251, of whom 155 surrendered after the offer was made.[14] Never-

---

[12] The Chief Secretary, Sir Alec Newboult, quoted in the *Straits Times* November 20th 1948.

[13] J. L. H. Davis, commander of the Force 136 mission in Malaya and intimate of Chin Peng, and Robert Thompson, former Chindit and future head of the British Advisory Mission in Saigon.

[14] In November and December there were 52 and 66 surrenders respectively and in January and February in 1950 the number fell away to 18 and 10, 28 in March, and below 10 for each of the last six months of the year.

theless the offer did help a number of guerrillas to get out of the jungle and, most important of all, provided a great deal of important detail hitherto unknown on the organisation of the MRLA.

An even more intractable problem in 1949 than the timing of surrender terms was that of 'protection money', its payment and prevention. To judge from the files it took the higher levels of government a couple of months or so to appreciate the size and dangers of the problem but at the end of September 1948 the Secretary for Internal Security set out some of the accumulating evidence that a number of Asian estates and mines, particularly in north and central Johore, were paying protection money to the guerrillas. Particularly strong evidence was building up against Chettiar owned estates. There was no doubt the practice was widespread and it seemed to be the reason why some areas were unnaturally quiet.[15] Gurney's original idea had been to take over the estates and put in European managers but it was soon obvious that on the scale on which protection money was being paid and the number of estates involved, this would be impossible. Nor were estates the only source of guerrilla finance. Bus companies were particularly vulnerable to attack and thus to extortion: and, again in Johore, it was believed that large sums of money were being paid in order that the buses should continue running. How much money was changing hands in this process will never be known although individual assessments may give some idea of the magnitude. In December 1948 the High Commissioner put it to a deputation from the Perak Chinese Miners' Association that payments amounted to as much as $100,000 a month—approximately what it was costing the government to provide special constables on the Perak Chinese mines—but, he noted, 'they shook their heads at the suggestion'.

One of the problems that had to be faced was whether exemplary punishment was worthwhile; and whether, in any case, the arrest of estate or mine owners would halt the flow of subscriptions. Even the temporary detention of Chettiars suspected of payment was soon enmeshed in the unpleasantness of attempted bribery of the investigating Indian police officer, to which the police alleged a Johore State councillor was party, and the

---

[15] The Chettiar community, itself part of the larger Indian community, were the recognised money-lending class. The normal practice so far discovered was an initial contribution which varied between $500 and $5,000, paid through the Chinese *kepala* (the Estates factor) followed by a levy of $1 per *pikul* of rubber produced.

improper intervention of a representative of the Government of India. In the case of the Chinese community there was a tendency, where possible arrests were pending, to fall back on bonds and statutory declarations that they would desist from paying protection money. The Commissioner of Police remained sceptical of their value and of the voluntary mutual insurance scheme which Gurney had discussed with the Perak Chinese miners. One of the results of this scheme, it was hoped, would be to show up the non-contributor as a payer of protection money. A point to which Gray added his comment, 'I am quite convinced that many Chinese would pay both protection and insurance money; and it is my opinion also that protection money is still paid in many cases where the mines themselves are guarded by SCs. The SCs are probably a means of keeping protection money at a low figure in these cases.[16]

To some extent the payment of protection money was tied in with the provision of special constables which, it will be remembered, was linked on the police side with the provision of prior information as a condition on which they were provided. The police argument was that it was illogical for government to provide further protection to estates that were already paying protection money; that it would be unwise to arm a large number of Chinese because of the difficulty of distinguishing loyal citizens from guerrillas; and that it any case it was difficult to persuade Malay special constables to remain on Chinese estates and mines, particularly where there were absentee managers. CPOs had therefore been instructed to provide special constables only when a request was made and they were satisfied the owner and staff were giving as much assistance as they could. Though logical enough it tended to perpetuate the vicious circle—no protection : no information : no protection. The case of a Chinese

---

[16] A supposition which tended to be confirmed by the CPO Perak 'For a period of about a month (after the meeting with the High Commissioner) the Chinese miners were serious in the matter and appeared keen on finding some solution to stop the payment of protection money but this keenness gradually faded out and there is no doubt at all that they are still paying the bandits, but with greater care and not as openly as before.' CPO to British Adviser Perak, February 22nd 1949. One favourable result, however, was the number of miners, planters and business men who came forward to give confidential reports of extortion letters or verbal demands received: reports which were negligible hitherto. This advantage, in turn, tended to be offset by the failure of the Liaison Committee who had so far given no information at all on either bandit activities or the payment of protection money. CPO *ibid*.

estate owner in Perak was perhaps a cautionary tale to those who thought twice about paying protection money. Having reported attempted extortion to the police, he found that they were unable to provide him with protection because there were no suitable quarters. The guerrillas then burned down his estate buildings to the value of $50,000 and the estate labour force disappeared. In the last analysis, the priorities of the Batu Arang Miners' Union was what counted. Most of its members, it was said, were in a position to give information but were afraid of guerrilla reprisals and preferred repatriation by government to death at the hands of the guerrillas.

In November 1949 a new policy towards those who paid protection money came, somewhat obliquely, into effect. In May, B. M. B. O'Connell, Deputy Commissioner, CID, had argued that it was impossible for a centralised government to compete in threats with an irresponsible Communist terrorist: 'They can outbid us every time.' O'Connell argued that in one form or another extortion was endemic

> It is farcical to suppose that Chettiars or capitalists except in possibly a few cases of potential community leaders, such as Tan Kah Kee, are Communists or will help the Communists unless they thought our regime was doomed to failure or unable to protect them. Peasants, *kulaks* and moneyed interests 'pay squeeze' in every country.

O'Connell was specifically concerned with the pending deportation of Chettiars but his argument of the damage that they could do to Malaya if they became antipathetic to the existing regime applied equally to the Chinese business community: and O'Connell's solution was to confiscate the moveable and immoveable property of those who, having signed bonds to discontinue payment on which an amnesty should be provided before May 1st, broke it by providing a voluntary contribution. In the event, the new policy as set out by the Secretary of Defence (in a letter to the Commissioner of Police, 3.11.49) was that anyone who came forward now and was prepared to make a clean breast to the police of past payment of protection money should not be detained so long as he really came clean and was prepared to assist police in any inquiries made.

With civil affairs a source of problems rather than solutions at the end of 1949, the renewed guerrilla offensive in early 1950, while it did not exactly catch the security forces off balance, nevertheless found the army far from at its best. After almost two years of insurrection the GOC, General Boucher, was on the point of leaving Malaya. Unlike a succession of French generals in Indo-China, there could hardly be any question of failure, but although the army had withstood the first impact, had succeeded in routing the main formations and had disrupted entirely the phases of the enemy attack, the guerrillas were still in existence and the hardest fighting as well as the heaviest casualties were yet to come. Boucher's appreciation of the military situation, February 1950, on the eve of his departure, was a rather bleak but realistic paper. The major problem was obviously shortage of troops. Apart from one armoured car regiment and an artillery field regiment operating as infantry, the GOC still had only thirteen operational battalions. And nearly all of these were badly under strength. Operating nominally on lower establishment (31 officers, 563 ORs, plus 43 first line reinforcements) many battalions had in fact been operating at least part of the time with only two or three companies of two platoons each. Compared with the nominal strength of 563, 1/Devon averaged 450 ORs between August 1949 and January 1950; 1/KOYLI, 463 between December and January; and 1/Suffolk, only 386. By way of comparison the GOC set out the number of troops operating in Palestine during the Arab rebellion in October 1938 alongside those of Malaya in 1950.

Palestine, 1938	*Malaya, 1950*
Force HQ	District HQ
2 divisional HQ	2 brigade HQ
5 brigade HQ	2 sub-district HQ
2 cavalry regiments	1 armoured car regiment
14 infantry battalions	17 infantry battalions
	1 field regiment Royal Artillery

and added the note 'the Arab rebels were no more formidable than Chinese bandits. They were not so numerous and not so well armed.' In any case Palestine was slightly smaller in area than the states of Johore, Malacca and Negri Sembilan. The country was hilly but open. It had good communications and was ideal for air action. A new battalion of the Malay regiment was coming into service in February 1950 but of the 17 battalions on hand, three were retraining and more would shortly have to be withdrawn for the same purpose. Ideally, said Boucher, one battalion in four should be retraining at any given time and, as all available military resources had been thrown in to support the surrender terms in September and October 1949, it might be deduced that the marginal effectiveness of many battalions was falling off rapidly. Then again there was the variable quality of the battalions. Given equal strength and training Gurkha and British units were considered to be of equivalent value but in practice there was a bias in favour of Gurkha battalions not only because of their adaptability to jungle warfare but also because they had a higher strength and a slower turnover. Malay Regiment battalions, having been raised quickly and committed before their full training had been completed, were assessed as half the value of a Gurkha battalion although when the target of one British officer per platoon had been achieved their value was expected to increase.

Roughly the same thing might have been said of the police jungle squads which were paramilitary units in effect; and here again a shortage was looming up. Suffering from an initial lack of training and having been at full stretch for a considerable period many of them had now to be withdrawn for rest and retraining. Approximately forty jungle squads at a time were likely to be affected—the equivalent in patrols of five companies of infantry—and they would be out of operation for three months.

Even before the Communist resurgence Boucher argued that he had had insufficient troops to press operations through to a successful conclusion. He gave three examples. The 5th (Perak) Regiment of the MRLA had been continuously harried by three battalions for several months. It finally evacuated Perak in August 1949 and took refuge in North-West Kelantan in a particularly inaccessible mountain area where there was little food. The advantage therefore was heavily on the side of the Security Forces, particularly since air supply was available, and if it had been possible to keep up this offensive the GOC said there was little doubt that the 5th Regiment would either have split up and disintegrated or withdrawn to Siam as a discredited force. Unfortunately, bandit concentrations and activity in Pahang which had been lightly held necessitated a quick redistribution of troops and the pressure had to be reduced. The 5th Regiment, though shaken, was still in the field and was planning to attempt to return North Perak. In Johore, continuous operations by four battalions had driven all major guerrilla units into the north-west corner of the state or into Pahang. In November 1949 it was decided that these could be dealt with by two battalions and the southern half of the state was therefore handed

THE ASSAULT RENEWED

over to the police. The result, said Boucher, was that gangs were now beginning to operate again in South Johore which was a comparatively soft area and where the *Min Yuen* were still proved to be in active support. Although reinforced by Singapore police it was again a source of anxiety. In Selangor, strong pressure in the north and south from August to November had broken up guerrilla concentrations; and when the Scots Guards were withdrawn for retraining early in November 1949 it was considered that the state could be held by one battalion of three companies. But by mid-January the main gang in South Selangor had returned to its old haunts and in North Selangor there were signs of guerrilla revival. It therefore became necessary to reinforce the area with four companies of infantry drawn in from outside: two from South Perak, two from Pahang.

Although the number of battalions needed in any one state varied according to the quality of communications as well as the number of active guerrillas, Boucher reckoned to maintain a ratio of approximately 5 to 1 or better when engaged with units such as the 5th Regiment in Perak/Kelantan or Chin Nam's company of the 12th Regiment in Pahang; but to achieve this density, as he pointed out, it was necessary with the number of troops then available to thin out in other areas where bandit activity had been temporarily subdued. Experience had shown, he added, that after a period the thinned out areas tend to revive: a disquieting feature which was likely to recur so long as the Communist executives in the *Min Yuen* remained intact.

The immediate answer to the problem was reinforcements and even when the fourth battalion of the Malay Regiment became operational in June 1950 Boucher considered that a further six battalions would be required as well as two additional squadrons of armoured cars and various supporting units. This, after some vicissitudes, was the figure for the number of battalions that was eventually accepted and implemented. Before considering how this came about it might be interesting to consider the curious interlude in which Chinese landings were reported in Thailand; and the way in which this underlined the need for reinforcements and reorganisation of Malayan intelligence services. In a startling dispatch on February 10th 1950 the High Commissioner told the Colonial Office that recent police intelligence reports gave strong indication that landings of Chinese Communists were now taking place on the east coast of Southern Thailand and that these were infiltrating across the border. Estimates were put at between 1,000 and 100 and a report from Songkhla (on the east coast of Thailand not far north of the Malayan border) referred to a party of eleven, all of whom were said to be staff officers of the China Red Army, who had been sent to Thailand and Malaya as agitators and instructors. A usually reliable source was quoted as saying that the CCP were building up a force of 2,500 (already up to 2,300) from the banishees and repatriates to infiltrate into Malaya via Thailand.

The latter part of this intelligence was the more credible. Efforts had been and were to be made to recruit Malayan Chinese who had returned to China for posts both for the Chinese Government and the Chinese Communist Party. But the reports of a Chinese landing were little short of sensational and on the strength of it, the first battalion of the Malay Regiment was deployed in north Malaya although it was about to move into Negri Sembilan where, with the police still 150 under strength, its presence was badly needed. Gurney's fears were thus realised. In January, discussing the question of a joint border operation with the Thais, he admitted that failure to carry it out, apart from leaving a very serious threat of armed guerrillas in the Betong salient, would be misunderstood by the Thai Government. At the same time, however, he warned the Colonial Office that a joint operation could not be mounted without serious prejudice to the internal security situation in the Federation.

The departure of the 1/Malay on this sortie thus opened up another breach; and, according to the British Ambassador in Bangkok (February 14th/18th 1950) it was little more than a wild goose chase. It was possible, said the Ambassador, that a very small number of Chinese Communists might have landed clandestinely on the east coast of Thailand though no, repeat no, proof was yet forthcoming from any quarter. Second, it was quite certain that Chinese Communists in large numbers had not, repeat not, landed in the above area. In any case he said the Thais were taking necessary action and the opinion of someone who was presumably on the spot, which the Ambassador shared, was that the calibre of informers and agents employed by the Kedah police to report on the border situation was very low indeed.

> It seems that none of these native agents are trained or regularly paid, information being obtained from certain specified individuals known to the Malayan police, who have occasion to cross the frontier or to mix with travellers. In such circumstances it is not surprising that reports furnished by these informants are only too

frequently unduly sensational and grossly arbitrary and consequently dangerous to rely upon.

The alleged landing of 2,000 Chinese Communists from Thai naval vessels, which can only be described as vicious nonsense but to which some credence appears to have been given is a good example of how mischievous such reports can be.[17]

To return to the matter of reinforcements, on January 17th, according to a cable to the Commissioner General (15.2.50), Gurney had told the Commander-in-Chief Far East Land Forces that additional forces equivalent to not less than three battalions were necessary. This was the figure that was passed back by the British Defence Co-ordination Committee, Far East, to the Ministry of Defence who also considered where this brigade (three battalions) could be found. According to the BDCC it appeared that no reinforcements could be expected from outside the Far East which therefore narrowed down the field to Hong Kong alone. Their recommendation was 26 Gurkha Infantry Brigade; and, if at all possible, they also wanted to strengthen the existing armoured car regiments to a level of four fighting squadrons from each of five troops; to raise the British Battalions to a higher establishment; and, on the long-term basis, to build up the communications, and particularly the telecommunications, network.[18]

The 26th Gurkha Infantry Brigade, consisting of one Scottish and two Gurkha battalions, duly arrived in Malaya in March, 1950. In April General Sir John Harding, Commander-in-Chief Far East Land Forces, was already asking for an additional brigade. This, it appeared from his appreciation for the BDCC, was needed as much to augment the civil structure as for its own sake. 'Our greatest weakness now,' said Harding, 'is the lack of

---

[17] In his previous dispatch the Ambassador had urged caution in accepting too readily probably exaggerated reports of insufficient native agents on the border. 'We have learned by experience here that at least some of the gentry are mainly interested in fomenting ill will between Thailand and Malaya.' The area in particular was largely Muslim and had been the subject of Malay irredentist claims, particularly those of the Pan-Malayan Islamic Party.

[18] An interesting but somewhat restrictive view of the army's function was given in the BDCC's observation—'Units and formations employed in anti-bandit operations in Malaya are seriously handicapped in carrying out their main peace-time task, namely preparation for war'. To this extent, therefore, battalions engaged in Malaya must be considered to have been wasting their time: a view which is somewhat surprising in 1950 although rather more fashionable 15 years later.

early and accurate information of the enemy's strength, dispositions and intentions.'

> For lack of information an enormous amount of military effort is being necessarily absorbed on prophylactic and will o' the wisp patrolling and jungle bashing and on air bombardment. Information services must depend almost entirely on the police who in their turn must depend on the confidence of the people, especially the Chinese, and the civil administration generally and its power to protect them and on a thoroughly efficient Special Branch organisation at all levels. Until the police force including the frontier force has been built up to a much higher degree of efficiency and confidence in itself, and civil administration has been effectively established throughout the country, troops are required for protective duties, screening operations and other defensive tasks.

For this reason, 'the need for more troops, in addition to 26 Brigade, must now be seriously considered as being the only means of giving the breathing space required by the civil and police authority to put in hand the decisive measures that they alone can take'.

The source of reinforcing Malaya by the second Brigade was the same as the first, Hong Kong. Not unnaturally both the Governor of Hong Kong and the Army Commander were apprehensive at the thought of having a second brigade removed, particularly as the second one that was ear-marked was the experienced No. 3 Commando Brigade. The final recommendation again lay with the BDCC and on April 20th they asked for the first Commando before the end of May and for the remainder to follow as quickly as possible, the whole move to be completed by mid-June. From Malaya's point of view there now seemed to be a proper sense of urgency and although the Brigade itself did not arrive until July, operations in the Briggs Plan began in June with the advantage of the heaviest, albeit limited, concentration of troops that had yet been assembled.

9

THE BRIGGS PLAN

Civil and military appreciations of the situation in Malaya show that, from the outset, 1950 was recognised to be a critical year. On the one side, there was the renewed assault by the guerrillas. On the other, a series of unresolved problems and areas of at least temporary weakness. Among the points made in Gurney's dispatch to the Secretary of State (12.1.50) was the admission that the political brains behind the Communist efforts remained for practical purposes untouched and unlocated. Recruitment for the MCP was likely to continue on account of Communist successes in China and the consequent closing of the repatriation door to Chinese who were detained in Malaya : a problem serious enough in itself without the expected and dreaded arrival of Communist consuls. For the second time, security forces were described as having expended their main effort and were now faced with having to operate with lesser numbers on account of the inescapable necessities of rest, training and leave. In the event, the year placed an almost insupportable burden on the police whose numbers of dead exceeded those of the army by almost two to one.[1] Gurney had warned London that no further appreciable expansion of the police force could be undertaken and that a period of consolidation was needed for the selection and training of NCOs and inspectors. Although Chinese police constables could now be recruited, few were expected as there were better prospects elsewhere. By the middle of the year the contracts of the ex-Palestine police sergeants would begin to run out, and, in addition, large numbers would be due for leave. The Malay Regiment was experiencing similar problems and its expansion

---

[1] The two incidents that involved heaviest casualties for the Malayan Security Forces occurred in February and March 1950. On both occasions Malay police and soldiers, although hopelessly outnumbered, fought with conspicuous gallantry and determination. For the police action at Bukit Kepong, Johore, see Tan Sri Mubin Sheppard's article, *The Sunday Times* (Malaysia), February 22nd 1970, p. 14. For the action of the Third Battalion the Malay Regiment and Malay Special Constables by the Semur river in Kelantan, see Short, Asian Communism, Pt. III, *The Asia Magazine*, November 20th 1966, p. 39.

had stopped with the formation of the fourth battalion for the same reasons as those which had halted police expansion.

Furthermore, Gurney had to admit that the problem of gaining the confidence of the Chinese community was unsolved. Here, an incipient dilemma was to be seen. Would self-government necessarily involve the withdrawal of protection against Communist China? That is to say, there were few doubts as to what would happen to those who had supported the Colonial Government when, rather than if, the Chinese Communists were to take over. With a more than fifty per cent Chinese population (the inclusion of Singapore subsumed) it was widely assumed that an independent Malaya would not be politically strong enough to withstand pressure from China even if it wanted to. A more specific problem to which Gurney referred was that the battle against Communism had still to be fought in the schools. It was of vital importance to bring Chinese schools under proper government assistance and control—but the Education Department had only one European officer who could speak Chinese, the cost of the necessary assistance was almost prohibitive, and there was a grave shortage of trained teachers, Malay as well as Chinese. In a later dispatch to the Secretary of State (24.2.50) Gurney again drew attention to the continued presence of thousands of detainees awaiting repatriation to China—'Their acquaintances who have given information against them are naturally hesitant so long as they see them still in this country and even of necessity being released'—and with their numbers likely to increase still further as government extended its effective administration and was able to classify, in particular, the numbers of Chinese squatters, this was likely to be an increasingly difficult problem.

In dealing with these problems the question that had first to be considered was the extent to which government could be strengthened—by itself or by selective reinforcement—and the purpose that would be served by additional military forces. In the opinion of the British Defence Co-ordination Committee the problem would never be solved merely by the provision of extra forces; but they agreed with Gurney that unless greater security could be created no substantial acceleration of the civil measures vital to the success of the campaign could be expected. In early 1950 therefore the purpose of increased forces was to permit

> (a) greater military activity to keep the guerrillas occupied and so permit civil measures to go ahead at a faster pace

and

(b) to increase the striking power available for destroying guerrillas in the field.

Both these purposes were somewhat diffuse; and a third was added by Sir John Harding, C-in-C Far East Land Forces, in his appreciation of the military situation in Malaya for the BDCC on April 9th 1950.[2] This was: to bolster slumping public morale

> My conclusion therefore is that although the military situation in itself may not warrant further large scale reinforcements, and additional troops will certainly not pay the full dividend of which they are capable until the civil administrative follow-up resources are much stronger, the need for more troops, in addition to 26 Bde, must now be seriously considered as being the only means of building up confidence quickly and so getting information, as well as giving the breathing space required by the civil and police authorities to put in hand the decisive measures that they alone can take.

In spite of the importance of raising local units Malayan resources were either insufficient or unavailable. The military value of the Malay Regiment, according to the C-in-C, was not high. It depended almost entirely on the efficiency and availability of British Officer leadership in which there was a serious deficiency both in quality and quantity. In Sir John's view local military forces as well as the police should be as fully representative of the people of the country in which they serve as they could be made.

> For that reason I suggested some time ago to the High Commissioner that consideration should be given to changing the title of the Malay Regiment to the Malayan Regiment and to opening it to Chinese recruits. He replied to the effect that there were constitutional and political objections to my suggestions, and that he thought the participation of the Chinese element of the population in the local defence organisation should be limited to the volunteer forces. I suggest that this question should now be reconsidered with a view to making arrangements to open service in the regular local forces to all elements of the population.

The C-in-C had certain specific proposals to make on reinforcements and improved communications; but in the last analysis

[2] Supra, pp. 229–230.

it might be regarded as a civil rather than a military problem.

> ... I cannot overemphasise the fact that the effective administration of the whole country is the only decisive answer to the elimination of the bandits. It has a direct effect on the number of troops required and the fundamental reason for my advocating plans being made for further reinforcements now is to give the civil administration a breathing space to strengthen itself and speed up its machine for rapid decision. From a military point of view quicker decisions and more rapid action in civil administrative field are essential.

Military opinion at this time, although somewhat equivocal regarding the purpose of additional troops, had no doubts as to the importance of civil government; and, without centurion overtones, it might be said that the provision of effective civil administration was now regarded as a military operation. How this was to be done and whether it might best be effected by a soldier were questions that began to be answered when, on March 21st 1950, the government announced the appointment of Lieutenant-General Sir Harold Briggs, as Director of Operations to plan, co-ordinate and direct the anti-bandit operations of the police and fighting forces. General Briggs had been a divisional commander in the 14th Army, a post-war GOC Burma, retired and living on the island of Cyprus. As Director of Operations he had the somewhat anomalous position of a soldier who was a civilian, directing military operations in support of a civil power. The appointment of a Director of Operations had apparently been asked for by the High Commissioner; and the reason discreetly advanced by Briggs himself was that the co-ordination of operations by Colonel Gray, the Commissioner of Police, had been detrimental to the efficiency of the police force which, in its expanded form required the Commissioner's full-time services. Briggs' appointment was in the nature of a compromise : an officer of the rank of Lieutenant General but in a civilian capacity, ranking equal to the Chief Secretary, with full powers of co-ordination of police, naval, military and air forces, which however, remained subject to their right of appeal to the High Commissioner in the case of the police, and to their respective commanders in chief in the case of the armed forces and in the event of any orders being given which were beyond their capabilities. At the special request of Field Marshal Slim, Chief of the Imperial General Staff, under whom he had served in Burma,

THE BRIGGS PLAN

Briggs agreed to undertake the task for a minimum period of one year. At the same time, 'for important private reasons', he put the maximum period of his tenure at eighteen months.

Briggs arrived in Kuala Lumpur on April 3rd 1950. A week later, on the basis of a rapid tour of the Federation and briefings in London and Singapore, he gave his impressions of the situation to the High Commissioner.

1. Our object was to eliminate the whole Communist organisation in Malaya before further measures could be initiated by Red China and to restore confidence in Malaya.
2. The morale of the Communists and the strength of their adherents increased in proportion to their successes, the influence of external events, and their propaganda. Their fighting strength was decided by the number of weapons they possessed. They relied for supplies, recruits and information on the Chinese population particularly in squatters areas but also in the populated areas in both of which they had their cells. These cells remained undetected and unscathed through denial of information. Chinese areas were widespread and close to the numerous objects of attack and most of them were outside the civil Administration which suffered through acute shortage of Chinese speaking officers. Communist propaganda, being more attractive and easier, was more effective than ours, which was weak. Many of our Press reports were inclined to help the Communist propaganda.

   Though Communist communications were poor, their informamation locally was good. The jungle was ideal for ambushes and 'snatch and grab' raids as it made surprise and a 'getaway' easy.

   Communists therefore had the initiative which had to be wrested from them.
3. Successes against bandit gangs, though essential to security and morale, were in effect only a 'rap on the knuckles'. It is at this 'heart' we must aim, to eliminate the Communist cells among the Chinese population to whom we must give security and whom we must win over. By so doing and removing the bandits' sources of supply and information the task of the Security Forces would be simplified and the enemy forced to fight for these in areas under our control. Thus only can the initiative be wrested from the bandits.
4. Control of the Chinese population would entail bringing it within the administration, a major task for the civil govern-

ment. It would mean taking officials from less important jobs, co-opting volunteers and 'oiling the wheels' of the State Administration. Speed in obtaining financial approval for emergency tasks must be made possible.

It must be realised that the Chinese are here for good and such land as they occupy must carry promise of a permanent title subject to good behaviour. Such a measure would give a feeling of security to the Chinese squatters and knock away the main plank for Communist propaganda.

5. Security of the population and the elimination of the Communist cells must be the primary tasks of the Police. Unfortunately our Intelligence organisation is our 'Achilles Heel' and inadequate for present conditions, when it should be our first line of attack.

Our information must come from the population or from deserters and, until we can instil confidence by successes and security among the population, our information will be worse than that of the Communists. We have not got an organisation capable of sifting and distributing important information quickly.

Police supervision and training has been inevitably weak owing to shortage of officers and its great expansion. Communications must be made sufficient to ensure perfect control.

6. The primary task of the Army must be to destroy the bandits and jungle penetration. They must also support the Police. The Air Force is particularly valuable for air supply of our forces and offensively against enemy morale. Owing to the invisibility of bandits in the jungle, killing is problematical only.

7. The need for the closest co-operation between the Administration, Police and Army requires joint headquarters at all levels.

8. Present operations proved, and the future side of the Administrative and Police tasks will confirm, that success everywhere at one time will not be possible. Furthermore, a real success somewhere is necessary to improve confidence and morale in Malaya. The fact that six more battalions are arriving in Malaya should allow the strengthening of selected areas by troops without undue risks elsewhere. The Administrative and Police potential would not permit any strengthening beyond such selected areas. Tactically the Southern States should be selected for this combined intensified action.

The guiding principle governing such priority areas must be that the Administration and the Police must be left so strong that when these extra troops are removed a recrudescence of terrorist activity can be prevented. The timing, therefore, must depend on the Administrative and Police 'build-up' which cannot be rapid.[3]

In effect therefore, Briggs was suggesting a long term plan to build up a comprehensive organisation as well as a short term plan which the doubling of troops in South Malaya might make possible. The Briggs Plan itself, as it was popularly known, was given in the form of a Report to the BDCC on May 24th 1950 and headed *Federation Plan for the Elimination of the Communist Organisation and Armed Forces in Malaya*. Recognising that the Communist armed forces in Malaya relied very largely for food, money, information and propaganda on the *Min Yuen*, Briggs argued that it was necessary in order to end the Emergency to eliminate both the *Min Yuen* and the MRLA. The first was primarily the responsibility of the civil authorities; the second of the Services, mainly the Army. The reason why the *Min Yuen* was able to exist and function in populated areas was largely because the population as a whole lacked confidence in the ability of the forces of law and order to protect them against gangsters, Communist extortion and terrorism. In consequence, information, which was essential if the *Min Yuen* and the bandits were to be eliminated, was quite inadequate. The difficulty was enhanced by the use of the 'cell' system in the Communist Party whereby members had little idea of the personalities or activities of corresponding cells. In the long run, Briggs argued, security, and with it confidence and information, could only be restored and maintained:

(a) by demonstrating Britain's firm intention to fulfil her obligations in defence of Malaya against both external attack and internal disorder;

(b) by extending effective administration and control of all populated areas which involves (i) a large measure of squatter resettlement into compact groups, (ii) a strengthening of the local administration, (iii) provision of road communication in isolated populated areas, (iv) setting up of police posts in these areas.

(c) by exploiting these measures with good propaganda, both constructive and destructive.

The outline plan, broadly, was to clear the country, step by step, from south to north. First, by dominating the populated

[3] *Report on the Emergency in Malaya* from April 1950 to November 1951, Kuala Lumpur, 1951, pp. 3–5.

areas and building up a feeling of complete security in them, with the object of obtaining a steady and increasing flow of information from all sources; second, by breaking up the *Min Yuen* within the populated areas; third, thereby isolating the guerrillas from their food, information and supply organisation in the populated areas; lastly, destroying the guerrillas by forcing them to attack the Security Forces on their own ground.

In order to achieve these objects it was planned that in all states

- (a) the Police Force will concentrate on fulfilling normal police functions including the obtaining of intelligence through its Special Branch organisation in all populated areas.
- (b) the Army will maintain in States in turn a framework of troops, deployed in close conjunction with the Police, to cover these populated areas which the police cannot themselves adequately cover. This will entail the setting up of a series of strong points whereon patrols will be based.
- (c) The Administration will strengthen to the utmost extent possible their effective control of the populated areas by increasing, duplicating or trebling as necessary, the number of District Officers and other executive officers 'in the field' to ensure that all populated areas are effectively administered; by making access roads to isolated, populated areas where necessary; by establishing police posts in all the populated areas brought under control; and by stepping up to the maximum extent possible within the limits of the manpower available in all areas where they are needed, the provision of the normal social services that go with effective administration, e.g. schools, medical and other services.

On this framework, the Army was to superimpose striking forces in each State in turn whose task would be to dominate the jungle up to about five hours journey from potential guerrilla supply areas. These forces would establish headquarters in populated areas, and would dominate the tracks on which the guerrillas relied to make contact with their information and supply organisation, thus forcing the guerrillas to fight, disintegrate, or leave the area. Increased offensive action by the RAF against guerrilla targets would be taken as and when reasonably reliable information was received.

In a sense, the role of the armed forces in the Briggs plan was to be that of a steam roller; but a steam roller whose purpose, in less sophisticated times, was that of an expensive but limited instrument in the construction of a permanent road. Like the steam roller, the Army would only be effective when the ground had been properly prepared; and this, apart from survey, materials and manpower, would also require effective co-ordination among the various authorities who were involved.

Before the first phase operation of the Briggs plan began on June 1st 1950 in Johore, the first three Directives had already been issued on Briggs' authority as Director of Operations. Directive No. 1 issued on April 16th, 1950 created a supreme Federal War Council and a chain of State and Settlement War Executive Committees. The Federal War Council was a small and manageable committee of half a dozen. It comprised the Director of Operations; the Chief Secretary; the General Officer Commanding; the Air Officer Commanding; the Commissioner of Police; and the Secretary for Defence.[4] It was the responsibility of the Federal War Council to produce policy and to provide all the resources that were required and which could be made available. The execution of policy and, as the Directive put it, of waging war in their own territories, lay with the State and Settlement War Executive Committees. These, in concept, were to be even smaller in number than the Federal War Council and comprised the *Mentri Besar* (or Resident Commissioner); the British Adviser; the Chief Police Officer; and the senior Army Commander, together with a full-time Secretary. Each committee was to appoint a secretary and chairman but, as the Directive put it,

> On the Civil side it is considered that the better course would be for the British Adviser to concentrate his efforts solely towards the prosecution of the campaign, since the *Mentri Besar* will have to administer the State and be responsible for making State resources available to the War Committee.

In Briggs' view, the civil administration of the Federation—eleven entities under a central co-ordinating Federal Government—could not be anything but slow in operation and completely unsuited to deal with an Emergency. In a sense, the War Executive system in the States and Settlements was a means of by-passing existing State administration; and the British Adviser, who had previously had little executive power, was now able to take a very active part in Emergency matters.

Thus, before operations actually began, a new framework was being created, and the existing framework was being strengthened. Meeting, roughly, every week, the Federal War

[4] To which Templer added the Director of Intelligence.

Council was now assisted by a Federal Joint Intelligence Advisory Committee and the practical outcome was the selection of Sir William Jenkin, formerly of the Indian Police Service, as adviser on Special Branch work and a recruiting drive for Special Branch Officers and particularly those who had experience in Indian Police or in Services intelligence. Additional administrative officers required on the ground—and Briggs had originally spoken of trebling their numbers if necessary—were obtained by raiding the less immediately important central government services and the Colonial Office had been asked to provide another 30 MCS officers. Of equal importance was the immediate need for English or Malay-speaking Chinese officers for work in Chinese village and squatter areas. Directive No. 2 provided for Chinese Affairs Officers at State level under direct control of the State and Federal Secretary for Chinese Affairs; and at District level for Junior Chinese Affairs officers responsible to the State SCA and the District Officer.

In the original Briggs plan squatter resettlement was taken as one among many examples of action that was required by the civil authorities. In the succeeding weeks the emphasis on resettlement increased and in the avalanche of decisions certain major political advances seem to have been subsumed. The most important of these concerned the Malayan Chinese. On the whole, Briggs was critical and rather unimpressed.

> The Chinese population is generally content to get on with its business even if it entails subsidising the Communists; nor is it willing generally to give any information to the Police Force for fear of reprisals until it is given full and continuous security by our Forces. The Chinese have always had a repugnance for joining Army or Police Forces; nor will they volunteer now at rates of pay lower than they can get in civil life, which are far greater than those earned by Malays. They are vocal and promise a lot, yet do nothing. Strangely enough compulsion is more acceptable than volunteering.

But he was also realistic.

> One of the most vital aims throughout the Emergency must be to commit the Chinese to our side, partly by making them feel that Malaya and not Red China is their home. Without their co-operation it will indeed be difficult to bring the Emergency to a successful conclusion.

Although its political significance may be debatable Briggs held that one of the most important duties of Chinese and Junior

THE BRIGGS PLAN

Chinese Affairs Officers would be the organisation of elections to choose committees and Chinese headmen for the village and squatter areas;[5] and even if the political inference of this is ambiguous—namely, a step towards direct Chinese participation in self-government—there was enormous political content in the simple heading *Chinese Village Guards* and the statement 'The time has come when selected Chinese should be recruited as Auxiliary Police and where necessary armed with shotguns to take their share in anti-bandit operations.' In practice[6] Village Guards composed entirely of Chinese were to be avoided 'until such time as the personnel have proven themselves and are considered thoroughly reliable'; but with the need to recruit more police of all kinds—regular, auxiliary, and special constables—more attention was being paid to the possibilities of Chinese self-defence as well as the need to attract them into various branches of the police force.

These, like many others, were latent rather than actual improvements when new military operations began in June. The denial of food to the guerrillas was something that could hardly be contemplated without resettlement of Chinese squatters. Even then, it was by no means easy, and when it was accomplished, there were other sources of supply, particularly logging camps and food lorries, so the introduction of prophylactic measures could not be expected to give a large return. On the whole, counter-guerrilla operations in the first phase of the Briggs plan were going to depend upon physical presence—for example, more armoured cars to protect food lorries and convoys—and clearer channels of command and would rely for their success on total domination of a limited area.[7]

On June 1st major military operations of the Briggs plan began in Johore.[8] Almost two thirds of the Army's available strength was now concentrated in the southern States of Johore, Negri

---

[5] 'It is essential that the local headman and committees understand as early as possible the responsibilities of their posts in order that information may be passed quickly to the proper quarter.'

[6] Directive No. 3, May 25th.

[7] Law also provided some constrictions. On June 1st 1950 the mandatory death penalty was introduced for 'anyone demanding, collecting or receiving supplies for guerrillas; and consideration was being given to mandatory imprisonment for the theft of rubber, copra and tin as well as the licensing and general discouragement of tapioca cultivation: indirect and direct sources of guerrilla supplies.

[8] The curfew in south Johore, however, did not begin until June 7th.

Sembilan and Southern Pahang. On August 1st intensive operations were due to begin in Negri Sembilan; and although Briggs had said at the outset that it was not practicable to forecast by which dates the States and Settlements would be cleared it was evident that the Army was working on a steam-roller timetable and that it was the intention to roll up—or flatten out—the Communist guerrillas in a massive drive to the north. It can be argued, however, and Briggs did so himself after the event, that this was a short term plan superimposed upon the major and long term programme to provide a framework for effective civil government and military operations. It was, Briggs argued, the result of the arrival of two infantry brigades and its purpose was to make a major effort in South Malaya and so to quicken up results there. To some extent this was a gamble—not that the rest of the country was thereby placed in imminent danger (although Briggs himself declared that it placed the unguarded areas in jeopardy)—but because it did not allow sufficient time for the weight of the army to be felt. It was not expected that substantial results would accrue from operations for the first two months but it was rather confidently assumed that the military presence would give increased security to the population and the result would be an increasing flow of information which would lead to more effective action by the remaining security forces. Against this, however, was the simple necessity of starting somewhere; the possibility that good results in one area would spread like ripples on a pool; and the fact that the direction of operations was out and away from the main British base in Singapore.

In the event, this crash programme failed. Or, as Briggs put it, the hope was not realised: which went to prove the necessity of the long term plan and that the Communist grip on the area was too firm.[9] During this period, said Briggs, certain facts were becoming more and more obvious.

The first was that the problem of clearing Communist banditry from Malaya was similar to that of eradicating malaria from a country. Flit guns and mosquito nets, in the form of military and police, though giving some very local security if continuously maintained, effected no permanent cure. Such a permanent cure entailed the closing of all the breeding areas. In this case the breeding areas of Communists were the isolated squatter areas, the unsupervised labour on estates, especially smallholders and

[9] *Report on the Emergency in Malaya*, p. 34.

Chinese estates without managers. Once these were concentrated there might be some chance of controlling the Communist cells therein. This showed clearly that a quick answer was not to be reckoned on.

The presence of large numbers of troops had not, in a matter of a few months, led to a notable increase in personal security or public confidence; neither did large scale patrolling on minimum intelligence lead to any notable increase in contacts in the first four months—over the country as a whole there was a dramatic and sustained increase from October onwards—although in local areas where resettlement had been completed Briggs maintained that there had been an immediate improvement.[10] In the non-priority areas enemy incidents increased considerably; and in the priority areas, after an initial drop, in Johore, at any rate, incidents again increased, partly due to the size of the resettlement problem there, partly due to the dispersal of the guerrillas into smaller groups and partly due to a weakness in operation of the military framework. The latter, according to Briggs, had already been 'adjusted' by the end of October but adjustment had still to be made to the fact that the guerrillas were now merging into a different background, mainly into unsupervised estate workers, and this again was a matter for civil government.

Most of the reasons which Briggs advanced for the slow progress of his plan up to the end of October were in fact to be found in civil measures—or their absence. Finance was mentioned as something that was forthcoming fairly freely and without great delay but which still entailed too much planning for the staff available. Current procedure entailed a considerable amount of work much of which ought to have been eliminated. There was always the danger that essential schemes might be seriously retarded and in some cases supplies had even been refused. While it was true that the High Commissioner could always exercise his reserve power this took time and was not politically desirable. The main difficulty lay in the shortage of trained civil servants on the ground. Reinforcements demanded from the United Kingdom were scantily met and only by untrained young officers. Leave for civil servants, though recently restricted, still proceeded on a quasi-peacetime basis while others were permitted to retire. The work of such officers as were on the ground, including the District and Administrative Officers, had been enthusiastic and

[10] Borne out by a decrease in incidents, by guerrilla efforts to hinder resettlement and by statements found in captured documents.

magnificent; but many of the officers who had been brought out of offices as an emergency measure were now reverting to their normal duties. In addition, the efforts to recruit Chinese executive officers had been handicapped by the political reluctance and slowness of State governments to appoint officers other than Malays. Technical departments were in most cases up to forty per cent understrength of officer establishments. Recruitment in England had run into serious difficulties while local candidates were practically unobtainable. The vital need for deportation of Communist detainees—'which, alone of any measure, would have the biggest effect on public morale'—had not perhaps been sufficiently appreciated by His Majesty's Government and none of the many alternative proposals made by the Federation Government had so far been acceptable.

From a practical point of view the removal of Chinese detainees from Malaya, and the consequent improvement of morale that was expected, would, by increasing public confidence, also increase the supply of intelligence. Hitherto, the Briggs plan had assumed that intelligence was a simple function of security and that it might be obtained by the physical presence of security forces. If, however, troops could not generate their own intelligence—and from the military point of view there was no doubt that intelligence was the key to successful operations—then it must be considered as a more complex equation in which intelligence equals confidence and this, in turn, was the product of information/propaganda/psychological warfare. The appointment in June 1950 of Mr. Alex Josey to the post of Staff Officer (Emergency Information) certainly helped to change the image of government and the public cause in at least one respect. Josey, who was seconded from the Department of Broadcasting and, somewhat ironically, was to be expelled many years later from a Malaysian Singapore on account of his neo-colonial activities, succeeded in arousing the anger of many Europeans with his broadcast reflections that the guerrilla war might contain elements of a struggle of the haves against the have nots; and that the sooner this was changed the better. With the boom in rubber prices created by the Korean war Josey made some pointed comparisons between dividends and bonuses on the one hand and wages on the other and even went so far as to suggest that such immoderate returns made a very good case for nationalisation of the rubber industry. This, perhaps, was not the change in its public image that the government required and although Josey seemed to succeed in breaking down certain of the military and outlaw stereotypes of the conflict—and perhaps, to this extent, diluting the concept of a colonial-revolutionary/egalitarian conflict—he was superseded in September 1950 by the appointment of Mr. Hugh Carleton Greene as Head of Emergency Information Services. With the appointment of Mr. Greene, head of the East European services of the BBC and future Director-General, information services now began to be expanded to include both propaganda and the varieties of psychological warfare.

As a means of generating intelligence on the one side and inducing surrender on the other, the role of the Emergency Information Services was of less immediate importance than the way in which the new war executive system worked, particularly in Johore. A number of Security Committees already existed in Johore but their place was now taken by what were called, in that State, War Committees. The principal differences were that they were executive rather than advisory; and that their numbers were reduced. On the State level there were four permanent members; the acting *Mentri Besar*; the British Adviser; the Chief Police Officer; and the Brigadier or Brigade Major. Others, variously in attendance, included the State Resettlement Officer; the Emergency Information Officer; the Chairman of the Regrouping Committee; and the Chairman of the Johore Planters' Association.[11] The main task of the State War Executive Committees was to agree on priorities and tasks in detail; but it is evident from the minutes of the Johore State War Committee that these were subject to central directives and at least in their formal meetings, do not seem to have been co-ordinated with police and army operations. Representative topics dealt with by the State War Committee included *kampong* guards; wireless telegraphy; intelligence organisation; detention camps; and the hours of curfew. Particular incidents were brought to its attention; authority to incur expenditure was given; opinions were expressed on various policy directives. At the District level there were some doubts about their anomalous position. The District War Committee had no legal status (it was thought unnecessary to provide for it since executive power was exercised through departmental channels); and it was simply a convenient body for rapid consideration of the action required. Any member could appeal to the State War Committee if his opinion was overridden and

---

[11] In announcing the disbandment of the Security Committees the Chairman of the Johore State War Committee showed particular solicitude for the feeling of the Johore Planters' Association whose members would not officially be included in the new committees.

departments which were not represented were under no obligation to accept decisions. On the State level it appeared that no practical difficulties had been experienced, nor had it been necessary to appeal to the Malayan War Council to settle a dispute. On at least one occasion the Director of Operations himself attended a meeting of a district War Committee; but while this may not have been as a result of differing interpretations or inaction—and indeed the files of the State War Committee as a whole in 1950 are comparatively tranquil—the question remains whether Briggs and Johore saw eye to eye on matters of fundamental importance: in particular, the extent and speed of resettlement.

These doubts persist on reading progress reports from the British Adviser in Johore and from his report of the Briggs plan in operation—'the Director of Operations was, I think, a little disappointed not to see visible evidence of any resettlement work'—onwards, there is little in his fortnightly reports to the High Commissioner on the subject of resettlement. Conceivably, this was because the British Adviser did not seem to think that it was very important: at least as a measure in itself. In a special paper 'On Some Civil Aspects of the Emergency in Johore—including Squatter Resettlement' the (acting) British Adviser argued that 'it would be a great mistake to assume that squatter resettlement is now anything but a temporary solution to the squatter problem and the stoppage of *one* source of bandit food and information'. The resettlement of some 30,000 squatters in Johore was, it was argued, a matter of comparative insignificance. Comparative, that is, to what might be called the 'total' Chinese problem. No particular solution to this total problem was advanced but the priorities were changed. Instead of resettlement the immediate need was to create an extensive intelligence network; and the implicit argument was that intelligence could be produced by good organisation. Elsewhere, the acting British Adviser had argued in favour of saturating resettlement areas with both detectives and under-cover agents: an argument which had been refuted by the Commissioner of Police both in principle and in practice.

In one important particular, however, the remarks of the acting British Adviser were prophetic

> Under the Briggs Plan the military role is jungle edge domination and jungle operations against the active terrorist gangs: to harry them, to kill them, to break them up. Never yet however—and we have had over twelve months bitter experience—has the departure of a gang left the ground clean as there remains mem-

bers of the armed labour corps, propagandists, subscription collectors who are to all, casual outward semblance, lawful citizens.

This was written in July 1950. In June and July guerrillas in Johore had been hit by military operations.[12] In August they were lying low; but a resurgence in September brought a fifty per cent increase in guerrilla activity as well as new tactics and organisation.

After initial successes, particularly in June when guerrilla communications were disrupted, and the capture of two large arms dumps north of Segamat yielded eighteen automatic weapons and 60,000 rounds of ammunition, results tailed off and some rather threadbare patches appeared in the blanket of army operations. In particular, Briggs criticised the ineffective and often dangerous 'fire-brigade' actions that were undertaken by army units in response to enemy attacks. Even more wasteful, were the cordoning operations which involved up to whole battalions and more to practically no effect. It was, however, revealing that Briggs described the most vital task of the Security Forces as the wresting of initiative from 'the Communists and their bandits' even if only in the States to which priority had been given. The purpose of his military operations may be seen in what were, for Briggs, two proven facts:

(a) bandit morale becomes badly shaken once they are continuously harrassed by ground and air action as their information becomes dislocated and they become more concerned with their own safety than with planning offensive action.
(b) The same effect is obtained if the jungle is shared with them. Their movement, supplies, information and security become increasingly difficult.

A dividend on the first month of intensive operations had been paid. It was not to be repeated for many months and the odds against the success of speculative patrolling, which was what jungle sharing amounted to in practice, were perhaps not fully appreciated as yet. The third task was that of giving closer security to the population; and while it might be argued that security forces were not sufficient for all three tasks, that argument, said Briggs, certainly in priority States, could hardly be justified. As Briggs himself admitted, insofar as this was part of a crash pro-

[12] Forty killed and ten surrendered: equal to the totals of the preceding five months.

gramme which detracted from the uniform strengthening of the administrative structure, this was a mistake that was corrected. In any case one could argue that one had to begin somewhere with something and, given an increase in available forces, this looked like as good a plan as any. However, with a possible reduction in the number of Army battalions available the emphasis was again on matters of civil policy.

From the end of June Briggs described external affairs as at their worst especially in Korea, and a World War seemed more imminent than it did before or has since. Great pressure was being put on Malaya to free troops both for Korea and NATO forces[13] although in fact there was a net increase in the military forces available. In particular, air operations increased considerably and there was a hundred per cent increase in offensive air support. In part, this was due to the arrival of a squadron of RAF Lincoln heavy bombers which began operations in March and was augmented by a squadron of RAAF Lincolns in August. More important for the ground forces engaged was the formation of an RAF casualty evacuation flight in Singapore which began helicopter operations in May to fly out the sick and wounded from jungle clearings. The latter half of 1950 also saw command reorganisation. Perhaps the most important was the appointment of Major-General R. C. O. Hedley, Commanding South Malaya District, as Deputy Director of Operations in the priority areas. This gave him supreme and immediate authority in South Malaya and foreshadowed further and undivided military control the following year when Brigadiers were translated into Assistant Deputy Directors of Operations and were responsible for operational control of their States or Settlements. Directive No. 1 had laid down that the civil administration, police and army should work in the closest collaboration and use combined joint operations and intelligence rooms wherever practicable down to the District level. Police and Army areas, however, did not always coincide. For example in Perak, the police headquarters was in Ipoh while the Army headquarters was some twenty miles away in Taiping. Within the police itself the organisation of intelligence gathering, collation and distribution was a source of continuing concern and was the subject of a Director of Operations directive in August which repeated the need for closer co-operation between the police and the army and suggested a working model for joint operational intelligence rooms.

One area of increasing strategic importance but one that was

[13] *Briggs Report*, p. 20.

THE BRIGGS PLAN

fraught with economic and social dangers was the periphery of Malaya's extensive plantation areas.

> Experience has shown that certain developed areas (other than squatter areas) in various parts of the Federation have been consistently used as supply bases or channels of supply to the bandits and that, owing to the dispersal of the persons dwelling in such areas and the lack of any local residents of any standing the efforts of the Security Forces to deny the use of the area to the bandits have been unavailing or only partially successful. In most cases these areas consist of smallholdings, small estates owned by absentee landlords with no manager in residence, and State or Crown land cultivated under Temporary Occupation Licence.

A new Emergency Regulation—17FA—gave State and Settlement authorities power to declare such areas to be 'controlled areas'. The purpose was to concentrate the residents of such an area at night in specific parts—labour lines for the most part—in an attempt to provide protection and to cut communications and supply lines with the guerrillas. A 'controlled area' could be anything between five and twenty-five square miles in area; but in order to concentrate the inhabitants in a few residential areas it would obviously be necessary to move large numbers of them. Anyone living outside a residential area could be compelled to move into it—or even to move outside the controlled area altogether—but a warning was given that the measure should be used only if it was essential for proper administrative control of the area and for the protection of the residents from terrorist domination. Difficulties seem to have been anticipated

> The new regulations will deny to lawful occupiers of land many of their normal rights and privileges and its use may cause them financial loss which they will not be able to recover in compensation from government. Further the administration of the regulation will inevitably give rise to unforeseen problems not all of which will be easy to solve. Lastly, the cost to government is likely to be considerable. For all these reasons state and settlement authorities are strongly advised to make use of the new regulation with the greatest circumspection.

and in the event, Directive No. 10 (January 26th 1951) laid down that regrouping and concentration schemes were to be planned and completed in three months. *Mentri[2] Besar* and competent authorities authorised by them could order owners or occupiers of land to construct buildings and wire fences without waiting for decisions on the incidence of cost.

An observer looking at the situation in Malaya at the end of 1950, both then and now, must have mixed feelings about the progress of the campaign, but it is difficult to overrate the importance of the Briggs plan both in its spirit and innovation. At the same time, the manifest pattern of insurgency and terrorism continued as before and although it could be argued that, for the first time, the battle was joined in 1950[14] there was still little knowledge of the enemy order of battle and the lines of battle had only begun to be drawn. Perhaps the most important change on the government's side was that the monolithic simplicity of 'killing bandits' was abandoned in favour of a geodectic structure which, although flimsy in its components, had infinitely more collective strength. In the War Executive system, Briggs had been concerned to forge a reliable weapon. It was designed for continual use; and when it jammed there had to be simple and immediate means of clearance. The Security Forces, to use a later analogy, now seemed to be no more than the warhead on a large and complex missile; but the doubt remained in Briggs' mind about the rest of the mechanism and the structure that was supposed to get it off the ground. In his progress report of November 1st 1950 Briggs went so far as to describe the Army and the RAF as 'the only really stable factors in this Malayan situation at present and upon them the main burden of maintaining the country's security depends'. His implied criticism became specific:

> During the last four months every effort has been made to overcome difficulties but, under increasing circumstances the limit has been reached. It becomes increasingly obvious that unless the Federation Government is placed on a war footing and the gravity of the situation is realised by HM Government, no quicker progress can be made and a still graver emergency will arise straining the morale of Malaya beyond breaking point.

His proposals for putting Malaya on a war footing were by

1. (*a*) His Excellency the High Commissioner presiding over the War Council with the Director of Operations as his Deputy, and the Council meeting at frequent intervals; (this has already been agreed to by the Officer Administering the Government);

[14] *Federation of Malaya Annual Report*, 1950, p. 5.

THE BRIGGS PLAN

   (b) handing over all Emergency matters from the State Governments to the War Council or State War Committees;
   (c) restricting the work of the Legislature as far as reasonably possible;
   (d) expediting the method of obtaining approval for Emergency expenditure;
   (e) postponing any major political changes;
   (f) curtailing leave, retirements or resignations during the Emergency.
2. Giving equal high priority to strengthening the Police potential both in the Uniform and CID branches, so that they can cope early with the tasks of anticipating and combating Communism under all conditions and with the minimum support of Military Forces. Speed is of the utmost importance.
3. Persuading His Majesty's Government of the gravity of the situation and requiring:
   (a) a firm and immediate favourable decision on the deportation of detainees;
   (b) a firm guarantee of financial support in the form of a fixed proportion of all expenditure on the Emergency;
   (c) production at the earliest moment of such specialists and technicians as have been asked of them, even if it is to the detriment of other territories or of the United Kingdom.
4. Publicising these measures, which should have an immediate heartening effect on the morale of the population of Malaya.

And he concluded

> There is no doubt that the success of the campaign should be definitely quickened by such measures on the civil side in particular as would make the task of the Police and Military easier to complete. The effect on the time-table will depend on the thoroughness and speed with which they are carried out. There cannot but be a speeding-up of at least several months in the whole time-table, though perhaps not so much as in the earlier phase.[15]

---

[15] *Report on the Emergency in Malaya*, pp. 47–48. In December (1950) Briggs and Watherston, went to London where together with Gurney, who was on leave, they had two meetings with Attlee, Bevin, Griffiths, Strachey and Slim. 'At least,' said Watherston, 'we were able to bring home the gravity of the situation and our need for much greater assistance.'

In its most important respect these proposals were very much the same as those which Gray, the Commissioner of Police, advanced at about the same time. In late November, it was announced at a meeting of the Federal Legislative Council that manpower was to be conscripted and that government office work was to be reduced to a minimum as part of the Federation's plan to step up the fight against Communist bandits. On December 15th Gurney announced the government's conscription measures which, at least in scope, put Malaya on a war footing. Government would now have the power to direct any man between 17 and 45 to perform military or police service. Engagement in employment was also controlled and so was the maintenance of labour for essential work. In law the government now possessed powers both for destroying support for the guerrillas as well as for regulating society. Those who served in the guerrilla supply organisation were now liable to be killed in law as well as in battle. Although challengeable in the courts, the government had power to prohibit 'seditious or inflammatory matter of any kind'. Frustrated by collective silence government now had power to resort to collective punishment: to impose a collective fine, to order the complete or partial closing of shops or the quartering of additional police on the inhabitants of any area who not only aided, abetted or consorted with guerrillas but who, in the government's opinion, suppressed evidence or failed to give information and did not have the courage or temerity to apprehend the guerrillas of their own accord.

Measures such as this, and the power to impose indefinite detention—qualified only by its serialisation in two-year periods—may suggest a welcome determination on the government's part; or else a note of something close to quiet desperation. The Emergency, said Gurney in December, must be brought to an end in 1951. So far, however, hardly more than one squatter in five had been resettled—12,000 in 82 resettlement areas—and no more than 3,500 Chinese had been committed to service in the Home Guard. Relations between the Colonial Government and an incalculable part of the Malay community had changed almost overnight when Muslim rioting in Singapore over the verdict in the Maria Hertogh case—a verdict that was considered to be racial as well as an affront to the Muslim religion—had brought Malay feeling to flash point. A few months later and the government professed to see the clouds lifting before they found themselves in the eye of the storm. At the end of the year the most that could be said was that the civil measures had not failed and that they gave some hope of success. But the political climate had grown worse, for not only was there little sign of a more general Chinese commitment to the government's support but the experience of Asia as a whole and of Korea in particular suggested to some at least that the Western position in Asia was about to be over-run.

COMMUNITY POLITICS

From the point of view of the insurgents their ultimate disadvantage and ultimate defeat lay in the fact that it was the insurrection of a Chinese racial minority. For various reasons the country was already divided before the fighting began; and, although revolutions are usually made by determined minorities, the weight of racial opposition together with the uncertainty of support from their own community were disadvantages that were never overcome. Having said this it must at once be added that, in quantitative terms at least, the size of the Chinese minority seemed to offer a fair chance of a successful insurrection.

In 1947, out of a total population of less than five million there were almost two million Malayan Chinese:[1] if to this was added the population of Singapore then Chinese outnumbered Malays; and, in any case, this was the largest proportion of Chinese to other inhabitants that was to be found anywhere in South-east Asia. With few exceptions the Chinese had maintained their existence as a separate community.[2] On grounds of religion at least there was little inter-marriage and with such a sizeable minority it would have been hard, for both sides, for them to be assimilated into a group that was only slightly larger. As a political entity the problem as far as Malaya was concerned was that of allegiance; and, as far as the Malayan Chinese were concerned, whether the Malayan Government was to be considered as their sovereign state. As far as the Malayan Government was concerned it could be argued, rationally, that the matter of the allegiance of the Malayan Chinese, which was in doubt, was the determinant of government policy. It could also be argued that the overwhelming evidence regarding the greater part of the Malayan Chinese was that, while Malaya provided the focus of interest for their working lives, their sentiments, ties and allegiance all lay with China. At least, this was the evidence from before the war. After the war, and the abandonment of what, from the

[1] Thirty-four per cent of the population compared with 49 per cent Malaysian and 15 per cent Indian. Total population: 4,908,000. Malaysians (including aborigines) 2,428,000. Chinese 1,885,000. Indians (including Pakistanis) 531,000.

[2] At the same time they were separate communities, such as Hokkien and Cantonese, divided by language and having no natural leader.

Chinese point of view, was the comparatively generous experiment of the Malayan Union the issue was in doubt; and thoughts of Chinese enfranchisement had in any event to be tempered by the consideration that this was largely a government of a federation of Malay states : states whose doubts and fears of the Chinese role were manifest from the constitutional level downwards.

Measures to meet the insurrection, as well as the insurrection itself, have therefore to be seen against the background of a plural society.

The Chinese

More or less permanent Chinese settlements in Malaya date back at least to the middle of the fourteenth century. By the early fifteenth century a somewhat diffuse tributary relationship had been established between Malacca and the Chinese empire; but as this thus excluded Siamese influence so, in turn, from the early sixteenth century Chinese political power was replaced by a succession of European outposts with the British lately succeeding to Portuguese and Netherlands empires. Accounts and profiles of the Malayan Chinese have tended to focus attention on the fortunes and enterprise of men and families who have brought the Chinese into positions of prominence in Malayan commerce, mining and industry.[3] On the whole, these accounts concentrated on urban activities and although there is no lack of information on Chinese labour as such, when broken down into categories it is either the experience of Chinese 'coolies'—and that notably in Singapore—or else in the mining and to a lesser extent estate 'industries' that is considered.

Accounts of the political characteristics of the Malayan Chinese agree that theirs was largely a self-contained society; and one which maintained the traditional views and characteristics of mainland China. What these are—or were—is perhaps best seen in a comparison. The British view and the British experience of government is based no less upon firm and ultimate sovereignty than on the more widely quoted belief in the rule of law. It is a view and experience of a society in which the warrior elements

[3] Foremost amongst them the works of Dr. Victor Purcell, *The Chinese in South-east Asia*, London, 1965; *The Chinese in Malaya*, London, 1948; *The Chinese in Modern Malaya*, Singapore, 1956; and *Malaya: Communist or Free?*, London, 1954. See also Purcell's first-hand experiences in the Malayan Civil Service, *Memoirs of a Malayan Official*, London, 1965. See also W. L. Blythe *The Impact of Chinese Secret Societies in Malaya*, London, 1969; M. Freedman, *Chinese Family and Marriage in Singapore*, HMSO, 1957; and Lea Williams, *Overseas Chinese Nationalism*, New York, 1960.

have been tamed and largely brought under public control. It is a government that is based formally upon elections, law and taxation; informally, upon a belief that public government demands public allegiance. In contrast, there is the Chinese view of government which, in turn, seems to be based upon a belief in a self-regulating society. In the Imperial Chinese system the lowest officials appointed by Pekin were the Sian magistrates, about 2,000 in number, who were responsible for districts of up to 100,000. Below that matters were left in the hands of the family and clan. A society in which elections were superfluous; taxation was a gambling hazard; and the law courts were a resort for civil rather than criminal proceedings. Although from 1877 onward the activities of the Chinese in Malaya were subject to increasing regulation it did not do for Protectors of Chinese to inquire too closely into the methods by which the 'Kapitan China' exercised his 'traditional' leadership of the Chinese community: although it would have been difficult, as a moral problem, to reconcile the nature of his authority with the nature of government as it was developing in late Victorian England. Government, for the Chinese, and particularly for those who did not live in the comparatively few large towns in Malaya, was often a matter of the immediate and physical power of a secret society which managed to combine mystical and mercenary functions as well as maintain a form of freemasonry and benefit society. Political organisations were almost always a reflection of the politics of mainland China and whether they were representatives of the *Kuomintang* or the Communist Party—though less in the case of the latter—their affiliations were largely external.

In any case it could be argued that it was meaningless to talk of 'the Chinese community' as if it were a single entity. And where traditional leadership may be considered relevant to a homogenous society it scarcely applied to a society which was divided, like many immigrant societies, by time of arrival and had been affected by the breakdown of authority during the war and the creation of rival authorities afterwards. The handful of MCS officers who were directly concerned with Chinese affairs after the war were careful to distinguish between the prinicpal groupings within that community. What these were tended to reflect the personal views of the official concerned but it was presumably on the basis of one such categorisation that Gurney described to the Colonial Office the groups within the Chinese community shortly after his arrival in October, 1948.[4] First, there were the

[4] October 8th 1948.

local born Chinese of at least two generations of residence in Malaya whose fathers were local born. Foremost amongst this group were the 'Straits Chinese', found in the old Straits Settlements of Singapore, Penang and Malacca. They were largely the products of English schools; they habitually spoke English; and their knowledge of the Chinese written language was likely to vary from slight to nil. Some were even unable to speak Chinese. Their feeling for China was only a sentiment and they would be helpless were they ever to return. They had married into families with a similar background and their relatives were to be found all over Malaya. They sought careers in the local professions and with European business firms. Many of them were clerks; and, with some exceptions, they were not among the extremely rich Malayan Chinese.

The natural loyalty of this group was obvious to Malaya : the only country where their children could grow up in the same social and cultural atmosphere to which they themselves had been accustomed. On this and other points they differed from the second group who, although local born and English-speaking, were Chinese of the first generation. Their fathers were immigrants; it was unlikely that they ever spoke English; and Chinese traditions were strong in the home. These families were apparently settling down in Malaya, with the children entering family businesses or becoming clerks. Knowledge of English gave them an opportunity of extending their business interests and was regarded as an asset rather than a habit.

From the point of view of the possibility of growth in Malayan consciousness, the behaviour of this group was more important than that of any other in local Chinese society. Recently established, it was more opportunist than those who had come to regard Malaya as their only home; and political parties based on China such as the KMT or, before its extinction, the China Democratic League, appeared to some to be the only appropriate organisation for protecting their class interests in Malaya from left-wing movements. In some parts of the country members of this group had already tried to control labourers through KMT contractors. English-speaking Chinese of the first generation were found in varying degrees of sympathy with the KMT : a tendency which necessarily hindered the growth of a genuinely Malayan consciousness among them. And Malayan Government policy which seemed to threaten the interests of this group was reckoned to increase their affiliations with China-based parties because they would look towards China for the protection of their communal as well as their class interests in Malaya. To this extent they were therefore potential Chinese nationalists and the extent to which they swayed between loyalty towards Malaya and loyalty towards China might be taken as an indication of the degree of confidence which first-generation Chinese had that their position in Malaya was secure. If all went well it was thought that they would in time become assimilated with the older group of local Chinese. If it did not, they might become the frontier force of the Chinese expansionist movement: whether Nationalist or Communist remained to be seen.

Group three were local-born and non-English-speaking Chinese of the first generation and these, said Gurney, could only be regarded as a menace and their outlook was a double threat to peace in Malaya. Within it, there were two sub-groups. First, businessmen of varying degrees of wealth. What has been said of the latent sympathies of group two could be said with much more emphasis of the members of this sub-group. Their outlook was described as 'entirely capitalist' as well as Chinese which meant that their affinities were with the KMT: the only party for Chinese businessmen in Malaya. They valued Malaya as a place for making money and as a safe place to live in. If the local government were unable or unwilling to maintain either of these conditions of their present political neutrality they would certainly look to China for help. The difference in outlook between this sub-group and newcomers from China was slight. Members of the second sub-group were thought to constitute an even greater menace which could not be stressed too frequently nor too urgently. These were the labourer-immigrants who still had as little in common with other Malayan communities as their fathers had. Their numbers were expanding in labour forces and squatter settlements and they could fairly be described as Chinese colonists in Malaya. They were hardy and prolific; and nothing could be done to convert them into Malayan citizens. Their outlook was entirely Chinese and as squatters they had spilled over the countryside on to land from which it was difficult to dislodge them. The squatter areas were described as 'Chinese colonies in Malaya' equipped with Chinese schools which intensified their Chinese outlook, and riddled with Chinese secret societies.[5] It was amongst this group, according to the Secretary for Chinese Affairs, that most of the guerrillas and their supporters were to be found; and while this was largely true, even if the main premises are con-

[5] Group 4 were newcomers born in China who were said to be similar to this group: 'only more so'.

ceded it would seem that this was, in part at least, based upon a fear of the unknown.

After the war, there is little doubt that the rural Chinese were, to the government, a comparatively unknown quantity. Before the war, each of the Settlements, the Federated States and Johore had one or more Protectors of Chinese. The Secretary for Chinese Affairs had his Secretariat in Singapore, was a member of the Legislative/Federal and Executive Councils of the Straits Settlements and the Federated Malay States and was consulted on all matters affecting the Chinese community. He was chairman of State and Settlement Chinese Advisory Boards, a member of the Chinese Consultative Committee, Registrar of Societies, Protector of Women and Girls, Controller of Labour and had subordinate Directors of Chinese Education. In the Settlements and States the Protectors of Chinese had similar functions, both advisory and executive.

Apart from advising on matters of Chinese customs and politics, recommending membership of public boards for councils and those who merited the receipt of honours, the Protector—or *Tai-jin* as he was called—served as a go-between for government and the Chinese. Government notifications to the Chinese were frequently in the form of circulars signed by the Protector of Chinese and sent to all Chinese clubs and bodies. As State officers they moved freely and their contacts were easily maintained. As Deputy Controller of Immigration, all classes including remote vegetable gardeners, woodcutters and fishermen would visit him once in two years to get a certificate of admission renewed. Committee men of societies would from time to time present themselves before him as Registrar. He inspected places of Chinese employment and the Protectorate afforded a special court for disputes involving Chinese where claims under the Labour Code might be heard and cases could be dealt with involving a special knowledge of Chinese customs, for example disputes about marriage, divorce, custody of children, adoption and so on. The Protector of Chinese was usually the Banishment Inquiry Officer. He also sat on State Councils, Sanitary Boards and Liquor Licensing Boards. As Protector of Women and Girls and of Children he had police powers and when the *Mui-tsai* ordinance was in force—which regulated the arduous conditions under which semi-adopted Chinese girls worked as family servants—he visited every house where there was a registered *Mui-tsai*. These executive functions not only gave the Protector of Chinese contacts with all classes, but made his office and function well known and appreciated by the Chinese to whom the *Tai-jin* represented the government as no other officer did.

That was the situation before the war. With the end of the war came the end of the Chinese Protectorate. In retrospect it would seem that its abolition was a serious mistake. In 1945 however, the cast of pre-war Malaya had been shattered and the interests of modern, rational and efficient government did not seem to require the existence of such a gigantic, paternal anachronism as the Chinese Protectorate. In pre-war days it had been an empire in itself. Now, its functions were redistributed and its powers of government which affected so much of the life of the Chinese community were to be taken over by government which recognised no particular communal characteristics. In the process, the compact with government for a large part of the Chinese community disappeared.[6] In a State where a large part of the population was regarded as transient the restriction on citizenship may have been justified. However, when the likelihood of return to China had been reduced the sense of allegiance to Malaya could be used as the criterion; and it makes for an interesting but perhaps interminable argument to consider which should have come first: citizenship or allegiance. What is a matter of fact, however, rather than speculation, is that one of the most important contacts between people and government had been broken. And where, for various reasons, the great majority of the Chinese population had no share in the government, for it to have lost touch with the Protectorate, paternalist and semi-feudal though it may have been, without a compensating advance towards citizenship, was another stage in the process of alienation.

Government too had lost contact: certainly its regulative and prophylactic powers declined. Instead of the circulars signed by the Protector of Chinese and sent to Chambers of Commerce, clubs and societies, there were now Press releases or a notification by the Public Relations Department: a more modern procedure, no doubt, but subject to the handicap that Chinese tended to treat everything that came out of the Public Relations Department as government propaganda. And impersonal propaganda at that. But the most dangerous vacuum was created with the lapse of the registration of societies: a function which was as important after the war as it had been in the 1870s when the Chinese Protectorate grew up. Communist associations in the form of

---

[6] Even when the office of Secretary for Chinese Affairs was created, its powers often reduced it to a nullity.

trade unions or the New Democratic Youth League and the strong-arm *San Min Chu Yi* Youth Corps of the *Kuomintang* took advantage of the lapsed regulations while in the north the Ang Bin Hoay Triad Society with its stock-in-trade of murder and extortion, flourished as it had not done for more than eighty years.

Politically, it could be argued that in many respects the Malayan Chinese were no further forward now than they had been ten or twenty years before—and were certainly worse off than they would have been under the constitution of the Malayan Union. Malayan Union citizenship would have been conferred automatically on everyone born and still normally resident in Malaya—including Singapore—and on everyone who, although not born in Malaya, had been resident there for not less than ten of the fifteen years prior to the Japanese occupation. Moreover, applications for citizenship might be made by anyone who had lived in Malaya for five of the eight years preceding his application. The only condition was that those who qualified by residence only were to affirm their allegiance to the Malayan Union. This, as Gullick points out, would have meant that most Malayan Chinese would have qualified by residence. As citizens they would later have votes and would thus outnumber the Malays on the electoral rolls: a prospect which united the Malay community in opposition to these proposals. Instead, under the 1948 constitution, where the entire Malay population became citizens, only about 350,000 Chinese qualified as citizens by operation of law.

It could also be argued, as indeed it was, that Malayan Chinese wanted to be loyal—but were the victims of discrimination under the Federation Constitution.[7] Be this as it may, and in spite of subsequent exaggeration, the Chinese community, although opposing the Federation Constitution, had shown little enthusiasm for the Malayan Union proposals and the question of citizenship had been insufficient, either negatively or positively, to create any lasting political party amongst them. After the insurrection began this was no longer a matter of academic interest and in response to early inquiries from the Colonial Office, Gurney outlined government's principal political objective of creating 'a genuinely Malayan Chinese Party'.

What we need to do is to encourage local-born and locally settled Chinese of intelligence and initiative who belong to one of the

[7] See, for example, *Kin Kwok Daily News*, Ipoh, March 8th 1948.

first two groups[8] and who have no previous political affiliations, to come forward as leaders in local Chinese society, reconciling differences of opinion, encouraging their more timid compatriots, and promoting good relations between the Chinese and the Malays. They would have strongest motives for doing this as their personal interests are vitally connected with the defeat of Communism. It is in the highest degree unfortunate that Doctor Ong, the most outstanding if not the only Chinese of this category who had shown real qualities of leadership had been murdered.[9]

The ideas on which a Malayan Chinese Party might be based were, according to Gurney, first, a revulsion against Communism; second, an appreciation of the principles of British rule and policy; third, the recognition of the connection between the morale of local Chinese society and internal security. These, no doubt, were admirable principles. But to build a party upon them was rather like making bricks without straw. Such a party as might be created on the basis of these ideas would, government recognised, have as its nucleus, those Chinese who were already Federal citizens or who were qualified to apply for citizenship. The others, at least for the time being, were excluded

> As you know, it would be politically impossible at present to make any attempt to widen the clauses of the Federation Agreement which laid down the qualifications for citizenship.

and the principal advantage of this sort of party was that it would not necessarily arouse the hostility of the Malays. Whether such a party could be created, and survive in this emasculated form, and whether it could continue in time of war remained to be seen. There was, of course, an obvious dilemma for its leaders. To co-operate with government and thus retain the seal of its approval: at the risk of becoming a government ancillary. Or to defend the interests of the Chinese community, whatever they were, at the risk of confrontation with and even suppression by government.

In the early days of the Emergency there was little sign of the emergence of representative Chinese leadership as a political advance that would compensate for their diminished prospects under the Federation Constitution. Mr. Tan Cheng Lock, as a political figure, survived the collapse of the Malayan Democratic

[8] See above, pp. 256–257.
[9] The murder of Dr. Ong Chong Keng, a member of the Legislative Council—1948—occurred when he was deceived into leaving his house at night to attend to a sick woman. Although a particularly treacherous murder it was not established as the work of the MCP.

Union, the quasi-popular front of the All Malayan Council of Joint Action and the abortive Malayan Chinese League. According to the Secretary for Chinese Affairs[10] the fact that the Malayan Chinese alone had failed to organise themselves into a communal organisation was because they were and are more interested in commerce. But once the insurrection which was largely and demonstrably Chinese had begun the Malayan Chinese were under increasing pressure to declare themselves or at least to decide for themselves which side was going to win. Government reports at least suggest a very fearful Chinese community in the early months of the Emergency; and even before the insurrection had begun they were dispirited not only by the Federal constitution but also what they took to be criticism of their community expressed by General Percival's retrospective dispatch on the Malayan Campaign[11] and from which they inferred that the British, in the past and at present, had no faith in the Chinese.

From June 1948 until the end of the year, the Chinese, at least on the constitutional level, underwent a sort of political anaesthesia. While expressions of public support for the guerrillas were perhaps not to be expected there were practically no condemnations of the terrorist activities either. In Singapore the prominent Chinese industrialist, Mr. Tan Kah Kee, called upon the Chinese to do their best to end lawlessness and restore normal conditions. He disapproved of all unnecessary disputes and violence and said that if the present disturbed conditions continued the labourers would be thrown out of employment and would have no money to remit to their families in China. Less influential but locally prominent Chinese could not afford even this ambiguous opinion and many of them disappeared from villages and smaller towns, leaving their businesses in the hands of their assistants, or else they stayed away from their homes after dark. The Secretary for Chinese Affairs, who provided a monthly review of the situation, argued that the Chinese were accustomed to acquiesce to pressure close at hand; that it did not occur to them to do anything about it; and that a very few could intimidate a great many.[12] The Chinese, he said, were under

[10] *Review of Chinese Affairs*, May 1948.
[11] Published in February 1948.
[12] Extract from note dated September 9th 1948: He instanced a gang which had regularly collected $10,000 a month from the inhabitants of Serdang village, near Kuala Lumpur, and that this went on until the police broke up the gang.

pressure the whole time and, willingly or unwillingly, were actively assisting the enemy. The extent of this assistance gradually became known: towns, villages, rubber estates, tin mines, businessmen, bus companies and other road transport in particular, and was estimated by the end of 1948 to be something like a quarter of a million dollars subscription per month to the Malayan Communist Party. Apart from this material assistance it is worth noting that the issue of Malayan Chinese allegiance—to Malaya or to China—was for a while put in question by an apparently mistaken report from United Press News which was reproduced by most of the Chinese papers in Malaya and Singapore to the effect that the Overseas Chinese Department of the Chinese Foreign Affairs Committee had opposed the Chinese Foreign Ministry's policy of encouraging Malayan Chinese to participate in resistance to Communist Party terrorism: action, which, it said, was tantamount to using Chinese against Chinese.

From London the situation looked rather different. In August, Sir Thomas Lloyd in the Colonial Office was asking Sir Alec Newboult, the interim Head of Government, 'Are we not gradually against our will being forced into the position of Europeans fighting the Chinese, or at least of Europeans and Malays fighting the Chinese?' If this danger were felt to be real both by him and by the Governor in Singapore, were there, asked Lloyd, any further measures which he could take to mobilise Chinese support behind us more effectively than hitherto? Possibly this was reaction to Newboult's public criticism of Chinese participation in the Emergency but in the meantime there had been little response to government needs for Chinese manpower—and this was becoming, for government, the criterion of Chinese allegiance.[13]

---

[13] In the review of Chinese Affairs for July 1948 fear seems to have been the principal handicap. A batch of recruits in Kuala Lumpur were reported as afraid to go to the local police station to be sworn in: they wanted the police to go to them at some other place and do it. The report added 'the open inconsistency of this unwillingness with their subsequent appearance on the streets with armbands and rifles does not seem to strike them'. 'Meetings were continually being held and correct speeches made but nothing seemed to happen for so long. In Johore Bahru recently the Batu Pahat representative said his town was peaceful and there was no immediate need for an auxiliary police force. Everything depended on the personality of the local Chinese leader. At Tapah, in Perak, there were 85 Chinese who had been accepted by the police and 43 who were awaiting acceptance. At Yong Peng, in Johore, 13 Chinese had been on patrol since August 9th; they were raised by a Chinese whose father was one of the early victims of terrorism and this was his method of avenging his parent.'

By the end of 1948 a *rapprochement* between government and the Chinese seemed likely on two counts. First, Chinese recruiting figures for various forces began to pick up by October; second, there were signs that the vacuum in Chinese political organisation was about to be filled. The position at the end of the year was that the large body of conservative Chinese businessmen who had been accommodated in the *Kuomintang, faute de mieux*, after the liberation, were once more without any other organisation with the exception of the Chambers of Commerce, the Chinese assembly halls and the Chinese Associations: all long-established organisations which had made little or no impression on government since the Emergency began. The new association would have the double function of strengthening the Chinese status in the Federation and taking the minds of its members, many of them former KMT supporters, off the rapidly deteriorating situation in China itself.

The initiative for the actual formation of the Malayan Chinese Association is a matter of some speculation. The first indication that steps were being taken was given by Gurney on December 19th 1948 in a telegram to the Colonial Office. The formation of a Malayan Chinese Association, he said, was being undertaken by leading Chinese; it was to be an association open to all who had made their home in the Federation with the object of co-operating with the government and with other communities in restoring peace and good order in this country. Rules were being drafted and were to be discussed with Gurney; but Chinese members of Legislative Council had undertaken to start to enlist support privately for this move in their districts at once. Gurney had mentioned the development to Dato Onn and was satisfied that it would be helpful in forthcoming Malay–Chinese conversation on long-term problems. Margaret Clark in her thesis[14] describes the Malayan Chinese Association in terms of an autonomous Chinese origination; but Lucien Pye in his unpublished study of the Emergency,[15] says that the initiative was taken by Gurney who approached Tan Cheng Lock; and this view appears to be borne out by Macdonald's telegram to the Secretary of State (April 19th 1949) in which he said that 'the High Commissioner has played, behind the scenes, a decisive part'. Whatever

---

[14] Margaret F. Clark, *The Malayan Alliance and its Accommodation of Communal Pressures, 1952–1962*, MA Thesis (unpublished), History Department, University of Malaya, 1964.

[15] *Lessons from the Malayan Struggle against Communism*, MIT (mimeo) n.d., p. 40.

the actual circumstances in which the proposals originated Gurney, in fact, attributed their success to pressure which was now being brought to bear upon the Chinese. 'They are, as you know, notoriously inclined to lean towards whichever side frightens them the more and at the moment this seems to be the government.' In particular, Gurney was trying to end the payment of protection money to the guerrillas: something, he said, which must clearly be demanded by public opinion and not merely by the government. Chinese public opinion had hitherto been silent on this point; but now that both extortion and police pressure had increased there was a natural revulsion of which full advantage could be taken. A month or so later (January 28th 1949) Gurney had the impression that three of the Legislative Council had 'retreated a little from their earlier intention to include as a prominent object the restoration of peace and order'. This was after a meeting with Mr. Khoo Teck Ee, Mr. Yong Shook Lin, and Mr. H. S. Lee on January 25th; and Gurney told the Chief Secretary that 'we must do all we can to keep them up to the mark of declaring themselves publicly on the side of law and order'.

The Malayan Chinese Association was thus born into a dilemma. Either it was a political and independent party, if only in embryo, or else it was the handmaiden of government. From the beginning it was asked to assist the police in the penetration of the MCP; to comment on CID classification of detainees; to arrange sureties; and 'to promote incidents of surrender'. Even the Emergency Chinese Advisory Committee found itself being asked to undertake an hortatory role and although it only met four times from April 1949 to February 1950 this infrequency, according to a later government report, was a reflection that the MCA had secured increasing recognition and consultation by other means.[16] The Advisory Committee did however provide an outlet for Chinese indignation; and while the judgement of the Secretary for Chinese Affairs, that the Chinese were now united on a basis of self-pity, was harsh it may have had some point. There were certainly plenty of occasions for such feelings which

---

[16] On the agenda of the first meeting of the Emergency Chinese Advisory Committee (April 5th 1949) were certain proposals for the registration of households including the provision of number plate and gong. The latter was to be used in 'two or three practices weekly in sounding the alarm so that constant practices by the squatters and cultivators would soon create in them a sense of unity instead of individuality and cowardice'—an unacknowledged and somewhat ludicrous Pavlovian experiment.

were investigated by Chinese community leaders. One example to which Mr. Tan Cheng Lock drew the attention of the Secretary for Chinese Affairs was that of a Chinese widow named Lee Moy, aged about 40, living at the Fifth Mile, Segamat, in the Seremban district, on her own land—about 20 acres of rubber. Her husband had died during the Japanese occupation and she had five children of whom the eldest was about 17 and the youngest about 7. She herself came to Malaya more than twenty years ago and she had no relatives or property in China, but in February 1949 they were all arrested and were to be deported to China: which, said Mr. Tan, was tantamount to a sentence of death on these six lives. In March, Mr. Tan went to the Malacca detention camp and interviewed detainees who had been removed there from Kajang in Selangor. Many of those who were removed from Kajang had dependants or husbands living outside this particular squatter area who had now, somehow, to resume contact. Children had been detained without mothers, mothers detained without children. From such pitiful cases as well as the prospects for those about to be deported who had neither family nor property in China could be seen what happened when the social fabric was torn into shreds and its effect upon the family: the most revered of Chinese institutions.

As far as positive co-operation with government was concerned, there were also impediments. In particular there were the difficulties facing Asian employers who wished to resist demands for protection money. In some cases estate labour was removed by the police and owners were denied entry which made it impossible for them to guarantee that there would be no illicit tapping. Owners applying for Special Constables, it was said, were often refused them by Chief Police Officers on the grounds that they had not co-operated in the past and estates in some areas were going out of production owing to lack of protection facilities. Much of the discussion in the Advisory Committee was concerned with detention; and here there was criticism of informers who laid information out of malice as well as of the organisation of detention camps which had turned them into nurseries for Communism.

Mutual recrimination, although muted on both sides, was the tenor of exchanges between government and the Chinese throughout 1949 and 1950. There were angry exchanges between Mr. Tan Siew Sin and the Attorney General in the Legislative Council on who should pay the costs of the Emergency: the British

Government or, with equal logic and fairness, said the Attorney-General, the Chinese community from whom the majority of the present terrorists came.[17] In August 1949 the Commissioner of Police expressed strong disappointment with the help received from the MCA in the matter of co-operation between government and the Chinese community; and shortly afterwards, in what might be considered an oblique attack on the Commissioner, Tan Cheng Lock and the MCA urged government to retain the services of two senior police officers after conflict on the alleged 'Palestinisation' of the police force. A prominent Singapore businessman, Mr. Aw Boon Haw, was for a while prohibited entry into the Federation largely, it was assumed, because of his criticism of government policy; and from local papers up to the national dailies such as the *Nanyang Siang Pau* in Singapore or the English language *Malay Tribune* there were constant reminders of the need to strengthen the legal political organisation of the people[18] and the argument that the present form of Federal citizenship was a bar to the growth of a Malayan national outlook.[19]

For articulate Chinese in general and for the leadership of the Malayan Chinese Association in particular it was a matter of explicit concern and, implicitly, it became the touchstone of Chinese association in the affairs of Malaya. Proposals were put forward for a Royal Commission to study the problems of Chinese citizenship as well as the immediate adoption of the Malayan Union citizenship provisions or something similar which would automatically make citizens of all those who had lived in the country for a certain length of time. The argument of the *jus soli* was the favourite of Mr. Tan Cheng Lock who always embodied it in his memoranda for visiting British Cabinet ministers and others. These memoranda, which were confidential, put the case for the removal of Chinese disabilities with a vehemence that was not found in the Chinese press. In the memorandum presented to Mr. James Griffiths, the Colonial Secretary, and Mr. John Strachey, Secretary of State for War, he described the position of non-Malays under the Federation constitution as that of political paupers—'dependent upon the charity of their British and Malay masters for whatever they want—even in the matter

---

[17] Proceedings of the Federal Legislative Council, May 19th 1949.
[18] *Nanyang Siang Pau*, September 12th 1949.
[19] *Tribune*, August 5th 1949. Mr. Tan Cheng Lock and his son, Mr. Tan Siew Sin, were the controlling interests in this paper. See also the MCA periodical *Malayan Mirror* for Mr. Tan Siew Sin's views.

of claiming their birthright'. The basis of this injustice, he argued, was that the whole population of Malaya with the exception of the aborigines, was of comparatively recent immigrant origin and yet, while the Malays were enfranchised as of right, about ninety per cent of the Chinese population were denied the right of citizenship by process of law and the acquisition of citizenship by application was extremely difficult if not practically impossible. Proposals had been made in April 1950 by the Communities Liaison Committee to make it easier for non-Malays to become Federal citizens but these, having been opposed by sections of the Malay community, had been amended by government to the point where they nullified the original.

In brief, Tan Cheng Lock argued that the anti-Chinese policy in Malaya which dated from the late twenties should be completely abandoned and reversed for the good of all concerned. It was a policy based on prejudice, fear and suspicion of the Chinese; one which they had done nothing to merit; which must naturally antagonise them; and would from the long-range point of view do infinite harm to the country as a whole and the cause of democracy. His point that whenever aliens were treated as citizens they became citizens whatever might be their religion or race may have been valid; his frustration and impatience may have been justified; but when he said that, generally speaking, the overseas Chinese made excellent, peace-loving and law-abiding citizens respecting the rights of the other inhabitants wherever they had settled in the Pacific he was arguing a general case which had little relevance to the immediate situation and when he added that for over 160 years the Chinese as a whole had proved themselves to be thoroughly and staunchly loyal to Malaya and to British rule, not only was it demonstrably untrue at the time but it also revealed the distance which divided him from, for instance, the bulk of Chinese peasant farmers who had no demonstrable feelings of allegiance whatever to the Malayan Government.

Judging from the opinion of many members of government there was little prospect of immediate help in ending the Emergency to be had from the Malayan Chinese Association and, in the matter of formal organisation, they seemed to be leaders without a party.[20] Tan Cheng Lock, in spite of his immense prestige with the Malayan Chinese which gave him great potential influence, was described as having an uncertain touch in

[20] For the ramifications of Chinese political/economic influence see Gullick, *op. cit.*, p. 112.

practical politics which diminished its effect on the course of events. In any case, it was argued that no political reform would make the slightest difference to the attitude of the Chinese businessman, miner, planter, labourer, peasant or squatter in Malaya[21] but if this was true then it seemed that there were only simple alternatives open to government: to bring less or more pressure to bear on the Chinese in order to secure their willing or unwilling co-operation.

The Chinese, with a few bloodthirsty exceptions, favoured less pressure. When a tribute was paid from the Legislative Council to the armed forces and the police, no Chinese member spoke in its support. The standard solution that was advanced, once the problem of at least partial Chinese commitment to the guerrillas had been admitted, was that of amnesty; and for some it was a long time before they discarded their view of the guerrilla as someone who was misguided or misunderstood.

The general principles that were raised and the terms of association that were set down were of the utmost importance for Malaya in the long run; but principles such as the Chinese squatter's right of self-defence raised more immediate problems than they solved.[22] Similarly, specific proposals such as more places for Chinese in the Malayan Civil Service, and the raising of Chinese armed forces, would founder unless the political objections could be removed.[23] Nevertheless, in limited areas and under the right conditions it was possible to raise, arm and rely upon Chinese defence forces. This was demonstrated by the Kinta Valley Home Guard: but it was a force raised by Chinese, of Chinese, and whose purpose was to defend Chinese property, namely Chinese tin mines in the tin-rich state of Perak. More to the point perhaps was that the force was comparatively well paid and, according to one description, it consisted of Chinese secret societies in uniform.

The Malays
If the insurrection had been supported by the Malay community

---

[21] *Straits Times*, May 15th 1950.
[22] A point that Mr. Tan made in his memoranda to Griffiths and Strachey and, later, to Lyttelton.
[23] The Chinese Secretariat papers include one from a prominent Methodist Chinese headmaster setting out the viewpoint of the Straits Chinese, many of whose points took in the Malayan Chinese as well. The Straits Chinese, he argued, were more indigenous than the Malays; but official policy had encouraged them to renew an almost lost allegiance to China.

to anything like the extent that it was by the Chinese it could not have been won by British forces. Considering the weight of this argument it is surprising that it was not used more often. Almost the entire rank and file of the police force were Malay. So were the Special Constables and, with the exception of Pahang in the first twelve or eighteen months of the Emergency, the states where there was a predominantly Malay population were unlikely, at least *en masse*, to give assistance to the guerrillas. In large part the Malays regarded this as the insurrection of alien Chinese and something to be resisted on racial as well as on political grounds. For some, the common political cause was more important than racial disparity but for the majority a successful insurrection was thought of in terms of Chinese domination, and the triumph of atheism rather than independence and Malay self-government.

Like the Chinese, the Malay community was divided politically : between the Sultans and the pattern of feudal loyalty on the one hand and the challenge of the more dynamic modern 'commoner' embodied in the mercurial Dato Onn, the Chief Minister of Johore and founder of UMNO, on the other. Onn, for the first time in the history of the Malay states, had challenged the authority of the Sultans on constitutional and political grounds; but in so doing the course of Malay nationalism had been diverted and, it was argued, the British stay in Malaya might be prolonged as a result of the dispute.

If, for various reasons, it was difficult for Malays to make common cause with Chinese at this point for the independence of Malaya it did not mean that they were satisfied with the way in which the Emergency was being conducted. On one issue—that of paying for the war—Malay and Chinese members of the Legislative Council spoke with almost the same voice and by the time the Emergency was into its second year Malay opinion was unsettled and increasingly critical. It was noted in *Majlis* (August 17th 1949) that according to the 1948 Annual Report the number of Malays in the Federation/Singapore fell short of Chinese by over 100,000. This, it said, was the result of placing the country under British 'protection'. The early reactions of Malay State governments to the problem of Chinese squatters has already been considered. By 1950 when government was seeking to regularise the tenure of squatters and tended to present the problem as a simple extension of administrative control the voice of Malay experience was heard as a reminder that squatters neither welcomed nor tolerated control however benevolent it might be.

> As I see it the root cause of the problem of the squatters is that this section of the people prefer to have their cake and eat it as well. They want to be the possessor of land, but will not accept or will not allow themselves to be bound by the usual commitments of the ownership of the land; they want to live their own lives, their way of thinking, their own customs. Why should they come under control when all these things are allowed them? They contribute nothing towards land taxes or anything that control requires.[24]

And yet, it seemed, everything was to be done for the resettled squatters.

> I note with interest paragraph 8 of the White Paper, which provides for such amenities as internal roads, drainage, access roads, health measures, security arrangements and assistance needed for moving and establishing themselves in new areas, including transport. I will comment on this point later on in my speech. Now, be it remembered that all these services are planned for people who have transgressed the law, broadly speaking. As I am a firm believer that prevention is better than cure, could not the government extend the same facilities, if not more, to the people who are with us? They have a better claim, surely? But unfortunately, most of them are left to their own devices. Must these people break the law before we recognise their existence? Must these people break the law in order to receive generous treatment from the government?[25]

To Malays, who were at least numerically bearing the brunt of resistance to the insurrection, it seemed that in every measure of social improvement Chinese were given priority over the Malays. Access roads, internal roads, health measures, transport, provision of tools and above all, padi cultivation in Malay areas were being passed over. In particular there was the need to provide land for demobilised Special Constables, both as a measure of improvement and as a recognition for their services; and now it seemed that even this was to give way to land for Chinese squatters. As Captain Hussein, Dato Onn's son, put it 'I agree that something must be done for the squatters. But I would like to warn

---

[24] Dato Haji Mohamed Eusoff, *Proceedings of the Federal Legislative Council* (Third Session), p. 117, April 19th 1950.
[25] *Ibid*, p. 118.

the government, with all sincerity, that when the programme is implemented, not to overdo it.'[26] In at least one analysis this was an insurrection in which foreign people were killing and murdering: a foreign army, not people of this country.[27] And even though the *Mentri Besar* of Perak was in favour of granting land titles in order that the squatters might put down roots this was clear warning to government that unwavering Malay support in what was now being presented as a case of Chinese rehabilitation should not be taken too much for granted. In the event, the need to recognise at least the equality of the Malay in economic advancement was one of the reasons which lay behind the creation of the Rural and Industrial Development Authority of which Dato Onn became chairman in the middle of 1950.[28]

Of all the criticisms that were made of government relations with both the Chinese and the Malay communities none was more telling than the fact that there was not a single Malayan to be found in the War Cabinet. The point was vented by Captain Hussein in April 1950. At the end of September it was announced that three Asians—Dato Onn, Mr. Leong Yew Koh, and Tungku Ya'acob—and one European 'unofficial'—chairman of the Pahang Planters Association—were to be members of the Federal War Council and that the broadening of War Executive Committee membership was also under consideration. In this, and the decision four months later, to introduce the 'member' system were to be found the most important political and constitutional advances towards self-government that Malaya had seen since the war.[29] They did not involve the whole Malay or Chinese communities in a constitutional political process nor did they lead to an obvious improvement in the conduct of Emergency operations but, taken together, they offered tangible evidence of an intention to proceed towards self-government even while a state of emergency continued. As far as the government was

---

[26] *Ibid*, p. 119. A year earlier (March 22nd 1949) Dato Onn had deplored government's policy of 'appeasement' of the Chinese and had warned that it would lead to trouble from the Malays.

[27] H.H. Tengku Abubakar.

[28] Another reason advanced by Gullick is that it was designed to prevent Dato Onn from going into demagogic opposition to the Malay 'establishment'. He also gives an incisive account of this phase of Dato Onn's career. Gullick, *op cit*., p. 114.

[29] For the most part it was Malayan members of the Executive Council who now became responsible for particular government departments: an approach both to independence and to cabinet responsibility.

concerned the introduction of the member system was one sector in an advance on three fronts. To Dato Onn it was evidence that not all European members of the Legislative Council treated Malayans as 'ignorant, uncivilised, and uneducated'. To an Indian member of the Legislative Council, Mr. Ramani, it meant that there was more to political advancement than 'looking at the tip of your nose'.[30]

[30] The Indian and possibly the European communities should properly be included in this account. In 1949 the Indian community was vexed by the question whether it was possible to have both Indian and Federal citizenship. Some very narrow distinctions were made by Mr. Ramani himself between nationality and citizenship and between allegiance and loyalty and it would seem that the visit of Mr. Nehru in 1950 helped to resolve the issue for many in favour of Malayan citizenship and allegiance. In the debate on the member system the opposition of European 'unofficials' to its introduction marked, in Gullick's opinion, the end of the pretensions of European commerce to influence major political issues. Ostensibly, at any rate, it was opposed on a matter of timing—and the opposition included Mr. H. S. Lee —but the suggestion that it should be deferred until the Emergency had ended was, at least, a conservative error. Conservative also in the sense of being accompanied by the remarks that it was 'forced on us by our Labour masters in the UK'.

SLACK WATER

At the beginning of June (June 4th) 1951, in a combined appreciation of the Emergency situation, Gurney and Briggs informed the Colonial Office that they had reached the turning point of the campaign. This was possibly—and almost prophetically—true; but it is equally true that, at this time, government lacked the impetus to carry its burden over the crest of the hill and begin the descent to victory. It was still an exhausting war and this was to be the year in which government lost its three most important officers; in which the battle reached its climax; and on the civil front, although in volume scarcely louder than a whisper, a year in which the first and only motion of no confidence in government's Emergency policy was tabled in the Legislative Council.

For no one was it a more exhausting war than for the police. Where, for British soldiers, Malaya represented a limited commitment of a year or two and where even long service Gurkhas went on leave, for the Malay policeman or Chinese detective there was only limited respite and no real escape from a campaign which was a mixture of armed rebellion and civil war. European police officers, like planters and miners, were at least able to get away at more or less fixed intervals but it was ironical that the most serious police crises developed while the Commissioner of Police was himself on leave. Gray did not return until the middle of July : according to some eye witnesses it was in this period that the Malayan police force began to fall apart. But whether or not one attributes this to Gray's absence and although the crises might have come in different form it is doubtful whether they could have been postponed indefinitely. This was certainly true of the conflict between Gray and the Director of Intelligence, Sir William Jenkin, on the question of whether there should be a separate and independent intelligence organisation although in this case there was the appearance of an unusual conjuring trick in which the acting Commissioner of Police was the unlikely assistant.

Sir William, a retired senior official of the Indian Police Service, was originally brought out to Malaya in May 1950 on agreement for one year to advise on the reorganisation of the CID. His purely advisory position did not prove very satisfactory and towards the end of 1950 proposals were formulated under which he undertook an executive role in the CID and was given the title of Director of Intelligence. In a confidential report, which was circulated to British Advisers after the event, it was said that under the proposals which were agreed with him he was given a special personal status for purposes of official precedence—but in taking charge of the CID he remained responsible to the Commissioner of Police. This, however, was the issue; and on May 18th, in Gray's absence, the acting Commissioner of Police informed all senior State police officers that the Director of Intelligence was personally responsible to the Federal Government alone and not to the Commissioner of Police for the discharge of his duties. The CID, renamed the Intelligence Bureau, would now cease to be responsible for criminal investigation and this function would pass to the uniformed branch.

It was almost a month before this considerable change was noted by civil government and matters did not come to a head until September 1st at a meeting between Gurney, Gray and Jenkin at King's House. An hour after the meeting ended Jenkin telephoned his resignation; and after the Colonial Office had delayed its reply in order that it should go to the Secretary of State for consideration they agreed that Gurney should not try to persuade him to withdraw his resignation. According to the Colonial Office at the various ministerial discussions great emphasis had been placed on the supreme necessity of securing intelligence of guerrilla movements; and that it had been agreed by all concerned that it was mainly through police channels that this intelligence should be obtained. The Secretary of State had apparently set great store by Jenkin's appointment and the improvement in the amount of information coming forward was a measure of Jenkin's achievement. Nevertheless, at the Malayan end, what was known as the 'Jenkin thesis' seems to have been unanimously opposed not only by Gurney and Gray but By Briggs, Keightley (C-in-C FARELF) and Morton, the Head of Security Intelligence Far East, while in Kuala Lumpur and in London it was agreed that Jenkin was, unfortunately, not far off a nervous breakdown.

This, as far as Gray was concerned, was a successful battle; but it was won in a campaign which, pragmatically at least, ended shortly afterwards in defeat. Curiously enough neither of the other two principal battles saw Gray obviously and openly defeated but on the first, the continuing controversy over the armouring of police vehicles, he suffered what was perhaps worse than a defeat: a series of unacknowledged retreats.

Standard guerrilla tactics and those taught by Force 136 to the war-time guerrillas are to stage an incident and then to ambush the relieving force. The physical characteristics of Malaya made this a particularly rewarding procedure for not only were all guerrilla attacks the occasion for police or Army action but the invariable movement by road of the security forces provided a constant as well as the largest quantitative target for guerrilla ambush. On uphill bends where a speed of 15 miles an hour would be hazardous an unarmoured truck or jeep was practically a sitting target; and where automatic weapons, Bren guns in particular[1], could be brought to bear from a concealed position overlooking the target the wonder was that there were not five or even ten times as many casualties. Properly staged ambushes would kill a dozen or more in a few minutes—sometimes an entire squad—and a large proportion of the total casualties suffered in road ambush was attributed to the driver being killed or severely wounded in the opening burst of fire. Some battalions and police jungle squads developed their ambush drill into a fine art but the chances of successful 'debussing' and counter-attack were obviously much higher if the vehicle could be driven out of the point of ambush. For convoys of vehicles, whether they were carrying troops or, later in the campaign, food supplies there were comparatively few problems—and few attacks where they were provided with an effective armoured car escort. But the small scale 'fire brigade' action or even the routine movement of patrols or police jungle squads by road was a considerable hazard and one certainly that it seemed possible to avert or reduce compared with patrols that were being ambushed on foot.

At the beginning of the Emergency the police had started from scratch and had ordered their first twenty-five armoured scout cars in September 1948. These did not arrive until February and March 1949: 25 Lynx armoured scout cars which were all that could be found of that type at that time in serviceable condition and with the necessary spares. There was at this time a manifest shortage of suitable armoured vehicles and a corresponding shortage of armour plate which might have provided a measure of protection. The insurmountable obstacles, however, to the provision of more armoured vehicles was the Commissioner of Police himself. It was widely believed that Gray's philosophy—possibly

[1] Some of which had by now been captured by the guerrillas.

born of his Palestine experiences—was that the police when ambushed in trucks should get out and fight. Gray's argument was that if armoured trucks came under fire those within would tend to stay put rather than leap out to engage the enemy. In a more sophisticated form, and in response to repeated requests from the Negri Sembilan State security committee in October 1949, the argument—which was essentially different—was advanced that the armouring of all police vehicles was neither feasible nor desirable.

(a) It is clearly not possible to armour or partly armour all police vehicles and any attempt to do so to a proportion of the fleet must lead to limiting police mobility.
(b) If any appreciable number of police vehicles are to be armoured or partly armoured a decrease in civilian morale must be expected.
(c) With the exception of two areas there is no police request for this measure.
(d) The more the police are protected or armoured the more likely are bandits to be driven to civilian targets. It is a police task to protect civilians as far as possible. So long as the police are taking the brunt of these attacks so long can we feel the task is being shouldered.

Not surprisingly the Negri Sembilan Committee rejected these arguments, particularly the mistaken one which opposed the armouring of all police vehicles. The Committee's argument had been for armoured driving cabs but even this measure was in the event rejected. The result was that for the first two years of the Emergency there was no protection whatever for police patrols and jungle squads travelling by road.[2] In Negri Sembilan, a month after Gray had said that the question of armour was not to be considered, an ambush was sprung on three police vehicles on the Jelebu Pass: the exact spot which the Security Committee had picked out as one of particular danger. The case against prevailing policy was put direct to Gurney by the British Adviser.

> It can be said without fear of contradiction that had the drivers of these vehicles been protected they would have been able to get through the ambush with relatively negligible loss. There

[2] It is asserted that in one State armour plating for a police vehicle that was provided by sympathetic and grateful planters was removed on instructions from police headquarters.

would undoubtedly have been some casualties but we should not have had seventeen dead and nine wounded nor would the vehicles have been totally lost and the number of Bren and Sten guns captured.

The almost inevitable result of this tragedy must be at least a temporary but dangerous loss of police morale and there will be no restoration of it until the police feel that they are being given a fair chance of fighting back. If soldiers can have this measure of protection without impairing their offensive spirit the civilian members of the State Security Committee cannot appreciate why similar assistance should not be given to the police. But as we have so far been unable to convince the Commissioner of Police, I am submitting the matter direct to Your Excellency.[3]

It was another four months before armoured personnel carriers —thirty-one altogether—were ordered for the police and by the time the last had arrived a fresh order was placed for another 60. This second order was placed in August 1950 and when the last of the deliveries was made in March 1951 it was again time for another order, this time for a further 59 armoured carriers. The process was repeated. Deliveries for this order were made in September and in October 1951 it was eventually decided to act on a large scale and orders were placed for a further 340. Even now this would scarcely have been sufficient for the 500-odd police jungle squads who were operating in 1950; considering that no armoured vehicles at all were ordered in 1949 the evidence suggests that police policy, which was virtually Gray's policy, on police armour was to provide too little and too late.

It would also seem that Gray's policy was changed for him. And that this was largely the result of outside pressure. At a meeting which was held with planters and miners on June 21st, 1951 Gurney agreed that armoured vehicles would be provided for police officers in dangerous areas and that he would take the matter up with the Commissioner of Police. Gurney appeared at first to think that vehicles available or on order would be sufficient and it took another two months before he raised the matter with Gray officially.[4] By this time there was a rising tide of dissatisfaction over the provision of armoured vehicles. Planters in Kedah and Negri Sembilan as well as in their central organisations, War Executive Committees and British Advisers were all

[3] December 13th 1949.
[4] On August 17th the Commissioner's secretary said that the matter had not yet been discussed between Gurney and Gray.

asking for more armour.[5] Letters to London were sent to the Prime Minister, the Leader of the Opposition, and the Colonial Secretary. Unfavourable reports appeared in the Press.[6] Questions were asked in Parliament. Gray now sought to distinguish the minor proposition; but still did not accept the major premise. Thus, he countered the arguments against providing armour especially for police lieutenants, the leaders of jungle squads, by saying that this would lead to a falling away in morale of the rank and file: and was in any case invidious. He showed that of a total of 36 European sergeants and subsequently police lieutenants who had been killed since the beginning of the Emergency only a half had been killed in road ambushes or the engagements that followed. Armour alone was not the only defence against ambush. The armouring of vehicles reduced their mobility. It definitely reduced the life of the vehicle, particularly the tyres. They were at some disadvantage in wet weather. More important in these particular cases was Gray's belief that the problem of transporting large numbers of police or troops about the country on their daily work had not yet been solved and that for the police there were many senior and experienced officers who took the view that it was difficult to be a good policeman if you shut yourself up in armour away from the public which was entirely without such protection. Gray did not refuse armour when it was thrust upon him. But in the last analysis it was impossible to move him from a singular and stoical concept of the Malayan policeman's lot which may be seen in this addition to a telegram to the Secretary of State which was drafted but not sent.

> There is a reluctance on the part of certain sections of the general public, as opposed to the Security forces, to accept casualties with the calm and fortitude which should be associated with the present emergency, particularly among the European population. Certain sections of the general public have caused unwarranted alarm in the past by their insistence on more and more armour and their outcries against the government and more particularly criticising the security forces. These vociferous demands by planters and unofficials are liable to lower the morale of the police force. Everything possible is being done to reduce casualties consistent with the policies set out above and the subject of armoured

[5] The British Adviser in Trengganu guessed that some 60 per cent of Security Force casualties were in vehicle ambushes.
[6] See for example *Sunday Express*, October 14th; *Scotsman*, October 26th 1950.

vehicles is constantly under examination but we cannot allow ourselves to be panicked and diverted from our main effort because casualties occur from ambushes on police vehicles.

The question was whether or not it was the duty of the police to expose themselves to danger for the public good; or to offer themselves as targets in a shooting gallery which would divert the guerrillas from other pursuits. If it was, then either the force would have to share the dedicated and selfless ideals of their Commissioner or else it must be prepared for inevitable demoralisation.

By the end of 1951, however (when Gray was on the point of leaving) the policy on armouring police vehicles had changed out of all recognition. The committee that had been set up to examine the question reported on December 16th on the optimum requirements: 900 troop-carriers, 200 escort armoured cars and 500 armoured individual transport vehicles.[7]

The question of armouring police vehicles, highly controversial though it was and still is the subject of bitter recriminations, may well have appeared to contribute to the demoralisation of the police force in 1950 and 1951. It was, however, only one of the increasingly severe strains upon the police force and its effective control: some of which must be mentioned before considering the issue which was finally joined in 1951 on whether the Commissioner of Police or the Director of Operations was the arbiter of Emergency policy. It has sometimes been argued that the particular problem which the Malayan police faced in 1951 was that of combining the para-military and the civil functions; and it was asserted, not least by the Colonial Office, that its mistake had been to neglect its civil role.

> Everything is being subordinated to anti-bandit operations . . . the operations room appears to be regarded as more important than the police station.
>
> In spite of a policy directive to this effect top priority has certainly *not* been given to the fulfilment of normal police functions in the populated areas.
>
> Recommendation of the Colonial Office, at the risk of a temporary slackening or even disruption of counter-guerrilla operations, was that this priority should be reasserted.[8]

This, while it may have been true in its parts, was certainly not the sum of the situation. Indeed, if criticism were implied, then it

---

[7] Less if the GMC scout car could fulfil both the second and third roles.
[8] Colonial Office to Officer Administering Government, December 22nd 1951.

should not be of the Commissioner of Police, who was more concerned than anyone at the growing importance of the paramilitary function, and who was anxious to reassert the importance of normal policing. Four tasks which the police had assumed were now occupying the greater part of the police effort. These were resettlement; the provision of jungle companies; the supervision of the special constabulary; and the manning and expansion of the country's main intelligence system. Gray himself identified the problems somewhat differently. At a conference with the Director of Operations and the Perak State War Executive Committee on August 28th, Gray explained why he was worried about the present state of the force. The reasons he gave were first that it was bottom heavy and lacked leaders. Second, that its efficiency was seriously impaired. Third, that morale was lower than it should be. Fourth, that a large part of the force was on static duties and thereby prevented from taking the offensive. Fifth, that static posts were now being overrun and that gains and losses of arms were approximately equal. In formal exchanges with Gurney, Gray always maintained that resettlement was not being held up through a shortage of adequately manned police posts. Gurney believed that it was; and on the evidence of this Perak conference alone there are a number of pointers that support Gurney's suspicions. For example, Gray agreed that resettlement schemes that were essential or had been planned in detail could continue: but that every effort had to be made to keep special constable requirements to a minimum. Special constables, he maintained, could not take over from the regular police. They were short of equipment and ammunition; their morale was lowered by inadequate training; and to top it off, the best special constables were going into the police force anyway. One ominous decision of this conference was that 'So far as possible existing police posts on individual mines/estates should not be closed down'. Another was that 'Completed regrouping schemes on mines/estates should be allowed to remain unless the police had very good reason for deciding that the approval they had formerly given should be withdrawn'. And third, 'Resettlement in essential areas must go on, but, where not considered immediately essential, it should be deferred until circumstances demanded it'. Eighteen months earlier the British Adviser in Pahang had reported 'We are limited by insufficient police in Pahang'; but more important in 1951 was the question of who was to decide on the provision of police posts for resettlement areas.

On this there was a good deal of tension between the Commissioner of Police and various State War Executive Committees. Sometimes States went ahead and built their police posts first and notified the police afterwards. Police headquarters countered by insisting on Federal control even in the matter of local purchases. In September 1951, all State and Settlement War Executive Committees were notified that in future as soon as it had been decided to proceed with a resettlement project the Chief Police Officer must in every case submit the proposal to the Commissioner of Police indicating the approximate date on which the police post would be required, the strength of personnel to man it, and whether or not the building of the post would retard other police building plans in the State or Settlement concerned. This meant, in effect, that the Commissioner of Police had the last word on all new State resettlement projects. Not surprisingly, there was strong reaction from the States themselves. For example, from the Resident Commissioner in Malacca who complained of 'vexatious delays',

> SWEC considers that it is in a better position to judge local needs within its own establishment than the Commissioner of Police.
>
> In the original concept of SWECs, decentralisation was the policy and it was the only practical answer to Settlement and State Emergency problems. That concept now appears to have been forgotten and ignored and we are gradually reverting to centralisation and its attendant disadvantages. I quote as an instance the farming out of Emergency financial control to departments which are completely out of touch with local Emergency policies.
>
> SWEC views with misgiving this divergence from previous policy which on the whole has worked well and accordingly requests a modification of the policy outlined in your letter.

The issues in police affairs were seldom clear-cut. Here, for example, there were really two questions. That of decentralisation was obvious, but there was also the question of whether States could, in effect, determine the quality of the means at their disposal. Not the least of Gray's problems was that of dilution: continuous pressure to make up the numbers of police with comparatively untrained special constables and also to use special constables as if they were the equivalent of regular policemen. But it is also clear from numerous reports that in 1951 the special constabulary was breaking down in various parts of Malaya. A report from the CPO Perak in March said that they were no longer an effective force in that State. Their discipline was steadily breaking down, desertions were increasingly frequent and in one week contingent orders contained 108 disciplinary cases, many of them prison sentences.

> The men are tired, disillusioned, consider they are underpaid and under-privileged. They feel acutely their inadequate issue of uniform and the inferior status accorded them in public esteem. All are anxious to get out and return to civil life. Under the terms of their employment this is at present denied them. As a result they seek to earn a prison sentence for misconduct (generally desertion, assault or other misbehaviour) as the sole means left to them of obtaining their release.
>
> In Perak special constables are used on estates, mines, vulnerable points in fixed installations as static guards. They are also placed in jungle squads alongside regular personnel, although their conditions of service and privileges are not the same. For instance, special constables do not receive non-operational rations; regulars do. There have been an increasing number of disquieting incidents where jungle squads and special constable posts have failed to stand up against enemy action, either permitting the enemy to pass their posts unmolested or, if attacked, tamely surrendering their arms and ammunition. In addition there have been cases of refusal of duty, incidents of the shooting of innocent people and of hysteria leading to panic firing for little or no cause. The lack of good leaders thrown up from the special constables is most marked, as indeed it is in the regular police. At present I cannot vouch for the reliability of the special constabulary in this contingent as an effective force at government's disposal in the present anti-guerrilla campaign.

Comparing them to German 'Landswehr' troops of World War I special constables were described as second or third line troops engaged in providing local defence: something that was clearly not a function of the police at all although, provided with police powers, these had frequently been abused. Another problem was that they had largely become the private armies of big estate and mine managements who, at the beginning of the Emergency, had raised from among their own labour forces a number of guards whom they incorporated in the special constabulary as soon as government assumed responsibility for their cost of upkeep.

These big managements have consistently fought the police for the control of the special constables posted on their properties; in Perak they have gone so far as to declare that it is a point of honour with them to look after the interests of their own men, retain them on their property, pay them extra emoluments in cash and kind, and provide them with married quarters (frequently at government's expense) while their wives and families are employed about the property. This viewpoint has embroiled OSPCs, OCPDs and SOSCs in continual contention with property managers and has been one of the most frustrating and heavy burdens which police officers have had to bear.

The proper administration, control and training of the special constabulary has now got beyond the powers of the regular police at all levels, especially at circle and district. Far too many organisational tasks have been thrust on these officers which seriously interfere with the performance of their proper duties. The time has now come when the special constabulary should be wholly detached from the police to form a separate organisation, distinctively uniformed, with its own command, administrative and training staff in adequate numbers and holding ranks commensurate with the size of the force on the same basis as in the armed services. The status of the force should be redefined in the light of its military function and all police powers withdrawn from its members.

Once relieved of the incubus of this unwieldy mass of pseudo-police, the regular police force could concentrate first on re-establishing its own discipline and training, and then on its essential tasks of combating crime and civil disorder, gathering intelligence and rounding up of *Min Yuen*, while the military take full responsibility for the conduct of the military campaign against the Communist armed forces, and the new force carries out second line guard duties. Static defence (with the exception of police stations) should be recognised for what it is—a military and not a police commitment.

From Negri Sembilan there came another report of low morale among special constables due to their poor conditions and it was considered fortunate that they did not have to resist sustained attack. A similar account was given from Pahang and here again it seemed to be a question not so much of the quality of the special constables but the degree of supervision and interest which was shown by estate managers. On the other hand, Malay Kampong Guards were described as a very real weapon and they had been responsible for eliminating a number of guerrillas as well as providing valuable information leading to the capture and elimination of others.

Low morale amongst special constables was a problem in itself but it was also a factor that contributed to declining morale amongst the regular police.[9] From Trengganu for example it was reported in September that the rank and file were tiring under the continual strain of the Emergency and that little or no effort was being put into Emergency work unless they were supervised by European or energetic Malay officers. The importance of leadership had been felt particularly in the police jungle squads, of which there had been some five hundred operating in 1950, some of them under the command of police lieutenants—many of them lately Palestine police sergeants—but the majority under the command of Malay police corporals. These jungle squads had never been properly organised on a military basis and were often no more than an *ad hoc* collection of men temporarily available from static duties who had been given no specialist training and who had learned mainly by bitter experience. It was this factor which made many of them into first class guerrilla patrols even though they lacked the most elementary equipment and often suffered their highest casualties in road ambushes before they had a chance of going into action. Their reorganisation into Federal jungle companies in 1951 may have been overdue but for some senior police officers the idea of forming such companies from police resources was a most unwise one.

Basically the problem was one of insufficient resources. The greatest difficulty that Chief Police Officers had to face was a serious lack of experienced supervision and of facilities for training the vast numbers of men under their command. Thus the CPO Negri Sembilan when called upon to provide 45 company commanders, all of whom should be able to speak fluent Malay and should have had previous military experience (in June 1951) was doubtful whether they could be found—far less the 45 officers who would be second in command. Many jungle squads were unpopular with the rank and file of the police; and although some States had achieved remarkable results there were complaints from the men that jungle squads were military formations: and if they had wanted to become soldiers they would have joined the army. Many of the jungle squads in fact contained large numbers of special constables and from the beginning of 1951 onwards they also contained small numbers of Malayan national servicemen who were drafted into them.

[9] When the two were grouped together.

In the event also it was decided to cut the raising of new jungle companies from 45 to 18, each of about 180 men, but, in spite of this, pressure on the police to expand continued and by August Gray and Briggs were in open disagreement. On August 10th, Gray set out his case in a letter to Briggs and to Gurney. The occasion was the Director of Operations' Directive No. 15 and the sentence 'Resettlement must continue'. Gray had asked that this sentence should be removed and on this, as on the policy of further police dilution, this time of special constables themselves, he had failed to reach agreement with Briggs. According to Gray the state of police efficiency was far from satisfactory and still decreasing.

> The reason for this state of affairs is clearly the vast expansion which has at all times outstripped the provision of leaders in each grade and has completely overwhelmed police training.
> Despite the recent decision to limit the number of jungle companies to be raised to eighteen I am alarmed at the further expansion in deployment and burden still being added in connection with resettlement and similar tasks.
> After long discussion, a reasonably full explanation of police difficulties and considerable pruning of civil plans, the new commitment in Perak alone is 450 men in 21 new police posts to be found within the next three months. These figures take no account of the increase required in certain regular police establishments in Perak due to resettled populations, or the need for additional police patrols to link up and visit new stations and posts.
> In Selangor contingent the proportion of regular police of all ranks serving in regular police establishments is only 56 per cent of the total personnel in these establishments. Of the 56 per cent more than half of them are men who only joined the force since the outbreak of the Emergency in 1948. They are very inexperienced.
> At no time during the past three years has the number of officers, inspectors and police lieutenants asked for by the Commissioner been granted : at no time has the reduced and authorised number been available. Despite this, commitments have been continually increased. The result is that the men now lack adequate leadership, supervision and training to an extent that is, in my view, dangerous.[10]

---

[10] The ratio of all police officers to rank and file was 1 : 40 but of Gazetted officers to men only 1 : 123.

Policing of the larger towns was now at such a low ebb that Gray doubted whether any outbreak of lawlessness, whether Communist inspired or not, could be quickly and effectively dealt with. Normal civil police duties were not in fact being properly undertaken although the total number of full-time and paid personnel of all types and grades was now over 62,000.

> With this position to face, any further police expansion is in my view unrealistic and indeed dangerous. A halt must be called even if it means stopping further resettlement. In considering these views, I hope that the enormous amount of work thrust upon the police in connection with auxiliary police, kampong guards, resettlement and regrouping schemes, food control and similar measures will not be overlooked.
>
> I do not wish to give the impression that the Force is done, but I do assert that it is heavily overstrained, and I cannot agree to further expansion and deployment into conditions of living and accommodation which in so many cases are nothing short of appalling. Morale and efficiency are difficult to keep up under such conditions and without better control and supervision than I can achieve with Force resources, disaster in many areas may ensue. Serious losses of arms during the past three months are a clear indication of the state of affairs and caused me much concern. The majority of these cases are directly attributable to lack of training and low morale.
>
> I therefore strongly urge that no further police expansion takes place for a period of at least six months and that this policy be made known to War Council SWECs and other appropriate authorities. The only exceptions to which I feel I must agree with reluctance are the minimum number of resettlement projects which have already reached a 'physical movement' stage, and cannot therefore reasonably be dropped without confusion. I am unable to agree that the moving of squatters or others into existing towns and villages is a measure which requires no further police expansion. Existing police stations are, in the great majority, of course, not able to undertake additional work.

The principal challenge to current and future government policy which this memorandum contained was the issue of resettlement. In the event that 'a change of police command is now wanted' Gray had said that he would raise no objections or difficulties; but when the confrontation took place between Gray, Briggs and Gurney, the Commissioner of Police was maintained while his policy was rejected.

His Excellency decided, after hearing the arguments put forward by the Commissioner of Police, that it was essential that the resettlement programme should go forward as planned. In coming to this decision, he emphasised that it was in the interests of the police themselves that the rural population should be brought under control; until they were it was impossible for an area to be properly policed. The additional commitments in new police posts and in personnel were not on present estimates serious in relation to existing police responsibilities.

On this issue, then, the critical decision was taken. But a second issue between Gray and Briggs was now building up. In his memorandum of August 10th Gray had referred to low morale in the Force: much of which stemmed from the European officers themselves who were confused by the large number of directives and orders, many of which had been amended or changed shortly after issue. Many, including responsible senior officers, he said, had told him that directives were not now taken seriously 'as they were found to be amended in a few days'. The evidence to support this was impressive but what was more important was how matters were to be resolved when the Commissioner of Police and the Director of Operations did not see eye to eye. 'Time and again,' said Gray, 'plans and expansions with which I have felt unable to agree have been forced upon me at the expense of police efficiency. I have done my best to implement these instructions, but now feel that the situation is getting out of hand and that breaking point will shortly be reached.' The initiative—if relations between the two men had not been cordial one might almost have said the offensive—was taken by Briggs who set out his views on police organisation and training in a memorandum dated October 22nd. It was justified by the interest which the Director of Operations had to take in these matters because of their vital influence on police efficiency, morale and operation. Training, said Briggs, had not kept up with the necessary expansion and in some ways organisation needed adjustment to cope with changed conditions. In future, priority had to be given to training without undue interference in operational efficiency.

Briggs' basic plan for reorganisation was to divide the police force into two categories: policemen and guards. Under the first heading he placed all men used in towns, villages, resettlement areas and regrouped smallholder and absentee landlord estate labour. It also included jungle companies and squads. For these a higher standard of training was necessary. Special constables on estates and mines however were purely guards and would be so for many months to come until they got much more training. Worse than that—they were purely static guards and although one would wish to see them more mobile there was at present little hope of that. These men did not need police training, but required intimate leadership, guard training, discipline and morale raising. Their training was of a military nature and was one which the Army could and would be prepared to undertake. As far as SCs who were actually operating with the regular police were concerned Briggs thought they should be trained and treated as regular police until they could be replaced. For the rest, special constables on estates and mines—'this heavy incubus on the police force as a whole'—should be State rather than Federal police or even made into a separate organisation altogether.

At Briggs' request Gray had circulated copies of this memorandum to all Chief Police Officers and a number of senior Staff Officers. The majority were not in favour although in one State it appeared that the CPO and senior State Officers approved the division unanimously. Gray himself referred to Briggs' proposals as a complete reversal of police policy which had been agreed by government; that it would be imprudent to attempt to distinguish between policemen and guards; and that 'the advantages which would accrue from your recommendations are not apparent to me'.

Many months later in a report on police affairs prepared for General Templer it was said that the framework of police organisation concentrated authority upon the Commissioner himself to an extent beyond his capacity and was not sufficiently adequate in senior ranks to ensure expeditious and efficient staff work. What had in fact happened was that the expansion of Headquarters had been outstripped by the increase in the numerical strength of the Force to a point at which it was no longer capable of meeting its heavy responsibilities. Furthermore, according to the report, and of equally serious consequence, preoccupation with a great weight of day-to-day administrative problems had resulted in a gap between Headquarters and Chief Police Officers.

Before accepting this opinion it is perhaps worth remembering the size of the Malayan police at this time. On January 1st 1950 the authorised regular establishment of the Malayan police was 16,600 officers and men. But when the number of special constables is added, almost 30,000 for whom the Malayan police were responsible, then the total exceeded that of the rest of the

Colonial Police Service put together.[11] In administration alone it is hardly surprising that there were bottle-necks: and this even assuming that the role of the police was clearly defined. When it was not, and when it was called upon to carry an enormous load of emergency operations as well as provide the infrastructure of counter-guerrilla activities, its short-comings are perhaps more understandable. Gray himself, at least on the evidence of a letter to the Chief of the Imperial General Staff, Sir William Slim, in November 1949 seems to have been not so much an empire builder as deeply concerned that counter-subversion, even in its armed form, was a matter for the police rather than the army.

In the early years of the Emergency, Gray had been the *de facto* Director of Operations. After Briggs' arrival, with the respective powers of the Director of Operations and the Commissioner of Police undefined, effective operation depended upon their agreement. By the end of 1951 the Director of Operations and the High Commissioner were commited to a policy which the Commissioner of Police said was impossible; and there was too much evidence of weakness in the police at all levels, as well as a disparity between commitments and resources, for it to have been able to execute emergency policy in its entirety. It did not perhaps matter so much that Police Lieutenants should kill one another or themselves in affrays and that mixture of boredom and bravado known as Russian roulette; that unsupervised special constables should turn check-points into toll gates; nor that occasional estate managers should abuse their special constables for so long without retribution. What was more important was that the making and execution of police policy at the centre should offer some remedy for demoralisation rather than contribute to it. When promotion to corporal was a matter that was still dealt with by Federal Police Headquarters rather than States it would seem that little had been done; and in 1952 Gray's successor found the back-log of promotion recommendations going back to August 1950.

Police affairs were important in themselves. Demoralisation meant that they were less effective both as a fighting force and in their normal role. But as far as the Emergency was concerned it was the police who were principally concerned with creating the infra-structure of the Briggs Plan; and upon them depended the ultimate success or failure of counter-guerrilla operations. Briggs realised that before the Army stood much chance of

---

[11] 46,587 compared with 46,216. Gray had given his figures in August as being 62,000 police of all categories.

making contact in significant numbers with the guerrillas their major source of supply, the Chinese peasant farmers, would have to be denied them. To do this it was not sufficient to issue directives or even to round up or transport the inhabitants of a given area, put them down in a new 'village', surround them with a single strand fence of barbed wire and call the finished job 'resettlement'. To seal off a community of a thousand or more Chinese, many of whom might be expected to have husbands, sons or brothers with the guerrillas ultimately involved their subjection to totalitarian processes of observation, searching and control if not the creation of a totalitarian state. To achieve it would mean villages of optimum size—those whose perimeters could be effectively patrolled—the building of chain link or double barbed wire fences, the trimming of vegetation or standing crops to a standard height, the replacement of paraffin pressure lamps with floodlights driven by electric generators, constant night patrolling of various kinds and, perhaps most onerous and distasteful of all, enough policemen and women to search most of the adult population every morning. This, of course, lays stress on the coercive aspect and does not take into account the necessity and the means to mount and sustain what was ultimately a series of some five or six hundred campaigns to convert a natural allegiance to the People Inside into a positive acceptance of and co-operation with government: or, at least, the withdrawal of voluntary support from the guerrillas.

In 1950, 1951 and even much later very little resettlement, or regrouping of estate labour, could be regarded as effective. To take only one criterion: unless and until there was effective food control then there were as many outlets from a resettlement area as there were holes in a sieve. This was not to say that the guerrillas were not put to an inconvenience: simply, that they had to walk further to get their supplies. The Chief Police Officer Selangor reported to the Commissioner of Police in September 1951,

> Thousands of Chinese of all walks of life are now living behind barbed wire and are expected to be policed by a handful of untrained men who are tied down by gate and perimeter patrol duties. Proper police work is well nigh impossible and duties in resettlement areas result in corruption, boredom and ill discipline. In addition there are vast problems concerning administration, health, education.[12]

---

[12] In one resettlement area thirty out of sixty-three police were committed every twelve hours to gate duty.

From Malacca the CPO reported that information, other than from paid agents, was practically nil; but that in dealing with the resettled Chinese ex-squatter population—'our main target' —morale *could* be considerably improved if more 'after care' action was taken by the local government.

In one of his earlier directives (No. 13, February 1951) Briggs had laid down quite elaborate plans for what he called the administration of Chinese settlements. These included the organisation of village schools, the provision of medical aid, and all the paraphernalia of social services that would provide a sort of instant welfare: community centres, community listening wireless sets, visits by mobile cinema vans, co-operative shops and Boy Scouts. Federation and State flags were to be provided for each settlement. The concept, however, was frankly custodial and although realistic, in that immediate co-operation with government could hardly have been expected, it was not until some measure of co-operation could be achieved that the resettlement areas could be counted a success. In the meantime, the pragmatic if conservative index of a village's affiliation could be seen in whether its Home Guard was armed or not. Briggs' February Directive laid down that as soon as the people of the settlement were ready for it a Home Guard was to be formed, not only to assist the police in the security of the settlement but also to deny food and contacts to active Communists and to ensure that no infiltration of Communist influence took place. In practice these comprehensive objectives were modified in a later Directive (No. 17, October 1951) and although by this time village Home Guards were to be formed immediately and were allocated to particular sections of a village, in practice also they were often unarmed. Stage I Home Guards simply watched the wire surrounding their sectors and reported any attempt at entry or wire cutting. In its critical stage, Stage 2, they reported to the police station for duty with police patrols and were armed with shotguns for the duration of the patrol only. Stage 3, when there must have been almost full confidence or, as the Directive put it, 'when these men are better known', selected Home Guards were allowed to take the shotguns to their houses so as to be more readily available for immediate action.

By the beginning of 1952 the physical resettlement of largely Chinese squatter families was four-fifths completed: some 400,000 people in some 400 new villages. It was soon to be admitted that speed had been achieved only at the sacrifice of other desirable features—'particularly the careful selection of sites for resettlement in the light of the means of livelihood of the settlers, the best use of available land, adequate access roads'—and it required a great exercise of imagination to assert that the people in the villages had now been brought under effective government control.[13] Everywhere there was a shortage of good European resettlement officers; and in too many instances the Chinese Assistant Resettlement Officers were reckoned to be of inadequate quality. What effective control there was of the resettlement areas therefore depended in many cases upon their first—and only—line of defence: namely, the police. And it was increasingly upon the battlefield of the resettlement areas and their approaches that the guerrillas chose to fight as their military efforts reached a crescendo in the second half of 1951.

This was to be the climax of the battle, as guerrilla attacks intensified both in incidence and strength. Reports from Perak in August 1951 showed that incidents had developed from terrorism committed by individuals and small gangs to large-scale attacks close to the settled areas in which twenty to thirty guerrillas took part, while intelligence reports of thirty to fifty were becoming common. For the guerrillas it would seem that necessity had first put a finer edge upon their attacks and then produced a measure of cumulative success. In Perak the deduction was that many of the attacks were being launched in order to maintain food supplies for large, deep jungle bases as the guerrillas were being hard hit by government food restrictions. It was also—and correctly—assumed that the guerrillas faced grave problems of arms and ammunition supply, and there was an interesting although probably fortuitous coincidence of attacks on special constable posts in South Perak and in Johore on a particular day in August 1951. In Perak there were in fact two well led groups whose primary object was the acquisition of arms and ammunition from the security forces; and where there was a shortage of automatic weapons guerrillas did not hesitate to ambush army patrols close to their bases in the hope of capturing them.[14]

The fact that the guerrillas were now prepared to bring the battle closer to the security forces and the inhabited areas can be seen as a mark of confidence or necessity; but it could also be taken as the first sign of success for the Briggs plan. First, there is a good deal of evidence to show that guerrillas recognised the challenge of resettlement and did their best to maintain their

---

[13] *Resettlement and the Development of New Villages in the Federation of Malaya 1952*, Paper No. 33, Federal Legislative Council.
[14] Police patrols tended to have fewer automatic weapons.

civilian contact in new and less favourable situations. Where in the past it was achieved voluntarily or with the threat of violence, violence had now to be increasingly overt and directed either against security forces or those who were reluctant to co-operate. This brought increasing risks and not only in the hazards of battle. In the second place the massing and movement of large bodies of men was thought unlikely to continue undetected either by 'friends or informers'. In one area of Perak it was reported that operational intelligence was already coming in at a greater rate than security forces could cope with; and where informed intelligence appreciations suggest that this was probably not true for the country as a whole nevertheless for the guerrilla it meant that the tide was going out; that he could no longer move among the people 'as the fish moves through the water'; and that when he was now forced to go close inshore he not only gave away his position but ran the risk of being caught in the shallows.

In conventional warfare an equally conventional expression is that enemy attacks are repulsed with heavy losses. Although guerrilla attacks were seldom spectacular enough to merit this description in particular cases, nevertheless the evidence for the year 1951 as a whole suggests that this, in effect, is what had happened. The number of major and minor incidents that was recorded did not show an entirely disproportionate increase compared to the last six months or so of 1950 but in casualties inflicted upon security forces, losses sustained by the guerrillas and, above all, in the number of contacts made, 1951 can be seen as the year in which the battle reached its peak. In 1950 there were less than 400 killed in the security forces; in 1951 more than 500. In 1950 650 guerrillas were killed; in 1951 almost 1,100. Most important, as far as the outcome of the battle was concerned, was the steady rise of contacts between guerrillas and security forces as the insurgent attack was stepped up to meet the challenge of the Briggs plan. Compared with the first half of 1950 the second half and the whole of 1951 saw two and three times as many contacts per month: an increase in tempo which was to bring heavy casualties on both sides. In April, August and October 1951 the security forces suffered their heaviest losses. In 1949 and 1950, with the exception of a month at the beginning, the middle and the end, the security forces averaged less than one killed per day. In these three particular months in 1951 the figure was doubled and for the first time the total figures for the year exceeded those for civilian casualties. For every soldier, policeman or special constable who was killed, however, there were two dead guerrillas—1,078 altogether—and another three hundred who had been captured or surrendered.

Impressive as these may be as scoreboard totals at the end of the year, the comparatively heavy casualties that were sustained day by day in what at best appeared to be a war of attrition was marked by receding public confidence. There was at this time the appearance of a never-ending conflict; and with no scent of victory in the wind certain basic premises of government policy were now called in question.

In a public form these doubts were expressed in the Legislative Council on September 20 1951, when a Malay member moved, 'That this Council views with grave concern the slow progress being made to end the Emergency and is of the opinion that the constant changes in directional control of operations can only lead to a further stalemate of events.' Inche Abdul Aziz, who moved the motion, argued that in three and a half years of war overall policies had been changed on a number of important occasions.

> Briefly, we have, under Major General Sir Charles Boucher driven the bandits deep into the jungle, and under Lieutenant General Sir Harold Briggs, we have tried with all our might to drive them out again. I realise, sir, that every commanding general is entitled to his own planning, and who are we to criticise him for his views? But, looking at the matter from the viewpoint of the layman, I am inclined to believe that all the chopping and changing of policy is as confusing to the public as it is to the bandit.

Inche Aziz complained first that the Legislative Council was as much to blame as anyone if the people of Malaya had been lulled into a false sense of complacency regarding the war. The country was at war, and apart from doubts about bewildering changes of strategy it looked as if it was a war that was conducted on a series of short-term contracts. Generals were employed, like civil servants, to fight a war for eighteen months.

> We cannot afford to employ generals for eighteen-month periods. We cannot accept plans which might be changed, altered or scrapped with each succeeding director of operations.

The seconder of the motion, Inche Nasaruddin, was even more critical. The people of the country, he said, were as near to chaos as ever a people could be. The two dangers that he saw were, first, that the slow progress in quelling the insurrection was a factor which might drag the country to financial ruin; and second, his fear that a bloodier war was in the making.

> Far from producing the opposite effect, the number of troops pouring into this country has been creating a feeling of suspicion on the part of the masses. They think—and are probably justified in thinking—that the signal for a bloodthirsty war is what they are seeing.

Since the Emergency began, top ranking officials had predicted that it would be over by 1949. What was wanted now was an assurance in the very near future from those who were directing the government campaign that the end was in sight.

These were the only two speakers who dealt in general criticism of government policy and when the motion was put to the vote it was supported by only four members, all of them Malays. In itself therefore, with 57 votes cast in opposition, the result might be taken as a vote of confidence—which was how the government chose to regard it—but it was hardly a matter of self-congratulation. In the first place it was—or should have been—disquieting to be reminded how much depended upon European planters whose morale could not altogether and indefinitely be taken for granted; not only among the 20 per cent or so who were over 50 but also in the middle age group, between 35 and 50, who in any case were difficult to replace but who were now having doubts about their future and security. Another reminder, this time on what 'public co-operation' meant to the ordinary man was given by Dato Haji Mohammed Yussof, one of the half dozen Malayan members who did not vote on the motion. There were those, he said, who usually blamed the public for not co-operating but when a headman went to the security forces it often took them a long time to arrive and naturally the guerrillas would not still be waiting.

> When the forces get there and find nothing, the Ketua (headman) or informer, instead of getting thanked, received curses, and, on top of that, is called names for taking the Security Forces away from the security and comfort of the police station. And in cases where information was given only on strong suspicion which may prove on investigation to be wrong, again the informer gets it on the neck. Well, if that is the sort of encouragement the public receives, co-operation cannot be expected.
>
> So, if we want the public to help, we should not only give them

a little more consideration for the time spent and for the public spiritedness in coming forward, but we must also remember the danger. If you live in a suburban place and you go to a police station, you are a marked man, and in a small place when you ask for the office of the CID, it became public news. The information is passed on from hand to hand at the risk of the informant. With this kind of treatment is it surprising that people feel a little diffident and reluctant to help even in doing what is considered a public duty?

As far as the government was concerned, however, public co-operation was all they asked for—or had to offer. 'Rallying round' was the expression used; and while it was nothing less than the truth to say that it was a matter of obtaining information so that the police could lay their hands on those who were breaking the law of the country—and it was asserted that the Emergency was primarily a police task—it was dispiriting to hear the Secretary of Defence argue that it was also, simply, a question of everyone rallying round and supporting measures which the government had taken to meet the present situation. Coupled with this were various remonstrances against the Chinese: so much so that what began as a motion of censure on the government seemed to have been turned into a motion of censure on the Chinese. The acting Chief Secretary, for example, hoped that there would be a more ready response than there had been up till then from Chinese to the call for police volunteers; and Gurney himself questioned the effectiveness of Chinese leadership.

> The question that Honourable Members should ask themselves in my opinion is whether enough is being done among that section of the Chinese population who are being victimised by this Communist attack to enable them to make up their minds to resist it. Is there adequate local leadership of the kind that they understand, to which they can look with confidence as providing the escape from their dilemma? In this vital field there are limits to what the government can do. It is a matter of morale, of confidence, of inspiration, in which these people must be provided with their own leadership every bit as active and forceful as that of the Communists.

Gurney's relations with the Chinese community had now reached their lowest point. A few days earlier, in a letter of considerable bitterness, he had written to the Colonial Office of more particular misgivings. As far as malicious reporting was concerned it related to one particular Chinese and his friends in Singapore; but, in general, Gurney said it was the Chinese who were doing their best to suborn all ranks of the police force 'and we know that many of our Chinese detectives receive more pay from other sources than they do from government and are completely unreliable'. It was this exasperating job of dealing with a lot of corrupt police and facing death from terrorist hands at the same time that subjected police officers to a very severe test: a test in which some of them had been demonstrably found wanting. The occasion for this particular letter was a draft reply to questions that were going to be put in the Legislative Council by Mr. Tan Siew Sin. Mr. Tan was to ask the Secretary of Defence what steps were being taken to allay public anxiety regarding recent allegations that persons held in police custody were subjected to physical violence; and, in view of this anxiety, to press the government to appoint a commission of inquiry. Gurney had privately informed the Colonial Office that he had been assured by his most senior officers—the Attorney General, the Commissioner of Police and the Director of Intelligence—that everything possible was being done to prevent the sort of occurrence of which Tan Siew Sin complained; but on both sides there was cause for criticism and in its public form much of the criticism of government arose from the allegations of police intimidation of witnesses arising from the sensational Watts-Carter case.

From time to time Special Branch reports mentioned areas of unnatural calm on certain estates and the inference was that protection or immunity was being bought from the guerrillas. On July 17th the trial opened in the Kuala Lumpur High Court of Jeffrey Watts-Carter, the former manager of a Perak estate, who appeared on ten charges under the Emergency Regulations of consorting with bandits, three of which carried the death penalty or penal servitude for life. He was not tried in Perak because of the high state of tension and prejudice over the case; and also, it was thought, because it was easier for the police to prepare their case in Kuala Lumpur. Conditions on the Watts-Carter estate were certainly remarkable. He himself drove around in an unarmoured car, police patrols on the estate were discontinued, and tappers were told that they had nothing to fear: which, in fact, proved to be the case. In his defence Watts-Carter claimed that he was never attacked because he treated his workers well. For the prosecution, tappers and former guerrillas gave evidence of a compact between him and local guerrillas.

In the event Watts-Carter was acquitted and cleared. What made the case particularly disturbing, however, was the weight of evidence that was brought to bear upon the police themselves. Brilliantly defended by Mr. David Marshall, a future Prime Minister of Singapore, most of the evidence of the prosecution was shown to have been rehearsed; and in their determination to make the case stick it appeared that police had manhandled and intimidated witnesses and that, in violation of the Emergency Regulations which permitted them to be held on suspicion for only twenty-eight days, some witnesses had been in custody for three months without being charged or tried.

As the *Straits Times* put the question, 'Do illiterate people know enough to realise when their rights are being violated?', it was one which had considerable ramifications. From the beginning of 1951 there had been considerable emotional turmoil in the Chinese community over government's manpower regulations and the prospect of compulsory military or paramilitary service for young Malayans. The first step was the registration for the 18–24 age group: a total of some 290,000. From this group it was intended to call up about 20,000 for a two-year period. The matter of selection was to be dealt with by boards; and irrespective of whether an appeal for exemption had been submitted, if a man was selected he had to report to a training camp (7–10 days) and from there was posted to a training centre for about three months' training. One point that was noticed was that the regulations were designed to take in the full 20,000—and only then was discharge possible if there was a successful appeal. There was thus the possibility that a man would have passed through the training camp and already be subject to the discipline of a training centre before he was declared exempt. This, to many, looked like an invitation to put their head in a noose; and to nervous, illiterate or semi-literate Chinese youngsters it was something to be avoided at all costs. Besides, there was the unhappy memory of the Japanese occupation when manpower registration had been the prelude to conscription for the Siam—Burma railway: another point which MCP propaganda was quick to make.

Having said this, further extenuation of the Chinese position on selective service could only be made if one rejected the **obligation** entirely or on account of a disparity between **rights and** obligation. In the event, only a handful—1,800—Chinese had been conscripted by the end of 1951, a quite disproportionate number of whom were from English schools. Of the remainder of those who were eligible, thousands fled from Malaya to Singapore, many from thence to Hong Kong and some to China itself rather than register at all and for those who remained there was almost no end to Chinese proposals for tempering the wind. The *Sin Chew Chit Poh*, for example (May 11th 1951) asked for exemption for students, skilled workers in agriculture, commerce and industry, and teachers as well as eldest or only sons. Mr. Tan Cheng Lock explained that the loyalty of the Chinese was to the family and locality rather than to the nation and to the idea of social justice as it was in Western thinking and pleaded for a more gentle process. The *Nanyang Siang Pao* (April 2nd 1952) asserted that the Chinese, when granted citizenship, would play an important part in the formation of an anti-Communist army and the *China Press* (March 25th 1952) was even more explicit and managed to square the circle at the same time when it argued that any call-up should be on a voluntary basis.

It is only fair to add that panic was reported earlier in the year when registration was announced among Tamil estate labourers as well as concomitant criticism by planters of what they called an 'ill-advised example of frenzied and panic-stricken legislation'. Nevertheless, the Chinese objections to anything like a call-up of young men were part and parcel of a generally unhelpful tone at least of the Chinese press at this time. Many of the objections, seen in the context of an infringement of human rights, would obviously be sustained: for example, the MCA's request that government should hear appeals of those who had been detained under Emergency Regulations for more than two years—but frequent reminders that government should win the people's co-operation and support as well as respecting their views and aspirations brought a reaction from those who thought that they should be concerned more with duties than with rights. At its worst, the unremitting and, on the whole, unconstructive criticism of the Chinese press put an anti-Chinese construction upon almost all significant acts of government policy. By the end of 1951 the inference stood in danger of becoming a fact as first Malay and then significant official opinion hardened against the Chinese. The Conference of Rulers, for example, returned to the theme of deporting Chinese as a solution to the Emergency (December 4th 1951; December 16th 1951) while Malay papers were increasingly loud in their objections to the behaviour of an alien community.

Gurney, one might have expected, was above communal differences, but the opinions which he wrote down himself in early October 1951 reflect his exasperation with the Chinese community as a whole.

> The attack of the MCP was always directed at the Chinese, to obtain their support through racial sympathy and intimidation. Three years ago it was made clear to the MCA leaders that unless they provided an alternative standard to which local Chinese could rally, the Communists would win. The answer was that the rural Chinese, the peasants, who are the real target, must first be protected. With the help of the MCA the whole vast scheme of resettlement has now been almost finished and labour forces regrouped. Into these settlements and into trade unions and into schools the MCP are trying hard to penetrate and are succeeding. If they are allowed to continue this unopposed by any Chinese effort whatever, the whole of the Chinese rural population will soon come under Communist domination. These people are looking for leaders to help them to resist. But what has happened?
>
> (*a*) the government wished to recruit up to 10,000 Chinese for service in the police. There was full prior consultation with leading Chinese, but as soon as the men were called up, the cry was all for exemptions, 6,000 decamped to Singapore and several thousands to China.
>
> (*b*) Everyone knows that the MRLA and *Min Yuen* are today being financed and supplied by Chinese. Everyone knows that with a few notable exceptions the Chinese themselves have done absolutely nothing to help their own people resist Communism, which is today rampant in schools and among the young uneducated generation. How many Chinese schools fly the Federation flag?
>
> (*c*) The wealth amassed by the Chinese in Malaya is enormous, and all of it will be lost unless something is done by the Chinese themselves and quickly. The British Government will not be prepared to go on protecting people who are completely unwilling to do anything to help themselves.
>
> (*d*) A feeling of resentment is growing up among all other communities at the apparent reluctance of the Chinese to help. These people live comfortably and devote themselves wholly to making money. They can spend $4 million on celebrations in Singapore but can spare nothing for the MCA anti-Communist efforts.

(*e*) Chinese labour forces lie wide open to Communism. There is no encouragement to them to join Trade Unions, which are mainly Indian-led.

Leading Chinese have contented themselves with living in luxury in Singapore etc. and criticising the police and security forces for causing injustices. These injustices are deplorable but are the fault not of the police but of these Chinese who know the truth and will not tell it. The longer this goes on, the more injustices there will be and the greater the opening to Communist propaganda.

Two days after writing this memorandum, on October 6th 1951, Gurney left Kuala Lumpur with his wife to spend the weekend at Fraser's Hill, a small hill resort sixty-five miles away. After picking up the vehicle escort at a nearby police station the convoy was led by a police land-rover; the High Commissioner's Rolls Royce was followed by a police radio van and a private car driven by the Attorney General; a police scout car brought up the rear. About twenty-five miles out of Kuala Lumpur the bonnet flew open on the wireless van which then had to stop and the escort commander transferred himself to the scout car. At this point contact was broken between Gurney and his effective escort and from here on the scout car was chasing the Rolls Royce at full speed in order to regain contact. Twenty miles or so further on the radio van, which was supposed to be the communications vehicle, broke down completely and as the Rolls-Royce entered the foothills beyond Kuala Kubu and began the ascent of the narrow, winding road its only escort was an open land-rover, completely unarmoured, and five Malay policemen who did not have an automatic weapon between them. A few minutes before one o'clock the two vehicles were approaching the Gap and the beginning of the one-way road to the peak of Fraser's Hill. For miles the Gap road provides almost perfect ambush positions as it winds around the side of a jungle-covered hill. Above and below the road are steep slopes, masked by thick jungle and distinguished by large clumps of bamboo. Strangely enough, since the Emergency had begun three years before there had never been an ambush on this particular stretch of road although it carried a fair amount of military and supply traffic. At a weekend there was nearly always a choice of attractive official targets and only five minutes before an Admiral from Singapore had gone by closely attended by two armoured scout cars. Four days earlier an armoured car troop of the 12th Lancers carried out a reconnaissance along the road and the day before a platoon of the Royal West Kents carried out a routine ambush drill which finished within a mile and a half of the point which Sir Henry Gurney's car had now reached. Above the road, a mixed platoon of guerrillas—thirty-eight men—were watching from ambush positions which extended for four hundred yards. They had been there, off and on, for almost a day and a half waiting for a good target to appear but had chosen not to attack some of the possible ones that presented themselves on the previous day: although the movement of vehicles and their contents was recorded in diary form.[15]

The sight of an open land-rover followed by a large saloon was perhaps too great a temptation to resist; and the odds were certainly very heavily in the ambushers' favour. Two Bren guns in the ambush position ensured that the vehicles drove into a storm of fire. In the police land-rover only a sergeant was left unwounded but he, together with the less badly wounded, continued to engage the guerrillas with their carbines and rifles. Behind them, with the driver wounded and the car halted, Sir Henry opened the door on the off side, stepped into the road and moved towards the overhanging bank. He reached it and fell dead into the deep gutter. In the car, in which thirty-five bullet holes were later counted, Lady Gurney and the High Commissioner's private secretary crouched unwounded. The firing continued for several minutes more, as the Bren gunner on the scout car, which had by now caught up with the official party, fought off the usual 'charging party' who had come down to pick up weapons from the wounded policemen. Then, at the sound of a bugle, the guerrillas withdrew.

One or two mysteries have still to be explained. After the event, every scrap of incidental detail acquired a new significance and Special Branch investigations took in the possibility that Sir Henry's visit was revealed in advance by the Chinese cook at his hill bungalow who ordered provisions from nearby Raub;

---

[15] According to one report the platoon was commanded by Chin Nam and was returning from a raiding expedition in the South over the hill to the fastnesses of Pahang. The ambush itself seems to have been part exercise and part speculation. They could conceivably have attacked one of the small but heavily armed troop convoys but perhaps did not relish the prospect of a fire fight with a platoon or more of Gurkhas. Similarly, a food convoy might have been attacked but if, as seems likely, the platoon had no local *Min Yuen* contact there was the problem of carrying off the food even if the ambush were a success. Perhaps the greatest risk of being ambushed was run by the occasional private car and ambulance which used the road.

or that there was a spy in the telephone exchange who was tapping the King's House line.[16] In spite of its careful planning and comparatively long duration, it is now evident that the ambush was not planned for the High Commissioner. At least, this information is derived from surrendered guerrillas although official MCP propaganda rather naturally took the credit for a well-planned and executed assassination. For a while, in fact, the guerrillas themselves thought that they had killed the Commissioner of Police; and, at the time, it was not realised that Sir Henry Gurney had met a rather careless fate.

The immediate result of Gurney's death was a frenzy of military activity in which whole battalions were drafted in to pursue and destroy his killers. In the early weeks of these operations, however, there was no evidence to show that contact had been made with that particular platoon. Stray parties of guerrillas who happened to be in the area, and must have wished themselves elsewhere, were bumped occasionally but for all intents and purposes there was nothing like a climax of retribution which would have demonstrated government's power to retaliate in kind. Retaliation of a different kind, however, was to be seen in the wholesale removal of the entire population of the Chinese village of Tras, the nearest to the scene of the ambush, an action which by no means exaggerated the wave of resentment of the Chinese community as a whole but which threatened to divert the course of government's Emergency policy.

Two months earlier, an important if not a critical decision for the campaign had been taken: that the resettlement programme should go ahead as planned. Resettlement, however, was perhaps the most difficult course that could be followed, involving as it did digging new foundations for almost the entire rural Chinese population. The question was now: would it be rescinded? Not only was there a shortage of police, without whom effective resettlement was impossible. Not only was it unpopular in that it appeared to reward the disloyal Chinese at the expense of loyal Malays. Was there now, with this latest outrage to constitutional government, a more drastic solution to be sought of the Chinese problem?

It was the worst of times. A month after Gurney's ambush

---

[16] Two of the exchange's test lines were found to be plugged in to King's House and the Maternity Hospital. Although the former may have been for the purpose of operational intelligence—the times and details of Gurney's movements—it was suggested that the two together, and particularly the nurses' quarters in the latter, might have been expected to provide interesting conversations.

the guerrillas inflicted on the security forces their heaviest weekly total of casualties. More important, government's Emergency policy appeared to have lost all direction by the end of 1951. Gurney's death was followed by Briggs' retirement in December and his death shortly afterwards; and if this were not enough, a new Colonial Secretary decided to remove Gray as Commissioner of Police. Increasingly powerful and vehement representations by Malayan estate interests had been made both in London and in Kuala Lumpur to effect Gray's removal and within a few days of receiving a delegation in Kuala Lumpur which declared that they had completely lost confidence in the police, Lyttelton decided that Gray must go.[17] At the same time, it might be argued that while it was patently not the best of times then, at least with the advantage of hindsight, there were good times coming. These removals and replacements meant that issues were resolved which, had they continued, would have become increasingly serious. Would resettlement have continued? Would Gray have been willing or able to carry it out? Who would have triumphed in the not altogether latent power struggle between Briggs and Gray? How would Gurney have dealt with the Chinese? These issues were now resolved : all the principals were removed.

[17] The planting interests who met Lyttelton on December 3rd at King's House were in a belligerent mood. They deplored the left wing influence in the Malayan press; suggested the establishment of summary courts; argued that the Trade Union Adviser's obvious antipathy towards employers was likely to provide opportunities for Communist infiltration into the Unions; and expressed the hope that politics—'unfortunately many local politicians were self-seeking and irresponsible'—would be kept out of the Emergency.

Second Opinions

NEW ORDERS (1): THE MCP

Nineteen-fifty-one, in its way, was just as bad a year for the MCP as it was for government. For both sides, the climax of the year came in October and while, on the government side, it was the head that was lost, for the MCP the change of policy in October followed severe convulsions in its body politic. These were the symptoms that showed that the MCP was in ideological trouble although the issues are perhaps best grouped around two names: Lam Swee and Siew Lau.

Lam Swee, it will be remembered, was the first major defector from the senior ranks of the Communist hierachy. His surrender in June 1950 was, in part, the result of an unsuccessful 'long march' from Johore in search of a secure base but it followed many months of deep dissatisfaction with MCP policy and particularly with the conduct of the Central Committee. The disintegration of guerrilla organisations in Johore as a result of heavy security forces attacks in September, 1948 began a series of mutual recriminations which lasted for almost two years. They started as criticism of the party leadership for their assurances of easy success, went on to question their competence and resulted in a state of wavering confidence throughout the rank and file. Leaders were criticised, sometimes quite openly, for 'officialism', for having special weapons, bodyguards, good food and clothing, watches, and the privilege of having their official and unofficial wives with them: privileges that were all denied to the rank and file. The political and military leaders in their turn blamed their subordinates for insubordination, 'extreme-democraticism', 'absolute-liberalism', 'wavering confidence', backbiting and so on. Political criticism from the rank and file now centred on four points. First, that there was no democracy in the party; the Central Committee had not been elected into office; neither had there been any election in the Party for as long as anyone could remember. Second, that Central Committee members, as well as the Secretary General of the Party, were cowards who dared not even disclose their names to the party members who, in consequence, had to render absolute obedience to people whose names they did not even know. Third, that most of the Central Committee members hailed from a bourgeois background : hence their 'degenerate behaviour' reminiscent of former Secretary General Loi Tak. Lastly, in view of the preceding point, there was a demand for a meeting of leaders from all States and Settlements to prepare for a Pan-Malayan Congress in order to elect a new Central Committee in accordance with rules and regulations of the MCP.

Most of the counter-accusations of the Central Committee turned on the question of loyalty. Leaders at the regional committee and regimental headquarters level, they said, not only failed to maintain discipline but, on the contrary, encouraged the attacks made by the lower ranks upon the Central Committee and even joined in themselves. Illegal meetings had been held to demand cost of living allowances as well as 'conditional obedience' to Central Committee orders; and the result, said the Central Committee, was that they were now treated in the same way as the enemy. Nevertheless, from June to November, 1949 several Central Committee members were deputed to investigate the matter and in January, 1950 two booklets were issued under the title 'General Summary of the Central *Politbureau* in reviewing the South Johore incident of general despondency and attack upon leadership.' By this time, the survivors of the 'long march' to the Tasek Bera swamp were on the point of open rebellion and it had been suggested that they should dispose with a Central Committee which had proved so corrupt and incompetent. Foremost among the critics was Lam Swee, former Vice-President of the Pan-Malayan Federation of Trade Unions, leading light in the South Johore Regional Committee and, for want of volunteers, Political Commissar of the Fourth Regiment, Malayan Races Liberation Army. Possibly on acocunt of his position Lam Swee was not 'eliminated' but was disarmed, placed under strict supervision and told to carry out self-criticism in order that he might admit his mistakes. He was also, formally, accused of being an 'internal spy'; and with the rather bleak future that this foretold Lam Swee escaped from the jungle in Pahang and surrendered at the end of June, 1950.

Within a month, the Central Politbureau issued another booklet, *The incident of Lam Swee going over to the enemy and betraying the Party* for circulation to the whole Party and this in turn led to the counter-attack : *My Accusation*[1] which was written by Lam Swee and distributed by the government in large numbers as a major propaganda item. On the one side there was a painstaking assemblage of evidence—incidents, significances

[1] Kuala Lumpur, 1951.

and precedents—for the indictment of Lam Swee; and on the other, an equally ponderous rebuttal which, together with the charge, suggests that the Chinese are the natural heirs of Marxist polemics. There were, nevertheless, damaging accusations laid against the Party based on first hand experience. The 'elimination' of an Indian guerrilla who, because of his confused state of mind, was likely to have fallen into enemy hands. The corruption of the Communist editor of the *Min Sheng Pao*. The Communist campaign to assert that Lim Ah Liang had been poisoned in prison. And the heroic but suicidel attack of Beng Kwang on Mengkarak police station: the result of his demotion after disagreement with 'Central' in 1949.

By the time Lam Swee's accusations were in circulation the MCP was not only in ideological trouble but had also to explain why it had ordered and carried out the execution of one of its very few, and probably its best, theoreticians. Siew Lau (Phang Yi Foo) was certainly one of the most intelligent and best read members of the Party. Formerly a school teacher he was well versed not only in Marx-Leninism but in the 'New Democracy' of Mao Tse Tung; and if his opinions were open to the charge of 'left-wing Communism'—what Lenin and the MCP leaders would have ridiculed as an infantile disorder—he seems, nevertheless, to have had the passionate sincerity of one of the Levellers of the English Revolution and, like them, he did not hesitate to criticise his leaders when they were in error. In June 1949, taking advantage of the absence of his superior, Siew Lau took the opportunity of convening a meeting of the Working Committee of the military sub-district which covered the whole of Malacca and part of North Johore to which he presented his theses. The Central Committee was not democratically elected by the Party members. It was wrong to start the armed struggle because the masses would not support the Party in such a policy. The Party did not fully understand the new democracy of Comrade Mao because in the MCP 'Programme for the People's Democratic Republic' issued by Central in January 1949 a totally wrong interpretation had been given to a proper economy based upon the New Democracy. New Democracy, Siew Lau argued, postulated equal distribution of land in the first instance in order to provide a strong attraction to the masses to support the Party against the capitalist-feudalists who owned most of the land. But the 1949 programme of the MCP stipulated that the large industries, which in Malaya meant rubber estates, would be nationalised as soon as the MCP captured political power. How, he asked, could the masses be induced to support a revolution which appropriated the rubber estates without the masses getting a share? Rubber estates, the argument continued, and other land should first be equally distributed among the masses: after which collectivisation would be introduced and through this process the land would eventually revert to state control. This was what Mao had proposed in China and it was through the appeal of land reform that the CCP had managed to mobilise the Chinese masses. In Malaya, however, by introducing terrorist activities, the Party had caused the masses much trouble and had thereby alienated their sympathies by robbing them of their identity cards, burning buses, slashing rubber trees, indiscriminate shooting at trains and the like.[2] Setbacks in Johore, in particular, were attributed to wrong Party leadership and lack of support from the masses, and Siew Lau concluded his propositions with the charge that 'Central' were 'horse Communists' driving the rest of the Party to their doom.

From now until the end of 1949 Siew Lau followed an independent line publishing pamphlets in which he continued to attack Party policy and as the guerrilla organisation was subject to increasingly heavy attacks in the course of the year he became more vehement in his denunciation of 'Central' for starting the armed struggle. In November 1949, with the support of his friends, he called a meeting of local guerrilla leaders in which he argued for a 'policy line of retreat' by dissolving the armed struggle, fading out the armed units and burying arms until the time was more propitious. Meanwhile, leaders such as himself and his friends should leave Malaya for further studies, presumably in a Communist country, in order that they should be equipped for another uprising in the future.

Siew Lau had been sufficiently persuasive for the meeting to have adopted his ideas and even to vote to raise funds which would enable him to leave the country. Meanwhile, faced with the evidence that was reaching them from the Malacca/North Johore area, the Central Malayan Bureau sent a representative down to investigate and to call Siew Lau and his associates to appear before a meeting of the Working Committee. This they refused to do and their Committee was therefore dissolved and then reorganised. Undeterred, Siew Lau sent a trusted friend to the secretary of the Malacca Special Committee in August 1950 to ask for financial assistance that would enable him and his friends to leave Malaya; but after a period of 'retrospection and recantation' his

[2] Which invariably produced random and therefore innocent civilian rather than military victims.

friend seems to have betrayed him and Siew Lau was deprived of his rank as well as his Party membership. In exchange, he and his wife and his follower were to be isolated in order that they could be won over and might continue as 'members of the masses who would not cause harm to the revolution'. Siew Lau, however, refused to recant, wrote 'A Thesis on the Equal Distribution of Rubber Estates in the Malayan Land Revolution'[3] and continued to criticise current MCP policy with a wealth of hagiographical quotation.

On May 15th, 1951 Siew Lau, his wife, Sow Wah, and his follower Siew Ping were executed by the Party. But within six months Siew Lau's heresy was to prevail.[4] In part, the Central Committee had itself to blame for broadcasting news of the Party's internal dissentions. Many who had never heard of Lam Swee or Siew Lau, nor pondered their arguments, were made aware of them by strident and probably self-defeating denunciations from 'Central'. And, while to the outsider it may have appeared that the revolution was devouring its children, for those who were within the Party not only were 'Central' under fire in respect of their origins but the infallibility of the Party line was now in question and had created something of an intellectual crisis. For the first time, as a result of Lam Swee's accusations, the Politbureau found it necessary to respond to 'enemy ideological attacks' and it was forced to defend itself against the charge that it had begun the war which was, therefore, 'neither a war of righteousness nor even a war of revolution but only an attempt on the part of a small minority of intriguers at terrorism to destroy peace and order'.[5]

---

[3] Addressed, in ignorance of the fact, to the friend who had betrayed him.

[4] Another critic of the party at this time, Lau Siew (not to be confused with Siew Lau) was also a former school teacher and a member of the wartime resistance. Again, the main criticism was of the undemocratic nature of Party leadership; in this instance, an early vote of no confidence in 'Central'. Lau, a State Committee member for Kedah/Penang, was eventually demoted to an assistant stencil cutter and provided with a defective Browning automatic but somehow managed to survive a report from the North Malayan Bureau that described him as an 'internal spy' and the request that he should be liquidated. (This request was made at the end of 1950. The Central Committee itself was on the move northwards at this time and the courier who was delivering the request, having failed in this important task and fearing the consequences, surrendered together with the documents.)

[5] *Pulverise the enemy ideological offensive and strengthen our ideological background*. Central Politbureau, August 30th 1951.

In its defence the Politbureau explained how British Imperialists had been trying to kill the MCP trade union movement during the 'peace period' and how the MCP was forced to adopt measures of self-defence. Comrades were adjured not to be so naïve as to believe that 'he who fired the first shot started the war' because the war had already been started by the British Imperialists even before the first shot was fired by the MCP. No doubt the war had started in a somewhat precipitate manner but under colonial rule it was impossible to make the full preparations and to get the right opportunity to strike. The war was going to be a long and arduous one, anyway, so there was no point in worrying about a small initial setback.

Overall, and making allowance for periods of comparative success, this initial setback promised to be distressingly permanent, and from this point (August 30th 1951) the MCP were on the defensive ideologically. For three years they had exploited every known and unknown grievance of the Chinese community but they were not always able to capitalise their successes. For example, government's manpower regulations tended to provide recruits for the guerrillas rather than for the security forces but once they were in the jungle many were speedily disillusioned. Reflecting on their fortune—if anything there was too much time for such reflection—it was becoming evident even to the 'horse Communists' not only that in three years they had failed to achieve any notable success but that the correctness of their original decision to begin the armed struggle could also be called in question.

An analysis of Communist propaganda[6] even in its early years shows that a great deal of the Party's effort was intended for internal consumption. Propaganda that was intended for tactical purposes suffered from millennial delusions and in the early days of the Emergency it was apparently expected that, in response to a flood of manifestos and appeals, the workers would leave their employment on estates and mines and withdraw to areas where they could provide food and other assistance for the 'Liberation Army'.[7]

[6] J. N. McHugh, *Anatomy of Communist Propaganda, July 1948–December 1949* Kuala Lumpur, 1950 (restricted). McHugh was the Director of Public Relations but was deeply concerned with the propaganda campaigns of both sides.

[7] Even where casualties were not claimed to have been inflicted as a result of direct action there was a suggestion that fate meted out its own justice. For example, it was reported of the 'six hundred red-haired pigs who arrived here from Palestine two months ago' that every one of them had fallen sick

NEW ORDERS (1): THE MCP

From the beginning the self-imposed task of MCP propagandists had been to show that their policy was in line with international Communism.

> The foundations of the MCP's creed are solidly laid in international Communism and Marxism-Leninism. No deviation is apparent. Since the outbreak of the armed revolt in Malaya the international aspect of Communism has been stressed, however much anti-British or local material may also have been included. Pains have been taken to present the Malayan situation as part of a world liberation movement, which in South-east Asia erupts in force of arms in Indio-China, Burma, Indonesia, China and to some extent in India. The objective of the Malayan revolution is a liberation of the people and establishment of a 'Democratic People's Republic'. This can only be achieved through the annihilation of the 'British Imperialists'.

With the increased success of the Chinese Communists, there had been a proportional strengthening of morale of the Malayan guerrillas—who described themselves in 1949, using the same Chinese characters, as 'The People's Liberation Army'—and from about the middle of 1949 there seems to have been less Marxist-Leninist theory in the content of the proliferating guerrilla news sheets. At the same time, these presented evidence of divergence of opinion within the MCP as to the significance and effect of the Chinese Communist victory in relation to the Malayan situation. Wildly optimistic hopes—for example that Chinese troops would liberate Malaya—were curbed by a Politbureau paper which stressed the importance of overthrowing British Imperialism by their own exertions: an argument designed to restrain the more impetuous from giving up the uncertainties of the Malayan revolution in favour of revolution triumphant in China itself. True, or ideological north may still have been in Russia—certainly she was represented as the leading progressive country in the world—but magnetic or affinitive north was to be found in China.

These factors taken together—alignment with Communist policy as laid down by the USSR, growing responsiveness to

of a tropical fever due to non-acclimatisation and excessive drinking of whisky. 'A clerk in the nearby tin mines said that he had seen about ten soldiers being carried away for burial daily. He added that the epidemic was continuing. The people said that British soldiers deserved such punishment because they had arrested people and burned down houses in many places'.

Chinese affairs, comparative failure of the Malayan revolution and doubts about the decision to begin the armed struggle, not to mention internal criticism—are probably sufficient to account for an impending modification of policy and do not depend on establishing a 'control' by which either the USSR or the Chinese People's Republic determined the policy of the MCP. Very little, in fact, seems to have been known and digested about MCP policy even by the end of 1954. At least, the presentation at the highest level of government was notably slight in spite of the way in which the nuances of policy were examined in order to prove the existence of a dominant Chinese connection. An Intelligence evaluation of MCP policy produced by those who specialised in intelligence and Communism *per se* stated bluntly, without date and without source, that

> As a result of this (the CCP victory in China), it was decided to delegate the practical conduct of the revolution in South-east Asia to Peking, and to apply the technique which had led the Chinese Communist Party to victory to the countries concerned. The Malayan Communist Party, which had not been making much headway with its armed insurrection, was therefore instructed to follow the Chinese example and to place itself in closer contact with Peking.

The actual Communist policy statement cited are a good deal more ambiguous. Liu Shao-Ch'i speaking in November 1949 at the Asian and Australasian Conference of the World Federation of Trade Unions had indeed said that armed struggles can and must be the main form of the People's Liberation Movements in many colonial and semi-colonial countries: although this did not mean that armed struggle did not need the co-ordination of other forms of struggle. However, what is described as a wider distribution of these views in a leading article in the Cominform journal[8] (January 27th 1950) gave as the lesson of the Chinese victory that 'the working class must unite with all classes, parties, groups and organisations willing to fight the Imperialists and their hirelings and to form a broad, nation-wide united front, headed by the working class and its vanguard, the Communist Party' but the formation of People's Liberation Armies under the leadership of the Communist Party was subject to the condition 'when the necessary internal conditions allow for it'.

Evidence of direct Chinese intervention in Malaya is, at best,

[8] *For a Lasting Peace, For a People's Democracy.*

NEW ORDERS (1): THE MCP

circumstantial.[9] In rather the same way direct Soviet encouragement of the Malayan armed struggle must be offset by changes in Communist policy in other parts of Asia which had a more or less direct bearing upon Malaya itself. For instance, Charles B. McLane in his invaluable study *Soviet Strategies in Southeast Asia*[10] points out

> A turn in the strategies of the Indian Communists in 1951, reflecting an altered view of the relevance of Chinese Communist experience in the colonial world, further reveals an impending shift in Soviet eastern policies. The importance of the turn is heightened by the fact that the CPI leaders had visited Moscow shortly before adopting their new course.[11]

Quoting an Indian Government source McLane says that a secret CPI directive late in 1950 asserted 'partisan war alone cannot ensure victory. It has to be combined with the other major weapons, that of strikes of the working class, general strikes, and uprisings in the cities led by armed detachments of the working class.' McLane adds 'the significance of the director does not, obviously, lie in any retreat from the strategy of armed struggle *per se*, but in the explicit rejection of the Chinese formula for armed struggle'. After the event, in November 1951, Zhukov told a Russian Orientalist conference that while the fruitful influence of the Chinese revolution could be detected in the colonial movements, 'it is risky to regard the Chinese revolution as some kind of "stereotype" for people's democratic revolutions in other countries of Asia'. Too mechanical an imitation of Chinese experience violated Lenin's thesis that each colonial revolution was distinctive and had to be considered in its own particular environment; 'peoples liberation armies', for instance, did not exist in all Eastern countries.

In its internal as well as in its western directed news and analysis Soviet writers continued to point to the brutality of the British campaign in Malaya and, conversely, to the heroism of the guerrillas; and as late as the auttumn of 1952 a Soviet student of Malaya continued to speak of the armed revolt there as 'the

---

[9] Hanrahan, *op cit.*, claims that in early 1950 'fresh groups of Chinese Communist cadres were introduced into Malaya from China on a regular basis, infiltrating by way of the Thailand border or coming in by boat from Hainan island. These men did much to revitalise the guerrilla commands and spurred the insurgents to greater efforts', p. 67. This is in no way borne out by evidence from Malayan sources.
[10] Princeton, 1966.
[11] *Ibid*, p. 452.

L

basic and highest form of struggle'.[12] Nevertheless, even the Chinese Communists themselves were showing signs of flexibility by the middle of 1951 when 'peaceful co-existence' began to be an acceptable theme. From this, and from the rest of the conflicting evidence, it would seem that unless one accepts that there was a line of communication that was and has remained entirely secret, the advice that was offered both by China and Russia to Malayan Communists was at best uncertain but that the trend was, if anything, towards a modification of the armed struggle.

At their most extravagant, assessments of the directives issued by the Central Committee of the MCP in October 1951 are that they 'virtually called off the shooting war'.[13] For over a year the Central Committee had been in the Mentakab area of Pahang and in this comparatively stable environment the Party was able to rethink its policy. Conferences were summoned and on October 1st the Party delivered its opinions on the course of the struggle so far and laid down its policy for the future. From the beginning, however, the Central Committee were on the defensive. They had, they said, overcome 'rightist opportunism' only to be hampered by 'leftist deviation'. Specific accusations that were made against the Party as a whole echoed the earlier ideological broadsides: 'extreme democratism'; 'egalitarianism'; 'libertarianism'; 'numbness with regard to the safe-keeping of Party secrets'; a lack of vigilance against 'empty theories'; and 'lop-sided emphasis upon the functional capacity on the question of cadreship qualification'—the Central Committee's retort to those who stressed the proletarian rather than the intellectual requirements for leadership.

Obviously what was needed was ideological retraining so that future errors would be avoided; and in identification of past errors Central Committee admitted that it, too, had made mistakes. As an analysis of the basis of its political support, actual and potential, Central was at least realistic. First, it admitted its mistakes in regard to the masses: specifically, that in December 1948 it was decided that the masses should be the sole source of food supply and that the decision that they were to be led forward by force consequently made excessive demands upon them.

[12] McLane, p. 397.
[13] 'Templer's predecessors had succeeded in subjecting the Communists to such pressure that they had virtually called off the shooting war four months before his arrival in Malaya and . . . his own success was mainly the natural consequence of Communist change of policy.' Purcell, *Malaya: Communist or Free?* London, 1954.

Second, that in its *Guide to the Anti-Resettlement Struggle*, issued in 1950, Central had 'caused the masses to suffer more losses and evoked their doubt regarding the correctness of Party leadership and even dissatisfaction against it'. In activities 'of destruction and sabotage' the Party had not considered the interests of the masses and committed the mistake of 'absolute emphasis upon the basic interests of the Revolution while discarding the existing interests of the masses', something that was 'contrary to the principle of free and voluntary masses participation' in the Revolution, thus making it impossible 'to further consolidate the link between the Party and the masses'.

A second mistake lay in the Party's attitude to the bourgeoisie. Here, the distinction should have been made between the 'incorrigible big bourgeoisie' and the 'exploitable medium bourgeoisie' and the latter, who should have been won over, had been antagonised instead.

With the recognition of these mistakes came a seven point programme for the establishment of a revolutionary platform, one of which, specifically, was that the united front was to be expanded. It was to consist basically of workers, joined by peasants, and united with the petty bourgeoisie. Medium capitalists were to be won over and no excessive demands were to be made upon the petty bourgeoisie in the 'workers and peasants struggle'. Most attention, however, was given to 'the masses' and the supreme criterion henceforth was to be whether Party tasks and policies, as well as activities, 'were supported and accepted by the broad sections of the masses'. Both the reaction of the masses and the urgency and importance to the Party of any proposed action should be carefully weighed before any action was initiated and the emphasis was upon 'legitimate forms of struggle' which included 'dilatory actions, evasions, and even playing up to the enemy and pretending to co-operate with them'. Struggles were to be carried out at appropriate and opportune moments. 'Blind and heated foolhardiness' was to be avoided. The emphasis was on 'regulated and moderate methods'.

Political activities were now, at least, co-equal with military action. The workers and peasants struggle was to be developed by means of illegal trade unions in the country and the infiltration and subversion of those that already existed legally in towns and villages.[14] Strikes were to be carried out but the purpose now,

[14] By taking virtually the whole Party into the jungle, the MCP had of course deprived itself of trained and dedicated members who would have been able to implement a policy of subversion.

in case of deadlock, was to end them under the most favourable conditions as soon as possible rather than to prolong the struggle.[15] Malay peasants were to be 'developed' by the Party and supported on the issues of freedom to sell *padi*, reduction of rents and interest and the allotment of land. The secret sale of *padi* was to be encouraged.

These were to be the political foundations for the Party's future policy but before considering the associated strategy and tactics, which could perhaps be inferred, it would be as well to look at the Party's new complexion and natural affiliation in order both to emphasise the change in policy and in order to put it into its proper perspective. The intelligence appreciation which has already been cited suggests that the October Directives were 'the first attempt to apply the Chinese Model to Malaya' and that they were made on instructions 'emanating from Moscow'. Leaving aside for the moment the question of a 'control' what is not in doubt is the importance of the Chinese experience. Mao, in the October Directives, is the specific, the panacea, the source of political wisdom whose course may be almost totally emulated. Considering how irrelevant was Soviet experience and how distant their problems and exhortations this is not surprising but the importance may be underlined—'the most important change in MCP policy so far—changing from the European form of Marxism-Leninism to the Asian form of Maoism'.[16] Chinese experience, after all and at the risk of stating the obvious, *was* more relevant than almost anything that had happened in Russia in the previous thirty or forty years; and before the Thoughts of Chairman Mao became a sacred book there was a great deal of Chinese experience that was comparable if not entirely relevant. What is important to note here is that in 1951 there were increasingly frequent references in Party propaganda to the history of the Chinese Communist Party and, as noted by C. C. Too, to two particular incidents. The first of these was the Ku Tien conference, held in Western Fukien in December 1929. The significance of this was the occasion of Mao's recognition that the Party had committed a grievous error in harbouring

---

[15] The tactic recommended in order to gain the workers' confidence was to start the struggle with minimum demands to ensure quick success and then to step up the demands in a series of struggles instead of starting with a big demand which the other side would not meet.
[16] C. C. Too, Head of the Psychological Warfare Service and the Federation Government's most knowledgeable and experienced officer on the history of the MCP.

'a purely military point of view', jubilance in winning and dejection at losing a battle, and 'an inclination towards warlordism' which isolated the Party from the masses. Second, was the spectacular event of The Long March: a study of which, Too believes, was soon to influence the Central Committee in a renewed trek northwards from Pahang to the sanctuary of the Thai border.[17]

Given the importance, and indeed the primacy of political considerations in the October Directives, the military decisions appear to be largely derivative. From now on, selective attacks only were to be made, mainly for morale and propaganda purposes although importance was also given to capturing weapons from the enemy. Activities such as stealing identity cards, slashing rubber trees, burning buses and the like were to stop.[18] Tactically, attacks were to be confined to platoon level and mainly ambushes were envisaged. Equal importance was given to the 'cultural level' of the rank and file and their awareness of the 'revolutionary experience' of the Peoples' Liberation Army in China. Units were to be rested and retrained and the tactical implications of this were reinforced by the logistic requirement that, while the masses were still the main source of supply, cultivation by the guerrillas themselves was to be stepped up as an auxiliary source, and to be given priority if necessary, while there was to be an extensive creation of food dumps. All this, in fact, amounted to a strategic decision that was of critical importance: to break contact and to develop jungle resources of space, concealment, food and, although this was something of a windfall, a new and at least potentially friendly population. It also meant that the political struggle had now begun.

[17] Somewhat ironically, the main source for this seems to have been Edgar Snow's *Red Star over China*. Numbers of copies of the Chinese translation printed in Shanghai in 1939 were recovered from guerrilla camps.

[18] Brimmell, *Communism in South-east Asia*, London, 1959, p. 327, includes 'burning Red Cross vehicles and ambulances' as prohibited activities but this was largely theoretical. Members of the Kuomintang and the MCA could be assassinated, but not members of the Malay parties: UMNO or the IMP. Brimmell reckons that this was a mistake: most of the leaders of the MCA should have been classified by followers of Mao as members of the national bourgeoisie to be won over to the Communist side.

13

NEW ORDERS (2): GOVERNMENT

The issue of new orders to the Malayan Communist Party in October 1951 coincided with a new government in London, the impending appointment of new men in Kuala Lumpur and, apparently, new policies all round.

In Kuala Lumpur the immediate aftermath of Gurney's death was what was virtually a plenary meeting on October 17th of Malayan interests, in which Asian members were very much in a majority, to discuss the Emergency situation. As a gesture this was no doubt desirable but perhaps it would have been expecting too much for such a meeting, even under the impact of the Gurney ambush, to have produced any radical solution for Emergency problems. In the event, it turned into something of a confrontation between the effective officers of government— the Director of Operations and the Commissioner of Police—and their Asian critics. Briggs, in reply to enquiries whether he had all the powers that he required, said that operationally he had full control[1] but this was qualified in regard to administration and training of the police: matters which sometimes had political aspects requiring consideration by the High Commissioner. He said that there had been disagreements between himself and the High Commissioner on one or two occasions only but maintained that these did not concern matters of first importance. He made no reference to differences of opinion with Gray but after further discussion it was agreed that there might be certain directions in which the powers of the Director of Operations should be given a more precise form and that he would make recommendations to government on this subject.

Continuing if not arising from this point was whether or not there should be a supreme commander.

Some persons present stressed the desirability of having at the head of affairs an officer—probably with preponderantly military

---

[1] Subject only to an appeal by local service commanders to their commanders in chief if he required them to undertake a task beyond their capacity, and to a similar appeal from the Commissioner of Police to the High Commissioner in respect of the police force.

NEW ORDERS (2): GOVERNMENT

rather than civil experience—who would be in complete control of operations as well as all the other functions of government.

These proposals, while they were a fair reflection of public impatience, ran into polite but powerful opposition from Malcolm MacDonald. In practice, he said, such a 'supremo' would find that he had to devote such a large proportion of his time to the consideration of political problems that he would be unable to give sufficient attention to the conduct of operations. Provided the High Commissioner and the Director of Operations were mutually compatible by temperament he considered that the system of dual control was better. Giving Indo-China as an example he said that in spite of the brilliance of General de Lattre de Tassigny a divided system of responsibility for civil and military affairs would have been preferable and that the dangers of relegating political considerations to second place were now becoming apparent. In the Federation, on the other hand, Gurney had observed the golden rule that political steps needed to be taken side by side with military operations and that frequently these operations might often be prejudiced if not accompanied by appropriate steps in the political field.

Discussion then turned away from the possible appointment of a supreme commander to the functions of the Federal War Council, the Advisory Committees of the War Council, and the position of the Federal Executive Council. At this point, Mr. M. V. del Tufo, the Officer Administering Government, announced that he already had in mind a proposal that the War Council should be reconstituted so that it should consist of the Federal Executive Council plus the present Federal War Council plus a few others to ensure wide representation. The War Council, thus reconstituted, would deal with major issues only and would in no way detract from the powers of the Director of Operations or add to his work.[2]

Among the conclusions noted on this part of the discussion was that the War Council should be reconstituted on a proper basis 'so that all communities and interests affected by the Emergency should be properly represented'. In the meantime, representations of a different kind were made in this meeting about the police and their treatment of the public, particularly the Chinese public, and this was extended to take in the behaviour of junior European

[2] The Advisory Committee to the War Council could continue in order to assist the Director of Operations if it was thought that it would serve a useful purpose. Obviously, this was now to be an ancillary body.

officers towards Asians in general. That there were neither sufficient Chinese police officers nor sufficient Asian officers as a whole on the staff of the Secretary of Defence was agreed; and insofar as the problem was still one of regaining the confidence of the Chinese community one solution put forward was that of restoring the old Chinese Protectorate. Here again MacDonald's authoritative statement ended the discussion: there could be no question of restoring the pre-war powers and duties of Protectorate officers although Chinese Affairs officers should be given sufficient status to take their rightful place in the Emergency campaign.

On the general subject of Chinese co-operation there was no recorded assent to MacDonald's suggestion of a 'Chinese Emergency Corps': a body to be at the government's disposal to make good deficiencies in the various units and services; and the Attorney General's suggestion that Gurney's death might be exploited throughout the country by the taking of some form of pledge against Communism—to be known, perhaps, as the 'Gurney Pledge'—also fell flat.

The record of this meeting, which was eventually transmitted to the Secretary of State in London, barely reveals the temper of the participants although it was perhaps more important for what was left unsaid. In an accompanying note del Tufo gave an idea of the underlying tension. Of the meeting itself he said,

> It was only after some persuasion that the three *Mentri*[2] *Besar* who were present were prepared to attend and the fourth (the *Mentri Besar*, Perak) who was invited refused to come. They felt that, as Chinese would be present, they would not be able to speak freely on the subject which was uppermost in their minds, namely, the complete failure in their eyes of the Chinese community to play its proper share in the effort to end the Emergency. There can be no doubt that this feeling that the Chinese are doing little or nothing to overcome what is, after all, predominantly a Chinese problem, is growing steadily among Malays and will become dangerous if it is allowed to develop unchecked. As it turned out, the expectations of the Malays were realised and no constructive proposals were put forward by the Chinese at the meeting.

Feeling against the Chinese was obviously running high at subsequent meetings. On October 25th at a meeting of the Conference of Rulers del Tufo reported that there was no doubt of a desire to see more severe action, including deportation on a large scale, taken against the Chinese. On the following day at a meeting of the *Mentri*² *Besar*, Resident Commissioners and British Advisers, at which MacDonald and Briggs were also present, del Tufo reported,

> There was clear evidence of the intensity of the Malay feeling against the Chinese and a number of proposals were put forward for pursuing a 'tougher' policy towards them, including operations under Emergency Regulation 17D, against 'black' areas, large-scale deportation and the sequestration of the property of persons who have committed specific acts of non-co-operation with the government, such as failing to supply information which must have been in their possession.

The recriminations under the stimulus of Gurney's death prompted one or two decisions and discussions that would be of significance in the future. Undoubtedly the most important of these was the reconstitution of the War Council which was to have the effect not only of giving it a broader base but, by opening it to nearly all members of the Executive Council who were not already members, at once gave them a measure of power and responsibility and associated them with government in the making of Emergency policy.³ Another matter of importance was the decentralisation of authority to State and Settlement War Executive Committees but here, as with Briggs' proposal that full executive authority should be delegated by the High Commissioner to the Director of Operations, it was as if the ground were being cleared or the way made straight for him who was yet to come.

In London, the decision who this was to be had still to be taken and was, as things stood, of critical importance. As far as the broad lines of Malayan policy were concerned there was little room to manœuvre, even for the colonial authority, and even if the British Government was unable or unwilling to cut the Gordian knot there was a strong feeling that the man who went to inspect it should have a sword at his disposal.

Some of this feeling was admittedly rather fortuitous. When the Secretary of State in the new Conservative Government, Oliver Lyttelton, arrived back from Malaya shortly before Christmas 1951 his invitation to lunch with the Prime Minister coincided with an earlier invitation to Field Marshal Mont-

---

³ del Tufo reported that Gurney seemed to have been considering changes such as this shortly before he was killed. It is also worth remembering that the Executive Council had never discussed Emergency matters at all.

gomery: from which the British Press inferred not only that Montgomery was to be the new High Commissioner in Malaya but even that he himself wished keenly for the appointment.[4] There is no doubt however that the new Conservative Government, and even perhaps the outgoing Labour Government, were thinking of a soldier to retrieve the situation in Malaya. According to Lyttelton again,

> My predecessor at the Colonial Office, Mr. James Griffiths, in a short talk when he handed over to me, confessed that the previous government were baffled by Malaya. Sadly he said, 'At this stage it has become a military problem to which we have not been able to find the answer'.

Lyttelton himself had decided that there had to be a general in charge of both military and civil affairs and his first choice was General Sir Brian Robertson, at that time Commander-in-Chief Middle East Land Forces. Robertson declined as apparently did Field Marshal Sir William Slim, but Lyttelton saw one or two more senior officers before Templer was chosen and flew to Ottawa to receive Churchill's approval.

The Conservative Government, both from its intentions and its previous record as an Opposition, proposed to put a high premium on restoring the situation in Malaya through force of arms. Lyttelton, for example, in Opposition had stressed the importance of more troops while generally and predictably Conservative attitudes were both tougher minded as well as limited to an immediate problem: the defeat of the insurrection. From the record of Parliamentary debates however it could not be argued that either Party had a well-defined policy for Malaya. In the early months of the Emergency there was a surprising concern with peripheral issues but after Mr. Gallacher, a Communist member, had discovered that the film of 'A Tale of Two Cities' had been withdrawn from exhibition in Malaya, and a politically incomprehensible question about ration scales for Dyak trackers, there were few meaningful exchanges or statements until the spring of 1949. In the meantime, there had been

---

[4] Lyttelton did not think that the job would appeal to Montgomery. The following day he received a letter—his only one—from the Field Marshal, which read: 'Dear Lyttelton, *Malaya*. We must have a plan. Secondly, we must have a man. When we have a plan and a man, we shall succeed: not otherwise. Yours sincerely (signed) Montgomery (F.M.). 'I may, perhaps without undue conceit,' Lyttelton wrote, 'say that this had occurred to me.' *Memoirs of Lord Chandos*, p. 379.

some desultory argument between Gallacher and the Labour left on the one hand and the government front bench on the other about the arrest of trade unionists; Mr. Stokes had voiced his doubts about fighting the Japanese in order to give Malaya back to rubber and tin interests; and for the Opposition, Mr. Butler did his best to make Party capital out of the government's alleged dilatoriness and inefficiency. There was some concern over banishment, dollar earnings and the supply of weapons and troops but, except for Mr. Gallacher, 1948 was not the year to be talking about Malayan independence. In the King's Speech of September it was said that lawlessness would be stamped out and when the question of Batang Kali[5] was raised there was an easy acquiescence of government in the Conservative argument that whatever was done there was in order to combat 'Communist murderers'.

On April 13th 1949 the government made its first Parliamentary commitment to Malayan independence: self-government, said Attlee, but no premature withdrawal. A Conservative member, Mr. Gilbert Longden, provided unusual support. The lack of progress, he said, was due to lack of native sympathy and for this reason he advised independence. Mr. Thorneycroft provided a more familiar Conservative view and urged support of the Dutch in Indonesia. By the middle of 1950 other Conservative members were prepared to urge the use in Malaya of Southern Rhodesians (presumably white) and the raising of a new force of 'Black and Tans'. The latter was apparently a serious suggestion, but in any case they would hardly have been necessary if one had accepted the Foreign Secretary's massively monolithic assertion (May 24th) that the local population were supporting the colonial authority. Two months earlier, in March 1950, the Prime Minister reaffirmed the objective of self-government for Malaya; but towards the end of the year, looking to the improbable future, one Conservative member wanted Britain to stay in Malaya permanently as an equal partner.

On the whole, Members seemed grateful for the fact that Malaya was still the principal dollar earner for the whole of the Commonwealth and did not question the continuing British presence or the need to defeat the insurrection before Malaya might attain independence. Mr. Lennox Boyd, for example, when it was announced that elections would be held in 1951 in the three main cities of Kuala Lumpur, Penang and Malacca, hoped that this would not interfere with the prosecution of the

[6] *Supra*, pp. 356–358.

war; but apart from those MPs who pursued their particular interests—for example in court martial figures or objection to the export of rubber to the Soviet Union—the level of argument tended to be somewhat parochial. In early 1951, the House spent almost as long debating whether or not young British soldiers should be sent to Malaya as it did on the situation in Malaya itself. It may perhaps have been justified. Certainly there was understandable concern with the former, more particularly when the government professed not to regard the Malayan campaign as subject to the rule of not sending troops into action under the age of nineteen. Particular actions or acts of policy, however, were seldom called in question. Government announced itself as being against a Royal Commission on the Chinese constitutional position in Malaya. Mr. Stan Awbery, with immediate knowledge of the country, complained that workers had no confidence in a moribund Malayan Labour Advisory Board. And when it was asked if it was true that senior European officers had dined with surrendered bandits at a Chinese Asociation dinner at Johore Bahru the government, still treating even surrendered guerrillas as untouchables, said certainly not with government permission.

Mr. Awbery was one of several members who had first-hand experience and a continuing interest in Malaya. Another on the Labour back benches was Mr. Woodrow Wyatt, who had numerous contacts in Malaya, among them the chief Trade Union Adviser, and whose pertinent questions indicated a firmer grasp than many on the Malayan situation.[6] There were, of course, other sources of information than Parliamentary debates and questions. Apart from business or professional interests some members had visited Malaya in a personal capacity to see the situation for themselves. Eden, for example, was early on the scene but Labour ministers were not always well received. In the course of a visit made by the Secretary of State for War, Mr. Strachey, in 1950, his treatment at the hands of European members of a Penang club brought outraged protests to Gurney from the Resident Commissioner there. The record of on the spot

---

[6] For example, on Chinese citizenship; disappointment that the Deputy High Commissioner was not a Malayan; and the assertion that it was police not troops that were needed. In response to his question why a number of Malays had been refused admission to the Malayan Civil Service there was the revelation that there was only one Malay officer in the senior ranks and that no non-European had been promoted since May 1949. There were, however, at least thirty or forty Malays in the MCS.

NEW ORDERS (2): GOVERNMENT

discussions, however, and the points made by visiting Cabinet Ministers, showed a more lively appreciation of the situation than replies to Parliamentary questions and it was for the benefit of first-hand impressions that the new Secretary of State for the Colonies, Mr. Oliver Lyttelton, visited Malaya in 1951.

This was both a reconnaissance and the beginning of a major reconsideration of policy by the British Government. When Lyttelton arrived in Kuala Lumpur it was to be met by a caretaker administration. del Tufo, the Chief Secretary, was now the Officer Administering Government. Briggs was on the point of departure, so was Jenkin, the Director of Intelligence. It was also a time of political uncertainty for Malayans themselves. As part of the consultative process Lyttelton was to see delegations from UMNO and the MCA but while the latter could still be identified with the views of Mr. Tan Cheng Lock, UMNO, moving in the direction indicated by recent readoption of the slogan, 'Malaya for the Malays', had lost its founder and leader in the process.

In a political report from King's House, Dato Onn's resignation from the presidency of UMNO was attributed to his exasperation with the conservative elements of his Party who were not prepared to make any further advances on the road to non-racialism. Onn had by this time found a new political home in the Independence for Malaya Party which, nominally at any rate, appeared to be an alliance of progressive interests and for a while included Mr. Tan Cheng Lock himself. Fears of this new Party, it was said, were both exaggerated and significant.

> It will be seen therefore that IMP has the support of the prominent leaders from the Chinese, Indian and Celanese communities, with, as yet, negligible support from the Malays, and that (although a few attended the inauguration meeting) it does not include any Europeans. In general terms the attitude of the Europeans towards IMP is that while the formation of a Party whose primary objective is to remove communal rivalry and provide a common ground on which all communities can meet is highly desirable, the timing and the methods employed are unfortunate, if not worse. Although Dato Onn in private conversation has said that the period set for reaching the goal is, in itself, of little significance, and is 'largely newspaper talk', nevertheless the public is bound to judge him by his statement that independence should be achieved in ten years. The planters,

miners and commercial men, who form the bulk of the European community, fear—perhaps unreasonably—that capital will no longer be safe, that there will soon be no place for them and that if independence (which they acknowledged to be the legitimate goal and inevitable) comes within ten years it can only bring in its train political and economic chaos and possibly even ruin to the Malays themselves. Moreover they have no confidence in Dato Onn, whom they regard as mercurial and wayward and they do not, of course, share the deep personal loyalty which he has inspired among a large section of his own people.

These were decidedly pessimistic political assumptions. Added to which there was a certain dichotomy between popular and formal political representation. It was recognised that Onn had next to no influential Malay support at this time and was in fact actively opposed by influential Malays, particularly the *Mentri² Besar* and the Rulers. Nevertheless, most of the unofficial Malay seats on the Legislative Council had been filled for the next two and a half years on the basis of Onn's recommendations and he himself occupied what had been recognised as the senior of the members' posts carrying precedence immediately after the three official members of the Federal Executive Council.[7]

Against this background of political uncertainty Lyttelton met the delegation from UMNO and the first encounter took place between a Colonial Secretary and the future Malayan Prime Minister, Tunku Abdul Rahman, the UMNO President. The first question that was put to the Colonial Secretary was whether His Majesty's Government still aimed at self-government for colonial territories; to which there was the assurance that there had been no change of government policy. From a discussion that followed on this question it was argued on the UMNO side that the Malays were losing faith in HM Government because they thought that the other races of Malaya were being given too favourable treatment; and in view of the bonds of loyalty to China which, they argued, were still very strong among the large mass of poorer Chinese in Malaya, it would hardly be fair to give the Chinese an equal share of managing affairs when self-govern-

---

[7] The report ended, 'The conclusion to be drawn from all this is that the precipitate announcement of the formation of IMP was a political blunder though not, let it be hoped, an irretrievable one. To the average Malay, Dato Onn is the daring young man who had launched himself from one flying trapeze and is reaching out for the other. Dato Onn is confident that he will catch it. Spectators—as always—are holding their breaths.'

ment came. Specifically, UMNO were concerned with government's alleged favouritism towards the IMP; the question of nationality; the slow rate of introduction of Malays into government service; lack of promotion for them in the police force; and lack of educational facilities in the rural areas. In short, their argument was that political and social respects of the Emergency were as important as the purely military campaign.

At the same time, however, UMNO were looking to the future, and were concerned with the political balance between the races when independence came. If, in the future, citizenship and political power were to be accorded to all Chinese, irrespective of their political allegiance, then this was a situation which, fraught with anxiety for the Malays, would be avoided if independence could be accorded without disturbing the *status quo*. This, in fact, was a suggestion put forward by the President of UMNO: that to help in the Emergency by encouraging the people of Malaya, the territory should be given independence under a Governor General, but without departure of the British Administration. This, he said, would put the people on their mettle and would be a valuable counter to Communist propaganda.

In view of the prevailing antagonism towards Malayan Chinese and the considerable dangers of alienating the Malay community, not to mention other factors, this was a tempting proposition. To have accepted it however would have meant that the British Government was committed to the idea of indefinite but probably permanent Malay political superiority, at least on the constitutional level. This, Lyttelton rejected in what was, arguably, the most critical decision for Malaya's political future. In the circumstances he agreed there could not, in any case, be complete equality for the Chinese because their numbers were smaller. Having said this, Lyttelton offered no other compromise: a united nation was the aim in which there must be equality for all loyal and patriotic citizens. As for the idea of early independence under a Governor General, Lyttelton stated and repeated that this would be impossible until there were more racial unity.

> The Secretary of State again said that the aim was clear and agreed; and to pursue it too fast would damage rather than advance the cause: the best way of maintaining the people's confidence in Britain and of opening the path to political, social and economic progress was by winning the Emergency.

To the Malays, and especially to the UMNO delegation, Lyttelton's views may have been cold comfort; but at least they were no source of gratification to the Chinese either. On some issues Malay and Chinese views were diametrically opposed. Where the Malays asked for a ban on further immigration, the Chinese asked for an immigration quota. Where Malays favoured large-scale deportation of Chinese, the Chinese asked that deportation, where it took place, should be far more selective; and while it could be argued that many of the fears of law-abiding Chinese had considerable substance—for example, that the Federation Government did not trust the Chinese as a whole—on at least one point the MCA delegation showed considerable political insensitivity in their suggestion that Chinese soldiers, presumably via Hong Kong or Taiwan, should be brought in to Malaya to fight the Communists.[8]

European interests who lobbied Lyttelton were, if anything, rather more short-sighted. According to Lyttelton's own account he was forcibly urged by the European community to take drastic measures: first, to bring down all the severity of the law upon those who could be found to be paying protection money; second, to dispense with the normal procedure and speed up the administration of justice through drumhead courts. Lyttelton's replies, again to judge from his own account, were impeccable.

> I refused both requests point-blank. On the first, I said that until the government could deliver its part of the bargain, which was to protect the citizen on his lawful occasions, it was mere cynicism to prosecute those who were protecting themselves in the only way open to them. 'At the point of a gun you would pay rather than be murdered,' I said, 'and so would I, and you know it.' Once we could provide reasonable protection the collaborators would be treated as traitors, but not before.
>
> I poured scorn upon the second proposal, against which my deepest beliefs were engaged. 'We stand for law and order,' I said. 'It is perhaps the greatest gift inherited that we can bestow on these peoples, and if we suspend the law because we are too incompetent to secure order, that is the end of us, of our mission and our ideals. Never, while I have anything to do with their

---

[8] The MCA delegation also put forward the rather dubious assertion that the effect of this would be to attract many Malayan Chinese to join the Security Forces. The effect on the Malays, if mentioned, was not recorded.

NEW ORDERS (2): GOVERNMENT

territory, will I agree to suspend the processes of law. Speed them up I will, if I can, but their principles must remain intact.'

At the end of his visit, after innumerable consultations and visits to the four corners of the country, and a trip to Hong Kong sandwiched in between, Lyttelton broadcast his impressions and offered a six-point programme for the future. First, he promised overall direction of civil and military forces against the enemy. Second, the reorganisation and training of the police which he described as urgent. Third, compulsory primary education. Fourth, a much higher measure of protection of the resettlement areas: to be achieved and achieved quickly. Fifth, the organisation of a Home Guard to include a large number of Chinese. Sixth, the refurbishing of the Civil Service. Some of the incidental points that he made seemed to be of considerable importance also.

> There must be sufficient armoured vehicles to enable both the Civil Authorities, the police, the planters and miners to move about their duties in vehicles which would enable them to hit back if they are attacked. I cannot subscribe to the theory that protecting a man from rifle fire reduces his fighting spirit.

The matter of a rapid increase in the number of government officers who could speak Malay and Chinese; the question of the appropriate weapons for issue to planters and tin miners; the officering of the Malay Regiment; a careful scrutiny of the propaganda system: these were all immediately comprehensible and might have helped to restore confidence. But the most important point to command a response from Malaya itself was the emphasis on a united Malayan nation: and that when this had been achieved the nation would carry the responsibility and enjoy the advantages of self-government. This had been implicit in the past but was now stated with considerable force. To it, was linked the prospect of another bargain. 'Today,' said Lyttelton, 'we had to place emphasis on the immediate menace. We must ask who are the enemies of these ideals? Who are the enemies of political advancement? What is delaying progress towards it? The answer is Communism. The answer is the terrorists. The answer is the *Min Yuen* and those who, partly from fear and partly from sympathy, create a passive but no less serious obstacle to victory. All these in greater or lesser degree betray our ideal and upon them must unite in visiting, under the law, the full severity which their betrayal merits. Only so will victory be gained.'

By combining forces, and overcoming their particularism, the communities of Malaya, and in particular the Malays and Chinese, would show that they were ready to proceed towards self-government. By defeating the Communist insurrection this progress would be assured.

This was Lyttelton's public offer. Privately, he was greatly concerned with Malaya's administrative tangle. Reading up his subject before he came to Malaya he recorded, 'It is evident that we were on the way to losing control of the country, and soon.' As a prologue to his Malayan inspection he had sat in on a conference of Governors of South-east Asian territories and colonies and recorded, privately, his sense of frustration at the end of the day: 'There was not enough said about action and nothing clearly proposed to put right the administrative tangle.' On Malaya proper, as seen from Kuala Lumpur, the view was even less promising.

> The situation was far worse than I had imagined: it was appalling. From a long life spent in administration, I could draw no parallel. I have had experience of the Brigade of Guards, the most highly perfected and disciplined human organisation of which I can think, great joint stock companies and government departments, all faced at times with dangers and difficulties in their various spheres, but I had never seen such a tangle as that presented by the government of Malaya. The last High Commissioner had been murdered five months before my arrival (sic), no successor had been appointed. There was divided and often opposed control at the top. Civil affairs rested in the hands of the OAG, military and para-military in those of Lt. Gen. Sir Harold Briggs. The two authorities were apparently co-equal, neither could overrule the other outside his own sphere. But what was each sphere? The frontiers between their responsibilities had not been clearly defined, indeed they were indefinable, because no line could be drawn to show where politics, civil administration, police action, administration of justice and the like end, and where para-military or military operations begin. Civil administration moved at a leisurely, peace-time pace.

The constitutional tangle, according to Lyttelton, was no less than the administrative and had been further bedevilled by the establishment of the Member system under which, it will be remembered, responsibilities for the different departments of government had been divided amongst nine Members, only three of whom were of the Malayan Civil Service. Whether this could, or indeed should, have been changed was open to question; but if he had to tolerate the complexities and delays of the constitutional position Lyttelton was not prepared to do the same for police organisation.

In retrospect, Lyttelton's views of police administration are severe and one or two of his statements rather surprising. It is, for example, unlikely that, having been given a rough estimate of sixty thousand, 'no one could tell me how they were disposed'; nor indeed that Malaya was a country the size of Wales. Nevertheless, the unresolved issues were obvious: the schism between the Commissioner of Police and Director of Intelligence; ultimate control of the police force; the question of armour. To these Lyttelton added the relationship between law and the police. Tan Cheng Lock had described Malaya as a police State. Lyttelton said that the position was intolerable.

> The government had wide emergency powers of mass arrest and detention without trial. It was estimated that perhaps 200,000 persons had been detained for less than 28 days; it was known that 25,000 had been detained for 28 days or more: of those, less than 800 had been prosecuted. Even after deducting the numbers of those who had been released or deported to China, there were at this time still 6,000 persons detained without trial. I judged that a properly trained police force would be able to make a great, even a startling, reduction in these numbers.

Having judged that 'the organisation of the police was in utter disorder', Lyttelton decided on drastic reorganisation.

> I secured the resignation of the Commissioner of Police, a gallant officer but not a professional policeman, and also of the Head of the Special Branch.

This is not altogether correct. Sir William Jenkin, the Director of Intelligence, had in fact resigned in October, when there was still a Labour Government in London, and this resignation had been accepted. Nevertheless he showed a capacity for on the spot action even if, as a result, Malaya was left with a caretaker government. Not only, by one means or another, had Gurney, Briggs, Gray and Jenkin been removed from office. del Tufo, who was acting as head of the government, was passed over not only as Gurney's successor but also for the new post which, as Lyttelton gives him credit for, he helped to create in negotiation with the Malayan Rulers: that of Deputy High Commissioner.[9]

When Lyttelton returned to London at Christmas he set about preparing a Cabinet paper. The gist of it, according to Lyttelton's published account, was that two authorities, one political and one military, with responsibilities ill-defined, and each with over-riding powers, had been the main reason for the appalling state of Malaya. The key to the problem therefore was that one man should be responsible for both civil and military sides of Emergency policy. As for the campaign itself it could not be won without the help of the population, and of the Chinese population in particular; and in order to win this support it was necessary at least to begin winning the war.[10]

The main effect of Lyttelton's conclusions was to narrow the field in which Gurney's successor was to be found. It was now more than likely to be a retired or serving soldier and even after the elimination of certain likely candidates the choice of Lieutenant-General Sir Gerald Templer was somewhat surprising. Templer was then fifty-three, a regular officer since the First World War, a wartime divisional and corps commander who had been badly wounded in the Anzio campaign. After a period as Director of Military Government in Western Germany, during which time the Burgomaster of Cologne, Dr. Konrad Adenauer, had been dismissed for general idleness and inefficiency, he had been Director of Intelligence at the War Office, Vice-Chief of the Imperial General Staff and, at the time of his appointment to Malaya, GOC-in-C, Eastern Command.

Templer arrived in Malaya in early February 1952; nothing

---

[9] One which caused acute difficulty, according to Lyttelton, with their Highnesses the Rulers: first, because it was necessary to change the existing constitution; second, because they all thought the holder should be a Malay. The strongest candidate for this post was undoubtedly Dato Onn. 'I knew, however, that only the highest administrative knowledge and experience would serve my purpose. I did not think that a Malay of the necessary calibre was available.' Chandos, *op. cit.*, p. 373.

[10] Lyttelton's main paper to the Cabinet was supplemented by appendices on Federal and State Councils; armoured vehicles; arms and equipment for the police; earth-shifting equipment; chemical defoliation of the jungle; language teaching; intelligence services; subversive activities; deception tactics; terms of employment of British officer and other ranks posted and seconded for service with the Malay Regiment; detention and repatriation; manpower and national service; tax evasion; finance; and extension of service beyond retiring age.

NEW ORDERS (2): GOVERNMENT

much happened until the last ten days of March. It had not been an altogether auspicious arrival. Unofficial members of the Legislative Council protested against the appointment, some even threatened resignation. In a unanimous recommendation they said that the new man should have been someone with local experience. MacDonald let it be known that he did not approve of a General as High Commissioner. The *Straits Times*, on learning of Templer's nomination, said it would have preferred a civil appointment and warned Templer that he would find morale difficult to restore after a long mishandling of the Emergency. Templer himself gave his first recorded opinion, with which most people would have agreed, that there was no clear cut solution to Malaya's problems and when, in his second reported sentence, he said that it was certain that with the support of the entire population he could lick the Emergency in three months, this was more of an axiom than a revelation. More than this, it suggested either an indecent haste or a recklessness and determination to achieve quick results that would most likely be achieved through the military dictatorship which MacDonald, for one, feared with a High Commissioner who was no longer a civilian.

In the event, however, and with one exception, it was the civil acts and intentions that stood pre-eminent in the early months of the Templer administration. Looking back it seems as if these were the months in which the political foundations of an independent Malaya were laid; and they were also the months in which one may discern a new tinge in the political complexion of the struggle itself. In London, the *Round Table*, a review of Commonwealth affairs which had largely ignored events in Malaya over the last three years, now gave a highly critical view of the situation.

> Hateful as it is, the MCP is a powerful movement, selflessly served by determined men and women, and compared with it other political movements are pallid and ineffectual. In fact, with the Communists in the jungle Malaya politically is an almost empty vessel, a vacuum waiting to be filled by the Communists should they break through the lid that is the Security Forces. Only the troops and police stand in between, but they have created and perpetuated, with the Emergency regulations and the government's attitude, conditions that stifle the growth of any alternative system to Communism. The few seeds and nuclei inside the vessel waste away in the rarified atmosphere.

For the writer of this article the only rival political forces in Malaya, apart from the Communists, were the IMP and the nucleus of Labour parties in the various States. Contemporary political developments were ignored; and the position of Dato Onn was enhanced accordingly. This was almost exactly what had been happening for the past two years. As long as Onn's political views bridged the difference between Malays and Chinese he was the only political figure to whom the Colonial Government attached any importance. Whether he was regarded as saviour or stalking horse is perhaps a moot point; but Gurney had put the problem squarely to Griffiths, the Secretary of State for the Colonies, as far back as June, 1950.

> His Excellency began by referring to the fundamental problem of achieving political agreement between the Malays and the Chinese. At present the Malay view of the recent proposals on citizenship put out by the Communities Liaison Committee was slipping. The point arose as to whether government should come out openly in support of these proposals and so lay the British open to the charge of selling the Malay birthright to the Chinese.

At that time it had been decided that the Communities Liaison Committee's proposals were not to be pushed by government and that the Malays should not be urged publicly to give ground to the non-Malays. Government's line was 'to emphasise in a general way the necessity for achieving agreement and unity' but sooner or later the issue had to be faced. In a general way this had been done by Lyttelton and it now fell to Templer to deal with the great political issue of Chinese citizenship.

Accumulatively, Templer's political programme may be regarded as the product of successive governments, High Commissioners and Civil Service advice. The decision, for example, to merge the Federal War Council in the Executive Council—which could at least be interpreted as a move in the direction of responsible government—had been proposed by the Colonial Office in January 1952 but its announcement by Templer was only one of what were regarded as many instances of decisive action. The announcement was made in the course of Templer's first speech to the Legislative Council on March 19th 1952. For the first ten minutes he was heard in silence. Everyone, said Templer, was affected in his daily life by the Emergency: there was no watertight compartment in which it could be separated from the normal peacetime processes of government. The thought that members of the Legislative Council would now be able to

NEW ORDERS (2): GOVERNMENT

play a greater role in framing Emergency policy evoked no recorded enthusiasm. Neither did the mention of restoring law and order as the principal task. The creation of a Malayan way of life was an idea that was received with similar coolness; and it might also have been indiscreet to applaud when Templer spoke of the necessity of ensuring that the regular police were trained in and were attending to their basic civil police duties. Nevertheless, when Templer went on to say that the armed forces must belong to the Federation as a whole, that they must contain at least elements of all the communities, and that one of his main objectives would be to start off a Federation army containing an entity open to all communities—the Federation Regiment—the Legislative Council broke into applause. The applause was repeated when Templer said that teachers should educate their children, whether in English, Malay, Chinese or Indian schools, in accordance with the social principles of Malaya's own way of life and not in accordance with the dogma of some country beyond the seas. Next he spoke on the question of land tenure and it is significant here that he regarded this as the most important problem concerned in resettlement.

> If these new agricultural communities are to be happy and enterprising they must have reasonable security in the tenure of their land. It will be our aim to ensure this for every community in the country and that aim will be vigorously pursued.

Templer's immediate objective, he said, was the formation of a united Malayan nation. It was an objective which was not to be hampered by the Emergency.

> I believe it right to ensure that truly responsible local government at the rural community and municipal council levels is firmly established and as quickly as possible. Not for one moment would I suggest that this should be postponed in any way at all because of so-called Emergencies upon us. On the contrary, it is all the more necessary because of the Emergency to press on with this measure. I firmly believe this from the bottom of my heart. I firmly believe in the principle of responsible local government by local people. I will do all in my power to foster this and the quicker we can start on it the better.

So it was with the whole range of subjects which Templer covered: recognition of the problems and a sense of urgency in dealing with them. From the beginning this was to be a political programme and a programme which he seemed to be starting on the right foot. It is hardly surprising therefore that he received an extremely good reception from the press. On the whole, Federation reaction to Templer's speech was that it was one of the most important and significant made by an executive in Malaya. From newspaper reports, it was the constructive nature of Templer's speech which most impressed them. The matter of land tenure, for example, lay at the heart of resettlement. The Briggs Plan, which had set out to put half a million squatters beyond the reach of the guerrillas had fallen short of its objective because amongst other reasons it could not guarantee to the resettled squatters security of tenure. Now this problem was publicly identified and there was at least the promise of action. Politically, Templer's programme was to achieve a united Malayan nation: an expression that was drawn from his Directive as High Commissioner, the means for the achievement of which was to be 'a common form of citizenship for all who regard the Federation or any part of it as their real home and the object of their loyalty'. The Directive itself had been made public and was again the subject of favourable comment. This was not to say, however, that the question of who did regard Malaya or any part of it as their real home and the object of their loyalty had thereby been settled; and ten days after Templer's speech in the Legislative Council there occurred the first of the visitations which became part of the Templer legend.

Whether it improved or detracted from his public image is perhaps another open question. The place was Tanjong Malim, some fifty-five miles from Kuala Lumpur and the event was a particularly bloody ambush of a party repairing a water pipeline that had been cut by the guerrillas. As on so many other occasions, no one in Tanjong Malim had heard anything, seen anything or knew anything of the event.[11] Descending on the town, Templer attacked its inhabitants with a violence of language which was to become typical but which has probably never been used, at least habitually, by Commissioners, high or low, in this century. The mildest charge was that of cowardly silence; and in retaliation Templer imposed a twenty-two hour curfew of indefinite duration. No one was to leave the town, schools and bus services were closed, the rice ration was reduced from five to three *katis* per person. Ten days later the prolongation of Tanjong Malim's punishment

---

[11] The event itself received widespread publicity in Britain because Michael Codner, the District Officer who was killed, had been one of the heroes of the 'Wooden Horse' escape from a German prison camp.

was made to depend on the result of a questionnaire addressed to the head of each household. More letters were distributed containing an assurance that reprisals need not be feared since absolute secrecy of information was assured (secrecy which may have been observed in principle but not always in practice in the past). The letters were placed in sealed boxes, the boxes were later opened by Templer in the presence of representatives from the town and desultory arrests were made. The curfew itself was lifted on April 9th.

For those who were waiting to see how and when Templer would remove the velvet glove and expose the mailed fist, Tanjong Malim seemed to confirm their worst expectations. Although it was not known at the time it now seems certain that in spite of the heavy incidence of guerrilla action in and around Tanjong Malim the particular event that brought such heavy retribution was accomplished, without prior knowledge from the town, by a mobile group of guerrillas who were reasonably certain that cutting the pipeline would bring a party of officials to effect its repair. Although a few *Min Yuen* and guerrilla supporters were arrested as a result of information laid there was nothing on the guerrilla unit itself. Nevertheless, and in spite of misgivings, the swingeing curfew at Tanjong Malim was, on the whole, applauded as evidence of firm and forceful action: of someone who would get things moving.

At first, however, it was assumed that the existing administrative machine was quite unsuited to swift or determined action. Not only would it peter out in the sands of the State government; but there was also the fundamental challenge to the Malay status quo. In London, both *The Times* and *Telegraph* suggested that Templer's power should be increased by short-circuiting the cumbersome States and sultans; and in the Malay press there were frequent suspicions that Templer was about to ask for the suspension of the Federation Agreement that governed relations between Britain and the nominal protectorates that comprised the Malay States. In May, 1952 the Attorney-General had in fact moved an amendment to the Federation Agreement in the Legislative Council: the effect of which was to confer citizenship on large numbers of Malayan-Chinese and safeguarded the rights of those who were already citizens. The amendment involved, as one Malay member of Council put it, a tremendous sacrifice by allowing members of other races to share the rights of Malays; but the interests of the country as a whole, he said, were foremost in their minds. When the question was put, the amendment was carried without dissent although the record itself scarcely reveals the astonishing political advance it marks. The following day (May 8th) the Village Councils Bill was given its second reading. The title of this, too, concealed the fact that it marked the enfranchisement of some 400,000 Chinese in resettlement areas which had been officially renamed 'New Villages'. This Village Charter, as it was called, was fairly described as laying the foundation of a new Malayan nation; elected Village Councils would administer villages directly, collect their own rates and taxes, employ their own staff and be completely responsible for their own budget and education. Asian members of the Legislative Council, particularly the member for Home Affairs, Dato Onn, were, however, critical of the overriding powers of European District Officers in the New Villages and there was a reminder from a Malay member that Malay *kampongs* were being neglected.[12]

Here again, the Village Charter was a culmination of government policy that went back far beyond the arrival of Templer; but again it stood to Templer's credit. What was entirely personal, however, was Templer's supercharged activity in a climate that was not traditionally conducive to violent exertion on the part of Europeans. Reporters on the English-language *Straits Times* stood back in amazement to describe the man who was out to see everything and whose descent from the 'Olympus of King's House' had set him apart from former Governors and High Commissioners. By the end of May Templer had visited every State since his arrival less than four months before and his tours, on the ground, were notable for the numbers of contacts that he made with the civilians of all races. Occasionally, there were remarks that looked rather silly in cold print—'Tell your people that I will hit them on the head if I find any more CTs in their district'—but for many these were offset by the range of his interests and his famous indictment of, at least by implication, the European community of Kuala Lumpur. At a Rotary International conference he attacked partygoers and the apathy of people who sat back and let others do the work for them. The Communists, he said, seldom go to the races, to parties, to cocktail parties or play golf: they work! 'Sir Gerald has scored a bullseye' said a leading Malayan trade unionist who, not long ago,

---

[12] In July the wide powers of District Officers were drastically reduced. To disallow any candidate the District Officer would first have to have the permission of the *Mentri Besar*; and he was not empowered to end the term of any Village Council member.

had been told by Templer that he would encourage trade unions to the fullest extent of his power—with the rider 'so long as they kept away from Communism'. At the Annual General Meeting of the Boy Scouts Association Templer was there to state his belief in youth movements: and to condemn youth movements that were run on racial lines. For those who wondered what they might do to help, not only in the prosecution of the Emergency campaign, Templer gave a list of 18 organisations which were in need of help ranging from the Auxiliary Air Force to youth organisations and taking in Blind Welfare, Blood Donors and TB Relief on the way.

Taking stock of the first few months of his achievements in Malaya, the most striking effect was Templer's political impact: he was not only there, but was most certainly seen to be there. Given that he had a favourable press, this was something that was achieved by his own activities rather than through assiduous press releases. In a word, Templer can be said to have energised the situation; with it there was a corresponding relief and realisation that something was being done. What this was, was sometimes intangible. The *Straits Times*, listing his achievements in June, 1952 gave him credit for the creation of New Villages out of resettlement areas; vast re-organisation of security forces (a reference to an integrated joint Services Police operational headquarters in Kuala Lumpur); the integration of Emergency and civil administrative duties; the brandishing of the mailed fist against fence-sitters (a reference to Tanjong Malim); new means of getting information from frightened people (the doubtful success of the Tanjong Malim ballot boxes); encouragement of youth movements; new life for the Rural and Industrial Development Authority; and a rapid development of adult education. Of his personal qualities there was no doubt: quick decisions, determined action, forthright statements. In Britain, rather than in Malaya, his activities had created some public concern[13] but in both countries both the actions and the man were very much in the public eye.

Templer himself, taking stock, laid down three priorities: (1) a sound police force; (2) gathering of information and other intelligence work; (3) telling people the truth about what was happening. They were to be followed as a plan of campaign and

---

[13] In reply to criticism of the Tanjong Malim curfew by Awbery and Shinwell, Lyttelton offered the disingenuous explanation, 'The rt. hon. Gentlemen must be aware that these measures are not primarily punitive'. 499 HC Deb. 5s., 1453–1455.

are obviously of enormous importance but, at the same time, they can be regarded as political tactics. The political strategy can be seen in the constitutional stage-setting of Templer's early months which was a culmination of British political decisions. The measure of the political revolution, in which a British Government proposed and a Malay people accepted the political and permanent presence of the Malayan Chinese, has so far only been considered in part.

14

BATTLE DEFINED

Political Definition
A few days before Templer's appointment as High Commissioner was announced in January, 1952, another announcement was made of equal significance for Malaya's political future. This was, in origin, a low level, *ad hoc* and local electoral alliance between the United Malay National Organisation and the Malayan Chinese Association. Its sources are somewhat uncertain; but it seems to have been born negatively, of a determination to ditch Dato Onn and his Independence for Malaya Party; and, positively, by an act of faith on the part of two communal parties.[1] From this modest beginning of a tactical alliance to fight the Kuala Lumpur municipal elections there came the formal alliance between the MCA and UMNO in 1953, joined by the Malayan Indian Congress in the following year, to create the Alliance Party which was to take Malaya to independence and provide the government for the first fifteen years of its existence.

After the event it can be seen that the Alliance was a success; Templer was a success; and the object of handing over independence to a non-Communist government in a country in which the Communist insurrection had been largely defeated was achieved. It may also be seen now that the Alliance provided both the framework and the spur for independence. It was, for example, known that Britain did not intend to hand over political power to one community alone and it was suspected that she favoured Dato Onn's Independence for Malaya Party. By winning nine of the eleven seats in the Kuala Lumpur municipal elections the alliance between UMNO and the MCA took on the dimensions of a major political force and, although it may be argued that the colonial government was in any case going in the same direction, formation of the Alliance proper allowed the political transition on what Britain regarded as acceptable conditions. Comparisons between Malaya and Indo-China suggest themselves. At least, it can be said that what was conceded by

[1] See Margaret Clark, *The Malayan Alliance and its Accommodation of Communal Pressures, 1952–1962*, unpublished M.A. thesis, University of Malaya, 1964, pp. 33–40.

way of developing independence was neither too little nor too late and must also be regarded as the political definition of a campaign which was now changing from that of a colonial struggle in which the people could have been united against an alien government to a struggle for independence in which the colonial government had become an accessory to an emergent nation.

In his first year as High Commissioner Templer introduced local elections, village councils, Chinese citizenship in which over half the Chinese population was enfranchised; a merger of the War Council with a more representative political organ, the Executive Council; and provided the first opening for Chinese in the ranks of the Malayan Civil Service.[2] In April 1954, three months before Templer left Malaya, it was announced that there would be a majority of fifty-two elected members in a Federal Council of ninety-eight; and in spite of loud complaints from the Alliance they had, as Gullick says, won on decisive points i.e. that there was to be an elected majority and an early election and Malaya was seen to be moving into the first stage of an orderly independence.[3]

The Economy
Economically, the Emergency was now well embedded in civil affairs as a financial if not a fiscal problem and a fall in the price of rubber and tin not only suggested retrenchment but underlined the economic problem of war in an underdeveloped society: how much was to be spent on the war itself and how much was required for the social improvement, much of it enforced, that was already under way?

Malaya until now might have considered herself lucky. In spite of considerable wartime neglect and devastation, her commercial economy had undergone an amazing restoration by the time the Emergency began and had scarcely been checked by the course of the insurrection. Since the Korean war began, and the United States, in particular, had begun an enormous expansion of its strategic stockpile, the Malayan economy had been borne up by

[2] Gurney had made successive attempts to persuade the Conference of Rulers to accept non-Malays into the MCS and to this extent had paved the way for Templer's success.

[3] This is not to say that all political squabbles were abolished. At one point—June 1953—Templer and the MCA were in open conflict over the question of MCA lotteries in the New Villages. Templer objected on the grounds that it gave their organisers political influence. The MCA claimed that they provided the wherewithal to finance their welfare projects: which were then discontinued.

the boom in tin and rubber prices. In 1950 the price of rubber rose from 1s. 3d. to a peak of 5s. 11d. per pound; and in the case of tin from £578 10s. to £1,300 per ton. This had meant a considerable increase in Malaya's export earnings—it continued to be the principal earner of American dollars for the entire Commonwealth—and in 1950 Malaya had a favourable balance on its overseas trade for the first time since the War.

Internally, the boom in commodity prices had allowed government to take the cost of resettlement, which had to all intents and purposes begun with the Briggs Plan in June 1950, in its stride. Similarly, the abnormal costs that were being borne by the rubber and tin industries could be absorbed as long as high prices were maintained but with the fall in the price of rubber in particular there were renewed demands for a pause in the measures which made resettlement and food control more effective.

Over the entire period of the Emergency the tin industry reckoned to have spent $30,000,000* in protective and security measures alone although there were a little less than a hundred attacks made on tin mines throughout this period—eighty of them in Perak alone. Rubber estates were more widespread and more vulnerable. Large estates submitted lists of 'grievous financial burdens' which had been imposed on the industry by the Emergency which included loss of crop directly or consequentially as a result of tapping being prevented or interfered with by activities of both the guerrillas and the Security Forces; abnormal expenditure on security measures; transporting labour to and from uneconomically centralised living quarters; field works done out of season or under conditions which made them unduly expensive; direct or consequential uninsured loss resulting from the destruction or damage of buildings, machinery and vehicles; and loss or damage of rubber trees themselves. In 1951 and 1952 the cost of defence measures on European estates (members of the Rubber Producers Council) was given as seven and a half million dollars per year; while the cost of other measures directly attributable to the Emergency such as the regrouping of estate labour lines averaged over eight and a half million dollars—£1,000,000 —a year.

Over the country as a whole the cost of the Emergency had risen steadily. In 1948 it cost $14,000,000; in 1949 $50,000,000; in 1950 $60,000,000; in 1951 $155,000,000; in 1952 $210,000,000; and in 1953 the cost was variously estimated at between $250,000,000 and $270,000,000. These figures, however,

* The figures quoted are for Malayan dollars.

revealed only part of the Emergency cost. They did not, for example, include expenditure on the police other than Special Constables and the Emergency establishment of Police Lieutenants. They did not include expenditure on the Malay Regiment. And they did not include the cost of maintaining British, Commonwealth and Imperial Forces in Malaya. When these costs were added it seems likely that, by 1953 at least, the real cost of the Emergency was something like £100,000,000 per annum—and probably more. In 1952, for example, estimates of expenditure on Malayan fighting services were £42,000,000. In 1954 the High Commissioner gave the approximate cost to Britain of Army, Naval and Air Force units engaged in Malaya as £550,000,000 per annum. Even Emergency costs within the Malayan budget itself did not take in items such as, in 1953, two and a half million dollars that went in acquiring 50,000 acres for the New Villages or the cost of building 430 New Village schools; and with a total, again in 1953, of £200,000,000—33 per cent of the estimated State and Federal revenue—spent on social welfare it is probable that most of the Malayan budget in one way or another was spent on Emergency projects.

Incredibly, the Emergency had barely affected overall production and by 1950, which it will be remembered was one of the worst years of the Emergency, rubber production reached an all-time record of over 700,000 tons. In 1951, when there was a reduction in both estate and smallholding output, guerrilla activity was only one factor involved.[4] In any event, as long as a small decline in volume was more than offset by a considerable increase in price there were no immediate problems but the vulnerability of the Malayan economy could be seen in the fact that on the 1948 volume of rubber exports alone the change of one cent per pound in the price of rubber meant a difference in gross income of about two and a half million pounds sterling per annum. By the beginning of 1951 inflation had become a serious problem, and was regarded by government as second in importance only to the Emergency campaign. By 1953 the price of rubber had dropped to its lowest point for three years and Malaya's rubber exports were the lowest since the war.[5] From

---

[4] The other factors were an unusually prolonged period of 'wintering', very heavy rainfall throughout the year, and absenteeism induced by the high level of tapper earnings. The only restrictive factor attributed to the Emergency was the economic disturbance of resettlement.

[5] In the previous eighteen months (up to July 1953) Malayan exports of rubber to America had fallen from 360,000 tons a year to exactly half that rate.

1950 Malaya had shown a budget surplus but 1952, 1953 and 1954 saw a total deficit of $262,000,000. To some extent this had been covered by outside loans—from the United Kingdom, Brunei and Singapore—and the government loan had been successfully floated within the country itself. Nevertheless, the recession in its various forms was beginning to have economic and political consequences. A strategic embargo on rubber exports to China closed down half the rubber mills in Singapore and threw 2,000 rubber workers out of employment. In 1953, with tin at about a third of its peak price, it was reported that more than fifty Chinese-owned tin mines had closed in Perak and that nearly 10 per cent of Malaya's tin mine workers had been dismissed.[6] There was also an element of political uncertainty which produced a reported uneasiness among the business community and the consequent decline in the incentive to engage in fresh industrial and commercial enterprise.[7]

Taken together these factors meant that for the first time the principle of economy had to be observed in Malaya. The costs of the Emergency had increased enormously—not only with resettlement but with a much heavier military machine—since the opening compaigns had been fought with a small number of troops and supporting arms backed by large numbers of poorly paid Special Constables. Now it was a matter of more troops, more planes, more expensive weapons and far more police officers. Costs, however, did not get out of hand and there was no question of the Emergency being won at any price. Nevertheless economy was the principal reason for at least one of Templer's London visits although, in the event, Templer seems to have been more successful than his predecessors in securing both troops and British logistic support. In expenditure, however, it was impossible to dissociate the military from the civilian costs; and in definition it meant that once again it was impossible to dissociate the military from the civilian function of government.

Order of Battle
(1) Guerrillas
The strength of the armed guerrillas in October, 1953 was estimated at 5,500. It had fluctuated around this figure for the past

---

[6] Less obvious was the restriction on prospecting for new tin deposits that was imposed by Emergency regulations.

[7] *Overseas Economic Survey, Malaya*, March 1951. HMSO London, 1952, pp. 3–6.

two years and even at the time the estimate was given, when the MCP casualty rate had risen to about 140 a month, it did not appear to be too difficult for them to obtain recruits, at the rate of some 1,600 a year, in order to replace the lower ranks of the guerrillas in all areas although, in fact, many of them were now compromised into joining.[8] The fact was that 7,000 guerrillas had been eliminated from the beginning of the insurrection up to the end of 1953—killed, surrendered, captured and those who had repatriated themselves—but there were still 5,000 armed guerrillas charted on the Special Branch wanted lists. Combined Intelligence Staff analysis suggested, however, that there should be an upward revision of this figure by 20 per cent which meant that at the beginning of 1954 there was an estimated guerrilla strength of 6,000 plus. Of the 5,000 or so of those whose location was known fairly accurately the greatest concentration of guerrillas was in three States, Pahang, Johore and Perak. Numerically, Pahang was the strongest although operationally it was perhaps weakest with large numbers diverted to the protection of the Politbureau. For three years or more the Politbureau—Chin Peng, Siu Cheong, Lau Lee—had been located in the Kuala Krau area of central Pahang. At the beginning of 1953 it moved north to the mountainous deep jungle area around the Cameron Highlands in north-central Malaya in order to improve its external connections via courier routes northwards to Thailand. At the time that the Central Committee moved north the MCP structure was reorganised so that operationally there was a Northern Bureau and a Southern Bureau, the latter being given permission to make its own decisions without reference to Central. This decentralisation, while it may have been effective tactically, presented considerable administrative problems. Theoretically, control of the MCP continued to be vested in the Central Committee although, in practice, it was directed by the much smaller Politbureau. Central Committee members were nevertheless deployed throughout the country where they doubled up as members of the various bureaux and State Regional Committees. They depended therefore upon the existing MCP organisation in the areas in which they lived both for protection and administration while their control function could only be effective through an elaborate communications network. Towards the end of 1953 it became increasingly obvious that the areas which contained Central Committee members and the centres of communication were of

---

[8] The principal limitation continued to be the availability of food and arms.

BATTLE DEFINED

great strategic importance to the MCP. The seven areas were identified as follows

(1) *The Cameron Highlands area.* This, for the obvious reason that it contained Chin Peng and two of the three members of the Politbureau. In addition, there was the Central Propaganda Department headed by Lau Lee, guard units and so on to a total of some thirty or forty people.

(2) *Kuala Lumpur* area. Although small in numbers, Kuala Lumpur was important as a centre of communications for the whole country as well as a political forum and weathervane for political trends. It was also the home of Yeong Kuo who, in spite of the fact that he held some independent ideas on MCP policy and had virtually decentralised himself, was the linkman between the north and the south.

(3) *Raub/Bentong area.* This had been the home of the Politbureau before it moved north to the Cameron Highlands. In it there was a well-organised system of open courier posts and accommodation addresses which handled mail and communications on behalf of the Politbureau both to other Central Committee members and to China. It was also the home of the north and south Pahang Regional Committees.

(4) *Penang/Province Wellesley.* The MCP Northern Bureau and MCP activity in south Thailand were controlled by Kwok Lau, a Central Committee member living on Penang Island. The communications system that enabled this control to be exercised was centred in the area—whether Penang or the mainland was not known—while *True News Press*, an important north Malayan flysheet for the MCP, was also found here.

(5) *The Betong area.* This geographical salient was the area through which practically all supplies between Thailand and Malaya passed as well as nearly all communications between Penang, Kedah, Perak and Thailand. It was recognised that it was an area that was under a considerable degree of MCP domination and was regarded as an important link between the MCP, the Thai Communist Party and even, it was thought, the Chinese Communist Party as well. Government intelligence in the area was poor.

(6) *The Tasek Bera.* This enormous expanse of swamp in Johore[9] was the site which had been chosen for the newly formed

---

[9] Actually in Pahang but both Government and the MCP resolved that it was more readily reached from the Segamat district of Johore.

Southern Bureau headed by the formidable Hor Lung, a Central Committee member, and the long-established *Battle News Press*.

(7) *The Kluang area*. Although not connected with the higher control of the MCP or its communications network this area contained the Johore State Secretariat and Press; and since the Johore guerrillas were reckoned, at least by government, to present a greater threat than those of any other State, their elimination would obviously be a considerable blow to the MCP and it had therefore to be considered a vital area.

These seven areas could hardly be regarded as guerrilla bases, either in fact or Chinese communist theory, which the guerrillas would have to defend at any cost but it did mean, paradoxically, that the stronger the organisation the more would be lost when it was disrupted. The more extemporary and flexible the arrangements and the more self-contained the units the greater was the chance of survival; but if effective action depended upon co-ordination then every link in the organisation was the source of potential danger.

Order of Battle
(2) Security Forces
The success or failure of the Security Forces depended, conversely, upon co-ordinated action. Immensely superior in numbers, fire power and logistic support they had, nevertheless, to bring these advantages to bear upon an elusive enemy and his largely invisible support groups. Co-ordination here, therefore, meant co-ordination between the various arms of government, between civil and military activities, between the bodies which produced and collated intelligence and those who acted upon it. Under Templer, the army order of battle moved up towards a maximum number of twenty operational battalions which, although highly important in themselves, had to be considered in relation to all the powers and effectiveness of government and, even as a spearhead, depended upon its shaft and the accuracy with which it was aimed.

As both High Commissioner and Director of Operations, Templer was the embodiment of an integrated Emergency policy. Beneath him, D. C. MacGillivray, who had been brought in from the West Indies, was Deputy High Commissioner in charge of civil affairs and General Sir Rob Lockhart was Deputy Director of Operations. The Director of Operations staff was reorganised early in 1952 to include a Combined Emergency Planning Staff comprising an officer from the MCS, the police and the Army; and to ensure effective co-ordination and liaison there was a section of this name with the same composition. In 1953 when Lockhart's term of service expired he was replaced by Major-General W. P. Oliver as Principal Staff Officer who was no longer a member of the Federal Executive Council and thus, paradoxically, had an executive rather than a legislative and quasi-parliamentary role. In 1954 General Sir Geoffrey Bourne assumed duty as Director of Operations when Templer left Malaya and combined this role with that of GOC Malaya. Hitherto the post of GOC had been separate and was held in 1952 by Major-General R. W. Urquhart and in 1953 by Major-General Sir Hugh Stockwell.

Military dispositions in the Army command structure tended to reflect the armed strength of the guerrillas. For example, in 1952, two Gurkha infantry brigades were disposed in Johore, one in the north and one in the south, which was the heaviest concentration of troops in any part of Malaya. A third Gurkha infantry brigade was located in the adjacent States of Negri Sembilan and Malacca and a fourth was allocated to Perak. Selangor and Pahang had a brigade each, one British the other Malay, while a North Malaya Sub-District took care of Kedah, Perlis, Province Wellesley and Penang. In 1953 Malaya was divided into three main areas for military purposes with formation headquarters in the north, south and east but in 1954 the Army withdrew from Kelantan, east Pahang and west Perak, where control was handed over entirely to the police and Home Guard, and used to reinforce the existing military framework elsewhere in Malaya. In each State a senior military headquarters was established alongside police contingent headquarters in the State capital and was responsible, through the State or Executive Committee, for military operations throughout that State. At the second level, a brigade or battalion headquarters was to be found near Police Circle headquarters at the administrative centre of the civil District and was responsible, through the District Executive Committee, for operations in the District. At the third level, infantry companies were deployed in each Police District where the company commander and his opposite number in the police, the OCPD, were charged to work in close co-operation.

Police Reorganisation
With Gray's enforced resignation as Commissioner of Police a

similar problem arose to that of replacing Gurney. Local conditions, it was argued, needed local men and for some the argument was reinforced by divisions between the old and the new in the Malayan police when Gray had originally been appointed Commissioner. Gray's task had been to create an enormously augmented Malayan police force and to keep it running until it was in danger of coming apart at the seams. Whoever the new Commissioner was he would have the job of cutting back and putting the machine together again: most important, perhaps, to reassert its primacy as police rather than force.

Gray's replacement, A. E. Young, was Commissioner of Police in the City of London when he was nominated by Lyttelton for the job. A former colonel in British Military Government in Germany and a future Commissioner of Police in Kenya, Young's genius lay in presenting the image of the ideal London bobby; and in transforming that ideal into a Malayan reality. He arrived at a time when, above all, the Malayan police needed someone to restore their confidence in themselves, when at least potentially law-abiding citizens needed sympathy and when, perhaps, the most immediate need was for a professional re-organisation of the entire force. Para-military and intelligence functions would, in fact, continue but the fact that the police force as a whole was organised on para-military lines had obscured its principal purpose: that of maintaining law and order.

When Young arrived in Malaya early in 1952 the Malayan Police was more than seven times as big as it had been in the immediate postwar years; a sevenfold expansion which had in fact taken place in less than five years. The obvious but not always appreciated fact was that the proportion of experienced police—that is to say those who had had a normal instead of a crash course of training—had been diluted to one-seventh of the original. Only a rapidly diminishing corps of experienced officers had known police conditions, either in Malaya or elsewhere, other than those that confronted them at the moment. This lack of other experience precluded the majority of the force from understanding the status, efficiency and responsibility of the police in terms of normal rather than abnormal standards. The majority of all ranks below superintendent had had no previous experience or adequate training; and, frequently in the lower ranks, since so many were conscripts or had enlisted as a result of conscription, no initial desire to be policemen at all.

The immense expansion of the Police Force had been necessary to the point where it could be argued that it had saved Malaya;

but, by way of vindicating Gray, Young reported shortly after his arrival[10] that the command of the Force had been prejudiced by the Commissioner's lack of authority, in particular regarding the promotion and discipline of his officers; and that until recently, it had been harrassed by external interference with the executive command of the Force. The command function was, therefore, through pressure of events influenced too much by expediency and insufficiently by principle. Under such circumstances it was not surprising that the Force lacked cohesion or that effectiveness depended more upon local leadership and enterprise than upon the ability of individuals to improvise, instead of upon a well-constructed standard of efficiency dispensed and ensured by the fabric of the Force itself.

> At present the Force has an organisation which is paradoxically inefficiently efficient. It is inefficient, because it has yet had no opportunity to adapt itself to its enormous responsibilities. It is efficient, because by the efforts and enterprise of individual officers, it has overcome so many of its problems, that ironically it is too frequently regarded as the well-established, organised and consolidated Service which it has yet had no opportunity to become.[11]

The immediate tasks, as Young saw them, were therefore to inspire leadership, to ensure confidence, to define command, to distinguish responsibility and to secure common and effective standards which would make common purposes possible. In short, to ensure that everyone was given a sufficient definition of his duty, a reasonable instruction and guidance in his task, and afforded the opportunity and time to fulfil it. In what were perhaps the two most memorable expressions in a notable report Young said that in the vital task of constructing a Police Force, it was not architects who were lacking but bricklayers; and that in the immediate need for the employment of force to control force it was of paramount importance to see that this did not obscure the more important requirement of the future, namely that the Police should be acknowledged as a Service rather than a Force. It was no exaggeration, said Young, that the task of the Malayan Police was the most difficult, the most dangerous and perhaps even the most important police responsibility in all the

---

[10] *An Appreciation of the Basic Situation by the Commissioner*, March 1952.
[11] ibid.

world: it was upon this that he reckoned that its duty would be fortified and inspired.[12]

To this mundane advice Young added the touch of showmanship that made 'Operation Service' such a spectacular and successful operation. In form this was a warning order followed by directives but the purpose was clear at the outset.[13] The aim was that the police should be both respected for their efficiency and zeal and esteemed for their kindliness and goodwill to the public. The effectiveness of the police depended more than anything else upon the regard of the public and their appreciation that the police performed their duties with tolerance and understanding. The proper regard of public for police and police for public led in turn to confidence and co-operation. It was, Young said, an ironic misfortune that because of the Emergency the police had been compelled in the course of their duty to protect the public from terrorism by force of arms and by the imposition of restrictive ordinances rather than by co-operation and trust. Operation Service was a six-month programme. The police must be prepared to deal with any such request sympathetically with the attitude 'We'll do it—what is it?'. Throughout Malaya emphasis was to be given to the distinction between the regular and the auxiliary police on the basis that the former was a fully trained Service owing obligations to the public whereas the latter was an armed guard enlisted primarily for the purpose of protecting the public during the Emergency.

Broadcasting on 'Operation Service' Templer said it would be a poor victory if, in rooting out terrorism, they were only to substitute one fear for another.[14] Law and order had therefore to be shown not to be the instruments of tyranny; and in this it was

---

[12] An article in the *Singapore Standard* (February 28th 1952) was a reminder that other than heroic virtues were called for if the police were to become effective. Not only, it alleged, was the police force largely untrained, but it was largely corrupt and was regarded by the people as something to keep away from. At the same time the war was a police action if ever there was one for not only were they in charge of operations, but it was they who got the information upon which every action against the guerrillas depended and it was they whose job it was to track down the *Min Yuen* whose destruction had become the key to the military problem. It was the police therefore who could gain the confidence of the humblest people by giving them protection and proving by their conduct that the government was the people's friend. Training alone could establish that confidence between police and people which could radically change the whole situation.

[13] Commissioner's Instruction No. 36 'Operation Service'.

[14] January 27th 1953.

the small touches as well as the rigorous re-training that would begin to change public appraisal. A new police badge that featured two clasped hands; a change of name in Malay for police stations from 'lock-up room' to 'police house'; and, at the end of December, 1952 the directive that police employed in ordinary street duty in urban areas throughout the Federation would no longer carry rifles :[15] measures such as these may not have endeared the police to the Chinese population but at least they helped to offset their public image as 'oppressors' which derived from their tasks of raiding and searching suspected guerrilla areas, the screening of individual suspects and the enforcement of curfews. If, as the *Nanyang Siang Pau* said, the fear which the majority of Chinese still had of government employees and the police was based not only on the traditional concept of the police that they had brought with them from China but also on their lack of understanding of the real duties of the police, then anything which helped to promote the image of service was important. More important at this stage because, in spite of an egregious report in the London *Times* that the Malayan Chinese Association had undertaken to provide as many Chinese recruits as the police could take in,[16] the fact remained that there were no more than eight hundred Chinese in a uniformed Police Force of some seventy thousand.[17]

The gaining of public confidence by the police was a long term process; and while this was Young's major contribution as Commissioner of Police his role was essentially short-term and self-liquidating. He had been seconded by the City of London for one year only and an assurance had been given that they would not be asked to extend the secondment. Young had asked for his successor to be appointed by September 1952 and when this was done, although not until the end of the year, while it could not be said that the battle had been won, the character of the Malayan police had undergone a radical change. When Young and Templer arrived it had been agreed that re-training was the first

---

[15] When police patrolled continuously in pairs one pistol between the two of them was deemed sufficient.
[16] *The Times*, July 9th 1952.
[17] *The Straits Times* (July 12th 1952) suggested that Templer's target was to recruit 2,000 young Chinese volunteers for the regular police. Shortly before his death it was said that Gurney had hoped to recruit up to 10,000 Chinese for police service. 'There was full consultation with the leading Chinese but as soon as the men were called up the cry was all for exemptions; 6,000 decamped to Singapore and other thousands to China'.

priority and Young brought out his own training officer from London as the first of a number of specialist appointments. By the end of the year the concomitant of this programme, namely a reduction in forces, was also under way. The Special Constabulary, although it may have been said to have saved the day, was not a trained police force and in December, 1952 it was announced that there was to be an annual reduction of 10,000 until the police force was reduced from an augmented strength of 75,000 to a regular force of 30,000. Vocational training and resettlement on the land were to be given to those who were discharged; and for those who remained the concept of static defence was abandoned in favour of Area Security Units which, unlike Special Constabulary, had no territorial limitations and could be used for offensive action on a Federal scale. On the administrative level Federal Police Headquarters was re-organised into five departments each with a Senior Assistant Commissioner in charge and a Deputy Commissioner (Field) was nominated to establish closer liaison between CPOs in the States and Federal Police Headquarters.[18] The latter was strengthened by the secondment of seven suitably experienced Army officers to fill posts for which qualified police officers were not available.

Despite this apparent underwriting of para-military operations Young resisted pressure to employ large police units and substantial police resources on 'temporary operations mainly of a military character'. 'Every additional operational demand made upon the police, particularly during the next three months, must be paid for in compound detraction from an early effectiveness, which we will surely achieve if we are afforded a necessary breather and opportunity: "Reçuler pour mieux sauter" '. With large numbers of police in being there was always a temptation to use them as so many extra bodies whether or not they were effective. Young and Templer disagreed at times whether the police should be used simply to augment numbers and there were disputes in which Young stoutly defended the interests and honour of his force. More significant than these differences were the difficulties that Young experienced on constitutional grounds. In particular, he complained that his efforts to speed up substantive promotion had met with much sympathy but no success— 'there are so many authorities to be consulted and convinced that promotions take months rather than weeks to effect'—and the

[18] Significantly, in this reorganisation of departments the security intelligence apparatus (Special Branch) was split away from the CID. Jenkin had proposed the change some months earlier.

delay was attributed to the fact that the Commissioner of Police was entrusted with too little responsibility and that his judgement had to be confirmed and checked by so many authorities. Similarly with two existing establishments for Singapore and the Federation Young believed that this was an artificial restriction, described the present position of the two Commissioners as partners in a three-legged race, and recommended a merger or at least a joint Police Force. In a quieter way, a problem which had plagued both Forces was being tackled. Too many of the 'old-time' Chinese detectives had had practically no training, some were themselves secret society graduates, and around quite a few there hung the unmistakable air of corruption. In Singapore, particularly, corrupt detectives were assassinated 'on behalf of the masses': a gesture which not only brought some genuine relief but increased the MCP's hold upon the Chinese public. Not only were detectives of this order a liability: they were also inefficient. Recruitment of Chinese into the uniformed Police Force was not a success but an increasing number of Chinese detectives and intelligence agents were under training and in operation by the end of 1952.

Intelligence
The first requirement for most military activity is that the enemy should be identified. Hitherto in Malaya the intelligence picture had suffered from too much fuzz—a dearth of information, and much of what there was, low grade, unreliable and probably stale—but now that the picture was becoming clearer nothing did so much to define the battle itself. Successful intelligence however is largely cumulative; and in this, as in other successes, the effort and experience of the past four years began to pay off.

In October 1952 the Deputy Director of Operations felt that the situation had changed so radically that an off the record talk was called for at which the Press would be taken into official confidence. In part, the situation had changed for the better because the MCP's October directives of 1951 had now been made known to practically all armed units and wholesale offensive actions had diminished accordingly. But at the same time it should be remembered that the Security Forces had continued to inflict casualties at a rate slightly in excess of the average figure for 1951: and this was something that called for further explanation. The most important reason, briefly, was intelligence. Higher grade information was being received from the public;

it was being more efficiently collated; and was therefore used more profitably.[19]

As far as collation was concerned this was done at the highest level by the Combined Intelligence Staff who produced their first paper in April, 1952. A small group, seldom exceeding four in number but occasionally augmented to produce a particular paper, it was principally civilian, preparing its papers on instructions of the Director of Intelligence, although the greater part of these were circulated to the Director of Operations' Committee. CIS subjects ranged from comparatively small areas ('Situation in Bukit Pelandok area of Negri Sembilan') to whole communities (Malay Participation in the present Emergency') and themes such as MCP recruitment; MCP finance; and penetration and subversion of labour and the Home Guard. With experienced members of the MCS and Chinese Affairs it provided an evaluation of government's strengths and weaknesses as well as analysis of guerrilla organisation.

An impressive though perhaps limited demonstration of what had been achieved by intelligence was provided in the CIS intelligence brief for phase one of Operation *Hive* that was mounted in Negri Sembilan in August 1952. This operation, in its first phase, was designed to inflict maximum damage/casualties to MCP armed units in the MCP district of Seremban and to disrupt the MCP political structure in the area. The Seremban district was the most important centre in the State of Negri Sembilan for the supply of money, food and recruits to the guerrillas. Overt MCP activity had not been exceptional; but

---

[19] I am indebted to Mr. G. C. Madoc, former Director of Intelligence, for this note on intelligence reorganisation. 'For re-organisation it was, and there were some innovations of importance: (a) Templer created a Director of Intelligence. The latter was responsible for Intelligence, but was not in charge of the Intelligence collecting machine—the Special Branch of the Police. (This sounds clumsy, but it worked awfully well. The Director of Intelligence and his CIS could "field" the many questions descending from on high, most of them requiring research. Thus Special Branch often was protected from problems that would have diverted it from its main task of collecting and collating intelligence.) (b) the Director of Intelligence was a full member of the D. of Ops. C'mte, ranking with the service commanders. (I heard many times that this was the first instance of the absolute importance of Intelligence being given full recognition. I know that was true of Malaya.) (c) a highly efficient Intelligence (Special Branch) Training School was established for the first time in Malaya. Not only did it train Special Branch personnel; it provided short courses for some executive officers of the Army, "General Duties" Police officers, and certain civil departments of Government.'

what was exceptional was the penetration of its organisation which had been achieved by government intelligence agents. In a restricted and top secret appendix to its main paper, where, because it was so highly sensitive, it was announced as a model only: 'figures and details quoted are fictitious', it announced.

> Of the persons detailed under section 'lower formation' in the main paper all except the six Executives 'starred' can be identified. It is estimated that 75 per cent of them can be arrested at any given time, if necessary. At least 20 of this 75 per cent are already in Special Branch pay and several operations are concurrently in hand to induce the promotion of such individuals and thus to raise the level of contact. So far Special Branch agents in these categories are in touch with one District Committee member and ten Branch Committee members.
>
> Special Branch penetrations of lower formations have reached a satisfactory stage and it has been possible to 'induce' promotion of police agents within the Communist organisation. Thus the level of penetration and contacts is being raised rapidly. Contact has also been achieved recently with two District Committee members, ten Branch Committee members and sixteen rank and file, including Party members.

In the Seremban district over fifty 'Executives of the Masses' were known to be operating and they were assisted by over two hundred food suppliers, subscription collectors, intelligence agents and the like.[20] All of them presented a more or less sitting target; and to judge from the evidence most of them were a liability to the MCP. There was always the temptation to arrest known agents, particularly where large numbers were involved, and thus destroy a considerable part of the civilian infrastructure. More intelligence would probably be available as well from interrogation. But there was also the prospect of even greater success if operations were postponed until there was a good prospect of eliminating the really important men: in this case both the military and the political State Representatives, the District Committee Secretary, the Commander/Political Commissar of an Independent Platoon as well as the armed guerrillas. For this reason, therefore, the CIS recommended that these four leading personalities should be made the principal individual targets; that teams of Special Branch, operational officers and surrendered guerrillas should plan specific operations to achieve their surrender or elimination; that penetration projects should be pushed forward with all

[20] Among them, sixty-two who were classified as intelligence agents.

possible speed; and that immediately prior to the beginning of the operation only selective arrests should be made to ensure maximum information at the outset.

Seremban, among the big towns of Malaya, was also exceptional in the number of *Min Yuen*, both who were known to and had been 'turned' by Special Branch but it was an outstanding example of the reason why the MCP had largely abandoned the towns for operational purposes. The vulnerability of large static organisations and the danger when one or more of the links was broken had led the MCP to write off the towns except as a means of serving the rural areas. One of the decisions contained in the October Directives was that open or aggressive activity in a town must only be carried out by 'special service squads' of the rural forces; and that any Party member or Masses Executive working in a town, if compromised, must at once go to the rural areas. No unified system of leadership was to be established, no committees to be formed, no resolutions formulated while every member of a town organisation had to be of a quality sufficient to become a Masses Executive. Anyone of lower qualifications had to be discarded. No cells were to consist of more than three members and each cell must be separately led either by a Party Branch, a Party Cell or an individual Party member. Each Party member should himself develop not more than two cells, while a Masses Executive must not be allowed to develop more than one. While young educated cadres were essential, and it was therefore most important to develop the organisation amongst Chinese Middle School students, and while underground trade unions, anti-British leagues and sympathiser cells might be established, it was clearly laid down that the objects of town organisation were to send cadres to the rural organisations and armed forces.[21]

Penetration of the MCP and *Min Yuen*, while it provided spectacular intelligence, was enormously difficult to achieve and tended in any event to be limited to the urban areas. In the comparative anonymity of large towns it was nevertheless easier to achieve than penetration at the levels which were closest to the armed guerrillas. The problem of how members of the public could send anonymous information had been considered ever since the beginning of the Emergency. At the village level it was

---

[21] Probably the most important event leading to this decision was the elimination of the entire Singapore Town Committee in 1950 which, it can be argued, prevented co-ordinated activity in this invaluable MCP base area for the next five years.

sometimes forgotten how much bravery or foolhardiness was involved in a Chinese peasant walking into a police station either in daylight or well-lit by night, and making a statement that involved his name or a signed deposition to a Malay police officer on the whereabouts of guerrillas in the neighbourhood or the presence of guerrilla supporters in the village itself. The placing of Special Branch agents and informers in new villages, particularly when they could be introduced under cover of a 'scrambling' operation, helped to overcome the dangers of transmitting information; but to be seen talking to a Chinese detective in a coffee shop was still an act that required a high degree of civil courage. Most new villages, at one time or another, seemed to have had some sort of guerrilla counter-intelligence organisation and the argument, 'We have agents in all the police stations, all government offices. If you give information to the police you are giving it to us and we shall kill you,' was particularly effective.

'Turning' operations, by which *Min Yuen* were first identified and then persuaded to act on Special Branch instructions were one way of overcoming this problem in the rural areas but until the same measure of effective and practically omniscient government could be established there, as in many towns, other intelligence sources had to be exploited to the full.[22] Apart from voluntary information and routine detective work a great deal of passive intelligence was built up from captured guerrilla documents. Packs full of papers, usually discarded in ambushes or found in jungle camps, revealed details of organisation, weapons, personalities, frictions—and contacts with the *Min Yuen*. Their translation,[23] evaluation and collation was a slow and painstaking process but one which began to show results in the early and middle 'fifties and was enormously helped by the recruitment of police officers in Britain and the secondment of two or three dozen British army officers as Military Intelligence Officers to work inside Special Branch and create the somewhat different product of operational intelligence. This, in turn, sometimes led to the jackpot prize: the ambush, killing or capture of a jungle courier. Apart from the importance of such an event and the discovery of what were usually high-level directives, couriers often revealed contacts or the contact points that were known as jungle

---

[22] Major-General Richard Clutterbuck gives some semi-fictional examples of how agents were recruited in an interesting chapter, 'Intelligence Agents —Fact and Fantasy'—of his book, *The Long, Long War*, London, 1966.
[23] Translation was the particular bottleneck.

post offices.[24] For routine matters, especially propaganda, the guerrilla organisation used the normal postal services: which, when their contacts and guerrilla relatives were identified, led to the interception of mail.

Operational intelligence, that is about armed guerrilla units, was much harder to come by. Cumulative information about guerrilla camps, their size and location, was of limited importance. So was aerial photographic reconnaissance once the guerrillas had learned not to attract attention by planting their crops in neat rows but to let them grow haphazard in aborigine fashion. Deep jungle patrolling, as the experience of the Special Air Service was to show, was of very little use when there was no specific information to go on. Even where troops and police were deployed in areas where there was a good chance of making contact—for example in the approaches to new villages—there was danger of a vicious circle developing: no intelligence meant no contacts and no contacts meant no intelligence. For example, an analysis of incidents in Perak for the period May 1952 to March 1953 indicated that the great majority of Security Force contacts with guerrillas had been by chance and not as a result of information; but even without the operational intelligence which was almost foolproof—that on a particular day at a certain time in a given area a probable number of guerrillas would appear for a specific purpose (to meet a courier, pick up food, etc.)—there was a chance that effective patrolling would, of itself, produce the contacts and raise the intelligence. The most valuable single source of operational intelligence was the surrendered guerrilla;[25] and a cursory

---

[24] Usually but not always the trunk or the roots of a particular tree: practically and statistically impossible to find by chance in a tropical rain forest.

[25] Particularly when he was used before his comrades realised he had probably defected. The most remarkable feature of surrendered guerrillas was their willingness to lead security forces back to their camps. For the British forces involved this 'betrayal' was a constant source of amazement; for the guerrillas it was perhaps some sort of 'renewal': or else surrender had brought a new perception of 'truth'. In her recent study of Vietnam and the United States, Frances Fitzgerald writes, 'And all modern Vietnamese parties have had to face the task of changing the nature of the "truth". Among people with an extremely pragmatic cast of mind, for whom values depend for their authority upon success, the task has implied a demonstration that the old ways are no longer useful, no longer adapted to the necessities of history.' *Fire In The Lake*, New York, 1972, p.22.

The Special Operations Volunteer Force of some 200 men was composed of surrendered guerrillas, led by Police Lieutenants, and used for both 'Q-force' as well as more regular activities.

analysis suggests that the greater the pressure, the shorter the food, the more intensive the harassment, the greater the likelihood of inducing a guerrilla to surrender.

Strategy and Tactics
Templer's strategic definition of the battle which, in a sense, had been developing since Briggs' analysis and plan two years before, did not immediately become apparent. From the minutes of the Director of Operations meetings and the Combined Emergency Planning Staff no great design emerges, at least in the first year, and in 1952, 1953 and 1954 large-scale and more or less conventional military operations were going on all over Malaya.

In 1952 Operation *Habitual* was mounted in the Kuantan area of East Pahang and South Trengganu, with approximately two battalions and the official result was given as severe disruption of the Seventh Regiment's armed forces and attendant supply organisation and an incident rate that fell to practically nil. Operation *Hive*, whose objective of destroying the guerrilla organisation in the Seremban district of Negri Sembilan has already been mentioned, was a three battalion plus affair and a somewhat similar operation, *Hammer*, in the Kuala Langat area of Selangor which started in October and continued into 1953 was officially said to have resulted in the virtual destruction of the Communist organisation in the area. According to police sources, however, this was not the case. The *Hammer* Operation was the result of selecting it together with other unconnected areas which had bad Communist histories and which contained strong MRLA units. The operational boundaries were based on major geographical features and the operational areas were kept as small as possible to enable the greatest possible impact through concentration of forces. Surprise was a major factor in the plan, forces were secretly developed and no overt preparation was permitted in the operational areas beforehand. The police view was that the *Hammer* Operation brought some limited success; but failed in the intended total destruction of their targets for the following reasons:

(a) The operational boundaries did not coincide with the operational boundaries of the Communist target and often encompassed too small an area. Consequently, the MRLA target was able to evacuate the area under attack and still remain within reach of its own supply and intelligence organisation.

(b) The emphasis on secrecy hampered preparation on the ground and frustrated the participation of the civil arm.

(c) The operation was mounted with scant regard for Special Branch preparation and as a result little information of operational value was forthcoming after the first onslaught.[26]

The *Hammer* Operation failed because full use was not made of all available forces; and a police view is that a desire for quick and spectacular results, which had an overriding influence on the planners, was responsible for many of the faults. It was not until new operational techniques were evolved, and Security Forces had been conditioned to wait for their successes, that successful results began to be achieved.

Another operational excursus was the mounting of deep jungle operations. In 1952 Operation *Helsby* against the guerrilla organisation in the Belum Valley of Northern Perak employed three squadrons of 22nd Special Air Service Regiment in the principal role; and a month later, in April, three SAS squadrons, again with support, explored deep jungle areas and aborigine cultivations in North-West Pahang. In 1953 operations centred on Pahang and seemed, in part, to have aimed at the elimination of Chin Peng and the MCP's Politbureau. Operation *Cato*, which started in March 1953 in the area north of Raub in Pahang (whose gold mine, incidentally, provided a major source of MCP income) was launched on the rather scanty intelligence of an MCP Central Committee meeting and although a large number of camps were found practically no contact was made. Operation *Matador* in June and July 1953 was another deep jungle operation, this time engaging elements of five battalions, but, in the official record, direct results were not spectacular. In July, a battalion of the 7th Gurkha Rifles was getting warmer in its search for Chin Peng by launching Operation *Sword* in the Bentong area of Pahang but it says much for the men about him that he was never betrayed.

In late 1953 until the middle of 1954 Operation *Galway/Valiant* was carried out in deep jungle along the spine of Malaya on the borders of Perak with Kelantan and Pahang. Another deep jungle operation, this was initially to be a reconnaissance of the area for guerrilla communications but when the presence of Chin Peng was suspected in the area, immediately to the east of the Cameron Highlands, elements of six battalions entered the hunt for him but he escaped again.

[26] R. J. W. Craig, MC. *A Short Account of the Malayan Emergency*, prepared for the Inspector General, Malaysian Police, 1966.

In July 1954 Operation *Termite*, in the deep jungle east of Ipoh in Perak, was the largest joint army/air operation that had been launched in Malaya.

Information indicated a considerable concentration of terrorists in the area who were living with the aborigines and who were protected by a well organised screen of aborigine informers and patrols. The terrorists were confident that normal Security Forces could not reach them undetected, and thus the only way to do so was out of the sky. The mission was to win over the aborigines and to disrupt and eliminate the terrorist organisations in the area. Selected targets were accurately bombed by the RAF and this was immediately followed by a parachute jump by three squadrons of the 22nd Special Air Service Regiment on to the target areas and suspected escape routes in the deep jungle. Ground forces then closed in. These consisted of elements of the First Battalion The West Yorkshire Regiment (the Prince of Wales Own), the First Battalion The Royal Scots Fusiliers, the First Battalion The 6th Gurkha Rifles and the Fifth Battalion The Malay Regiment, supported by a company of the First Battalion The Malay Regiment, one troop of 'B' Battery First Singapore Regiment Royal Artillery, two platoons of the Police Field Force, one platoon of a Special Operation Volunteer Force and eighty armed aborigines. The majority of the forces employed were supplied by air throughout the operation and much troop lifting and casualty evacuation was carried out by helicopters. Many traces of recent terrorist occupation were found including several dumps, a large number of camps and many cultivation areas. In view of the disappointingly small number of actual contacts with the terrorists, resulting in only fifteen eliminations, it must be assumed that the majority of them had moved out of the area before the operation started. Owing to the bombing and the disturbance created by the Security Forces it was some time before the frightened aborigines could be contacted.

The most optimistic assessment of Operation *Termite* was that it had thoroughly disrupted the guerrilla organisation: for the time being. It was however necessary for Security Forces to continue operations in order to cover the establishment of a jungle fort from which protection could now be offered to the aborigines: and this was a very long-term operation. It represented nevertheless one of the major developments—deep jungle operations—which, a few years before, had been considered largely out of the question except for specialist units.

Army Tactics

By the middle of 1954 Malaya was covered with a military framework within which the greater part of operations were conducted. The deployment was one battalion to every police circle, with battalion headquarters at police circle headquarters and a detachment of not less than a company in strength covering the circle as a whole. It had been established much earlier that apart from distance the nature of the country made the company the largest tactical entity that could conveniently be handled by one person in the battle area.[27] A reserve of one

---

[27] 'Reflections of a Company Commander in Malaya.' Major R. E. R. Robinson, The Devonshire Regiment. *The Army Quarterly*, October 1950. Other public sources on service experience up to the end of 1954 are:

'Royal Marines in Malaya,' by Major W. R. Sendall, RM. *The Navy*, July, 1950.

'Some Account of an Operation in the Malayan Jungle,' by Lieutenant-Colonel K. H. Clark, RAMC. *Journal of the Royal Army Medical Corps*, Vol. 94, No. 6, June 1950.

'Tactics in Malaya,' by Major J. L. Hilliard, 10th PMO Gurkha Rifles. *Army Quarterly*, April 1951.

'A Subaltern's War in Malaya,' by Major P. E. Crook, OBE, RWK. *British Army Journal*, January 1953.

'Some Personal Observations on the Employment of Special Forces in Malaya,' by Captain J. M. Woodhouse, MC, Dorset Regiment. *Army Quarterly*, April 1953.

'Parachuting in Malaya,' by Captain D. D. Ranft, Royal Signals. *Army Quarterly*, July 1953.

'Operation Metcalf,' the Story of a Raid on a Terrorist Camp in Malaya, by Lieut.-Colonel W. D. H. Duke, MC, The Gordon Highlanders. *Army Quarterly*, October 1953.

'A History of 1st Battalion the Worcestershire Regiment in Malaya 1950–1953'. Extracts from *Firm*, 1954–56.

'Malaya—Time for a Change,' by M. Harvey. *The Army Quarterly*, April 1955.

'Jungle Crusade.' *Royal Air Force Review*, February 1950.

'A Supply Dropping Mission in Malaya,' *Royal Air Force Quarterly*, October 1950.

The principal books, for the main part based on first-hand experience, are:

A. F. Campbell. *Jungle Green*. London, 1953.
Oliver Crawford. *The Door Marked Malaya*. London, 1958.
A. J. S. Crockett. *Green Beret, Red Star*. London, 1954.
M. C. A. Henniker. *Red Shadow Over Malaya*. London, 1955.
R. C. H. Miers. *Shoot to Kill*. London, 1959.
J. B. Oldfield. *The Green Howards in Malaya*. London, 1953.
Tom Stacey. *The Hostile Sun*. London, 1953.
J. W. G. Moran. *Spearhead in Malaya*. London, 1959.

See also War Office Library Book List 537, *Operations in Malaya, 1948–1960*. (5th Issue, August 1962), and Gregory Blaxland, *The Regiments Depart*, London, 1971, pp. 73–131, for much interesting detail.

BATTLE DEFINED

company per battalion was earmarked for Federal operations but the emphasis now was on battalions staying in an area long enough for them to feel that they were disputing it on equal terms with the enemy.[28] Battalion performance varied enormously. As a whole, the outstanding performances were recorded by battalions of The Gurkha Rifles but although some British battalions were notably accident and ambush prone others, for example solid County Regiments such as the Suffolks and the Royal Hampshires, turned in notable performances. This was now a war which was to take in not only half the Line Regiments and all the Gurkha battalions of the British Army, but seven battalions of the Malay Regiment, battalions of The King's African Rifles and other African Regiments and, what was probably the most spectacular, a single battalion of the Fijian Regiment.[29]

Although obviously idiosyncratic—for example, locally raised battalions of The Malay Regiment had an obvious advantage when operating in their home territory—army success generally depended upon the way in which they were articulated into the general civil/military framework. On a tactical level publication of *The Conduct of Anti-Terrorist Operations in Malaya* in 1952 provided every platoon commander with an indispensable handbook. Contents were unspectacular—background to the country, the enemy and government forces, the characteristics and format of jungle operations—but it represented, in immediate action drills, patrolling and ambush situations, the distilled experience of the past four years and is still used as a basic manual on Malayan jungle fighting. In it, the size of the fighting unit is firmly identified as that of the platoon, the section and even the sub-section of two or three men.

Royal Air Force
In 1953 a new dimension was given to the RAF role in the Emergency operations. Three years earlier in May 1950 a casualty evacuation unit had been formed and helicopters were introduced for the purpose. In 1951 fifty-five casualties had been lifted out of the jungle by helicopter and in 1953 there was a

---
[28] The Officer Commanding The First Battalion The Worcestershire Regiment, noting the Battalion's move to Selangor in September 1951, wrote, 'This was the fourth major move since arriving in the country, and it was a great pity that the Battalion had to leave an area which they had now got to know thoroughly and in which recently they had had notable success'.

[29] Australian ground forces took part in later Emergency operations.

tenfold increase which reflected not only on the increasing number of deep jungle operations but also on the more widespread use of helicopters. Up to 1952 only five small S.51 helicopters were available and their role was limited to that of air ambulances. The immense possibilities that helicopters offered began to be realised when a helicopter wing was formed in 1953 which had under its control an RN squadron of S.55s as well as an RAF squadron of S.51 machines. The larger S.55s were largely responsible for the total number of 14,000 troops who were lifted in the course of the year and in 1954 another squadron was added: although this was equipped with the smaller S.51 machines instead of the larger troop carrying aircraft which were called for.

It was not until 1954 that Air Headquarters, Malaya, moved from Singapore to Kuala Lumpur and established its air staff adjacent to HQ, Malaya Command. Hitherto tactical headquarters had been established at Kuala Lumpur although the airfield there had not always been available either for air strikes or for air supply drops. These tasks, which had been performed since the beginning of the Emergency, continued and while there was no question of the increasing importance of supply dropping missions—long-range patrols which needed to be supplied every fifth day would have been impossible without them—it was not altogether certain how effective air strikes on guerrilla locations had been. When RAF heavy bombers zeroed in at night on to an electronic homing device that had unwittingly been introduced into a guerrilla camp, the results were spectacular. At other times they were a matter of conjecture. In a notably optimistic paper that was produced in February 1950 the AOC Malaya claimed that, despite the small weight of attack, it was known that at least a hundred to a hundred and fifty guerrillas had been killed as a result of air strikes.[30] It was also claimed that many of the contacts between Security Forces and guerrillas had been brought about as a direct result of disorganisation caused by air attacks; and that many surrenders had also been engendered by air strikes.

Surprisingly, Gray, the Commissioner of Police, confirmed at the time that air strikes had contributed more than any other factor to the number of bandit surrenders; but whether air attacks could disrupt guerrilla organisation or whether they had caused anything like the number of casualties claimed was

---

[30] *Air Support in the Malayan Campaign against Communist Insurgents.*

another matter. In fact, when it came to a tactical role the RAF could only make a small contribution.

The Army had asked three questions:

(a) Can the RAF take over an area and deny it to the enemy, on similar lines to the area prescription on the North-West frontier of India and in Palestine?
(b) Can the RAF encircle and cut off an area whilst ground troops are attacking inside?
(c) Can the RAF drive bandits out of an area towards stops placed by the ground troops?

The answers to (a) and (b) were negative; and to (c) the answer was that something could be done but only on a limited scale. In part, this was due to the scarcity of aircraft at the time: three strike squadrons (one Tempest, one Spitfire, one Brigand) and a squadron of eight Dakotas that were used for air supply communications and air lifts.[31] With the arrival of RAF and RAAF Lincoln bombers the pattern of attack on guerrilla camps changed, but it is perhaps more important to see how the incidence was reduced.

In 1952 the RAF attacked nearly 700 targets, flew nearly 4,000 offensive sorties and dropped over 4,000 tons of bombs. In 1953 less than 300 strikes were made and 2,300 sorties were flown. Conversely, there was a 30 per cent increase in parachute supply drops from 1,500 to 2,000 tons of supplies dropped to jungle patrols and police posts. In 1954 the quantity of supply had gone up by over 40 per cent on the previous year. By and large the RAF was now committed to an ancillary rather than a primary offensive role: locating the enemy by tactical and high-level photographic reconnaissance and supplying, evacuating and sometimes transporting the ground forces who were launched against what must often have appeared to be a tempting aerial target.[32]

Royal Navy
In February 1952 the gunboat HMS *Amethyst* appeared thirty miles up the Perak river to bombard a suspected guerrilla camp.

---

[31] Two squadrons of Sunderlands were used primarily for coastal reconnaissance but could be diverted to provide a rather improbable strike force. Harvards were also diverted from training purposes and for sheer noise took some beating. They were, by inference, the stated cause of at least one guerrilla surrender.

[32] Also psychological warfare: leaflet dropping and 'voice' aircraft, *infra*.

Two years later a new *Daring* class destroyer worked its way up nine miles of the Johore river for the same purpose. These were two of the more spectacular events in a series which, in 1952 for example, totalled thirty-nine bombardments by destroyers, frigates and minesweepers. Most of them were coastal and by 1954, except for a bombardment by the six-inch guns of the cruiser HMS *Newfoundland* in the Kedah peak area after the CPO Kedah had been ambushed and killed, the withdrawal of guerrillas into the deep jungle meant that only occasionally were targets within range of naval guns. Apart from an element of surprise warships provided little more than convenient gun platforms and their employment as mobile artillery was subject to the limitation of all offensive shelling in the Malayan campaign: imprecise co-ordinates and an uncertainty which way the guerrillas would move which made it a matter of harassment rather than destruction.

Like the RAF the Navy was also used for troop landing: occasionally coastal but more often using landing craft, launches and experience on riverborne operations. In the air, Naval helicopters were first into the troop carrying business and occasional air strikes were launched from aircraft carriers that were visiting Malayan waters. The Navy's principal role however was to maintain the territorial definition of the campaign by its coastal patrols. In 1952 over a thousand craft were stopped and searched; and in spite of the rumours of coastal landings, Russian submarines and the like there is still no evidence of either men or weapons being landed by the guerrillas on Malayan shores.[33]

Frontiers
The Navy had, in fact, sealed Malaya off on three of its four sides; but while its greatest effort was on the east and west coasts the border problems were greatest in the north and the south. Southern problems were dealt with by the Straits Control Organisation[34] which was aimed at Communist/guerrilla supply lines

---

[33] Nor is any evidence of intercepted supplies or landings such as characterised the Algerian and the second Vietnamese wars.

[34] The Straits Control was exercised through 'The Straits Control Committee' and a 'Joint Control Authority' and was set up in March 1953 as a result of negotiations between Singapore and the Federation Government and a conference that was held in Singapore in September 1952. Apart from the control point which scrutinised approximately 80 boats a day the most interesting feature was the 5 pairs of fixed-beam searchlights. Except in very heavy rain craft crossing the beams showed a distinct silhouette to watchers on either side.

between Singapore and the mainland of Malaya which used innumerable small craft and equally numerous Chinese fishing *bagans*—wooden fishing huts built alongside fish traps and above the comparatively shallow water—were to be found in the Straits of Johore. This was a frontier that was open to naval interdiction and with constant patrolling and the use of powerful land-based searchlights guerrilla lines of communication were seriously affected. They were still possible both by sea and across the narrow thread of land that constituted the causeway between Singapore and Malaya. Here, at either end of the causeway, control was constant and if men and supplies sometimes slipped through it was on a very small scale.

The Thai Border
For most of its three hundred and seventy miles Malaya's northern border with Thailand, which included three large salients of Thai territory, runs through thick jungle. Then as now there are two road and two rail routes linking Thailand and Malaya which cross the border but any number of established smuggling trails. Population in the border areas varied. On the Malayan side the Malays who were largely antipathetic to the guerrillas. On the Thai side was the Betong salient, 80 per cent of whose population of 12,500 were Chinese and who, for one reason or another, largely supported the Communist Party. In appearance this was an open frontier and although it was impossible with the Security Forces ranged on either side of the border to prevent incursions of men or the supply of weapons and materials, in fact it was open only to the point at which the MCP, their Thai supporters, armed guerrillas and *Min Yuen* either wanted to or were able to collect and move supplies into Malaya. In 1951 and 1952, after one of Thailand's periodical coups, it was estimated that about two hundred small arms, mostly automatic, some home-made hand grenades and ammunition came across the frontier.[35]

More important than this potential source of supplies and reinforcements—although this was an unsolved problem and one that had always to be considered together with the possibility of a change in the political alignment of Bangkok and even the enormous possibilities that were open to China should she decide on active intervention in Malayan affairs—was the steady build up of Malayan guerrillas along the border as they considered

---
[35] Occasional Madsen sub-machine guns, originally supplied to the Thai Navy, and .38 automatics bearing Thai Navy markings were recovered from guerrillas in Malaya.

it prudent to move out of other parts of Malaya. In April 1952 it was estimated that 200 guerrillas were on the border. In August 1953 the figure had risen to 540 and although they were comparatively quiescent not only did they present a particular problem in that they were able to slip across to the comparative sanctuary of Thai territory if the attention of Malayan Security Forces became too pressing but it was soon to be the moving but definite location of Chin Peng and the Central apparatus. On the Malay side of the border there were, in the western sector alone, over a thousand police, including Special Constables, while on the Thai side there were some three hundred men of the Ninth Police Division actually on the frontier itself. Thai politics had for long ensured the invulnerability of Communist organisations, whether indigenous or foreign, and when, eventually, the law was passed outlawing the Communist Party the potential of the Thai Police was reckoned to be low due to a lack of training, equipment, adequate legal powers and Chinese speaking personnel. Police pay was inadequate, thus opening the way to corruption; many of their senior officers were actively engaged in politics; and their intelligence system was almost non-existent. Within their limitations however the Thai Police of the Ninth Division did all in their power to co-operate with Malayan forces but it was in Bangkok that an understandable absorption in politics detracted from the possibilities of effective action in the south.

Formally, and after a good deal of prompting from the British Embassy in Bangkok, a Thai-Malayan border agreement had been concluded in 1949 which was supposed (*a*) to prevent guerrillas being able to escape from the police of one country by crossing the frontier into the other and (*b*) to enable either police force to investigate without delay reports reaching them of wanted men or of concentrations of terrorists in adjoining areas of the other country. Materially, this agreement provided for the crossing of the frontier by police patrols engaged in counter-guerrilla operations subject to the condition that they should normally be accompanied by a police officer of the other country —although this was waived in favour of early liaison where this was initially impossible—restriction in the numbers of a patrol to thirty-five—although two or more patrols might operate in conjunction when prior permission had been obtained—and the proviso that arrests should be effected by the national police in their respective countries. In effect this meant the exclusion of military patrols from Thai territory and a restriction of photographic reconnaissance to the Malay side of the border only.[36] The principal drawback to mounting anti- guerrilla operations in the border area, and one of the main deficiencies in the border agreement itself was intelligence. This had already begun to be remedied by the cross-posting of liaison officers but in August 1952 a big step forward was taken with the establishment of the Frontier Intelligence Bureau at Penang and this led to the establishment of a combined Malayan/Thai Special Branch team at Songkhla, with posts at Sadao and Betong in South Thailand and a series of joint Thai/Malayan Police Field Force operations against guerrilla targets. By the end of 1954 co-operation between Thai and Malayan forces had increased considerably and in spite of areas of particular sensitivity Malayan guerrillas could no longer rely on finding sanctuary once they were over the Thai border.[37]

Standard Operations

In the GOC's appreciation of the situation—October 1953—intelligence and food control were described as decisive weapons in anti-guerrilla warfare. In order to apply these throughout Malaya a framework of battalions deployed by companies now covered the inhabited areas. Day to day operations by framework companies based on short-term information, local knowledge, and knowledge of the terrorists in the area were the most profitable way of getting kills and accounted for about 80 per cent of the guerrilla casualties including a fair proportion of surrenders. Guerrilla casualties, however, including surrenders, were spread evenly over the country so that a damaging blow was seldom dealt to a particular MCP organisation and, almost

---

[36] In February 1952 the terms of the agreement were extended to permit the use of landing fields on both sides of the frontier by aircraft of the RAF and Royal Thai Air Force. However, there were no well-established Thai air bases in the vicinity of the border and only three serviceable air fields in the entire country.

[37] A small number of revolvers and Bren guns had been presented to the Thai police in 1949; but it was difficult to persuade the Commissioner of the Ninth Police Division to accept further assistance which might be considered to be charity and a reflection on the adequacy of Thai resources. It was made known, however, that practice ammunition, tinned jungle rations, five hundred pairs of jungle boots and four new lorries would be acceptable as a gift. Another area of sensitivity, particularly in view of the past and future irredentism in what were largely Malay speaking border provinces on the east coast, was the operation of Malayan intelligence agents on the Thai side of the border.

without exception, the upper echelons had not been engaged. In any case, the Army, while it had frequent success in its mosquito hunts, was not sufficient to deal with the breeding grounds; and in order to do this had to be integrated in the highly elaborate, extremely complex standard type of food denial operations.

These were based on a previously prepared intelligence plan and were aimed at a specific MCP district. They did not produce rapid results but were the only method which promised to clear up an area permanently and had proved to be the most successful way of dealing a concentrated and sometimes devastating blow at the total guerrilla and Communist organisations in a particular area. They had produced a higher proportion of surrenders than any other form of operations but, as they needed to be sustained for a period of three to six months, troops engaged were therefore committed for long periods with a consequent loss of flexibility. The purpose of a food denial operation was to destroy a specific guerrilla target by the interruption of its supply lines and a complete stoppage of its supplies so that the guerrilla, weakened by hunger, was induced to surrender or be captured or killed by Security Force action on information. It was designed for inhabited areas where civil and Security Force effort could be concentrated and intensified food control combined with vigorous Security Force action against the guerrilla target. Its essential feature was the complete stoppage of guerrilla supplies.[38] In the normal area that was covered by a District War Executive Committee it was recognised that food control could not be completely and continuously effective in view of the limited resources available; but in a food denial operation the guerrillas had to be cut off completely from their supplies and this task had first call on the Security Forces available.

The operation was normally mounted in three phases. Phase one was a preliminary period of one to two or three months in which intelligence was built up. Phase two saw the beginning of the operation itself with an intensification of food control and Security Force pressure. Phase three was designed to exploit the enemy's loss of morale and the increased flow of intelligence by Security Force ambushes, patrolling and attacks on located camps. In phase one the Special Branch, assisted by military intelligence, prepared the target intelligence which was required to mount the operation. Security Force action in the area was often necessary

---

[38] A very important exception was where Special Branch had intelligence agents among the food suppliers. Then, a loophole would be left deliberately to attract guerrillas to points well covered by intelligence.

to force the guerrillas to move and thus to increase the flow of information. In phase two the operation itself began with a concentration of SF and the occupation by them of the New Villages and labour lines. At the same time the simultaneous arrest of as many known food suppliers as possible caused maximum disruption to the guerrilla supply lines; and the lifting of surplus stocks of foodstuffs and the application of intensified food control measures was designed to prevent alternative sources of supplies. If, as a result, the guerrillas were cut off from all supplies a situation was created in which they would be starved into surrender or else obliged to move into areas of the Security Forces' choosing. As the information available from surrendered guerrillas and other sources increased, phase two merged into phase three when the main SF effort was switched more and more to ambushes, attacks on camps and other action to eliminate the guerrilla target.

In all this the Army played an important part but it was one that was part of a larger play. Apart from stirring up intelligence in the initial phases, destroying food dumps, patrolling and ambushing, all of which could be done independently, their most important role was as a striking force in the final phase when they were launched against known targets. How these targets became known was as a result of an integrated civil and military effort and it is worth remembering that food denial operations were always the responsibility of a District War Executive Committee. In any case the Army was expected to assist indirectly in the gathering of intelligence by advising and helping in the improvement of the local defences, in the training of the Home Guard, and in assisting police and Home Guard on the gate and field checks which prevented supplies passing at the individual level.[39]

On the purely civilian level food denial operations were accompanied by outbreaks of supercharged administration. All departments of government were ordered to make their presence felt in the area and senior officials instructed to visit all schools, public health facilities, estate labour lines and all agricultural and drainage projects. The most detailed administration and regulations naturally concerned food itself. Additional food inspectors were posted in to purchase all surplus rice, orders were issued to whole-

---

[39] Apart from putting on a demonstration of armed strength—positions for guns and 3 inch mortars that fired into the jungle were to be in or near inhabited areas—morale and information were to be encouraged by the use of bands, medical aid, team games and other forms of contact with the local population.

salers and retailers, checks were made of surplus ration cards, periodic checks in conjunction with the police were made on stocks of rice and what might be called tactical commodities not only in shops but in all private houses as well. People living inside food restricted areas had to buy their food from within the area from one of a small number of licensed shops. Rubber tappers and manual labourers were not allowed to take food out of their villages for a midday meal, thus causing considerable hardship, and in particularly bad areas an Operational Rice Ration was introduced that was little more than half the normal ration.

By the time Templer left, in June 1954, instructions for food denial operations which also included the role of police, Special Constables (operating as Area Security Units), Home Guard, information services and psychological warfare had been issued in standard form by the Director of Operations. Not surprisingly, no more than two such operations could normally be mounted by a State at any one time but in spite of the fact that they were to increase in complexity they were now the standard and most effective planned operation against a guerrilla target and its support organisation.[40]

White Areas
Counter-insurgency, to be effective, begins by taking Chu Teh's aphorism that the guerrilla moves among the people as a fish swims through the ocean—and turns it back upon itself. Food denial operations, New Villages and all the civil measures that were designed to assert government control over all populated areas did not succeed in draining the ocean but it at least began to create the shallows in which the guerrillas might more easily be seen and caught. By imposing massive control, however, as was done in food denial operations, there was always the danger that it would create such bitterness and hostility as to make it self-defeating; and the problem remained of how to lighten the burden once the object of destroying the guerrilla organisation had been attained, and how to provide some sort of prize that would both encourage co-operation with and lighten the burden of government. The solution was found in the concept of the White Area.

White Areas were defined as those in which certain Emergency regulations, such as food restrictions and curfews, could be sus-

---

[40] The actual area of the operation depended on the guerrilla target chosen. It was particularly important to establish its normal operational boundary but normally the area was no larger than that of an MCP District.

pended because the Emergency situation had so improved that their continuance was no longer necesary and their relaxation was a justifiable risk. The policy began in September, 1953 when part of the central district of Malacca was declared 'White' and in the next two and a half years White Areas were extended to include almost half of the entire population. The introduction of a White Area meant the suspension of all local restrictions on food and other 'tactical' articles, the lifting of curfews and the decontrol of roads, and the optional ending of rice rationing. There was no general dismantling of defences in White Areas but Home Guard units were reduced to a cadre of ten to twenty young, picked volunteers. Similarly, there was to be no uncontrolled dispersal of labour forces that had been regrouped; but, subject to a Special Branch appreciation, details of resettlement that had been carried out and a brief Emergency history of the area, the Director of Operations Committee would consider the proposal to declare a White Area.

An important factor in considering such proposals was the degree of co-operation between the inhabitants and government: something that was both a local and a national function. The question that might be asked after the event was whether, judging from reports, this was being eroded or even destroyed if not at the national level then at the level of one of the two principal communities.

Criticism of Templer
Templer in Malaya is perhaps best remembered for the aphorism that it was a battle for the hearts and minds of the people. He is also however the subject of violent attack by the distinguished Chinese scholar Dr. Victor Purcell and although the conflict between the two—rather one-sided in its public aspect— is probably not sufficiently important to require separate analysis it is useful in that it provides the most articulate criticism of government's Emergency policy at this time and raises the question whether Templer created a police state in Malaya; whether this was consonant with winning the hearts and minds of the people; whether his policies were effective in the matter of counter insurgency and in the larger political task of creating a viable basis for independence.

Malaya: Communist or Free?[41] may be taken as a book that is written from the liberal standpoint. It might, alternatively, be regarded as the pro-Chinese view of the Emergency; or it might,

[41] London, 1954.

on a lower level, be taken as evidence of a personal vendetta. Its author was not only the authority on the Chinese in Southeast Asia, but had considerable experience of Malaya as a senior member of the pre-war Chinese Protectorate and a colonel in the post-war British Military Administration. Badly wounded as an infantry officer in the First World War he was not without practical experience of military affairs and his urbanity, wit and distaste for everything pretentious made him, as his memoirs reveal, the most charming of literary companions.[42] With every expectation of balanced judgment the very wide range of his charges is therefore more disquieting. Perhaps the most serious was that the Templer regime, like no other administration that Malaya had ever known, cut at the very roots of civil organisation. There were many others:

> Steps towards self-government were nothing but window-dressing.
>
> Malaya early in 1954 was politically one of the most backward territories in the British Empire.
>
> Owing to the Emergency controls, potential leaders were either under lock and key, behind barbed wire, or in exile.
>
> If the present policy was continued, the situation in Malaya would in time not differ materially from that in Indo-China and would be just as hopeless.
>
> The official substitute for self-government under the Templer regime was charity and uplift.
>
> The political side was to be subordinate to the non-political.
>
> There was no human activity from the cradle to the grave that the police did not superintend.
>
> The real rulers of Malaya were not General Templer or his troops but the Special Branch of the Malayan Police.
>
> What General Templer had ordered was virtually a levy *en masse*, in which there were no longer any civilians and the entire population were either soldiers or bandits.
>
> The means had become superior to the end.
>
> Force was enthroned, embattled and triumphant.

Continuing Purcell's specific charges, they are that Emergency regulations suspended basic civil rights; that the Legislative Council was much less representative of the people than the old Russian *duma*; and that, bearing this in mind, the incessant talk of justice, democracy, representative institutions, welfare, service, partnership of the community, winning the hearts and minds of

[42] *Memoirs of a Malayan Official*, London, 1965.

the people, was so much hypocrisy. The inference was that talk of independence for Malaya was a sham : it was, for Purcell, no more than a measure of self-government by easy stages within the present century. Political reform had therefore been relegated to the role of psychological warfare and, more comprehensively,

> What was so terrifying about the regime was not its harshness or its brutality, but its bankruptcy of imaginative resource, its stultifying reliance on threadbare platitude, its complete lack of all mental content. It was a terrifying combination of crassness and voodoo.

All these charges are, incidentally, laid in the introduction and not in the text of Purcell's book. In the text itself he levels two historical charges against the British administration : the almost complete failure to teach the people to govern themselves; and turning Malaya into a plural society. When he turns to the post-war period his singular opinions are replaced by singular facts. For example, an idyllic picture of the situation in 1950 with the Briggs Plan going steadily ahead, immediate improvement in areas where resettlement was completed, decrease of incidents, and what he calls 'the gradual disappearance by resettlement of the guerrilla supply bases', the visible improvements in civilian morale and a further increase in the flow of information.[43] The situation in 1951 that Purcell presents is too good to be true.

> Wherever resettlements were completed, the original terrorist and extremist organisations were disrupted.

This is remarkably misleading. There was very little resettlement that was 'completed' in 1951. Barbed wire fences were lacking, perimeter lighting was lacking, and, with their absence, one cannot pretend that any sort of security had been given to a New Village. The only hindrance to the guerrillas was that they might have to walk further to get their supplies and information.

The situation described by Purcell is the one observed in his visit to Malaya in August and September, 1952 at the invitation of the Malayan Chinese Association. It was one of 'restlessness, friction, anxiety, widespread corruption and a general feeling of discontent'. The essentially civilian atmosphere of pre-war Malaya had vanished, he wrote, and a fashionable barbarism was taking its place. That this essentially civilian atmosphere might be an

---

[43] He is also careless with his figures both for numbers of regular troops and the cost of the Emergency and, more surprising for the author of the 'Myra Buttle' books, he misquotes G. K. Chesterton.

unavoidable casualty in a country undergoing insurrection is not a point that Purcell considered, although 'fashionable barbarism' is sufficiently disquieting in itself, and it is this impression on Purcell's sensibilities that suggests an atmosphere very different from European official sources, whether civil or military. Perhaps the most interesting charge, certainly as far as Templer was concerned, was that 'so far no answer had been found to the terrorist campaign'. This is curious. Particularly when one bears in mind the success of resettlement which Purcell postulates for 1950 and 1951. Could it be that Templer, on his own, had undone all this good work? That the War Executive system had ceased to function? That there was no approach to a solution? That is, even assuming that there was one answer to the problem.

From errors of policy to faults of character, there is an easy transition. Templer needed no colleagues or associates; he required only instruments of his will. 'What made his venom so blood-freezing was that it had no detectable undercurrent of humour or self-criticism.' 'No detail was too small for his attention' (this is taken to be a fault). Comments upon personality are, of course, legitimate. It is hard to understand the regime of Genghis Khan, Adolf Hitler or Torquemada without some reference to the personality factors involved. Purcell's fear, which one must assume to be genuine, was that

> where there were no truly representative institutions consisting of duly elected members, for example, Parliament, the kind of leaders who would obey this call (Templer's call for leadership) would include many petty führers anxious to exploit the situation and exercise arbitrary authority over their fellows under the High Commissioner's umbrella.

Templer's violence of language was a fact. So were many of the accounts of violent interviews and encounters. The instant removal of a portrait of Dr. Sun Yet Sen. The exaggerated remarks to a future Minister of Agriculture.[44] But the exaggeration that Purcell offers suggests what is almost a caricature of the situation in which one must assume that Templer was identified in thought and in policy with every expression of benevolent but semi-literate soldiers provided in a semi-novel *Jungle Green*[45] to which the Malayan Chinese Association took such sensitive but violent exception. Similarly, one wonders why Templer should be burdened

[44] Described as 'a rat' after an unflattering first hand report of the Coronation.
[45] Arthur Campbell, *Jungle Green*, London, 1953.

with the vulgar errors of the visiting American, Judge Douglas;[46] and anyone with experience of Ireland in the post-war troubles would wonder whether there were any comparisons to be made between police and Army in Malaya and the infamous Black and Tans in Ireland.

A Police State?
There are, in fact, so many specific opinions and details to which objection may be taken as might seem to invalidate a large part of Purcell's argument. On the whole his criticisms of the advances of Central and Local Government are valid; but much of the rest suffers from cheap jibes, confusion of the issues and charges that would be thrown out of most courts. Nevertheless, the most powerful argument which Purcell uses is in fact taken from a local source: an excerpt from a speech of Mr. Tan Cheng Lock in December 1953 in which he alleged that Malaya in many respects had become a Police State; in which the power of the Executive had been tremendously increased at the expense of the individual; and that the minor benefits that an autocratic form of government, like the one in Malaya, conferred on the country, could never compensate for the spiritual degradation which it involved.

Part of Purcell's argument must have been based upon conversations that he had when he was in Malaya; with those middle-class Chinese for example who spoke to him with such vehemence about Templer's 'raids' and his vituperation which included some of the General's victims who had refused to take his insults in the proper spirit and who regarded them as an affront to human dignity. Where they were mute, Purcell was articulate; where they were mild, he was voracious. In the Legislative Council, for example, Chinese and Malay criticism, although focussing on the iniquities of detention was notably tempered by discretion. Newspapers, and in particular the English-language *Straits Times* were more outspoken on particular aspects of long detention: which was only one of a number of disturbing legal features. Most of them stemmed from the fact that captured guerrillas were liable to the death penalty. In practice those who volunteered information and abandoned their former principles—in the extreme case of taking up arms against their former comrades—were not prosecuted. At the end of 1953 over a thousand guerrillas had been captured but the total number

[46] In an article entitled 'Jungle Treachery' in *Look Magazine*. Purcell cites them on page 241.

of those who were hanged throughout the entire Emergency was 226. The death penalty was becoming increasingly rare; when it was imposed on a woman it was often a matter of great concern.

The best known case was that of Lee Meng, known popularly as 'the grenade girl', who was arrested in 1952 and charged with being in possession of a hand grenade.[47] At the time of her arrest she was not armed and all the evidence was given against her by surrendered guerrillas from Perak. In this State, trial was by an English judge assisted by two assessors and in September, in her second trial, she had been sentenced to death by the presiding judge who declared himself in agreement with the European assessor after the two assessors, the other an Asian, had disagreed among themselves. At the first trial two Asian assessors had found her not guilty; but the judge disagreed and a retrial was ordered. Lee Meng's appeal against the verdict at this trial was dismissed on the split decision of the Appeal Court in Kuala Lumpur and in February 1953 she was refused permission by the Privy Council to appeal against her death sentence. In the event, and after fifty British MPs had signed a petition for clemency and the Hungarian Government had offered in exchange for her a British business man serving a term of thirteen years' imprisonment for alleged espionage, the Sultan of Perak in the State Executive Council commuted the sentence to life imprisonment and Lee Meng eventually returned to China.

The most obviously disturbing feature of this case was, as the *Straits Times* noted, the impression that in Malaya authorities ordered retrial after retrial until they secured a conviction.[48] The second feature, which Purcell notes,[49] is that if Asians had had the same right as Europeans—the right to trial by members of their own community—Lee Meng would not have been convicted. A third feature may be added: the difficulty of securing conviction in an open court when a verdict of guilty might have involved the death sentence for the Asian assessors as well as for the accused. Lee Meng was one of the most ruthless and capable members of the *Min Yuen* in Ipoh. The case against her was built up on the interrogation of surrendered and captured guerrillas

---

[47] Noel Barber in his exciting book, *The War of the Running Dogs*, London, 1971, gives an account of Lee Meng and presents her as 'the virtual boss of the Communist courier network, p. 165.

[48] *Straits Times*, March 2nd 1953. While believing that, for a number of reasons, the death sentence should not be carried out the editorial insisted that Lee Meng was not wrongfully convicted or denied justice.

[49] *op cit.*, p. 126.

BATTLE DEFINED

who affirmed her responsibility, amongst other things, for ordering a number of executions by guerrilla Special Service squads. Had it not been for the skilful and pertinent defence arranged by the Seenivasagam brothers of Ipoh[50] a judicious amount of publicity and inflation into an international issue the Lee Meng case might have attracted less attention.[51] But a second case, this time involving an apparently less culpable woman guerrilla, showed that government had neither learned much from the Lee Meng case nor had any moral scruple about sentencing women guerrillas to death. In this case an eighteen-year-old girl, Lee Ah Tai, was sentenced to death for the crime of consorting with armed bandits: although, in the event, sentence was reduced to ten years' imprisonment by the Federal Court of Appeal. Not long after, the death sentence was passed on a guerrilla convicted of carrying a revolver but on appeal to the Privy Council in July 1954 the sentence was quashed and the effect of the ruling was to recognise than an intention to surrender lawfully excused a guerrilla possession of a revolver or other weapons.

As with legal decisions, so with acts of policy that reacted on public confidence: the mailed fist was not entirely concealed. Emergency Regulation 17D which provided for collective punishment—it was perhaps the most unpleasant and notorious of all Emergency Regulations—was rescinded by Templer and upon inspection it may be noted that it had been used less frequently by Templer than by Gurney who had introduced it. Nevertheless, curfews, threats and punitive actions against recalcitrant

---

[50] A contributory factor to the subsequent remarkable political alignment in Ipoh in which the People's Progressive Party, consisting largely of the Seenivasagam brothers, was based upon a solidly Chinese electorate.

[51] There are other, less well known, features to this case. As part of her defence Lee Meng claimed that she was looking after two young children, her nephew and niece, who were apparently the children of a Central Committee member whose wife was dead. There was apparently unnecessary obstruction when her lawyer asked for their whereabouts; but it also appeared the police were fearful for their safety and had moved them to Kuala Lumpur in the care of a social welfare children's home. Second, she was shunted from Taiping to Alor Star—without the knowledge and to the express dissatisfaction of the British Adviser, Kedah—and thence to Johore Bahru. Finally, when her sentence was commuted to life imprisonment, the police were so anxious to have information of the courier routes which she supervised that they proposed to move her to a special interrogation centre for three months. This was rejected on the grounds that while government might be satisfied that it was properly conducted, it would be almost impossible to convince the public either in Malaya or elsewhere that information was not obtained by questionable means.

villages were continued by Templer and clashes with the Malayan Chinese Association, for example over the book *Jungle Green*[52] and the ban on MCA lotteries in New Villages for political reasons had as a sequel Templer's disclaimer in his farewell address that he was anti-Chinese.

One returns therefore to Purcell's charges. Was Templer anti-Chinese? Was he a dictator? And did his attitudes and policy hinder the success of the Emergency campaign? To appreciate the irony of the first question one has to remember Gurney's exasperation with the Chinese in his last days as High Commissioner; and substitute for this Templer's pragmatic optimism about the Chinese and their position and future in Malaya. It was shown in citizenship and the arming of Chinese Home Guard. In answering the second question one might perhaps be influenced by the image of the *Daily Mail* and *Daily Telegraph* Man of the Year but the answer would still seem to be no: although, with the powers of a Cromwell at his disposal, he often looked like the Lord Protector, albeit in his English rather than his Irish role. Perhaps in the end Templer stands or falls on two counts: the future pattern of Malaya and the course of battle which he directed. Purcell, who was deeply concerned with the political future of Malaya, believed that unless the Emergency powers were surrendered and certain risks were taken there was no reason to hope that there would be such freedom of speech, association and of the press as would allow the emergence of popular leaders. When he takes Ceylon as his model of the decolonised state and of the decolonising process one feels a certain fall of confidence; and one wonders in any event who were the popular leaders, the shadowy perhaps almost mythical figures, who had 'failed to emerge' by 1954. And what of those who had emerged? Dato Onn? Tan Cheng Lock? Colonel H. S. Lee? Tunku Abdul Rahman? Mr. Tan Siew Sin? Were they all to be consigned to the dustbin of history even though they took Malaya into independence and one of them remained Prime Minister ten years and more later? No Asian, says Purcell, had yet arisen to assume the role of a national leader. The vacant position, he says, was artificially filled by General Templer. This may have been true; but while it is true that he was a transitional leader it is also true that he was, simply, a leader.

Templer's methods, according to his critics, would lose the war. When he left Malaya, it was clear that the battle was being won. Guerrilla numbers were still very high but, although it still

[52] A. F. Campbell, *Jungle Green*, London, 1953.

appeared to be intact, the guerrilla organisation was about to crack. 1953 had clearly been the breakthrough year.[53] Large numbers of the guerrillas had been eliminated. Their vulnerability, notably in the matter of supplies, had been demonstrated and it was now a matter of exploiting their weakness rather than using military strength. For the guerrilla it was a problem simply to continue to exist.

[53] In his sometimes embarrassing panegyric (*Templer in Malaya*, Singapore 1954) Professor C. Northcote Parkinson begins each chapter with a quotation from Henry V. Overall, one from Julius Caesar might have been more apposite: 'There is a tide in the affairs of men which taken at the flood leads on to fortune.'

Course of Battle

15

THE NEW VILLAGES

At the end of 1951 the insurrection was neither more nor less than when it had begun. Guerrilla warfare continued : but the guerrillas themselves had never succeeded in transcending their limitations. In order, therefore, to deprive them of their support, and after a number of *ad hoc* experiments, government had decided that the only method which was at all effective was a concentration of the suspect rural population in properly laid out villages garrisoned by the police and enclosed by perimeter fences.[1]

If resettlement had been absolutely perfect three well-defined zones would have been in existence.[2] The first, the fortified area, would have contained a population which was completely under the rule of the Administration and securely protected by the police while it was inside that zone. Beyond that there would have been a second, unfortified area, a kind of no-man's land where a part of the population worked and where they came under the domination of whatever forces happened to be there at the time. This, the police would have controlled by means of patrols, ambushes and attacks on the enemy's organisation. Beyond it again would have been the third zone, the jungle and the jungle fringe, which might equally well be described as a no-man's land but which was mainly dominated by the guerrillas through their greater knowledge of the country. Here were the main guerrilla forces with varying but general support of the aborigines and it was this territory within which security forces would operate.

---

[1] During 1952, 56 additional new villages were established, bringing the number to 509 with a population of 462,000. There are some discrepancies for the total figures. Corry *infra* lists 439 New Villages as of September 1954. In May 1953 the Director of Operations Staff gave a figure of 535 New Villages with a population of 563,000 plus 84 NVs that had been planned. Kernial Singh Sandhu *infra* takes a figure of 513,000 transferred to New Villages between 1950 and 1960 and adds to this 650,000 who were 'regrouped' on estates and mines: 'The resettlement of about 1,000,000 —86 per cent Chinese—rural dwellers into more than 600 compact "new" settlements.' Whatever the exact figure, a round number of half a million resettled represents the largest and perhaps the most important social engineering project in South-east Asia since the war.

[2] This argument is largely based upon a paper by B. S. Davis, Secretary for Chinese Affairs, Perak. *The Briggs Plan and Resettlement*, Feb. 1952.

Ideally, therefore, the population would have been entirely cut off from the enemy when it was inside the settlements; protected to some degree while at work; and separated from the main forces of the enemy by the operations of the Security Forces. Or, to put it another way, a wedge would have been driven between the population and the administrative-cum-supply branch of the guerrillas and they, in turn, would have been separated by a less tangible wedge from their military forces. The result should have been that the guerrillas would be forced either to attack in strength to obtain supplies or to disperse into such small groups that unified command would have been impossible. The nearer this ideal was approached the quicker would victory be obtained. Perfection, however, could not be obtained without unlimited forces and an arrangement of the population which accorded entirely with operational strategy; but neither of these could be obtained except at the expense of the entire economy.

The most notable achievement of the Briggs Plan had been the establishment of a boundary between the guerrillas and the population: the perimeter fence, which was the only tangible frontier in the campaign and the existence of which, to some degree, localised what had previously been an almost ubiquitous battle line. Behind it lay the main source of the enemy's supplies. It was a frontier that was by no means impenetrable and in its rear the guerrillas had their own agents and supporters: for while it had been in the process of establishment they had not been slow to recognise its existence and to take steps both to render government's aims ineffective and to turn certain features to their own advantage. When the population was concentrated, government could administer them all easily. At the same time the guerrillas could tax them more easily. To control the population behind the fence was a main object of the enemy both as a strategic necessity and as a matter of prestige; and the methods he used were penetration, infiltration, propaganda and terrorism. The elements inside the fence which he relied on were convinced supporters, relatives of guerrillas, those who met them in the course of their work, the hired men, the terrorised and those who hoped to return to China before they died. Chinese, in the main, so the Chinese Affairs officers argued, would rarely betray or refuse to help members of their own family and that feeling might be extended to all members of their own clan. It was, however, only members of the first class who had gone out of their way to help the enemy if contact was made difficult. Any measure that tended to eliminate the guerrilla supporters within or to cut off contact with the enemy outside would strengthen government's position and contribute to victory. The more obvious measures were the strengthening of the perimeter fences, a better training of the garrisons and an increase in the Home Guards whenever reliable people could be found. It was better still, however, to prevent the enemy from reaching the population at all by aggressive action outside the perimeter fences.

With the exception of town workers living in resettlement areas on the edge of the larger towns the greater part of the population of the resettlement areas either worked on estates, mines or vegetable gardens without protection or else passed through relatively unprotected areas on their way to work. This, the inner zone, was dominated by whatever forces happened to be in it at a particular time. For eight hours a day workers were in areas in which they were likely to be within range and power of the guerrillas. Although their position was better than before resettlement, when the period of possible domination was a full twenty-four hours, it was clear that they worked with at least the tacit agreement of the guerrillas; that the guerrillas demanded a *quid pro quo*; that the workers paid for this privilege in information, cash and supplies; and that, if they did not, they paid with their lives.

It was obvious that this section of the population, with few exceptions, would do very little to help government and would help the guerrillas at least to the extent that ensured the continuance of life. As any action inside the perimeter wire on behalf of government would be interpreted as hostile to the guerrillas, they would do nothing except under the excuse of compulsion; and while there were elements among them who assisted government, there was no doubt that the majority would not help government or even stop helping the guerrillas until the chances of contact with them were considerably reduced.

It was in this inner zone, too, that guerrillas made contact with their agents inside the perimeter wire. The MCP's District and Branch structure, consisting of uniformed men, directed the *Min Yuen* from the fringe of the outer zone although, as the eyes, ears and general providers for the uniformed guerrilla forces they had usually to remain in or near a populated area. The *Min Yuen*, consisting of the plain-clothes branch of the MCP operating with identity cards, had to dominate and convert the rural population. The taxes they gathered were regarded as the most permanent source of income; and domination of the rural population was a necessary preliminary to the domination of the whole country.

Resettlement, imperfect though it was, had gravely upset the guerrillas' plans; but it had not, however, greatly affected the numbers of those whom they dominated.

In December 1951, for example, the Sultan of Kedah, speaking on behalf of the Conference of Rulers, had told Lyttelton that resettlement, at best, was only a qualified success. How—and if—these qualifications were to be lifted was something that was to occupy at least the next three years, probably six, and, arguably has been a continuous and continuing problem ever since. Ultimately it may be said to have involved the welfare, contentment and allegiance of half a million uprooted Chinese peasant farmers whose natural affiliations lay with the guerrillas and whose experiences had done little or nothing to modify their inbred Chinese antipathy to government.

Practically, and from the government point of view, perhaps the most critical period was that of the actual resettlement. In the early phases too little thought had been given to the physical problems, too little attention had been paid to the site itself and the whole project would often get under way in an atmosphere that ranged from sullen hostility to outright violence. By the end of 1951, with resettlement firmly in the hands of the State War Executive Committees, something like a standard pattern began to emerge. In Perak, for example, a paper by the chairman of the South Perak SWEC gave a good idea not only of the pattern itself but also of the lessons that had been learned. In general it underlined the importance of pre-planning and co-ordinated action. Resettlement that had taken place in the early years of the Emergency had largely been a matter of sweeping up squatters from one area and putting them down in another. With the realisation that the resettled squatter was there to stay for a very long time more attention was paid not only to the land itself, to ensure that it was capable of development, but also to the physical process of resettlement. First, squatters in an area to be resettled were defined—'agricultural' or 'industrial'. Next military parties were sent round to paint numbers on every squatter house in the area—and thus to count houses and approximate numbers—and sketch maps were prepared. The use of troops was essential, not so much for the security they provided but for their transport and the ready-made organisation that an army company provided. Before the actual move took place, however, a survey team could mark out a village site for two hundred houses in three or four days; and if post holes were dug at the same time the squatters, having been collected at first light, started building the barbed wire or mesh perimeter fence as soon as they arrived at the new site. It was important that the squatter should have brought his old house, or as much of it as he wanted to move, with him (for which army transport was provided) and in practice it usually took from seven to ten days for the new houses to be built. In the meantime they were housed in army tents, and, in addition to a disturbance or house grant of $70 a small subsistence grant was paid to resettled peasants who were temporarily deprived of their means of livelihood.[3] In South Perak it was reckoned that a New Village comprising agricultural squatters needed four acres per family and village densities were planned on this basis. It was fortunate that, in Malaya, land was available on this scale; and also that the decision that land should be available for squatters had been taken at the Federal level.

On December 1st 1951 government announced its policy of granting permanent title to squatters by all States and Settlement Governments, except Kelantan, which meant in practice that Chinese squatters in resettlement areas would be given titles to the land which they occupied. In practice, also, the granting of land titles was held up at State level, often through a shortage of Land Office Collectors, and there were frequent reports from District as well as Chinese Affairs Officers of misunderstanding among Chinese New Villagers about the terms on which they were to hold land and a reluctance to commit themselves and their resources to what seemed to be unknown hazards. Initially, the main difficulty lay in making contact between government and the New Villages and explaining the terms on which land was offered. Here, there were variations between States but the normal term was thirty to thirty-three years—except in Johore where the term was twenty-one years—and express conditions could be imposed to restrict the right to transfer or otherwise deal in land and to ensure that it was used for certain defined purposes.[4]

[3] The amount tended to vary with the State. In Kedah the disturbance grant ranged between $100 and $300 and the subsistence payment was $15 for an adult ($7.50 for a child) for up to 6 months.

[4] 'No question has been more deeply misunderstood and consequently misrepresented locally than that of the issue of titles to land to the resettled inhabitants of the New Villages—whether over house-lots within the villages, or over agricultural land outside. The prevalent misconception is that it is almost impossible to get a title to land in the Federation unless one is a "son of the soil"—and this definition would probably now include a federal citizen. Thousands of Chinese and other aliens are pictured as pleading in vain for titles to the lands they occupy which hard-hearted State Govern-

Surprisingly, MCP propaganda did not make much out of the issue of land tenure. In fact, the whole campaign against resettlement, having reached its peak around the middle of 1951, began to fall away in favour of other themes. A booklet issued by the Selangor State Secretariat of the MCP at the beginning of 1952 admitted that the 'no removal' campaign could never develop into a mass struggle or prevent resettlement, but that propaganda could still be made on the lines of demands for increased allowances, supplies of building materials and cultivating implements, transport facilities and compensation for damaged property. Grievances such as taxation, restrictions on movement, and occasionally a poor water supply or inadequate medical facilities were other targets which government was expecting the MCP to develop as well as any evidence of corruption or exploitation. For somewhat fortuitous reasons there seems to have been more MCP propaganda directed towards Malay resettlement in the mid-fifties than on the state of the Chinese New Villages; but the prospects of disaffection through careless administration were always there to be exploited and turned to practical advantage for the *Min Yuen* and, ultimately, 'The People Inside'.[5]

In part, bad resettlement was a product of bad co-ordination between government services; and the situation that existed before an integrated effort was made was, as the Resettlement Supervisor in Kuantan reported, one in which there was 'unlimited scope for modification and reconstruction in these projects'.

> An assessment of the units in existence conveys rather vividly the fact that little physical supervision; a dearth of specialised advice; a considerable lack of forethought were employed by the authorities who actually established these New Villages. Of the eight fenced areas in Kuantan district, not less than five were inside the

ments, actuated by favouritism towards one community, refuse to grant them. Any concessions now being made are presumed to be of very recent origin, and to have been dictated by the Central Government.' *A General Survey of New Villages*, by W. C. S. Corry, CBE, Government Printer, Kuala Lumpur, 1954.

[5] The name which Chinese New Villagers gave to the guerrillas. Undoubtedly the most brilliant, although imaginative, reconstruction of a disaffected Chinese New Village and its incompetent, corrupt administration is given in Han Suyin's *And the Rain My Drink*, London, 1956. The setting is fictitious as well as some of the generalisations implied but some remarkable insights are provided from Miss Han's experience as a doctor in Johore and her marriage to a Special Branch officer.

boundaries of a mining area—clearly defined by the Regional Planning Committee—yet, no record exists to indicate that the Mines Department were consulted, and indeed enquiries proved the fact, prior to establishing these New Villages.

Furthermore records clearly indicate that not one unit was projected with the assistance and advice of all departments concerned—emphasis being placed on the importance of Health, Agriculture, Drainage and Irrigation and Public Works. In fact, two New Villages were actually functioning before the local Health Department was informed.

The general location of sites is bad, with indication that water supply, agriculture and permanency were apparently never considered. These failings have caused the local inhabitants to be, in far too many cases, grouped, regrouped, settled and resettled. This indication of government administration has provoked a sullen subjection to the changing whims and fancies of successive powers (District) with the appalling result that East Pahang natives are very definitely anti-government, and unco-operative in all issues.[6]

This report, coming well after the formulation of the model South Perak resettlement plan, showed how much the fortunes of resettlement depended upon local administration. Some of the specific problems could be solved. Proper preparation, including job-classification, could be made before actual moves took place. Co-operation between security and resettlement departments seemed to be an elementary precaution. And an overall policy which related the New Villages to administrative units, such as a Town Board, was obviously needed.

On the ground, however, there was an equally obvious shortage of qualified administrative staff. In the South Perak report, the chairman of the War Executive Committee said that they had never had sufficient staff to deal really efficiently with the problems that had faced them; and apart from a senior member of the MCS who was needed as Resettlement Officer, particularly for financial matters, Chinese staff appeared to be the key to the whole problem : 'and it was in this respect that we were woefully short'.

Our staff consisted of two Chinese Town Board Health Inspectors, one Chinese English-speaking Detective, and as many Chinese Civil Liaison Officers as the military could supply; this was usually

[6] Resettlement Supervisor to District Officer, Kuantan, May 2nd 1952.

one per camp but sometimes less. The CLO's primary function was of course to help the military but they were able to do a lot of work for us in their spare time.

In the opening days as many Chinese speakers as can be found can be used with profit. There is so much to do that it is probably impossible even to obtain a really adequate staff. Malayan Chinese Association could possibly help with this although our local branch is not very active.

Once a camp settles down a little, two Chinese officers per Village are probably adequate—we rarely had more than one. Of these officers one is needed to run the shop and office and keep the various documents up to date while the other answers queries and is generally in charge. A Health Inspector who is usually a competent officer with a good grounding in health matters is very suitable for this job.

Ultimately I feel one Chinese Liaison Officer should be left in each camp after it has reached the completion stage. His main job will be to act as government's representative, deal with the Village Committee, help the villagers in their relations with the Malay Police, organise a village Home Guard as a sort of adjutant, and generally help in forming the village into a stable and happy community. In addition to this Liaison Officer per village, each District should have a Chinese Affairs Officer who can be directly responsible to the District Officer and can exercise a degree of supervision over a number of villages.

Even where Chinese Liaison Officers were acting as *de facto* MCS District Officers—a point not without political implications —another area in which Chinese help was essential to the success of a New Village was in its school. By contemporary standards there were serious deficiencies in Malayan education, both Chinese and Malay, but while Malays and children of Indian estate labourers had been provided with free education the Chinese had been left to develop their own educational system. Chinese schools were traditionally run by a committee drawn from community leaders in the town or village which the school served and were largely financed by the school fees collected from the parents. If the standard reached was considered sufficiently high by the Department of Education a grant in aid of five, seven or ten dollars per annum per pupil was handed out according to the standard reached; but even in the case of a school receiving the highest grant in aid it was often only barely enough to meet the teacher's salary unless the school was fortunate in having some very wealthy patrons. Thus, at the end of 1950, and after six months of the Briggs Plan, the Secretary for Chinese Affairs in Johore reported that the largest school in Muar was a month in arrears with its master's wages—and this was the least of the problems of Chinese school teachers. As a result of government economies in the early 1930s there had been practically no facilities in Malaya for training Chinese teachers and the result was that in most cases well-trained teachers in Chinese schools were China born and China educated, poorly paid, having no pensions or provident funds to look forward to and no security of tenure. Out of some 270 Chinese schools in Johore, only 100 had reached a sufficiently high standard at the end of 1950 to qualify for a grant in aid—which, apart from indicating the level of education, meant that, in practice, the Education Department could exercise little control except in matters of health. In 1952 the enrolment in New Village schools increased from 29,000 to 47,000 but, even so, at the end of the year with over 500 New Villages in existence less than half—234—had their own schools.

This was, however, an area of increasing expenditure from Federal, State and private sources and not least important, as far as government was concerned, was the need to teach teachers how government worked as well as to explain it to the New Villagers in adult education classes. In education as in practically all the services that began to be provided in the New Villages, only part of the cost, although nevertheless a substantial one, was borne by government. In public health, as in education, the New Villages focussed attention on the absence of government commitment to the extent that in April 1952 the Malayan branch of the British Medical Association called the New Villages, with their threat of epidemics, a new risk to public health, condemned the gross inadequacy of medical services and alleged that resettlement had been unsupported by any medical plan and had little or no regard for health. Government gradually began to assume responsibility for the health of the New Villages, but as late as 1954 the British Red Cross and St. John's Ambulance still had almost sixty medical teams visiting the New Villages.[7] In the absence

---

[7] Some idea of the hazards—and the dilemmas—of these unarmed and unescorted ladies is given in Barber, *op. cit.*, pp. 200–201. Sir David Watherston points out, 'These Red Cross and St. John nurses not only visited the New Villages, but they lived in them, gaining the confidence of the people, the women in particular. This provided an antidote of sorts to the attempts to form Communist cells. They travelled from village to village, unescorted,

of government commitment, however, Templer did his best to co-ordinate voluntary help and within a few days of arriving in Malaya he had taken the initiative that resulted in a Co-ordination Committee being set up under the chairmanship of the Chief Secretary which produced monthly progress reports to the end of 1953 on work that was being done in the New Villages by all unofficial organisations.

Much of the work was done by Christian Missionary Societies and, fortuitously, the reduction in the numbers of missionaries in China meant that more were available to work with the Malayan Chinese. Most of them specified in their reports that their work was evangelistic as well as medical or educational and although this may possibly be considered an ulterior motive it is hard to avoid the conclusion that without the work of these voluntary associations the New Villages would have rotted away. Between them, the obvious and the secular, such as the Malayan Chinese Association who were organising help to fellow Chinese, as well as the religious and little-known, such as the Evangelise China Fellowship, together helped to give a semblance of welfare and social services that did much to alleviate the harsher realities of resettlement.

The welfare of the New Villages, however, was a continuing problem and although there was constant attention to what was officially designated 'after-care' the situation in many New Villages fell away so badly that by the end of 1955 the Inspector-General of the Home Guard complained that shocking conditions were having a bad effect on the efficiency of his men. In the multitude of government reports from all sources and at all levels there were the same terms which had been used to describe slum clearance and evacuees in a generation of reports and blue books in Britain; and in some villages it seemed that no matter how much money was pumped in nothing would improve their squalid conditions.

How long the problem continued can be seen in the fact that in 1960, long after the Insurrection was over, the New Villages were included in the government's Rural Development Plan; but in the meantime, although there was perhaps a link between social

but were never ambushed. If a man came in with a wound, they dressed it and did not ask questions. They did a magnificent job.' A scheme for Police Health Visitors/Nursing Sisters was also introduced. 'Templer felt Police were entitled to the same privileges as the troops and would be happier knowing that their families were being cared for in their absence.' M. I. Lawrence, *Nurse*, May 1966.

squalor and political alienation, the expenditure on Chinese New Villages had been a subject of much unfavourable attention from the Malay community whose amenities, is was argued, were far less yet whose allegiance to government was something that was taken for granted. A full-scale report on the New Villages had been ruled out for political reasons : most important of which was the need to maintain a balance between Malay and Chinese development; and for many Malays a Chinese insurrection was bad enough without the additional insult of vast expenditure upon what they took to be an essentially alien community. In any case, there seemed to be no end to resettlement; and as the numbers of those resettled grew so did the numbers of those who had still to be resettled. In theory, resettlement was selective and was carried out as a security measure after careful logging by police and State governments of incidents in squatter areas. In practice, by far the greater part of the Chinese rural population was moved into New Villages but, even so, there were still 100,000 Chinese who had not been grouped into New Villages at the end of 1954; every one of whom was liable to divert expenditure from the Malay *kampongs*.

From the point of view of government expenditure would be justified if it removed a source of guerrilla support; but, in any case, it was argued that the New Villages were themselves an indispensable experiment in democracy. One of the weaknesses of the Malayan administration was the lack of local authorities at the lowest level. Where, in England, there were the Parish Councils or in Africa a Native Authority which was responsible for the small, detailed work connected with their particular area, in Malaya there was only the Town Board which, for various reasons, was unsuitable for the majority both of New Villages and *kampongs*. In a memorandum from Johore the Secretary for Chinese Affairs[8] argued that the village had for hundreds of years been a vital unit in China and therefore local government based in the Chinese village or settlement was the logical answer in Malaya. His first argument, apart from practical advantages, was that racial harmony would be encouraged in villages where there was a mixed population; and while this was of limited

---

[8] R. G. K. Thompson. Later Secretary for Defence in Kuala Lumpur and then head of the British Advisory Mission to South Vietnam. His book, *Defeating Communist Insurgency*, London 1966, apart from illuminating comparisons between the Emergency and the beginnings of the Second Vietnamese War, is the clearest statement of counter-insurgency principles and practice that one can find.

application the general argument that it would provide education and political development—was sustained.

> The workings of Municipalities, State and Settlement Councils, the Federal Legislative Council and the Member system are far above the heads of dwellers in villages and settlements, and even although some may acquire the right to vote in due course they are not likely to display the least interest in the franchise or for democracy in action, because they have had so little, if any, personal contact with it. If, however, the ordinary person can see exactly the same system working in his Village (or Settlement) Board as works in the Councils, then he will have a better chance of understanding democracy and his own responsibilities in democracy. Furthermore if the normal method of appointment to Village Boards is by popular election in which every resident adult has a vote and is himself eligible for election, no matter if he be alien or not, then the effect will be to teach those aliens who are not yet Federal citizens or subjects of the Ruler the advantages of democracy and their civic responsibilities under it.

In May 1952 the introduction of the Village Councils ordinance had also introduced the New Villages to the powers, perils and responsibilities of representative government. The power of the District Officers in selecting local representatives was soon reduced, the Ordinance extended to cover Malay *kampongs* as well as Chinese New Villages and by 1953 New Villages were gradually being absorbed into normal District administration and were no longer an Emergency priority. In February 1953 Templer set out the general priorities of a District Officer in which 'continuing to raise the standard in the New Villages until they had reached a position that could be considered to be properly settled' was the last on the list; but while improvements to Malay *kampong* life were considered to be more important, the inauguration and guidance of elected Local Councils took precedence over both.

By the time Templer left in July 1954 there were two hundred Village Councils in existence, most of them popularly elected, and all of them with power to impose limited local taxes and rates, to repair, maintain or build roads and other village amenities, and to undertake capital projects in their areas if the money was available. The Federal Government provided grants in aid in the ratio of one dollar for every two dollars they collected; and an annual budget and estimate were prepared. As a measure of introducing self-government about a million inhabitants of

New Villages had elected Councils by the end of 1955; and government was reported to have been delighted at the success of the plan to develop a democratic spirit among the New Villages.[9] At about the same time newspaper articles were also appearing which asked whether the position of the New Villages had really improved and suggested that there was a conflict between economic needs and security requirements.[10] Comparing losses and gains it was obvious that limitations had been put on both the area and quality of squatters' land; but, this on one side, perhaps the most serious inconvenience was the separation of the New Villager from his pigs and his market garden and the burden of carrying fodder and manure backwards and forwards. Constraints imposed by resettlement on agriculture had inevitably increased the smallholder's dependence on wage employment: hence greater exposure to fluctuations in wages and loss of security were the result.

This being said it was still arguable whether, given the opportunity, New Villagers would leave at the first opportunity;[11] and although it was a fact that for years there were disappointingly few applications for permanent title either to house sites or smallholdings this did not mean, as the article alleged, that those who saw in the introduction of 'civilised amenities' a vast improvement in the squatter's lot were, in fact, wrong. When the Emergency was over the most astonishing feature of the New Villages was the extent to which they held together. In place of the anticipated dispersal and general break-up of the New Villages the great majority of them continued and many of them grew considerably in size.[12] In a number of villages the wire fences remained for years, presumably because it was too much trouble to take them down, and continued to provide somewhat defective ammunition for those political combatants who saw in this continued proof of rural concentration camps. In the last analysis it was the perimeter fence that separated the guerrillas from their actual or potential supporters in the New Villages. It is, however, a crude analysis and the mere existence of a fence was no more than an acceptable hindrance if the villagers, for whatever reason, had a mind to help the People Inside. Security of a New Village,

---

[9] *Straits Times*, November 9th 1955.
[10] *Straits Times*, December 1st, December 2nd 1955.
[11] This, it was argued, was the implication of an International Bank Mission report in 1954. The Corry Report also considered that this was a likelihood.
[12] Kernial Singh *infra* gives a figure of only 6 New Villages known to have been abandoned out of 480.

absolute or relative, ultimately turned upon comparatively technical factors such as perimeter lighting,[13] the intelligence organisation within the Village and the quality of its Security Forces, whether police or Home Guard, but the condition was that other factors could be taken as being equal. From the administrative point of view Templer put his name to the following set of criteria whether or not a New Village could be considered to be properly settled.

1. The provision of at least a modicum of agricultural land, preferably just outside the wire, though in any case close at hand, for the agricultural population of the village.
2. A reasonably adequate water supply.
3. A Village Committee, or preferably a Village Council, which functions reasonably well.
4. A reasonably friendly and co-operative feeling in the village towards government.
5. A school to accommodate at least the vast majority of children, and adequate teachers' quarters.
6. A village community centre.
7. A reasonably flourishing Home Guard, i.e. one that has at least reached Stage II as defined in Director of Operations' Instruction No. 9, dated 14th August 1952, with an adequate village defence scheme and proper arrangements for the security of arms and ammunition.
8. Long-term land titles covering house plots and agricultural holdings.
9. Efficient perimeter wire, illuminated by night in the case of priority 'A' villages. In these latter cases, the inhabitants should be given the chance of having their own electric light in their houses at a fixed charge.
10. The beginnings of certain activities such as Scouts, Guides, Cubs, Red Cross, etc.
11. A reasonably friendly relationship between the police and the inhabitants.
12. A place or places of worship.
13. Trees along the main streets and round the *padang* and school.
14. Roads of passable standards with side drains.
15. Reasonable conditions of sanitation and public health.

[13] In February 1952, out of 350 New Villages, only 19 had perimeter lighting. In 1953 there was a standstill in perimeter lighting—not supplying it to 24 villages had resulted in a capital saving of $700,000—and it was still under consideration for some New Villages as late as 1955.

Even when the 'reasonable standards' outlined above have been achieved the village cannot be left entirely to its own devices. Interest and pressure will have to be kept up.[14]

From a security point of view the New Villages were faced with two hazards: first, the number of 'natural' guerrilla supporters that it might contain; and, second, the ease with which New Villagers might be contacted by guerrillas during the day when they were working away from the villages. Initially, New Villages were as good—or as bad—as their resettled population and, in the absence of screening operations, the good were mixed in with the bad and the contest for allegiance was on. Inevitably, very many New Villages provided their quota of *Min Yuen* whose job it was to organise the collection and transmission of supplies whether it was bags of rice or herbal medicines thrown over a poorly constructed perimeter fence at night—particularly one that was unlit—or the carrying of rice, clothing or other supplies in the morning when the tappers, peasant farmers and others went to work in the surrounding area. Nevertheless gate searches could make it extremely difficult, particularly when a specific food denial operation was in progress, to smuggle out even small quantities of rice although it was concealed in bicycle frames, padded brassières or in the false bottoms of pig manure buckets.

[14] Applying these criteria to the New Village of Salak South, five miles outside Kuala Lumpur, and the subject of a social and economic survey by A. F. and D. Wells, of the University of Malaya in 1953, this was obviously not a village that could be considered to be properly settled. The New Villagers were described as unco-operative, lacking in institutions and social amenities—no community centre, no school, no Home Guard, Boy Scouts, clubs or Women's Institutes—and little or no attempt at community development either by the Village Committee or by government officials. The Village Committee had not been set up until March 1953, nearly eighteen months after the beginning of resettlement, and among the committee there was dissatisfaction and the feeling that they had not been properly chosen. The fact that they were hand-picked by the Resettlement Office may have been a disadvantage; but one wonders whether there was any other way of choosing councillors or whether anyone was really 'suitable', i.e. did not have too much work to do. It was probably unrealistic to apply the standards of established representative government to Chinese peasant farmers but the committee's argument that they had neither authority nor responsibility and could take no effective steps to deal with shortcomings, e.g. bad roads or water was at least one that deserved to be taken seriously. Kernial Singh Sandhu provides some useful details and distribution maps of New Villages in his article, 'The Saga of the Malayan Squatter', *Journal of South-east Asian History*, March 1964. There are interesting—and saddening—comparisons between the New Villages and the strategic hamlets in Vietnam in Milton Osborne, *Strategic Hamlets in South Vietnam*, Cornell University 1965 (mimeo).

In the village of Semenyih, twenty miles from Kuala Lumpur with a population of 5,000, four-fifths of whom were Hakka-speaking Chinese, gate searching had been going on for three years before, in September 1955, it was intensified in anticipation of a security operation that was brought forward to the middle of January 1956. Semenyih had more than doubled in size since the Emergency began and a large part of its new population were the unfortunate Chinese villagers who had been burned out of Kachau.[15] More than four-fifths of the entire population worked as rubber tappers on surrounding estates, but it was reckoned that there were very substantial earnings, no unemployment, no outward signs of poverty and that the village presented a generally prosperous and thriving appearance.

It was surrounded by a wire perimeter fence, a little over three miles long, which was floodlit during the hours of darkness and in which there were four gates constantly guarded by Security Forces. Through one of them, the Kachau gate, some 2,500 tappers—over half the working population of the village : 60 per cent of whom were women—left every morning to go to the tapping areas which were anything from one to five miles away. Because of the curfew tappers could not leave their homes before 5 a.m. and could not, strictly speaking, pass through the perimeter fence until 6 a.m. There was no means of ensuring that they should present themselves at the gates in a steady stream and, in fact, they were much more likely to arrive in irregular groups. Then there was the difficulty that, owing to the geographical distribution of the tapping areas, more tappers wished to leave by the Kachau gate than by the other three gates put together. There were also material difficulties. The searching booths that had previously existed were falling to pieces. The searching had to be carried out during the hours of darkness for, during the month of January, the sun did not rise until shortly before seven o'clock and the pre-dawn period of twilight was extremely short. The lighting on the perimeter fence, which was the only lighting available, was normally extinguished at half-past five.

Under the Emergency Regulations, and subject to the provision that no woman was to be searched except by a woman, anyone leaving or entering the area within the perimeter fence or found in the area outside the fence might be searched by any police officer, soldier or Home Guard while engaged in food denial operations under orders of the District Home Guard officer. This power to search seemed to exist irrespective of any ground of

[15] *supra*, pp. 163–166.

suspicion which might be attached to any individual against whom it was exercised and also to imply the power to use any physical force that might be necessary to give it effect.[16]

The intensification of searching in September soon began to create discontent and on one day in November the tappers at the Kachau gate forced their way through in such a mass that no searching at all was possible. At this time searching was entirely in the hands of the police, including a number of women Special Constables and Home Guard searchers. But in early January 1956 a Gurkha Provost Company was brought in and assumed control of the gate searches. From the very beginning the searches that were carried out by the Military Police met with extremely strong disapproval and opposition on the part of the tappers concerned. This took the form of displaying reluctance, at times amounting to physical resistance, to going into the searching booths and outbursts of shouting which generally began with the women and spread to the men. By the middle of January 1956 after a series of complaints were lodged with and by political parties in Kuala Lumpur and a great deal of unfavourable publicity of the order of an eight-column banner headline which read 'Striptease Riles Village', the morning searches in Semenyih had practically turned into a riot and occasioned a Commission of Enquiry which began work on the spot almost immediately.

The Commission's Report was published in April.[17] Materially, it revealed that numbers of Villagers objected to effective searching; that some women searchers showed little consideration where women tappers had to dress and may well have been extremely offensive; that some of the temporary searching booths were semi-transparent; that some Special Constables and troops regarded the proceedings as a peep-show; and that on one particular day hardly anyone was able to get to work. The Commission's Report would also seem to be remarkable for its sym-

---

[16] It was a criminal offence punishable with a fine of $1,000 or imprisonment not exceeding three years or both to take any food or supplies into or out of the area enclosed by the perimeter fence without permission of the District Officer. It was also a criminal offence punishable with a fine of $5,000 or five years' imprisonment or both to be found in possession of food or supplies without permission of the District Officer in a very considerable area of country surrounding, and immediately outside, the perimeter fence. Except under conditions prescribed by the District Officer the movement of food or supplies on any of the four roads leading out of the village area was also prohibited.

[17] *Report on the Conduct of Food Searches at Semenyih.* Government Printer, Kuala Lumpur 1956.

pathetic attitude and notably well-etched picture of the burdens on a New Village as it went to work; the reaction against a routine that had suddenly become intolerable; and what food denial meant in effectiveness as well as discomfort. But perhaps its primary—and permanent—importance was a reminder of the conflict between civility and operational requirements.

> These events have to be viewed in their historical setting. For over seven years now the public have had to submit, and on the whole have submitted with most praiseworthy willingness, to a growing measure of interference with their personal liberties as a result of the Government's efforts to put an end to the present Emergency. This interference has been more acutely felt than elsewhere, though it has not been more real, in the case of that section of the population who have been compelled to live in the so-called New Villages. It has been supposed, and there are clearly grounds for this, that some of these people have been in sympathy with the terrorists and are disposed to assist them. There have been difficulties of race and language in the way of enabling them to appreciate that they are regarded as an integral part of the community as a whole. By nature and by upbringing many of them are intensely independent and individualistic. Most of them, until they came to live in the New Villages, were accustomed to live in isolated family groups and to rely on their own efforts and undoubted industry to maintain themselves and their families, a disposition which was strengthened by their experience during the late War when they are said to have been treated with a certain lack of sympathy by the occupying power. It is not suggested that life in the New Villages is altogether repugnant to them. Indeed there are indications that many of them welcome it. But for many of them coming to live in a community has in itself invoked an effort of adaptation and though it has enabled government to do more for them than in the past in the way of providing social services it has also exposed them more than in the past to what may be called normal interference with their lives and activities on the part of government. In the circumstances it is not surprising that at times they should show a certain impatience with the continuation year after year of additional restrictions which, however necessary, they may in some cases find difficulty in appreciating. Nor is it surprising that when as at Semenyih there is a sudden intensification of the incidence of these restrictions their habitual patience should fail them at least temporarily.

The causes for specific discontent were that

> In the first place, personal searching involves an extremely drastic interference with what is generally accepted as the sanctity of the person. It is true that it is an interference to which the individual may from time to time be subjected in the interests of the enforcement of law and there is no reason to suppose that at Semenyih it was not called for as a necessary element in the operations against the terrorists. Nevertheless, it is something unpleasant and it is something to which normally an individual would only expect to be subjected in the most exceptional circumstances. To expect thousands of people to submit to it morning after morning irrespective of whether there are grounds of suspicion against them individually is to put a very severe strain on their patience and understanding. It is not a question of degrees of modesty. It is a question of a very drastic interference with human dignity. No useful purpose is to be served by making general statements as to the character of the Chinese who are probably neither more nor less modest than anybody else. To appreciate what was involved it is only necessary to ask the question 'What would have occurred had a similar operation been carried out, and carried out daily, in relation to a large number of female operatives, proceeding to their work in England?'

> Apart from this on one particular day there had been substantial economic loss and there were certain unsatisfactory features regarding the way in which the searching was carried out. These, according to the Commissioner, contributed to, though they were not to be regarded as the main cause of dissatisfaction to which it gave rise.

> What has been said may be shortly summarised. The incidents which occurred at Semenyih in the first half of January this year were the direct result of the tightening up of the system of food control in and round the village which took place as a result of the substitution of military for police control. If it be accepted that such measures of food control are an essential part of the operations necessary to bring to an end the present Emergency, and, if it be accepted that intensification of these measures was necessary for operational reasons in Semenyih in January, it was probably desirable that the forces used should be military rather than police by reason of the difference in nature between military discipline and the more flexible discipline of the police. There can, however, be no two ways about it that this intensification caused very great popular opposition and dissatisfaction. To some

extent this may have been stirred up by Communist agitators but its main grounds were the increased interference with the personal liberty and economic activities of the people.

The actual incidents which occurred, deplorable as they were individually, were not in themselves important nor were they numerous when viewed in relation to the magnitude of the operation as a whole. They were, however, of importance as symptoms of a very real and substantial measure of dissatisfaction. The likelihood of causing such dissatisfaction is, of course, no reason why measures necessary in the public interest should not be undertaken. *Salus populi suprema lex*. It is, however, a matter which must be taken into account when such measures are embarked upon and this is clearly more so now than it was in the earlier stage of the Emergency.

This is clear from the public interest which was aroused by the subject matter and the conduct of the present Inquiry. For that, the Press was largely responsible by reason of the great amount of space it devoted to reports which perhaps tended to emphasize certain human aspects of the matter likely to appeal to its readers. It is plain too that members of the Malayan Chinese Association played some part in encouraging the people to give voice to their complaints. It is thought, however, that both the Press and the Malayan Chinese Association may have served the public interest here for at the very lowest their activity has led to the holding of the present Inquiry which, again at the very lowest, has afforded the people concerned an opportunity to give public voice to their grievances and has enabled a number of incidents unsatisfactory in themselves to be seen in their proper setting and proportion.

As an image of the Semenyih affair the gentleman who was asked to remove his shirt and trousers, and who subsequently complained, was presented as 'some sort of village Hampden'. From the point of view of security Semenyih, and the affair itself, look rather different. As the Commissioner noted, the District as a whole had for long been notorious as the scene of operations for the 'Kajang Gang' and in the month preceding the village incidents nineteen guerrillas had been killed or captured in the area. From the middle of October 1955 onwards there had been sixteen guerrila incidents in an area of four square miles surrounding the Village and these included the murder of a Chinese rubber tapper who was found tied to a tree and who had been shot twice and stabbed in the throat. In the six months preceding the Inquiry twenty residents of Semenyih were convicted for various food offences, nine for curfew offences, and some two tons of food had been found hidden in various parts of the area. During the first few days of January some twenty tappers leaving the area for work had been found in possession of carbide, valve rubbers and lighter flints, all of them presumed to be destined for the guerrillas. While the Inquiry was in progress a woman tapper was caught taking out a large quantity of Chinese drugs and two days after the hearing of evidence had been concluded two guerrillas were killed about a mile and a half from the Kachau gate. There was thus little doubt about the contact between Semenyih and the guerrillas. It was, however, doubtful at the time to what extent there were genuine grievances and to what extent they were the product of the local *Min Yuen*. Later in the year a paper by the Combined Intelligence Staff[18] suggested a new perspective on the affair. In July 1955—that is to say well before the intensification of food searches—a report which was admitted to be from an untried source was received of a meeting between guerrillas and the Semenyih *Min Yuen* at which the supply question was discussed and it was decided that the *Min Yuen* themselves should create trouble at the gate, complain of ill-treatment by the Security Forces, and that the Village Committee should be requested to approach the authorities with similar complaints. Later information showed that a member of the Village Committee was, in fact, a member of the *Min Yuen*: something that was by no means exceptional.

In some Villages it was said that practically the whole Committee was on the MCP side and, more particularly, numerous cases were established where individual members, including chairmen, were active members of the *Min Yuen*. It was, therefore, particularly difficult to decide whether what might otherwise have been quite innocuous requests—proposing the establishment of a co-operative store, complaining about food regulations, and asking that night school students should have curfew passes—were genuine or not and it was vigilance on this scale, multiplied by five hundred for the number of New Villages, that was required in the constant but, for the most part, peaceful battle for the New Villages.

Home Guard
Whether, in these circumstances, it would ever be possible for

[18] *MCP Penetration and Subversion in New Villages and other small Communities.* September 1956.

New Villages to provide their own security; or whether, by entrusting New Villages with their own defence security might somehow be engendered was at once the theoretical and practical problem that was involved in the expansion of the Home Guard. In 1951, when the Resettlement Plan was getting under way it was decided that in any area all males between the ages of eighteen and fifty-five could be conscripted into the Home Guard where it was considered necessary. Malays from the old Kampong Guard predominated but Chinese provided about 40 per cent. To relieve the police, the Home Guard was placed under a Civil Defence Department for training and organisation and a small permanent staff was provided. In December 1951 Lyttelton ordered complete reorganisation and in 1952 it was decided to make the Home Guard a separate Department of Government with an Inspector General and a small Headquarters Staff under the Ministry of Defence. Senior officers including Major-General E. B. de Fonblanque were recruited from the British, Indian and Australian armies but, as with Special Constables where the leavening of former Palestine Police Sergeants had not in itself been sufficient, the point of critical importance was to provide proper training for the rapidly increasing numbers. In July 1951 there were 79,000 Home Guards but in 1953 the numbers went up to almost 250,000 although by the end of the year the figure had dropped to 210,000. Even so, the greater part of the Home Guard were still largely untrained and although it could be argued that priorities were right and that it was more important to train the volunteer nine or ten man Operational Sections which operated in support of Police and Army and of which there were 400 by the end of 1955—the equivalent of ten Infantry battalions —the presence of Home Guard was not necessarily to be equated with the security of a New Village.

Originally, it was intended that Home Guards should not be formed in a New Village unless and until the security of that Village could be provided by the police or Army. Home Guards were to take over responsibility in three phases. In stage one the New Village was divided into sectors, each being the responsibility of a head man and his Home Guard. Their main duty was to watch the wire; to make sure that it was not approached from either side; and, somewhat optimistically, 'to report the presence of any Communist agents in their sectors'. At this stage they were unarmed but in stage two they reported to the police station for duty with police patrols in their own sector and drew shotguns for the duration of the patrol. In stage three 'when these men are better known' the original instruction was that Home Guards might be permitted to take shotguns to their houses so as to be more readily available for immediate action in defence but ultimately stage three meant that Home Guards were entirely responsible for the defence of their own Villages.

By the end of 1953 the Home Guard was fully responsible for the defences of 72 New Villages, as well as for the defence of most Malay *kampongs*; but as far as total security was concerned there were two serious hazards. It was recognised that because of the length of the perimeter wire—often extending to several miles —no Home Guard could defend it completely from penetration and that what was needed was a secure command post and standing patrol together with an alarm scheme wherein the Village was covered by a network of defended posts which would hinder or prevent the exit of the attackers. Home Guard actions in 1953 resulted in guerrilla casualties of 33 dead, 64 wounded and 65 captured or surrendered. Their own casualties were 43 killed, 7 wounded and 8 captured. As long as action could be anticipated this was at least an antidote to boredom but the routine involvement of Home Guard in gate searches and road checks was reckoned to be a soul destroying job in urgent need of relief. In October, 1953 it was decided that no Home Guard other than members of Operational Sections would be detailed for daytime duties on more than three days in any given month and that normally such duties would be limited to a maximum period of four hours. Nevertheless, the objective and the trend was a move towards small numbers of Operational Sections rather than a large number of static ones. Operational Sections of nine or ten men were formed from volunteers from the static companies and were paid and fed when on operations. At the beginning of 1954 there were almost 400 of these sections which were largely Malay, however, and, with very few exceptions, they were not organised in New Villages. Nevertheless, by September 1954 largely Chinese Home Guards had taken over defence of 129 out of 323 New Villages and the entry of a Village into stage three of the Home Guard defence scheme was of sufficient importance to deserve a formal ceremony. It meant, in fact, that the Home Guard Commander, himself a New Villager, was entirely responsible for the defence of his Village. Police and Area Security Units might be operating from or around the Village, but, in the first instance of attack, it was the Home Guard Commander who, on a prepared and rehearsed defence plan, mobilised the Village defences.

As with Village Councils so in Home Guards there was an element of risk. Very occasionally a Home Guard Commander might disappear with his weapon and ammunition. In one New Village in Perak Home Guard members spent their evenings on duty posting Communist slogans in the Village; other New Village Home Guards were either known or strongly suspected to have 'non-aggression pacts' with the local guerrillas; and there was a small but steady trickle of lost weapons. Sometimes the Home Guard post would be overwhelmed by prior arrangement but the figure of 103 weapons lost up to November 1954 out of a total of 89,000 issued seemed to vindicate rather than to condemn the decision to arm Villages and *kampongs* in their own defence.[19]

The second and more important hazard to Home Guard security came not at night when they were inside their perimeter defences but when, during the day, they were in the field farming, tapping and unarmed. Among Home Guard casualties could be reckoned those who were murdered during the day for no other reason than that they were loyal and effective Home Guards; but the fact that Home Guards could be and often were intimidated and suborned during the day cast doubts on their effectiveness at night. Some areas were particularly prone to Communist penetration. In Johore, for example, as late as 1956 it was alleged that MCP influence was so widespread amongst Chinese in the Home Guard that Special Branch coverage of all affected units was impossible. In one New Village there ten Home Guards were members of the *Min Yuen* while seven MCP members formed two Home Guard party cells. In Perak, too, the Combined Intelligence Staff said that many of the New Villages in phases two and three of Home Guard responsibility could be attacked under conditions of no resistance from the Home Guard: and the fact that there had been so few attacks was because the New Villages were such an important source of supply that it was thought expedient to leave them in peace rather than to invite restrictions by staging attacks. In May 1956, therefore, the Home Guard was entirely reconstructed both in theory and practice. It was decided that the defence of New Villages was to be entrusted to Chinese Operational Sections: and that these Sections were to be recruited from those inhabitants who were not field labourers and who were not, therefore, subject to guerrilla pressure by day.

[19] Where guerrillas were prepared to pay for their ammunition there was a standing and not always resisted temptation for very poor members of the Home Guard to sell their shotgun cartridges.

THE NEW VILLAGES

By the end of August 1956 two-thirds of the total authorised strength of 400 New Village Operational Sections had been established; and the remainder of the Chinese Home Guard were, at the same time, being stood down and employed on unarmed duties only within the Villages.

BATTLE FOR THE MIND

The Emergency was, in the words of Gurney as well as Templer, a battle for the hearts and minds of the people. In crude terms popular allegiance might be manipulated, manufactured or natural. In the first instance it was a matter for government's Emergency Information Services and the varieties of psychological warfare. Until Briggs became Director of Operations, propaganda and Emergency information generally had been one of the responsibilities of the Department of Public Relations, but the arrival of Briggs in 1950 led to the decision to intensify both the psychological warfare campaign against the guerrillas and the use of propaganda in attempting to raise the morale of the public and inducing them to provide information. When the British Government were asked to provide an officer with experience of wartime propaganda Hugh Carleton Greene, later Director-General of the BBC, was seconded to the Malayan Government for one year. His first report on conditions was not encouraging.

> Reliance had been placed to a great extent on leaflets and the possibilities of the direct spoken word, broadcasting and of films had for various reasons been comparatively neglected. Little use had been made in propaganda of surrendered bandits or the detailed intelligence about the terrorists and their organisation available to the police. There was too much general exhortation and not enough local detail, too much dwelling on bandit acts of terror (which was only calculated to help the other side) and not enough of the points where the enemy was weak. The physical problem of distribution, of getting the printed propaganda material both into the jungle and into the hands of the general public in the rural areas had not really been tackled. Communist leaflets and posters were a more common sight in the countryside than government leaflets and posters in spite of the millions that were printed. Interrogation of bandits who surrendered in the summer and autumn of 1950 showed that very few of them had ever seen any government propaganda material.[1]

[1] Report on Emergency Information Services, September 1950–September 1951.

In general, and at least until 1951, MCP propaganda was reckoned to be far superior to that of government. Far too much government propaganda was on too high a level altogether: 'stringent controls' and 'redeeming friendship', for example, did not have an immediate public impact.[2] In Negri Sembilan a State Emergency Information Officer was experimenting with various propaganda forms; but apart from the dubious value of forging letters to guerrillas from their families and inciting others to murder their superiors before surrendering, government officials were not always assisted by events.[3] For example, when it was critically important to stress that surrendered guerrillas were well treated the physical assault by a British officer on a surrendered guerrilla who had failed to find his previous camp was of no help whatever. According to some District Officers in 1950, ninety per cent of government's poster propaganda was discredited; and specific objection was taken to strong arm methods. Cinema slides were an innovation although the slogans were sometimes dubious.[4]

One of the most interesting recruits at Federal level was Lam Swee, former political commissar of the Fourth Regiment who began working for government in March 1951; but the bulk of propaganda output, in order to be effective and speedy, had to be devised at State and District level. States were given their own Emergency Information Officers, together with a full-time Chinese assistant, and in practice most of the work was entrusted to Chinese Affairs officers.

The task of the Emergency Information Services, as laid down by Carleton Greene, was

(1) To raise the morale of the civil population and to encourage confidence in government and resistance to the Communists with a view to increasing the flow of information reaching the police.

(2) To attack morale of members of the MRLA, the *Min Yuen* and their supporters and to drive a wedge between the leaders and the rank and file with a view to encouraging defection

---

[2] Difficulties of translation are not always appreciated, for example 'sitting on the fence', when literally translated, left many Chinese listeners baffled.

[3] 'Black' propaganda, i.e. manufactured by government but purporting to be from Communist sources, became an operation on its own. It is a highly sensitive area of inquiry and no assessment has been attempted.

[4] 'If your son is a bandit, he is your worst enemy.' 'The only good bandit is a dead one.'

and undermining the determination of the Communists to continue the struggle.
(3) To create an awareness of the values of the democratic way of life which was threatened by international Communism.

but the fundamental problem was how best to achieve these ends in a country where the majority of the population was illiterate, where four main languages were spoken and where the enemy— or rather the enemy armed units—was in the jungle.

As far as operational propaganda, i.e. the second purpose was concerned, experience had shown that the two strongest propaganda weapons in government hands were, first, surrendered guerrillas and second, rewards. For the first two years or so of the Emergency, government had probaly failed to make adequate use of surrendered guerrillas; and Carleton Greene's argument was that in any ideological war it was the convert and the deviationist who would have the most effect both on his former comrades and on those who had been influenced in any degree by the ideology in question.

> This showed itself to some extent during the German war—but still more plainly since international Communism became the enemy. Wherever the free world has been engaged in any form of psychological warfare against Communism it is the convert and the deviationist who have been recognised in the Communist world as the most dangerous enemies, because these people understand the Communist mentality and method as no one else can. Malaya is no exception to this rule.

Once they had surrendered the most effective forms of surrender propaganda were those produced by former guerrillas. Letters written by surrendered guerrillas describing their reasons for surrender and their treatment by government were reproduced in leaflet form in their own handwriting together with photographs. These were left on jungle paths, in guerrilla camp sites, dropped from the air by the million and distributed in areas where the *Min Yuen* was active and where there was direct contact with guerrillas. For dramatic effect and impact, however, personal appearance lecture tours by surrendered guerrillas in rural areas where they were well known were the most impressive.[5] News of these tours

[5] After one of the first appearances of Lam Swee in a rather bad area of Kluang a tapper came up to him and in sight and hearing of about two or three hundred other tappers seized him by both hands, burst into tears and said: 'I'm so glad you came out. Men like you can help to finish

and of what was said by ex-guerrillas got back into the jungle through the *Min Yuen* with remarkable speed. And the appearance of surrendered guerrillas in areas where they were known did more than anything else to undermine the Communists' own propaganda line that surrender meant torture and death.

One of the aspects of surrendered guerrillas that never failed to impress European observers was the willingness and enthusiasm with which most of them turned on their former comrades. Instead of rather shamefaced explanations of why they surrendered many guerrillas launched into vehement denunciations of the MCP and guerrillas in general and particular: something which helped to overcome the impression, while there were still few of them, that they were no more than 'running dogs'. Their presence, however, often provoked violent reactions from the guerrillas themselves; but although ambushes were staged there was never a sufficiently impressive retaliation to discourage SEPs from their propaganda tours.[6]

What was discouraging, at least in the first place, was the uncertainty of the SEP's position as far as government was concerned. Borderline cases between capture and surrender were sometimes prosecuted in spite of strenuous representation from Chinese Affairs and Information officers; and although in one particular case it was possible to represent a binding-over for three years as an acquittal there were anxious moments for SEP teams in the area as well as those who were directing them. Nevertheless, the use of surrendered guerrillas for propaganda purposes had considerably simplified the whole vexed question of surrender terms.

> For government to announce that surrendered bandits would not in any circumstances be prosecuted would amount to an amnesty—and the psychological moment for an amnesty will not come until government is so clearly on top that the public announcement of an amnesty might hasten the end by leading to mass desertions. At the same time surrender terms hedged in by reser-

this thing off. They killed my son six months ago.'

J. B. Perry Robinson gives an account of a later tour of SEPs (surrendered enemy personnel) and their experiences; and a most imaginative reconstruction of a guerrilla's state of mind when he had surrendered. *Transformation in Malaya*, London, 1956, pp. 47–53.

[6] Apart from adequate protection the success of a tour was reckoned to depend upon: an adequate and effective supply of accompanying leaflets; importance of preliminary briefing by the local Special Branch; a well-timed itinerary; differentiation in treatment for different types of areas; and exchange of views between SEP teams in different parts of the country.

vations would probably repel rather than attract. The policy since the formation of Emergency Information Services has therefore been to let surrendered bandits, through the written and spoken word, explain what *has* happened to them in government hands and what their comrades can therefore *expect* to happen to them if they surrender. There has been a strict avoidance of government *promises*. SEIOs (State Emergency Information Officers) have been instructed that there must not be promises even by implication.

Even before Templer arrived the 'battle for the mind' was being fought on many fronts. As head of the Emergency Information Services Carleton Greene had doubled the number of cinema projectors and public address systems in order to amplify word of mouth propaganda; and in a pre-transistor age, when battery radios were a luxury, the first five hundred community listening sets had been installed—in many areas providing the only regular means of communication—and another seven hundred receivers were being distributed in Chinese resettlement areas. Whether or not they were to be used for Emergency purposes was, in the first instance, disputed. According to Carelton Greene, the Director of Broadcasting had presented a paper on Community Listening which bore no relation whatever to the Emergency; and, in the case of the Chinese programmes, specifically stated that 'direct anti-bandit propaganda is undesirable in the early months of the service to this audience'. This was rejected on the grounds that the main objective of the Community Listening programmes, which would provide access to quite a new audience, must be to help to end the Emergency. The latter view was accepted and extended so that the overriding purpose of the Community Listening programmes was to keep the audience informed of the progress of the Emergency and of government measures and to raise their morale so that the flow of information was increased and aid to the guerrillas diminished. 'The long-term educational aspect must not be lost sight of but, in present circumstances, it must inevitably take second place.' From then on, there was a separate controller of Emergency Broadcasting while on the regular programmes of Radio Malaya the output of anti-Communist programmes—critical accounts of collectivisation, conscription and other internal events in China—was increased.

In general, government propaganda became more popular and more effective. It ranged from SEP concert parties with mouth organists, dramatic monologues and a sort of Victorian melodrama performed by ex-guerrillas, to the sophisticated news and feature films of the Malayan Film Unit. As head of Emergency Information Services, however, Carleton Greene had also influenced government policy on the rewards that were offered for information leading to the capture or killing of guerrillas. These now ranged from $2,000 for the rank and file up to $60,000 for Chin Peng[7] and a rather belated thirty per cent increase for bringing in guerrillas who were alive rather than dead.

In spite of all this, however, there was no immediate and spectacular improvement; and if the Kuala Pilah area of Negri Sembilan was any criterion, government propaganda to Chinese labourers on estates and mines in 1951 could be reckoned a failure. A Special Branch report, describing arrests made among the *Min Yuen* said that they

> seemed to be completely ignorant of the government's fight against the bandits. They had no knowledge of Security Forces' successes in areas close to their own area, nor did they appear to know that bandits had been surrendering. It should be noted out of nine persons arrested only three could read and understand a paper. In fact it appeared obvious that as far as they were concerned government propaganda was not reaching them.

The situation, nevertheless, may not have been so bad as far as effects on the guerrillas themselves. It was, for example, known in December, 1952 that over the previous eighteen months twenty-three guerrillas had been executed in Kedah alone for being potential deserters or suspected spies; and as the incidence of contact, both actual and potential, between guerrillas and the various forms of government propaganda increased so the MCP was forced to divert more of its propaganda resources into countering government propaganda and strengthening its own ideological basis. Thus, from the latter part of 1951 onwards—and specifically to refute the charges made by the defector Lam Swee and his booklet *My Accusation*—the volume of guerrilla counter-propaganda suggested that government information/propaganda was beginning to make its mark.[8]

For operational purposes government propaganda could be divided into strategic and tactical types. Strategic propaganda was written around particular themes that were, nevertheless,

---

[7] Eventually raised to $250,000 = £30,000.
[8] The Party's official reply entitled 'Smash the Enemy's Ideological Attack and strengthen the Ideological Front' was published in a number of editions together with follow-up literature for study sessions.

thought to be of general application. A quarterly report on psychological warfare in 1954 gave the following examples of strategic leaflets

  (i) *'Where does all the money go?'* Exploiting the MCP's present financial difficulties.
  (ii) *'Why work against the interests of the masses?'* Emphasised that there is no longer any moral justification for staying in the jungle. The struggle is useless and lost.
  (iii) *'It is dangerous to carry a pistol or carbine.'* By saying that the Security Forces are liable to shoot those so armed first it is hoped that the leaflet will cause panic amongst lower-ranking leaders.
  (iv) *'One of your comrades has been killed in this area.'* A theme to exploit kills with the minimum of delay.
  (v) *'Do you need medical assistance?'* A theme to exploit the situation when it is definitely known CTs have been wounded.

These last two examples of 'strategic' leaflets were, of course, adaptable to tactical needs. In March 1954, the Operations Division of the Information Services was transferred to the Director of Operations staff; and at the end of the year the Secretary for Defence assumed full control. Throughout that year it was estimated that fifty per cent of the guerrilla propaganda effort was directed to counter-propaganda and the evidence of the effect that government propaganda was having continued to mount. In Pahang, for example, between June and September, 1953 it was claimed that twenty-three guerrillas surrendered as a result of reading government pamphlets and five having heard broadcasts from 'voice' aircraft.[9] While it is hard to believe that these were always examples of cause and effect, and that other factors did not supervene, more detailed interrogations of high-level guerrillas who surrendered were often encouraging. For example a very well-known Malay guerrilla, Osman China, first thought of surrender when he read in the Information Services periodical *New Path News* that a particular friend of his had been killed. This may not have been a particularly skilful piece of propaganda—although experience suggested that the closer

---

[9] Mostly RAF Valettas for 'blanket' coverage with Austers used for pin-point targets. Messages were both recorded—including a famous one from Templer, in Chinese—and, occasionally, live. Quality varied; but some surrendered guerrillas said that even garbled messages made them uneasy. Hardier characters merely remarked that the dogs were barking. Night broadcast flights tended to be at the expense of day flights.

it was to the truth the more skilful it was—but improvements in technique and style at least increased the chances of success.

Surrender themes, often in cartoon and comic-strip style, may have continued to appear rather crude but one improvement noted was that they were now treated with sympathy instead of bombast and ridicule. The importance of group photos showing the latest guerrillas to have surrendered *together* with those who had surrendered in earlier years was recognised as well as the importance of being able to read leaflets without actually picking them up : this for the benefit of wavering guerrillas who were still in operational groups. Wrapping paper with propaganda themes was supplied free in areas where guerrillas were known to be obtaining their supplies. Fixed searchlight beams, parachute flares and hand sirens were all tried as direction-finding aids in solving the very real problem of guerrillas who wished to surrender but did not know which way to go; while safe-conduct passes were distributed by the million.[10] In areas where it was thought that there were guerrillas who were willing to surrender, given favourable circumstances, local cease-fires were arranged. In Johore, Mount Ophir was, in August 1954 the retreat of a rather weakened, battered guerrilla unit. The area was heavily bombed, strafed, shelled and patrolled : and then all troops were withdrawn. The withdrawal was announced by 'voice' aircraft with the explanation that the object was to permit guerrillas to surrender in safety. Three took advantage of the lull and came out and surrendered. At the end of the cease-fire period of four days battle recommenced and, on information from surrendered guerrillas, two more were killed and one surrendered. This, although not the first local cease-fire, was the first to be successful.

Increasingly, in the middle and later years of the Emergency, government propaganda was directed against individuals. As a group, guerrillas in the jungle cultivation areas had been singled out for special deliveries on account of their comparatively static position and the amount of time it was assumed they had on their hands. Most unnerving, perhaps, for the guerrilla was to hear a 'voice' aircraft speaking to him by name : in this case after a contact with Security Forces.

> A day or two later the aircraft again broadcast to us. This time the broadcast was directed at me and Tan Piow calling us by

[10] Which were, unfortunately, no guarantee against the occasional ambush and killing of a guerrilla who was making his way out to surrender.

name and said that both of us no longer had a leader and our livelihood would be very difficult. Make haste to leave the jungle or else we will face danger if we hesitate. Surrender to the government for we will be well treated. But I was frightened to leave then as Tan Piow was with me.

For some time it was thought inadvisable to mention the name of potential surrenderers for fear of prejudicing their chances. It was found, however, that the mention of names, either by 'voice' aircraft or in leaflets, tended to make guerrillas act quickly although they were in continuous danger until they did come out. A surrendered guerrilla meant, quite often, that there was a situation which could be exploited. Either the guerrillas were under heavy pressure: constantly on the move, unable to make contact with the *Min Yuen* or to find their food dumps, suffering from starvation, sickness or possibly even with wounded men on their hands; or else, whether or not they were aware of being hunted, the fact that one or two guerrillas were ready to surrender seemed, according to many who had surrendered, to make itself felt particularly in small groups. In 1953 when the number of guerrillas who surrendered rose to 372 (previous figures were 1952: 257; 1951: 201; 1950: 147; 1949: 251) there were several cases of one or two SEPs being used to bring in another six or ten guerrillas. Had these particular operations been mounted simply with the idea of killing guerrillas it was possible that only one or two would have been killed—or so it was argued. Those who were concerned with psychological warfare were often really interested in a different type of operation which aimed at surrenders rather than kills; and although there were some notable failures it was, at least from the intelligence point of view, better to have surrendered guerrillas than dead ones.

Subversion, Alienation and Integration
The formal opening of the MCP 'Peace Offensive' is usually taken as May 1st, 1955: the date of the pseudonymous *Ng Heng* letter in which it was announced that the aim of the MRLA was nothing but a peaceful, democratic and independent Malaya and that, as a political party, the MCP would be willing to hold a round table conference to ensure peace and independence. The origins and consequences of this proposal will be considered later, together with its climax in the Baling talks; but, in a sense, the October Directives of 1951 had already helped to transfer the struggle on to the political plane: political, that is, in terms of

influence. Insofar as propaganda was concerned with manipulating the news—which it seldom did although Carleton Greene, for one, was critical of the overly-cautious attitude towards the release of news of Emergency incidents—it might influence opinion; and there were long disquisitions on how to overcome such embarrassing facts for the Malayan-Chinese as the priority of conscription over citizenship. By impeding open guerrilla access to Chinese peasant support, and by resettlement in viable New Villages, even when properly administered and self-governing, government had not thereby necessarily enlisted Chinese support for the campaign against the guerrillas. To a large extent both sides were still competing for influence over the unaffiliated mind; and in this the MCP was once again searching for an acceptable cause. With the Armed Struggle in abeyance a new basis of support was required: one that required public sympathy and acceptance. And if it was not possible to win support on a Malayan basis then there was still much profit to be gained from a return to the Chinese theme.

On the government side propaganda, rather like diplomacy, was to make the purpose of HMG understood and, if possible, accepted. In practice, while it had many operational successes, it was still only engaged around the periphery of public confidence and when it came actually to making contact with the Chinese community and the Chinese mind it was surprising to see how senior government officers fell back on the assumption that this was and would remain almost impervious to conventional analysis and understanding. 'The secret society complex' wrote a Secretary for Chinese Affairs 'is the most powerful factor in the whole Chinese organism.' Portentous questions and arguments were set out: 'Can they discard their traditional attitude towards government and politics and accept a principle of collective responsibility, based, in the final analysis, on the individual conscience?' Could three major obstacles—intense racial pride, the power of their organisation ('the framework of the KMT is still with us'), their attitude towards government—be overcome? Convinced how little they knew of Chinese secret societies it was hardly surprising that at the end of 1954 the Combined Intelligence Staff recommended a thorough investigation; reassuring, however, that inquiry was recommended rather than action.

Chinese Secret Societies
Nearly all the Chinese secret societies in Malaya were derived from the Triad Society (*Hung Lee*). Its political activities in

China began with support of the overthrown Ming Dynasty against the Manchu conquerors, continued in support of open rebellion in the nineteenth century and, with other societies, combined in the Revolutionary Alliance which assisted Dr. Sun Yat-sen to power in the Chinese Revolution of 1911. In Malaya it could be argued that secret society activities had been just as important. In 1825 secret societies conspired with the Siamese to overthrow the colonial government in Penang. From 1851 on there were secret society disturbances, riots and killings—as Roman Catholic converts became independent of society protection—and in the 1870s it was the activities of Chinese miners and their secret societies which led to British intervention in the Malay States and to the transformation of Malaya. In the nineteenth century its importance both as a political and a social structure could hardly be overestimated.[11] In Malaya in the 1950s, however, it seemed as if the MCP and the secret societies were two elements in a system of countervailing power. In December 1953, for example, the acting SCA reported that it was becoming increasingly evident that the more the Communist menace receded, the more the *Wah Kee* (a secret society) engaged in unlawful activities.[12] Many of the *Wah Kee* groups had committed themselves to the government side but, at the same time, they had taken and were taking advantage of their position for material profit. In Selangor at least the MCP recognised the strength of the secret societies.

> The masses are more influenced by the secret societies than by the Revolution whose forces are not so deeply rooted. In the circumstances, therefore, if we try to purge them hurriedly, and take

[11] 'It must be remembered in those days if you were a Chinese leader at all, it had to be a Triad or Tokang leader. None the less it was clear that the British had very much to learn about the underground machinery of Chinese social life before they could completely govern their newly-acquired protectorate.' Purcell, *The Chinese in South-east Asia*, London, 1965, p. 266.

[12] The societies usually had high-sounding ideals: brotherhood, charity and mutual aid. In rare cases powerful leaders had adhered to these ideals and had succeeded in maintaining peace and good will among their members. In most cases, however, societies degenerated into protection organisations or closed shops amongst groups of workers. In the large towns the tendency was for the control groups in the societies to specialise in gambling promotion and collection of protection money from shop-keepers, hawkers and more or less organised vice. In the coastal areas societies took care of smuggling activities; while societies organised by labourers were to preserve occupational rights and privileges for their members.

over the reins of these organisations immediately, it will be like trying to attain an object today when it should be obtained tomorrow, and it will result in the two forces having conflict with each other. And as their force is strong and more deeply rooted than that of the Revolution, it will be more to their advantage. The result of such a conflict will possibly be our own displacement . . .

If, as this opinion seemed to show, the MCP had failed to win over the masses where the secret societies had control, then it was faced with almost the same problem as government itself. If the MCP were to alienate the leaders of the secret societies sufficiently, then they were likely to use their power against the Party to deny it access to the masses. Government, on the other hand—or so the Secretary for Chinese Affairs argued—must not alienate the *Wah Kee* and other societies to such an extent that it lost their co-operation against Communism. The Malayan-Chinese secret societies could be regarded as a pre-constitutional or extra-legal form of political organisation. Effective in the nineteenth and the first half of the twentieth century they had now to withstand the political but still extra-legal challenge of the MCP; and it was sometimes argued that, in spite of their differences, this was the characteristic form of political activity among the Malayan Chinese.[13] It could also be argued that, sociologically, the Malayan Chinese were in a state of transition. In 1931 only 30 per cent of the Malayan Chinese population had been born either in Malaya or in Singapore. In 1947, however, the figure stood at over 60 per cent and this radical transformation was confirmed over the next ten years when, by 1957, over three-quarters of the Malayan Chinese had been born in Malaya and Singapore. Nevertheless, the links with China remained. In 1955 remittances from Malayan Chinese to their families in China were over a million dollars per month;[14] but, apart from this tangible affinity, sympathy and support for China—the new Communist China—was reckoned to be at least potentially equivalent to support for the MCP/MRLA in Malaya.

[13] W. L. Blythe has now written a definitive study of Malayan Chinese secret societies: *The Impact of Chinese Secret Societies in Malaya*, London, 1969.

[14] Remittances were made through the Bank of China and its branches in Malaya. The Director of Intelligence and the High Commissioner disagreed on their estimates of the Bank's activities. Madoc complained of the KMT professional intelligence pedlars who wished to discredit the Bank. MacGillivray thought this rather a complacent attitude.

Chinese Schools

Nowhere among the Malayan Chinese was potential support for the MCP greater than in the Chinese schools. To begin with there were twice as many children at school in the 1950s as there had been before the war: a large part of them Chinese.[15] Second, was the long-standing tradition of autonomous Chinese education in Malaya; and its tradition as a forcing house of radical ideas, both Nationalist and Communist.[16] Third, was the fact that education in China had always had a political bias.

> Since the Han Dynasty for more than two thousand years students have always had an official career in mind. There is an axiom in China that the students of today are the rulers of tomorrow.
>
> Politics being the science and art of government it just didn't make sense to tell the Chinese student not to concern himself with politics. It was the justification of his very existence.
>
> The Confucian classics which form the staple of its education are preoccupied with questions of good government. After the Revolution in 1911 the Confucian classics were scrapped in favour of modern text books. But the students inherited a political bias as well as the prestige of their predecessors.[17]

Fourth, since the time when Ming Hung Wu had driven the Mongols from the throne of China, there was the mystique of the alliance of scholars and peasants: the two classes upon which all Chinese government rested. Students, as embryo scholars, were essential to the workings of government: if they withdrew, no system could work.[18] Lastly, it could be argued that Com-

---

[15] Purcell hazards the guess that the increase is largely accounted for by the numbers in Chinese vernacular schools paid for in the main by the Chinese community. Purcell, *The Chinese in South-east Asia*, p. 281. For the Chinese Middle Schools, numbers went up from less than 5,000 in 1947 to more than 40,000 in 1957.

[16] In 1794 Captain Francis Light, the founder of Penang, observed 'They have everywhere people to teach their children, and sometimes they send males to China to complete their education'. Purcell, *op cit*. p. 244. Purcell notes that after nothing had been done to provide universal free education in Engish the Chinese community was surrendered to Chinese nationalism and, in effect, to Communism for this was more and more disseminated through the influence of poorly paid (and therefore Leftist) teachers so many of whom were employed in the Chinese vernacular schools. *Ibid*. p. 278.

[17] *Straits Times*, June 8th 1955. The article, anonymous, was said to be by a China-born Chinese who had lived and worked in Singapore for more than forty years.

munism was the most exciting idea—and in some cases probably the only excitement—that Chinese schools in Malaya offered, particularly to over-age students.

In 1954 Chinese schools took on the dimensions of a major political problem of the Emergency. The trouble was seen to begin in Singapore and started in opposition to registration for national service. It was estimated that 98 per cent of those who were liable to registration did, in fact, register—much to the Singapore Government's surprise—but the opposition mounted in three Chinese schools and, after permission to stage a demonstration had been refused, lorryloads of Chinese students attempted to converge on Government House; the police dispersed the crowd of about four hundred with comparatively little violence at first but, after it had re-formed, at the cost of stone-throwing on one side and a baton charge on the other. The result of all this was eight Chinese students arrested and charged in court and some unfavourable press comment, particularly from the Chinese-owned *Singapore Standard*. A motion was rushed through the Students' Union in the University of Malaya, then based on Singapore, and the upshot, in the words of the Singapore Intelligence report, was,

> to give the students a distorted view of their own importance, and at the same time to alienate a considerable body of moderate opinion in the town, which was misled into thinking that the police had used excessive force

—a situation that was not unknown elsewhere in more recent times. Chinese leaders, acting through the Chinese Chambers of Commerce, tried to restore order when eight hundred students barricaded themselves in one of the Chinese high schools overnight; but escalating student demands—complete exemption from national service, a full inquiry and punishment of police officers—led to a breaking off of relations between the Chamber of Commerce and the embattled students. Revolutionary fervour ebbed away, after another mammoth sit-in, when Chinese schools were closed a fortnight in advance of their normal holidays; and a number of the most disaffected students made their way to China by sea.

These disturbances presented a disproportionately large political problem. First, there was the threat to public order; second, and perhaps more important, was the problem of determining the

[18] See for example C. P. Fitzgerald, *The Birth of Communist China*, p. 26.

nature and extent of Communist involvement. The sheer efficiency of the demonstration—particularly the use of girl students as an embarrassing vanguard—and the organisation of follow-up meetings, together with escalated demands, exaggerated rumours and collection of funds for the wounded and the decision to celebrate an annual anti-government school holiday: all these were considered significant and the conclusion drawn was that not only had MCP influence been the dominating factor but that it was more than probable there had been a high degree of Chinese People's Government influence behind the students' campaign.

It had been known since 1953 that the MCP had succeeded in infiltrating three Chinese schools in Singapore; and the day before national service registration had begun the MCP had issued a special supplement to their *Freedom News* which opened the attack and from then on a variety of pamphlets, posters and cartoons were distributed over the name of the Anti-British League which had existed in Singapore intermittently and in various manifestations since the Emergency began. Nevertheless it was agreed by the Singapore Special Branch that not all the troublesome students were Communists by any means; that there was only a very small hard core of sympathisers in each of the schools; and that the factual evidence of direct Communist instigation was to be found in only one single instance and three uncorroborated secret source reports. Of the student ringleaders at least four had been previously mentioned as having some Communist connections but it was not clear whether these connections went beyond the 'sympathy' that was adduced in the main piece of factual evidence. Out of twenty-five thousand Chinese students in Singapore it was hardly surprising that a few hundred should have reckoned themselves supporters of Chinese Communism; but it was alarming that their influence should have been so pervasive[19]. As for remedying the situation the pessimistic but factual conclusion was that as long as the Chinese community provided most of the money for the Chinese schools it was difficult to see how any great control could be achieved. The Singapore school disturbances provided no clear-cut answer to the question whether they were a result of MCP inspiration and organisation or a matter of more or less spontaneous combustion. To the question, 'How was the MCP going to mobilise support?' the answer was that in Singapore on the sensitive issue of Chinese

[19] One rumour was that draftees were to be sent immediately to Indo-China. Circulated at a time when the battle for Dien Bien Phu was at its height, this had an obvious effect.

conscription the Singapore Government had almost done the job for it.

In Malaya, 1954 disclosed evidence of Communist organisation in Chinese middle schools that more than fulfilled the worst suspicions. As in Singapore, where acid had been thrown in the face of a Chinese headmistress, Malayan Chinese students had been capable of spectacular acts of violence in the past. In 1951, for example, the murders of the headmasters of the Chung Ling High School, Penang, and the Chong Hwa Middle School, Klang, had been arranged by their pupils with local 'killer squads'. In Penang there was a long history of Communist involvement in Chinese schools, dating back to well before the war, and when, in 1949, the Anti-British Alliance was set up as an MCP support organisation, the Seventh Branch (out of eighteen) was devoted to student activities. These activities included opposition to government and to teachers and school management committees on various domestic issues, publicising the successes of the MCP, carrying out such demonstrative acts as raising the red flag and supplying information to and acting as a courier organisation for the MCP. It was organised into a number of sympathiser cells of two or three members each, coming under the school control body of the Anti-British League which, in turn, was controlled by the MCP's Penang Town Committee. The particular group responsible for the murder of the Chung Ling High School headmaster, David Chen, was broken up by police action in late 1952 and was not re-formed. By this time the October Directives were having their effect and the 'Seventh Branch' ceased to engage in overt action. Two years later the Combined Intelligence Staff admitted that little was known of MCP activities among Penang students but it was assumed that it was using the contacts and influence that had been built up by the Seventh Branch. The Penang experience was repeated in Selangor where, after the murder of the Chinese headmaster in Klang, the Students' Union, which was under MCP control and was also connected with an Anti-British League, was broken up by police action; and when the MCP resumed its work among Klang students in 1952 overt action was avoided. Cells of MCP sympathisers were re-established in three Klang Middle Schools under the personal direction of a State Committee Member and District Committee Member in the vicinity but it was this connection that helped to make their presence known and the cells were again broken up by the arrest of members in 1954.

As long as clandestine groups of Chinese students existed they were liable to discovery and even penetration, in the case of older students, by police agents; and as long as they engaged in overt action, whether it was murder or simply the raising of the red flag, they at least advertised their existence and their members were open to arrest. By the middle of 1954, however, a new phenomenon had appeared: groups of Chinese students with a common interest in Communism and opposition to government's education policy, who were not actively breaking the law. Technically their existence may have been illegal but insofar as they were the continuation of the Kuala Lumpur study groups that had been founded in the early 1950s, while they may not have been harmless, they would have benefited rather than suffered from police action. In Kuala Lumpur the organiser of the Students' Union was known to be in touch with a member of the *Min Yuen* and, through him, with a member of the Selangor State Committee's propaganda section; and it was with the intention of disguising its student membership that the name of the Students' Union was changed to that of the Anti-British League. But it would have been difficult and probably foolish to take action of any kind against groups which had no known MCP connection—as was the case with the Klang Students' Union in 1954—and the discretion with which the newly-named Anti-British League in Kuala Lumpur refused to distribute pamphlets attacking the government's education policy that were provided by the Klang Students' Union—on the grounds that it would draw down government suspicion of MCP action—showed how difficult it was even to trace political activity once it was almost entirely submerged.

The Pontian Case
A revelation of this proliferating proto-political activity was provided in August 1954 when a member of the South Johore Regional Committee was killed and MCP documents were recovered on student organisation in the Pontian district of Johore.

> An instruction issued by the Gelang Patah-Pontian District Committee in July 1954 stated that as its Pontian branch contained a high percentage of students among its party members, it should concentrate its political activities on the students. In carrying out these political activities, the instruction continued, the old-style method of running an illegal Masses Organisation assisting the Party's 'military and public propaganda activities', was to be

abandoned, and the new technique of setting up legal public organisations secretly controlled by Party cell members adopted. As the Pontian district was earmarked for student activities, recommended types of legal organisation were: Old Boys' Associations, Basketball Teams, Stage Clubs, Singing Clubs and Literary Societies, the most promising types being those the least likely to attract government attention. In order to cultivate the goodwill of the students, the instruction advocated the imparting of uplifting advice to the unindustrious and the proffering of assistance to those in difficulty or trouble. In addition, leadership was to be given 'in any legitimate struggle'—e.g. in demonstrations against unsatisfactory school administration and teachers and exposure of corruption in the press and launching of drives against 'depraved literature'. These and other laudable methods were to be pursued to 'unite the masses'.

A working plan for the second half of 1954 included 'gray activities' which were described as contacting the masses by means of picnics, excursions, moonlight parties, debating societies and essay competitions; and if this seemed a rather hopeful and random collection the results had been amazingly successful for, on the basis of these documents, the following legal organisations, each controlled by a Party cell member, were first detected and then broken up:

(1) The Sin Sang Basketball Group—formed by the Pontian MCP cell leader with a membership of thirty.
(2) Various student groups in the Pei Chun Middle School, Pontian—directed by MCP cell members, and including art study groups, essay competition groups and a reading circle.
(3) The Bin Chong Old Boys' Association, Pontian.
(4) The Bin Chong Night School, Pontian, with a membership of fifty plus formed at the suggestion of an MCP cell member.
(5) The Chi Chih Night School, Ayer Baloi, founded by the headmaster of the day school who had been made an MCP Branch Committee Member.
(6) The Hung Chi Basketball Team, Ayer Baloi—started by the Branch Committee secretary.
(7) Various afternoon and evening classes for poor children in Pontian started by students of the Pei Chun Middle School that included one Party member and one probationer Party member.

Several conclusions may be drawn from this evidence. But

perhaps the most important fact is that all these groups originated in one man: Lau Choon Toh. Lau had been a member of the MPAJA from 1942 to 1945. In 1946 he became a member of the Pontian 'People's Committee' and also a member of the Ayer Baloi Chi Chih Primary School Committee. Although a Communist supporter Lau did not join the Party until about 1953, nor did he become a guerrilla in 1948. Instead, he lay low at the beginning of the Emergency and did not engage again in pro-Communist activities until 1950. In that year he used his position as member of the School Committee to bring about the employment of three teachers of pro-Communist background at his school: two of whom had been provided with false diplomas by Communist authorities in China. Together with these three teachers Lau set up an Anti-British League at his school and succeeded in recruiting fifteen members, most of them from the Pei Chun Middle School in Pontian. What is remarkable about his activities up to this point is that they continued without any assistance from the MCP which, at the time, was interested in the 'Masses Organisation' purely as sources of supply. Lau's Anti-British League, on the other hand, occupied itself only with the study of Communist doctrines.

As might have been expected, however, the MCP began to interest itself in Lau's organisation after the policy change of October 1951 had reached the South Johore Regional Committee: that is, in late 1952. Soon afterwards the MCP's Pontian District Secretary established contact with Lau and took over the direction of his organisation. Lau himself was made a Party member, but found inadequate as a Branch Committee Secretary, which was the post offered him. This post was then allotted to one of the pro-Communist teachers taken into Lau's school, and another school teacher was made the third member of the Branch Committee. In addition to this amalgamation, a new Party cell was formed for political work, made up of three of the student members of Lau's organisation. In accordance with Party practice in running Masses Organisations, each of these cell members was made responsible for one cell of the Anti-British League. When it was decided, in accordance with the October Directives, to abandon working through the Anti-British League the result was the proliferation of legal organisations, which, while they may have been weakened in revolutionary fervour, nevertheless involved many more people and reached a wider audience which, in turn, might be expected to become generally sympathetic towards Communism.

'Defend Racial Culture'

Even when the feeling about unpopular issues had begun to die away—most notably Chinese resettlement and national service registration—there was still enough doubt about the future of the Malayan Chinese, their insecurity and the future course of government policy which the MCP could use for capitalisation purposes. Although apparently of general application the policy line, 'Defend Racial Culture', in practice meant 'Defend Chinese Culture' and, in particular, Chinese education. To the Malayan Chinese the problem of education was essentially a problem of culture. In 1951 a report on Malay education (the Barnes Report) had recommended inter-racial national primary schools: a scheme which 'would be seriously weakened if any large proportion of the Chinese, Indian and other non-Malay communities were to choose to provide their own primary classes independently of the National School'. Purcell argued that the committee, both in composition and in its report, were strongly pro-Malay and anti-Chinese; and as a result of considerable Chinese criticism a second report was commissioned from an American educationalist and a Chinese UN official. The Fenn-Wu Report took a pluralistic approach to Malayan education but the result was that Chinese education and culture were reckoned to be inextricably bound.

> To most Chinese in Malaya, Malayanisation is anathema, in view of the absence of a culture or even a society which can as yet be called Malayan. The first point in the Secretariat's announcement appeared to envisage elimination of Chinese schools and the relegating of the Chinese language to inferior status, with the ultimate result, if not the present purpose, of the extinction of Chinese culture in Malaya.

When it came to executive action Malayan Government favoured the first of these two reports, i.e. it supported the principle of national schools; but for the moment this had little effect on the structure and political activities of the Chinese Middle schools. Even the Fenn-Wu Report had suggested that the Malayan Chinese should set their own house in order; that there was no real advantage for Chinese culture in maintaining the forms or indeed the methods and content of schools in China; and that foreign politics in any form should be eliminated from Chinese schools, while text books should be introduced that were suitable for Malayan use.[20] The weaknesses of Chinese middle schools

[20] Purcell, *Malaya, Communist or Free*, p. 158.

have already been noted. They stemmed from the depressed and uncertain employment of their teachers, a general absence of money, capricious, fearful and often inactive management committees, variable but rather low standards and the determination to remain Chinese both in form and content. The latter was also their strength and, together with the tradition of political activities, was to be a continuing problem for government.

Hsueh Hsih
As a problem it was encapsulated in the idea and practice of *Hsueh Hsih*. In origin a Confucian analect—'How delightful it is to study and practise frequently'—it had, for the classical Chinese scholar, a respectable connotation implying hard work, diligence, and the desire to study deeply—qualities that were all held in high regard by the Chinese. As a political format the scholar-gentry political association or 'study societies' were part of the reform movement in China at the end of the nineteenth century; and as combined student-soldier revolutionary study societies were instrumental in the 'Double Tenth' revolt of 1911.[21] In 1938 Mao Tse-Tung introduced *Hsueh Hsih* amongst the rank and file of the Chinese Communist Party and it was henceforward understood that 'study for action', the unity of theory and practice, was essential to the success of Communism. According to Special Branch, the *Hsueh Hsih* method of indoctrination had been used in varying degrees in Malaya since 1938; but in 1955 the system was introduced on a major scale by the Singapore Chinese Middle School Students' Union. When this union was eventually dissolved by the Singapore Council of Ministers in September 1956 and several of its leaders were arrested, the *Hsueh Hsih* campaign was cited as an example of organisation policy and behaviour that closely followed that of Communist student bodies elsewhere. In format it was larger than the Communist cell—according to the New Knowledge dictionary, published in China, between eight and fifteen people meeting once a week—and in practice, according to a not very sympathetic Special Branch paper.

> The student must study as a member of a group and he is constantly subordinated to group pressure. The group is controlled by experienced *Hsueh Hsih* group leaders and the new student is taught not to differ from, or stand up against, the group.
> The first lesson that they teach the newly recruited student is

[21] A point that was omitted in the Special Branch study of the problem.

that he must never differ from the views of the group, neither must he ever stand up against the collective views that are expressed.

In such collective *Hsueh Hsih* study, the 'joint decision' and the 'majority view' are all important. Individual deviationist views are quickly suppressed and eradicated by forceful and humiliating criticism.[22]

In January 1955 thirty-six 'observers' from Chinese middle schools in Singapore attended a conference in Kuala Lumpur of the Pan-Malayan Students' Federation; and from subsequent accounts it appears that the *Hsueh Hsih* system was introduced to Malaya at this date. Overt demonstrations were impressive but inconclusive. For example, there was a rash of political picnics where Chinese Communist songs were sung and in September the *Yang-Ko*, with particular Chinese Communist associations, was danced *en masse* on the golf course at Fraser's Hill: an event which was, no doubt, of immense symbolic significance but of little political import. By the end of 1955, forty-five song books had been proscribed under Emergency Regulations or the Undesirable Publications Ordinance and government had turned its attention to the diffuse and rather absurd problem of non-political picnics as well as the reform of the middle schools. The aim that was laid down by a committee of the Chief Secretary that was considering the matter was to make those who were the directing force behind student troubles expose themselves. Whenever evidence of subversive activity among teachers or pupils existed in such a form as to enable police action to be taken, this was to be done. School Management Committees were to be encouraged to provide such evidence. Whenever evidence of Communist sympathies among teachers was substantiated—although not in the form that would enable police action to be taken—administrative action to remove the teacher was to be taken by invoking the education ordinance to withdraw or withhold the teacher's registration. Whenever evidence of Communist sympathy or deliberate indiscipline among pupils was substantiated—although again not in a form that would enable police action to be taken—the headmaster, with the backing of the Management

[22] In an analysis of the stages in which the student became involved with the study group—which might extend throughout the last four years of secondary education—it was reckoned that even during stage one the potential recruit had received lessons on all the points of the MCP's Manifesto: particularly the United Front programme.

Committee, should expel the pupil. When there was an unwillingness to take such action the Management Committee was to be supplemented by the addition of government officers.

In August 1955 twelve pupils from the Chung Ling High School in Penang were arrested. Some of them were found to be in possession of proscribed literature. One was fined $300 or a month's imprisonment, five were released and excluded from Penang under the Emergency Regulations and the rest were released unconditionally. Similar repressive action was taken in Johore Bahru against five pupils—including a girl of twenty-one and three boys of twenty[23]—after the School Management had invited police action but were unwilling to commit themselves to any action for fear of reprisals. In this case, the pupils were expelled by the Management Committee: but only after the threat of dilution with government nominees. More positive government measures recommended included priority in the government training of Chinese school teachers, the enforcement of the teacher/pupil ratio, and the superannuation of over-age students. Culturally, efforts were made to provide patriotic songs but these did little more than reveal the difficulties of producing government inspired culture that was acceptable to anyone other than the Special Branch.[24]

[23] There was a large number of over-age pupils in the Chinese Middle Schools: up to early and even mid-'twenties.

[24] It was not surprising that one notably pathetic effort had never been reported as being included in a school concert. The artistic danger here could be compared with the appalling didacticism of the ideologically correct artist: even though the latter had the marginally better line 'Who knew that when the dog had gone the monkey would come to take its place?': a genial comparison of the Japanese and the British.

ABORIGINES AND THE DEEP JUNGLE

One of the options that is open to the insurgent is to call off the insurrection, insofar as it involves attacking the enemy and disrupting his organisation in the inhabited area, and, if local conditions permit, to withdraw to comparatively inaccessible parts of the country and there set up a new base. The disadvantage is, that by breaking contact, he loses the initiative and ceases to influence the course of events. The advantage is that he continues to survive.

In 1949, after the first wave of attacks had failed, the MPAJA withdrew their forces in order that they could be rested, regrouped and retrained; and in 1950 and in 1951 the second and by far the more serious wave of attacks kept government forces at full stretch. For reasons that have already been considered the MCP decided that on account of their losses, and lacking a firm foundation of support, they would once again withdraw: this time to deep jungle bases. Effectively, this policy was put into operation in 1952—when the October 1951 Directives had filtered down to the lower levels—and, in spite of some initial setbacks, two years later, in 1954, all the evidence pointed to the development of safe base areas throughout the length of Malaya. In the North, the Perak/Kelantan Border Committee and the Kedah/Penang Joint State Committee; in the centre, the Perak State Committee, the North and South Pahang Regional Committees, the Negri Sembilan State Committee; and in the South, the South-Malaya Bureau and the North and South Johore Regional Committees were all seeking to establish themselves in the deep jungle. Under the new plan, base areas were thought of not as fixed camps but as safe areas supplied by numerous small and well camouflaged cultivation plots which were to be opened up in virgin jungle. Tactically and practically their purpose had not changed: recuperation, training and expansion of the armed forces and reindoctrination of the Party's cadres. Strategically, and more hopefully, they were to serve as operational bases from which forces could emerge to capture Security Force posts in inhabited localities and thus establish the elusive phase two of the Liberated Area. As a preliminary, State Secretariats were instructed to organise Work Forces, consisting of from ten to fifteen men, whose task was to establish cultivation plots and to stockpile food. These Work Forces were given the target for 1952 of accumulating sufficient stocks of food to maintain one MRLA platoon for twelve months in each base area. At the same time the State Regimental Command had to recruit one additional MRLA platoon each in order to enable a unit of this strength to be withdrawn into each base area.

Deep jungle bases were not, however, self-sufficient in food. The individual, and even the individual European, could, if he was determined, survive on jungle fruits and primitive trapping but only for a limited period; and where bodies of men were concerned this meant an impracticably low level of subsistence. Hill rice, vegetable gardens and, most important, tapioca could all be cultivated given time; but for clothes, medicine, implements and a great deal of their foodstuffs, particularly oil and salt, the guerrillas were dependent upon outside supplies. This fact, and the fact that MCP district organisations could be and were being broken up meant that even deep jungle guerrillas were vulnerable on this side. In the event, however, the results of security force operations directed specifically against base areas had not been up to expectations; and experience had shown that when deep jungle operations had concluded, the guerrillas soon reassembled in the same area and resumed their activities unless subject to constant harassment based on good local intelligence.

> It would thus appear that the chances of rendering a base area inoperative or of eliminating any significant number of the terrorists within it by means of large-scale direct attack are remote, and that prolonged offensive patrolling by small units is more promising. Clearly the earlier in the development of a base area that such operations are commenced, the less opportunity the terrorists will have of developing a series of defended camps and foodstocks enabling them to subsist for long periods in the face of continuing attacks.[1]

By the end of 1954 it was reckoned that MCP District Organisations, which were one of the two main sources of supply for deep jungle bases, had proved to be remarkably resilient to pressure from the Security Forces. On the other hand, consider-

[1] CIS Paper, *The MCP's Jungle Base Areas*, August 18th 1954.

able success was claimed for government efforts to win over the Malayan aborigines who were the indigenous inhabitants of the deep jungle. Within a few days of the beginning of the Emergency a group of some ninety aborigines had sought refuge in the Segamat district of Johore claiming that their settlement had been attacked by guerrillas. This, although a somewhat unusual event, prefigured the importance as well as the isolation of the aborigines in the insurrection. Relations between the aborigines and Chinese guerrillas, particularly during the Japanese occupation, were often good; and by a judicious blend of friendship and terrorism on the part of the guerrillas government was faced with a situation at the end of 1953 in which it was estimated that the guerrillas dominated almost the entire hill population of the country from Negri Sembilan and South Pahang right up to the Thai border: a total of perhaps some thirty thousand people.

In 1948, and for many years thereafter, the aborigine population of Malaya was a matter of more or less informed guesswork.[2] Three years later the estimate had risen to at least a hundred thousand; but the critical figure, as far as the Emergency was concerned, was the number of aborigines to be found in the deep jungle. In point of fact, very few of these aborigines had been found—by government—and no Emergency action was taken until early in 1949. In February 1949 the District Officer, Kinta, was reporting that some of the aborigines in his part of Perak were suspected of helping the guerrillas; and if they continued to assist them the problem was serious enough to necessitate either their removal altogether from the hills or else they would have to be 'chased around and probably out of the country'. In extenuation of this kind of big game policy—capture/stampede—it could be and was said that District Officers had far too many other commitments to give serious thought to what did not appear to be an immediate problem. Nevertheless, when government discovered on closer investigation that their officers were quite often the first Europeans that had been seen in aborigine areas for ten years or more it was recognised that the immediate need was to find out a great deal more about a people in whom interest hitherto had been anthropological rather than political.

One of the first moves was to take on a major in the Civil

[2] In the census of 1947 the number was put at thirty-four thousand; but many of the more settled aborigines were recorded as Malays rather than aborigines and, on the other hand, many of the remoter jungle areas with considerable aboriginal populations were not visited at all.

Liaison Corps, P. R. D. Williams-Hunt, as Protector of Aborigines. Williams-Hunt had impressed the Chief Secretary as a competent archaeologist with a marked flair for ethnological work and a determination to spend his life working among aborigines for, like many other government officers, Williams-Hunt identified himself closely with the interests of his charges. Apart from commercial exploitation aborigines had been subject since the Emergency began to many examples of insensitive treatment by government who reacted in much the same way to this problem as they did to that of the Chinese squatters. In December 1949 the problem was discussed at King's House but the only effect of this meeting was that both the police and the Army bowed out of the scene. The problem was one of control or rather an approach to it that would yield intelligence from the aborigines. Gurney argued that the only objection to the establishment of military or police posts in the deep jungle was the difficulty of maintenance; but Gray, the Commissioner of Police, said that it would be impossible for the police to take on this new commitment—a commitment at which the GOC also demurred.

The possibility remained of creating *ad hoc* forces; and in this Perak led the way with the Perak Aboriginal Areas Constabulary (PAAC) that was formed in March 1950 and consisted predominantly of Malays with some Indians and aborigines and European officers. The commander of this unit, J. A. Hyslop, was the State Protector of Aborigines and a former Force 136 officer and their work, including the building of two jungle forts, prefigured later government policy.[3]

1950 was, however, distinguished by more spectacular failures of government aborigine policy. On the basis of little knowledge of the aborigines themselves but increasing fears of the importance of their co-operation with the guerrillas, States were left to seek their own solutions which, in practice, tended to be the same solution as that of the squatter problem: resettlement. In various States, particularly Kelantan, aborigine groups were rounded up and brought into more accessible areas. The result, to quote a Protector of Aborigines, was nothing short of disastrous,

[3] An opinion, after the event, by the Deputy Director of Operations was that it had been a failure: 'impossible to provide certain equipment, trained specialists and a guaranteed supply of officers'. It continued to be opposed by the police; but under Colonel Young the police took over responsibility in 1952 and it became a Police Jungle Company.

It was unfortunate that there was no trained anthropologist at the time who could have given advice to the government, or, if there was, his advice was ignored. Used to living up in the hills in a comparatively cool climate the aborigines could not stand the heat of the plains; neither could their stomachs get used to an abrupt and complete change of diet (from tapioca and fresh meat to rice and salt fish). Used to living a natural, energetic life, the men clearing and planting, hunting or fishing, and the women digging tubers, collecting wild foods or simply looking after the family, they could not adapt themselves to a life of idleness. Day after day they could do nothing but gaze longingly through the wire at the jungle beyond. Hundreds died because of the sudden mental and physiological shock to their systems; hundreds more just ceased to have the will to live, and died also. Yet other hundreds, in one instance a whole Resettlement Camp, crept through the wire at night, deftly avoided the sentries and fled back to the jungle.

The GOC and Williams-Hunt were soon at odds on policy, the latter complaining of the wrong way to evacuate aborigine communities that was often followed by the Army, in particular Gurkha battalions; and even where aborigines were resettled, at least one Chief Police Officer did not want any responsibility for aborigines 'squatting around his bases'. The police, in particular, seemed to have been exasperated by the aborigines, whom they regarded as rather squalid children, and the point was made that they had the mentality of six-year-olds. In part this seems to have been because the control of aborigines was described by Gurney as 'a bottomless pit as far as man-power was concerned'.[4] Nevertheless, by the beginning of 1951 control of the aborigines was third on the list of government priorities and half a million dollars had already been set aside to supply resettled aborigines. The support of aborigine evacuees presented problems of its own and even when they were not removed to alien areas the government was enmeshed in a problem of air supply. For many groups this was eventually discontinued on the grounds of shortage of aircraft and policy officially changed from one in which aborigines sat around waiting for tinned milk to fall out of the sky to one in which they were supposed to become self-supporting. But the question still to be answered was whether resettled aborigines would ever become self-supporting. The experience of Kelantan

[4] Malaya War Council, January 22nd 1951.

over two years from March 1951 suggested not. When the rice drops stopped those who remained in the camps almost starved.[5]

Apart from the perils of resettlement, with its dubious compensation of air supply, aborigines were subject to another experimental and highly dangerous government policy: namely air attack. This, it seems, had two functions. First, it was assumed that by bombing roughly a thousand yards away from known aborigine clearings the aborigines would be driven out of areas in which government wished to deny their support to the guerrillas. Second, with rather less respect for propriety, clearings which were obviously supporting far more people than the number of aborigine huts indicated, were to be bombed in order, speculatively, to kill the guerrillas and frighten the aborigines away. Williams-Hunt had complained of this policy in 1950 but at the end of 1951, with aborigine food cultivation for the guerrillas an increasing problem, one still found the Chairman of the Kelantan State War Executive Committee suggesting that, as the RAF considered the aerial spraying of sodium arsenite to kill cultivation to be too dangerous to its own personnel, the cultivation areas should be attacked with high explosive including a percentage of delayed-action bombs.

Kelantan and Kuala Lumpur were often at odds on aborigine policy. What was originally a matter of State policy was now, in effect, contested at the Federal level and Briggs, as Director of Operations, as well as E. B. David, the Secretary of Defence, were explaining to Kelantan that the deliberate bombing of aborigines was 'a very major question of policy which required to be referred to the Federal War Council' and that it was not a measure that they could undertake on their own. Similarly, on the matter of the resettlement of aborigines, Briggs' opinion was that the Kelantan scheme had generally proved abortive; while repeated reports from the Adviser on Aborigines, in Kelantan and elsewhere, said that large numbers of resettled aborigines were dying.

---

[5] One extraordinary incident involved the Commissioner of Police. 'Owing to CT Incident Batu Katak, Temiar have moved. Signal sent to CP requesting tomorrow's air drop made at DZ (Dropping Zone) Oboe (Kuala Betis) instead of DZ Roger (Batu Katak). CP refuses to alter drop. Urgently request you to instruct drop at DZ Oboe tomorrow as do not want drop in middle of jungle where no Temiar are and bandits sitting. Please deal with this urgently and signal that you will accede to request.' Development Officer Kelantan to D. of Ops. July 19th 1951. In the event, it took a telephone call from the Director of Operations to switch the job to the new DZ.

I have given some thought lately to this problem and feel that what we have done is ill-advised and on such a small scale is not to be worthwhile. Total resettlement will never be possible.

I consider that the best we can ever do is to give them a measure of mobile security, thereby doing our best to gain their support and preventing the establishment of food *ladangs* for bandit use.[6]

As it happened, the sporadic bombing of aborigines was still going on in the middle of 1954, at which time it was decided quite clearly (in a D/Ops Instruction) that only guerrilla rather than aborigine clearings could be attacked from the air. At about the same time—July 1954—a new policy was introduced of rehabilitating resettled aborigines, i.e. that they should be allowed to return to the jungle; and this, in effect, was the end of resettlement. In its place, government services were now going to the aborigines in their original locations; and by combining more intensive medical treatment, which involved doctors in overnight stays, proper training facilities to enable aborigines to get a fair return from their produce—both of which were urged by MacGillivray, the Deputy High Commissioner—with the establishment of jungle forts a new phase had begun not only in government's aborigine policy but also in the battle for the deep jungle.

In November 1953 Templer told the Conference of *Mentri*[2] *Besar* that he had been constantly thwarted and disappointed by events and circumstances in solving the problem of aborigines. On one point at least his judgment seems to have been at fault in that he refused initially to approve schemes in which jungle forts were to be supplied by air;[7] and although this was obviously prompted by a sense of economy in the use of aircraft—and possibly by unreliability in bad weather—the fact was that by the end of 1953 all seven jungle forts that had been established were now supplied by air.[8]

Internal reorganisation of the Department of Aborigines took place at the end of 1953. In effect, it meant that the problem was to be dealt with on a Federal rather than a State level; and the appointment of two Protectors of Aborigines who divided up

[6] D/Ops Note on the Aborigine Problem in Perak, September 9th 1951.
[7] Minute to Deputy D/Ops, July 4th 1952.
[8] Templer's argument was that the military or police posts should have been on a main road. Earlier experiments with jungle posts had involved less orthodox methods of supply; equally unusual guerrilla ambush; and the signal 'Elephants are indefensible'.

the country between them. Subordinate staff were increased, training courses set up and, in general, a much more intensive effort was made by government to win over aborigines.[9] Reorganisation was in itself insufficient; and to some extent it begged the question of what government's policy was going to be. Insofar as it concerned the jungle forts, the first of which had been established in Perak and Pahang, it suggested, with its emphasis upon medical teams and trading posts, a rather more sympathetic approach than hitherto. But the principal purpose of the jungle fort was 'domination' of the surrounding area; and although it was patently too much for a platoon of between thirty-six and forty-five men to be expected to dominate the jungle in a fifteen-mile radius from the fort—six hundred and seventy-five square miles—even those two thousand-odd aborigines who lived, as it were, under the protective umbrella of the forts had been of little use in building up the intelligence picture of guerrilla location and movement. One short-lived member of the Department of Aborigines to whom Templer took an immediate dislike and who was dismissed within a fortnight of arrival, had argued for the need to discover roots of the aborigines' spiritual life before any action was taken; and although this in a sense relegated it to the status of an academic problem it would seem that not until this advice was in fact taken and government not only acquired patience in dealing with the aborigines but also the imagination to see how things looked through their childlike eyes that the foundations of its success were laid. This, however, was not the only reason. As well as reorganisation, in December 1953 Bah Pelankin was killed in the Raub area of Pahang; and the considerable influence of this uncharacteristically ruthless aborigine who had thrown in his lot with the guerrillas was thus removed.

In breaking up their organisation and in eliminating the

[9] R. O. D. Noone, who was subsequently appointed Adviser on Aborigines and Director of Museums, succeeded Williams-Hunt (who had died tragically, having slipped and been impaled on jagged bamboo) and had formerly been on the staff of the Director of Intelligence. His brother, Pat Noone, who had lived, married and died among the aborigines, had become something of a legend. See Dennis Holman, *Noone of the Ulu*, London, 1958. John Slimming, a former Malayan police officer, who became an Assistant Protector of Aborigines, gives an evocative account of his journeys to a jungle fort in *Temiar Jungle*, London, 1958. See also his *In Fear of Silence*, London, 1955, a novel which has the authentic 'feel' of ambush. Richard Noone has now written an affectionate and entertaining memorial for his brother, *Rape of the Dream People*, London, 1972. Chapters 8 and 9 deal particularly with his own experiences during the Emergency.

guerrillas from the deep jungle—which was the ultimate purpose—government was thus faced with several distinct but related problems. Insofar as it was a contest for the allegiance of aborigines government was at a disadvantage in that the guerrillas had established themselves well before. Quite a number of the MCP had been known to the aborigines since pre-war days as itinerant traders, *jelutong* tappers and the like; and close relationships had been established during the Japanese occupation when, by a policy of fitful but indiscriminate slaughter, the Japanese had succeeded in terrifying aborigines and cementing their friendship with the guerrillas. When the Emergency began and the Communists returned to the jungle many of their old aborigine contacts were led to believe that they were still fighting the Japanese and therefore they co-operated once again.

> Gradually, however, they learned the truth as told to them, which was that the Chinese had beaten the Japanese, and were now fighting the Europeans. What were they to do? A pre-war European Government had been defeated and driven out by the Japanese; the Chinese had in turn driven out the Japanese; now the Europeans were back in power again, and the Chinese were fighting them also. Who was going to win this time? The Europeans had lost before, and the Chinese guerrillas from the jungle had won against the Japanese. Perhaps they would win again. Thus reasoned many of the jungle people; whatever they might think the answer was quite simple. The Europeans were remote, the Chinese were sitting on the house-ladders so they must help the Chinese for two good reasons :
> (*a*) because they were armed and demanded their co-operation. No one else did.
> (*b*) because on form at least they stood a good chance of defeating the Europeans.

This was the situation before Security Forces began to penetrate the deep jungle in any numbers. In addition, the guerrillas very often went to great lengths to enlist aborigine support. Some units maintained liaison officers who spoke the local aborigine dialect but their greatest and institutional success lay in the formation of the *Asal* Clubs. In name alone it had an immediate advantage. For years, the Security Forces and government outside the Department of Aborigines, referred to the various aborigine tribes simply as *Sakai*. This was a fairly derogatory term, implying the status of a near slave, and was deeply resented by the aborigines themselves. *Asal,* from the Malay word for origin or source, was not only closer to the word 'aborigine' but also implied a different relationship. In return for practical assistance in crop planting, health and hygiene the aborigines extended their own cultivation areas, provided couriers, porters and guides, collected information on Security Force activities, purchased supplies for the guerrillas —if necessary from the jungle fort trading posts—and helped to influence neighbouring tribes in the guerrillas' favour. As a result

> The Communists' domination of these hill peoples was so tight at one stage that probing military patrols could penetrate, and for days traverse and reconnoitre an area in which there were terrorists, and return to base having found no signs of them; only 'friendly' aborigines. They had perfected an early warning system, a 'screen' of aborigines which surrounded their bases which was so efficient that it reported every move of the 'enemy' and enabled them to take evasive action long before the soldiers arrived on the scene. The domination of the hill population was by no means complete. It was strongest in the areas closest to their bases. Influence over the surrounding communities was exerted through the medium of the *Asal* Clubs. *Asal* teams consisting of Chinese leaders and their aborigine counterparts, with a mixed escort of Chinese and armed aborigines, were continually on the move through the more distant areas, holding meetings at the houses of important headmen and disseminating propaganda.

The establishment of jungle forts as well as disrupting MCP plans for jungle bases—for example the North Pahang Regional Committee's base—also made life more embarrassing for the aborigines. Before analysing their characteristics Noone had argued that they had no desire to be dominated by anybody; and this was reinforced by the following factors:

> (a) a fervent love of freedom to live their lives as they always had done and a resentment of outside interference;
>
> (b) whilst they may succumb temporarily to threats of violence, they can take swift retaliatory action if the safety of the group is not endangered;
>
> (c) an intense sense of loyalty to the group, extended through the kinship system to relatives wherever they may be;
>
> (d) mutual responsibility for action taken, also extended through the kinship system;
>
> (e) a quick appreciation of the value of material assistance if it would benefit them.

Nevertheless with government forces and guerrillas competing

ABORIGINES AND THE DEEP JUNGLE

for their support isolation was no longer possible and a new policy was necessary to ensure their freedom and the minimum inconvenience in carrying on their normal life.

The solution which they hit upon may best be described by quoting an actual example; the first case which came to our knowledge when the situation was developing along these lines in south Kelantan. One of the early Forts to be established was Fort Brooke in this area. Prior to setting it up, the aborigine Chairman of the local ASAL Club was one Penghulu Pangoi, an energetic old man with the interests of his people at heart. He had been cultivating extensively for the Communists in the upper reaches of the river on which the Fort was to be built. His sons and other young men of the group had been trained and armed, and on behalf of the Communists he held considerable authority over all other groups down the river. At that time he was supporting, and acting as screen for, a high level camp just over the range from the source of the river.

When the SAS Regiment arrived in the area to establish the Fort, Pangoi sent some of his men as spies to see what was going on. They stayed with another related headman named Menteri Awol, whose cultivation was close to the Fort. When news got back to Pangoi that the soldiers appeared to be building a Fort which was to be occupied permanently from then on, he not unnaturally became very worried about his own position, and that of his group. What was he to do now? He sent messages to all the communities along the river inviting them to a meeting in his longhouse. The notables, including Menteri Awol, duly arrived and unknown to the Communists or to the soldiers, the meeting was held. It lasted for three days and nights, and this was the final outcome :

(a) That Pangoi would continue to support the Communists, as before.
(b) That Menteri Awol would give his support to the government.
(c) Neither was to give any information to either side which might endanger anyone in either of the two aborigine factions.
(d) Neither was to give any information to either side which might result in a fight between the Communists and the soldiers (because the aborigines would be blamed)
(e) Both factions were to warn each other if either the Communists or soldiers moved against them.

(f) All the other communities were to remain strictly neutral and maintain that they knew nothing about anything if anybody asked them.

(g) If, in the long run, the Communists won the war, Pangoi was to ensure the safety of Menteri Awol and his people; similarly if the government won, Awol would ensure that nothing befell Pangoi.

The effect of this pact, for such it was, was that they had backed both horses in the race, and whichever one was the winner they would not be the losers. This form of double insurance became the pattern to be adopted subsequently by all hill groups finding themselves in the same awkward position. To them it was the natural solution since kinship ties and the doctrine of mutual responsibility bound them together up and down the valley, and beyond, and it was of paramount importance to safeguard their independence and preserve their way of life. Throughout the length and breadth of the main range similar pacts spread rapidly, wherever the government made a permanent base. The system is still being followed along the Thai frontier, where the Communists are trying desperately to maintain their grip on the last batch of aborigines under their influence. On the face of it, it would seem impossible to persuade the hill people to throw their weight into the government side of the balance. In the event, it was not quite so impossible as it seemed; had it been so, the Communists might still be ensconced in strength in the deep jungle.

The reorganisation of the Department of Aborigines at the end of 1953 meant that it became totally responsible for administration, education, welfare, medical facilities and the conduct of psychological warfare. In addition, it now had the task of collecting intelligence by setting up a network of agents. In two months the Department grew from under twenty to over two hundred personnel and, with effective forces deployed in the jungle, a small team of officers in Kuala Lumpur was responsible for the conduct of a combined civil-police-military campaign and had, as its principal arm, the Special Air Service Regiment whose CO was the chairman of this control team. In the first phase of operations there were, by 1955, a total of ten jungle forts manned by the Police Field Force and a base not only for the SAS Regiment but field assistants from the Department of Aborigines. The forts were supplied from the air—where possible an airstrip was built that would enable a Pioneer aircraft to land—and they were vulnerable on this count as well as to a company-sized attack had the guerrillas ever been able to muster that many men and to approach undetected. In the event, however, no serious attacks were launched. With a secure base, aerial reconnaissance first helped to pinpoint cultivation areas—and thus the communities responsible for them—and a rapid survey on foot helped to determine the location, tribe, numbers, name of headman and circumstances of all local communities. Armed with this basic information the next step was to gain confidence : which was the most difficult task of all.

> In these initial stages, of all the tactics used to win them over, the trump card was undoubtedly our ability to explode the propaganda which the Communists had been slowly injecting into them. In one area for instance on asking to whom the aircraft dropping supplies in the next valley belonged the hillmen were told that they were Communist aircraft from China. A few weeks later in the same area there was a major operation whilst two forts were being constructed. The hillmen asked why it was that the jungle was now swarming with European soldiers. They were told 'because Communist soldiers have captured the towns, the government has been driven out, and all the Europeans have fled to the jungle'.

To counter these opinions with reality a hundred headmen were brought out to Kuala Lumpur by helicopter, 'plane, on foot, by truck and by train.

> Here they were given a three-day 'Civics Course' during which they were taken round the town, shown the government offices, and also the Valettas on the airstrip which they recognised as those they had seen in the jungle. In order to impress them with the might of government, they witnessed a huge parade at the Police Depot; and also a demonstration of fire power by mortars and armoured cars. After a feast and a ceremonial dance they returned to their various river valleys, thoroughly enlightened by what they had seen and impressed with the power of government. News travels quickly in the jungle.

Perhaps the greatest of the positive attractions which government offered to aborigines were the medical clinics. In one year alone the ten forts between them treated over fourteen thousand new aborigine patients; and as many aborigine medicine men trained as Medical Assistants they were able to more than double the range of the remedies for poor hygiene, minimal nutrition and the high incidence of disease, particularly yaws. More and more families made their way towards the jungle forts and were treated by government as refugees while their new cultivation areas, opened up close to the forts, matured. On discovering that they were provided immediately with rations, that government were prepared to continue this up to a period of nine months, and that they would not be locked up, let alone killed, as a result of seeking government protection, aborigine confidence in the guerrillas waned. There were still, however, considerable handicaps to be overcome before these shifting opinions could be translated into useful intelligence. 'River Valley' pacts were still operative. Aborigines had an almost pathological dread of any fighting, shooting or killing anywhere near their settlement. They still wanted to be left to their own devices. And, with the best will in the world, they had great difficulty in appreciating numbers above about five or six: in their own dialects they only counted up to three.[10] Nevertheless, those living under the influence of the forts now began to assist government more openly and could afford to leak more accurate information provided they did not contravene the terms of the pact. For example, if they knew of a guerrilla camp far away from their area in which there were only Chinese not directly supported by any aborigines then they would inform the fort. On occasion they were even prepared to act as guides if they could be suitably disguised as soldiers in jungle green; but their sense of collective responsibility never allowed them to admit the presence of a guerrilla camp within their own territories.

> This principle of collective responsibility for the group area had other interesting angles from the intelligence point of view. When we were hurriedly collecting basic data on the various communities, we also investigated the question of hereditary areas and plotted them on the one-inch maps. As the information grew these maps took on the appearance of a neat jigsaw puzzle, almost every inch of jungle belonging to one headman or another. Occasionally, we discovered a patch of territory not claimed by anyone. All neighbouring headmen hotly denied that it formed part of their territory. Nine times out of ten there was a Communist camp there. No one would claim the area because they might be held responsible for the existence of the camp.

Ultimately, aborigines seemed to be subject to the same rules of

---

[10] They are much disturbed by death and are liable to vacate their tribal grounds entirely on the death of a headman. One of their most endearing taboos is that they do not laugh in the presence of butterflies: who are believed to be the spirits of their departed dead.

confidence and morale as the more sophisticated races: the quantity and quality of information given was in direct proportion to the military successes in the area. More kills produced bigger and better intelligence from the tribes. More accurate information in turn led to more kills. In the collection and processing of intelligence there were other similarities: in this case, accentuated. A basis of trust and confidence was essential before aborigines would pass on any information: and this was something that could be immediately undone by the sudden transfer of a fort commander or a field assistant. An Aborigine Research and Interrogation Section on the jungle edge twelve miles from Kuala Lumpur was built on the pattern of an aborigine village with a large Temiar longhouse as the centrepiece which was used for detailed interrogation for those who were brought out, usually by helicopter, from the deep jungle. One of the particular problems that was dealt with here was the membership of the *Asal* Clubs.

We became aware of the existence of the 'river valley' pacts at an early stage of the campaign, but to get the names of the *Asal* Club members was a difficult task. Although in most cases we were able to identify the group and its headman (Chairman of the Club), it was not so easy to find out who were the other members. Who would own up to have a near relative in the *Asal*? Captured documents, reports, diaries, etc. helped to a certain extent, but the Chinese system of writing down aborigine names led to confusion. Here again the basic data we had collected earlier usually gave a clue. Wherever possible the family trees of headmen had been compiled both for record purposes and to enable an investigation into their kinship system. The ramifications covered a wide area and included all remembered relatives of a given headman. Having compiled the table and checked the kinship terms, the next step was to ask the headman concerned where all these people were, by going through the list one by one. Embarrased silences and such replies as, 'I don't know, he no longer lives here', usually indicated which were the *Asal* members. Armed with these leads, skilful interrogation at the Centre completed the picture of these Clubs.

Having identified the membership the next thing was to try and locate them on the ground. Although we knew their general areas of responsibility we wanted to pinpoint them as a prelude to establishing contact through the pro-government groups. To begin with this information was almost impossible to get. In one area an *Asal* Chairman named Chawog broke the local pact by murdering two pro-government aborigines for giving information about him. This so incensed the friendly groups that within a week they shot him in the act of stealing a pro-government headman's wife. In this case the subsequent disintegration of the *Asal* led to the final elimination of the Communists it had formerly supported.

In other areas our first move was to ask the pro-government headmen to try and persuade their relatives in the *Asal* to seek government protection. Many meetings were held between the two factions, but they could not be convinced that they would not be killed if they fell into our hands. Having lost the support of the bulk of the uncommitted hill population, the Communists at this time were desperately trying to prevent the defection of the *Asal* Clubs; their last source of food and information. They were told that we knew all about them and that they would be killed if they went anywhere near the Forts. The story of Chawog was twisted and quoted as an example of government's duplicity. So, although we had established contact with the numerous clubs, we could not persuade them to come out. Even a widely publicised declaration of fair treatment and a guarantee that they would not be killed had no effect at that time.

In one area of Perak we were in negotiation with the *Asal* for over two years before the leader eventually surrendered with his people. This was Kerinching, a very intelligent and cunning man. When the proposition was first put to him at a meeting with pro-government headmen, he demanded a supply of food, cloth, axes, salt and knives as a token of good faith. This was duly supplied from our welfare store. At all subsequent meetings similar gifts were sent in the hope of enticing him out. We even sent him an expensive Malay *kris*, but to no avail; he wanted further time to consider the matter. Finally, word came from the pro-government headmen that Kerinching would come out, but he was worried because these headmen had reported him to government. Because they had thereby broken the pact he asked them to pay $400/- to him on receipt of which he would come out. The money was produced, further gifts were sent, and a large meeting and feast was held; unknown either to the Communists or the Fort nearby. Our hopes were high. Back came the pro-government emissaries without Kerinching and minus the money. On being paid the money after the feast, he had agreed the debt had been squared but had changed his mind about coming out. Before they could catch him, he was off into the jungle. A year later he did come out, but only because new operations in the area made it too hot for him and his health was failing.

In other places we were luckier, negotiations terminated satisfactorily. But the *Asal* headmen always tested us out first. They would send out one or two of their people to live with the pro-government headmen and when they saw that they were well treated (they were treated like lords on such occasions) they would send out some more, and eventually came out themselves. Not that they always severed their connections with the Communists on coming out. Some of them continued to supply food for a time, but we knew this was happening; it helped to pinpoint the location of the remaining camps.

Slowly but surely, for one reason or another, but basically because the areas they were living in became operationally too hot for them, the *Asal* Clubs disintegrated and their members surrendered. Government kept its word. No action was ever taken against any former *Asal* member, even the armed hostile ones. On several occasions, however, the Department had to intercede on their behalf and get them released from police lock-ups where they had been placed by some misguided police officer. A special instruction was later brought out to the effect that no action was to be taken against aborigines seeking government protection and that they were to be handed over to the Department immediately on surrender.

Breaking contract between guerrillas the aborigines was by no means the same as breaking up the guerrilla organisation itself. Nevertheless, from the middle of 1954 onwards an exploitable situation was being created in the deep jungle in which, even in this vastness, the guerrillas were beginning to be isolated. At the beginning, this situation was not exploited to the full. In his review of the Emergency situation at the end of 1954, the Director of Operations said that it was 'regrettable that our operations to disrupt the three main deep jungle bases are slowed down by the inability of the War Office to provide the second SAS Regiment requested in July 1954'. It was to be another two years before a small experimental unit was to be raised with the same function as the Malayan Scouts—the SAS under their local title—but in the meantime the number of 'hostile' aborigines had dwindled to a few hundred.[11] Some disagreements on policy continued

Even during this enlightened period mistakes were still being

[11] The figures given seem to have been rather notional. For example, thirty thousand at the end of 1953 but only two thousand in October 1954.

made that did not help to win over the jungle people. The destruction of aborigine cultivation from the air with chemical sprays was not very well received by the communities with upturned faces below, who had spent months clearing and planting the hillsides. This idea was eventually abandoned on realising that it is physically and chemically impossible to destroy tapioca. A square half-inch of the tuber casually dropped on the ground will sprout and grow. Neither did the bombing of the deep jungle result in anything except dead animals and a serious doubt about government's real intentions.

but the deep jungle was no longer the guerrillas' invincible ally.

Evaporation

NEGOTIABLE TERMS?

By 1955 'armed struggle' was rather unfashionable in the Communist world. On reading the omens it would seem that this general policy change dates back to 1954 or even earlier but in 1955 it was obvious that events in Malaya, as well as in the rest of the world, provided a favourable climate for some sort of negotiations. At Bandoeng, in Indonesia, the Afro-Asian Conference in April had seen the Chinese Prime Minister Mr. Chou En-lai take a surprisingly moderate line on colonialism, peaceful co-existence and the allegiance of the Nanyang Chinese.[1] More particularly, as far as Malayan Chinese might be concerned, and specifically on the issue of dual nationality, he hoped the Chinese living overseas, after making their choice, would 'increase their sense of responsibility towards a country whose nationality they have chosen'. Other indications that a peaceful settlement in Malaya was favoured have been noted by C. C. Too. At the second conference of the Communist and Workers' Parties of the British Commonwealth held in London in April 1954 a report entitled *Malaya Fights for Freedom* had been submitted by the exiled Lim Hong Bee that favoured, among other things, a provisional coalition people's government formed by all patriotic parties to achieve full national independence. The MCP *Freedom News* in Singapore had translated this report and appended one of the six emergency resolutions of the conference that urged an immediate cease-fire and negotiations with the 'genuine representatives of the people of Malaya' in order to attain peace. In August 1954 a Malayan delegate to the Council of World Democratic Youth in Peking was quoted as saying

> The campaigners of Malayan liberation have constantly declared that they are willing to undertake peace talks to bring the Malayan war to an end if the basic rights of national independence and

[1] Some of the points made in Mr. Chou's resolution on world peace were: respect for the sovereignty and territorial integrity of all countries; abstention from aggression, military threats, and interference in other countries' internal affairs; recognition of the equality of all races and nations; and respect for the right of people to choose freely their own way of life and their political and economic systems.

self-determination of the Malayan people are maintained. This peace offer is ardently supported by our youth and ignored by the colonialists.

By November 1954 a guerrilla news-sheet produced in the Kedah/Penang area carried this report in English together with approval of the Geneva Conference on Indo-China as an example of how 'disputes can be solved justly by peaceful means' and how 'respect for national independence, democratic freedom and territorial integrity of the oppressed nations' provided 'a successful solution of a colonial war by peaceful means'. The British in Malaya were specifically urged to follow the French example in Indo-China.

Malaya itself was now approaching a critical phase in its approach to independence. In early 1955 it was announced that the first Federal elections would be held in July and the leader of the Alliance, Tunku Abdul Rahman, suggested at the same time that terrorists should be offered an amnesty if they were to surrender. In May the Alliance manifesto was published and contained, among other things, a proposal that a general pardon should be offered to terrorists. What would have been a straightforward Malayan initiative, reinforced by success in the Federal Council elections, was now complicated by the MCP's own initiative in which it sought to identify itself with the cause of Malayan independence. In a letter dated May 1st and posted from South Siam an 'announcement of the representative of the MRLA general headquarters' was received by leaders of the Alliance and other political parties in June over the pseudonym 'Ng Heng'.[2]

This was the beginning of the MCP's peace offensive. The aim of the MRLA, so the letter said, was nothing but a peaceful, democratic and independent Malaya, which it hoped to achieve by peaceful means if possible. To attain independence it was necessary to end the war, abolish the Emergency Regulations, hold national elections in a peaceful and democratic atmosphere so that all political parties, organisations, and individuals who genuinely strove for peace could hold a round table conference to reach a unanimous agreement in conformity with actual conditions in Malaya for peace and independence. While the MRLA was willing to take the proposed amnesty, unsatisfactory as it was, as a basis for peace negotiations it would be an illusion to attempt to

[2] Conceivably so that responsibility might be disclaimed if this initiative was ideologically unsound.

force the MRLA to surrender. Owing to difficulties in arranging a meeting in the jungle, the MRLA was willing to send its representatives to Kuala Lumpur to make arrangements if a safe conduct was given. Government's answer could be given over Radio Malaya. Government's reply was that if the Communists genuinely wished to end the Emergency they could take advantage of the present liberal terms of surrender: the government itself was not prepared to bargain.[3]

Sir Cheng Lock Tan, the leader of the Malayan Chinese Association found it difficult to say whether he agreed with the government's reply; but a Selangor State councillor, Mr. Tan Tuan Boon described the government's reply as a grave error: 'Communism cannot be defeated by force of arms'. With an overwhelming electoral victory behind him, in which the Alliance won fifty-one of the fifty-two elected seats and polled 80 per cent of the votes cast, Tunku Abdul Rahman, as Chief Minister, now made good the offer of an amnesty, beginning in September, but promised there would be no negotiations with the MCP.[4] By the end of September, however, the Tunku had agreed to meet Chin Peng 'but only Ching Peng and only to clarify amnesty arrangements'. Nevertheless, the closer the MCP came to a meeting with government, the more difficult it was to categorise peace 'negotiations' and to distinguish them from arrangements for a surrender. At preliminary meetings that were held on the Siamese border Chen Tian, head of the Central Propaganda Department

---

[3] According to Sir David Watherston 'The letter signed "Ng Heng" was not sent—clearly deliberately—to the Government direct. By great good fortune, a copy received by the UPAM in KL was passed on to us at once. We knew there would be other copies and certainly one or more with the left-wing Chinese press.

If it had been published it could have led to public demand for negotiations before we had time to point out the implications that this would involve, i.e. recognition of the MCP and acceptance of them as equals at a negotiating table.

We had a hectic three or four days—McGillivray had just left for London and I was OAG—exchanging telegrams with the Colonial Office after the proposals had been analysed, and we were able to publish the MCP's offer and the Government's reply before any other copy of this letter had come to light.

Our fear was the one you express, that the public would be willing to pay a higher price for peace than was desirable, taking the long-term view.'

[4] Of the one and a quarter million who registered as electors over 80 per cent were Malays and only 11 per cent Chinese. It was reckoned that threequarters of the six hundred thousand eligible Chinese were too apathetic to get themselves put on the roll. Gullick, *op. cit.* p. 118.

of the MCP, handed out statements to newspaper correspondents in attendance that suggested, amongst other things, that an international commission should supervise any peace agreement which might result from the coming meetings.[5] With some truth the MCP claimed that 'genuine public opinion expressed in the press' was against the methods proposed by the Federation government, through the amnesty, to end the war. Before the confrontation between Malayan leaders and the MCP the majority of local Chinese newspapers, particularly the *Nanyang Siang Pau*, which had the largest circulation, were generally in support of the MCP's terms and acceptance of the MCP as an equal party.

On the eve of the talks the MCP issued a manifesto sub-titled *Struggle for the materialisation of the independence, democracy and peace of Malaya* which set out, in Leninist terms, the minimum programme. Item one was an end to the war through negotiations for reasonable terms and the repeal of the Emergency Regulations. Equal status was to be accorded to all political parties; but apart from this there was hardly anything to which one could, *prima facie*, take exception: more particularly, as the terms seemed nearly all to have been borrowed from the Alliance electoral campaign programme, reinforced, somewhat surprisingly, with particular emphasis on cultural and economic relations with Britain. The manifesto ended by pointing out that the programme was only an interim one to suit 'the present common demands of all communities and all strata in Malaya'; that 'the Communists always never want to hide their longterm aims of fighting for people's democracy and socialism'; and offered the reminder that this was 'not a programme for a people's democracy or socialism' but only one suitable for the present practical conditions of Malaya and the only way to settle the relations of Malaya and Britain.

'Practical conditions' demanded, in the first place, the recognition of the MCP and it was with this outward display of confidence that the MCP triumvirate emerged from the jungles of North-east Kedah in December 1955. On the eve of the Baling talks the MCP had announced that a Malay, Musa bin Ahmad, was now Chairman of the Central Committee and an Indian, R. G. Balan, was Vice-Chairman. The former had not hitherto been reckoned to be among the two or three most important

---

[5] The Korean armistice, the Geneva Conference and the Bandoeng meeting were cited as evidence of a world movement for peace and anticolonialism: from which Malaya ought not to be excluded.

Malay members of the MCP and was not a member of Central Committee; the latter had been in detention since the beginning of the Emergency. Neither of them accompanied Chin Peng, the Secretary General, at Baling although there was a semblance of a more national representation in the inclusion of Rashid Maidin, a Malay; the third member was Chen Tian, head of the MCP's Central Propaganda Department.[6]

On the other side were three elected national representatives. Tunku Abdul Rahman was now the Chief Minister of the Federation Government. Dato Sir Cheng Lock Tan, although not the most senior Chinese member of the Cabinet, was a recognised leader of the Malayan Chinese; and the third member was Mr. David Marshall, the Chief Minister of Singapore.

The confrontation at Baling began on December 28th, lasted more than eight hours, and was spread over two days. Popular hopes were high; the fact that talks were taking place at all was considered something an an achievement; and there were great expectations that a peace settlement of some sort would result. Whether or not the door was open to a negotiated peace was hardly considered—although the government disclaimed any such idea—and there seemed to be enough, although perhaps only slight, discrepancies in some of the Chief Minister's preliminary statements to suggest an opening that might be enlarged by careful negotiation. Thus in his opening remarks, having first affirmed his willingness to discuss questions of peace, Chin Peng referred to a past statement of the Chief Minister: 'that if we (the MCP) stopped the Armed Struggle our Party could then enjoy equal status so that we could fight for independence by constitutional means'. This, while it may have been the MCP's assumption, was certainly its aspiration. According to the Chief Minister, who replied, he had, in the course of various speeches, said 'I want you to come out, so that we could fight together for independence for Malaya by constitutional means'. What was now under discussion was whether the MRLA and MCP were interested in accepting the terms of the government amnesty and whether 'they genuinely intend to be loyal to the Government of Malaya and give up their Communist activities'. Simply to be anti-British was not sufficient to show that one was loyal to Malaya.

> The position is this: that today the people in Malaya, one and all, regard the Communist activities as something entirely foreign

[6] The prinicpal conducting officer was John Davis, Chin Peng's wartime comrade and leader of Force 136 in Malaya.

to the Malayan way of life. They regard the Communist Party as belonging to a power outside this country and consider its members give allegiance to that foreign country and not to Malaya. Therefore, it is necesary for you to prove and to convince the people that it is not so, that your duty, your loyalty, your love, your everything belong to this country. That is the position; that is why I said in this letter 'those who show that they genuinely intend to be loyal to the Government of Malaya and to give up their Communist activities will be helped to regain their normal position in society'. Once you have joined this society, taken your place in society, as I said before, there is no difference between you, I or anybody else.[7]

Loyalty to Malaya was to be the ultimate criterion. In the meantime, the immediate problem was what was to happen to the MCP and the immediate issue was that of recognition. For the MCP there seemed to be some small glimmer of hope for the future, at least in Singapore, in Mr. Marshall's suggestion that it would be for the government of the day to consider whether the Party could be formed at some future date, whether it was called Communist or something different; but for the moment it was clear that the Communist Party would not be recognised and, as its dissolution was unacceptable to the MCP negotiators, the discussions could well have ended at this point.

Neither side however appeared to have been anxious to take responsibility for breaking off the discussions there and then. After three hours of inconclusive argument on recognition the third session began with probing questions from Chin Peng whether or not the British Government had given a full guarantee for independence to Malaya. The Tunku assured him that the High Commissioner had given this in the Legislative Council and that the target date was August 31st 1957. Independence, he said in reply to a further question, included responsibility for internal security; and after a short interval in which the recording apparatus was checked to see whether these entirely Malayan conversations were being overheard, Chin Peng brought the discussion back to the question of recognition.

Challenged by the Tunku to say whether, with a predominantly Chinese membership, the MCP could claim to be the nationalist party of the country, Chin Peng countered with the argument, half question, half supposition and wholly disingenuous, 'What would happen if only Federal citizens or those who were

[7] Tunku Abdul Rahman, verbatim report of the Baling Meeting, p. 6.

happy to become Federal citizens were allowed to join the Communist Party?' The answer, again, was that loyalty to the country had to be proved first : which raised the further question of what happened to those members of the MCP who took advantage of the amnesty? These terms were, in fact, set out in the amnesty and were repeated by the Chief Minister: they would be held in special camps rather than in prison for as long as was necessary to carry out the investigation with the aim of effecting a signed declaration not to engage in activities that would be prejudicial to the interests of Malaya and Malayans. Those who surrendered would be helped to rehabilitate themselves in society; those who wished would be given every facility to return to China.

Again, these terms were unacceptable to Chin Peng and when the talks resumed on the following day there were only two hours left before the Tungku had to return to Kuala Lumpur *en route* to London and talks on the final stages of Malayan independence. The position had been made clear on both sides but, whether for propaganda purposes or the apparent advantage of having an agreement about something that might be the subject of future bargaining or emendation, Chin Peng set out the MCP's position in this way

> The present government, although it is a popularly elected government, still is not an independent government. (Marshall: Tell him we recognise that fully.) Under such circumstances, therefore, when we bring out our suggestions we have got to have regard to this situation. If these popularly elected governments of the Federation in Singapore have self-determination in matters concerning security and national defence, then all problems could be solved easily. As soon as these two governments have self-determination in internal security and national defence matters, then we can stop the war immediately.

This would seem to have been a dubious card to play. Tungku Abdul Rahman fastened on to the possibility immediately

> *Tungku*: Is that a promise? When I come back from England that is the thing that I am bringing back with me.
> *Chin Peng*: That being the case, we can straightaway stop our hostilities and also disband our armed units.

As an unconditional statement of MCP policy this must surely have been regretted and was, in any case, not to be honoured. In fact, it was subject to conditions. First, the unspoken premise: that the MCP was established as a legal political party. Second, when the exact meaning of their intentions was probed and the Tunku inquired: 'Would you ask for any terms before you throw down your arms?'

> *Chin Peng*: This question is very simple. The answer is very simple. If the MCP is recognised, if members of the MCP are not subject to detention and investigation, they can throw down their arms at once. The question of weapons can be solved easily. (Interpreter: I don't know what they actually mean by that.)
>
> The downing of arms does not mean that the arms will be handed in (repeats) is not equivalent to the handing over of arms to government. May I repeat: the downing of weapons is not equivalent to the handing over of weapons to government.

The two positions seem comparatively clear, and also the distance separating them, but from this there issued the statement signed by both sides that was immediately issued as a press release.

> As soon as the elected governments of the Federation obtain complete control of internal security and local armed forces, we will end hostilities, lay down our arms and disband our armies. It does not amount to accepting the present amnesty terms.

It seems surprising now that this statement was agreed. Bearing in mind the intentions of both sides which had not been concealed hitherto this was a meaningless form of words and although, months later, there were linguistic arguments about 'surrender' and 'cease-fire', the real argument was not so much whether the Chinese expression for laying down arms implied surrender but whether the surrender was to be unconditional. In what may be taken as a more definitive statement Chin Peng had said,

> If only the MCP is recognised; if only we are not subject to restriction of our liberty, it is possible for us to surrender our weapons.

But here, even if the word 'surrender' is ambiguous, there can be no doubt that it was conditional on recognition of the MCP.

Compared with this, other questions, such as where the investigation of MCP members would take place, were rather academic. Even on a close reading—on the whole, the exchanges make more sense when treated with a certain detachment—there is a surrealist quality to some of the dialogue[8] but at least the political prospects were stated with unexpected clarity. For the Tunku, recognising the strength and support of Communism in Malaya, it would be impossible to control the MCP if it were to come out of the jungle and be allowed to organise as a *bona fide* political party.

> Therefore if you do not come out to surrender, we would rather not accept you in our society. If you want to have peace in this country, one side must give in—either we give in to you, or you give in to us. Two ideologies, yours and ours, can never work side by side. That is my frank opinion.

For Chin Peng, the principle of investigation implied surrender, which was unacceptable; and when he described it plainly as 'humiliation' it is tempting to assume that it would have been an unbearable loss of face. Partly for this reason there is still the bare possibility to be entertained that the MCP would have emerged from the jungle had they been allowed to disperse *before* they were subject to inquiry, investigation or whatever process was devised. At the same time, there is a feeling that the Baling talks were intended by the MCP as a political demonstration and it was not only because they failed to achieve a settlement that they were described as part of the 'rigorous' peace offensive.

As a political demonstration they were certainly impressive for both sides. Although they were seldom expressed at the time there were fears that an amiable and perhaps rather slow-thinking Chief Minister would be outwitted by the nimbleness and tactical skill of Chin Peng. In the event, any tactical triumph belongs to the Tunku. But at least to one observer after the event the most impressive quality was his passionate concern for the welfare of his country. Where, it must be admitted, Dato Sir Cheng Lock Tan's argument—'Why waste money unnecessarily on the Emergency'—was limited in appeal—no humanitarian consideration, no appeal to reason or justice—there are passages of the Tunku's transcript which will stand not only as the epitome of Malayan patriotism but an epigraph of decency and justice. Much the same could be said of the Chief Minister of Singapore, Mr. David Marshall, whose forensic skill exposed the weakness of his

---

[8] Chin Peng: 'Reporting to the police has a touch of surrender.'

opponents' argument. As a national party, the pretensions of the MCP were also exposed: an impression that was not removed by the silences of the MCP's Malay delegate. Chin Peng himself was still impressive. Much fatter than when the Emergency began, but with a certain puffiness and colour that was a result of years in the deep jungle, he had conducted his case skilfully.[9] For the first time the Chief Minister of the Federation had encountered, in him, his principal political opposition and understood not only the size of the challenge but also the political dimension of the Emergency.[10]

Nevertheless there were signs over the next few months of an uncertain political touch compared, at least, with the former determination that there should be no negotiated peace except one that involved the surrender of the MCP. As a popularly elected leader in a country within measurable distance of independence the Chief Minister was in a position of obvious political strength. At the same time, the hope that the MCP could be persuaded to lay down its arms and thus, for the time being, end not only the fears and the terrorism but also the enormous public and private inconveniences of the Emergency created a certain pressure for the recognition of the MCP as a political party. As an elected leader, too, it was proper that the Chief Minister should consult the wishes of the people; but in the early months of 1956 policy, as expressed, veered away from 'mobilisation of the people' and 'national mobilisation' to a question 'What did the people want him to do?' and willingness to accept foreign offers of mediation. These, presumably, included Chinese offers; and the Chinese element in the insurrection was emphasised by Mr. Tan Siew Sin who reportedly 'stunned' members of the Legislative Council with his suggestion of a mission to Peking for exploratory talks about persuading the MCP to give up its armed struggle. Shortly afterwards Tan received a letter from the MCP, this time posted in Penang and signed by Chen Tian, requesting a

---

[9] The degree of isolation had been marked when the preliminary negotiations were held: Chen Tian's unfamiliarity with push-button handles on car doors.

[10] 'Chin Peng really taught me what Communism was. I had never really understood and appreciated its full meaning. When I was briefed on Communism by the British experts I always felt that they were interested in making a bad case against the Communists. But there in that room in Baling Chin Peng taught me something I shall not forget. He taught me that Malayan Communism can never co-exist.' Harry Miller, *Prince and Premier*, London, 1959, pp. 192–93.

NEGOTIABLE TERMS? 469

resumption of peace talks and the repeal of the Emergency Regulations.[11]

This request was immediately rejected by the Chief Minister and, instead, discussions began in the new Emergency Operations Council to intensify the 'People's War' against the guerrillas including, so it seemed, a consideration of national service. A few days later two more notes from the MCP were received explaining their aims and announcing a reshuffle of the Central Committee so that Malays, Chinese and Indians were all represented. And although this was countered with the announcement of a new all-out 'People's War' against the terrorists within the next four weeks, a few days later the Chief Minister announced that he was prepared to meet Chin Peng and to offer 'more liberal' terms in an effort to end the Emergency. The conditions, however, were that there should be a fixed agenda; that there were to be no negotiations; and that the guerrillas would still have to lay down their arms and come out of the jungle. It is difficult to see how the original terms could have been liberalised in any significant way but, by this time, Peking radio had announced the MCP's offer to re-open the Baling talks,[12] and in September, 1956 the MCP sent a formal request to the Chinese Communist Party Congress in Peking asking for international mediation to bring peace to Malaya: although this did not, in the event, mean, as the Tunku suggested, that they could not fight on much longer and were appealing to outside powers to mediate on their behalf.

In any event it was domestic rather than foreign representation that mattered. The MCA/UMNO Alliance was no longer the only political party in the field. Further to the left the Labour Party's attitude to the MCP was more equivocal; and its Selangor division had urged the Tunku to meet Chin Peng and to end the Emergency immediately. In July 1957, a few weeks away from independence, the Malayan TUC also urged that peace talks should be opened; and in the meantime the MCP, in yet another letter, received this time by a Chinese communal organisation in Perak, had suggested the conditions for a negotiated peace. These were that its members should be given privileges enjoyed by citizens; that they should have freedom to participate in elections and stand as candidates; and that there should be a guarantee

[11] A similar letter was received by the MCA Headquarters in Kuala Lumpur.
[12] This was taken as evidence of a direct link between the MCP and China but could just as easily have been based upon public as upon private sources.

that political as well as armed members of the MCP should not be punished. With the achievement of independence on August 31st there was now a marked increase in the MCP's peace proposals and in November 1957, after a direct proposal from Chin Peng, the Chief Minister agreed to a preliminary meeting and the border town of Kroh was chosen as a site for possible talks. The Tunku had inferred from Chin Peng's letter that the MCP had accepted the principle of surrender but, as doubts increased, and after a government ultimatum, another letter was received from Chin Peng stating that he was prepared to send two emissaries for preliminary talks but that the question of surrender did not arise.

Thus ended, after two years, the possibility that peace could be negotiated in advance of a military settlement. On the whole, the MCP's campaign for a People's United Front had met with little overt success. Nevertheless as long as both the MCP and the Emergency Regulations were in existence there was always the possibility that the public would pay a higher price for peace than would the government. The MCP, provided it could conserve its dwindling strength, was not averse to continuing the Emergency. The surrender terms that had been offered by government would prevent the MRLA and the *Min Yuen* from emerging into civil life, free and apparently respectable, and therefore able to take an influential part in political and labour activities. The Party leaders considered that a very cautious demonstration of military activity would keep their casualties low and at the same time might persuade the public and the government that the MCP could not be destroyed by military measures and that peace would have to be sought upon Communist terms. Directives recovered on the death of Yeong Kuo, the Vice-Secretary-General of the MCP, in August 1956 had stressed the importance of developing 'legal' United Front activities that were directed from the jungle although in his monthly reports the Director of Intelligence seemed more concerned with Communist influence in Singapore where, for example, the Communist penetration of the new People's Action Party and the 'Middle Road' Trades Unions was likely to have some influence on Malayan affairs.[13] In Malaya itself the Labour Party, the Party Ra'ayat formed by Ahmad Boestaman, of pre-Emergency API fame, and the revised Islamic

[13] In April 1956 the PAP journal *Petir*, in an article which bore a marked resemblance to the new MCP line, carried a strongly worded attack on the Chief Minister of the Federation declaring that his policies were not in conformity with the wishes of the Malayan people.

party *Persatuan Islam Sa-malaya* of Dr. Burhanuddin, were all sympathetic to recognition of the MCP but there was, at this time, no evidence of any direct penetration by the MCP.[14] Whether the latter could get its Party executives *out* of the jungle in sufficient numbers to organise a secret party structure for penetration and subversion of these parties or any other legal organisations was a problem second only to that of the continued existence of the MRLA and its supporters.

[14] After his maiden speech in the Legislative Council in December 1957 Mr. Seenivasagam, leader of the People's Progressive Party and defending counsel for Lee Meng in the 'Grenade Girl' case, was accused by the Chief Minister of taking Chin Peng's side and inciting the people to open rebellion against the government.

FIGHT TO THE FINISH

At the end of 1955, in his annual review of the Emergency situation, the Director of Operations was in a notably cheerful and confident mood. There was, he said, every prospect in the coming year of inflicting severe and even crippling casualties on the Communist terrorist organisation. Conversely, on any 'objective' reading of the situation the MCP must have felt that its military capabilities had dwindled away and its political fortune, rather than depending on a successful outcome of the armed struggle, now turned upon an unlikely transition to peaceful co-existence.

From a peak figure of 8,000 armed guerrillas in 1951 the MRLA at the end of 1955 was reduced to some 3,000 men: having lost approximately 700 men in the course of the year. Guerrilla incidents had fallen from a maximum of 500 to 65 a month; civilian casualties from over 80 to 12; and Security Forces casualties from over 100 to 15. The MCP/MRLA command organisation had retreated to the Thai border; its north-south communications had been broken; and, at least from the government point of view, the insurrection had died away to the point at which almost half the population were living in areas that were reckoned to be free from armed guerrillas. Captured documents revealed the MCP's concern for the destruction of so many of its cultivation areas, the weakness of the *Min Yuen* intelligence support—which meant that regular MRLA units had been diverted to gather intelligence—and increasing doubts about the reliability of the *Min Yuen* itself.[1] In South Selangor, with the active support of the local population, the entire MRLA forces had been eliminated; but it was in Pahang that the Director of Operations claimed the outstanding military success of the year that had resulted in the virtual destruction of the MCP in four-fifths of the State and the creation of the largest 'White Area' in the Federation.

The Pahang Experience
Successes in Pahang were a result of major food denial operations

---

[1] Where possible the balance was to be redressed by squads of 'Little Devils': boys and girls of ten and upwards who smuggled food, bought supplies and reported on the presence of Security Forces and 'spies'.

that had begun as far back as 1953. Before then, operations in the State had been aimed at MRLA units. While these produced a high rate of elimination over the whole State there was little change in overall MCP activity but with the introduction of long-term food denial operations the situation changed. For these operations there were three criteria. First, that the target should be of great strategic importance to the MCP. Second, that it must be in an area favourable to Special Branch penetration, i.e. where the MCP were in contact with the *Min Yuen* and where a Special Branch team was present on the ground. Third, that the destruction of the target must lead towards another important MCP organisation. Thus, the destruction of the Bentong District Organisation also severed the MCP federal deep jungle courier route and the high-level outside courier organisation. The destruction of the two Raub districts not only eliminated four MCP branches but also destroyed one of the proximate Independent Platoons, forced another to vacate its chosen operational area and closed half the supply lines to the North Pahang regional deep jungle base. Lastly, the destruction of Lipis West District eliminated a group of seventy in seven months and also closed down all the remaining Pahang supply routes to the North Pahang jungle base, broke up the Unity News Press and Department of Malay Work and extensively widened the breach in the MCP's federal courier routes. Where operations had been aimed at other kinds of targets—for example armed units or the Battle News Press—not only had they been unsuccessful but they had also resulted in a general MCP move out of the target area and a consequent drying up of information.

At this, and indeed at almost every stage of the Emergency, effective operations were based on intelligence. This applied even more to food denial operations where intelligence in depth was required not only on the MCP formations but on all their actual and potential sources of supply. The great weight of preparing this intelligence in an operational form rested on the Contingent Special Branch Organisation. Their target in the first place was likely to be an MCP District, possibly two, and once an outline plan describing the target, the numbers of Security Forces needed and the estimated time for the first phase had been drawn up and approved by SWEC the planning began for Phase One: the critical part of the operation but one in which it was possible that not a shot would be fired.

Generally, the easiest section of the plan to complete was the MCP order of battle: its Armed Work Forces, Independent

Platoons, jungle courier organisations, presses, cultivation units, bodyguards, headquarter units and the like. Similarly, there was nothing esoteric involved in the area survey which had to be completed: simply painstaking and exhaustive study. Topographical information listed and described all inhabited areas; communications included ferries, jeep tracks, air strips, landing zones and estate telephones; population figures by race as well as industrial and agricultural details which gave approximate harvest dates for rice-growing areas and the location of timber-cutting concessions. The second part dealt with all manifestations of guerrilla/Communist activity over the past year.

Guerrillas who were considered to be of vital local importance were the subject of special study by the Contingent Research Section. Files were built up to give all known characteristics and weaknesses that might provide an opening for 'winning over or elimination' although, in the event, large files were built up for two District Committee members in Pahang but operations failed to dislodge them. A more likely opening was through guerrilla relatives and contacts and here the Special Branch Headquarters prepared up to date lists and a 'black' register listing Special Branch directed approaches to the relatives or contacts of known guerrilla waverers. Few of these approaches were expected to develop into actual target operations but on occasions there was an almost geometrical progression.[2]

In addition to the 'natural' contacts that a guerrilla would make with family or friends he would at some time or other make contact with his affinitive supporters: the *Min Yuen*. Key working charts of the entire *Min Yuen* organisation within the target area were therefore drawn up showing the cell organisation, its central figure and its 'director' within the jungle. All the work done by the individual cell, its method of operation and, most important, whatever was known of its system of contact with the armed guerrillas was charted and prepared from indexed evidence from all sources: SEP/CEP statements, captured documents, agents' reports and so on. Alongside it there was a Strategic Supplies Chart, comprehensive almost down to the Khrushchev level of

[2] After many attempts over several weks by Raub Special Branch to get an old Chinese mother to persuade her local guerrilla son to surrender, she suddenly said that he was prepared to surrender privately the next day. She was briefed to tell the son to urge his sick Branch Committee Member to accompany him. Which she did and both surrendered in secret. They then led Security Forces back to their Branch headquarters where a Branch Committee Secretary was captured. He, in turn, led an Army patrol to the District HQ camp where all its five occupants were killed.

trouser buttons but, from experience, concerned particularly with gold, sewing machines, battery operated radios, watches and everything connected with printing and duplicating as well as the obvious medicines and explosives. When items were found in guerrilla camps—or, more surprisingly, watch repair slips and the like were recovered—they could then be traced to particular shops in the area which were thus identified as conscious or unconscious guerrilla supply points.

By the end of Phase One of a food denial operation Special Branch would first have achieved maximum penetration of the *Min Yuen* organisation within the target area. Second, it would have selected inhabited areas from which practically all supplies would be prevented from reaching the MCP by means of rigid food denial measures. Third, it would have selected killing grounds where the *Min Yuen* would be directed and controlled by Special Branch itself. It would also have completed lists of *Min Yuen*, known and suspected Communist sympathisers and those who were providing the guerrillas with supplies. On the first day of Phase Two the planned arrests, selected and prepared for in Phase One, took place in one sudden operation. The entire identified *Min Yuen* organisation was arrested; and the arrests were synchronised with the removal of all 'surplus' food and the imposition of rigorous food denial measures.

In the Pahang experience, for approximately two months after these arrests there was a lull in operational information. The MCP District Organisation would be concentrating its efforts on the rebuilding of the shattered *Min Yuen*; and in the meantime the MRLA units did their best to live off their food dumps and what was left of their jungle cultivations while they waited for Security Forces pressure to relax. Now was the time for the Security Forces to attack known MRLA Headquarter Organisations, ambush known courier routes and destroy deep jungle cultivation: all with the aim of breaking up the Headquarter units, keeping MRLA units and particularly their leaders constantly on the move and, most important, destroying the organised routine direction of Armed Work Force activities. The lull would end when the MRLA units had exhausted their food dumps and attempted to resume their regular food supply contacts with the *Min Yuen*. It was at this point that the *Min Yuen* food supply, now thoroughly penetrated by Special Branch, began to provide the last, fatal support for the MRLA units as they emerged from the jungle.

The Pahang experience, although by no means standard

throughout Malaya, was common to areas that had had the resources to plan carefully and to mount major food denial operations. As the pattern of events in Phase Two became clearer operations against adjoining MCP districts often became necessary. Here it was important that DWEC and their supporting forces kept their balance so as to move into any gaps that might appear and the importance of forward planning was to be a step ahead of the MCP so that maximum damage could be inflicted before effective counter-measures, for example building up new District Organisations, could be taken. Not until the District Organisations were destroyed could the major MRLA/MCP units be dealt with.

By the end of 1955 successes in Pahang had begun to open up a gap between the northern and southern branches of the MCP/MRLA organisations. Not only was one of the three deep jungle bases disrupted but a large wedge had been driven into the centre of the enemy's position. In addition the main courier routes on the eastern side of the central mountain range had been cut so that the MCP was forced to try and repair their communications by diversion through North Selangor. The result of this victory was to enable government to concentrate on extending the Pahang breach southwards and westwards, coupled with the disruption of a second deep jungle base, and to this end priority was given to operations in South Pahang and North-east Negri Sembilan. If success could be achieved in these operations then the forces were to be released either to extend the breach northwards and westwards into Perak or else to continue operations southwards into Johore.

But the MCP's position was perhaps not as bad as it seemed. Its District Organisations in Johore, Perak and Kedah were still relatively intact; and, although now functioning in binary form, Chin Peng in the north and Hor Lung, the commander of the South Malayan Bureau, both planned to develop the *Min Yuen* in Perak and Johore. In this they were assisted, unfortunately but perhaps inevitably, by the restrictions that were placed on operations by the political requirements of the amnesty.

It is possible to exaggerate but from an operational point of view it could be argued that the amnesty which was declared on September 9th 1955 and finally withdrawn in February 1956, the long drawn out approach to negotiations with the MCP, the resulting uncertainties and, most important, the reduction of Security Forces pressure on the MRLA and the *Min Yuen* combined to produce a considerable setback to the counter-insurgency campaign. At best, it was a mixed blessing. Sixty surrenders under amnesty terms were effected between September and December 1955; but until the outcome of the desultory negotiations was known no new food denial operations were mounted nor any others which could in any way be regarded as punitive and thus liable to alienate potential support. The result, apart from an outbreak of aggressive incidents in Johore and the lifting of SF restrictions in November 1955 notwithstanding, was that for almost six months guerrillas were able to build up jungle stockpiles of food and supplies to counter anticipated food denial operations in the future.

Summing up the situation for the country as a whole, operations experience during 1955 confirmed that:

(a) The basic targets for operations against the terrorists are their static District and Branch organisations on which the Malayan Communist Party hierarchy and offensive platoons rely for their supply.

(b) The line of the main mountain range in Malaya and of the main road and rail communications to the west of it does in fact represent the spine of the Communist Terrorist organisation, and the Malayan Communist Party's districts away from it should be regarded as secondary to those which straddle it.

(c) The best method of clearing large areas of Communist Terrorists is to project success from one cleared Malayan Communist Party District to the next. This should achieve a snowball effect, which not only gives each operation a firm starting point which it would not have if conducted in isolation but also produces the best chance of preventing infiltration back into a cleared area, as the masses organisation in cleared areas would have been broken up.

(d) From a Security Force point of view, food denial provides the only reliable means of obtaining information, contacts and eliminations. Furthermore, on the evidence of the Communist Terrorists themselves, food denial is the most telling weapon being used against them.[3]

The Federal Plan for 1956 was therefore to maintain maximum pressure in central Malaya with the object of establishing a White Area belt across the Federation to Malacca and the west coast; and when this had been achieved to project success simultaneously

[3] Director of Operations, *Review of the Emergency situation in Malaya at the end of 1956.*

northwards through central Selangor and south Perak and southwards into Johore. Throughout 1956 Security Forces kept hammering away to open up the gap but for various reasons it did not open easily. Emergency operations were now settling into a pattern of individual duels in which a District War Executive Committee was pitted against an MCP District. A great deal depended upon the initiative of the particular DWEC and there was always a danger that the standard framework operations would become a matter of routine: to the point where, a year later, the Director of Operations had to remind individual DWECs that framework operations were intended to be offensive rather than defensive. At the same time, some DWECs at least could claim that they just did not have the forces to mount effective operations of any kind. On occasions, mistakes were made in mounting food denial operations[4] but in some areas there was no self-generating intelligence, not enough Security Forces to upset the MRLA and established District Organisations and a situation where, in fact, the military/political threat was not being contained.

This was a situation that could be found in 1956 in the Tapah District of south Perak. It was a fairly representative Malayan cross-section with a Chinese population employed in tin mines, in rubber estates and in logging who lived on estates, in villages and in small towns. In the past it was thought that their support of the guerrillas was produced by fear; but now it was believed that, with the lack of government success against the guerrillas and in part as a result of MCP propaganda, its support had become voluntary.

There was, to begin with, no effective food control whatever. In many of the twenty-five regrouped estate areas there was simply a wire fence surrounding the labour lines with no guard at all and the wire merely served as a nominal demarcation for food control measures. Area Security Units were stationed on certain estates with resident European managers; but there was no set policy regarding effective gate checks. The majority of the tin miners lived within one of the eight towns or ten New Villages; but in twenty-nine more or less self-contained mines in isolated areas labourers lived in wired-in settlements which, again, were completely unguarded. The result of all this was that only a very small percentage of the population was subject to regular and intensive food checks. Five of the towns offered no

[4] In Malacca Operation *Sodium* failed, according to the Director of Intelligence, because it went straight into Phase Two.

FIGHT TO THE FINISH

barrier or threat whatever to the potential food smuggler while in the New Villages, where checks were made at irregular intervals, the shortage of women searchers made it ineffective.

It is therefore possible for a regular and systematic supply of food to reach the Communist Terrorists from any one of these New Villages, regrouped estate areas and isolated tin mine *kongsis* whenever an order is given for delivery to those members of the masses who are working for the CTO.

In eighteen months from January 1955 there had only been seven surrendered guerrillas; morale was high among the two hundred-odd guerrillas in the area; and it was impossible to envisage surrenders caused by hunger.

This high state of morale has a further deleterious effect upon the gathering of information. The well-fed Communist presents a picture of self-confidence and courage to those tappers and labourers he accosts during their working hours. Solicitations made towards them are difficult to resist as both they and the Communists are fully aware of the paucity of control that exists within the residential area occupied by the workers. It has been found in the past that when there are insufficient police or military seen by the labourers a sense of omnipotence is attributed to the Communists which lends itself to an overriding fear of disclosing the fact that he has been seen, met or encountered. Thus, under those conditions reports of Communist Terrorist presence is usually related second or third hand to the Special Branch officer concerned; whereas in contrast to this, in areas dominated by troops the apparent security afforded by their presence leads to a greater flow of information.

In part, this 'sense of omnipotence' could be attributed to the fact that there was only one full battalion in the area.

This battalion, whilst carrying out its important role of patrolling and ambushing in close rubber, is insufficient, numerically, to make even a dent upon the hard shell of the well-entrenched CTO in this circle—and it labours manfully—its strength depleted by the very nature of the terrain it occupies and by the many small Armed Work Cells who present a will o' the wisp target—their movements unknown and their resting places interchangeable. Their mobility offers them the greater security.

In this situation—an insufficiency of troops and police on the ground—the conclusion drawn by the Head of the Special Branch

Contingent was that until further resources were made available it would be virtually impossible to do more than hold and contain the known enemy 'while he feeds and supplies and strengthens himself both physically and morally'. In effect, therefore, this was the same sort of situation as there was when the Emergency began. Security Forces were not making contact. There was no food problem for the guerrillas, no effective control of the civil population and not enough intelligence. Guerrilla food supplies were not large: but they did not have to be. The intelligence network was better: but it had to be better still to find the smaller numbers of *Min Yuen* as well as the wary, experienced guerrillas who were now tending to avoid direct contact with their supporters in the civilian population when there was the slightest doubt about their reliability.

Concentration of Forces
Over the country as a whole, however, compared to the beginning or even the height of the Emergency, the ratio of Security Forces to armed guerrillas had now increased enormously. This was less the case with the Army where there were now eighteen or nineteen battalions operational out of twenty-two[5] than with local forces made up of police, Special Constables and Home Guard. Drawn from these three categories in 1955 there were almost a thousand jungle squads in existence[6] and this does not include the static units of Malay Kampong Guards and Chinese Home Guard units in the New Villages. Moreover, the mobility of the Security Forces was increased still more by the availability of helicopters; and in spite of the disappointing performance of the British Whirlwind Mark IV helicopters in Malayan conditions thousands of troops and police a month were being lifted by helicopter. Between them, in 1956, two squadrons of medium helicopters lifted over 25,000 troops: the equivalent to positioning by air every soldier in Malaya once during the year. Tactically this introduced a new dimension into operations, that of leap-

[5] Six British, six Gurkha and six Malay regiments, one Federation/Reconnaissance regiment (that was open to all races) plus the Fijian and various African battalions. The first Australian infantry battalion arrived at the end of 1955 together with a squadron of the New Zealand SAS.

[6] 556 Area Security Units composed of Special Constables; 400 Mobile Operational Sections of the Home Guard; 27 Police Special Squads; 19 sections of Police Aboriginal Guards; and a Police Field Force of 3,000 who provided, amongst other services, garrisons for the jungle forts and a police framework on the Siamese frontier.

frogging, in which, for example, the same patrol could be used to overtake and ambush the guerrilla unit it had contacted and which might otherwise have escaped.[7]

Nevertheless, with MRLA units deliberately lying low there was a notable decrease in contacts from almost a thousand in 1954 to 560 in 1955 and the average time that a soldier spent on patrol before seeing a contact made was estimated at a thousand hours: and that did not occur until he had already been on patrol for four hours. In ambush, either from deduced or informed guerrilla intentions, a soldier spent on average three hundred hours before contact was made and in this case the contact did not occur until he had already been in an ambush position for twenty-four hours.

Amongst other things these figures indicated the immense outlay of men and time that was needed on more or less speculative patrolling; and was one of the reasons why the hunt was given up of the Independent Platoons *per se*. This, it will be remembered, had been one of the objectives for 1955—elimination of the six most aggressive Independent Platoons—but by the middle of 1956 the Director of Operations stated specifically that the Independent Platoon was not vulnerable to sustained Security Force action because

(a) it would always take avoiding action, and
(b) it had no 'outside contacts' whom Special Branch could penetrate.

Operations in fact continued against Independent Platoons, the enemy's main striking force, and the chances of success were greatest when, as in the case of the Third Independent Platoon in northern Negri Sembilan they were forced to turn over to *Min Yuen* work or else, as in the case of the Fifth Independent Platoon, they were pinned down to two MCP Districts which were then made the target for a major food denial operation.[8]

Of even greater importance than the decision to abandon the

---

[7] Perfected, however, by Gurkha battalions in the Borneo operations of the second Emergency: the confrontation with Indonesia.

[8] If comparisons between jungle and naval warfare are ever extended, independent platoons will probably feature as powerful enemy strike forces which, like the Bismarck for example, could do immense danger if unlocated. There was little doubt of the Security Forces' ultimate ability to destroy them; and their lines of movement could be predicted; but in the end, like the Bismarck, an intelligence tip-off provided the vital or rather mortal clue.

chase of the Independent Platoons was the announcement at the same time, in July 1956, that there was to be a new system of allotting Federal priority to certain operational areas. This system had in effect begun earlier in the year in Selangor, Negri Sembilan and Pahang; and in these three States, together with supporting operations in Johore and Malacca, all agencies—civil, military, police and Home Guard—had been given top priority: if necessary at the expense of less important operations. This was a notable modification of framework operations but States, or rather SWECs, did not always seem to appreciate the distinction. In any case, both systems had their protagonists. Framework operations usually allowed battalions to stay put in the areas with which they became remarkably familiar. The alternative permitted a heavy concentration of forces such as could be seen in an operation planned against the MCP organisation in the Central District of Selangor. In this District there were only two active MCP Branches, one at Ampang, the other at Cheras, and a total charted strength of sixteen in both Branches. For this operation, admittedly more difficult than many others because of proximity to the capital, Kuala Lumpur, and the consequent impossibility of effective food control, the minimum requirement was one battalion—plus two extra companies for framework operations in the adjacent areas—together with Home Guard operational sections and police units. The operation required a minimum of six months.

In the case of the Third Independent Platoon, mentioned above, it was almost a year until Tan Fuk Leong, whose inspiring leadership was acknowledged, was killed in a bombing raid: but as a result of an intelligence operation. In February 1956 the Seventh Independent Platoon which had newly moved into a camp in a swamp west of Kluang in Johore had been the subject of an air attack that had resulted in the death of its Political Commissar, Goh Peng Tuan, and thirteen other members of the platoon but, again, this had been a result of information obtained by Special Branch.[9] The same was true of the death of Yeong Kuo, the Vice-Secretary-General of the MCP—in August 1956. This, to date, was the MCP's most serious loss both ideologically and organisationally but, again, and newspaper reports notwithstanding, this was not an accidental encounter. A third loss, Ah Ho, State Committee Secretary of Negri Sembilan—seemed

[9] An account of this operation is given by the late CO of the First Battalion South Wales Borderers. Richard Miers, *Shoot to Kill*, London, 1959.

to support the argument that high-ranking members of the MCP/MRLA were the main targets for the Security Forces whereas, in fact, the successes had been almost fortuitous.

Food Control
Routine successes, however, could be expected from standard food denial operations; but these, in turn, depended upon the success of food control. Over the years a number of experiments in this had been tried that allowed both efficiency and flexibility. Nevertheless effective food denial had almost always depended upon rigorous measures and was the Emergency Regulation that bore most heavily upon the people. Particularly in the countryside; but although there were few if any effective food control measures in towns, on occasions those that were introduced threatened ruin to provision stores and food shops. In January 1954 when the 'squeeze' was being put on Layang Layang in Johore, nineteen out of twenty-one provision stores were closed for the course of the operation and only one rice dealer was allowed to trade. In the 'food prohibited areas' in the country— in rubber estates for example where guerrillas might be expected to make contact—the mere possession of food at one time carried a penalty of up to five years' imprisonment and five thousand dollars fine.[10] As a burden on everyday life the operational rice ration was even worse. This was introduced in the course of specific military operations: a ration of three: two and a half: two *katis* of rice per week for men, women and children. 'Just enough to keep a person in good health,' said a government spokesman; 'leading', said the Chinese Chamber of Commerce in Johore (Senai), 'to fifty thousand half-starved people, many of whom were too ill or too weak to work'. When even this was considered insufficient to interrupt guerrilla supplies it was coupled, as in the Bahau/Jelebu area, with a house curfew from 7 p.m. till 6 a.m.; and, although it was exceptional, when these

[10] How to decide whether food was supplied voluntarily or not—and the consequences—was a continuing problem. In 1953, directives from the Commissioner of Police pointed out that 'the mere supplying of food to CTs is no longer considered sufficient grounds for detention: there must be clear evidence of willingness to assist and of the absence of duress'. As the CPO Pahang remarked, 'It will be appreciated that for Special Branch to prove that the supplying of food was "voluntary" is extremely difficult'. Even when known guerrilla food suppliers were arrested in a food denial operation many of them were released as Committees of Review were unwilling to make orders of detention on less than two independent sources of evidence that supplies were on 'an aggravated scale'.

measures had not produced favourable results the entire labour force—four hundred plus—of Glendale Estate, Bahau, were removed elsewhere and workers from outside the State (Negri Sembilan) took their place.

As it was the single measure that gave most hope of success in Emergency operations so food control became government's biggest problem. Strategically, and indeed in commonsense, it was realised that it was impossible to impose completely effective control throughout the country and sometimes even in small areas but the Emergency Regulations, seen from a distance, seem to have become almost obsessive. Templer had tried to get SWECs to use their discretion in allowing estate labourers to take food out with them to work—something which, at least in 1953, they refused—but at the same time he had suggested to the Chief Justice that food offences be regarded as extremely serious and pressed for deterrent sentences, preferably imprisonment. Roughly from this time onwards food control measures became more effective—and more rigorous. In addition to the protected movement of food, whether in convoyed lorries by road or rice farmers bringing in their harvest under Special Constable escort, there was a mounting burden of restrictions both on shopkeepers and consumers. Food denial operations meant in practice a reduction in the number of shops that were licensed to sell restricted articles, the control of eating shops, the banning of tinned Quaker Oats—a guerrilla emergency ration—and the restriction in individual houses of quantities of tinned meat, fish and cooking oil. This in addition to Operational Rice rationing, the communal cooking of rice and the solemn ceremony of a Tin Puncturing Order to ensure that their contents could only be kept for a limited period. Before long, there were differences of opinion, even within SWECs, between Army and police on the one hand and civil authorities on the other how far and how long the Operational Rice ration should be imposed: the argument of operational desirability versus humanitarian considerations and the effect on civilian morale. There was also the danger in food control of spawning a vast and repressive bureaucracy and a government that was utterly remote from the people both in its intentions and its observances. In the mid-nineteen fifties half the retail and even more of the wholesale trade in foodstuffs was subject to proliferating restrictions. As for the individual, some idea of their previous stringency may be had from the relaxation of certain Emergency Regulations in June 1956.

People passing through restricted or prohibited areas can now carry a reasonable quantity of drugs or medicine if they can produce a certificate showing they need them. Those travelling with children under two years of age can take food for the children. Typewriters are no longer restricted. Articles and vehicles carrying restricted goods or foodstuffs may pass through prohibited areas without formal permits from District Officer or Supplies Department. They are allowed to pass on producing a written record or manifest. A *Mentri Besar* or resident Commissioner however can still prohibit any foodstuff in a particular area and can order the destruction of prohibited crops.

In any case by the middle of 1956, after eight years of the Emergency and for the moment discounting the MCP's efforts both to create and to capitalise upon a situation of uncertainty, there was a growing weariness with the burden that was imposed by all these civil restrictions; which, in turn, made their working less effective. In May 1956, therefore, the Chief Minister announced that a number of food control measures would be lifted, that midday meals could again be taken outside New Villages, that curfew hours would be reduced and control of movement relaxed in what were to be called 'Selected Areas'. The first Selected Area in Perak involved some thirty-five thousand people in the Taiping district and, in addition to the measures announced, the number of retail, rice and restricted goods dealers was also increased. This was followed in July—and itself followed representations from the local Malayan Chinese Association—by partial lifting of the ban on eating shops in Kluang and a restoration of fifty per cent of the usual allocation of rice to eating shops and food hawkers.

At the same time as these relaxations were being introduced it was decided to tighten up existing organisation and a new Emergency Food Denial Organisation was set up under the former British Adviser, Negri Sembilan, Mr. M. C.ff Sheppard. Its most important innovation was large-scale widespread central rice cooking, in which families collected and took home cooked rice to which they added their own embellishments, and this allowed the Operational Rice ration to be doubled.[11] Food denial operations were later to be redoubled in intensity in order to clear particular areas; but for the moment it was recognised that even operationally 'the support of the people has become an increas-

---

[11] Cooked, compared to uncooked, rice does not keep and is much bulkier.

ingly important factor in the prosecution of the Emergency'.[12] Nevertheless, complete success in achieving the Federal aim of clearing the centre of Malaya had not been achieved. In Negri Sembilan and Selangor Security Force pressure had split and scattered the guerrillas into elusive and unrewarding targets that were considered to be unsuitable for continued large-scale operations after the end of the year. From January 1957 therefore Federal priority operations began against numerically greater and more concentrated guerrilla targets in South Perak and North Johore. The objective was to produce a 'White Area' from Tapah in the north to Kluang in the south by September 1st 1957. For a while this, the date of forthcoming Malayan independence, became a target, for even the approach to independence was reckoned to be having an adverse effect on the conduct of operations. The reduction in the British content of police, Special Branch and the Malayan Civil Service was of the order of twenty-five per cent; the abolition of the post of British Adviser had led to certain problems of chairmanship of the State War Executive Committee; and no Commonwealth troops were expected to be able to take part in food denial operations once independence had been achieved.

By the beginning of 1957 the rate of guerrilla elimination which had been falling steadily over the previous years, stood at about an average of one per day. Sometimes this rate was increased by a chain of events in a particular area and there were hopes that a psychological reaction—for example to the new constitution or to independence—would lead to a crumbling away of the guerrilla organisation. Politically, this was a vain and somewhat naïve hope for at about the same time the MCP's aim had shifted to allowing its four hundred ranking members to survive and to leave the jungle as free men and the potential leaders of a Communist state. The situation was thus nicely balanced. On the one hand, after severe losses over the past two years, the MRLA was reduced to some two thousand members, including fourteen independent platoons,[13] and their losses had been the indirect but logical result of major food denial opera-

---

[12] D/Ops, *Review of the Emergency Situation in Malaya at the end of 1956.*

[13] These may have existed largely in name. Many of them seem to have broken up to reinforce Armed Work Forces, decimated Districts and Deep Jungle Bases. A surprising decision, says Madoc, was when they buried their Brens. 'I cannot now remember when that happened, nor the reason; but it made a great difference to the effect of CT ambushes.'

tions. On the other hand, the complexity of these operations meant that government's resources were now sufficient only for two at any particular time; and while they were undoubtedly the best means of breaking into the MCP/MRLA organisation, an operation could be expected to last the better part of a year. At the same time it was recognised that the guerrillas now had the measure of standard food denial operations and the instruction that MCP District or Branch areas which the guerrillas had difficulty in maintaining might be abandoned, together with a halt to guerrilla recruitment, meant that it was going to be harder still to break into the Communist organisation. Unless the tempo of Emergency operations could be speeded up it was reckoned that the enemy organisation might well not be decisively defeated for some three or four years and that 'very likely the residual problem would tend to become less and less soluble by military means'.

The interaction of civil and military events had already been seen in Singapore in October 1956 when five battalions from the Federation had been diverted to the island because of civil disturbances and had been out of action for three weeks. On a less dramatic level the conduct of the Emergency had moved into the hands of the Emergency Operations Council, headed by the Chief Minister, and a certain slackening of administration of the New Villages and a plea for overdue land titles, both of which contributed to publicise the discontent, were a reminder, if one was needed, that New Villages were still the battleground and the touchstone of the Emergency. But for all practical purposes the initiative now lay wholly with the government and it was obvious that the MCP was completely outplayed and could do little but wait for the government to make mistakes which might still allow it to snatch victory out of the jaws of defeat. Nevertheless, the policy of keeping itself to itself might conceivably pay a future dividend. In the north and across the border into Thailand the policy of not stirring things up had ensured a comparative sanctuary; and the Thais, disclaiming all responsibility for the presence of Malayan guerrillas, are reported to have said that the guerrillas sought sanctuary 'like gentlemen'. As long as it did not move, or was not seen to move, the MCP/MRLA did not provide government with intelligence; and with almost every elimination the result of information, about half of it direct information on future movements, Special Branch was still in need of first priority for both money and manpower.

An additional source of intelligence, and one which to a certain extent short-circuited the established Special Branch network, was now being provided by the more or less 'committed' Chinese Home Guard sections. In 1955 there had been a great deal of criticism of the wisdom of arming Chinese New Villages in their own defence and the very high rate of comparative loss of weapons had led to demands, mostly European, that the Chinese Home Guard be disbanded.[14] Instead of succumbing to pressure every effort had been made to improve morale and raise their standard of training although it was realised that Chinese Home Guards were simply a sample of the people in their own villages.

> If as a whole the village is cowed by the terrorists, or is sympathetic towards them, the Home Guards inevitably reflect that sentiment—they cannot strike out a line for themselves without placing their own lives, families and livelihoods in jeopardy. To disband units would not only encourage inefficiency in other units (since the Chinese dislike having to serve), but would also admit failure in a delicate experiment to weld the Chinese Home Guard into a thoroughly reliable force. Such a step would be a first-class victory for the Communists.

In 1955, in almost every case of loss of weapons, there had been evidence of collusion or unwillingness to fight. In 1956, however, when a major guerrilla raid was made on Chinese Home Guards in the New Villages of Kulai and Scudai in Johore, with the obvious aim of intimidating them, they fought back hard although it was clear that many of the villagers themselves had assisted the guerrillas.

In several ways, this was one of the most hopeful signs for the future of the Emergency. Not only did this have a heartening effect on other Chinese Home Guards but, whereas the loss of the leader of an MRLA unit was known to have surprisingly little effect on the rest, it was also known that when a population turned against the guerrillas it was a critical point for many of them, both for their morale in general and whether or not they decided to surrender. Conversely, perhaps the biggest boost to the morale of the Chinese Home Guard was the formation of four hundred Operational Sections in 1956. The result, in brief, was that in place of large, unwieldy masses (many of them

---

[14] Chinese Home Guards lost one hundred and thirty-eight weapons in 1955: out of a holding, however, of fifteen thousand; compared to five weapons lost by the Malay/Indian/Aboriginal Home Guards: out of a total holding of fifty-five thousand.

FIGHT TO THE FINISH

inevitably guerrilla sympathisers) carrying out a static defence, there were now in each village one or more trained and uniformed volunteer Operational Sections who carried out a mobile defence both inside and outside the perimeter wire.

During 1956 one guerrilla out of every five still in the jungle was killed, captured or surrendered. At the end of the year there were a little over two thousand guerrillas still known to be in the jungle of whom almost eight hundred were in Perak, four hundred and fifty in Johore and over a hundred in both Selangor and Negri Sembilan. Perak and Johore were the two States in which concentrated food denial operations began although it was not until the end of the year that the results could be seen. In the meantime, a 'White Area' belt was established across the country in August and henceforth every reasonable risk was taken in extending it in both directions. Insofar as this depended upon food denial operations it was bought at the cost of much heavier imposition on the civil population. At times, life came to a standstill. Where guerrillas were known to be on the verge of starvation curfews of up to thirty-six hours were imposed in addition to operational rice rationing and all the paraphernalia of restrictions of which mention has already been made. More important, there was ever greater concentration of forces. Thus, in an operation to destroy the Gemas Bahru Branch in Johore, three battalions plus an infantry brigade HQ, five Area Security Units, two Police Special Service Groups and a Special Operational Volunteer Force, comprising ex-guerrillas, was assembled. The plan was to destroy the easy sources of supply for the North Johore Regional Committee and the South Malayan Bureau in the east of the area and to drive them to the west where Special Branch coverage was better and there was thus a greater chance that they would be destroyed. In the event, in a climactic operation which lasted five weeks or so, no guerrillas were killed but the maintenance of pressure of all kinds, including psychological warfare and complete local food denial plus the continued presence of Security Forces on the ground, broke guerrilla morale and their will to continue the struggle. The concentration of Security Forces, both on patrol and in ambush, meant that the guerrillas, even though possibly lucky or clever enough to escape the decisive engagement, were continually forced to move. As a result:

(a) their RVs with Masses Executives, Food Suppliers, Couriers and others were upset or complicated;
(b) they were no longer free agents to decide when or for how

long they would live alongside a particular food dump or jungle produce area and thus their rations were affected and/or they were caused to carry disproportionate loads;
(c) any physically weak or maimed members became increasing burdens on them.

Maintained for many weeks on end this process not only wore down at least the weaker members to surrender point but also, during the frequent moves and splits it imposed upon them, gave unusual opportunities to break away and surrender. This, in fact, was what happened. The hard core and the leader himself ultimately surrendered not primarily because their own morale was destroyed but because they realised that their organisation was disintegrating. Psychological warfare proved to be a particularly valuable weapon to ram this home: each defection was a further strain on the morale of the remainder, quite apart from the tactical value to the Security Forces.

Nevertheless, this type of operation required the selection of a target area sufficiently small or manageable to permit its complete domination. And, in the event, no more than twelve guerrillas were eliminated: one captured and eleven surrendered. For the first nine months of the year over the country as a whole the average surrender rate was never more than thirteen a month while the total number of eliminations varied between twenty and forty. With every prospect of stalemate and, in fact, an unsuccessful race against time to destroy the greater part of the Communist organisation by September 1st 1957 there began, instead, their almost miraculous disintegration in the key states of Perak and Johore.

In part the phase of the 'mass surrenders' may be attributed to relentless military pressure and in part to burgeoning public confidence with the achievement of independence. In public statements Tunku Abdul Rahman, now Prime Minister of an independent Federation of Malaya, hinted that extraordinary developments were under way but it was not until July and August 1958 that details were given of the operations that led to the surrender of a hundred and twenty guerrillas in Perak and another hundred and sixty in Johore including Hor Lung, the head of the South Malayan Bureau. Some of the details of both these operations must still be considered classified; but in Perak the avalanche began moving when a European motorist picked up five guerrillas who later induced the remaining members of their group to surrender. From then on, mixed parties of surrendered guerrillas and Special Branch officers disguised as guerrillas used jungle letter-boxes and couriers to locate other groups who were then talked into surrender, were disarmed or, in one case, killed. In fact, the majority of the hundred and nineteen who were classified as surrendered enemy personnel were captured : and many of them openly said that they came out because they were caught unawares or tricked—otherwise they would have fought to the last. The attitude of many after their capture certainly bears this out. Some of them were learning English and Malay in order to prepare themselves for political and Trade Union activities when they were released; others were inquiring about identity cards, State and Federal citizenship; and a third group took it upon themselves to keep the rank and file true to their principles. In practice this meant no films and no hair 'perms'. The arguments of a woman, newly surrendered with a male comrade, why he should induce others to surrender were equally interesting.[15]

In Johore, the number one guerrilla in southern Malaya, Hor Lung, was the first to come out. Forced out of his jungle base in South Pahang, having lost contact with all his units and with a bodyguard whom he no longer trusted, Hor Lung walked into a police station near Segamat in North Johore, in his vest and underpants, and surrendered. In four months he brought out another hundred and sixty Communists, twenty-eight of whom rated as 'hard core'. The financial reward was enormous; the damage to his nerves considerable. After it, there came the agony of the killing grounds in South Johore. The Regional Committee Secretary, Ah Ann, was one who was betrayed and shot : together with his wife. There were others who died in harrowing circumstances.

At this time also there were seventeen CTs in the south of the Pengerang peninsula. There were also five in the north in the White Area of Mersing, one in Lukut Branch and a 'confinement' group of three in the area of Bay Twelve, one of whom was under sentence of execution.

---

[15] The MCP Armed Struggle was a total failure and by prolonging the Armed Struggle it would mean causing greater sufferings among the masses and the MCP/MRLA would sustain increased loss in personnel, reputation and prestige. The realisation of the revolution would only be possible by means of an open, legal and peaceful struggle. In her opinion the People's Progressive Party that was centred on Ipoh was directing its political activities on the same or very similar lines to those of the MCP. The difference was only in name.

On November 9th Regional Committee member Ah Fun despatched a relief and execution party of six CTs north to make contact with the confinement group and the one member of Lukut Branch. One CT was executed on the way, one was killed by 2/7 Gurkha Rifles and one subsequently surrendered.

After this, operations speeded up. On November 28th the Branch Committee Member of Pengerang, Leong Tung Seng, was killed and on December 3rd, one female of the relief party was killed and another slightly wounded. The pregnant woman apparently died in childbirth for we discovered her body, and nearby, on the same date, the body of Chow Chong. Chow Chong was a CT under sentence of execution and it was assumed he had been executed by his comrades.

On December 4th the last member of Lukut Branch surrendered, and on December 5th a member of nine platoon was killed on the edged of the Punggai swamp.

This last kill persuaded the Regional Committee Member Ah Fun that his position was hopeless and the whole remaining group in the south (nine CTs) came out and surrendered on December 12th.

By the end of 1958 the situation had changed out of all recognition. In the whole of Johore there were four known guerrillas left. In Negri Sembilan only two. Half of Perak was a White Area and a total of five hundred guerrillas had surrendered in the course of the year. Major guerrilla incidents had been reduced to an average of one a month and the total Security Forces casualties for the year numbered twenty-nine. The shooting war was now almost over.

It had been announced publicly that August 31 1958 was the target date for the end of the Emergency; and in the hope that many of the guerrillas and their supporters would surrender the *Merdeka* surrender offer of September 1st 1957, which was due to end at the end of the year, was three times extended and did not eventually close until July 31st 1958. As has been seen already, 1958 produced an avalanche of surrenders and although these included 'hard-core' guerrillas they depended heavily upon the initiative of Hor Lung in Johore and another, lesser-known, initiative in Perak. To this extent they must be considered fortuitous and by 1959 the total number of surrenders hal fallen away to 86.

1958 had, in fact, seen the end of the MRLA as an organised military force and the point at which armed Communism ceased to be the major threat to the security of Malaya. At the end of the year there was reckoned to be no further need of a separate Director of Emergency Operations; and on the retirement of Lieutenant-General Cassels the post was occupied, *de facto*, by the then Chief of Staff to the Federation Armed Forces, Major-General Brooke. Similarly, in the War Executive Committees, a permanent staff was no longer necessary and meetings were held at longer and longer intervals.

Even now, however, there were still weaknesses in the operational structure. In Kedah, for example, it was reckoned that no major operations were worthwhile until administrative conditions in the northern part of the State had been improved.[16] Intelligence was still a problem; and, in Perak, in operations against the 9th Independent Platoon, it was decided to withdraw nearly all security forces to allow Special Branch to reconstruct its coverage of the area.

The border with Thailand had now become the major residual problem of the Emergency, at least as far as operations were concerned. The formation of a Border Security Council, with the Prime Minister as chairman, and a Border War Executive Committee based on Alor Star, the Kedah State capital, improved the organisation on the Malayan side of the border although it did not prevent, and may indeed have hastened, the drift of MRLA forces across the border. On October 1st 1959 the estimated overall strength of MRLA forces was 698, of which 243 were in the Federation and the rest north of the border. Six months later, on March 1st 1960, the total had fallen to 609 of whom only 117 were still in Malaya.

Those guerrillas who remained on Malayan soil were now in some of the least known and most inaccessible areas of deep jungle where they owed their survival to 'support groups' of aborigines. For many, the measure of support increased as they married aborigine wives and, insofar as they lived like aborigines, 'represented a target that was almost impossible to eliminate by conventional military or police methods'.[17] In early 1956 the suggestion that a fighting force of aborigines should be raised to deal with this problem was turned down as impracticable; and it was doubted whether aborigines could be trained to fight. By the end of the year, however, it had been agreed to raise four

[16] In particular because of the difficulties of food denial in a major rice-producing state.

[17] Paper *The Senoi Pra'aq: A Brief History and Description*. Senoi Pra'aq HQ, Kuala Lumpur (22.2.66).

sections of ten men, paid and administered by the Department of Aborigines and trained by the 22 SAS Regiment.

A year later this new force, the *Senoi Pra'aq*[18] was established with three squadrons of 60 men each and for operational purposes was attached to and under the command of existing battalions. In 1958, its first year of operations, results were disappointing, largely because it was restricted to a reconnaisance role, but in February 1959 it was presented with an ideal target: a group of eight guerrillas, with two attached groups of 'hostile' aborigines, which had been impervious to Police and Army operations for the last four years. In the third week of the *Senoi Pra'aq* operation the first guerrilla was captured together with the headman of one of the aborigine groups. Shortly afterwards, three more guerrillas were captured, two surrendered and the last two were killed in ambush. By the end of 1959 and after the killing of three more guerrillas, among them a Regional Committee Member, after a three-day running battle the *Senoi Pra'aq* had been responsible for eliminating more guerrillas in that year than any other Commonwealth or Federation unit in Malaya.[19]

By the beginning of 1960 the military campaign in Malaya had been reduced to the level of mopping-up operations. In southwest Pahang and the Pahang-Trengganu border area a handful of eliminations, including RCM Ah Tian who was shot by a British Army officer on leave hunting wild boar, was sufficient to turn Pahang into the seventh 'all-White' State and Priority I operations now shifted to the Thai-Malayan border and combined operations with the Thais.

By this time, the whole of south and central Malaya were considered to be 'white' and free from terrorists while large parts

---

[18] 'Fighting Aborigines'. *Senoi* is the Temiar and Semai word which both tribes use to describe themselves compared to other peoples. *Pra'aq* is also common to both tribes and is a corruption of the Malay *perang* or 'war'.

[19] Apart from local knowledge, *Senoi Pra'aq* successes were based upon speed of movement and phenomenal carrying capacity. Each Squadron could split itself up into 12 independent sections and thus search large areas of jungle very quickly. By carrying 16 days rations—which could be stretched further—compared to the normal infantry's 5–7 days—the number of telltale air drops was reduced considerably. With 16 days rations, arms and equipment a *Senoi Pra'aq* trooper was carrying a weight nearly equal to that of his own body. Even then it was reckoned he could still move faster than soldiers or police. Recruitment was on a month to month basis. Officers carried no rank and NCO's were elected by the men. Discipline was rather unconventional. Any shouting or show of temper, both of which aborigines consider to be the height of bad manners, was likely to result in a man handing in his uniform, equipment and weapon.

of north Malaya were either 'white' or 'selected' areas. Approximately 100 guerrillas were still on Malayan soil but incidents had fallen away to a dozen in 1959, less than thirty contacts had been made and combined civil, police and military casualties were down to a dozen or so. In 1960, there were no military, police or civil casualties at all.

On both sides, the political picture was becoming clearer. The Alliance Government, with another landslide electoral victory in 1959—although losing control of two east coast states—was on the brink of an unqualified military and substantial political victory. Its refusal to compromise with the MCP, its attainment of independence, electoral ratification, the inheritance of an effective administrative machine and substantial Commonwealth military assistance, together with a prosperous economy, high standards of integrity and considerable political competence, were the elements of its success. More than this, the elements had been fused in a successful although comparatively unconventional struggle. Instead of the colonial struggle, in which political differences are submerged, this had been first and foremost a political contest. In its course had occurred perhaps the greatest defeat of militant communism in Asia since the war; and a country, in which there was no lack of racial tinder, had been spared the horrors of an overt civil war.

On the other side, the Malayan Communist Party had largely been destroyed and had destroyed itself. Retreating now, bodily, to the refuge of a foreign country its members might cling, pathetically, to the 'Minimum Programme' and pin their hopes on eventual recognition as a legal party, or a change of political fortunes, but in the meantime they were a self-evident failure; as revolutionaries, as the vanguard of the proletariat, and as the party of national independence. On July 31st, 1960 the State of Emergency which had lasted for twelve years was declared at an end and the Federation of Malaya had passed through its first ordeal of political independence.

CONCLUSIONS

In the course of this study of the Malayan insurrection I have felt, as Mr. A. J. P. Taylor has written, that the prime and humble duty of the student of contemporary history is to establish the elementary record before it is dissipated. What I have attempted is a record of an insurrection, some indication of how and why it was launched, and how it was withstood. The parallel account, which overlaps at many points, is how Malaya became independent. This I have not attempted although others may discern in this political process critical factors which I have omitted. Neither have I intended to produce a manual of counter-insurgency; and, for this reason, have spent almost as much time on the difficulties of government as I have on its successes.

Origins
Historically, it is the origins of the insurrection that still seem to be the most interesting. While I have rejected the plain economic argument that seeks the causes of the insurrection in intolerable conditions and repressive government policy and have instead sought the sufficient cause in the aspirations and decisions of the Malayan Communist Party, yet this still seems to me to be the basis of a fascinating if not fruitful argument. Conceding that economic conditions had begun to improve by the time the insurrection began perhaps one should seek in this confirmation of de Tocqueville's argument that revolutions begin almost precisely at the point when economic conditions begin to improve. To say this however seems to me to isolate a condition rather than a cause of revolution. It is conceivable that if improved wages and conditions had been the cause as well as the occasion of industrial action in Malaya that conflict might have been avoided. If the purpose of industrial action, however, as conceived and co-ordinated by the Malayan Communist Party, was to overthrow capitalist government at its source, then it would seem that conflict was probably inevitable.

Another revolutionary factor that may have been common to South-East Asia at this time, and which is picked out in the

CONCLUSIONS

case of Indonesia, is the age of the combatants; and the suggestion here is that this was in fact the revolution of one generation against another.[1] To some extent this may have been true in Malaya, although at the beginning of the insurrection at least there were surprisingly large numbers of middle-aged guerrillas, and it seems a more important observation that by 1945 the majority of the Malayan Chinese had now been born in Malaya. Even this seems to be a physical rather than a political fact and the question of primary allegiance, whether to Malaya or to China, was indeed largely metaphysical and, as a fact, something that awaited demonstration. As far as the instruments of insurrection are concerned another point of lateral comparison between Malaya on the one hand and either Indonesia or Indo-China on the other, is the number and availability of weapons in 1945. In the case of Indonesia large numbers of militia had been trained and provided with weapons by the Japanese. In the case of Indo-China vast numbers of weapons were available from various sources at the end of the war.[2] In Malaya, however, Japanese discipline on the whole was far better and they were, in any event, disarmed by British forces within a comparatively short period. One does not want to exaggerate the point, and in fact large numbers of weapons had been buried by the anti-Japanese guerrillas, but the easy and general access to weapons with its promise of a genuine arming of the people was not one of the problems that the returning colonial government faced in Malaya.

Nevertheless the postwar military and colonial administrations were ill-equipped to withstand an insurrection. In particular their weakness lay in their relationship with and knowledge of the Chinese community and, having abandoned the 'special relationship' implied in the pre-war Chinese Protectorate and having, at the same time, been unwilling or unable to augment the number of Chinese speaking officers in other departments of government, this weakness now centred in the police and the intelligence services. In August 1947 Mr. O'Connell, the Director of the CID, wrote

---

[1] Benedict R. O'G. Anderson, *Java in a Time of Revolution*, Ithaca, 1972. Also J. R. W. Smail *Bandung In The Early Revolution, 1945–1946*. Ithaca, 1964.

[2] J. T. McAlister argues that it was political organisation and not weapons that was the primary support of the Viet Minh's military operations; but by March 1946 32,000 weapons had been made available to the Viet Minh north of the 16th parallel by the Japanese and Nationalist Chinese. *Viet Nam The Origins of Revolution*, New York, 1969, pp. 246–55.

> We are fighting a battle based on Chinese psychology, with, say at the very most, 400 persons who have some idea of what the Chinese does and what the Chinese thinks and some 9.600 persons who are right outside the picture. The machine was built to fight a quite different battle.

In the event the police, as a force, were hard put to deal with the wave of violent crime, the communal disorders, and the continuing political fracas that affected all three communities. For the most part however the fears of a colonial government were that there might be a form of Malay insurgency and with the continuing disorders in Indonesia, and the evidence of colonial crisis there, this loomed as a very large possibility. In that event eight or nine battalions of infantry might have been enough to defeat many times that number of untrained insurgents in pitched battles; if that had been the latter's intention. In 1948 it was not; and the threat came from a different quarter. Once the guerrillas had merged into the jungle and the rural population an entirely different force was needed.

When, and before, this happened, one of the unspoken assumptions of the insurgency was that there had been a reduction not only in colonial, i.e. British, power but in authority; and after the psychic as well as the physical impact of the fall of Singapore it was not altogether surprising that many believed that the pre-war colonial cast had been shattered. In its place there was now the pretension of the Malayan Communist Party: that, as their wartime title proclaimed, they represented the Malayan people. If one accepts this simple premise then, whether or not it deserved to succeed, the insurrection was legitimate and of about the same order as the Viet Minh in Vietnam if not the nationalists in Indonesia.

Personally, this argument seems unacceptable save on the Communists' own terms: that they are the repository and best judges of the people's interests and the executive of the popular will. There are undoubtedly many for whom the MCP spoke after the war, many who benefited from the militancy of trade unionism and many for whom the distant and uncertain prospect of independence, and in the meantime effective exclusion from Malaya's political processes, was quite unacceptable. It was not a time when democracy flourished. In its absence, and in the favouritism, weakness and repression of its preparatory school, there were alternative claims to authority and allegiance—and those of government were correspondingly reduced.

In principle, one must concede that the insurrection could have been averted. Before it reached the stage of open insurrection the problems for government were those of sedition, intimidation and criminal conspiracy: none of them easy to establish and most of them by today's standards rather obsolete. By the standards of the day there may well have been different appreciations of the problems, depending whether one was in the Colonial Office in London or King's House in Kuala Lumpur—not to mention a lonely estate road in Johore or a side street in Sungei Siput—but even if, in the absence of incriminating evidence, as in Northern Ireland today, Sir Edward Gent had been persuaded to use the Banishment Ordinance earlier, i' is hard to say whether this would have averted or precipitated the insurrection.

When it came the government might, although there is no evidence that it did, consider itself fortunate that it had not declared the MCP illegal—and that the MCP had struck first. If their political campaign had confined itself to destruction of the *Kuomintang* and what might be thought of as the Old Believers among Malayan Chinese one may wonder in retrospect what government would have done in this event. And if the MCP had continued to dominate the Malayan trade unions to the point where practically the whole of organised labour would have responded favourably to some later call for action, more particularly if the Malayan Government had been unable to withstand the egregious advice from London to admit Communist Chinese consuls, then it is possible to imagine that the longer time that passed, the stronger the MCP and the revolutionary infra-structure would have become: perhaps to the point where the government would have lost the battle before it had begun. As it was, in June 1948 the Party was well over the threshold of violence. From the evidence it would seem incontrovertible that the MCP had, as a matter of policy, been prepared and had prepared its followers for the armed struggle and that this was to be contingent on the banning of the Party. In the event, the violence of Sungei Siput and the *Min Sheng Pao* editorial of June 15th, the belated police raids which followed and the disappearance of the last open members of the MCP produced a synchronised state of emergency on both sides. It was in this way that the insurrection began.

Course
Perhaps the most remarkable feature of the insurrection, certainly in the perspective afforded by time, is the fact that government continued to govern. Although absent in part at the outset and

constrained at times until the end of 1951, nevertheless it did not withdraw and leave significant parts of the field to its opponents. At the worst it was always contending with the MCP who, except in the case of the original Chinese squatters and the aborigines, had neither the intiative nor the ability to provide an alternative system of government rather than temporary if at times benevolent exploitation. It is hard to exaggerate the importance of this para-normality: what, in practical terms, Sir Robert Thompson has called the ability and the determination of government to continue to record births, marriages and deaths. For one thing it created at least the impression of stability and this both encouraged and was reinforced by the fact that, for the most part, District Officers, police, planters, tappers, peasants and miners remained where they were in spite of often continuous danger.

As far as the representatives of government and capitalist enterprise were concerned it would seem that their continued existence depended upon the inability of the insurgents to muster sufficient numbers sufficiently quickly to drive them out. In part this would also seem to have been a self-imposed disability on the insurgents' part who were either unwilling or unable to give up their internecine feud with the *Kuomintang* members of their own community and made the critical mistake of dividing their forces and objectives. Government was thus fortunate that the guerrillas never attained the mass or momentum that would have enabled them to overwhelm particular towns or areas and that they did not divert even more of their forces and effort from the principal task of dealing with the sources rather than the manifestations of insurrection. For a year and more the army were under the temptation to go after the main force guerrillas and were often in the hope of forcing decisive action upon them; but even when times were at their worst in 1950 and 1951 there was never anything like a battalion-sized target nor, and this was perhaps more important, the prospect of suffering devastating and often enormous ambushes of whole columns that were such an appalling feature for French forces in the first Vietnamese war. Critical fire-power in Malaya, on both sides, was thus limited to small arms; and although artillery and even heavy bombers were occasionally employed it was for the most part on a speculative basis rather than support for the crude, counter-productive principle of prophylactic fire that was, until countermanded by General Westmoreland, such a disfiguring feature of the second Vietnamese war.

Apart from this absence of escalation in the type and dimension of warfare in Malaya it may be noted that troops did not suffer the urban outrages of Palestine, Cyprus or Algeria and, perhaps in part for this reason, their discipline did not break down. The regular Police, too, were a disciplined force while the government itself made it possible for guerrillas to surrender and soon gave up exacting the full penalty from those who did.

Operationally, Malaya confirms—and of course provided the basis for—Thompson's deductions of the general principles of counter-insurgency;[3] but I have found it a problem to distinguish what is particularly significant although, overall, it might be permissible to pick out the importance of the Police and the New Villages. In the first instance it is the opinion of many that the country was saved by the fortuitous arrival in 1948 of the Palestine Police. With them came the Palestine Commissioner of Police, Colonel Gray, whose task it was to expand the Malayan Police to unprecedented numbers, hold them together, and withstand the first and second guerrilla offensives. His successor, Colonel Young, from the City of London, had the entirely different task of reconverting the Police from a para-military to an essentially civil function. Here again it seemed fortuitous that the two men arrived when and in the sequence that they did; and when government was beginning to run out of steam at the end of 1951 one may note the removal of its three principals: the High Commissioner, the Commissioner of Police and the Director of Operations. Fate on one side, however, it can also be argued that the basic decisions that were taken and arrived at were essentially sound.[4] At the very beginning it was not a fiction that the

---

[3] (1) The Government must have a clear political aim: to establish and maintain a free, independent united country which is politically and economically stable and viable.
    (2) The Government must function in accordance with law.
    (3) The Government must have an overall plan.
    (4) The Government must give priority to defeating the political subversion not the guerrillas.
    (5) In the guerrilla phase of an insurgency, the Government must secure its base areas first.
    Sir Robert Thompson, *Defeating Communist Insurgency*, London 1966, pp. 50–57.

[4] A contrary opinion is that of Mr. G. C. Madoc, former Director of Intelligence, and I am again indebted to him for this note 'Right from 1950 we thought Briggs was wrong in planning to "roll up" the CTs from the South. If for no better reason than that Johore contained perhaps the most powerful, best supported, MCP; and that the whole government machine needed to practice and gain experience on a less powerful target.'

army was acting in support of civil power. Within two years, although this much time may have been a luxury, Briggs' basic analysis and prescription had set the pattern that was to be followed through to a successful conclusion. By this time resettlement into New Villages had already begun, although in many ways, 1949 had been the year of the locust, and it was possible to see the outline of an exceptionally effective plan. In a permanent framework of military operations, a completely integrated civil and military administration and a proper appreciation of what was required in the New Villages may be seen the blueprint for success.

Negatively, perhaps the most important decision, *faute de mieux*, was that there could be no reliance on the illusions of air power: from the beginning to the end military power had to go in on foot. Even with ground forces, and the eventual concentration that sometimes provided a ratio of over fifty to one, it was recognised that it was possible to have too many—and too many who were not properly trained. Too much logistic support was never a subject of complaint; but in retrospect and comparison it may also have been an advantage that Malaya was not overwhelmed by foreign aid as well as foreign troops. In general, and if one omits the colonial structure and the presence of British and Commonwealth troops, there was very little foreign interference in the Malayan insurrection: a point which sometimes seems the more remarkable bearing in mind that it was largely a Chinese insurrection. China, in the form of the People's Republic, provided little more than fitful encouragement for the insurrection; and, for the guerrillas, the absence of any contiguous source of support meant a critical difference compared at least to the insurgents in post-war Vietnam.

Other things being equal it is perhaps obvious that the key to counter-insurgency in Malaya was intelligence. In particular, it was a matter of Chinese sources of intelligence and, to be even more specific, surrendered guerrillas who were, incidentally, unlikely to give up as long as it was commonly believed that prisoners were tortured to death. Apart from this the guerrillas were most vulnerable in the matter of their communications—their absence of radio meant not only a lack of communications but also of surprise and initiative—and once a courier route or line of communication became known it was possible, in a sort of Minotaur plan in reverse, to trace the higher formation back along the line and thus to eliminate it. On occasion these lines of communication were penetrated as a result of speculative patrolling; but while, for the army, the temptation was always there to fight the regular units of the MRLA the only way in which one could be certain that they would fight, disintegrate or leave the area was to cut them off from all supplies, recruits, intelligence and support or else, when Special Branch had done its work, to allow them that controlled access which would almost guarantee the first contact of a successful ambush. Even where the problem involved aborigines rather than New Villages or regrouped estate labour, it was still a matter of locating the enemy and the way to do this was essentially the same : intelligence that was produced by patience, skill and, on the part of those who gave it freely, a sense of increasing confidence.

The Nation
It is, I think, improper for a non-Malayan to suggest which of the two events—the defeat of the Communist insurrection or the attainment of independence—was the more important in form or in time for the future of Malaya. The struggle against the one was also the birth trauma of the other; and a conclusion or principle that may or may not emerge from the preceding pages, but an idea, perhaps a commonplace, that became a conviction in the course of writing, is that the successful outcome of the insurrection, in the course of which Malaya became independent, could never have been achieved by a single community. Insofar as this account has any purpose other than the historical it is the hope that it is not too archaic to have seen the end of the insurrection in terms of the triumph of multi-racialism. Ultimately it may be that the dead were all on the same side. If that is so, then in 1960 the greater part of the living were also on the same side of an independent and united country.

As far as the various communities are concerned the more obvious features of this account are that the largely Chinese insurrection was met by largely Malay resistance; that the Chinese among the civil population suffered the heaviest casualties; among the security forces the heaviest casualties were suffered by the regular and auxiliary Malay police. And that in spite of the jagged edges which appeared between the Chinese and Malays the differences were reduced rather than exploited : to the point where a British Government insisted on, and Malay and Chinese leaders accepted, a multi-racial basis for independence. This was the outcome rather than the inception of the process of independence. To the Chinese it was part of the realisation that a one stage, China-type revolution had failed and that a Chinese insurrection was unable to transcend its limitations. At the beginning, however, for those Chinese who did not support the guerrillas the question that was still to be answered was what would happen when the British left? How soon were they going and what state would the country be in when they went? To make it worthwhile for the Chinese to take risks was the fundamental and long term problem facing the Federal Government in framing its Chinese policy. In the meantime the short term problem was to make it not worthwhile for the Chinese not to take risks. But in the last analysis the solution to both problems was the same: confidence. When Chinese Home Guard sections were fully armed or when a British battalion, in the mortal peril of ambush situations, was prepared to let the first shot be fired and the trap to be sprung by the accompanying surrendered guerrilla, these were expressions of confidence on one side. When no attempt was made to use the thousands of weapons in the hands of Malay Home Guards, Special Constables, Police and soldiers for a final solution to the Chinese problem, this may be seen as confidence on another side. When the Chinese, whether as Home Guards, political leaders, detectives or as the sources of information, took their lives into their hands by supporting government, this, too represented confidence.

Mutual confidence, however, particularly between the Malay and the Chinese communities, was something which, at the beginning of the insurrection, was something that manifestly did not obtain. It would almost certainly not have been possible for Britain, acting as a colonial government, to have resisted a united demand for independence but at the outset neither a colonial government nor Malay political leaders were in much of a hurry for independence while the radical and militant wings of both Malay and Malayan Chinese nationalism were enthralled to alien powers, the one to Indonesia, the other to China. Where these provided a surrogate passion, the more moderate bulk of both nationalist forces lacked the confidence which, had it been turned against the colonial government, would have made it the victorious ally of the Communist guerrillas. Malay nationalism was mobilised in UMNO by Dato Onn and, although it continued and flourished after Onn had left, it was not a party that was in a hurry for independence. Neither the Malay nor the Chinese communities could be certain on what terms independence would come. Both feared the preponderance of the other and made the implicit assumption that in a fairly evenly balanced society the extremist elements would triumph in both groups. Put more briefly, there was little prospect at that time that an independent Malaya would emerge as a politically viable state.[5]

Nevertheless, in the turmoil and kaleidoscope of post-war British colonial experience both communities were entitled to their particular fears; and if the Chinese feared that the British Government would have been prepared to see the Malay States become independent in some form, the example of Palestine for the Malays and their fears of a thrusting immigrant community were enhanced by the arrival of administrators and policemen who might have been tempted to believe that they were taking part in a repeat performance. That Malaya, unlike Palestine, was not torn apart by community conflict may again be regarded as a piece of good fortune as is the fact that, unlike Vietnam, it was not ravaged in the attempt to destroy the insurgents. More particularly, however, it should be seen as a reflection of the collective good sense of the Malay community who, although in this study may well seem to have been forgotten, were nevertheless the central and the largest component of counter-insurgency. Now that this account is free of the sanction or stigma of being the official history it may seem more credible to refer to the immense, patient help of the Malays in withstanding not only the insurrection but also the temptation to make out of it permanent political capital; to the deceptively simple but extraordinary political skills of Malaya's first political leaders; and to the energy and courage of those leaders of the wartime Malay resistance who took part in counter-insurgency, some of whom are today leaders of the Malaysian Government.

In what is perhaps rather a romantic view the Communist insurrection in Malaya is a story from which no community and few individuals emerge badly. Malay soldiers and police, Commonwealth and particularly Gurkha soldiers, European planters, miners and government officers, and the civilians of all communities who were in frequent and sometimes constant danger ultimately resisted the demands of an embattled minority. Even the Chinese guerrilla, capable of hideous cruelty as well as calculated ferocity, possessed a tenacity which made many fight to the end and which took as many more up to and often past the point of death by starvation. Their commitment to Communism and its variants which, if it was not idealism, represented conspicuous devotion had been sufficient to maintain only a few

[5] A. Short 'Nationalism and the Emergency in Malaya' in Michael Leifer (ed.) *Nationalism, Revolution and Evolution in South-East Asia*. Hull Monographs on South-East Asia, No. 2, 1970, pp. 43–58.

hundred along the Siamese borders in the early 1960s; but they continue to present themselves as the radical alternative to government as long as there are political causes that will support them.[6] In the event, Indonesian confrontation, Chinese propaganda and even the revived horrors of a communal outburst might have been the causes but have failed to be the occasions for renewed insurgency over the past ten years. Compared to the early and even mid-1960s the situation in Malaya now looks more ominous with the staging of some effective border ambushes and evidence of revived armed propaganda units as far south as Ipoh.[7] For the moment, however, and in spite of propaganda to the contrary, the Communist Party of Malaya has not been able to begin a second phase of the armed struggle and may still be digesting the lessons of its failure in the first. Governments, presumably, are doing likewise.

[6] See e.g. Justus M. Van Der Kroef *Communism in Malaysia and Singapore: a contemporary survey*. Martinus Nijhoff, The Hague 1967. Frances L. Starner 'Communism in Malaysia: a Multifront Struggle' in Robert A. Scalapino (ed.) *The Communist Revolution in Asia*. Prentice-Hall Inc., 1965, pp. 221-55. A Short 'Communism, Race and Politics in Malaysia', *Asian Survey* December 1970, Vol. 10, No. 12, pp. 1081-89.

[7] Government of Malaysia, *The Path of Violence to Absolute Power*. Kuala Lumpur, November 1968. Government of Malaysia, *The Resurgence of Armed Communism in West Malaysia*. Kuala Lumpur, October 1971. A Short, 'The Communist Party of Malaya: in Search of Revolutionary Situations', *The World Today*, December 1970, pp. 529-35.

APPENDIX

CASUALTIES, INCIDENTS, CONTACTS

	Total 1948	Total 1949	Total 1950	Total 1951	Total 1952	Total 1953	Total 1954	Total 1955
TERRORISTS KILLED	374	619	648	1078	1155	959	723	420
TERRORISTS CAPTURED	263	337	147	121	123	73	51	54
TERRORISTS SURRENDERED	56	251	147	201	257	372	211	249
TOTAL ELIMINATIONS	693	1207	942	1400	1535	1404	985	723
TERRORISTS WOUNDED				649	596	291	212	161
TOTAL TERRORIST CASUALTIES	693	1207	942	2049	2131	1695	1197	884
REGULAR POLICE KILLED	45	104	148	116	65	10	6	8
REGULAR POLICE WOUNDED	73	93	161	191	113	9	21	17
SPECIAL CONSTABLES KILLED*	37	51	134	192	106	19	19	21
SPECIAL CONSTABLES WOUNDED	42	72	138	217	134	34	52	32
AUXILIARY POLICE WOUNDED	4	5	22	46	31	10	16	11
AUXILIARY POLICE KILLED	7	9	32	72	36	29	28	18
MILITARY FORCES KILLED	60	65	79	124	56	34	34	32
MILITARY FORCES WOUNDED	92	77	175	237	123	64	65	43
TOTAL SECURITY FORCES KILLED	149	229	393	504	263	92	87	79
TOTAL SECURITY FORCES WOUNDED	211	247	496	691	401	117	154	103
TOTAL SECURITY FORCES CASUALTIES	360	476	889	1195	664	209	241	182
CIVILIANS KILLED	315	334	646	533	343	85	97	62
CIVILIANS WOUNDED	149	200	409	356	158	15	31	24
CIVILIANS MISSING	90	160	106	135	131	43	57	57
TOTAL CIVILIAN CASUALTIES	554	694	1161	1024	632	143	185	143
INCIDENTS { MAJOR			1744	2333	1389	258	293	206
{ MINOR			2995	3749	2338	912	784	575
TOTAL INCIDENTS	1274	1442	4739	6082	3727	1170	1077	781
CONTACTS			983	1911	1868	1407	993	565

	1956	1957	1958	1959	1960
TERRORISTS KILLED	307	240	153	21	13
TERRORISTS CAPTURED	52	32	22	8	6
TERRORISTS SURRENDERED	134	209	502	86	29
TOTAL ELIMINATIONS	493	481	677	115	48
TERRORISTS WOUNDED	115	59	33	4	48
TOTAL TERRORISTS CASUALTIES	608	540	710	119	
REGULAR POLICE KILLED	5	2	1	1	
REGULAR POLICE WOUNDED	9	2	4	8	
SPECIAL CONSTABLES KILLED	12		2		
SPECIAL CONSTABLES WOUNDED	17	6	2		
AUXILIARY POLICE KILLED	8	3	1		
AUXILIARY POLICE WOUNDED	6	3			
MILITARY FORCES KILLED	22	6	7	1	
MILITARY FORCES WOUNDED	47	22	13	1	
TOTAL SECURITY FORCES KILLED	47	11	10	9	
TOTAL SECURITY FORCES WOUNDED	79	33	19	10	
TOTAL SECURITY FORCES CASUALTIES	126	44	29		
CIVILIANS KILLED	30	22	3	3	
CIVILIANS WOUNDED	36	7		3	
CIVILIANS MISSING	26	2		6	
TOTAL CIVILIANS CASUALTIES	92	31	3		
INCIDENTS { MAJOR	102	40	13	4	5
{ MINOR	333	150	77	8	
TOTAL INCIDENTS	435	190	90	12	5
CONTACTS	486	303	186	27	21

BIBLIOGRAPHY

BOOKS, PAPERS AND MONOGRAPHS

Allen, James de V., *The Malayan Union*, Yale Southeast Asian Monograph Series No. 10, 1967.
Anderson, Benedict R. O'G., *Java in a Time of Revolution*, Ithaca, 1972.
Barber, Noel, *The War of the Running Dogs*, London, 1971.
Blaxland, Gregory, *The Regiments Depart*, London, 1971.
Blythe, W. L., *The Impact of Chinese Secret Societies in Malaya*, London, 1969.
Brimmell, J. H., *Communism in South East Asia*, London, 1959.
Campbell, A. F., *Jungle Green*, London, 1953.
Chandos, Viscount (Oliver Lyttelton), *The Memoirs of Lord Chandos*, London, 1962.
Chin Kee Onn, *Malaya Upside Down*, Singapore, 1946.
Chin Kee Onn, *Ma-Rai-Ee*, London, 1952.
Clark, Margaret F., *The Malayan Alliance and its Accommodation of Communal Pressures 1952–1962*, M.A. Thesis (unpublished). History Department, University of Malaya, 1964.
Clutterbuck, R., *The Long Long War*, London, 1966.
Cowan, C. D. (ed.), *The Economic Development of South-East Asia*, London, 1964.
Crawford, Oliver, *The Door Marked Malaya*, London, 1958.
Crockett, A. J. S., *Green Beret, Red Star*, London, 1954.
Cross, Robert and Thatcher, Dorothy, *Pai-Naa*, London, 1959.
Donnison, F. S. V., *British Military Administration in the Far East, 1943–1946*, London, 1956.
Fitzgerald, C. P., *The Birth of Communist China*, London, 1964.
Fitzgerald, Frances, *Fire in the Lake*, New York, 1972.
Gamba, Charles, *The Origins of Trade Unionism in Malaya*, Singapore, 1962.
Gullick, J. M., *Malaya*, London, 1963.
Gurchan Singh, *Singa—the Lion of Malaya*, Kuala Lumpur, n.d.
Han Suyin, *And the Rain my Drink*, London, 1956.
Hanrahan, Gene Z., *The Communist Struggle in Malaya*, New York, Institute of Pacific Relations 1954 (mimeo)

Henniker, M. C. A., *Red Shadow Over Malaya*, London, 1955.
Holman, Dennis, *Noone of the Ulu*, London, 1958.
Holman, Dennis, *Green Torture*, London, 1962.
Kathigasu, Sybil, G. M., *No Dram of Mercy*, London, 1954.
Kroef, Justus M. Van der, *Communism in Malaysia and Singapore : a Contemporary Survey*, Martinus Nijhoff, The Hague, 1967.
Lam Swee, *My Accusation*, Kuala Lumpur, 1951.
McAlister, J. T., *Viet Nam The Origins of Revolution*, New York, 1969.
McLane, Charles B., *Soviet Strategies in Southeast Asia*, Princeton, 1966.
McVey, Ruth D., *The Calcutta Conference and the South-east Asian Uprisings*, Ithaca, 1958 (mimeo).
Means, Gordon P., *Malaysian Politics*, London, 1971.
Miers, R. C. H., *Shoot to Kill*, London, 1959.
Miller, Harry, *Prince and Premier*, London, 1959.
Miller, Harry, *Menace in Malaya*, London, 1954.
Moran, J. W. G., *Spearhead in Malaya*, London, 1959.
Oldfield, J. B., *The Green Howards in Malaya*, London, 1953.
Osborne, Milton E., *Strategic Hamlets in South Viet Nam*, Ithaca, 1965 (mimeo).
Overstreet, Gene D., and Windmiller, Marshall, *Communism in India*, University of California Press, 1959.
Parkinson, C. Northcote, *Templer in Malaya*, Singapore, 1954.
Perry Robinson, J. B., *Transformation in Malaya*, London, 1956.
Purcell, Victor, *The Chinese in South-east Asia*, London, 1965.
Purcell, Victor, *The Chinese in Modern Malaya*, Singapore, 1956.
Purcell, Victor, *Malaya: Communist or Free?*, London, 1954.
Purcell, Victor, *Memoirs of a Malayan Official*, London, 1965.
Purcell, Victor, *The Chinese in Malaya*, London, 1948.
Pye, Lucian, *Lessons from the Malayan Struggle Against Communism*, M.I.T., n.d. (mimeo).
Renick, Roderick, *Emergency Regulations of Malaya: Background Organisation, Administration and Use as a Socialising Technique*, unpublished M.A. Thesis, Tulane University, 1964.
Scalapino, Robert A. (ed.), *The Communist Revolution in Asia*, New York, 1965.
Sharpley, Cecil, *The Great Delusion*, London, 1952.
Slimming, John, *In Fear of Silence*, London, 1955.
Slimming, John, *Temiar Jungle*, London, 1958.
Smail, J. R. W., *Bandung in the Early Revolution, 1945–1946*, Ithaca, 1964.

BIBLIOGRAPHY

Spencer-Chapman, F., *The Jungle is Neutral*, London, 1957.
Stacey, Tom, *The Hostile Sun,* London, 1953.
Stenson, M. R., *Industrial Conflict in Malaya*, London, 1970.
Stenson, M. R., *Repression and Revolt*, Papers in International Studies, South-East Asian Series, No. 10, Ohio University, 1969 (mimeo).
Stenson, M. R., '*The 1948 Communist Revolt in Malaya: A note on Historical Sources and Interpretation. A Reply by Gerald de Cruz*'. Institute of Southeast Asian Studies, Singapore, 1971 (mimeo).
Thompson, Sir Robert, *Defeating Communist Insurgency*, London, 1966.

ARTICLES

Blake, D. J., 'Compilation, Chronicle or History? A Review of Chalres Gamba, "The Origins of Trade Unionism in Malaya" ', *Malayan Economic Review*, October 1963.
Clark, Lieutenant-Colonel K. H., RAMC, 'Some Account of an Operation in the Malayan Jungle', *Journal of the Royal Army Medical Corps*, Vol. 94, No. 6, June 1950.
Crook, Major P. E., OBE, RWK, 'A Subaltern's War in Malaya', *British Army Journal*, January 1953..
Duke, Lieutenant-Colonel W. D. H., MC, ' "Operation Metcalf", the Story of a Raid on a Terrorist Camp in Malaya', *Army Quarterly*, October 1953.
Harvey, M., 'Malaya—Time for a Change', *The Army Quarterly*, April 1955.
Hawkins, Gerald, 'Marking Time in Malaya', *International Affairs*, January 1948.
Hilliard, Major J. L., 'Tactics in Malaya', *Army Quarterly*, April 1951.
Kernial Singh Sandhu, 'The Saga of the Malayan Squatter, *Journal of South-east Asian History*, March 1964.
Parmer, J. N., 'Chinese Estate Workers' Strikes in Malaya in March 1937', in Cowan, C. D. (ed.), *The Economic Development of South-East Asia*, London 1964.
Ranft, Captain D. D., 'Parachuting in Malaya', *Army Quarterly*, July 1953.
Robinson, Major R. E. R., 'Reflections of a Company Commander in Malaya', *Army Quarterly*, October 1950.
Sendall, Major W. R., RM, 'Royal Marines in Malaya', *The Navy*, July 1950.

Sheppard, Tan Sri Mubin, 'The Police Action at Bukit Kepong, Johore', *The Sunday Times* (Malaysia), February 22nd 1970.

Short, A., 'Asian Communism, Pt. III', *The Asia Magazine*, November 20th 1966.

Short, A., 'Communism, Race and Politics in Malaysia', *Asian Survey*, December 1970, Vol. 10, No. 12.

Short, A., 'The Communist Party of Malaya : in Search of Revolutionary Situations', *The World Today*, December 1970.

Short, A., 'Nationalism and the Emergency in Malaya', in Leifer, Michael (ed.), *Nationalism, Revolution and Evolution in South-East Asia*, Hull Monograph on South-East Asia, No. 2, 1970.

Starner, Frances L., 'Communism in Malaysia : A Multifront Struggle', in Robert A. Scalapino (ed.), *The Communist Revolution in Asia*, New York, 1965.

Stenson, M. R., 'The Malayan Union and the Historian', *Journal of Southeast Asian History*, Vol. 10, No. 2, September 1969.

Wohlstetter, Roberta, 'Cuba and Pearl Harbour : hindsight and foresight', *Foreign Affairs*, July 1965.

Woodhouse, Captain J. M., MC, 'Some Personal Observations on the Employment of Special Forces in Malaya', *Army Quarterly*, April 1952.

Yeo Kim Wah, 'A Study of Three Early Political Parties in Singapore, 1945–1955', *Journal of Southeast Asian History*, Vol. 10, No. 1, March 1969.

'A History of 1st Battalion The Worcestershire Regiment in Malaya, 1950–1953'. Extracts from *Firm*, 1954–56.

'Jungle Crusade', *Royal Air Force Review*, February 1950.

'A Supply Dropping Mission in Malaya', *Royal Air Force Quarterly*, October 1950.

PUBLIC PAPERS

Federation of Malaya

    Annual Reports, 1948–57

    Corry, W. C. S., *A General Survey of New Villages*, Kuala Lumpur 1954.

    Legislative Council, *Proceedings*, 1948–57.

    Labour Department, *Annual Reports*.

    Trade Union Adviser, *Annual Reports*.

    Trade Union Registry, *Annual Reports*.

    Report on the Conduct of Food Searches at Semenyih, Kuala Lumpur, 1956.

Great Britain

HMSO
Callwell, C. E., *Small Wars, their Principles and Practice*, 1906.
Federation of Malaya : Summary of Revised Constitutional Proposals, Cmd. 7171, 1947.
Malayan Union and Singapore : Statement of Policy on Future Constitution, Cmd. 6724, 1946.
Malayan Union and Singapore : Summary of Proposed Constitutional Arrangements, Cmd. 6749, 1946.
Labour and Trade Union Organisation in the Federation and Singapore, Colonial No. 224, 1948
Overseas Economic Survey, Malaya, March 1951, 1952.
House of Commons, Debates, 1945–57.
House of Lords, Debates, 1945–57.

Malaysia
The Path of Violence to Absolute Power, Kuala Lumpur, 1968.
The Resurgence of Armed Communism in West Malaysia, Kuala Lumpur, 1971.

INDEX

*Compiled by Norman Knight, M.A.,
President of the Society of Indexers, and Valerie Chandler,
B.A., A.L.A.A., M.S.Ind.*

bis after a reference number indicates that the item is mentioned twice quite separately on the same page, and *ter* three times; *passim* denotes that the references are scattered throughout the page numbers indicated; *qv.* stand for *quod vide* ('which see'); *q.* stands for 'quoted'.
Subheadings have been arranged in alphabetical (not chronological) order. The method of alphabetical arrangement is word-by-word.

A

Abbreviations used, list of, 15–6
Aborigine Research and Interrogation Section (near Kuala Lumpur), 453
Aborigines, Malayan (indigenous inhabitants of the deep jungle)
  air attacks on, 444, 445; Asal Clubs, 447–8, 449; census, 441; characteristics and culture, 446, 448–50, 452–3, 494*n*
  cultivation areas, 451, 452; death and starvation, 444–5; effect of jungle forts, 448; family and group loyalty, 448–50, 452, 453; government policy towards, 441–56 *passim*
  Operation *Termite*, 367
  Police Aboriginal Guards, 480*n*; reaction to Japanese Occupation, 441, 445, 447; rehabilitating resettled aborigines, 445; relations with guerrillas, 367, 391, 441, 444, 447–55 *passim*, 493;
  relations with Security Forces, 367, 440–3 *passim*, 449–56 *passim*, 493–4; resettlement, 442–4; welfare, medical and other government services, 445, 446, 450, 451–2
Abubakar, H. H. Tengku, *q*, 273*n*
Administration, Civil (*see also* Civil Service; High Commissioner, *and* Officer Administering Government)
  Lyttelton concerned about tangle, 334–6; suffers through shortage of Chinese-speaking officers,
232, 235; Templer's programme, 341–3
Army, the (and RAF), 'the only really stable factors'—Briggs, Nov. 1970, 250
  organisation in 1953, 353; proper function, 285; property destruction and, 154
  reinforcements asked for by Boucher and Gurney, 226–30
  tactics (1954), 368–9, 377; training, 300, 393
  reinforcements arrive (2 infantry brigades) (1950), 242
  strong points and striking forces (Briggs Plan), 238
  two-thirds concentrated in Southern States (June 1950), 241–2
  uncertain how to deal with Malay insurgents, 209
Arrest and detention, *see* Detention
Advisory Committees (Detainees), 159
African troops, 369, 480*n*
Afro-Asian Conference, Bandoeng, 459
Agricultural Department, and opening up of forest reserves, 175
Ah Ann (MCP Regional Committee Secretary), 491
Ah Fun (MCP Regional Committee member), 492
Ah Ho (State Committee Secretary of Negri Sembilan), 482–3
Ah Tian (guerrilla), 494
Air Headquarters, Malaya, 370
Air strikes, 153, 370, 444, 445
  100 per cent increase (1950), 248
Air supplies
  to aborigines, 443–4; to Security Forces, 370, 445, 450

INDEX

Airforce weakness, 114, 502
Alexander, Albert V. (Minister of Defence, 1948), 135
Aliens Enactments and Ordinances repatriation procedure under, 184
All Malayan Council of Joint Action, 262–3
Alliance Party (*see also* Rahman, Tungku Abdul), 345, 460, 469, 495
Ambushes
 Army, 153, 167
 jungle ideal for, 235
Amethyst, HMS, 371
Ambushes, casualties, 280–1; guerrilla tactics and, 205, 277–8, 294, 321; Gurney's death, 303–5; road and rail, 211–2; Security Force tactics, 277, 278, 481; Tanjong Malim, 340–1
Amnesty for surrendering bandits, 221–2
 offer of (1955), 460, 461, 463, 465, 466; withdrawn (1956), 476–7
Ampang (Selangor, typical guerrilla camp at) 97–8
Ang Bin Hoay Triad Society, 260–1
Angkatan Pemuda Insa'af (API— 'Youth Movement for Justice'), 38
Anti-Bandit Month (1950), 215, 216–8
 counterblast to, 219
Anti-British Leagues, 362
 Klang, 431, 432; Kuala Lumpur, 432; Penang Anti-British Alliance, 431; Pentian, 434; Seventh Branch of Anti-British Alliance, 431; Singapore, 430
Anti-Japanese Army, *see* Malayan People's Anti-Japanese Army
Anti-Japanese National Salvation Associations, 21, 22
'Anti-Japanese Programme' (MCP, 1943), 23
Anti-Japanese Union, 24, 29
API, *see* Angkatan
Appeal Court (in Kuala Lumpur), Lee Meng trial, 384–5
Area Security Units of Police Force), 358, 413, 478, 480 *bis*
Armed Work Forces (MCP), 473, 475, 479, 486*n*
Armies, private, *see* Private armies
Armoured cars
 Briggs Plan and, 241; lack of (1948), 135, 150; Lyttelton recommends more, 333; police use of, 277–81, 333

Arms and armour
 Communist shortage limits action, 350*n*; Communist supplies from Thailand, 373; limited to small arms, 500; Lyttelton's recommendations, 333, 335; remained from Japanese, 497; Security Forces' guns captured by guerrillas, 278–9, 294
 Security Force provision, 277–80
Army, the (*see also* African troops; Australian troops, British troops; Conscription; Ferret Force; Fijian Battalion; Gurkha troops; Indian Army; Malayan Security Services; *and entries under* Operation — e.g. Operation Hive), 133–9
 acts in support of civil power, 123; Batang Kali the only blot on their conduct, 169; criticisms of, 154–5, 155–6, 169; emergency responsibilities, 336, 339; expansion needed, 225, 349
 operations of, 136–9, 500
Asal Clubs (Chinese and aborigine groups), 447–8, 449, 453–5
Aziz, Inche Abdul
 moves motion in Legislative Council on the Emergency, 296

B

Bah Pelankin (pro-guerrilla aborigine), 446
Bahau (Negri Sembilah), 483–4
Bakar, Abu (police SPO), killing of, 220
Balan, R. G. (delegate to Empire Communist Conference (1947)), 44
 arrest of (1948), 60, 91; detained for ten years, 92*n*; the great strike promoter, 92; power of, in Perak, 66; Vice-Chairman of Central Committee, 462–3
Baling talks, 462–8, 469
Bandits, *see* Guerrilla forces
Banishment orders (*see also* Deportation), 72, 92, 178, 184, 188; British subjects and, 72, 73; laws regarding, two different, 74
Banishment Ordinance, 72, 76, 499
Bank of China, 427
Barber, Noel (author of *The War of the Running Dogs*), 384*n*, 399*n*

INDEX

'Barnes Report, the', on Malay education, 435
Base areas (MCP), see Deep jungle bases (MCP)
Batang Kali (Selangor), 327
  prisoners shot in, 166–9
Battle News Press, 352, 473
Batu Arang, Selangor
  colliery strikes in, 20, 99; guerrillas converge on (1948), 99, 100, 102, 137; squatter evictions, 182
Batu Arang Miners' Union, priorities of, 224
Batu Caves (Selangor)
  compensation lacking for Mawai's settlers from, 198n
  disastrous meeting of MCP and MPAJA at (1942), 22, 38
BDCC, see Defence Coordinating Committee
Bekok (Johore), guerrilla activities in, 109
Belum Valley (Perak), Operation Helsby, 366
Bentong area (Pahang)
  District Organisation destroyed, 473; guerrilla activity centre, 351; Operation Sword, 366
Betong area (on Thai border), guerrilla activity centre, 351, 373–4
Bin Chong Night School (Pontian), 433
Bin Chong Old Boys' Association (Pontian), 433
Bin Seng Rubber Milling Factory, burning of (1948), 55
Blythe, W. L., 255n
Boestaman, Ahmad (founder of Party Ra'ayat), 470–1
Border Security Council, 493
Borneo, constabulary and Dyaks from, in Ferret Force, 132, 133
Bose, Subhas Chandra, his INA, 210
Boucher, Major-General Sir Charles (GOC Malaya), 120
  assurance of sufficient forces by, 149; criticised in Legislative Council, 296; fixation of, with guerrilla reinforcements, 136; on help from police and 'civil', 139; on Malay Regiment, 225–6; Paper on Security Situation . . ., A, by, with Col. Gray (April 1949), 136–7; on reinforcements needed (1950), 226–7
'Boucher Promises More Toughness" (report), 137

Bourne, General Sir Geoffrey (Director of Operations and GOC Malaya), 353
Boyd, Lennox (British M.P.), 327
Brazier, John A. (Trade Union Adviser), on Federations of Trade Unions, 66–7
Bren guns
  captured by guerrillas, 278–9; used by guerrillas, 277
Brigand squadron, 371
Briggs, Lt.-Gen. Sir Harold (Director of Operations, qv.), 202
  aborigine policy, 444–5; announces turning point of Emergency (1951), 275; appointment (1950) specially requested by Field-Marshal Slim, 234–5; criticised in Legislative Council, 296, 322; Home Guards set up, 293, 412–5; impressions of, about situation (April 1950), 235–7; and jungle squads, 287; meetings with Cabinet Ministers in London (1950), 251n; on need for closer cooperation between police and army (1950), 248; opposes Jenkin, 276; police organisation, 287–91; propaganda and psychological warfare, 416; proposes that Director of Operations has full executive control, 325; and resettlement in Johore, 246; responsibility for military and para-military affairs, 334, 501-2; retirement of, 306, 329
Briggs Plan, the, 231–53, 288–95, 340, 381, 391–2, 501–2
  began (June 1950) with the heaviest troop concentration yet assembled, 230; Directives under, see Directives; failure of first crash programme, 242–3; outline of, 237–9
British Advisers
  favour armouring police vehicles, 278–80; Gurney's discussions with (1949), 187–8; meet to discuss Chinese, 325; post abolished, 486
British Association of Straits Merchants, 118n
  representations by (1947), 73
British Communist Party, CCP and, 44
British Defence Co-ordination, see Defence Co-ordination

s

518　INDEX

British Government
　policy on Malaya (1948–52), 325–9; policy on Malayan independence (1953), 327, 345, 464, 504; questions asked on armouring police vehicles, 280; three requests from—Briggs plan (1950), 251
'British Imperialism'
　denounced, 50–1, 55, 56–7; 108, 314, 315; 'fascist rule of' (*Min Sheng Pao*), 60, 61
British Medical Association. Malayan Branch, 399
British Military Administration (Post-War Malaya), 380
British personnel reduced, 486
'British Presence', 327, 331, 459, 462
British Press
　on Montgomery as High Commissioner, 325–6; reports on armouring police vehicles, 280
British regiments in Malaya, 113–4, 369
British troops, 326, 327, 328
　limited commitment, 275; officers recruited for Home Guard, 412
British view of government, 255–6
Brooke, Major-General (de facto Director of Emergency Operations), 493
Broome, R.N., and Ferret Force, 132
Brown, George (now Lord George-Brown)
　on Batang Kali killings, 168
Bukit Kepong (Johore), police action at (February 1950), 231*n*
Buildings, British destruction of, 153–4
Bukit Serene (Johore)
　conference on recognition of China (November 1949), 214; conference on squatters (1948), 178–9
Burhanuddin, Dr (of Persatuan Islam Sa-malaya), 470–1
Bus Companies, vulnerable to 'protection money', 222
Butler, R. A., 327

C

Calcutta Congress of CPI (1947), 48
Calcutta Youth Conference (1947), 45–8
　belligerence towards colonial rule,
46; 'Emergency', the, was it bred there?, 48–9
Callwell, Col. C. E., *Small Wars . . .* (1906), 138*n*
Cameron Highlands (north-central Malaya, guerrilla activity centre, 350, 351, 366
Campaign, the, *see* Operations
Campbell, Arthur, *Jungle Green*, 368*n*, 382, 386
Carleton Greene, Hugh (Head of Emergency Information Services), 245, 416, 417–8, 420, 425
Cassels, Lieut.-General (last official Director of Emergency Operations), 493
CCP, *see* China Communist Party
Cease fire
　arranged to aid guerrillas who want to surrender, 423; urged by *Freedom News*, 459; versus 'surrender', 466
Ceylonese community, supports IMP, 329
Casualties
　among civilians, 295–6, 472, 495, 503; among guerrillas, 295–6, 349–50, 359–60, 375–6, 472; at Semenyih, 410–1—caused by air strikes, 370; caused by Home Guards, 413; among Security Forces, 231*n*, 280–1, 295–6, 305–6, 472, 492, 495, 503; among Home Guard, 413, 414; lifted by helicopter, 369–70; Special Constables, 127
Censorship, 141–2
　books proscribed, 437, 438; introduction of, proposed (1949), 159
Central Committee of MCP, 84, 206
　admits errors, 318–9; 4th Plenary session of (1948), 49–53; 5th Plenary session of (1948), 49, 55–9; general criticisms of, 309–13; 'liberated' areas decided by, 104; place of, in MCP, 350–1; position (1955), 471; representatives, 462, 469
Central Enlarged Conference, and the case of Loi Tak, 42–3
Chambers of Commerce, Chinese, 118*n*, 127, 260, 265, 429
Chandos, 1st Viscount, *see* Lyttelton
Changkat Jong (Perak)
　pre-war irrigation scheme at, 201, 204
　resettlement problems (1950), 202

INDEX

Chawog (*Asal* Chairman), 453–4
Chemor (Perak), Union office raided by police (1948), 92
Chen, David (murdered Chinese headmaster), 431
Chen Tian (Head of MCP Central Propaganda Dept.), 461–2, 463, 468–9
Chettiars
and 'protection money', 222–3
Chi Chih Night School (Ayer Baloi), 433
Chiang Kai Shek, his defeat by Communists (1948), 156
Chief Police Officers
conference of, in Kuala Lumpur (1948), 161; intelligence centres attached to HQs of, 140; of Pahang, on operations (December 1948), 139; of Selangor, on need of reinforcements, 139; Police Jungle Squads, problems for, 286; Special Constabulary and, 283–5, 286, 290
Chief Secretary, Acting, comments adversely on Kachau tragedy, 166
Chin Nam (guerrilla leader), 206, 304
Chin Peng (Politbureau member), 43, 53
at Baling Talks, 461–8; attempts to capture him, 366, 421; Chou En Lai's letter brought back by (1947), 44; location of, 350, 351, 374; plans for *Min Yuen*, 476
China
British recognition of People's Republic (1950), 213–4; Communist successes (1949) boost Malayan guerrillas, 187, 201; conflict with, possible, 83; effect of withdrawal of protection against, 232; influence in education, 427; political influence and intervention in Malaya, 315–8, 320, 321, 468, 469, 502; receives conscription evaders, 301, 302—and disaffected students, 429; repatriation to a 'war-worn', 191; view of government, 256
China Communist Party (CCP), 53, 228; 'bases' essential for long-term war, 207; Congress (1956), 469; example of their victory, 156; influence of, 19–20, 21, 315–8, 320; Loi Tak's contacts with, 43–4; MCP's contacts with (1947), 44; provides false teaching diplomas, 434
China Democratic League (CDL), 54, 87, 88, 257
China Press, 167–8, 301
China Red Army, the, 228
'China solution, the' (= *Repatriation, qv*)
Chinese, Malayan (*see also* Sino- and Squatters, Chinese), 254–70, 503–6
alienation of, by Regulation 17D, 191, 192; allegiance of, 38, 53; alternative names of, 143; apathy about election (1955), 461*n*; Asal Clubs, 447–8, 449, 453–5
'Back to the land' movement among, 203; Briggs on the, 240; Chinese consuls, appointment of, 214–5; conscription, 300–1, 302, 314, 354; constitutional position, 328, 330–1, 338, 341–2, 344, 459; control of, essential, 235–6; co-operation needed, 324, 336, 425
corrupt detectives, 299, 359; criticised for not helping Emergency effort, 324; criticisms of Templer, 383; deportation, 141*n*, 324–5, 332, 335; economic conditions, 302, 303, 330
education of, 398–9, 428–38 *passim*; family loyalty, 301, 392, 408; first victims of Trengganu terrorism, 151–2; Government writ did not run for rural (1948), 173; guerrilla activity, 291–5, 314
'hold the commercial life in their hands and are becoming also a resident peasantry', 179; Home Guards, 413, 488–9; importance of, 147; inexhaustible labour supply of, 28; Malay integration with, rare, 26, 209–10
number of China-born Malayan Chinese, 427, 497; Police Force and Intelligence work, 359, 497; population increase, 203; problem of gaining their confidence, 232; relations with Gurney, 298–303, 338, 347*n*; relations with police, 298–9, 302, 323–4, 357
remittances to China, 428 *bis*; repatriation of, *see* Repatriation; resettlement of rural, *see*

Chinese Malayan (*continued*)
  Resettlement; response to MCP propaganda, 314; return to China, 301, 302, 429, 466
  secret societies, 425–7; self-reliant character of, 180; sex-ratio change among, 203; State governments' attitude towards rural, 195–201, 202; students used by MCP, 362
  support IMP, 329; thought China's success (1947) had ended Malaya's need for revolution, 53; 24 shot at Batang Kali, 166–9; unpopular, 324–5
Chinese Affairs Officers (State), 324, 398, 417, 419
  appointed under Briggs Plan (1950), 240; duties of, 240–1
Chinese Association, *see* Malayan Chinese Association
Chinese Chamber of Mines, 127
Chinese consuls, problem of, 214–5, 216, 231
Chinese employers, 92
  showdown welcomed by, 32
Chinese estates, absence of special constables on, 127
Chinese People's Republic, British recognition of (1950), 213–6, 220
Chinese press, unhelpfulness of (1950), 301
Chinese Protectorate, 260, 324, 380, 497
Chinese Village Guards, 241
Chong Hwa Middle School (Klang), 431
Chou En-Lai
  MCP's letter from (1947), 44; on world peace (1955), 459 and *n*
Chow Chong (guerrilla), 492
Christian Missionary Societies, 400
Chung Ling High School (Penang), 431, 438
CID, *see* Criminal Investigation Department
CIS, *see* Combined Intelligence Staff
Citizenship (*see also* Constitution, *and* Racialism)
  and the Chinese, 260, 261, 268–9, 331, 341; and the Indian community, 274; Templer's suggestion, 340
Civil Defence Department, 412
Civil Service, *see* Malayan Civil Service
Civilian control, 139–48
Clark, Margaret (author), 265

Codner, Michael, 340
Coldstream Guards in Malaya, 219
Collective punishment, 385–6
Colonial Office
  Gurney informs about Chinese, 298–9; Gurney informs about Regulation 17D (January 1949), 189; Gurney informs about violence, 299; High Commissioner unable to act without its authority (June 1948), 71, 74; optimism of (March 1949), 146; police rôle and, 281; Trade Union ordinance and 72, 74
Colonial Police Service, *see* Police Force
Colonial Secretary of State
  delegation to, of 'all Malayan interests', 118; perturbed by alarmist reports (1948), 85*n*
Combined Intelligence Staff, 140, 360, 414, 425–7
Combined Intelligence Staff Summary, 101
  quoted (July 1948), 99, 109
Cominform
  directives of, 53; Yugoslavs, did they represent, at Calcutta?, 48
Comintern's Far Eastern Bureau, 20
Commando Brigade, No. 3
  arrives in Malaya (1950), 230
Commissioner General for South-East Asia, *see* MacDonald
Commissioner for Labour, *see* Labour
Commissioner of Police (*see also* Gray, Young), 67, 73–4
  his authority in relation to that of the Director of Operations, 291, 322–3, 333, 353; on improved labour situation (1948), 76
Committee of Review Advisory Committees, 188–9
Communalism, drift towards, 156–60
Communications network and supply routes (MCP) (*see also* Supplies, Communist), 350–1, 472, 473, 502–3; between Singapore and Malaya, 372–3; between Thailand and Malaya, 373
Communism (*see also* Hsueh Hsih *and* Soviet Union), 315, 320, 459, 463–4, 467
  Malayan, *see* Malayan Communist Party; policy changed after German invasion of, 21
Communist associations, 260–1
Communist influence, growth of (1947), 78

INDEX

Communist International, 2nd Congress of (1922), 19
Communist Party of Malaya, *see* Malayan Communist Party
Communist and Workers' Parties of the British Commonwealth. 2nd Conference (1954), 459
Communists outside Malaya, *see* Asian Communists
 Chinese Communist Party; India, Communist Party of; Soviet Union; *and* Thai Communists Communities' Liaison Committee, 269
Compensation under Regulation 17D, 190, 198
Conduct of Anti-Terrorist Operations in Malaya, The, 369
Conference of Rulers
 attitude to Chinese, 301, 324; Deputy High Commissioner's position, 335–6; non-Malayans in Civil Service, 346; oppose Onn, 330; resettlement criticisms, 394
Conscription (*see also* National Servicemen), 300–1, 314, 425; starts November 1950, 252; to Police Force, 302, 354
Constitution (*see also* Citizenship; Independence; *and* Malayan Government)
 Chinese position, 328, 330–1, 338, 341–2, 344, 459; Lyttelton concerned about tangle, 334–5
Consuls, problem of Chinese, 214–5, 216, 231
Contingent Research Section, 474
Contingent Special Branch Organisation, 473
Corporal punishment, *see* Flogging
Corry, W. C. S., British Adviser, Pahang (author of *A General Survey of New Villages*), 396, 403n
Council of World Democratic Youth (1954), 459–60
Counter-terror, approach to a, 160–9
CPI, *see* India, Communist Party of
CPOs (*see* Chief Police Officers)
Creech Jones (Colonial Secretary, 1948), 163n
Crime Regulations *and* Law and Justice (*see also* Emergency)
 in towns, 288; Lyttelton's plan, 327; murders, political, 88, 92–3; police task, 285; wave of crime in 1947, 498, 499
Criminal Investigation Department (renamed Intelligence Bureau), 80, 275–6
Cuban analogy, 88–90
Curfews
 in the Bahau/Jelebu area, 483; in Johore (south), 241n, 245; at Semenyih, 406; at Tanjong Malim, 340–1; reduced, 485; suspended in 'White Areas', 378–9; tightened, 489
Current Situation in Malaya, The (MCP document), 50
 Sharkey responsible for?, 52–3

D

Dakota squadron, 371
Dalforce (Dalley's Chinese army), 79–80
Dalley, Lieut.-Colonel John (head of MSS), 126
 analyses security position (June 1948), 80–3, 115, 116; career of, 79–80
David, Edgeworth
 indictment of Regulation 17D by, 190–2
Davis, J. L. H.
 and Ferret Force, 132, 133, 221n; Force 136; resistance contact with Chin Peng, 463n
Death penalty, 141, 383–5
 extension of mandatory, 241n
Deep jungle bases (MCP)
 aborigines and, 439–56; affected by Security Forces, 448, 455, 476; bombing of, 455–6; cultivation in, 439, 440; purpose, 439–40; reinforced, 486n
Deep jungle operations (Security Forces), 136, 137, 226, 364–9 *passim*, 439–40, 476–83 *passim*
 domination of jungle, 238, 246, 247
 (*see also* Jungle forts *and* Police jungle squads)
Defence Co-ordination Committee in Singapore, 117, 139–40, 202, 229, 232
 believe that civil as well as military measures are necessary (1950), 232; 'Briggs Plan' reported to (May, 1950), 237
del Tufo, M. V. (Officer Administering Government), 323, 324–5, 329, 334–5

'Democratic People's Republic' (Malaya), 315
Department of Aborigines, 445–6, 450
Department of Malay Work, 473
Department of Public Relations responsible for propaganda and Emergency information, 416
Deportation
  of Chinese, 211, 324–5, 332, 335; of Indians, 211; mass or selected, 178–9; no 'general policy of', 176; right of, 141n
Deputy Director of Operations, 352–3
Deputy High Commissioner (see also MacGillivray, D.C.), 328n, 335–6
Detainees, 232, 267
  appeals by; deportation of Communist, vital, 244; number of (1948), 184; objections to women and children as, 183, 189; release and resettlement of, 201–2; resettlement of, 197–9; six, 12 and finally 24 months, 184; thousands of, awaiting repatriation (1950), 232
Detention camps, 142, 180, 189, 245
  a 'forcing house for Communism', 193
Detention, 301, 335, 385 (see also Emergency Regulations No. 17)
  collective, 188; for squatters unwilling to return voluntarily to China, 179
Detention orders, 142, 179
Devonshire Regiment, 1st Battalion, 113, 225
Directives (Briggs Plan), 248 bis
  No. 1 Police and Army collaboration, 248; No. 2 State Chinese Affairs Officers, 240; No. 3 Chinese Village Guards, 241n; No. 10 (January 1951), Regrouping and concentration schemes, 249
Director of Intelligence, 276, 360, 360n (see also Jenkin, Sir William and Madoc, G. C.)
Director of Operations (see also Bourne, Briggs, Brooke, Cassels, and Templer)
  annual review (1955), 472; annual review (1956), 477, 486
  his authority in relation to that of Chief Secretary, 234; Commissioner of Police, 291, 322–3; of High Commissioner, 322–3, 325, 334, 336; and of; Officer Administering Government, 334
Deputy President of Federal War Council, 250; Malcolm MacDonald on job of, 323; position no longer needed, 493; staff organisation, 352–3; on units in Malaya, 113–14
District Officers (DO), 153, 175, 342 bis, 402, 407, 441
District War Executive Committees food denial operations, 376, 377, 476; versus MCP District, 478
DO, see District Officer
Dobree, C. T. W., Asst Police Commissioner
  Kachau tragedy uncovered by, 163, 165 and n
Dominion Estate (Selangor), attack on (1948), 163, 164
'Double Tenth' revolt (1911), 436
Dual nationality
  of Chinese, 459; of Indians, 274n
Dunlop, General (GOC Singapore) on squatter locations as enemy areas, 178
Dyaks (from Borneo)
  Ferret Force's use of, 132

E

Eastern Exchange Banks Association, 118n
Eden (Robert) Anthony (later Earl of Avon), 328
Education
  adult education, 343, 399; Barnes Report, 435; Communist activities in schools, 302, 362, 428–38; Fenn-Wu Report, 435; lack of, in rural areas, 331
  Malayanisation in schools, 339, 435; New Village schools', 348, 398–9, 404; of Chinese, 198–9, 428–38 passim; primary education, 435; shortage of trained teachers, 232
Education Department—only one Chinese-speaking European office, 232
Elections
  Federal (1955), 460, 461; local (1952), 346
Elphil Estate (Perak), murders in (1948), 93

INDEX

Emergency, the state of (Communist insurrection, 1948–60) (*see also* Commissioner of Police, Director of Operations, High Commissioner, Intelligence services, Security Forces), 5, 43, 56, 70
annual review by Director of Operations (1955), 472; (1956), 477, 486; all emergency matters to be handed over to Federal War Council or State War Committees—Briggs Plan (1950), 251; attempt to put it into perspective (1949), 144–8; beginning of, 80, 83, 469–9; Communist pattern of attack, 95–113; counter-insurgency principles, 501
Declaration of (18 June 1948), 90, 93–4; discussed in Legislative Council, 296–8; ends (1960), 495; evaluation of Malaya in, 160–9; expenditure, obtaining approval for, 251; finance and economy, 267–8, 283, 346–9, 496
forces' insufficiency during first 4 years of, 149; foreshadowed by the Resistance (1941), 24; Government consultations preceding (1948), 65–8; 'must be brought to an end in 1951'— Gurney, 252; no Chinese consul to be appointed for duration of, 216; policy change after Gurney's death, 305, 306, 325
reasons why it 'is dragging on' (1949), 187; regulations introduced by Gurney, 140–3; responsibility for, 65–94; turning point (1951), 275; unsettling effect of, 157
Emergency Chinese Advisory Committee, 215, 266
Emergency Information Services, 416–22 *passim*
Emergency Operations Council, 469, 487
Emergency Regulations (*see also* Curfews *and* Detention *and* Food control), 218; abolition required by MCP before peace, 460, 462, 468–9, 470; and civil rights, 380; books proscribed, 437, 438; collective punishment, 385–6; death penalty for guerrillas, 383–5
gate searches, 405–11, 478–9; relaxation of Regulations (1956), 484–5; 'Selected Areas', 485, 494–5; stifle political growth, 337; tin mines, 349*n*; 'White Areas', 378–9; No. 17 (*see also* Detention), 159; No. 17A ('controlled areas'), 249; No. 17D, 188, 189, 193 *ter*, 197, 201 *ter*; No. 17E (May 1949), 194; No. 17F (August 1949), 194 *bis*
'Empire' Communist Conference, London (1947), 44
Employers (*see also* Property management)
'bloody-minded or incompetent', 32; Chinese, 32, 92
ER, *see* Emergency Regulation
Essential Regulations Proclamation, Emergency measures taken under (June 1948), 141–3
Estates and planters (*see also* Property management for entries covering both Estates and Mines)
attitude to armoured police vehicles, 278 *n*, 279–81; and conscription, 301; defence forces armed and paid for by, 126; force Gray's removal, 306; and Government policy (1951), 297
Malayan State Owners' Association, 127; managers in jeopardy (1948), 106; nationalisation recommended by MCP, 311–2; New Village workers' problems, 406–11; protection or immunity bought from guerrillas?, 267, 299–300; rubber industry affected by Emergency, 346–9; use of Special Constables, 284–5, 290, 291
European community
attitude to casualties, 280; attitude to IMP, 329–30; criticised by Templer, 342; on protection money, and drumhead courts, 332; security of their property, 122; to be shown as not invincible (1948), 87; three estate managers murdered (16 June 1948), 93
'Evangelise China Fellowship', 400
Eviction orders by State rulers, 194
Exco, *see* Executive Council
Ex-Comrades' Association
continuing organisation of MPAJA, 25; unhelpfulness of (1945), 36
Executive Council, 323, 325 *bis*
banishment cases to be reviewed

524 INDEX

Executive Council (*continued*)
  by, 178; Extraordinary meeting of (June 1948), 76–7; merges with War Council, 338, 346; Morib camp condemned by member of (1948), 182; its power criticised, 383; reaction of, to Squatter Committee report, 194–5; suspected guerrillas and, 184
Expenditure on Emergency, 251 *bis*

F

Facer, H. H., 7
  and banning of MCP, 75–6; on subversion in Malaya, 73
Federal Committee on the Squatter Problem, *see* Squatter Committee
Federal Court of Appeal, 385
Federal Government (*see also* Administration, Civil; Constitution; Executive Council; High Commissioner: and Legislative Council)
  administrative system, 402; clash with Perak State, 181–2; coalition suggested, 459; constraint of, 149–169; disadvantages of, at start of insurrection, 120
  Emergency policy meeting (1951), 322; maintenance of, 113–48; Member system, 273–4, 334–5, 402; no Malays in War Cabinet, 273; political advances criticised, 380–1, 383
  policy regarding strikes, 30; possible examination of records by, 6; reluctant to take action against suspects, 183; War footing recommended (1950), 250; withdraws approval of this book's publication, 5; its writ did not run for rural Chinese (1948), 173, 175
Federal Joint Intelligence Advisory Committee, 240
Federal War Council, 212, 273, 323, 338, 346
  appeals to, 246; assisted by an Intelligence Advisory Committee, 239–40; composition of, 239; Emergency matters to be handed over to—Briggs Plan (1950), 251; High Commissioner to preside over, 250
Federation Agreement, 341
Federation Plan for the Elimination of the Communist Organisation ... (the 'Briggs Plan' *qv*), 237
Federation Regiment, The, 339, 480*n*
Federations of Trade Unions, State (*see also* Pan-Malayan)
  action against, proposed, 67, 71–2; condemned by visiting British trade unionists (1948), 31; 'desperation' of (1948), 66–7; Government's policy regarding, 30–1, 67; 'MCP had betrayed', 51; registration refused (1948), 93, 108
Fences (*see also* Gate searches), 173, 250, 391–406 *passim*, 413
'Fenn-Wu Report, the', on Malayan education, 435
'Ferret Force', 132–3
  Malay one needed, 209; officer's 'troubled conscience', 161
Fijian Battalion, 369, 480*n*
Financial Times, on fighting near Kuala Lumpur (July 1948), 136
Flogging proposed, 76, 77
Fonblanque, Major-General E. B. de, 412
Fong Feng, General (of CCP Central Committee), 44 *bis*
Food denial operations, 238, 246, 375–9
  cease for amnesty, 477; guerrilla counter-measures, 475–6; method of operation (in Pahang), 472–6; mistakes, 478; resettlement and, 241; results, 486–7, 489
Foo Chee Hwa (guerrilla leader), 110
Food control (Emergency Regulation), 375–9
  importance to Security Forces success, 483–5; relaxed (1956), 485; in resettlement areas, 292; at Semenyih, 408; in the Tapah District, 478–80
Food Denial Organisation, set up (1956), 485
Food supplies, Communist (*see also* Supplies, Communist, Rice and Tapioca)
  aborigine help, 447–8; deep jungle bases, cultivation in, 439–440, 475; food dumps, 321, 475, 477; gate searches in New

INDEX 525

Villages, 405–11, 478–9; shortage forces guerrilla attacks, 294; shortage limits guerrilla action, 350*n*
'For a Lasting Peace, For a People's Democracy!', Cominform paper (1947), 45
Force 136 (of Special Operations Executive, 1943), 23 bis, 24*n*, 277
  officers' killing suggested (1945), 34; officers of, and Ferret Force, 132 bis, 133*n*
Forestry Department, and opening up of forest reserves by peasants, 175, 176
Fort Brooke (Kelantan), 449–50
Fort Dickson (HQ of Malay Regt.) Ferret Force based upon, 133
Forts, Jungle, see Jungle forts
Framework operations (Security Forces), 156, 478, 482
Freedman, Professor M., 255*n*
Freedom News (MCP), 430, 459
Frontier Force, 134–5
  police control of, 134–5
Frontier Intelligence Bureau, 375

G

Gallacher, W. (Communist M.P. in Britain), 326–327
Galloway, Lieut.-General (GOC Malaya)
  and garrison reduction, 78, 113; on strongest timely action (1947), 78
Gate searches, 405–11, 478–9
Gelang Patah-Pontian District Committee, 432
Gemas Bahru Branch (MCP in Johore), 489–90
General Labour Unions
  all-purpose associations, 28; control over registered, 90; democracy lacking in, 30; demonstration of their power (1946), 28–9; established in all states, 29; impregnable till T.U. Ordinance is passed, 75; political power of, 30
Gent, Sir Edward (High Commissioner)
  accused of not having won Asians' confidence (June 1948), 118, 122–3; assistance to police asked for by banishment policy of (1948), 70*n*, 72, 449; complains of inadequate Intelligence (1948), 85; despatch to C.O. (June 1948), 59
  difficulties of his position (1948), 73; European representatives' meeting with (June 1948), 72–6; father of the Federation (FMS), 120; meeting with MacDonald and Gimson (1948), 85*n*, 114–7; and squatters, 177; recalled, but dies in air-crash en route, 119; views of, on crisis (1948), 70, 72
Gimson, Sir Franklin (Governor of Singapore, 85*n*), 114
Glen (steamship) Line, 118*n*
Glendale Estate (Bahau), 484
Glossary, 15–16
Ganapathy, S. A. (Indian Communist leader), hanged (1949), 210
GOC Malaya, see Boucher
Goh Peng Tuan (Political Commissar of the MCP Seventh Independent Platoon), 482
Government, see Federal government
Government Forces, see Security Forces
Governor General, 331
Governors of South-east Asian territories and colonies, Conference attended by Lyttelton, 334
Gray, Col. W. N. (Commissioner of Police, qv, 121, 126
  appointment's results, 131*n*, 140, 141, 501; bans further evictions without Federal authority (1948), 181; bleak account of situation (1950), 219–20; defends operations under Regulation 17D, 193; co-ordination of operations by, 234; directive to, re destruction of houses, 153–4
  disagrees with Briggs and Gurney on resettlement, 288–9; disagrees with Briggs on jungle companies, 287; disagrees with Briggs on police organisation, 287–91; disagrees with Jenkin on intelligence organisation, 275–6; Lyttelton's criticisms, 335
  MCA criticised by, 268; opposes use of armoured vehicles, 276–81; Paper on the Security Situation, by, with GOC (April

S*

526 INDEX

Gray, Col. W. N. (*continued*)
1949), 146; on para-military and civil functions of police, 281–9, 291, 442; on 'protection money', 223; removed as Commissioner (1951), 306, 335; war footing proposals similar to Brigg's (1950), 252 activities' of the MCP, 433

Griffiths, James (Secretary of State for the Colonies), 268, 326

Gua Musang (Kelantan), 109, 111 guerrillas' brief capture of, 102–4, 137, 207

Guards (*see also* Kampong Guards) auxiliary police work, 356; Briggs' recommendations, 289–90; used by property management, 284, *bis*; Village, 241

Guards, Brigade of, arrival of 3 battalions (October, 1948), 135, 139

Guerrilla Forces, 95, 104, 107, 209–10, 218; *see also* Casualties among guerrillas; Deep jungle bases; Food supplies, Communist; Independent Platoons; Malayan Communist Party; Malayan People's Anti-Japanese Army; Supplies, Communist; Surrendered enemy personnel
  activities, in and around New Villages, 391–4, 405; amnesty and, 220–1; basic requirements of, 97; camps for, 97–8; Chinese opinion and, 147; communications poor but information good, 235; denial of food to, *see* Food denial
  denying food and support to, 202, 238; difficult to identify, 160–2, 223, 246–7; executions within the force, 313, 421, 492; 5th (Perak) Regiment of, 226, 227; 4th and 5th Regiments' tribulations, 104
  independence and peace policy, 460–71 *passim*; Johore forces receive setback (1948), 309, 310, 312; killer gangs unlikely to surrender, 221; KMT and MPAJA, 133n; Lam Swee as Political Commissar of the 4th Regiment, 310
  major incidents reached their peak (September 1950), 211; MRLA ceases as an organised military force (1958), 492–3; one major incident a week (1949), 204; tenacity of, 505; registration disrupted by (1948), 143
  relations with aborigines, 367, 391, 441, 444, 447–55 *passim*, 493; reports of low morale (1949), 111; resurgence of (1950), 206–30, 231; Siew Lau's recommendations, 312; strength (1950), 213
  strength and location (1951–4), 349–52, 366, 367, 373–4, 386–7; (1955), 472; (1956), 480–2 (1956–60), 486–7, 489, 494, 495; (1960), 505–6; tactics, 277, 321, 500; successes against, a mere 'rap on the knuckles' (1950), 235; 10th Regiment eliminated (1949), 210; 12th Regiment of, 227; weapons captured and lost by (1948–50), 212

Gullick, John M., 261, 273n, 274n, 461n

Gurkha Infantry Brigade, 26th, arrival of (March 1950), 229

Gurkha Rifles, 6th, First Battalion, 367

Gurkha troops in Malaya, 93, 110, 353, 366, 369
  bias in favour of, 226; Ferret Force's use of, 132; not to be used for strike breaking, 74; reduction of (1947), 78; regiments named, 113–4, 229; special constable mistakenly killed by (1949), 162

Gurney, Sir Henry (High Commissioner), 121, 123, 140
  aftermath of his death, 322, 324, 325 *bis*; announces turning point of Emergency (1951), 275; attitude to police use of armoured vehicles, 279–81; attitude to political and military co-operation, 323
  and the Chinese community: Chinese in the MCS, 346n, he describes groups within community, 256–9; he favours Malayan Chinese Party, 261–2; his relations with the Chinese, 298–303; on Chinese citizenship, 338; reports on MCA, 265–6
  Colonial Office notified by (January 1949) of Regulation 17D; Conference with *Mentri Besar* and British Advisers (1949), 187–8; disagrees with Gray on police organisation, 289, 291; disagrees with Gray

INDEX

on resettlement, 228–9; in discussion on aborigne policy, 442
Dispatch No. 1 (January 1949) to Colonial Secretary, 144–5; emergency regulations introduced by, 140–3; Kachau burning admitted wrong by, 166; Kedah Mentri Besar's letter to (November 1948), 180–1; killed in ambush, 303–5
meeting held by, to discuss squatter problem (1949), 196; opposes appointment of Chinese consuls, 214, 216n; opposes Jenkin, 276; his schemes for squatter problem, 201; on violence to people in police custody, 299

H

Hailam Kang, security operations at (1948), 110
Haji Mohamed Yusoff, Dato, 272n speaks in Legislative Council on public co-operation, 297–8
Harbour Board, see Singapore Harbour Board
Harding, Gen. Sir John (C.-in-C. FARELF)
asks for additional brigade (1950), 229; opposed to recognition of Chinese Government (1950), 215; on 'slumping public morale', 233
Harvards, 371n
Harrison & Crosfield, defence forces recruited by, in Singapore, 126
Healey, Dennis (Defence Secretary), on Batang Kali shootings, 168
Hedley, Brigadier (GOC Johore), 123, 124n
appointed Deputy-Director of Operations (1950), 248; promoted Major-General and GOC South Malaya (1950), 248
Helicopters, use of, 367, 369–70, 372
Hertogh, Maria, case of (Singapore, 1950), 252
High Commissioner (see also Deputy High Commissioner, also Gent, Gurney, Templer)
the position of its authority, 322–3, 325, 334, 336; to preside over Federal War Council, 250
High Court (in Kuala Lumpur), Watts-Carter Case, 299–300

Hill people, see Aborigines
Ho Ah Chung (of Harbour Board Labour Union), 55
Ho Chi Minh, arrest of, 20
Home Guards
Briggs' Directives, 293; Chinese Sections, 252, 270, 413, 488–9; Lyttelton's plan, 333; New Village work, 393, 400, 404, 411–5; Operational Sections, 412, 413, 414–5, 480n; reconstructed (1956), 414–5; responsibilities, 353; 'White Areas' units reduced, 379
Homes, destruction of, see Buildings and Property
Hong Kong:
fate of, 216; reinforcements for Malaya from, 229, 230
Hor Lung (Head of MCP Southern Bureau), 352
plans for *Min Yuen*, 476; surrenders, 59n, 490
Hsueh Hsih (Chinese study societies), 436–7
Hung Chi Basketball Team (Ayer Baloi), 433
Hyslop, J. A. (Perak State Protector of Aborigines), 442
Hung Lee (Triad Society), 425–6

I

Identity cards, see Registration, national
IMP, see Independence for Malaya Party
INA, see Indian National Army
Incident of Lam Swee going over to the enemy . . . (MCP publication), 311
Incorporated Society of Planters, 118n, 183
Independence (see also United Malaya, 156, 232
achieved (1957), 470, 503; attitude of population, 271, 329–30, 504–5; British MPs attitudes, 327–8; effect on Security Force operations, 323, 486; first Parliamentary commitment (1949), 327
Lyttelton's view, 333–4; MCP and guerrilla policy, 460–71 *passim*; multi-racial basis, 503; security and national defence, 465, 466; Templer's work for, 337, 380–1

528　INDEX

Independence for Malaya Party favoured by British Government? 331, 345; members not to be guerrilla victims, 321; purpose of Party, 329–30; UMNO and MCA attitude, 345
Independent Platoons (MCP), 473, 481, 482, 486
India, Communist Party of, 47–8, 317, 329
Indian Communism in Malaya setbacks to (1949), 210–1
Indian community, 274n
Indian Empire, its liquidation sets example, 37
Indian National Army, influence of, 32, 210
　officers recruited for Home Guard, 412
Indian Navy, mutiny in (1945), 46
Indians, Malayan, 274n
　banishment orders and, 72; cadres of, if attacked, to be transferred to other States, 57; Chinese strikers backed by (1948), 54; inexhaustible labour supply of, 28; vulnerability of estate labourers, 211
Indonesia, example of, 156
Industrial unrest (see also Strikes), 60
　employers partly to blame for?, 66
Intelligence agents (MCP), see Min Yuen
Intelligence Services
　(see also Combined Intelligence Staff; Jenkin; Madoc and Special Branch Contingent)
　aborigine information, 452–3; achievements against MCP, 360–3, 366, 375, 487, 488; Briggs Plan and, 244; difficult to get information on guerrillas, 222, 223–4, 230; evaluates MCP policy, 316; failure of (1947–8)? 77–90, 85–6, 88, 137, 145, 155, 229–30
　food denial operations, 375–9, 473–5; good in Perak (1948), 111; Gurney's death investigations, 304; Hsueh Hsih study, 436–7; key to counter-insurgency, 502, 503
　MacDonald urges new organisation (1948), 85; Malayan-Thai team, 375; MCP's superior to British (1950), 211; Military Intelligence Officers, 363; MSS' divorced from police's, 86

New Village security, 403–4; police take over manning and expansion, 275–6, 282, 285; protection racket reports, 299; re-organisation leading to successes, 359–63; Templer's plan, 343; Thai border work, 375 bis
Intelligence (Special Branch) Training School, 360
Intelligence Summary, see Combined Intelligence
Internal Security Committee, functions and meetings of, 122, 139
International Union of Students, 45
Intimidation (see also Violence), 31, 66 bis, 85n, 176–7
　evidence of, hard to obtain, 74, 90; firmness needed in dealing with (1948), 72; by murder (1948), 87; of witnesses makes law a farce, 75, 90
'Invulnerability cults', 151
Ipoh (Perak)
　killer squads close to (1950), 219; police headquarters in, 20 miles from Army HQ, 248
Irregular (government) forces, 132–4; jungle squads, 165
Ishak bin Haji Mohammed, detention of, 143
Islamic Party (Persatuan Islam Sa-malaya), 470–1

J

Jalong (Perak)
　houses burnt in, 162
Japanese invasion of China (1937), effects of, 21
Japanese occupation of Malaya (1941–5)
　aborigine reaction, 441, 445; Chinese land settlement and, 204; Chinese reaction, 300, 408; few weapons left after, 497; resistance to, 21–5, 127n, 204
Java and Sumatra, 'reign of terror' in (1948), 84
Jelebu (Negri Sembilan), 483–4
Jelebu Pass (Negri Sembilan), guerrilla ambush on police vehicles, 278–9
Jenkin, Sir William (Director of Intelligence), 275–6, 329, 335, appointed as adviser on Special 360

INDEX

Branch work, 240; resignation of (1951), 335
Johore
  API youths trained in guerrilla warfare, 143; army strength weak in, 114; Briggs, did he and, see eye to eye on resettlement?, 246; Briggs Plan, operations began in (1 June 1950), 239, 241; A British Adviser's paper on the Briggs Plan (1950), 246-7; British officers' killing suggested (1945), 34; Chinese schools, 399; clearance of squatters in, 187
  Commissioner-General's visits to, 123; guerrilla activities in, 109, 111, 161-2, 227; guerrilla organisations disintegrate, 309, 310, 312; guerrilla strength, 101, 350, 352, 489, 491; Gurkhas stationed there, 353
  'liberated areas' in, 188; the 'Long March', 309, 310, 321; mass surrender of guerrillas, 490-1; MCP activity in, 476; MCP influence Home Guard, 414
  Min Yuen, active in, 227; mobilization haphazard in (1948), 96; notorious Scudai/Pontian area of, 26; operations in, 138; planters ask for Gent to go, 119
  police reinforced in (1948), 76; Pontian Case, 432-4; 'population half-starved', 483; and resettlement of squatters, 198, 199, 202; riots in (1948), 91
  Security Force concentration (1957), 486; Security Force weak in, 213; South Johore Regional Committee, 432, 434, 439; squatters, its attitude to, 197-200; 30,000 squatters in (1950), 246; unrepresented at Gurney's installation, 121; violence in (1947), 27; (1948), 92-3, 161-2; Working Committee meeting of Siew Lau, 311, 312
Johore Bahru
  Chinese, 264n; students arrested, 438
Johore Planters' Association, 245n
Johore Squatter Resettlement Committee, 198
Johore State Liaison Committee
  advisory rather than executive, 123-4; composition of, 123

Johore State Secretariat and Press, 352
Johore State War Committee, 245
Johore State War Executive Committee, 245
Joint Control Authority, 372n
Joint Intelligence Advisory Committee report (1950), 212
Joo Lim Saw Mill, attempted arson at (1948), 55
Josey, Alex (Staff Officer, Emergency Information), 244-5
June Resolutions of the Central Politburo (1949), 208
Jungle forts
  built by PAAC, 442; effect on MCP and aborigines, 448; principal purpose, 445, 446
Jungle squads, *see* Police jungle squads
Jungle warfare, *see* Deep jungle bases (MCP) *and* Deep jungle operations (Security Forces)
Junior Chinese Affairs officers, 240
  duties of, 240-1
Justice and the law, *see also* Appeal Court; Emergency Regulations; High Court; Police Force, 332-3, 339, 383-5

K

Kachau (Selangor) ('Little Yenan') burnt down on orders of OCPD Kajang (1948), 162-6
Kajang (Selangor)
  detainees from, 267; first operation under ER 17D carried out in, 189; hotbed of guerrilla activity, 100, 101-2, 110; OCPD of, orders destruction of Kachau, 162-6
'Kajang Gang' (notorious guerrillas), 410
Kampar (Perak), terrorist attack in, 206
Kampong Guards
  cause police extra work, 288; given $10,000 reward (1949), 209; success against guerrillas, 285-6
Kampongs
  defended by Home Guards, 413; expenditure diverted from, 401; guerrillas in, 208-9; Town Boards not suited to, 401; Village Councils introduced, 402

INDEX

'Kapitan China', 256
Kedah
  Army in, 353; asks for armoured police vehicles, 279–80; attitude of, to Chinese cash crops, 195, 197; border-state problems of, 134–5; British Adviser's warning on squatters, 179
  clearance of squatters in (1949), 189; CPO Kedah killed, 372; deep jungle bases, 439; liaison between Army and police negligible, 154; MCP activity, 476
  Mentri Besar's letter to Gurney (November 1948), 180–1; MRLA casualties and recruitment in, 213; police informers of low calibre, 228–9; police and Mentri Besar disagree over squatters, 153; police paramilitary operations in, 131
  police posts closed (1948), 106, 114, 138; resettlement of squatters, its attitude to, 197, 202; resettlement opposed by, 197; resettlement subsistance grant, 395n; riots (1947), 76; Security Force and intelligence problem, 493; Sultan of, 394
Keightley, Gen. Sir Charles (C-in-C FARELF), 276
Kelantan, 104, 111
  aborigine policy, 442–4, 449–50; border-state police problems of, 135 *bis*; deep jungle bases, 439; five new police stations authorused (December 1948), 131
Kemaman (Trengganu), refugees in (November 1948)
Kerinching (*Asal* leader), 454
Kernial Singh Sandhu, 391n, 403n, 405n
Khaw Kai Boh (Perak Security Officer), his report (1948), 86
Khoo Teck Ee (member of Legislative Council), 266
'Killer squads'
  pamphlet left on victims' bodies by, 107–8
Killing grounds in food denial operations, 475, 491
King's African Rifles, The, 369
King's House (High Commissioner's home), telephones tapped, 305 *bis*
Kinta (Perak)
  aborigines and guerrillas, 441
Kinta Valley Home Guard, 270
Klang (Selangor)

Communist involvement in Chinese schools, 431; Students' Union, 431, 432
Klapa Bali estate (Perak), strikes and evictions on (1948), 92
Klian Intan (Perak),
  violence in (1947), 27
Kluang, OSPC, his account of a Johore tragedy, 162
Kluang area (Johore)
  food restrictions relaxed, 485; guerrilla activity centre, 352; Lam Swee's propaganda, 418n; Security Forces activity, 353
KMT, *see* Kuomintang
Kongsi house system, the, 203
Korea, pressure to free troops for (1950), 248
Kota Tinggi (Johore), 114
  guerrilla activities in, 109, 110
KOYLI, 1st Battalion
  strength of (1950), 225
Kroh (Perak), 470
Ku Tien Conference, Western Fukien (1929), 320–1
Kuala Krau (Pahang), 207
  guerrilla attack on (1949), 206; police station attacked (1948), 96
Kuala Langat (Selangor)
  Operation *Hammer*, 365–6
Kuala Lumpur
  Air Headquarters, Malaya, moved there, 370; Chinese consul in, 214; guerrilla activity centre, 351; HQ, Malaya Command there, 370
  insurgents prepare to filter into (1948), 136; MCP activity among students, 432; municipal elections (1953), 345; Students' Union changes name to Anti-British League, 432
Kuantan (Pahang)
  cause for alarm in (July 1948), 149; New Villages, 396–7; Operation *Habitual*, 365
Kulai (Johore), 488
  guerrilla stronghold (1948), 109, 110; major guerrilla raid, 488
Kuomintang (Chinese Nationalist Party), 20, 21, 24n, 108
  allegiance to China, 256, 257, 258; banditry in its irregular forces, 24; conflict with Communists, 26, 88; government's overthrow (1949), 214; guerrillas kill three members, 99–100

INDEX   531

Johore leaders shot dead (1948), 93; loss of mainland China by, its effect, 201; Malayan Chinese support for, 37 MCP target, 321n, 499, 500; *San Min Chu Yi* Youth Corps, 260–1; secret societies, 425; supporters, 265
Kwok Lau (Central Committee member), 351

L

Labour, Commissioner for, 65, 66 bis
Labour, Deputy Commissioner of, his Situation Report (November 1948), 182
Labour in Malaya (*see also* General Labour Unions)
 blacklegs, murder of, 87; Commissioner for, *see* Commissioner for . . .; defended in Legislative Council (1948), 68, 69–70 'estates controlled by' (1947), 32: (1948), 91; lawlessness of, 68, 72, 74–5; post-war immobility of, 28; pre-war tranquility of, 28
Labour movement
 Communist penetration of, 146
Labour Party, 338, 469, 470–1
Lam Chun Fuk (Secretary of a Labour Union), 55
Lam Swee (defector from Communist hierarchy), 110, 206, 309–11, 417, 418n, 421
My Accusation, 310–11
Land hunger, 174, 177
Land Office fees, 196
Land tenure, 195, 339, 340, 395–6, 403, 404
Langkap (Perak), murder in, 205
Language and literacy problems, 408, 417, 418, 421
Langworthy, H. B., Police Commissioner, resignation of, 120
Lattre de Tassigny, Marshal J. de (Commander in Indo-China), 323
Lau Choon Toh (MCP organiser in Johore), 434
Lau Lee (Head of Central Propaganda Dept.), 350, 351
Lau Mah (guerrilla leader), killing of, 206
Lau Siew (MCP member, critic of Party leadership), 313n

Lau Tong Tui (*see also* 'killer squads'), 95
Lau Yew (President of MPAJA Ex-Communists' Association), 96
Law and justice, *see* Justice and the law
Lawlessness (*see also* Intimidation *and* Violence), 178
Layang Layang (Johore), 483
Lee, Col. H. S. (member of Legislative Council)
 meets with Gurney, 266; opposes the member system, 274n; on violent crime, 77, 218n
Lee Ah Tai (girl guerrilla), 385
Lee Meng (*Min Yuen* 'grenade girl'), 384–5
Lee Moy (Chinese widow), 267
Lee Soong (MCP delegate at Calcutta), 49, 52
Legislative Council
 Commission of Inquiry rejected (1948), 68, 70; debate on the crisis (1948), 66, 68–71, 93; Emergency discussed (1951), 296–9; independence promise, 464; Indian pro-Gent motion tabled in (1948), 119; MCP condemned in (1948), 93; paper on the squatter problem (1950), 201; restricting work of— Briggs Plan (1950), 251; Templer's appointment opposed by, 337; Templer's first speech in, 338–40
Leng Goan (of CCP), 44
Lenggong (Perak), Communists set up own government in, 204
Lenin Publishing Press, propaganda by (1948), 108–9
Leonard, G. R. (long-range jungle group), 133n
Leong Tung Seng (MCP Branch Committee member), 492
Leong Yew Koh
 his motion against appointment of Chinese consul (Perak), 315; named as member of Federal War Council, 273
Leow Cheng Chi (of CCP), 44
Le Tam (Vietnamese delegate to Calcutta Conference), 46
Liaison Committee, lack of information from, 223n
'Liberated areas', 188, 207, 208
'Liberator' (U.S. Bomber: B.24) helps Force 136
Liew Yau (MCP and MPAJA), 101

INDEX

Liew Yit Fan (MPAJA and MCP), arrested (1948), 60, 93
Lim Ah Liang, 311
Lim Hong Bee (writer of *Malaya Fights for Freedom*), 459
Lima Blas estate (Perak), riots and evictions on (1948), 92
Lincoln heavy bombers, 371 arrival of (1950), 248
Lipis West District (Pahang), 473
Listowel, 5th Earl of (Secretary of State for Colonies), 135
'Little Devils' (ten-year-old spies and smugglers), 472*n*
'Little Yenan', *see* Kachau
Liu Shao-Ch'i (CCP), 316
Lloyd, Air-Marshal (AOC), Gent's dismissal and, 119
Lloyd, Sir Thomas (in the Colonial Office), 264
Local Defence Committee, 188
  Combined Intelligence Staff responsible to, 140; meetings of, 121–2, 134; recommendation on squatters, 183
Lockhart, Gen. Sir Rob (Deputy Director of Operations), 352–3
Loi Tak, Sec.-Gen. of MCP (1942), 22, 79*n*
  alias of, *see* Wright; career of, 39–40; contact with CCP, 44; criticism of, 40–1, 310; defection of, 41–2
Long March, The, 309, 321
Longden, Gilbert (Conservative M.P.), 327
Lotteries banned, 346*n*, 386
Lukut Branch (MCP in Johore), 491–2
Lumut (Perak), Sungei Siput's squatters removed to (1948), 182
Lyttelton, Oliver (Secretary of State for the Colonies; later Lord Chandos)
  chooses Templer as High Commissioner (1952), 325–6; criticises Police Force, 334, 335; Emergency policy, 326, 333; 'Gray must go', 306; Home Guard re-organised, 412; meets planters, 306*n*; meets Rahman, 330; *Memoirs of Lord Chandos* (1962), *q*, 326*n*; plans for a united Malaya, 330–6; six-point programme of (1951), 333; UMNO and MCA delegation to, 329, 330; visits Malaya (1951), 329–33

M

MacDonald, Malcolm (Commissioner-General for South-East Asia), 71, 73
  and action against squatters, 178–9; against Templer's appointment, 337; on appointment of Chinese consuls, 214, 215–6; 'burgeoning confidence of' (1949), 145; confrontation with Gent (June 1948), 116–7
  considers number of terrorists underestimated (1948), 86; costs of the Emergency, 267–8; Gent's dismissal and, 118, 119; Internal Security Committee and, 139; MCA and, 265
  meeting with Gent and Gimson (June 1948), 85*n*, 114–7; self-government promised by (1949), 156; suggests Chinese Emergency Corps, 324; visit to China (1948), 107*n*
MacGillivray, D. C. (Deputy High Commissioner), 328*n*, 336, 352, 445
Machap (Malacca), Communist stronghold, 32
Madoc, Guy C. (Director of Intelligence), 8, 360, 486*n*, 502*n*
Majeedi detention camp (Johore), 110, 197
Majlis (FMS newspaper), nationalist views of, 157, 271
Malacca
  Chinese settlements, 255, 257; detention camp, 267; first 'White Area' in, 379; Gurkhas stationed there, 353; labour problems in, 32; MPAJA nearly driven from (1941–5), 99; Working Committee meeting of Siew Lau, 311, 312
Malay and Indonesian Communists (MSS document), 84
Malay bandits (*see also* Guerrilla forces), 208–9
Malay Mail
  public executions idea supported by, 159
Malay Nationalist Party (MNP), 25, 38, 143
Malay Regiment, 139, 225–6
  additional battalion of, 134, 225, 227; advantage when in home territory, 369; Brigade Group (2nd) raised (1949), 144; Fifth Bn. of, 367; First Bn. of, 228,

INDEX

367; 'half the value of' Gurkhas, 226; halting of expansion (1950), 231–2; HQ of, 133*n*; officering of, 333; seven battalions involved, 369
3rd Bn's action by Semur river (March 1950), 231*n*; transport shortage, 140
Malaya
  Communist Party of, *see* Malayan Communist Party; defence of northern frontier, 134; government of, *see* Federal government; increase in number of battalions in, 135–6, 236; independence of, *see* Independence; Southern States for intensified action (1950), 236; war footing, Brig's proposals for putting Malaya on (1950), 250–1
Malaya Command, Headquarters of, 370
'Malaya for the Malays' (UMNO slogan), 329
Malaya Tribune, on Chinese rights, 158
Malayan Chamber of Mines, 118*n*
Malayan Chinese Association (MCA, loyalist body), 187, 197
  anti-guerrilla efforts, 269, 302; detention protest, 301; controversial dinner, 328; food searches, 410; forms Alliance Party with UMNO and Malayan Indian Congress, 345; foundation of, 265–9; guerrillas' attitude to, 321*n*; help for States' resettlement from, 196, 199–200; leaders speak out against banditry (1950), 218*n*; Lyttelton's visit and, 329; New Village work, 398, 400; Purcell's visit and, 381; reception of Arthur Campbell's *Jungle Green*, 382, 386
Malayan Chinese League, 262–3
Malayan Civil Service
  and the Chinese, 256, 270, 346; Lyttelton's plan, 333; Malays discriminated against?, 328*n*, 331; shortage of trained civil servants, 240, 243
Malayan Communist Party (MCP, *see also* Anti-British Leagues; Armed Work Forces; Central Committee; Guerrilla Forces; Masses Executive; *Min Yuen*;

October Directives (1951, Politbureau)
abandons town for normal operations, 362; activities in schools, 302, 362, 428–38; armed struggle begun by (1948), 65, 72; banning of, impracticable?, 75–6, 77, 120; British reoccupation (1945) not opposed by, 34, 35
cash in on farmers' insecurity, 204; CCP's contacts with, 44, 87; Central Committee of, *see* Central Committee, Chinese racial composition of, 19; Chinese secret societies a problem, 426–7
Chinese subscriptions, 264; communications poor but information good, 235; concentrates its struggle in the masses, 33, 208; condemned in Legislative Council (1948), 69, 93; control of Labour Unions by, 29
declared illegal (1948), 94, 96; declining support for (1947), 54; delays political progress, 333–4; designation of, changed, 104; destroyed (1960), 495
District Organisations, 440, 476; foundation of (1930), 20; ideology, 309, 311, 313, 463–4, 467; independence and peace policy, 424, 460–71 *passim*
insurgents and organisation largely unscathed (1949), 211; insurrectionary instructions issued verbally, 58; insurrectionary manifesto of (1 May 1948), 55; Lam Swee's accusations, 309–11; legality of (1945–8), 25
and 'liberated areas', 207–8; members disappear, 499; mobilisation of (1948), 95–8, 183; murder list of, 142*n*, 206, 210; New Village activities, 393
Northern Bureau, 350; objectives of, 21, 78–9, 81–2, 95–109; Plenary Meetings of, *see* Central Committee; PMFTU's May Day programme taken over by, 86; policy, 315–8, 320, 321
policy change (1951), 309; policy criticised by Siew Lau, 311–3; *and* by Lau Siew, 313*n*; Pontian Case, the', 432–4; position in 1973, 506; post-War political record of, 37–9

534 INDEX

Malayan Communist Party (*continued*)
recognition question, 461–8 *passim*, 495; 'represents the Malayan people', 498; resistance to Jap. invasion by, 21–5
rural work, 362; Singapore Labour Union created by (1945), 28; Southern Bureau, 350, 351; State Regional Committees, 350; twenty-four 'martyrs' of, 168; violence benefits (1948), 27, 58; when insurrection was decided upon by, 120

Malayan Democratic Union (MDU) Communists infiltrate, 25; Tan Cheng Lock survives its collapse, 262–3

Malayan Estate Owners' Association, 127

Malayan Film Unit, 420–1

Malayan General Labour Union directed by MCP members, 29; foundation of (1930), 20

Malayan Government, *see* Federal Government

Malayan Independence, *see* Independence

Malayan Indian Congress, 345

Malayan People's Anti-British Army, 104

Malayan People's Anti-Japanese Army (MPAJA), 22, 23 (*bis*), 24–5, 99; ex-Service Comrades' Association declared illegal (1948), 49; phased mobilisation, 96; fights KMT resistance rather than Japs, 24*n*; lays down most of its arms (1945), 35; members re-registered and mobilised (1948), 59, 86; tactics, 277; withdraws to deep jungle bases, 439

Malayan Races Liberation Army, *see* Guerrilla Forces

Malayan Scouts, *see* Special Air Service

Malayan Security Services (MSS), *see* Security Forces

Malayan Union, 120, 121, 255, 261, 268

Malayan War Council, *see* Federal War Council

Malays, 270–4
attitude to Independence, 503–5; attitude to the Independence for Malaya Party, 345; banditry by, 208–10; citizenship rights, 269; fears and grievances about Chinese, 84, 157–8, 331, 332, 400–1; integration of guerrillas with Chinese rare, 209–10; land tenure problem and, 195–6, 204; 'Muslim first and Communist second', 210; praised for part in the Emergency, 505; Thai border Malays antipathetic to guerrillas, 373

Mao Tse Tung
collectivisation, 312; influence on MCP policy, 320–1; introduced Hsueh Hsih, 436; 'New Democracy', 311, 312; rebels' strategy derived from works of, 103

Marshall, David (Prime Minister of Singapore)
at Baling talks, 463, 464, 467–8; defends Watts-Carter, 300

Martial Law, demanded by many Europeans and Asians (1948), 123

Marxism-Leninism, 315 *bis*, 320

Masses', 'The, 57–8, 311–2, 318–9, 321 *bis*

Masses Executive, 361, 362

Masses Organisation, *see Min Yuen*

Mawai (Johore), squatter resettlement in, 197–9

Maxwell, Sir George (former Chief Secretary), *q*, 127*n*

May Day
MCP manifesto (1948), 55, 86; processions banned (1948), 55

MCA, *see* Malayan Chinese Association

McLane, Professor Charles B., *Soviet Strategies in South-east Asia*, 316

MCP, *see* Malayan Communist Party

MCS, *see* Malayan Civil Service

McVey, Ruth, on Calcutta Conference, 46 *bis*

MDU, *see* Malayan Democratic Union, 25*n*

Mengkarak police station, 311

Menon, V. M. (T.U. Legislative Councillor), quoted (1948), 68, 77

Mentri Besar (State rulers)
authority, 342*n*, 485; hostile to Chinese, 324–5; Gurney's discussions with, 187; oppose Onn, 330; in Perak favour granting land titles to squatters, 273

Merdeka surrender offer (1957), 492

Military, the, *see* Army and Royal Air Force

INDEX

Military Intelligence Officers, 363
Miller, H., *Menace in Malaya* (1954), 93, 101
  Prince and Premier (1959), *q* on Communism, 468*n*
Min Sheng Pao (Malayan Chinese paper), editorial, 499
  Government action against, proposed, 67 *bis*, 93; MCP takes over (1948), 60, 93; sedition, difficult to prove its, 74
Min Yuen ('Masses' Organisation) (*see also* Guerrilla forces; Masses Executive), 24, 111–2, 213 *bis*
  activities of, 227 *bis*; delaying political progress, 333–4; eradication of, necessary, 237, 238; financed by Chinese, 302; New Village activities of, 395, 405, 411, 414
  reprisals by (1950), 218; responsponsibility of police, 285; in Seremban, 362; studied in food denial operation, 474–5; unlikely to surrender (1950), 221; weakening (1955), 472; why it was able to exist and function, 237
Mines and miners (*see also* Property management for entries covering both Estates *and* Mines favour use of armoured police vehicles, 279; tin industry affected by Emergency, 346–7, 349; use Special Constables, 284–5, 290
MNP, *see* Malay Nationalist Party
Montgomery, Field-Marshal Lord, 325–6
Morib camp for squatters, 182
Morton, John Percival (Head of Security Intelligence Far East), 276
Mount Ophir (Johore), cease-fire, 423
Mountbatten of Burma, Admiral Earl, 23
MPAJA, *see* Malayan People's Anti-Japanese Army
MRLA (Malayan Races Liberation Army), *see* Guerrilla Forces
MSS (Malayan Security Services), *see* Security Forces
Mui-tsai ordinance, 259
Murders, political, 88, 92–3
Musa bin Ahmad (Chairman of Central Committee), 462–3

N

Nan Chiao Jih Pao (Left-Wing daily), warning from (1950), 216
Nanyang Chinese, 459
  Malaya the national home of?, 121*n*
Nanyang General Labour Union founded (1926), 20
Nanyang Siang Pau (newspaper), 268, 301, 357, 467
  military and police warned by, 168
Nanyang University, Singapore banned publication by, 168*n*
Narayanan, P. P. (Trade Union leader), quoted (1948), 69
Nasaruddin, Inche, second motion on the Emergency in Legislative Council, 296
National registration, *see* Registration
National Servicemen (*see also* Conscription)
  considered, 469; drafted into jungle squads, 286; opposition to registration in Singapore, 429–31
Nationalism (*see also* Racialism), 143, 157
  Indonesian example of, 156; resurgence of Asian (1947), 78, 156
NATO, pressure to free troops for use with (1950), 348
Navy, the British, *see* Royal Navy
Negri Sembilan
  attitude of, towards rural Chinese, 195–6, 197, 202; Briggs Plan, operations begin in (August 1950), 242; British Adviser and Mentri Besar, of *q*, 195–6; clearance of squatters in (1949), 189, 195–6; deep jungle bases, 439
  difficulty in forming jungle squads *qv*, 286; favours armouring police vehicles, 278–9; guerrilla situation, 476, 486, 489, 492; Gurkhas stationed there, 353; jungle squad work unpopular, 286
  morale low among special constabulary, 285; Operation *Hive*, 360–2, 365; propaganda against Communists, 417, 421; resettlement of squatters and, 202 *bis*; State Security Committee meeting (October and November 1948), 179

INDEX

Negri Sembilan estates
  MPAJA nearly driven out from (1941–5), 99; only one Chinese auxiliary policeman on, 128; pamphlet left on victim's body, 107–8; two murders on (1948), 92
Nehru, Jawaharlal, 274*n*; on Malayan Government's folly (1949), 210–11
New Democracy (of Mao Tse Tung), 311, 312
New Democratic Youth League, 26, 66, 260–1
  declared illegal (1948), 94; Indian labourers' contact with, 92
New Path News (Information Services periodical), 422
New Villages, *see under* Resettlement
Newboult, Sir Alec (interim Head of Government), 264
  assumes administration (July 1948), 120; repatriation *qv* favoured by, 184, 188
Newfoundland, HMS, 372
Newspapers, government control of (1948), 141–2
Ng Heng letter, 424, 460, 461*n*
Ninth Police Division (Thai Police), 374 *bis*
Noone, Pat ('of the Ulu'), 446*n*
Noone, R. O. D. (Adviser on Aborigines and Director of Museums), 446*n*, 448

O

O'Connell, B. M. B. (Director of CID), 497–8
  on accommodation for detainees, 193; his solution to protection money racket, 224
October Directives (1951)
  alter MCP policy, 309, 434; China used as model, 320; deep jungle bases result, 439; political implications, 321, 424–5, 431; Security Forces change tactics, 359; town activities curtailed, 362
Officer Administering Government, *see* Del Tufo, M. V.
Officers Commanding Police Districts, responsible alone for property destruction, 154
Officers Superintending Police Circles, Special constables allocated by
Oliver, Major-General W. P. (Principal Staff Officer), 353
Olsen, F. A. (long-range jungle group), 133*n*
101 Special Training School, Malaya, 21
Ong Chong Keng, Dr, murder of (1948), 77, 262
Onn Dato (President of UMNO), 56
  and IMP, 345; and Malay nationalism, 504; and the MCA, 265; challenges authority of Sultans, 271; Communism's eradication urged by (1948), 69, 77
  criticises power of European District Officers, 342; combines with 'British Imperialists', 56; dangerous press publicity protested against by, 142*n*; Gent urged to go by, 119; on government appeasement of Chinese, 273*n*; Gurney's appointment protested against by, 121
  independence views of, 329–30; member of Federal War Council, 273, 274; his position in politics, 338; proposed as High Commissioner (1948), 158; State Liaison Committee member, 123
  suggested as Deputy High Commissioner, 336; UMNO leader, 124; warns against treating Malaya as a colony, 157
Onn, Capt. Hussein, 272–3
Operation *Cato*, 366
'Operation *Frustration*', 183–5
Operation *Galway/Valiant*, 366
Operation *Habitual*, 365
Operation *Hammer*, 365–6
Operation *Helsby*, 366
Operation *Hive*, 360–2, 365
Operation *Matador*, 366
Operation *Service*
  police public relations programme, 356–7
Operation *Sword*, 366
Operation *Termite*, 367
Operational intelligence, 363, 364
Operational Rice Ration, 378, 483, 484, 485, 489
Operational Sections (New Village defence forces), 412, 414–5, 488–9

INDEX

Operations, 136–9
  approach a counter-terror at the start, 160–9; campaign's anticipated phases (1949), 144–5; deep jungle, *see* Deep jungle operations; food denial, *see* Food denial operations; 'framework', *see* 'Framework . . .'; intensive, 242, 247; patrols, 136, 161, 162, 167, 247; squatter areas, 189–96; sweeps and drives, 136, 137–9
Osman China (surrendered guerrilla), 422
OSPCs, *see* Officers Superintending Police Circles
Overseas Defence Committee, Emergency guidance by, 145

P

PAAC, *see* Perak Aboriginal Areas Constabulary
Padi, *see* Rice
Pahang
  approach to absolute power in, 122; Army brigade there, 353; bandit concentrations in (1949), 226; Central Committee conferences held, 318; deep jungle bases in, 439; destruction of MCP through food denial, 472–6; exempted from discontinuance of ER 17D (June 1949), 193
  guerrilla activities in, 109–10, 208, 209, 350; guerrillas, freedom from (1959–60), 494; jungle forts, 446; Kampongs in, 208–9; 'liberated areas' in, 188; and the Long March, 309, 321; morale low among Special Constabulary, 285; Operation *Cato*, 366
  Malay loyalty to Sultan of, 209*n*; operations in, 139; propaganda results, 422; reports of insufficient police, 282; SAS operations, 366; troops needed in, 138;
Palestine (1938)
  fears that Malaya would become a second, 121; Malaya (1950) compared with, 225
Palestine police in Malaya
  contracts begin to run out (1950),
231; influence of, 268, 277–8, 286, 412, 501
Paloh (Johore), 110
Pangoi, Penghulu (*Asal* Club Chairman), 449–50
Pan-Malayan Congress, 310
Pan-Malayan Federation of Trade Unions (PMFTU), 54, 66, 210
  action against, proposed, 67–8; grievances exploited by, 66; MCP and its May Day programme, 86; proscribed (1948), 60; raids on branches of (1948), 71; registration refused (1948), 93; Singapore meeting of (1948), 66
Pan-Malayan Students' Federation, 437
Pan-Pacific Trade Union Secretariat, Shanghai, 20
Pantai Remis (Perak), Emergency settlement at, 200–1, 202
Paper on the security situation . . ., A (1949), 146
Parit (Kedah), air-strike (unauthorised) on, 153
Parkinson, Professor C. N., in Singapore, 175*n*
Party Ra'ayat, 470–1
Patrols, *see under* Operations
Peace moves (*see also* Amnesty), 459–71 *passim*; Baling talks, 462–8, 469
  'loyalty to Malaya' criterion, 463–4, 465; 'no negotiated peace', 461, 463, 468, 470; MCP claims to negotiate, 460–1, 462, 469; signs of MCP interest, 459–60
'Peace Offensive' (MCP) (1935), 424, 460, 467
Pearl Harbour analogy, 88–90
Pei Chun Middle School (Pontian), 433 *bis*, 434
Penang
  Army activity in, 353; attitude of, towards rural Chinese, 195; Chinese groups, 257; Communist involvement in Chinese schools, 431; deep jungle bases, 439
  MCP activity in Penang/Province Wellesley, 351; move for secession from FMS (1949), 158; registration of all residents in (December 1948), 142; revolutionary fervour of, 31
Pengerang (Johore), 491–2

538 INDEX

'People Inside, The' (a name for guerrillas), 396 bis
People's Action Party, 470, 470n
People's Liberation Armies and movements, 316, 317
  Chinese, 321; Malayan, 314, 315
People's Progressive Party, 385n, 491
People's United Front (MCP campaign), 470
'People's War' against guerrillas, 469
Perak
  administrative no-man's-land in, 174; Adviser on Chinese Affairs, assessment of; squatters by (September 1948), 174–7, 203; border-state problems of, 135; carries motion against appointment of Chinese consul, 215; Chief Police Officer's review (1950), 219–20
  Chinese 'jungle squad' working in guerrilla uniform in (January 1949), 133; CID in (1947), 80; clearance of squatters in, 182–3; deep jungle bases in, 439; eighty-five strikes in (1948), 92
  Farmers' Association and Sago Workers' Union, 204; Federal 'admiration for its initiative', 181; Federal authorities' clash with, over resettlement, 181–2; guerrillas active in (1948), 100–1, 108–9; guerrillas' activity (later), 294, 295, 364, 414, 476; guerrillas' strength, 350, 489, 492
  Gurkhas stationed there, 353; intelligence problem (1958), 493; jungle forts, 446; Lee Meng trial, 384–5; mass surrender of guerrillas, 490–1
  mining land squatters, problem of, 200; Operation Helsby, 366; Operation Termite, 367; police and army headquarters 20 miles apart, 248; police para-military operations in, 131, 132
  rejects appointment of Chinese consul (1950), 215; report on Special Constabulary, 283–5; resettlement, 394, 395, 397–8; resettlement problems for police, 287; Security Force concentration, 486
  security situation deteriorates (1950), 218–21; squatters' resettlement, its attitude to, 197, 200–1, 202; supervision of mines' protection, 128; tin mines closed, 349; Watts-Carter Case, 299–300 Perak Aboriginal Areas Constabulary, formed 1950, 442
Perak Rubber Workers' Union, offices raided by police (1948), 92
Perak State Squatter Committee, report of (1949), 177
Percival, General, 263
Perimeter fences (see also Gate searches), 173, 391–406 passim, 413
Perimeter lighting, 403–4, 406
Perisoc (Malay political organisation), 80
Perlis, 353
  border-state problems of, 134–5
Persatuan Islam Sa-malaya (revised Islamic party), 470–1
Petir (People's Action Party journal), 470n
Phang Yi Foo, see Siew Lau
Pioneer aircraft, 450
Piratin, Philip (Communist M.P.), 163n
Planter, The, on Anti-Bandit Month (1950), 217–8
Planters and estates, see Estates and planters
Poh Lee Sen, guerrilla stronghold, 109, 110
Police Aboriginal Guards, 480n
Police Field Force, 367
Police Force (see also Area Security Units; Auxiliary Police; Chief Police Officers; Commissioner of Police; Special Constabulary; Thailand Police Force
  aborigine work disliked by, 443; Army greatly outnumbered by, 114; counter-guerrilla operations, 291–2, 297–8, 374; criticisms of, 154–5; deaths' ratio to Army's, two to one, 213
  elimination of Communist cells the primary task of, 236; Federal Headquarters, 358; Field Force operations, 375, 450, 480n; Frontier Force controlled by, 134; functions of, 281–2, 285, 288, 290–1, 354
  improved conditions suggested (1948), 73; increased arms, personnel and equipment, 144; information services depend almost entirely on (1950), 230; Lyttelton's criticisms, 334, 335; Malays predominate in, 271

INDEX

morale and discipline problems, 130, 219, 275, 279–93 *passim*, 299, 353, 359; Palestine Police influence, 268, 277–8, 286, 412, 501; promotions, 291, 331, 358–9; public relations, 323–4, 356–7; raids on open members of MCP, 499
relations with Chinese; with MCA, 268; with recruits, 264*n*, 298–9, 302; reorganisation and expansion, Briggs' plan, 287–90, 291–2; Templer's plan, 333, 339, 343; Young's job, 353–9; resettlement work of, 287–9, 292, 305,, 391
shortage of officers, 236; search, detention, etc., powers of, 141; strength of (June 1948), 129; later, 237, 290; Thailand border work, 374–5; three main problems for, 131
training, 333, 339, 357–8; training problems, 283, 286, 287, 289–90, 322, 323; treatment of Chinese by, 323–4, 357; use of armoured vehicles, 277–81; Young recommends merger with Singapore Police Force, 359
Police jungle squads, 131, 150–1, 226, 277–84 *passim*
Briggs' plan, 289–90; Perak Aboriginal Areas Constabulary becomes a Police Jungle Company, 442*n*
Police Special Squads, 480*n*
'Police state,' Templer's creation?, 383–7
Politbureau (MCP), 350, 351, 366, 462
'battles of anihilation' directed by (1949), 212
Political Line of the Party, The (MCP document), 50
'Pontian Case, the' (Johore), 432–4
Populated areas, Min Yuen active in, 237, 238
Press, British, 280, 341, 386
Press, Malayan (*see also Singapore Standard and Straits Times*)
Left-Wing influence, 306*n*; on gate searches, 410; reaction to Templer, 340, 341, 343, 383; recognition of the MCP, 462
Press, Malayan Chinese, *see China Press; Nanyang Siang Poh; Sin Chew Chit Poh*
Press, Malayan Communist, *see Battle News Press; Freedom News; Min Sheng Pao; True News Press; Unity News Press*
Printing Press Act (June 1948), 141
Private armies, formed from Special Constabulary by property managements, 284
Privy Council, 384, 385
Programme for the People's Democratic Republic (MCP, 1949), 311
Propaganda, Government (*see also* Psychological warfare)
among aborigines, 451; 'black' propaganda, 417*n*; media and techniques, 416–24; Lyttelton's view of its importance, 333; *My Accusation*, by Lam Swee, 310, 421; rewards or bribes to surrender, 418, 421
Propaganda (MCP), 220, 310–1, 314–5, 320, 321, 331, 417
against resettlement, 396; against surrender of guerrillas, 419; Central Propaganda Dept., 351; in Chinese schools, 430; Communist strength dependent upon, 235; counter-propaganda, 421, 422; *Incident of Lam Swee* ... 310; increase of (1948), 65, 66; killer squads, 107–8; on Japanese occupation, 300; leaflets and posters, 416; peace moves, 461–2, 465
Property, destruction of, 153–4, 183, 190
Property management (covering both Estates and Mines. See also separate headings)
Briggs' plan for use of special constables, 290; fears about Independence, 329–30; police work, 282; private armies, 284
'Protection money' paid to Communists, 127, 128, 222–4
Protection money
cost to industry, 347; employers' difficulties, 267; Europeans urge drastic measure, 332; Gurney tries to stop, 266; in New Villages, 393; 'payments amounted to $100,000 a month', 222; Watts-Carter case, 299–300
Protector of Aborigines, 442, 445–6
Protector of Chinese, 259–60
Province Wellesley
Army strength there, 353; MCP activity, 351
Psychological warfare (*see also* Propaganda *and* Surrendered

540 INDEX

Psychological warfare (*continued*)
  enemy personnel), 371*n*, 378, 416-38, 489-90
Public confidence in Government (*see also* Department of Public Relations; Emergency Information Services; Propaganda; Government
  apparent injustice decreases confidence, 385; Chinese confidence, 425, 504; heavy casualties effect on, 296; in police, 356*n*, 357
Public co-operation
  with administration, 379, 380-1, 404, 408; with guerrillas, 291-5; with police, 297-8, 356-7, 359, 362-3
Public Relations Department, 260
Pulai (Johore), 111
  surrender of occupying rebels at (1949), 103
Purcell, Dr Victor (author of *Malaya: Communist or Free?*, and *The Chinese in South-East Asia*)
  on British help to MPAJA, 24; on Chinese in schools, 428*n*, 435; on Chinese secret societies, 426*n*; criticisms of Templer and his Emergency policy, 318, 379-87; on rule by British or else by extortioners, 29; writings on the Chinese and on the MCS, 255
Pye, Lucien (author), 265

Q

'Q-force', 364*n*
Quaker Oats (tinned), banned, 484

R

RAAF, *see* Royal Australian Air Force
Racialism (*see also* Chinese, Malayan)
  culture, 435;
  hindrance to integration, 408; and Independence, 503; Malayanisation, 339, 435, 464; racial balance, 401; UMNO attitude, 329, 330-2

RAF, *see* Royal Air Force
Rahman, Tungku Abdul (Prime Minister of the Federation Government)
  at Baling talks, 461, 463-8; meets Lyttelton, 330; suggests amnesty for terrorists, 460, 461
Rajagopal, M. P.
  on 'denial of a living wage', 70 and *n*
Ramani, Senator R., 69*n*, 274
  on employers' attitude (1948), 69-70; on 'the new despotism', 159-60
Rashid Maidin (MCP representative at Baling talks), 463
  delegate to 'Empire' Communist Conference (1947), 44
Raub/Bentong area (Pahang)
  guerrilla activity centre, 351; MCP members eliminated, 473, 474*n*; Operation *Cato*, 366
Red Cross, 399 *bis*, 404
Regarding Decision on Struggle Strategy (MCP document, 1948), 57
Regarding the Peasant Struggle (MCP document), 59*n*
Registrar of Trade Unions, 65, 66
  raid on PMFTU's HQ suggested by (1948), 67
Registration
  Chinese squatters in remote areas, 176; national, 142, 142-3
Regulation 17D, *see* Emergency Regulations
Reinforcements, *see under* Army
Repatriation of Chinese, 147, 181, 184
  China's revolution's effect on, 201; errors in, 191-2; preferred to guerrilla reprisals, 224; voluntary, 183, 184
Report on the Emergency in Malaya (1950), 251*n*
Resettlement of aborigines, 442-5
Resettlement of Chinese, 173-205, 291-5, 302, 305, 391*n*, 394, 397-415
  agriculture problems, 403, 406-11, 414; Briggs Plan and, 240; changes (1956), 487; China's Communist successes, effect on, 201; cost, 348
  education and, 398-9, 404; failure of (1949), 201; Federal point of view, 177-8; lotteries banned, 346*n*, 386; *Min Yuen*, 395, 405, 411, 414

INDEX

'New Villages', 342, 391*n*; number of those resettled, 184*n*, 201, 252; physical process of, 292, 394–5, 422–4; police rôle and problems, 282–3, 287–9; Purcell description of 1951 position, 381
purpose and set-up, 391–415; security of action depends upon (*see also* Security and Defence), 188; site, choice of, 394–5, 396–7; social and welfare services, 397, 399, 400; States unanimous in accepting principle (1949), 201, 202; States' action, 176, 180–1, 186–7; 'a temporary solution', 246; 'Resistance' movement to Japanese (1942–5), 21–5
'hot-house for Malayan Communism', 23, 25*n*, 204
Restricted Residence Enactment, 72
Rhodesians, Southern, suggested use of (1950), 327
Rice
grown by Chinese, 204; official control of, 137, 377–8, 484; peasants supported by MCA on freedom to sell, 320; rationing of, 379, 485, 489; shortage of, during the war, 204
Ritchie, General (C-in-C), Gent's dismissal and, 119
'River Valley' pacts, 449–50, 452, 453–4
Robertson, General Sir Brian (C-in-C MELF)
declines post of Supreme Commander (civil and military) of Malaya, 326
Robinson, J. B. Perry, *Transformation in Malaya* (1956), *q*, 122, 419*n*
Round Table, *q*, on administration, 337
Royal Air Force (*see also* Air and Special Air Service)
air-strike arranged by DO of Kedah, 153; arrival of squadron of Lincoln bombers (March 1950), 248; Briggs Plan for, 238; Emergency rôle, 369–71; increase in (1949), 136
Operation *Termite*, 367; Thailand border work, 375*n*; use of, 137; value of, 326; its weakness, 114
Royal Australian Air Force, 248, 371
Royal Hampshire Regiment, notable performance of, in Malaya, 369

Royal Navy
coastal operations by, 150, 372; Emergency rôle, 371–2
Royal Scots Fusiliers, First Battalion, in Operation *Termite*, 367
Rubber industry, 346–9
'case for nationalisation of', 244; MCP try to bring it to standstill (1948), 86; state of the industry (1947), 78; workers a target for Communism, 31; world demand for, 28
Rubber Growers' Association, 118*n*
Rubber Trade Association of London, 118*n*
Rubber Workers' Union, a cover for MCP, 92
Rule of law, the, departure from, 160
Rulers, Conference of, *see* Conference of Rulers
Rural Development Plan (1960), 400
Rural and Industrial Development Authority, 273, 343
Russia, *see* Soviet Union
Ryves, Harvey (MSS officer)
on MCP's campaign (1948), 86

S

St John's Ambulance, 399 *bis*
Sakai (Security force term for aborigines), 447
Salak South (outside Kuala Lumpur), 405*n*
San Min Chu Yi (Youth Corps), 26, 260–1
Sarawak, Malaya's resettlement a model for, 173
Scots Guards, prisoners shot by patrol of, 166, 168
SCs, *see* Special Constabulary
Scudai (Johore), major guerrilla raid on (1956), 488
Second World War, *see* World War II
Secret societies, Chinese, 256, 258, 425–7
Secretariat, Federal, unnecessary expansion of, 175*n*
Secretary for Chinese Affairs, 259, 260*n*, 263–4
his report on resettlement (1950), 202
Secretary of State, *see* Colonial Secretary
Security and defence of resettlements (*see also* Gate searches; Home

Security and defence of resettlements (*continued*)
  Guards; Kampong Guards; Perimeter fences; Perimeter lighting), 333, 381, 392, 403–15 *passim*
  police rôle and problems, 282–3, 287–9
Security Forces (*see also* Army; Director of Operations; Home Guard; Police Force; Royal Air Force; Royal Navy; Security and defence of resettlements; Special Constabulary), 79, 140
  air power lacking, 502; casualties in, *see under* Casualties; chief problem of—to identify the enemy, 160, 223, 246–7; Chinese members, 332*n*; deep jungle operations, 364–9 *passim*, 439–40, 476–83 *passim*; Director's powers reduced, 140; failure against MCP, 337; Gent accused of having ignored their warnings, 118
  intelligence review's lurid forecasts (June 1948), 83–4; internal reports of, 79–80; Lyttelton's policy, 326, 333; organisation (1953), 352–3 (1956); 480–2; praised for their work, 505; relations with aborigines, 367, 440–3 *passim*; 449–56 *passim*, 493–4; removal of squatters by (1948), 182–4, 187; staff shortages in (1948), 85
  Templer's work, 338–44, 365, 378, 484; Thai border work, 373; 'warhead on a complex missile', 250; 'Seditious or inflammatory matter', power to prohibit, 252
Seenivasagam brothers (of the People's Progressive Party), 385 *bis*, 471*n*
Segamat (Johore)
  aborigine settlement in, 441; guerrilla arms dumps captured (June 1950), 247
Selangor
  army brigade there, 353; Chinese secret societies, 426–7; clearance of squatters in, 182, 189; concentration of Security Forces, 482; guerrilla situation, 227, 472, 476, 486, 489; MRLA strength in, 213; operations in, 138, 365–6; police numbers, 287; report on Chinese resettlement, 292; State Secretariat of the MCP, 396; police flying squad in, 131; and resettlement of released squatters, 202; Staff Officer Operations, on Kachau tragedy, 163; typical guerrilla camp in, 97; violent crimes in (1948), 87–8, 92, 99–100, 101, 162–6
Selangor State Committee of MCP, reorganised for armed struggle (May 1948), 59
'Selected Areas', 485, 494–5
Self-government, *see* Independence
Semenyih (Selangor), gate searching, 406–11
Semur river (Kelantan), action beside (March 1950), 231*n*
Senoi Pra'aq (fighting aborigines), 493–4
SEPs, *see* Surrendered enemy personnel
Seremban (Negri Semibilan)
  gaol flooded with detainees (December 1948), 142, 184; murder at (1948), 99; Operation *Hive*, 360–2, 365
Settlement War Executive Committees, 283
17D, *see* Emergency Regulations
Seventh Branch (of Anti-British Alliance, Penang), 431
Sharkey, Lawrence (Australian Communist) and the Malayan insurrection, 52–3
Sheppard, M. C. (Head of Emergency Food ff. Denial Organisation), 485 ff
Siam, *see* Thailand
Sian magistrates, 256
Siew Lau (Phang Yi Foo, executed MCP member), 311–3
Siew Ping (executed with Siew Lau), 313
Sin Chew Chit Poh (newspaper), on conscription, 301
Sin Sang Basketball Group (Pontian), 433
Singapore
  Air HQ Malaya moved from (1954), 370; Chinese consul in, 214; Chinese groups in, 257; Chinese schools problem, 429–31; Communism in, 20–22, 470; Communist Central Committee wiped out (1942), 22; constabulary seconded for Ferret Force, 133; defence forces recruited in, 126; fall of (1942) a factor in insurrection, 34;

INDEX

General Labour Union created (1945), 28, 29; loans made by, 349; Muslim rioting in (1950), 252; police problems, 349; receives Chinese evading conscription, 301, 302, 357n; revolutionary fervour of, 31; Straits Central Organisation, 372n

Singapore Chinese Middle School Students' Union, 436

Singapore Federation of Trades Unions, 54

Singapore General Labour Union created by MCP (1945), 28

Singapore Harbour Board Labour Union, 55; serious strike at (1948), 54

Singapore Regiment Royal Artillery, 1st, 'B' Battery, 367

Singapore Standard, 356n, 429

Singapore Teachers' Union education proposal by, X, 216

Singapore Town Committee, 57 betrayal of, 38, 55, 362n

Singapore Workers' Protection Corps, objects of, 55

Sino-British Treaty (1943), 158

Sino-Malay enmity, 84, 157–8

Sino-Malay Goodwill Committee, *see* Communities' Liaison Committee

Sino-Malay massacres, 26

Siu Cheong (Politbureau), 350

Slim, Field-Marshal 1st Viscount (Chief of the General Staff) meets Briggs and Watherston in London (1950), 251n; requests appointment of Lt.-Gen. Briggs qv, 234–5; suggested as High Commissioner (1952), 326

Slimming, John (Asst Protector of Aborigines, author of *Temiar Jungle* and *In Fear of Silence*), 446n

Slump and consequent Immigration policy (1931–2), 203

Socfin estates (Slim River), industrial trouble on, 66

Societies' Ordinance, 67

Some Civil Aspects of the Emergency in Johore . . . (1950), 246

South-East Asian Communists, and violence, 44–5, 46–7, 48

South-Malaya Bureau (MCP) deep jungle base, 439

Soviet Union
Communist policy, 315–6, 317; influence and intervention in Malaya, 315–8, 320, 321, 372; South-east Asia's insurrections and, 44–5, 83, 85n

Sow Wah (wife of Siew Lau), 313

Special Air Service (Malayan Scouts) deep jungle work, 366, 367, 449, 450, 455; New Zealand squadron, 480n

Special Branch, *see* Intelligence services

Special Branch Contingent, 473

Special Constabulary, 176
in action by Semur river (March 1950), 231n; arming of, 126, 127–8; Briggs' plan for, 290; casualties in, number of, 127; estates' use of, 223, 284, 285, 291; Gray's attitude, 282; jungle squad work, 480n; land provided for, 272; low morale, 282, 283–6; mainly Malays, 126, 271; mines' use of, 284; pay of, 126; police use of, 282–7 *passim*; raising of, 124–9; Thai border work for, 374; training of, 125, 129; value of, 101, 106; Young reduces, 358

Special Operations Volunteer Force, 364n, 367

Special Service Corps (*see also* 'killer squads'), 95, 99 bis

Spencer-Chapman, Lt.-Col. F. W., Training School organised by, 21

Spitfires, use of, 103n, 114, 136, 371

Squatter areas, 188
blacklisting of the most dangerous, 189; Communists dependent upon, for information, 235; operations against, by police and army, 189–96

Squatter Committee, Federal (*see also* Perak State Squatter Committee)
composition of, 185–6; measures of, to supplement Regulation 17D, 189; report of (January 1949), 179, 187, 194, 196

Squatter Problem in the Federation of Malaya in 1950, 201

Squatters, Chinese (*see also* Resettlement), 183
arrest of, 124n; bandits' contact with, 187; camps for, *see* Detention camps; classification of, 232; deportation of, *see* Deportation
detention of, *see* Detainees; dislike control, 271–2; Federal or State

Squatters, Chinese (*continued*)
  matter?, 181–2; five groups of, 175–7; land titles for, 236, 272–3, 340
  morale low, 293; numbers of, resettled, 293–4; physical process of resettlement of, 394–5; problem of, 137, 147, 153, 173–205; repatriation of, *see* Repatriation; resettlement of, *see* Resettlement; right of self-defence, 270; settlements, 258
State Federations of Trade Unions, *see* Federations
State governments
  Squatter Committee recommendations and, 186, 188; varying attitudes of, to rural Chinese, 195–201
State Liaison Committee, 123
State War Executive Committees, 239
  all Emergency matters to be handed over to Federal War Council or to—Briggs Plan, 251; attitude to police posts, 283; control resettlement, 394; favour armoured police vehicles, 279–80; a reliable weapon, 250
States, the
  defence of, 282–3, 285; demand for restoration of their former status, 157
Sten guns, captured by guerrillas, 278–9
Stenson, M. R.
  on General Labour Unions, 29, 33*n*; *The 1948 Communist Revolt in Malaya* (1971), 56*n*
Stockwell, Major-General Sir Hugh (GOC Malaya, 1953), 353
Stokes, Richard (British M.P.), 327
Strachey, John (Secretary of State for War), 268, 328
'Straits Chinese', 257, 270*n*
Strikes, 317
  crescendo of (1948), 32–3, 54–5, 86–7, 91–2; Government policy regarding, 30; Johore (1948), 91; Perak (85 in 1948), 92; political capitalisation of, 31; Singapore general strike (1946), 29
Straits Control Organisation, 372–3
Straits Times, The, 26, 127*n*
  on Anti-Bandit Month (1950), 217; on Chinese education, 428*n*; clemency suggested by (1948), 220–1; on detention, 383; on Lee Meng trial, 384 *bis*; on New Villages, 403*n*; pro-Gent letter in (1948), 119; on Templer, 337, 342, 343, 357; on Trengganu terrorists, 151*n*
Strategic Supplies Chart, 474–5
Struggle for the materialisation of the independence, democracy and peace of Malaya (MCP manifesto), 462
Students' Unions
  Klang, 431, 432; Kuala Lumpur, 432; Singapore, 436; University of Malaya, 429
Suffolk Regiment, 1st Battalion
  notable performances, 369; strength of (1950), 225
Suicide squads of ex-killer, 87 *bis*
Summary trials, pressure for (1949), 159
Sun Yat-Sen, Dr (Chinese leader) (1866–1925)
Sunderland flying boats, 114, 371*n*
Sungei Patani, police in, 131
Sungei Remok estate (Selangor)
  explosions mistaken for ambush at, 167, 168
Sungei Siput (Perak), 499
  evictions of Chinese squatters from (1948), 181, 182, 183; guerrilla strength in, 111; murders in, 88, 92, 93, 96, 204–5; resettlement of squatters, 186; terrorists take to the hills, 87
Supplementary Opinions of the Central Politburo on Strategic Problems in the Malayan Revolutionary War, 207
Supplies, Communist (*see also* Food supplies, Communist)
  from Chinese resettlement areas, 292–4, 351, 392, 405–11; deep jungle provision, 238, 440, 473
Supplies, Air
  to aborigines, 443–4; to Security Forces, 370, 445, 450

T

Tai-jin, the pre-war (Protector of Chinese), 259–60
Tai Tong Rubber Factory, sit-down strike at (1948), 54–5
Taiping District (Perak), 485
  Army headquarters in, 20 miles apart from police HQ, 248
Tam, Le, *see* Le Tam

INDEX

Tan Cheng Lock, later Sir Cheng Lock Tan, 157
against conscription for Chinese, 301; asks for Gent to be reinstated, 119; at Baling talks, 463, 467; citizenship for Chinese, 268-9; criticises police, 268; investigates harsh treatment of Chinese, 267; 'Malaya is a police state', 335, 383; MCA work, 265, 269, 329; makes anti-Communist speech (1950), 218*n*; on surrender offer (1955), 461; survives politically, 262-3
Tan Fuk Leong (leader of MCP Third Independent Platoon), 482
Tan Kah Kee (Chinese industrialist), 263
Tan Kan (a Labour Union President), 104-6
Tan Piow (guerrilla), 423-4
Tan Siew Sin, 267, 299, 468
Tan Tuan Boon (Selangor State Councillor), 461
Tanjong Malim (near Kuala Lumpur), 340-1, 343
Tapah District (south Perak), 264*n*, 478-80
Tapioca growing, 440, 456
  erosion of soil from, 204
Tasek Bera (Johore), 310
  guerrilla activity centre, 351-2
Taxes
  paid to Government, 396; paid to guerrillas from New Villages, 392, 393
Tempest squadron, 371
Templer, Field-Marshal Sir Gerald (High Commissioner)
  aborigine policy, 445; achievements, 318*n*, 346; achievements criticised by Purcell, 379-87; appointed High Commissioner and Director of Operations (1952), 326, 336-7; battle strategy, 365; 'character', 382-3; his food denial instructions, 378, 484; lays foundation for Independence, 337; leaves Malaya (1954), 346; political programme, 338-44; propaganda broadcast, 422*n*; public health efforts, 399-400
Temporary Occupation Licences, 175, 176, 195, 249
  Perak prefers Mukim Register to, 200

Terrorism (*see also* Counter-terror Guerrilllas *and* Violence), 206
Chinese the first victims of, 151-2
Thai Communists, 374
Thai-Malayan border agreement (1949), 374
Thailand
  air bases in, 375*n*; Border Security Council, 493; British Ambassador on 'a wild goose chase', 228; Chinese Communists reported to have landed in (1950), 227-9; frontier, 142, 180, 374
  guerrilla sanctuary, 487-93; Malayan guerrillas in South, 213; MCP activity in, 350, 351, 373-5, 450, 494; Police Force, 374-5
Thompson, Sir Robert, 132, 221*n*, 401, 500, 501
Defeating Communist Insurgency (1966), q, 212*n*
Thondar Pandai, 32
Thorneycroft, Peter (Conservative M.P.), 327
'Three stars', *see* Guerrillas, MPAJA
Tin industry (*see also* Mines and miners *and* Property management), 346-7, 349
  miners a target for Communism, 31; world demand for tin, 28
'Tin Puncturing Order', 484
'Toilers of the Far East', 1st Congress of (1922), Malaya unrepresented in, 19
Too, C. C. (Head of the Psychological Warfare Dept.), 7, 320-1, 459
  quoted on MCP, 54
Town Boards, 397, 401
Trade Union Adviser, government, 65, 66 *bis*, 306
  on Balan's power, 45
Trade Union Amendment Bill (1948), 60, 67, 71
  enactment of (June 12), 91; principal provisions of, 91; restoration of deleted subsection, 72, 73, 74, 76
Trade unions (*see also* Federations of trade unions *and* General Labour Unions)
  arrest of members, 327; British Imperialists hinder, 314; Chinese association, 260-1; Chinese, not encouraged, 303; Government policy not to encourage revival of, 159*n*

546 INDEX

Trade unions (*continued*)
MCP penetration and domination, 302, 499; in Singapore, 470; Templer's attitude to, 342–3; underground, 362
Trades Union Congress, London, Adviser's letter to (1946), on condition of Malayan Unions, 30
Trades Union Congress, Malaya, urges peace talks (1957), 469
Tras (Pahang), 305
Trengganu (*see also* Kuantan)
Metri Besar of, is cabled not to expect troops, 152; mines incidents in (August 1948), 150–1; possible 'liberated area', 152*n*
Trengganu
Special Police morale low, 286
Triad Society, 425–6
Tronoh (Perak)
homes burnt as counter-terror, 162; murders in, 205
Trotskyism, 19
True News Press, 351
'Twelve stars', *see* Guerrillas, KMT

U

Ubaidullah, S.O.K., tables pro-Gent motion, 119
Ulu Yam Bahru (Selangor)
killings at (1948), 100; villagers' accounts of Kachau burning, 167
UMNO, *see* United Malay National Organisation
Undesirable Publications Ordinance, 437, 438
Unions, *see* General Labour Unions *and* Trade Unions
United Malay National Organisation, 26, 124
forms Alliance Party with the Malayan Chinese Association and Malayan Indian Congress, 345; members not to be guerrilla victims, 321; Onn's resignation, 329; policies, 329, 330–2, 504
United Malaya, 331, 333, 339
United Planting Association of Malaya, 73, 118*n*, 461*n*
United Press News, 264
Unity News Press, 473

Urquhart, Major-General R. W. (GOC Malaya, 1952), 353
Utusan Melayu (Singapore newspaper), extreme nationalist views of, 157
q pessimistically on achievement of self-government, 156

V

Valetta aircraft, 451
Veerasenan (Indian Communist leader), shot (1949), 210
Vietnamese Communist Party, 53
Vietnamese wars, 184
Malayan no analogy to, 160
Village Councils, 342, 402–3, 404, 411
Village Councils Bill (1952), 342
Village Guards, 241
New, *see under* Resettlement
Violence (*see also* Terrorism) (1947 and 1948), 25–8, 31, 59–60
Government inquiries into (1947), 32; Johore (1948), 92–3; MCP endorses use of, 51, 58, 59, 79; public inured to (1948), 77; Security forces, 160–9; Selangor (1948), 87; Singapore's increasing (1948), 55; Southeast Asians and, 44–5, 46–7; Suicide squad of ex-killers formed (1948), 87

W

Wade, General (GOC Malaya), succeeded by Gen. Boucher (1948), 136
Wah Kee (Chinese secret society), 426–7
Wahi Annuar (insurgent leader), surrender of, 209
Wallich, W. A. (Chamber of Commerce chairman)
denounces campaign 'originating outside this country' (1948), 68–9; police sufficiency questioned by, 75; Secretary of State denounced by (1948), 76
Wan Ali (bandit insurgent), killing of, 209
War Councils *and* Executive Committees, *see* Border Security

INDEX

Council; Federal War Council; Settlement War Executive Committees; State War Executive Committees
War footing, Malaya on a (1950), 250–1, 252
Warships, use of, 372
Wartime guerrillas, *see* Malayan People's Anti-Japanese Army (MPAJA)
Watherston, Sir David (Chairman of Internal Security Committee), 122, 189, 216*n*, 399, 461*n*
  backs David's attack on Regulation 17D, 192–3; Kachau burning disapproved by, 166; meetings with Labour Cabinet Ministers (December 1950), 251*n*; protests against Chinese consuls, 215
Watts-Carter, Jeffrey, 299–300
Weng (Perak), evictions from, 180
West Yorkshire Regiment (the Prince of Wales Own), First Battalion, 367
White Areas, 378–9, 477, 489
Williams, Professor Lea, 255*n*
Williams-Hunt, P. R. D. (Protector of Aborigines)
  appointment, 442; death, 446*n*; opposes air attacks on aborigines, 444; opposes resettlement policy, 443
Wohlsletter, Mrs Roberta: 'Cuba and Pearl Harbour' (1965), 88–90
Worcestershire Regiment, 1st Battalion, Officer in Command, 369
Work Forces, in deep jungle bases, 440

World Federation of Democratic Youth, 44, 45
World War II, anti-climax of its ending, 34
Wright (alias of Loi Tak, *qv*), 41, 50, 53
Wyatt, Woodrow Lyle (British M.P.), 328

Y

Ya'acob, Tungku (member of Federal War Council), 273
Yeong Kuo (Vice-Secretary General of MCP), 39, 351, 470, 482
Yong Peng (Johore), 264*n*
Yong Shook Lin (member of Legislative Council), 266
  speaks out against banditry (1950), 218*n*
Young, A. E. (Commissioner of Police), 353–9, 501
Youth movements
  API, 38; Boy Scouts Association, 343; encouraged by Templer, 343; used by Communists, 433–8
Yugoslav 'resistance', parallel to, 24*n*
Yugoslavs at Calcutta Congress and Conference (1947), 47–8

Z

Zhdanov, Andrei, his plea to Communist parties (1947), 45, 47
Zhukov, E. M., 317

Date Due